PENGUIN REFERENCE BOOKS

THE PENGUIN DICTIONARY OF
NINETEENTH-CENTURY HISTORY

John Belchem is Reader in History at the University of Liverpool. His recent publications include *Industrialization and the Working Class* (Scolar, 1990), *Class, Party and the Political System in Britain, 1867–1914* (Blackwell/Historical Association, 1990) and *Popular Radicalism in Nineteenth-Century Britain* (Macmillan, 1996).

Richard Price is Professor of History at the University of Maryland, College Park. He is a frequent contributor to scholarly journals and the author of three books: *An Imperial War and the Working Class* (Routledge, 1972), *Masters, Unions and Men: Work Control in Building and the Rise of Labour 1830–1914* (CUP, 1980) and *Labour and British Society 1780–1980* (Croom Helm, 1986).

Richard J. Evans is Professor of History and Vice-Master of Birkbeck College, University of London. He is a Fellow of the British Academy and of the Royal Historical Society. His book, *Death in Hamburg: Society and Politics in the Cholera Years, 1830–1910*, won the Wolfson Literary Award for History in 1988 and is also published by Penguin.

D0263319

The Penguin Dictionary of

Nineteenth-Century History

Edited by

John Belchem and Richard Price

Advisory Editor

Richard J. Evans

PENGUIN BOOKS

Published by the Penguin Group
Penguin Books Ltd, 27 Wrights Lane, London W8 5TZ, England
Penguin Books USA Inc., 375 Hudson Street, New York, New York 10014, USA
Penguin Books Australia Ltd, Ringwood, Victoria, Australia
Penguin Books Canada Ltd, 10 Alcorn Avenue, Toronto, Ontario, Canada M4V 3B2
Penguin Books (NZ) Ltd, 182–190 Wairau Road, Auckland 10, New Zealand

Penguin Books Ltd, Registered Offices: Harmondsworth, Middlesex, England

First published by Basil Blackwell Ltd 1994
Published in Penguin Books 1996
1 3 5 7 9 10 8 6 4 2

Contents

Contributors

Edward Acton
University of East Anglia
Lawrence P. Adamczyk
Western Montana College
Steve Amann
University of Maryland
Peter Bailey
University of Manitoba
Tony Barley
University of Liverpool
D. W. Bebbington
University of Stirling
John Belchem
University of Liverpool
Steven Beller
Georgetown University
Robin Betts
University of Liverpool
Tom Bottomore

John Breuilly
University of Manchester
Patrick Buckland
University of Liverpool
M. G. Carroll
University of Liverpool
F. L. Carsten
London
Malcolm Chase
University of Leeds

Gregory Claeys
*Royal Holloway and Bedford
New College,
University of London*
J. S. Cockburn
University of Maryland
James E. Cronin
Boston College
John Davies
*Liverpool Institute of Higher
Education*
Richard Dellamora
Trent University, Ontario
Simon Dentith
University of Liverpool
David Dutton
University of Liverpool
James Epstein
Vanderbilt University
Charles Esdaile
University of Liverpool
Henry Finch
University of Liverpool
Humphrey J. Fisher
University of London
Gordon Fletcher
University of Liverpool
R. A. Foley
University of Cambridge
Robert Friedel
University of Maryland

Sheridan Gilley
University of Durham
J. M. Golby
The Open University
Robert G. Greenhill
London Guildhall University
P. E. H. Hair
University of Liverpool
John L. Halstead
University of Sheffield
June Ellen Hargrove
University of Maryland
Sylvia Harrop
University of Liverpool
Elizabeth Harvey
University of Liverpool
Roger Hausheer
Wolfson College, Oxford
John Haywood
Lancaster University
E. P. Hennock
University of Liverpool
J. Hibbs
University of Central England
Edward Higgs
*Wellcome Unit for the History
of Medicine, Oxford University*
Pat Hudson
University of Liverpool
Luke Jensen
University of Maryland
David J. Jeremy
*Manchester Metropolitan
University*
D. S. Johnson
Queen's University, Belfast
Barbara Kaplan
University of Maryland
Simon Katzenellenbogen
University of Manchester
Gerry Kearns
University of Liverpool
Liam Kennedy
Queen's University, Belfast

George O. Kent
University of Maryland
Timothy Kirk
*University of Northumbria at
Newcastle*
A. V. Knowles
University of Liverpool
Robin Law
University of Stirling
Rohan McWilliam
University of Essex
Luke Martell
University of Sussex
Gerald Martin
University of Pittsburgh
John Martin
University of Maryland
Kathleen Martindale
York University, Toronto
Rory Miller
University of Liverpool
John Molony
University College, Dublin
Graham Mooney
University of Liverpool
Robyn Muncy
University of Maryland
Kevin Murphy
University of Maryland
Bryan D. Palmer
Queen's University, Ontario
Terry Parssinen
University of Tampa
Simon Pepper
University of Liverpool
B. Marie Perinbam
University of Maryland
Roy Porter
*Wellcome Institute for the
History of Medicine*
Richard Price
University of Maryland
Roger Price
University of East Anglia

Martin Pugh
University of Newcastle upon Tyne
Michael C. Pugh
University of Southampton
Alice E. Reagan
Northern Virginia Community College
A. N. Ryan
University of Liverpool
S. J. Salter
University of Sheffield
Gail Savage
George Washington University
Sally Sheard
University of Manchester
Richard J. Soderlund
Illinois State University
John Springhall
University of Ulster at Coleraine
Brian Stanley
Trinity College, Bristol
Paul Sturges
Loughborough University
Alan M. Suggate
University of Durham

Donald Sutherland
University of Maryland
Michael Tadman
University of Liverpool
David Thistlewood
University of Liverpool
Maria Todorova
University of Florida
Barrie Trinder
The Ironbridge Institute
Geoffrey Tucker
Wirral Metropolitan College
Geoffrey Tweedale
University of Sheffield
Pamela J. Walker
Carleton University, Ottawa
Joel H. Wiener
City University of New York
R. I. Woods
University of Liverpool
Robert J. Young
University of West Chester, Pennsylvania
Madeline C. Zilfi
University of Maryland

Acknowledgements

We would like to thank Richard Evans for his sage advice on the headword list in the planning stages of this book. At Blackwells, Alyn Shipton and Jason Pearce have provided technical and other guidance in efficient, patient and helpful manner. Most of all, however, we wish to express our gratitude to Martha Kanya-Forstner for her valued assistance at a late and hectic stage in checking many obscure facts and dates connected with the entries.

John Belchem and Richard Price

Introduction

———◆———

This dictionary of nineteenth-century world history is intended to provide a handy guide for the general reader who needs a quick reference to some of the most common themes, events and personalities of that age. It serves as a first point of enquiry for all aspects of political, diplomatic, military, social and economic history, and provides overviews of the artistic and cultural history of the period. It does not pretend to be comprehensive, if only because we know more about the nineteenth century than any previous century and our knowledge continues to expand at an alarming rate. Interest in the nineteenth century, an age of remarkable transformation, reflects the nearness of the period to our own: still close in time, the nineteenth century initiated and bequeathed much that is familiar in the modern-day world.

If we were to be transported to the beginning of the nineteenth century, however, the world about us would look entirely unfamiliar. The ways people thought, dressed, lived would be strange and alien; they moved on foot or in horse-drawn carriages; they dwelt, in the main, in small settlements and were closer to the land; their loyalties were to families, tribes, local communities. Monarchs and central governments – where they existed – were distant bodies, playing little role in the day-to-day lives of ordinary people. Queen Victoria, the most venerable of nineteenth-century monarchs, scarcely registered with the people of rural Oxfordshire, hardly the most remote part of the empire, until the 1880s, by which time her Golden Jubilee was approaching. At about the same time, Italian peasants were only just beginning to understand that *Italia* referred to their country rather than to the wife of their king. And only in the last part of the century did the idea of *France* replace the sense of regional belonging for most French peasants. Ironically, these traditional local identities often withstood the shock of displacement: much of the migration of the nineteenth century, whether from countryside to town or across the seas to new lands, took place within chains and networks which enabled newcomers to settle and adjust alongside earlier arrivals from their own village, locality or region. These examples point to the different rates of change within the century. Until the latter third or so of the century, there was much that would have been familiar to men and women of an earlier age. But there was much also that would have been unfamiliar, and contemporaries of the early nineteenth century were acutely conscious – as their fascination for statistics evinced – that they were living through a period of bewildering change. The pace of change was rapid and exponential, evident in every sphere of activity from population growth to changes in the nature of scientific knowledge and research. When the century opened, Europe was already in flux, jolted into change by the industrial revolution and the French Revolution. By 1900, these 'dual revolutions', to use Eric Hobsbawm's memorable phrase, had swept inexorably across the globe, rendering the world very different from what it had been a few decades before.

In itself, the industrial revolution was not particularly cataclysmic or dramatic: in the 1840s over 75 per cent of manufacturing in Britain, the first industrial nation, remained in unmodernized industries, little affected by the use of steam power. However, the industrial revolution marked an epochal change, initiating the ongoing process of economic growth that was to transform the Western world, undermining in the process Britain's industrial pre-eminence as new industrial nations (Germany, the United States, Japan and others) applied the latest technology and mass-production systems. Unlike the experience in earlier historical periods, economic growth in the nineteenth century proved cumulative and self-sustaining, enabling a decisive break with 'traditional' or 'pre-industrial' patterns of behaviour. Thus, population was able to break loose from the material constraints – the 'homeostatic pre-industrial demographic system' – which had previously held it in check. As rising numbers no longer precluded a secular rise in prosperity, population increased unchecked – birth control was not to become common until the twentieth century. With the growth in population, the locus of economic growth shifted from agriculture to industry, prompting a fundamental change in attitudes, beliefs and culture.

At the basic material level, the people's well-being, previously in the hands of God and the weather, came to depend on the fluctuations of the industrial trade cycle. Here, as in several other respects, the revolutions of 1848 marked the watershed. Famine prices and high unemployment throughout Europe led to the last major outburst of 'pre-industrial protest', riots provoked by catastrophic disaster, by poverty in the midst of scarcity and dearth. Britain, however, escaped such disorder. In this industrial economy, material well-being was determined by the trade cycle, the worst downturn of which had occurred a few years earlier when poverty had prevailed in the midst of unparalleled abundance and glutted overstocked markets. In this new and bewildering form, distress was socially divisive, widening the gap between rich and poor, the 'two nations', vexing the consciences of Christian philanthropists.

As the material facts of life seemed no longer attributable to fate or a supernatural being, religious belief withered. The Western world continued to think of itself as religious, an image reinforced by its missionary zeal elsewhere in the world, but faith diminished. Cyclical fluctuations notwithstanding, industrialization heralded man's victory in the age-old contest with nature. It was now possible to dream of controlling the forces of nature, of conquering the vast distances that separated the parts of the world and of exploiting and manipulating the resources of the earth. The opening of the western parts of the United States, and the exploration of the interior of Africa, were enormously disruptive for the indigenous inhabitants and were achieved with a full measure of force and rapine, but they were also standing examples of the power that could now be deployed to do things that had been impossible before.

Indeed, there was a strong sense that material progress was an unending prospect, despite the gloomy tenor of the 'dismal' science of political economy. The enormous increases in economic production came to be regarded as the governing condition of economic life, the register of the 'progress of the nation', banishing the devastating experiences of famine and decay that had dominated earlier centuries. Naturally, the blessings of this enhanced materialism were neither unqualified nor unquestioned. The pursuit of material wealth was accompanied by growing criticism of its inequitable distribution, its ecological cost and its aesthetic and cultural consequences, arguments which were to shape twentieth-century debate.

In politics the legacy is no less ambivalent. For example, the nineteenth century bequeathed both 'liberal' nationalism and 'right-wing' patriotism. Having been stirred by impact with the French Revolution, nationalist aspirations gained intellectual respectability and political weight in the early nineteenth century. Adopted by the intelligentsia, the demand for self-determination was reinforced by the hasty invention of national tradition, by the construction of a distinct cultural or 'ethnic' identity (and history), usually on the basis of language. Like the liberals, nationalists looked to redraw the map, to banish absolutism and dynastic boundaries, but linguistic culturalism lacked politico-geographical precision, serving to provoke much subsequent conflict. As such, nationalism was increasingly open to appropriation by the right, 'patriots' who stood forward to defend not only the territorial integrity of the *patrie*, but also its ethnic purity, a political misapplication of the new scientific racialism. But internationalism, very much a minority creed, also acquired its culture and tradition in the nineteenth century, with such festivals and icons as May Day and the red flag.

The political map of the world as it currently exists was both prefigured and created in the nineteenth century. Several changes – most notably the unification of Germany and Italy in the 1860s and 1870s – owed as much to political pragmatism as to nationalist ideology. The modern version of the United States may be said to have been created only with the victory of the north over the south in the Civil War of 1862–5 – a war, incidentally, that has some claims to be the first of the modern wars at least in the extent of its slaughter and destruction. Similarly, the creation of independent South American countries in the 1820s from the decaying Spanish Empire was a product of localist tensions prevailing over the more romantic notions of a wider Central and South American unity. These revolts are also noteworthy as being the first examples of internal nationalist revolution against European domination.

Independent Latin America apart, nationalism was normally manifested in the world beyond Europe through formal empire and imperial domination. After their Civil War, the United States set about subduing the large political federations of the native-American Indians in the west and south-west. This was the period of the 'Wild West', romanticized beyond recognition by twentieth-century Hollywood, but now being rewritten by historians in terms other than the relentless and natural expansion of the frontier.

The interior of the United States had been penetrated by Europeans since the sixteenth century, but the African and Asian continents (with the significant exception of India) had previously been only peripherally exposed to European politics. Although knowledge of exotic cultures was a feature of eighteenth-century Europe, it was not until the next century that a full exploration and intervention occurred to disrupt indigenous political entities of which Europeans were generally only dimly aware. Following the Crimean War, for example, Russian military expansion pressed east across the vast reaches of Siberia into Asia proper and south towards India: between 1868 and 1873 the huge independent khanates of Khokand, Samarkand, Khiva and Bokhara were absorbed. Similarly, the great empires of western and central Africa, with their sophisticated political forms, were wrenched apart under the combined assault of trade, the Bible and the flag, European imports made effective by the machine-gun. The European powers then proceeded to redraw the political boundaries of the continent at the Berlin Conference of 1884, bequeathing a troublesome legacy for the independent states of present-day Africa.

If imperialism – to which we shall return – was the major theme of world international relations, democracy, or rather manhood suffrage, was its equivalent in domestic politics. Economic and social change led to political tensions, as evinced by the linguistic confusion as the old social vocabulary of ranks, orders and estates gave way to a new language of class. This was a time of intense political debate about fundamental issues: the boundaries of the political nation and the principles of inclusion and exclusion; the respective responsibilities of the individual and the state; the structural parameters of political authority; and the mechanisms to facilitate political change. Much of the debate was gender-exclusive, since politics itself was generally defined as a male 'public' sphere, out of bounds for women, whose proper role remained at home, the 'private' sphere celebrated in the new ideology of domesticity. By the end of the century, however, these 'separate spheres' were under fierce attack from a variety of feminist (and other radical) positions. In these and other areas the nineteenth century established the discourse of debate which has continued to shape present-day political argument.

At the time, of course, the level and nature of political debate varied across the globe, but there was a certain internationalization of politics that flowed from European domination. By the end of the century, ideals of (male) democracy were being widely discussed in the non-Western world, either as a path to modernization (as in China) or as an embarrassment to the imperialists, turning the words of the West against its political domination (as in India and west Africa).

The growing universality of political themes illustrates a further distinctive feature of the nineteenth century: the powerful pull of integrative forces. The world grew smaller, intellectually and physically, as knowledge increased of the scientific and physical processes that underlay nature, drawing its component parts tighter together in increasing interdependence. The transport revolution is one obvious example of this. Throughout the century distances shrank: the voyage across the Atlantic fell from a matter of weeks to a matter of days as steam replaced sail. Transatlantic messages could be sent almost instantly from the 1860s by undersea cable, which by the end of the century covered the globe. Rail drastically reduced the time and effort expended on internal travel, making London and Edinburgh, Paris and Marseilles, accessible within the day. The east and west coasts of the United States were joined by the first cross-continental railway, constructed between 1862 and 1869, a development which began the real opening of the west. At a more prosaic level, the introduction of trains to seaside resorts in Britain in the 1860s and the invention of an efficient bicycle in the 1880s effected a veritable revolution in leisure-time possibilities for ordinary people. Such gains apart, improved transport tended to accentuate the division between social classes, adding a geographical dimension, absent in the pre-industrial city, to social segregation. The tram confirmed the new topography, enabling the more fortunate citizens (including the burgeoning numbers of clerical and white-collar workers) to move out to suburbs, while the poor were left trapped in inner-city areas, rapidly 'made down' into slums. The shortening of the lines of communication around the globe was mainly a European and North American phenomenon. The stately caravans of Arabia, central Asia and Africa continued to dominate inland transportation: they were little affected by the railroads that began to push into their interiors from the 1890s – the Trans-Siberian railway was begun in 1891 and not completed until 1916. But there were few, if any, parts of the world that remained untouched by this Eurocentric development.

This brings us back to the relationship between imperial and local powers and cultures. Global interdependence was integral to the political and economic domination of European civilizations, as their imperial power reached out from metropolitan Europe to the farthest corners of the world. The exact nature of this relationship, however, was a complex process of interaction and reciprocity between the dominant and subordinate groups. Historians of those parts of the world that were under European rule now seek to reconstruct an indigenous past, a history separate from European premises, perspectives and prejudices, but this is a difficult historiographical project. The very concepts that inform the metanarratives of history continue to flow from European paradigms. Indian history is a case in point: dominated by ex-government officials until independence, it continues to be written within frameworks such as state formation and modernization. These processes, although privileged in European historiography, are not necessarily appropriate for an understanding of the indigenous Indian dynamic (rather than that of British India) in the history of the Indian subcontinent. But exactly what other organizing principles can provide the narrative framework for these histories is still a question that few historians have ventured to approach. Thus, even the writing of the histories of non-Western peoples in the post-colonial era bears the discursive legacies of that past.

The distorting lens of the conqueror extends to the invention of history itself. It has recently been argued that the story of Maori origins owed more to the inventions of anthropologists that, for their own reasons, Maoris chose not to challenge, than it did to historical fact. Similarly, in east Africa, the impact of European presence on African structures included the actual invention of the notion of the 'tribe'. Viewed from the other end, imperialism penetrated deep into the culture of the imperial nation, not least through hastily invented traditions in national celebration of imperial grandeur, festivities that attracted considerable popular support.

It is our hope, then, that this dictionary will convey to the reader some sense of the complex nature of the changing world of the nineteenth century. Our own presumptions have shaped our choice and selection of entries, although each contributor has been free to write the entry as she or he saw fit. We have tried to make this dictionary accessible to the general reader and to balance three considerations that reflect the current realities of historical knowledge and enquiry. First, the well-established themes, topics and personalities continue to be represented. Here there is a distinct European and male bias in accordance with the dominant factors projected at the time, a historical legacy unchallenged by traditional historiography, with its narrow focus on political events and personalities. We have chosen not to ignore this reality: a book designed for the general reader must include the kinds of references that she or he will still most frequently encounter. However, in the second place, we have tried to reflect recent changes in the historiography of the period. The shift in emphasis from high politics towards the social processes of history has resulted in a more inclusive scholarship. The history of women, for example, is proving an immensely innovative and fertile field of enquiry, joining such venerable partners as economic and social history as a distinct historical subdiscipline. We have felt it important that these kinds of changes be echoed in this dictionary, so we have tried to balance the more traditional topics with those that now occupy the attention of the specialist historian. Thus, for example, we have quite deliberately not included every nineteenth-century president of the United States in order to make room for prominent African-American and native-American figures. We have also restricted most biographical entries to 150 words – even for the most important Western politician – so that we could maximize our inclusive range. A further historiographical development – which we referred to earlier in a slightly different context – is reflected in our third consideration: the effort to ensure a fair representation of the world beyond Europe. We do not claim to have escaped the ethnocentrism of European-based history writing, and the majority of entries refer to the European–North American axis. But we have tried to include themes, topics and persons important to the internal history of non-Western countries as well as those which relate to the imperial experience.

The use of the dictionary is quite straightforward, but certain features demand explanation. The first concerns periodization. There are more than a few nineteenth centuries; many historians treat 1789 (the French Revolution) or 1815 (the final defeat of Napoleon) as its beginning and 1914 (the outbreak of the First World War) as its end, although others have found it ending in the 1880s. There could be endless debate about which dates are most appropriate, but we have chosen to stick quite closely to the calendar dates of 1800 and 1900 because this dictionary is preceded by one on the eighteenth century and followed by one on the twentieth century. Persons who lived in both centuries have been included if their main work occurred in the nineteenth century, and excluded if they are mainly eighteenth-century or twentieth-century figures. Thus, neither Tom Paine nor Lloyd George features in our dictionary, even though both lived in the nineteenth century, because we feel that, taking their lives and work as a whole, they are more (in the case of Paine) eighteenth-century or (in the case of Lloyd George) twentieth-century figures. But, by the same token, Napoleon and Joseph Chamberlain are included in our entries. Naturally, individual contributors have been free to range beyond these dates when they felt it appropriate.

Our treatment of the cultural and literary themes of the period also demands explanation. The constraints of space did not allow us to include all the individual painters, musicians, writers and other cultural figures who warranted inclusion; nor would it permit us properly to treat the many artistic themes and movements that flowed through the century. But to leave the dictionary with no representation of the cultural history of the nineteenth century (and it was a century when culture flowered) would have been equally inappropriate. Thus, we decided to include large entries on the cultural disciplines – architecture, music, painting, the novel, sculpture and so on – and on some movements that crossed disciplines like romanticism. It should also be noted that those fields are well served by established reference books and thus this dictionary could most usefully provide a broad overview and a guide to further enquiry.

The organization of the entries is broadly consistent. The first sentence is generally definitional except where it is considered unnecessary; cross references are in small capitals, with the letter under which the entry is alphabetized a large capital; in most cases there are references for further reading for all entries over 300 words and selected references for those under 300 words. Word and spelling usage has followed the conventions in the particular field – thus, the African entries use the indigenous rather than the Anglicized spellings, and similarly with the Asian entries. But we have Anglicized the names of European monarchs. The dating of the Russian entries follows the Gregorian calendar. Since individual entries could not be included for every significant figure of the nineteenth century, an index of people has been provided as an alternative route into biographical information.

John Belchem
University of Liverpool

Richard Price
University of Maryland

A

Abbas Hilmi II (*b* Alexandria, 14 July 1874; *d* Geneva, 20 December 1944)   Khedive of Egypt (1892–1914). He succeeded his father, MUHAMMAD TAWFIQ PASHA, in 1892, ten years after the start of the British occupation. Unlike his submissive father, Abbas used the palace to rally nationalist sentiment. His attempt to appoint a prime minister without consulting Britain resulted in a humiliating scolding that compelled him to forgo open confrontation, but raised his stock among Egyptians. He was a generous patron of Egypt's new literati, many of whom published their first anti-British tracts with his support. On a visit to Istanbul in 1914 he made no secret of his sympathy for the YOUNG TURKS' anti-British position. In December 1914 Britain used the opportunity of his absence to declare Egypt a protectorate and Abbas deposed. Forbidden to return to Egypt, he spent his last years in Switzerland.

P. J. Vatikiotis, *The History of Egypt from Muhammad Ali to Mubarak* (Baltimore, 1986).

MADELINE C. ZILFI

Abd al-Qadir, amir (*b* Guetna, Algeria, 6 September 1808; *d* Damascus, 26 May 1883)   Leader of the Qadiriyya religious brotherhood and Algerian resistance hero. Although Algeria was technically a province of the Ottoman Empire, native elements organized around the Qadiriyya order and, led by Abd al-Qadir, offered the only sustained resistance to French colonization efforts. Unlike movements elsewhere in Africa, the Qadiriyya under Abd al-Qadir did not make Messianic claims. Abd al-Qadir's successes against vastly superior European arms led the French to employ increasingly brutal methods in order to put down the revolt and salvage their invasion. In 1847, pressed by the French and an assortment of local enemies, Abd al-Qadir surrendered to the

French. Imprisoned in France for five years, he settled in Damascus, where he added to his already considerable reputation by rescuing thousands of Christians during the Druse-Maronite disturbances of 1860.

MADELINE C. ZILFI

abolitionism The movement for the emancipation of American slaves, abolitionism can be divided chronologically into two main divisions. Old-school abolitionism was characterized by an emphasis on gradual emancipation, best typified by the American Convention for Promoting the Abolition of Slavery, founded in the 1790s. Its favourite project was the American Colonization Society, (1816), which sought to end slavery by sending African-Americans to Africa. Though it attracted the support of Henry Clay, almost all free African-Americans rejected the assumption that they could live and find equality only among their own race. In 1831 Nat TURNER led a sensational slave revolt in Southampton, Virginia, slaughtering fifty-seven whites and sending shock waves throughout the south. Turner was captured and hanged, and as the south closed ranks around the central institution of its society, northern abolitionists realized the futility of the gradualist approach.

Informed by religious revivals of the time which held that salvation was a matter of personal choice, the resulting new-school abolitionism rejected colonization and gradualism. More uncompromising and radical, this approach was best typified by the American Anti-slavery Society (founded in 1833 by William Lloyd GARRISON) and its demands for the immediate abolition of slavery.

The abolitionist movement split in 1840. Garrison believed that abolitionists should rely on moral suasion and join forces with other reform movements, including women's rights, while his opponents urged concentration on the single issue of slavery, using political means when necessary. This latter branch of the movement found political expression in the LIBERTY PARTY and later in the radical wing of the Republican Party. Impeded by some northern businessmen who believed that abolitionist agitation disrupted trade with the south and by an often indifferent northern public, abolitionist agitation was partially rewarded when Abraham Lincoln issued his EMANCIPATION PROCLAMATION in 1863.

See also SLAVERY (UNITED STATES).

Gerald Sorin, *Abolitionism: A New Perspective* (New York, 1972).

KEVIN MURPHY

abortion In nineteenth century BIRTH CONTROL debates abortion figured prominently, but the extent to which it contributed to declining levels of fertility is difficult to determine, since the practice was usually illegal and therefore screened from public enquiry. For a woman, abortion represented some means of control over her own body. However, illegality and lack of medical guidance concerning abortion techniques and abortifacients meant that women ran extraordinary risks if they wished to regulate their own fertility. A number of quack options were available. Abortion could be attempted by taking mineral- or metal-based poisons, the quantity of which would hopefully be enough to kill the foetus but not the mother. Lead pills, nitrobenzene and arsenic, perhaps only available at a local level, were used for their toxic impact upon the blood. Irritation of the bowels often induced contractions: the result of ingesting plant decoctions such as ergot of rye, savin, squills, slippery elm or various iron compounds. Household implements such as hat-pins, needles and pencils would also be used. Knowledge of available methods was part of traditional folklore and information networks, was passed on by abortionists, or became increasingly popular through thinly veiled newspaper advertisements and chemists.

Oral evidence suggests that abortion was not the cultural norm throughout non-industrial regions. The economic advantages of having a large family persisted well into the twentieth century, and in some cases women derived a strong social status from having large numbers of children, especially sons. In western Europe and the urban areas of north-eastern America, however, the socio-economic forces prevalent later in the century made a smaller family preferable. All artificial means of birth control were officially castigated by the medical profession until the last third of the century. However, the fact that the middle classes not only had access to superior medical advice, but could also afford mechanical contraceptives, has led recent commentators to suggest that abortion, in Britain at least, was largely a working-class practice. For America, it was considered to be an upper- and middle-class phenomenon, related to the growth of materialism and restricted to the Protestant population.

Angus McLaren, *Birth Control in Nineteenth Century England* (London, 1978).

GRAHAM MOONEY

Act of Union, Irish (1801) The Irish Act of Union abolished the Irish parliament and united the kingdoms of Great Britain and Ireland, giving Ireland generous representation at Westminster, and (eventually) establishing free trade between the two countries. Since 1782 the Irish parliament had enjoyed considerable independence from Britain. However, in the 1790s Britain, at war with revolutionary France, was alarmed at instability in Ireland, where the unrepresentative, Anglican parliament was challenged by the United Irishmen, demanding an Irish republic. Rebellion by United Irishmen in 1798 and French landings there determined Britain to force union on an initially reluctant Irish parliament which finally accepted, largely because of the union's anticipated benefits. The union was besmirched less by corruption than by the failure to carry CATHOLIC EMANCIPATION, the promise of which had secured Catholic acquiescence. The union lasted until 1921 and was as much an attack on the Protestant ascendancy as on the 'Irish nation'.

See also IRISH UNIONISM.

G. C. Bolton, *The Passing of the Irish Act of Union* (London, 1966).

PATRICK BUCKLAND

Adams, John Quincy (*b* Braintree, Massachusetts, 11 July 1767; *d* Washington, DC, 23 February 1848)   President of the United States (1825–9) and leading American diplomat of the early nineteenth century. He was one of the first to think of America as a continental empire. Early in his career he led the delegation that negotiated the TREATY OF GHENT (1814) which ended the War of 1812 between Great Britain and the United States. As secretary of state during the Monroe administration, he was instrumental in the American acquisition of Florida (Adams-Onis Treaty, 1819). In 1823 he formulated the MONROE DOCTRINE, which formed the basis for American foreign policy for the rest of the nineteenth century. Elected president by the House of Representatives after the election of 1824 failed to produce the necessary electoral majority, Adams served one frustrating term as president because his opponents controlled Congress. He then returned to Washington in 1831 as a congressman, where he spent much of his later career battling the 'gag rule' (1836–44) imposed on abolitionist petitions.

Samuel Flagg Bemis, *John Quincy Adams and the Foundations of American Foreign Policy* (New York, 1949).

ALICE E. REAGAN

Addams, Jane (*b* Cedarville, Illinois, 6 September 1860; *d* Chicago, 21 May 1935)   American welfare reformer and pacifist. She graduated from Rockford Female Seminary in 1881, and like many other members of this first generation of college-educated women, spent nearly a decade wondering how to satisfy her ambition. In 1889 she and her friend Ellen Gates Starr (1859–1940) founded Hull House, soon to become the world's most famous social settlement. Located in a working-class neighbourhood in Chicago, this residence for middle-class women and men was intended to bridge the deepening chasm between America's rich and poor. Over time Addams and her settlement colleagues translated that purpose into numerous, creative social-welfare intiatives, which catapulted her to national leadership of movements for child welfare, industrial regulation and immigrant protection. A prolific author as well as an activist, Addams was awarded a Nobel Peace prize in 1931.

Allen Davis, *American Heroine* (New York, 1973).

ROBYN MUNCY

Addington, Henry, first Viscount Sidmouth (*b* London, 30 May 1757; *d* Richmond, 15 February 1844)   English statesman and Tory prime minister. An uninspiring placeman who rose to prominence through close friendship with William Pitt (1759–1806), and then acquired the premiership himself (1801–4) when the king and the Commons, wary of Pitt's aloofness, put their trust in his very mediocrity. His rigid Tory principles were later applied to the point of infamy when he served as home secretary during the troubled years of 1812–22. While refusing to intervene to alleviate economic distress – he wrote an ode to Adam Smith (1723–90) eulogizing *laissez-faire* – he was ruthless in deploying the resources of the state, through the mechanism of 'alarm', to crush the radical challenge, a policy of repression which culminated in the SIX ACTS. He was unswerving in his Toryism, and his last speech in the Lords was against Catholic emancipation and his last vote against the Reform Bill of 1832.

Philip Ziegler, *Addington* (London, 1965).

JOHN BELCHEM

Adler, Victor (*b* Prague, 24 June 1852; *d* Vienna, 11 November 1918) Founding father of Austrian social democracy. He was born into a middle-class Jewish family in Bohemia and moved to Vienna as a child. He studied medicine at Vienna University and became involved in the politics of the Austrian labour movement. His newspaper *Gleichheit* (Equality) campaigned for the formation of a united mass party which would bring together the moderate reformists and Marxist radicals in the movement, and this was achieved with the formation of the Austrian Social Democratic Workers' Party (SDAP) at the Hainfeld 'Unity' Conference of 1888–9. This early compromise was reflected in the development of a distinctive 'Austro-Marxist' school of politics and ideology which occupied a place between Bolshevism and reformist social democracy. As party leader Adler was instrumental in preserving party unity in the face of left-wing opposition after the outbreak of war in 1914. He joined the Austrian government in October 1918 but died shortly afterwards, before the declaration of the first Austrian republic.

TIMOTHY KIRK

Adowa, Battle of (1 March 1896)   The Battle of Adowa marked the defeat of Italy by the forces of the emperor MENELIK II of ETHIOPIA during the late-nineteenth-century SCRAMBLE FOR AFRICA. Following the Berlin Conference (1884–5) – and with British consent – the Italians occupied the Ethiopian territory of Massawa in February 1885, later seizing the neighbouring Red Sea coast, advancing inland and instituting an arms blockade. Defeated by the Ethiopian emperor Yohannes IV (c.1839–89) at Dongali in January 1887, the Italians successfully counter-attacked, occupying Asmara, later establishing (1890) the Red Sea colony of Eritrea. Recognizing Italian claims to Eritrea in return for acknowledgement of his imperial Ethiopian sovereignty, Menelik concluded the Italo-Ethiopian Treaty of Wichale (May 1889). Treaty agreements likewise permitted Ethiopian access to French and Russian arms transmitted through territory claimed by the Italians. Treaty ambiguities and conflicts in the Amharic and Italian texts, however, later led to disputes, in the wake of which the Italians attacked the Ethiopians at Adowa, in Ethiopia. The Italians sued for peace on 9 April 1896.

Harold G. Marcus, *The Life and Times of Menelik II: Ethiopia 1844–1913* (Oxford, 1975).

B. MARIE PERINBAM

advertising   Providing information about merits claimed for various products and services, from being something of a novelty, began to gain acceptance as a commercial weapon that, in an age of emerging mass production, could regulate consumer demand. Traditional forms of advertising conducted by sandwich-board men, wall posters or by street sellers in open-air markets gradually became obsolete in Britain, following the abolition of advertising (1837), stamp (1855) and paper (1861) duties on newspapers. Most advertisements appeared initially in newspapers and pictorial magazines, like the *Illustrated London News* (established 1844), and were aimed at middle-class audiences. A sample of some 3,500 advertisements taken from selected English newspapers at fifteen-year intervals from 1810 to 1855 showed the most important category to be auctioneers (with 16 per cent of the total), followed by retailers (with 13.6 per cent), legal and public notices (with 11.7 per cent) and situations vacant, property sales and publications (over 7 per cent each). Surprisingly, considering the volume of criticism they attracted, medical advertisers accounted for only 6.5 per cent of the total.

The British advertising industry was transformed beyond recognition from 1851 to 1914, as fully modern American-style agencies replaced the early Victorian space brokerages and advertising agents. Consumer choice began to expand for the working class, initially limited to advertisements for such utilitarian products as washing and cleaning fluids, or food additives such as sauces, relishes and meat extracts. By the 1880s rising real incomes were reflected in advertisements for sets of furniture offered on credit terms, ready-to-wear clothes for men and paper patterns and sewing-machines (*see* SEWING-MACHINE) for women. Soap manufacturers, like Pears, and patent medicine vendors, like Beechams, were the heaviest advertisers of the 1890s.

T. R. Nevett, *Advertising in Britain: A History* (London, 1982).
Thomas Richards, *The Commodity Culture of Victorian England: Advertising and Spectacle, 1851–1914* (London, 1991).

JOHN SPRINGHALL

aestheticism As a term aestheticism did not become current in English until the mid nineteenth century, while its European equivalents have only slightly longer histories. It denotes a belief in the self-sufficiency of art, founded on the perception of sensuous perfection independent of moral, political or other non-aesthetic considerations. In cruder versions aestheticism appeared under such slogans as 'l'art pour l'art' or 'art for art's sake'.

Aestheticism as a doctrine had its roots in German philosophy at the end of the eighteenth century and the beginning of the nineteenth century. Here, and especially in the philosophy of Kant (1724–1804), the aesthetic (a term only recently coined in German from a Greek root) was advanced as an area of value where the beautiful and the non-practical were supreme. Equally, Schelling (1775–1854) insisted upon the formal distinctiveness of the art work. This emphasis upon the separately beautiful, and its opposition to the merely practical or utilitarian, was to mark aesthetic theory throughout the nineteenth century. Furthermore, this opposition implicated aestheticism in debates, especially in France and England, about the social value of art and the relationship of the beautiful to the useful.

In France it is possible to trace a line of aestheticism, in artistic practice as well as in theory, from the early nineteenth century onwards. German aesthetic ideas were diffused by such writers as Madame de Staël (1766–1817); but it was Gautier (1811–72) who, in the preface to *Mademoiselle de Maupin* (1835), first gave polemical expression to some distinctive themes of aestheticism by denying any useful value to art. The aesthetic practice of the American writer Edgar Allan Poe (1809–49), in the 1830s and 1840s, was also influential on French writing; Poe was perceived as subordinating all other considerations to the supreme aesthetic one of formal perfection. There is thereafter a clear line, especially in poetry, in which the aesthetic was perceived as the privileged means of apprehending value; from Baudelaire (1821–67) through Mallarmé (1842–98), Verlaine (1844–96) and Rimbaud (1854–91) poetry was understood as at once an escape from the world of actuality and an implicit critique of it. Aestheticism in this respect can be considered a forerunner of characteristic twentieth-century notions of the artistic avant-garde, in which artistic distinctiveness is achieved by a combination of criticism of dominant bourgeois values and an artistic practice marked by self-conscious formal experiment and, often, difficulty.

In England aestheticism gained most prominence, and some notoriety, in the aesthetic movement of the 1880s and 1890s, though this movement had antecedents going back to the English romantics. There is a line of poetry, for example, which runs from Keats (1795–1821) in the 1810s and 1820s, through the early poetry of Tennyson (1809–92), and the poetry of Pre-Raphaelitism, especially MORRIS, in which the vividly imagined world of art was counterposed to the valuelessness of the actual and the everyday. Equally, in the art criticism of John RUSKIN the beautiful was mobilized as a category against the deadening actuality of contemporary industrial society. More particularly, in the writing of Walter Pater (1839–94) aestheticism received its finest and most influential statement. In *The Renaissance* (1873), for example, aestheticism emerged not only as a doctrine about art but almost as an ethical position as well, in which the value of beautifully formed sensory perception became supreme. Pater thus concluded by urging the sensitive individual to 'burn always with this hard gemlike flame'. Pater influenced a range of writers late in the century, including Wilde (1854–1900), Dowson (1867–1900), Lionel Johnson (1867–1902), Symons (1865–1945), the early W. B. Yeats (1865–1939) and George Moore (1852–1933). Wilde's brilliant aphorisms captured the spirit of late-nineteenth-century aestheticism. When he wrote 'There is no such thing as a moral or an immoral book. Books are well written or badly written', or 'All art is quite useless' or 'Art never expresses anything but itself', he gave extreme expression to views that were a development of long-standing opinions about art and were widely shared – though perhaps more widely ridiculed or condemned.

In the writings of Oscar Wilde aestheticism could appear like dandyism; in the English poets of the 1890s, influenced by French poetic models as much as English ones, it emerged as fine, sophisticated but fugitive lyrical poetry. In all cases aestheticism took its stand on the self-justifying value of the beautiful against the moral or didactic requirements of contemporary bourgeois society. But only in the aesthetic reflections of William Morris, following those of John Ruskin, did this commitment to the beautiful become a militant aesthetic and finally a political crusade against the ugliness and exploitation of late-nineteenth-century English society.

See also ARTS AND CRAFTS MOVEMENT.

R. V. Johnson, *Aestheticism* (London, 1969).

SIMON DENTITH

Afghanistan Traditionally Afghanistan has been a loosely defined, isolated and usually unstable political unit organized and administered along tribal lines. The reach of the national government, whether from Kandahar or Kabul, was limited by tribal and clan loyalties that contributed repeatedly to the traditional instability of the region. Prior to the mid nineteenth century, the region rarely influenced world history, and then it was only due to the intensification of Anglo-Russian rivalries as the century progressed. Russian expansion into the Merv region and simultaneous British expansion in the Punjab gave it a diplomatic and strategic significance. Eventually it was these neighbours, in cooperation with Persia (Iran), which defined the territorial limits of Afghanistan in a series of international agreements. The understanding behind them was a need to preserve Afghanistan as a buffer state between the Russian Empire and British possessions in India. British claims to the Sisten region defined Afghanistan's western border in 1872; the Anglo-Russian Agreement of 1873 by and large defined the northern border at the Oxus River; and the Treaty of Gandamak, in 1879, defined the border of southern Afghanistan.

Much of the modern history of Afghanistan has been bound up with the fortunes of the Durrani clan, which has provided most of its rulers since the eighteenth century, and the Pushtun people which comprises approximately half the population. In a multi-ethnic and multilingual population, which includes large Uzbek, Tadjik and Turkoman units, the Pushtun dominate. Although virtually the entire population adhered to Islam, there were additional lines of cleavage based on Sunni–Shiah rivalries and a long history of Sunni domination.

See also DOST MOHAMMED, SHER ALI.

Suhash Chakravarty, *From Kyber to Oxus* (Delhi, 1976).

ROBERT J. YOUNG

Africa, Scramble for In the nineteenth century Africa was partitioned between seven European powers, England, France, Germany, Italy, Belgium, Portugal and Spain. Emerging from a series of long-standing and complex relationships, African–European political and economic pressures date back to as early as the fifteenth century, when the Portuguese first sailed down the western coast of Africa. Given this long history, no one explanation for the scramble for Africa will therefore suffice; and in both Africa and Europe causations, explanations, justifications and rationalizations can be found along the full length of the historiographical spectrum.

Among the explanations from the European perspective, however, was the competition (hence 'scramble') between the seven European states for their political entitlement – as they perceived it in the 'Age of Empire' and 'New Imperialism' – to the control of African territories, including peoples, raw materials, markets and investment opportunities. To this extent most European states had the support of domestic interest-groups including merchants, military and missionary lobbies, as well as scientific and humanitarian associations. From the African perspective, an important factor was the creation of dependent African and Afro-European communities and political economies competing for European commerce. Shifting European diplomatic relations, together with the late-nineteenth-century European economic decline, combined to create instabilities in these increasingly dependent African political economies. Anticipating business and strategic losses in several of their African commercial and political enclaves – for example Egypt (an autonomous province of the Ottoman Empire), or in west or southern Africa – some western European governments and private interest-groups urged initiatives designed to protect existing and future business and politico-strategic interests.

Triggering the scramble – and subsequent partition – was King Leopold II (1835–1909) of Belgium, who had advised European powers to be on the look-out for spoils in outlying areas. Under the guise of an international organization (the International African Association), he initiated claims (1879) to a personal African 'empire' in the Congo basin (see INDEPENDENT CONGO STATE). Leopold's initiatives were followed by the unexpected French protectorate over TUNISIA (1881) and the British ocupation of EGYPT (1882), both designed, among other things, to protect European interests. Equally unexpected were German measures (1884) to acquire territory – in Namibia (German southwest Africa), Cameroon (German Kamerun), Togo (German Togoland) and ZANZIBAR – while in west Africa, British and French competition converged on control over the resources of the Niger river basin (see NIGERIA). Fearing that European conflict and competition in Africa could threaten the peace, thereby restricting future African opportunities, Bismarck, the German chancellor, convened the CONFERENCE OF BERLIN in December 1884.

Initially intended to control rather than to extend the scramble for Africa, the conference achieved limited objectives, only securing free trade and navigation rights along the Niger and Congo river basins. With respect to the latter, the sovereignty of Leopold's Congo Free State was recognized, in reality a misnomer as, in collusion with Belgian bankers and financiers, the king simply transformed the 'state' into a privately owned chartered company for rubber and ivory production. Terms and conditions restricting future claims to 'effective occupancy' were likewise established. Despite modest short-term goals, the conference, however, secured significant long-term gains by establishing a legal international framework for further action and the resolution of conflict in African–European affairs. Most importantly, given that these latter could ignite smouldering European conflicts, the conference integrated Africa into the structure of international law, with the exception of ETHIOPIA and LIBERIA which, never officially colonized, remained on the periphery of international relations throughout most of the nineteenth century. As a consequence, the scramble was thus more or less contained, if not always controlled, including the Anglo-French conflict threatening war at Fashoda in the Sudan, in 1898 (*see* FASHODA CRISIS). Although most of Africa had come under European control by 1903, territorial claims were not ratified until the Treaty of Lausanne (26 July 1923).

Although it affected the lives of millions of Africans, they were not consulted during the scramble and subsequent colonization of their continent. Ironically, during the scramble and wars of 'pacification' or conquest, many Africans provided support systems for European armies, merchant, missionaries, investors and scientific explorations. Many others, however, resisted for decades both before and after, and were partly responsible, in some instances, for delays in colonial policy settlements and implementations (*see* ALGERIA, 'UMAR IBN SAI'D TAL, ALMAMI SAMORI TURAY). Had the transportable Maxim gun, and the QUININE prophylactic against malaria not been developed, it is debatable whether Europeans could have been successful in their scramble and colonization of Africa.

Raymond Betts, *The Scramble for Africa* (Lexington, Mass., 1972).
John Lonsdale, 'The European Scramble and Conquest in African History', in R. Oliver and G. N. Sanderson (eds), *The Cambridge History of Africa*, vol. 6 (Cambridge, 1985), pp. 680–766.
Thomas Pakenham, *The Scramble for Africa 1876–1912* (New York, 1991).
B. MARIE PERINBAM

African-Americans During the nineteenth century the life of African-Americans underwent vast change. The African-American population expanded from 1,002,000 in 1800 to 7,760,000 by 1900. Most of these individuals were ex-slaves who lived in the south. Before the Civil War approximately a quarter of a million free African-Americans lived in the north and another quarter-million lived in the southern states. By 1860 approximately 4 million slaves lived in the south. The African-American population of the United States was the only slave population to reproduce itself in the western hemisphere during this period.

Regardless of where they lived, free African-Americans faced great discrimination in the ante-bellum period. In the north they lived in segregated housing and were often limited to certain occupations, such as barbers, fishermen or day labourers. Only Massachusetts conducted desegregated schools and permitted African-Americans to sit on juries. Only the most northern New England states permitted black suffrage before the war. Despite these difficulties, northern African-Americans formed their own churches (African Methodist Episcopal and Baptist), their own fraternal groups (such as the Masons) and self-help societies. Most free African-Americans in the north lived in urban areas, where there was safety in numbers. Many of their leaders, such as Frederick DOUGLASS, Martin Delany (1812–85) and Sojourner Truth (1777–1883) were vehement in their attacks on slavery, going further than white abolitionists in their calls for emancipation and equal rights (*see* ABOLITIONISM).

Southern free African-Americans also faced heavy discrimination, and like their northern counterparts, often lived in urban areas for safety. At the same time, however, many were skilled artisans who competed with white urban labour for jobs, causing much discontent. Some of these southern free African-Americans were mulattos, especially those in cities such as Charleston and New Orleans. In these areas the 'free people of colour' often owned some property and received educations from their white relatives. A few such individuals even owned slaves themselves. Whatever their status, free African-Americans in the south faced great scrutiny and lived under strict legal codes, for many whites feared they might incite discontent among the slaves. Slaves lived an even more controlled existence (*see* SLAVERY (UNITED STATES)).

Emancipation (1863) brought many changes for African-Americans in the south (*see* EMANCIPATION PROCLAMATION). Refusing to work under the old gang system of plantation labour, they negotiated a new system, sharecropping, where they split their crops with the white landowner. In the cash-poor south, however, many African-Americans soon fell victim to the crop-lien system where they borrowed money from planters or merchants at high rates of interest to pay for supplies before the crop was harvested and sold. Once they fell into this system, few ever got free of it. Although the federal government passed the Southern Homestead Act (1866) to provide cheap federal land for the ex-slaves, most could not afford it.

At the same time, southern African-Americans founded their own institutions, because they wanted autonomy from whites. Many joined the African Methodist Episcopal or Baptist churches when missionaries arrived from the north after the Civil War. They also founded their own schools and colleges, such as Hampton Institute, Howard University, Tuskegee Institute and Atlanta University, with the help of religious benefactors. African-American parents insisted that their children attend school, and husbands wanted wives to stay at home with the children, as they attempted to gain more control over their families. On some plantations families relocated their cabins away from white homes to escape prying eyes.

During the late nineteenth century African-Americans, regardless of location, still faced great prejudice. Although the fourteenth and fifteenth amendments to the constitution granted them the right to vote and other basic civil rights, African-Americans north and south continued to face housing and job discrimination. In the north they continued to hold low-paying jobs, and in the south most remained agricultural labourers. Only the tobacco industry employed many southern African-Americans. Southern African-Americans also faced growing white attacks on their civil and political rights.

Although the Civil Rights Act of 1875 outlawed segregation of public facilities such as transportation and restaurants, the supreme court declared the law unconstitutional in 1883. After this ruling, southern communities began to pass the first of the Jim Crow laws that created segregation in the south. By 1900 African-Americans had been reduced to second-class citizenship by these laws, which created separate streetcars, rest rooms, and drinking-fountains. In addition, southern states soon mounted an attack on African-American voting rights. In 1877 Georgia established a poll tax to make voting more difficult, and South Carolina followed during the 1880s with the confusing Eight-Box Law. After African-Americans voted for the populists in large numbers during the late 1880s and early 1890s, southern Democrats disenfranchised them with literacy tests and other such devices.

See also FREEDMEN'S BUREAU.

Ira Berlin, *Slaves without Masters: The Free Negro in the Antebellum South* (New York, 1974).
Leon Litwack, *North of Slavery: The Negro in the Free States, 1790–1860* (Chicago, 1961).
—— *Been in the Storm So Long: The Aftermath of Slavery* (New York, 1979).

ALICE E. REAGAN

Afrikaners Referring to twentieth-century descendants of South African whites of Dutch heritage, the term 'Afrikaner' has been applied more specifically since the turn of the century to those who speak Afrikaans, a Dutch-derived language. Non-white Afrikaans-speakers, many of whom are descendants of Afrikaner and non-white unions, are known as 'Coloureds'. Until the Anglo-Boer Wars (1880–1, 1899–1902), Afrikaners were known as 'Boers', the Dutch word for 'freeburghers', or farmers owning their own land. It was, roughly speaking, their Dutch ancestors who settled the CAPE COLONY in 1652 under the aegis of the Dutch East India Company. Afrikaner antecedents were likewise responsible for establishing the TRANSVAAL and ORANGE FREE STATE, two nineteenth-century Boer republics. They were later involved against the British in the ANGLO-BOER WARS, and joined the newly created Union of South Africa in 1910.

Gwendolen M. Carter and Patrick O'Meara (eds), *South Africa: The Continuing Crisis*, second edn (Bloomington, Ind., 1982).

George M. Frederickson, *White Supremacy: A Comparative Study in American and South African History* (New York, 1981).

Leonard M. Thompson, *The Political Mythology of Apartheid* (New Haven, Conn., 1985).

B. MARIE PERINBAM

Agassiz, Jean Louis Rodolphe (*b* Môtier, Switzerland, 28 May 1807; *d* Cambridge, Massáchusetts, 12 December 1873) Swiss pioneer in palaeontology and geology. Descended from a Huguenot family, he published a landmark five-volume work on fossil fishes (1833–44) which excited interest in the study of extinct life. He began exploring glaciers in the 1830s, while professor of natural history at the University of Neuchâtel. He experimentally proved that glaciers moved and that an ice age had existed over a vast area of the earth. Invited to lecture in Boston in 1846, Agassiz remained at Harvard for the rest of his life. He became known as a strong opponent of Darwin's theory of natural selection and as an innovative educator who introduced field-work as a component of natural-history education.

Edward Lurie, *Louis Agassiz: A Life in Science* (Chicago, 1960).

BARBARA KAPLAN

Agrarian League Founded in February 1893 in opposition to the trade-liberalization policies of Chancellor CAPRIVI, the Agrarian League was a right-wing pressure group for agrarian interests. It was led by Prussian *Junker* nobles (*see* JUNKERS) but had attracted a mass membership of 250,000 by 1900. It exercised influence through financial contributions to right-wing political parties and was a major force behind the introduction of higher tariffs on agricultural imports by Chancellor Bülow (1849–1929) in 1902.

S. R. Tirrell *German Agrarian Politics after Bismarck's Fall* (New York, 1951).

S. J. SALTER

agriculture European and North American agriculture was revolutionized during the nineteenth century. So too was farming in almost all other countries which came into Europe's commercial orbit. The key changes were: property relations, technology and transport and the rapid emergence of an international market.

Few pre-industrial cultivators had a concept of private property in land in the modern sense. The ENCLOSURE of open fields, and the elimination of feudal concepts of land tenure and of personal service owed to one's lord, a long-established process in Britain, gathered pace elsewhere in Europe. The social stratification of rural Britain into large landlords, their tenant farmers and landless wage-labourers was complete by mid-century, except in marginal upland areas. The French

Revolution was a powerful force for change in the lands of Napoleonic conquest as well as France itself, where the peasantry was established in control and ownership of the soil. In Prussia, by contrast, the feudal lords (the *Junkers*) themselves became capitalist farmers, and the former peasantry wage-workers. Though the conditions and pace of change varied considerably between regions as well as countries, elsewhere in Europe peasant farming generally shifted from subsistence to market production. As commercial relations penetrated villages there emerged a class of farmers or peasants producing for the market and increasing numbers of landless wage-workers (who also migrated in large numbers to industrial communities elsewhere in Europe and America, and also, in Britain's case, to the colonies). In the United States and British colonies native populations were displaced from what authority disingenuously regarded as 'free land', and were replaced by white owner-occupier farmers. (Only in India were native cultivators left undisturbed, except for stringently administered systems of land taxation).

The centrality of technological change to nineteenth-century farming practices can be exaggerated. Except in his native Prussia, the chemist Liebig's (1803–73) work on artificial fertilizers (1841) had limited economic impact: English agriculture (the most techically advanced by the 1860s) depended instead on heavy manuring and on the import, from the 1840s, of massive quantities of guano (sea-bird excrement) and, from the 1870s, of naturally occurring nitrates, both from South America. Virgin lands were still cleared by axe and fire. Human and animal power massively exceeded steam, even on the largest English farms, and changes in hand tools (for example the scythe replacing the sickle) could be more significant than introducing mechanical implements – with the important exception of the North American grain harvest. In the second half of the century, however, the extension and intensification of transport systems had a fundamental impact, together with innovations in food processing. Bulk-carrier shipping made international trade in fertilizers economically viable, and by the 1870s enabled the North American prairies to undercut English and German grain producers. Simultaneously, the latter were exposed to the competition of southern Russia and Hungary via the pan-European railway network. By 1894 the price of wheat was around only a third of its 1867 level. Canning made possible the export of Argentinian beef, and from the 1870s REFRIGERATION brought Australian and New Zealand meat to Britain.

An international market emerged as transport made possible agricultural specialization on an unprecedented scale. World agriculture became increasingly linked to the needs of advanced industrial countries, since European agriculture was inadequate to support the increasing proportion of the population which was no longer engaged in farming. Protective tariffs only partly excluded imported foodstuffs, while the government of the most urbanized market – Britain (where by 1901 only 3.5 per cent of the population was engaged in agriculture) – operated a policy of FREE TRADE. Colombian tobacco, Bengalese jute, South American coffee, Ceylon tea, Danish bacon and Dutch margarine joined American grain and colonial wool and meat on the docksides of Britain.

Thus advanced industrial nations shrugged off dependency on their domestic agriculture. (The IRISH FAMINE was the last occasion that anywhere in western Europe or the English-speaking world was decimated by harvest failure and starvation.) However, the capitalization of agriculture depressed general living standards for landless rural workers, while the world market was intensely vulnerable to overproduction and sudden competition. The GREAT DEPRESSION in agriculture of the final quarter of the century was 'essentially a depression of the staple national and international food-crops' (Hobsbawm). Thus its impact, severe in Britain, was greatest on the arable sector. Improved transport and food processing enabled dairy and other specialist farmers (for example soft-fruit growers) to prosper, as did commercially orientated peasant farmers elsewhere in Europe.

C. M. Cipolla (ed.), *The Fontana Economic History of Europe*, vol. 3: *The Industrial Revolution* (Glasgow, 1973), pp. 452–506.

E. J. Hobsbawm, *The Age of Capital, 1848–1875* (London, 1975), ch. 10.

MALCOLM CHASE

Aix-la-Chapelle *see* CONGRESS SYSTEM.

Albert, Alexandre Martin (*b* Buxy, 27 March 1815; *d* Melle, 27 May 1895) French worker and politician. He was brought into the provisional government of 1848 by Louis BLANC as a genuine worker – he was a mechanic by trade; but he was hardly typical, however. A member of the most important secret societies of the 1830s, he participated in the abortive risings of 1832, 1834 and 1839 as well as in the successful one of February 1848. He was imprisoned at Belle-Ille, for signing a proclamation overthrowing the Constituent Assembly in May 1848 (another failed insurrection). He was amnestied in 1859 and returned to Paris to work for the gas company.

DONALD SUTHERLAND

Albert, Francis Charles Augustus Emmanuel (*b* Schloss Rosenau, near Coburg, 26 August 1819; *d* Windsor, 14 December 1861) Prince consort of England. Second son of Ernest (1784–1844), duke of Saxe-Coburg-Gotha, he was tutored in the principles of constitutional monarchy by Baron Stockmar (1787–1863) in preparation for marriage to VICTORIA in 1840. Although 'unEnglish', he personified many of the values later associated with Victorianism: hard-working and serious of purpose, he cared little for rank or aristocratic pursuits but took a keen interest, as the Great Exhibition of 1851 evinced, in practical improvement through science and industry. He enjoyed the friendship of Peel but was unpopular with politicians and the establishment in general, as his rapid mastery of all things British led to fears of his active intervention. He was indefatigable in the promotion of the arts, science and social reform, but his work undermined his strength, leading to an early death from typhoid fever. The Albert Memorial aside, his most fitting monument is the South Kensington complex of educational, artistic and scientific institutions, financed from the Great Exhibition surplus.

JOHN BELCHEM

Alexander I (*b* St Petersburg, 24 December 1777; *d* Taganrog, 1 December 1825) Tsar of Russia (1801–25). The son of Tsar Paul (1754–1801), he was educated on the insistence of his grandmother Catherine the Great (1729–96) by a radical Swiss tutor, a follower of Rousseau, in the spirit of the French Enlightenment. During the first half of his reign he instigated a number of reforms. On the prompting of his chief adviser, Count M. M. Speranski, (1772–1839), he established a council of state, whose members, appointed by him, were to suggest legislative improvements. He reorganized the government ministries and suggested the introduction of an elected state duma and representative forms of local government. He founded a state school system and a number of universities. He proposed the emancipation of the serfs in the Baltic provinces without land, while certain categories of Russian landowners were encouraged to free theirs with land. He granted a constitution to Poland, and abolished torture and lightened censorship.

His foreign policies were dominated by relations with England and Napoleon, culminating in the War of 1812 (*see* BATTLE OF BORODINO) and by the expansion of territory into Bessarabia, Finland and the Caucasus. In the second part of his reign he became a mystical reactionary, inspired the HOLY ALLIANCE and revoked many of his earlier reforming proposals. This changed mood was typified by his appointment as chief minister of Count A. A. Arakcheev (1769–1834), a cruel and blinkered despot, and the establishment of the Military Colonies, which were intended to combine the benefits of the army and farming but failed in both. He was a complex personality, virtuous to Jefferson, glorious to Castlereagh, a Sphinx to Pushkin (1799–1837) and exasperating, inconsistent and untrustworthy to most of his contemporaries. His death heralded the abortive revolt by the DECEMBRISTS.

Alan Palmer, *Alexander I, Tsar of War and Peace* (London, 1974).

A. V. KNOWLES

Alexander I, prince of Serbia   *see* KARAGEORGE.

Alexander II (*b* St Petersburg, 17 April 1818; *d* St Petersburg, 1 March 1881)   Tsar of Russia (1855–81). The son of Nicholas I, he succeeded to the throne during the Crimean War. He was known as the 'Tsar-Liberator' for the long-awaited emancipation of the peasants in 1861 (*see* SERFDOM) and the freeing of Bulgaria from the Turks in 1878 (*see* RUSSO-TURKISH WAR), and his reign witnessed wide-ranging attempts to modernize Russian social and political life. Important changes were made in local government in the countryside (*see* ZEMSTVA) in 1864 and the municipalities (1870). Autonomy of the universities was guaranteed (1863), universal military service introduced (1874), alterations in the judicial system made (1864), including trial by jury in criminal cases, and Russia's chaotic financial systems overhauled. To 'crown the edifice', an elected, representative assembly with consultative powers was to be introduced, only to be forestalled by his death.

Although all the reforms were enthusiastically supported by Alexander and influential sections of public opinion, and were ably carried out by liberal ministers and officials, they created considerable opposition from both conservatives and revolutionaries (*see* POPULISM (RUSSIA)). Several attempts were made on his life, culminating in his assassination by the terrorist Narodnaia volia (People's Will). That his reforms little changed the police or civil service was to have far-reaching consequences. His foreign policy was largely one of non-intervention, except in the case of the Turkish massacre of the Bulgarians, the Polish uprising of 1863 and the intensification of the conquest of the northern Caucasus. Albeit a sincere and modest man he was never widely popular and his death was marked by general indifference. To some, though, including the French ambassador, he was 'a great tsar and deserved a kinder fate'.

W. E. Mosse, *Alexander II and the Modernization of Russia* (London, 1958).

A. V. KNOWLES

Alexander III (*b* St Petersburg 26 February 1845; *d* Crimea, 20 October 1894)   Tsar of Russia (1881–94). He was the second son of Alexander II. The memory of his father's assassination and the influence of Pobedonostsev (1827–1907), eminent jurist, senator and, from 1880, procurator of the Holy Synod of the Russian Orthodox Church, ensured his domestic policies were unashamedly reactionary. All opposition was removed, censorship intensified, police powers increased, education stultified and Russification of national minorities expanded, especially with regard to Jews (*see* JEWS AND JUDAISM). Most of the positive results of his father's reign were nullified. He pursued a protectionist economic policy which resulted in a rapid expansion of industry and increase in exports, especially grain. Attempts were made to ease the awful working and living conditions of the peasantry and industrial workers which served only to assist the spread of social democratic and Marxist ideas. His foreign policies were generally peaceful and saw a rapprochement with France.

A. V. KNOWLES

Alfonso XII (*b* Madrid, 28 November 1857; *d* El Pardo, 25 November 1885) King of Spain (1874–85). The eldest son of Isabella II (1833–68), he came to the throne in 1875 in the wake of the collapse of the first republic thanks to a combination of the political activities of the conservative leader Antonio Cánovas del Castillo (1828–97), and a military coup on the part of General Martínez Campos (1831–1900). Under the influence of Cánovas, Alfonso presided over the establishment of a political system that provided stable government by means of the so-called *turno pacífico* and kept the army out of politics by satisfying the social, political and professional concerns that had led it to indulge in numerous *pronunciamientos* in the period 1814–68. Determined to avoid the mistakes that had led to the overthrow of his mother, Alfonso accepted the role of a constitutional monarch and for a time Spain enjoyed exceptional – if deceptive – stability.

CHARLES ESDAILE

Algeria Invaded by France in June–July 1830, Algeria was annexed in October 1870 as a 'white settler' French overseas territory. It was incorporated into the French civil administration seven months prior to annexation, the ultimate goal being 'L'Algérie française', or a French Algeria. Accordingly, by the latter part of the nineteenth century, French citizenship and civil rights were extended to almost all Europeans, about 476,000 in 1871 and 553,000 by 1903. Only Algerians integrated into the body politic through FRENCH POLICIES OF ASSIMILATION, intermittently applied, qualified for these privileges.

French conquest replaced approximately three centuries of Ottoman administration, and resistance to it recurred throughout the greater part of the nineteenth century. Particularly offensive to Algerians, most of whom had been Muslims since about the eleventh century, was their subordination to the protocols of Christians ruling through a secular state, French civil law and a secular educational system. Equally threatening was their loss of land to white settlers. Although Louis Napoleon set aside nearly 3 million acres of land in 1866 for white-settler and colonizer ownership and/or use, by 1900 nearly 4 million acres had been appropriated (almost 6 million by 1930), some by dubious means, others illegal. Across a century of revolt, resistance and uprisings, the most important of which were the Great Insurrection (1832–47), under the leadership of the sultan ABD AL-QADIR, and the Great Uprising of 1871, millions of Algerian mujahidin, 'those who fight in holy war', lost their lives.

Once established, French administrative policies were implemented on the basis of assimilation, or the extent to which local populations had narrowed the cultural and political gap between themselves and the French. For example, in arid southern regions occupied almost entirely by Muslims, a predominantly military administration ruled indirectly through local dignitaries such as bachaga, agha, qadi and shaikh implementing Islamic law (see INDIRECT RULE). In mixed communes (commune mixte) with European minorities, Muslims were granted only limited participation in municipal elections, leaving local affairs in the hands of qadi and indigenous notables applying Islamic law. Finally, in European-dominated communes, the French system of communes (communes de plein exercise, or municipal government), including laws and electoral systems, was applied with little modification. Only assimilated Algerians forswearing Islamic law were granted full civil rights.

Possessed of considerable capital and a skilled and unskilled labour force, 'L'Algérie française' mostly thrived for the greater part of the nineteenth century; growth rates were not to any degree paralleled in the 'other Algeria', where landlessness and declining food production impoverished thousands. Thus by the latter part of the nineteenth century, when the Muslim population was eight times larger than the European, only 37 per cent of the national wealth was in Muslim hands, according to official French estimates. For the same period, according to the same sources, only 6.9 per cent of Muslims were urban dwellers, rising to 7.6 per cent in 1906. A large percentage of rural dwellers, now landless and working as khamma, or sharecroppers, and agricultural labourers, eked out a harsh and penurious livelihood.

Jamil M. Abun-Nasr, A History of the Maghrib in the Islamic Era (Cambridge, 1987), pp. 119–58.

Charles-Robert Ageron, Histoire de L'Algérie contemporaine 1830–1970 (History of Contemporary Algeria) (Paris, 1970).

Charles André Julien, Histoire de l'Algérie contemporaine: la conquête et les débuts de la colonisation 1827–71 [History of Contemporary Algeria: The Conquest and the Beginnings of Colonization 1826–71] (Paris, 1964).

B. MARIE PERINBAM

Ali Mohammed, Sayyid (b Shiraz, 20 October 1819; d Tabriz, 9 July 1850) Persian theologian and founder of Babism. Of the many movements that arose in reaction to Western domination and Qajar misrule, that of Ali Mohammed, a young merchant and student of religion, was the most lasting. In 1844 he challenged orthodox Shi'ism with the declaration that he was the 'Bab' or 'Gateway' to the Twelfth Imam. More radical messages followed, including his claim to be the

Imam himself and, later, the 'Mirror' of God. The movement quickly gained adherents, called 'Babis', and the Bab was briefly imprisoned in 1845. In 1847, as his disciples fanned out across Iran, he was imprisoned again and held for three years. In 1850 he was assassinated, apparently by one of his own adherents. In the struggle that followed, several prominent Babis established Baha'ism, which soon eclipsed Babism by confining Ali Mohammed's role to that of a 'foreteller' of God's Chosen One, Baha-ullah (1817–92).

Peter Avery, *Modern Iran* (New York, 1967).

MADELINE C. ZILFI

All-German Workers' Association Founded in Leipzig in May 1863 under the leadership of LASSALLE, the All-German Workers' Association (ADAV) was the first German labour party in that it claimed to represent workers as a class and saw itself as a purely political organization. It broke with an earlier tradition of engaging in many kinds of associational activity, being dedicated to political agitation. It was highly centralized, vesting much authority in its leaders, Lassalle and later Johann Baptist von Schweitzer (1833–75). Its major principles were government on the basis of universal manhood suffrage and state-supported producer co-operatives. It favoured Prussian leadership in Germany. By Lassalle's death (August 1864) there were 4,600 members, concentrated in Hamburg, the Rhinelands and Saxony. By the end of 1865 the figure was 5,500. Internal dissent in 1866–7 led to a breakaway group forming the Lassallean ADAV, helped by Lassalle's former patroness, the duchess von Hatzfeldt (1805–81). The ADAV increased to over 7,000 members by late 1868. It expanded into trade-union organization, although it did not think strikes and trade unions could achieve much.

Dissent within the ADAV, mainly over Schweitzer's leadership and pro-Prussian policy, led some to leave in 1869 and help found the Social Democratic Workers' Party (SDAP) (*see* EISENACH CONGRESS). By now Marx and Engels opposed the ADAV. The ADAV remained the larger party, however, with 21,000 members in 1870 and 15,000 in 1875; it gained 60,000 votes in the Reichstag elections of 1871 and 180,000 in 1874. These were concentrated in Prussia and the Hanseatic cities. Quarrels between the ADAV and the SDAP subsided from 1873 as both had to recognize the permanence of a Prussian-dominated Germany, the antilabour character of its government and the problems of economic downturn. In 1875 the two parties merged to form the Socialist Workers' Party.

Helga Grebing, *The History of the German Labour Movement* (Leamington Spa, 1985).

Gary Steenson, 'Not One Man! Not One Penny!' German Social Democracy, 1863–1914 (Pittsburgh, 1981).

JOHN BREUILLY

Alsace-Lorraine   Territories in north-eastern France annexed after the FRANCO-PRUSSIAN WAR (1870–1) by the victorious Germans, who claimed that they were historically and ethnically German. The region had a substantial German-speaking population and industries useful to the German economy. It was integrated into the German Empire as a *Reichsland* (Elsass-Lothringen), but enjoyed no local autonomy until after the turn of the century. The annexation of Alsace-Lorraine was an important factor in Franco-German antagonism before the First World War, and the region was returned to France by the Treaty of Versailles. It was again declared part of Germany after the defeat of France in 1940 and finally reverted to France after the Second World War.

TIMOTHY KIRK

American Civil War   *see* CIVIL WAR, AMERICAN.

American Federation of Labor   Growing out of the Federation of Organized Trades and Labor Unions, the American Federation of Labor (AFL) was founded by Samuel GOMPERS in 1886. The AFL under Gompers stressed 'pure and simple unionism', reflecting a belief in the basic virtues of the capitalist system as opposed to the more reform-minded approach taken by the KNIGHTS OF LABOR or the radical attitude of Eugene V. DEBS. Gompers once said, 'At no time in my life have I ever worked out a definitely articulated economic theory.' Instead, the AFL concentrated on the immediate objectives of improved wages, hours and working conditions to secure for labour a greater share of capitalism's material rewards.

Mirroring Gompers' belief that the industrial unionism of the Knights was inherently unable to cope with the challenges that labour faced in the late nineteenth century, the AFL focused on concrete economic gains rather than utopian ideas or political entanglements. Gompers believed that labour should seek political protection rather than social change through legislative action. The AFL did not ally itself with the Socialist Party or any independent labour party, holding that labour should 'reward its friends and punish its enemies' in both major parties.

The AFL was organized as an association of autonomous national trade unions, each limited to skilled workers in a single trade. Its tactics were boycotts, negotiations and strikes when necessary. By 1890 AFL membership had surpassed that of the Knights of Labor; in 1900 it was 500,000, and by 1920 it peaked at 4 million. Though the AFL was by far the most powerful and important American labour group by the end of the nineteenth century, it never represented more than a fraction of the nation's workers because of its emphasis on skilled trades.

Stuart Kaufman, *Samuel Gompers and the Origins of the American Federation of Labor* (Westport, Conn., 1978).

KEVIN MURPHY

Ampère, André Marie (*b* Lyons, 22 June 1775; *d* Marseilles, 10 June 1836) French mathematician and physicist, a key figure in laying the foundations of electrical science. The young Ampère early showed himself to be a prodigy, especially in mathematics, and taught himself largely through his avid reading. His early exposure to the great eighteenth-century *Encyclopédie* was combined with a strong Catholic upbringing to produce a distinctive philosophical approach in his later work. In 1803, after teaching in the provinces, Ampère became a teacher of mathematics at the École Polytechnique in Paris. He quickly achieved some success both as an educator and a scientist, making modest contributions to mathematics and chemistry. It was, however, the announcement of the discovery of electromagnetism in 1820 that directed him to his greatest work, the creation of the foundations of electrodynamics. Through a careful combination of experiment, mathematics and theory, he established the basic rules for the physical (especially magnetic) effects of electric circuits, publishing the results in 1827.

ROBERT FRIEDEL

anarchism The theory that conceives of society without government, anarchism contends that social order can be achieved without obedience to central authority and by free co-operation between individuals and groups. Anarchism was a product of the nineteenth-century debate about the inherent nature of man and the most appropriate principles of social organization. Anarchists believed that relationships between people were naturally harmonious and were brought into contention only by the intrusion of alien, external forces which if removed would allow the spontaneous generation of co-operative social organization. Although anarchism came to be associated in the public mind with bomb-throwing terrorists and to be synonymous with disorder and chaos, it was in fact a theory that saw humans as essentially good and peaceful, and most variations of the theory eschewed violence. Indeed, the roots of modern non-violence associated with Gandhi and Martin Luther King lie in the anarchist thought of people like Kropotkin and Tolstoi.

Anarchism shared certain characteristics with liberalism and socialism. In common with liberalism, it placed the individual at the centre of its political theory against the intrusions of the state or other forms of central authority. Unlike liberalism, however, it did not believe that competitive market relations and private property were the natural consequence of individualism. Anarchism shared with socialism a repudiation of the economic exploitation of capitalism, but unlike socialism it rejected the idea that the state was a necessary agent of social and political emancipation. Although anarchism and socialism were closely associated in people's minds, and for some of the nineteenth century were political allies, the differences between the two movements went beyond a simple disagreement over the role of the state and reflected profoundly different assessments of the nature of human personality and society. Anarchists believed that harmony and co-operation were the natural order of things; socialists believed that these qualities had to be constructed and that only then could the state wither away. Politically, anarchism was impeded by its distrust of authority and it never seriously challenged socialism for the leadership of the labour and trade-union movements in Europe.

The first person to formulate anarchist theory was William Godwin (1756–1836) whose *Enquiry concerning Political Justice, and its Influence on Morals and Happiness* was published in 1793. Pierre Joseph PROUDHON was, perhaps, the most important anarchist thinker who attempted to reconcile anarchism's tendency to emphasize local community with the large-scale organization of modern industry. He was the first to formulate anarchist economic and social strategy, and was the originator of the idea of workers' control of industry.

Mikhail BAKUNIN represented the revolutionary strain in anarchism and argued that only by revolutionary violence could the fetters of state control be broken. It was under Bakunin that anarchism posed its most serious challenge to Marxism within the international socialist movement. The two groups had maintained an uneasy alliance until their differences over the role of the state came to a head within the FIRST INTERNATIONAL following the PARIS COMMUNE in 1872. Bakunin's supporters were expelled from the International and turned to terrorism.

Peter KROPOTKIN, Bakunin's successor as leading anarchist spokesperson, believed that anarchism would come to dominate social organization through a process of natural evolution. Kropotkin was an anarcho-communist whose concept of mutual aid returned anarchist thought to the focus on co-operative labour that Proudhon had formulated. By the end of the century there were many different kinds of anarchisms, from Count TOLSTOI's religio-mystical variety to anarcho-syndicalism which argued the necessity for direct action by workers against capitalism through strike action that would culminate in an expropriatory general strike.

George Woodcock, *Anarchism: A History of Libertarian Ideas and Movements*, second edn (London, 1986).

RICHARD PRICE

Anatomy Act (1832)   With the advance of medical training in Britain, the gallows no longer provided a sufficient legal supply of cadavers for dissection and teaching purposes, leading to a black market for corpses obtained by 'resurrection men' and other body-snatchers. The solution proposed by a parliamentary select committee in 1828 – that the bodies of paupers dying unclaimed in workhouses, hospitals and other public institutions should be sent to the surgeons – gained considerable approval a few months later with the scandalous revelations that Burke (1792–1829) and Hare (1790–1860) had murdered their victims to sell their bodies for dissection. Although the first Anatomy Bill was withdrawn in 1829 after the bishops in the House of Lords objected to the want of provision for the Christian burial of the remains, this was only a temporary set-back and legislation, suitably amended, was finally passed in 1832. Such a utilitarian solution to the pressing needs of medical science was applauded by liberals and advanced radicals – the Anatomy Act established the earliest centrally funded and administered inspectorate of the Benthamite calendar of nineteenth-century administrative reform – but it horrified popular radicals (most notably Henry Hunt and William Cobbett) and old-fashioned paternalist Tories. It was an issue which adumbrated the divisions over the NEW POOR LAW and other 'reforms' of the 1830s. For all its efficiency and rationality, the 'Dead-Body Bill' was a blatant piece of discrimination against the poor, offending against deeply held popular attitudes towards death, burial and the human body. Previously the dreaded punishment for murderers, dissection was feared henceforth as the final punishment for the poor.

Ruth Richardson, *Death, Dissection and the Destitute* (London, 1988).

JOHN BELCHEM

Anderson, Elizabeth Garrett (*b* Aldeburgh, Suffolk, 9 June 1836; *d* Aldeburgh, 17 December 1917)   First woman doctor in England. She resolved to pursue a medical career in 1859 after a troubled period during which she made the acquaintance of Elizabeth Blackwell (1821–1910), the first American woman doctor. She studied privately and, in 1865, took the examinations of the Society of Apothecaries. With the support of her father, she set up a private practice in London. In 1871 she married James Skelton Anderson, and together they had three children. Although she regarded her medical career as primary, Anderson took an interest in a wide range of women's issues. After her husband's death in 1907, she joined her daughter Louisa in the militant campaign for women's suffrage. Her life embodied a practical feminism, providing an exemplar of how a woman could pursue a demanding career, enjoy a happy family life and engage in political activism.

Jo Manton, *Elizabeth Garrett Anderson* (London, 1965).

GAIL SAVAGE

Andrássy, Julius [Gyula], Count (*b* Košice, Slovakia, 8 March 1823; *d* Volosca, Istria, 18 February 1890) Hungarian statesman. He studied law, and in 1847 was elected to the Hungarian diet. During the 1848 revolution he was a supporter of Louis KOSSUTH's independence movement. On his return from exile (1848–58) he became a close supporter of Francis DEAK, and was a leading figure in the COMPROMISE OF 1867. Andrássy became Hungary's first prime minister in 1867; foreign minister of Austria-Hungary from 1871, he worked for closer ties with Germany, and an understanding with Russia over the EASTERN QUESTION. He played a leading role in the CONGRESS OF BERLIN. Austria-Hungary's occupation of Bosnia-Hercegovina led to his resignation in 1879, but not before he had brought about the Austro-German Alliance. The leading principle of Andrássy's career was the utilization of the 1867 Compromise to Hungarian advantage, within the Habsburg Empire and, through the preservation of the latter's great-power status, in Europe.

STEVEN BELLER

Anglo-American War (1812–1814) *see* WAR OF 1812.

Anglo-Boer Wars (1880–1, 1899–1902) The Anglo-Boer Wars were fought to prevent the independence from Britain of the TRANSVAAL and the ORANGE FREE STATE, two independent Boer republics. Ever since the British annexation of the Cape Colony in 1815, Anglo-Boer relationships were often conflictual, involving, at one time or another, the controversial use of the English language and civil law, land policies, recurrent missionary charges of African domestic slavery in the Transvaal (outlawed in 1838), and political enfranchisement for UITLANDERS in the Transvaal Boer republic. In leaving the Cape Colony between 1835 and 1843 to form the two Boer republics, the more than 12,000 Boers (voortrekkers, or 'front runners') were expressing their frustration with British rule. The two breakaway Boer republics were accorded independence in 1852 (Transvaal) and 1854 (Orange Free State). Conceivably, events could have remained relatively unchanged for some time had not diamonds been discovered in Griqualand (Orange Free State) in 1867, and gold in the Witwatersand (Transvaal) in 1886.

The first Anglo-Boer conflict, more a Transvaal rebellion than a war, was marked primarily by President KRUGER's attempt to recover the republic's independence, surrendered to the British in April 1877, in the wake of financial and administrative disorders, and in return for protection against the Zulu chief Cetshwayo. Following a wholly unnecessary disaster for the British at Majuba (February 1881), William E. Gladstone, the British liberal prime minister, restored their independence under British suzerainty at the Convention of Pretoria (1881), a restriction removed in 1884.

The second Anglo-Boer conflict, a full-blown war, involved both breakaway republics. In addition to the Boer grievances outlined above, many of which still remained unresolved, the republics resented the Cape Colony's annexation of Griqualand in 1879–80, a territory which they both claimed. The electrifying effects of this annexation on the Boers culminated in an Afrikaner nationalism, virtually non-existent before the 1870s. Between 1895 and 1899 two attempts were made to bring the breakaway republics back into the British sphere of influence. The first, an abortive plot in December 1895 to replace the Kruger regime with a more pro-British one (*see* JAMESON RAID, RHODES), the second a less direct political pressure. So irritating were these covert and overt attempts to intimidate that, in October 1899, the two republics declared war on Britain. Concluding with the Treaty of Vereeniging (May 1902), they were brought under British imperial rule, 'cutting a deal' for the recovery of their independence in 1907. In 1910 the two former Boer republics, and the British Cape and Natal colonies were joined in the Union of SOUTH AFRICA.

More an Anglo-Boer struggle for power – over control of South Africa and its rich resources – than a war of independence from Britain, the wars also involved Blacks and Coloureds (*see* AFRIKANERS), many of whom provided support systems for both the British and Boer armies, many more suffering the effects of scorched-earth policies and concentration camps. Believing to no avail that their efforts would be rewarded with a greater share in the region's political and economic development, many also took up arms in support of the British, while others occupied deserted Boer farms in the mistaken expectation that alienated lands would be restored.

P. Warwick, *The South African War: The Anglo-Boer War* (London, 1980).
—— *Black People and the South African War 1899–1902* (Cambridge, 1983).

B. MARIE PERINBAM

Anglo-Chinese Wars (1839–1841, 1857–1858) The first Anglo-Chinese War, commonly called the first Opium War, arose out of the attempts of the Chinese government to suppress the growing traffic of opium into China (*see* OPIUM TRADE). From the end of the eighteenth century opium produced in India was shipped illegally into Canton as British merchants tried to prise open the China market. In March 1839 the distinguished official LIN TSE-HSU arrived in Canton to enforce the imperial ban on the import of opium. Failing to recognize the British superintendent of trade, Elliot (1801–75), an opponent of the opium trade, as a possible ally, Lin ordered the surrender of all opium and confined the British community to their factories (warehouses) where they were besieged for several weeks. Their opium was confiscated, burned and then thrown into the Pearl River. Further pressure in Canton led to the withdrawal of the British community to Hong Kong.

In Britain the leading opium merchant Jardine (1825–1905) led a campaign demanding government compensation for the opium merchants. The cabinet decided that such compensation should be extracted from the Chinese government. A British expeditionary force was sent to south China to enforce compliance with the demand for compensation. The foreign secretary, Palmerston, was confident that a blockade of the coast would force the Chinese government to yield. Elliot disagreed, favouring a direct attack on the forts off Canton. After fitful, unsuccessful negotiations the British extended their operations up the coast to the Yangtze, and the emperor, faced with the loss of Nanking, was forced to accept defeat. The TREATY OF NANKING (1842) followed.

The British soon found the trading concessions extracted by this treaty insufficient, and in the 1850s pressed for revision. Representatives of foreign governments in China still did not have access to the Chinese government. Britain wanted a resident minister in Peking and the opening of further TREATY PORTS. The Chinese rejected any treaty revision.

After the crew of the *Arrow*, a Hong Kong vessel flying the British flag, had been arrested in Canton and charged with piracy, the British, later joined by the French, used the issue to extend their treaty rights. After Anglo-French attacks up the coast the Chinese were forced to sign the TREATY OF TIENTSIN (1859).

Jack Gray, *Rebellions and Revolutions: China from the 1800s to the 1980s* (Oxford, 1990).
A. Waley, *The Opium War through Chinese Eyes* (London, 1958).

JOHN DAVIES

Anglo-French Commercial Treaty (1860) The tariff duties that remained on foreign goods after 1846 affected mainly trade between Britain and France. The Anglo-French Commercial Treaty, also known as the Cobden-Chevalier Treaty, freed the main items of exchange between the two countries: wine, brandies and fine silk goods from France and coal, iron and other industrial goods from Britain. The economic effects of the treaty were limited; it did not greatly increase trade between the two countries, although it did cause the destruction of the Coventry ribbon industry. The treaty helped end a growing political tension between Britain and France and inaugurated a general movement towards lower tariffs. The first of eight 'most favoured nation' treaties that Britain negotiated in the 1860s, the treaty served as a model that other European countries followed until the revival of PROTECTIONISM in the 1880s.

Barrie M. Ratcliffe, 'The Origins of the Anglo-French Commercial Treaty of 1860: A Reassessment', in Barrie M. Ratcliffe (ed.), *Great Britain and her World* (Manchester, 1975), pp. 125–51.

RICHARD PRICE

animal sports and cruelty   It was in Britain that the first organized movements protesting against cruelty to animals were set up. At the start of the century most animal sports involved violence, blood and betting. The sports ranged from animals being baited by humans (for example cock throwing, which consisted of throwing missiles at a tethered cock until it was dead) to animals fighting between themselves (cock-fighting and dog-fighting) or being baited by other animals (bull-baiting and badger-baiting). In large towns sports such as cock-fighting took place on a regular organized basis. In 1800 Newcastle upon Tyne had seven cockpits where fights took place on most days of the week from January to June. But many of the blood sports were associated with rural seasonal festivities. Throwing at cocks was a traditional Shrovetide activity while the Stamford bull-running took place annually in November.

Movements condemning cruelty to animals grew in the early years of the nineteenth century. The Society for the Prevention of Cruelty to Animals was formed in 1824 and part of its energies were taken up with attacking popular blood sports. Between 1800 and 1829 ten bills dealing with cruelty to animals were presented to parliament but they met with little success. Eventually, a Cruelty to Animals Act was passed in 1835 which outlawed all sports involving the baiting of animals and, in addition, it was made an offence to keep cockpits. Nevertheless, the tradition of these sports was such that it proved difficult to enforce this legislation, although the new borough and county police forces played an important role, if not in eliminating these sports, at least in driving them under cover. Although never entirely eradicated, animal blood sports by the end of the century were the exception rather than the rule.

See also HUNTING.

R. W. Malcolmson, *Popular Recreations in English Society 1700–1850* (Cambridge, 1973).

J. M. GOLBY

Anthony, Susan Brownell (*b* Adams, Massachusetts, 15 February 1820; *d* Rochester, New York, 13 March 1906)   American reformer and suffragist. Following the example of her Quaker father, she began her career as a schoolteacher. Soon she became involved in a number of reform movements, especially temperance. Angered when male temperance workers refused to allow her to speak in public, she organized the Women's State Temperance Society of New York in 1852. Often touring as a lecturer for this cause, she also worked for abolition. During reconstruction, Anthony and her allies urged Congress to include women in the fourteenth amendment, and when this proved unsuccessful, she founded the National Women's Suffrage Association, which worked for WOMEN'S SUFFRAGE. During the 1872 presidential election, as part of a nation-wide plan, she was one of a number of women who attempted to vote. Later in her career she was president of the National American Women's Suffrage Association.

Kathleen Barry, *Susan B. Anthony: A Biography of a Singular Feminist* (New York, 1988).

ALICE E. REAGAN

anthropology Although the term came into use in the seventeenth and eighteenth centuries, the true origins of anthropology as a coherent and increasingly institutionalized subject concerned with the scientific study of humanity lie in the nineteenth century, and in particular in the Darwinian revolution (*see* DARWINISM). The proposal that humans had evolved along with other plants and animals led to a concern with placing humanity, and different human populations, into their 'place in nature'. Anthropology, seen as the natural history of mankind, brought together both the study of social customs and human physiology and anatomy. Under the influence of books such *The Origin of Species* (1859) and *The Descent of Man* (1871), the first syntheses and the most influential nineteenth-century anthropological works were explicitly evolutionary (*see* EVOLUTION). This often involved tracing the history of mankind from simple or primitive conditions through to the development of complex societies and civilizations.

This work saw the establishment of the principal components of modern anthropology, including the development of a time-scale for human evolution; the discovery of the first fossil evidence for humans (for example Neanderthals and *Pithecanthropus*); confirmation of the close anatomical similarity and evolutionary relationships between humans and apes (for example Thomas HUXLEY's *Man's Place in Nature* (1863)); and the documenting of the variety of human social customs and cultural forms. These very diverse lines of evidence were used primarily to support generally progressive models of human development, such as those for politics and economics espoused by Herbert SPENCER, or for mental condition (for example James Frazer's (1854–1941) *The Golden Bough* (1890–1915)), or for legal systems (for example H. L. Morgan (1818–81)); or for cultural practices and social organization (for example E. B. Tylor (1832–1917)).

Although evolutionary ideas remained significant in physical or biological anthropology, the end of the nineteenth century saw the abandonment of grand evolutionary schemes in social and cultural anthropology both as the variety of human social life became clear and progressive views of evolution in general became untenable.

R. A. FOLEY

Anti-Corn Law League The most famous exercise in 'pressure from without' in early Victorian Britain, the Anti-Corn Law League owed its origins in Manchester 1838 to a change in tactics by middle-class radicals. With the nation ill-disposed towards further constitutional reform, the frustrated radicals decided to campaign not for the ballot but for the repeal of the CORN LAWS, the symbol of aristocratic misrule. It was an inspired change of direction, enabling BRIGHT and COBDEN to transform a political movement into a moral crusade, promising not only new markets and prosperity but also international fellowship and peace through FREE TRADE. In promoting the 'mission of industry', the league attracted substantial subscriptions with which it transformed the machinery of extraparliamentary politics – three and a half tons of tracts were dispatched from Manchester via the new penny post every week.

Although keen to project a cross-class image, the league failed to enlist significant working-class support as the Chartists, by no means uniformly hostile to free trade, regarded the league with suspicion, fearing a repetition of the 'delusion' of the Reform Bill agitation. After the disturbances of 1842 the league abandoned attempts at cross-class alliance in favour of 'electoral pressure', an avowedly middle-class policy to register and convert voters, to whose numbers provident free-trade supporters were to be appended by the purchase of 40 shilling freeholds. Although historians dispute the impact of the league on the timing of repeal, these new tactics – which would have made the Corn Laws the main point of contention at the next election – may have restricted PEEL's room for manœuvre, denying him the opportunity of delaying repeal until the issue became non-controversial. The league claimed repeal as a victory, but it took no part in framing the legislation of 1846.

N. McCord, *The Anti-Corn Law League* (London, 1958).

JOHN BELCHEM

anti-Semitism A word coined by the German Wilhelm Marr (1818–1904), in 1879, 'anti-Semitism', broadly defined as persecution of or discrimination against Jews, was not new, having been present in some form throughout European history. The late nineteenth century did see, however, the development of novel forms of Jew-hatred, which were to put anti-Semitism on a new and eventually lethal level. At the beginning of the century the predominant form of anti-Semitism was the religious, Christian anti-Semitism, which labelled the Jews as killers of Christ, encouraged anti-Semitic myths of ritual murder and desecration of the Host and held that the non-Christian Jews could not be full participants in the 'Christian' states of Europe. In some countries (for example the Habsburg Empire) this persisted in the form of informal discrimination even after formal legal emancipation. The harshly anti-Semitic policies of the Russian Empire throughout the century were deeply influenced by the religious anti-Semitism of the Russian Orthodox Church.

The nineteenth century also inherited an anticlerical anti-Semitism, inspired by the Enlightened critique of organized religion (as in the thought of Voltaire (1694–1778) and Kant (1724–1804)). This attacked Judaism as a religion of superstitions, which enslaved the morally autonomous individual. From this came a left-wing anti-Semitism, which, allied with an economic anti-Semitism aimed at the prominent place of Jewish bankers in the emerging capitalist economy, led to a radical, socialist anti-Semitism, especially strong in France, as in the works of Alphonse de Toussenel, Bruno Bauer (1809–82) and the young Karl Marx. This socialist anti-Semitism, though weakened, was still extant in 1900.

The most potent form of anti-Semitism arose on the nationalist right, partly as a response to the identification between the success of liberalism and the achievement of Jewish emancipation (in Germany by 1866–71, in the Habsburg Empire by 1867). This took three main forms: economic, cultural and racial. In economic terms Jews were regarded as part of the liberal-cosmopolitan forces working against national economic power and cohesion. In cultural terms (exemplified by Richard Wagner (1813–83)) Jews were regarded as alien to national customs and traditions, and hence their cultural productions could only be poor, and corrupting imitations of the 'authentic' national spirit. This still left the theoretical opportunity for Jewish individuals to 'overcome themselves' and become truly part of the nation.

Eventually, however, the adoption of theories of racial anti-Semitism, such as those of Marr and Eugen Dühring (1833–1921), blocked even this possibility. By such theories, Jews were biologically fated to have a destructive impact on European national cultures, and hence no one of Jewish descent could be admitted into the national community. This was by far the most radical and absolute form of anti-Semitism, and also, with its pseudo-scientific, quasi-Darwinian character, the most modern and ultimately the most dangerous.

Political anti-Semitism, which embraced some or all of the above forms at one time or another, emerged in the aftermath of economic crisis after 1873, and the ensuing weakening of the liberal position in central Europe. In the late 1870s Marr and others started to blame German economic and political problems on Jews, and this theme was taken up by Adolf Stöcker (1835–1909), preacher to the Prussian court, who became the main leader of the German anti-Semitic movement.

For the next two decades anti-Semites achieved occasional political success in Germany, but nothing major. In the Habsburg Empire, however, the Christian Social Party, led by Karl Lueger (1844–1910), captured municipal office in Vienna in 1895–7, and the various nationalist parties elsewhere in the empire, notably the Czech and Polish, also used anti-Semitism to harden nationalist support. (The Magyar establishment, after the ritual murder trial of Tísza-Eszlár in 1882, cracked down on political anti-Semitism in Hungary.)

While the worst anti-Semitic excesses took place in Russia, with waves of pogroms from the 1880s, the most famous anti-Semitic affair was the DREYFUS Affair, which dominated French politics from 1898 to 1900. Although at the time there appeared a serious threat to the liberal values of the French state, the outcome of the affair was a devastating defeat for the conservative and anti-Semitic Right. In Germany, similarly, political anti-Semitism seemed a fading force by 1900, but in other ways the values of anti-Semitism had been absorbed by the ruling classes, to survive as a terrible force in the twentieth century.

See also JEWS AND JUDAISM.

Jacob Katz, From Prejudice to Destruction: Anti-Semitism, 1700–1933 (Cambridge, Mass., 1980).
Peter Pulzer, The Rise of Political Anti-Semitism in Germany and Austria (London, 1988).

STEVEN BELLER

Anti-socialist Law (1878) Exceptional legislation passed by the imperial German Reichstag and Bundesrat, which came into force on 21 October 1878, the Anti-socialist Law stemmed from BISMARCK's determination to crush the newly formed socialist party and was intended to suppress socialist activity. An earlier draft of the law, introduced after an assassination attempt on the life of Emperor William I, had been rejected by the liberals and CENTRE PARTY in the Reichstag, and the law was passed, with the support of the conservative parties and the right-wing National Liberals, only after a second assassination attempt. The law banned socialist political parties and meetings, and forbade the publication of newspapers expressing socialist views and the collection of funds for the furthering of socialist activity. It was administered by the police forces of the federal states, most harshly in Prussia. Many socialists were imprisoned or chose exile. Significantly, the law did not prohibit the candidature and election of socialists to the Reichstag and it failed to prevent their election in greater numbers during the 1880s. By 1890 it had become clear that the law had been a political failure and, when the Reichstag refused to renew it, it lapsed.

See also SOCIAL DEMOCRATIC PARTY (GERMANY).

V. L. Lidtke *The Outlawed Party* (Princeton, NJ, 1966).

S. J. SALTER

Arabi Pasha *see* URABI PASHA, AHMAD.

architecture In the nineteenth century architecture was subject to continuous debates about stylistic identifications appropriate to the age, and historical and exotic models available for emulation and perfection by advanced Western civilizations. Key phrases in the subject's literature include 'Victorian eclecticism', 'Battle of the Styles' (NEOCLASSICISM versus GOTHIC REVIVAL) and 'expression of new materials' (referring to iron and glass – in fact ancient materials newly available in unprecedented scale and quality). Earlier practice had featured a choice between classical and picturesque treatment for categories of building considered worthy of an architect's attention: great residences, places of worship, modest houses within schemes for estate improvement. This strictness of alternative is explained as respecting either an intrinsic logic of form, structure and proportion (in the classical) or an extrinsic logic of architecture as scenery (in the picturesque). However, by 1800 there had arisen a tendency to interrelate these – a classical language might be employed for pictorial or decorative effect (that is romantically), while the irregular forms of a picturesque romanticism might be stylized (classicized) for, say, publication in a pattern book prior to general deployment.

Fonthill Abbey (1796–1813) by James Wyatt (1746–1813) is a fine example of this hybridization in Britain, while the University of Virginia, Charlottesville (1817), a display of classical themes and variations by Thomas Jefferson, is the result of the architect's having acquired stylistic understanding from published sources. The removal of the stark classical–picturesque alternative prepared the way for admission of 'exotic' styles, as for example in the Royal Pavilion, Brighton (1815–21), in which John Nash (1752–1835) combined Indian and Muslim detailing, the regularity of Georgian planning and the novelty of cast-iron construction. It was partly the new technology— unencumbered by such stylistic associations—that encouraged ideas of styles as applied form and decoration. Being extrinsic, they were adaptable. The United States Capitol, Washington, DC provides a history of such adaptability: its original and undistinguished first building (1792–1828) in Georgian, by William Thornton (1758–1828), was inventively restyled in Classical Revival (1814) by Benjamin Henry Latrobe (1764–1820), and again substantially enlarged, reclothed in

Second Empire style and complemented with commanding cast-iron dome (1851–65) by Thomas Ustick Walter (1804–87).

Throughout the century alternatives multiplied, for while purists continued to regard the principal idioms as mutually exclusive it became increasingly acceptable to substitute and intermix them. In 1818 John Soane (1753–1837) offered the church commissioners model churches 'clothed' in Greek, Renaissance or Gothic. Soon architects' repertoires included Chinese, Egyptian, Flemish, Florentine, Grecian, Norman, Roman, Stuart, Tudor, Oriental, Venetian and several other styles (*see* Richard Brown, *Domestic Architecture* (1841)). An increase in building types considered worthy of design (factories, warehouses, poorhouses, schools, hospitals and other public facilities) fuelled the diversity. Styles were not merely mixed but synthesized, as for example by Pierre François Henri Labrouste (1801–75), the elevations of whose Bibliothèque Sainte-Geneviève, Paris (1842–50) assimilate a wide range of archaeological referents without quoting any specifically.

Labrouste's use of such modern devices as heating systems was a conscious tribute to an industrial age. This typified the beginnings of the celebration of functionalism, in which the human uses of a building, or its special means of construction, or its functioning parts, would be 'expressed' as equalling or exceeding the significance of elevational arrangement. An early example of the expression of 'use' is to be found in the Opéra, Paris (1862–75) by Jean Louis Charles Garnier (1825–98) in which special provisions were made to accommodate the 'social theatre' of seeing and being seen, parading and display, associated with opera-going. A contemporaneous, uninhibited revelation of new materials is evident in Oriel Chambers, Liverpool (1864–5) by Peter Ellis (1804–84), who used iron not only structurally but also as exterior cladding (with Egyptianate decoration) for this prototype multistorey office block.

Railway stations both respected and rejected this tendency. Most were great sheds of iron, competing to attain ever more impressive roof spans over their platforms, and thus expressing the structural principles that facilitated them, while perversely expressing historicism in the styling of their main halls and principal frontages. For example, Euston Station, London (1835–9) comprised a train shed by Robert Stephenson (1803–59), and classical waiting-rooms, hall, courtyard and ceremonial Greek Doric propylaeum—the famous 'Euston Arch'—by Philip Hardwick (1792–1870) and Philip Charles Hardwick (1820–90). In competition, Saint Pancras Station (1863–5) comprised an engineering structure by W. H. Barlow (1812–92) and R. M. Ordish (1824–86), spanning a previously unparalleled 243 feet, and magnificent Gothic hotel and ancillary buildings (1868–74) by George Gilbert Scott (1811–78).

The rapid 'evolution' of iron structures was evident at the Paris International Exhibition (1889) by the 385 feet span of the Gallerie des Machines by Victor Contamin (1840–93) and C. L. F. Dutert (1845–1906). This exhibition housed both the the widest span and the greatest height in built constructions—the famous Tower by Gustave Eiffel (1832–1923) rising to 1,000 feet. These are examples of a genus of structures categorized as both architecture and engineering, epitomized in the Crystal Palace, London (1850–1) by Joseph Paxton (1803–65) (see MUSEUMS). When iron gave way to steel in the later years of the century, it became possible greatly to exceed the old records of height by means of skeleton construction, as in the Home Insurance Company Building (1883–5), the first true skyscraper, by William Le Baron Jenney (1832–1907) (see CHICAGO SCHOOL), though it must be noted that another vital enabler of high-rise building was the electric elevator, developed in 1880 by Charles William Siemens (1823–83) and Werner von SIEMENS.

Such diversity characterized a century of architectural change dominated by technological innovation and stylistic antagonism. If the great achievements of architectural engineering typify the former, the latter is exemplified in powerful contrasting images: for example the Altes Museum, Berlin (1822–3) by Karl Friedrich Schinkel (1781–1841) and the decorative detailing of the Houses of Parliament, London (1840–65) by Augustus Welby Northmore Pugin (1812–52).

See also ARTS AND CRAFTS MOVEMENT, ENGINEERING.

Roger Dixon and Stefan Muthesius, *Victorian Architecture* (London, 1978).
Robin Middleton and David Watkin, *Neoclassical and Nineteenth Century Architecture* (London, 1987).

DAVID THISTLEWOOD

Argentina The first region of the Spanish Empire to achieve emancipation was Argentina. Local forces in Buenos Aires successfully repulsed British invasions in 1806–7, but in 1810 the city's elite refused to recognize the authority of the Spanish provisional government, gaining the support of many creoles in the interior. Six years later the CONGRESS OF TUCUMÁN formally declared independence.

Consolidating the new nation was difficult. Upper Peru (see BOLIVIA), PARAGUAY and the Banda Oriental (see URUGUAY) remained separate, while intense conflict arose between *unitarios* in Buenos Aires and federalists in the interior and the other riverine provinces. By the 1820s, a decade of bloody civil wars, Buenos Aires retained little authority over the provincial *caudillos*, an impasse that was only partially resolved by ROSAS, governor of Buenos Aires (1829–32, 1835–52).

The economy of the pampas around Buenos Aires expanded steadily after the opening of foreign trade, initially on the basis of exporting cattle hides and salted beef (*charqui*), and then from the 1830s with wool production. Rosas's rise symbolized the growing influence of the creole landowners (*estancieros*) who gained from the southward expansion of the frontier at the expense of nomadic indigenous peoples. Buenos Aires's increasing wealth and its determination to control Argentina's external trade, however, continued to exacerbate conflicts with other provinces. After Rosas's fall Buenos Aires refused to recognize the authority of the Argentine Confederation, which in 1853 adopted a liberal constitution favouring foreign trade, investment and immigration. The country was not reunited until Bartolomé Mitre (1821–1906), governor of Buenos Aires, defeated the confederation at Pavón in 1861. Mitre then ratified the 1853 constitution (with some amendments) and initiated the development of national institutions like the treasury, army and legal system.

Despite these struggles economic growth continued. Wool exports rose from 7,558 tons in 1850 to 65,704 in 1870, and the *estancieros* introduced many innovations. The first railways were constructed and European immigrants attracted by colonization schemes in littoral provinces like Santa Fé. In 1879–80 General Julio A. Roca (1843–1914) completed the 'Conquest of the Desert', driving into Patagonia the 'Indians' who had continued to threaten settlement in the pampas. Roca then became president, consolidating the rule of the oligarchic Conservative Party. The city of Buenos Aires was federalized, resolving the constitutional problem of the capital's status.

During the 1880s the economy grew rapidly. Foreign (chiefly British) investors proved keen to finance both the national and provincial governments as well as forming new banking, railway and public-utility companies (9,000 miles of track were open by 1893); 650,000 immigrants (chiefly Italian and Spanish) arrived in the decade. The frenzy of speculation was temporarily ended in 1890 by a revolt against President Juárez Celmán (1844–1909) and the BARING CRISIS, which necessitated a restructuring of Argentina's external debt. However, by 1900 the infrastructure built before the crisis had stimulated renewed export growth (now concentrated on grain and meat), and Argentina's return to prosperity was epitomized by its adoption of the GOLD STANDARD in 1899.

Jonathan C. Brown, 'The Bondage of Old Habits in Nineteenth-Century Argentina', *Latin American Research Review*, 21(2) (1986), 3–32.
David Rock, *Argentina, 1516–1982: From Spanish Colonization to the Falklands War* (London, 1986).

RORY MILLER

aristocracies For most of the medieval and modern periods aristocratic elites exerted an abiding influence on European history. Land was the main form of wealth; from possession of land flowed power: when individuals or groups happened to gain power or come into money without a base in landholding, they quickly grounded both in the ownership of land and, where possible, the acquisition of hereditary titles. Such was the norm until very recently. As late as 1750 landed elites – and especially those with recognized claims to noble status – were economically and politically dominant in nearly every country in Europe. By 1900 that situation had drastically changed and landed power was much diminished. It was further reduced in the aftermath of the First and Second World Wars; and by 1945 it was primarily a memory.

What might be called the long nineteenth century, from 1789 to 1914, was the moment when aristocracies lost their historic accumulations of land, wealth and power or when, at the least, wealth held in land ceased to be the sole key to political power. The process began, of course, with the French Revolution and the famous events of the summer of 1789. 'La Grande Peur' (the Great Fear), which swept the countryside while the king and his opponents manœuvred for advantage in Paris and Versailles, was a peasant uprising prompted in part by fear of brigands and of the army, but also by a deep desire to sweep away the privileges of the landed elite. Characteristically, therefore, peasants invaded châteaux to steal and destroy documents purporting to support seigneurial claims. Such actions were effective and irrevocable: hence on the night of 4 August nobles in the National Assembly rose up one after another and renounced their feudal rights.

The struggle over land and power in France was bitter, but the outcome was not in doubt after 1789. Napoleon made the revolutionary land settlement permanent in France – while exporting it to the lands he conquered – and even during the Restoration the best the former nobles could get from the sympathetic regime was an indemnification. To be sure, noble landowners still owned roughly a sixth of the land in the 1880s, but they never truly regained their previous wealth or influence. France became, and remained, a largely peasant society.

In other nations the struggle over land and the political rights of nobles proved more difficult, and the outcomes less clear-cut. In Prussia, for example, feudal power was ended through the reforms imposed after defeat at the hands of the French. Serfs were freed of legal obligations to their owners, non-nobles were allowed to purchase estates, and positions in the army and bureaucracy were opened to competition based on merit. In exchange for personal freedom, however, the serfs ceded land to the nobles and their share of farming land actually decreased. Nor was the political power of the nobles really eclipsed, particularly in the east, where the JUNKERS continued to monopolize political power. In 1879, moreover, the landed estates forged an alliance with a section of the industrialists which afforded them protected markets for grain and privileged access to positions in the state apparatus. Throughout the entire imperial period, the *Junkers* received preferential treatment both economically and politically.

Elsewhere, ambiguous outcomes were also the norm. Noble power was curbed in the Habsburg Empire in several stages from the 1780s to 1848; in Russia the serfs were not freed until 1861. But the peasants did not usually secure control of the land in central and eastern Europe, except in areas like German Austria where small-scale peasant production was already established. Even in England, aristocratic and gentry control over land continued. Perhaps the only country to witness a genuine land redistribution was Ireland, but even there it was facilitated by a government policy that handsomely rewarded the former owners.

That nineteenth-century efforts to curb aristocratic power had such mixed results has led scholars to reassess the role of landed elites in the period. It is hard, given the tenacious grip of landed elites on agricultural property and their over-representation in the state, to speak of the nineteenth century as the 'Age of Capital' or the era of bourgeois advance. It can even be argued, as Barrington Moore has claimed, that the key to modern political development is the role of the landed elites. Still, it would be a mistake to overestimate the success of landed, aristocratic elites in the nineteenth century. They fought an impressive rearguard action against forces that undermined their power, but by 1900 Europe was fast becoming an urban society and agriculture was everywhere in decline. Thus, their economic role was much diminished. The GREAT DEPRESSION of 1873–96 was particularly hard on large landowners, who emerged from the crisis heavily in debt or, in some cases, with their estates sold off. The economic viability of agrarian elites came increasingly to depend on their ability to merge with other kinds of money: by marrying off their progeny to families with industrial or financial wealth, by entering business themselves or by lending their names and titles to non-agricultural enterprises in return for a share of the profits. In sum, it was increasingly difficult for aristocrats to resist the forces of democracy and capitalism, and where they did, as in Russia, they were doomed.

David Cannadine, *The Decline and Fall of the British Aristocracy* (New Haven, Conn., 1990).

Arno Mayer, *The Persistence of the Old Regime* (New York, 1981).

Barrington Moore, *The Social Origins of Dictatorship and Democracy* (Boston, 1966).

David Spring, *European Landed Elites in the Nineteenth Century* (Baltimore, 1977).

JAMES E. CRONIN

aristocracy of labour The term 'aristocracy of labour' was commonly used by late-nineteenth-century radicals and adapted by historians to describe the upper strata of the Victorian working class, a group defined by their skill, relative economic security and distinct culture and values. The concept is most commonly used in reference to British labour, but has also been applied to other WORKING CLASSES. Some modern historians have observed that the craft exclusiveness of labour aristocrats furthered the fragmentation of the Victorian working class, thereby contributing to the quiescence of the post-1850 labour movement. The acceptance by labour aristocrats of liberal values and ideology also played a role in stabilizing Victorian society and securing broader middle-class hegemony. Yet, if labour aristocrats accommodated themselves to ascendant industrial capitalism, their ties to the middle class and liberalism were complex and marked by ambiguity.

Respectability, independence and SELF-HELP lay at the core of the labour aristocracy's culture and values, linking it to the middle class. However, labour aristocrats transformed these values in subtle ways to meet their own needs. They embraced the ostensibly individualist virtue of self-help, for example, but pursued it collectively through co-operatives, an institution with Owenite roots. Similarly, although the attainment of independence set the labour aristocracy off from the unskilled multitudes below, it also freed them from patronage from above. In short, the adherence of the labour aristocracy to middle-class liberalism entailed a process of negotiation rather than outright capitulation, and while allowing for greater social cohesion it also created new sources of tension.

Those tensions were present at the workplace, as well, where the uneven development of British capitalism ensured that the craft control of SKILLED WORKERS came under regular challenge from employers. In a context of vulnerability, the enforcement of craft exclusiveness allowed labour aristocrats to limit such threats to their independence and establish a base of strength for future working-class organization.

Robert Gray, *The Aristocracy of Labour in Nineteenth-Century Britain* (London, 1981).

RICHARD J. SODERLUND

Armenian Massacres In the early nineteenth century the Ottomans took to calling the Armenians of the empire 'the loyal community' because the behaviour of this minority contrasted with the violent separatism of Ottoman Greeks, Serbs and Bulgars (*see* OTTOMAN EMPIRE). But by 1878 the Greek example, Russian encouragement and a growing sense of their own identity led to nationalist demands by the Armenians. As revolutionary bands stepped up operations to carve out a state in Anatolia, Ottoman reaction was fierce. In 1895 and 1909 thousands were slaughtered in bloody rampages in cities as well as in the countryside. The highest death toll occurred in 1915: between

300,000 and 500,000 of a total population of 1.5 million Armenians perished when the Ottoman regime, fearing Russian advance, deported Armenians in the east into the interior. Thousands died of famine and disease, but most were massacred by Ottoman irregulars, chiefly Kurdish tribesmen, but also including Turks.

MADELINE C. ZILFI

Arnim, Heinrich Friedrich, count von (*b* Berlin, 23 September 1791; *d* Berlin, 28 April 1859) Prussian statesman and diplomat. During the 1848 revolution in Prussia (*see* REVOLUTIONS OF 1848) he played an important role as adviser to FREDERICK-WILLIAM IV, encouraging the king to grant concessions to liberals and to support the cause of German unity under Prussian leadership. Between March and June 1848 he was foreign minister of Prussia in the liberal government appointed by the king following the revolutionary upheavals in Berlin. During his period in office he pursued a 'revolutionary' foreign policy, reversing the policy of co-operation with Russia and Austria. He sought (without success) French and British support for the creation of a German national state and for the restoration of an independent Poland. After the suppression of the revolution in Prussia, he continued to support the idea of German national unity.

ELIZABETH HARVEY

Arnold, Matthew (*b* Laleham, Middlesex, 24 December 1822; *d* Liverpool, 15 April 1888) English poet, literary critic and educationalist. The son of Thomas Arnold (1795–1842), headmaster of Rugby School, he wrote lyrical and narrative poetry of a meditative and philosophical cast in early life. His literary and political criticism won him a prominent place in Victorian and twentieth-century cultural debates, advocating the value of 'disinterestedness' and 'sweetness and light' in place of what he saw as the excessive sectarianism and partisanship of his contemporary intellectual and social environment. *Culture and Anarchy* (1869) in particular proposed an ideal of culture, the study of the 'best that has been thought and written in the world', as an antidote to the narrownesses of the three classes in English society. His working life was spent as an inspector of schools, and he advocated the values of classical and liberal education for the middle classes. In later life he sought to rescue Christianity from assaults on its truth by arguing the supreme value of the Bible as poetry; by the same token he came to advocate the value of poetry as spiritual resource and consolation.

SIMON DENTITH

art galleries *see* MUSEUMS.

Arthur, Chester Alan (*b* Fairfield, Vermont, 25 October 1830; *d* New York, 18 November 1886)   President of the United States (1881–5). Early in his career as a lawyer he won a case that led to the desegregation of the New York City streetcars. A long-time New York political operative and ally of Stalwart Republican leader Roscoe Conkling (1829–88), Arthur became head of the New York customs house in 1871. Despite his personal honesty, he became embroiled in a patronage scandal that led to his removal by President Rutherford B. Hayes (1822–93) in 1878. Seen as a martyr by hard-line spoilsmen, he joined the 1880 Republican presidential ticket as vice-president to appease the Stalwarts. When President James A. Garfield died from complications following an assassination attempt in 1881, Arthur became president. As chief executive, he proved an able administrator who supported the passage of the Pendleton Act (civil-service reform) and the creation of a modern steel navy. He also vetoed the Chinese Exclusion Act (1882).

Thomas C. Reeves, *Gentleman Boss: The Life of Chester Alan Arthur* (New York, 1975).

ALICE E. REAGAN

artisans   *see* SKILLED WORKERS.

Arts and Crafts Movement   The latter half of the nineteenth century saw a tendency in architecture, design and DECORATIVE ARTS which was opposed to industrialized production and concerned to regain contact with medieval craft practices deemed natural, creative and dignifying of the artisan. The complex origins of the Arts and Crafts Movement include the writings of John RUSKIN, especially *Seven Lamps of Architecture* (1849) and 'On the Nature of Gothic' in *The Stones of Venice*, volume 2 (1853), and hence had a close affinity with GOTHIC REVIVAL architecture. The movement's great motivating force was the practical idealism of William MORRIS, generating a constant succession of publications on art, architecture, industry and socialism allied to tangible standards in furniture and decoration. These inspired enterprises both commercial, for example Liberty & Co. (founded 1875), and idealistic: Ruskin's Guild of St George; the Century Guild (1882–8) formed by Arthur Mackmurdo (1851–1942); the Art Workers' Guild (founded 1884) formed by *inter alios* William Lethaby (1857–1931); the Guild of Handicraft (1888–1907) by Charles Robert Ashbee (1863–1902); and the Arts and Crafts Exhibition Society (1888–1914); besides the American Art Workers' Guild, Providence, Rhode Island (1885) and the Chicago and Boston Arts and Crafts Societies (both 1897).

Prominent architects included Philip Webb (1831–1915) whose Red House, Bexleyheath (1859–60) for Morris was seminal; Mackmurdo;

Lethaby – whose house Avon Tyrrell, Ringwood (1891–3) was exemplary; Ashbee; Charles Voysey (1857–1941); and others who worked for the practice of Richard Norman Shaw (1831–1912). Representative Americans included Henry Richardson (1838–86) and especially Frank Lloyd Wright (1867–1959) whose Winslow Residence (1893) is comparable to the work of Scottish architect Charles Rennie Mackintosh (1868–1928) and of the Belgian Henry van de Velde (1863–1957) in forming bridgeheads with modernism. Notable designers include Mackay Baillie Scott (1865–1945) (architecture, furniture, decoration) and Christopher Dresser (1834–1904) (silversmithing, glass) who, like Owen Jones (1809–74), wrote standard grammars of ornament and decoration.

Margaret Richardson, *Architects of the Arts and Crafts Movement* (London, 1983).

DAVID THISTLEWOOD

arts and literature

Africa

Literary styles, art forms and the purposes for which they were intended frequently varied from from one region to another, and in a number of instances were influenced by local religions and domestic ideologies. Most African literature in this period was oral. Establishing chronological boundaries for African arts and literatures have proven problematic, if only because the data hardly lend themselves to European periodization. Yet across the centuries, changing literary and aesthetic styles and contents usually reflected innovations produced internally and externally. For example, in response to pre-colonial internal innovations, the emergence of a new sovereign political entity, or state, usually produced corresponding changes in both the literary and the visual arts. Or, in response to changes externally produced, such as the introduction of Islam during the second millennium AD, many literatures reflected the new ideology; writing (in oral cultures) became the function of many literary elites. Similarly in the wake of the SCRAMBLE FOR AFRICA and subsequent colonization, many arts and literary forms reflected changes at work in people's lives. A new genre of written literatures appeared, together with literati, and a new Christian art. Thus instead of establishing chronological boundaries, we may more appropriately speak of African pre-twentieth-century classical or traditional arts and literary forms, bearing in mind that they changed in response to internal and external exigencies.

Generally speaking, both African visual arts and literary theory worked with signs, that is symbols contextually construed conveyed meaning to those embedded within the culture producing those signs in the first place. As part of religious and cosmological beliefs, this theory operated on the assumption that signs possessed catalytic powers, literally and metaphorically, depending on the circumstances. It was believed, for example, that a word, not including banal conversation, could become a catalytic word-sign, or dynamic sign-phenomenon with an existence of its own, capable of producing change depending on the circumstances and skill of the speaker-narrator-actor. Or in the case of visual arts, to take another example, an initiation mask was a catalytic mask-sign laden with meaning for young initiates and their adult initiators. In other words, word-signs and mask-signs in the mind-mouth of an experienced 'smith' could be empowered through the 'forge' of ritual, ceremony, divination, oathing and so on. Under certain contractual circumstances, relationships bound by the word or the mask were inviolable.

Usually the sign theory required its own social actualization. Because of the extraordinary powers believed to be embodied in the minds, mouths and personalities of the 'smiths' who had 'mastered' the signs' catalytic powers, many societies put distance between their members and these 'smiths'. For example, in parts of west Africa, societal members traditionally eschewed marriage into *jeli* (French *griot*), or bardic, lineages. Similar distancing occurred elsewhere where 'masters of the word' were known by different names. Less powerful, mask-sign-makers sometimes experienced similar distancing.

Powerful literary media frequently employed by word-smiths included myths and legends found, for example, among the Mande (Mali) and Yoruba (Nigeria), as well as the secret graphic signs used, for example, by the Dogon (Mali). In addition to explaining a people's identity, oral myths and legends were constantly in the process of 'becoming', and being revised, edited and updated in the mouths of their actor-narrators. By constantly and selectively incorporating past data-as-remembered, oral myths/legends could become quasi-histories. Thus like the European historical treatment of past data-as-written, African quasi-histories were always 'contemporary'. Less powerful literary media, but not lacking in social significance, included stylized mockery (for example among the Fulbe of west Africa), and the catalogue of continent-wide stories, riddles and fables, as well as proverbs, mottoes and slogans. With respect to visual arts, usually three-dimensional, the most commonly used media included rock surfaces (north African and Saharan rock art), pottery and wood (for example masks, heads, figurines, carved doors). Ivory was also used. Among three-dimensional metal workers, iron and copper alloys were most common.

Chiefly at courts, choreographed and stylized epic poems prevailed over the popular literatures, such as the epic poetry of the nineteenth-century court of the Ganda Kabaka, or great chief, in Uganda, or that of the Segu Bamana. Also part of sub-Saharan Africa's literary genre was the 'drum literature', repeated by 'talking drums' imitating the human voice. Although it was a means of communication, a sacred and secret drum literature was also 'spoken' at initiation ceremonies, chiefly among forest peoples. In Islamized regions, such as north and east Africa, as well as the Sahara, an Islamized literature – written and oral – appeared early in the second millennium AD. South of the Sahara, similar literatures developed from the sixteenth and seventeenth centuries in the western Sudan. By the eighteenth and nineteenth centuries, a full-blown Islamized Swahili (east Africa) written and oral literature had also emerged. Most Islamized literatures – written and oral – consisted of praise songs, epic poems, chronicles, histories and theological treatises. In Ethiopia, Amharic chronicles, theological literature and histories appeared from the early part of the second millennium AD, at least, continuing into the nineteenth century. Added to these were religious texts and treatises written in Arabic by the nineteenth-century Islamic reformers, of whom UTHMAN DAN FODIO (Hausaland) and 'UMAR IBN SA'ID TAL were but two examples.

René A. Bravman, *Islam and Tribal Arts in West Africa* (Cambridge 1974).
Daniel F. McCall and Edna G. Bay (eds), *African Images: Essays in African Iconology* (New York, 1974).
Wole Soyinka, *Myth, Literature and the African World* (Cambridge 1976).
Jan Vansina, *Children of Woot* (Madison, Wisc. 1978).
Frank Willet, *African Art* (London, 1971).

B. MARIE PERINBAM

China and Japan

There are striking contrasts in the development of the arts and literature in China and Japan in the nineteenth century, which symbolized and reflected the contrasting responses of China and Japan to external pressure from the West. In China this was, politically, a period of internal rebellion, foreign aggression and the decline of the CH'ING DYNASTY, and the arts and literature reflected this decline and intellectual stagnation. The Ch'ing emperors had adopted and encouraged Confucian culture, which had always highly valued painting and calligraphy as part of a scholar's education. But by the nineteenth century Chinese art was largely derivative. The artistic standards of the distant past dominated, ancient models being considered far superior to contemporary works. These ancient models were slavishly copied; the resulting work often showed technical competence but little originality or liveliness. During the TAIPING REBELLION the great Ch'ing pottery at Ch'ing-t'e Ch'en in Kiangsi, which had produced the great porcelain of the Ming and Ch'ing periods, was destroyed. Although the industry was revived after the suppression of the rebellion, the products, while demonstrating great technical skill, were inferior imitations of earlier ware. By the end of the century art and literature, like the social, economic and political systems of China, were moribund, having failed to respond positively to the challenge of the West and to changing political and social conditions.

In contrast to the strong resistance in China to Western influences, in Japan there was a general, at times naively uncritical, enthusiasm to copy and adopt all things Western, particularly in the later part of the century after the MEIJI RESTORATION. The arts and literature were caught up in this movement. In literature Japanese novelists strove, not always entirely successfully, for greater social and political relevance. Painting and architecture were also influenced by Western forms, but this interaction was characterized by tension and ambiguity, symbolizing the relationship of Japan to the West. In architecture, Western styles and practicality were often adopted for public buildings, but foreign influences were resisted in domestic house-building, where traditional Japanese styles continued to dominate. A similar ambivalence spread across painting and the arts, prompting a reaction among Japanese nationalists who sought to locate the roots of Japan's growing strength firmly in its own traditions. Hence, enthusiasm for all things Western gave way to an attempt to resuscitate popular interest in indigenous artistic traditions and genres. The classical Noh drama was revived, as were flower-arranging and the tea ceremony, while the more ardent nationalists extolled the virtues of sumo wrestling and kendo, the art of fencing. Tension remained, but the ambiguity towards Western forms injected a vigour and vitality lacking in Chinese art and literature.

W. G. Beasley, *The Modern History of Japan* (London, 1963).
C. P. FitzGerald, *China: A Short Cultural History* (London, 1950).

JOHN DAVIES

India

In India the political chaos which followed the collapse of Mughal authority in the eighteenth century was mirrored in the parallel decline of the traditional dependence of the arts upon court patronage. Although glimmers of the rich tradition of miniature painting survived in isolated courts such as Kangra, and beautiful courtly poetry in Persian or Urdu was still composed in equally isolated courts, the traditional wellsprings of Indian culture were running dry. The nineteenth century was not noted for significant developments in the arts although by the century's end there were signs of new stirrings. However, in terms of literature, and especially vernacular literature, India produced its first internationally renowned poet, RABINDRANATH TAGORE. This was a century when India opened its heart and talents to the West, and was deeply influenced by and began to assimilate the English literary tradition. The Indian mind was stimulated by often conflicting new ideas and concepts that flowed in from the West.

The nineteenth century saw a steady expansion of institutions patterned after English models, institutions which prepared Indians for service in the East India Company's bureaucracy while fostering the development of an Anglicized elite. Administrative centres such as Calcutta, Madras and Bombay soon harboured an Indian elite population increasingly Anglicized in language and taste. This development was paralleled by the equally significant growth of vernacular education at the hands of Christian missionary organizations. Each in turn was to have a significant impact on literary trends by the end of the century.

Also significant were the advocates of the 'Hindu Reformation' in Bengal during the early decades of the century, including RAM MOHAN ROY, although they were not consciously attempting to stimulate vernacular literatures. While they wrote in English to reach the elites of Bengal and elsewhere in India, they also had to utilize the vernacular in order to foster reform among the masses. Numerous translations of Sanskrit religious texts into the vernacular served as a further stimulus to the use of Bengali for literary purposes. Indeed, the prose that flowed from the pen of Ram Mohan Roy represented some of the first modern Bengali literature. The use of vernacular languages elsewhere in India served as a medium to reach the rapidly expanding urban middle classes, which led to the development of other Indian languages into literary tools. The growing use of vernaculars, particularly Bengali or Hindi, by elites also found expression in short stories and plays which were deeply influenced by Western forms. The simultaneous development of newspapers, magazines and journals during the latter part of the century rapidly expanded an audience for such works and generated literary formats which had not previously existed in India.

The emergence of bicultural, bilingual literary figures was a distinguishing feature of India's intellectual and artistic community as the century ended. Individuals such as Rabindranath Tagore drew on the imagery of the Indian countryside while composing his most notable work *Gitanjali* in English. He paid due homage to the English romantic poets and the Bengali bards, and in the process was able to present Indian literary works that appealed to both Indian and English audiences. Indeed, *Gitanjali*, which was translated into all the major languages of western Europe, where it found an appreciative audience, marked the arrival of Indian literature on the world scene. Meanwhile, his other works, written in colloquial Bengali, were to have a deep impact on modern Bengali literature.

In painting, there was a similar synthesis at work although it was never as successful as in poetry and prose literature. Moreover, the dynamic of rising nationalism after 1885 probably did not provide the stimulus in the arts that it did in literature. However, beneath the surface the pictorial arts were poised to capture a vitality that would be revealed in the opening decades of the twentieth century. The rediscovery of India's architectural and artistic heritage, which was manifested by the notable shift of Calcutta painters such as Abanindranath Tagore (1817–1905) to Indian themes and techniques, presaged the arrival of the great Indian painters such as Jamini Roy (1887–1972) on the scene. Many like Abanindranath were involved in the rediscovery of the pictorial traditions of Indian courts as well as folk arts. They were no less members of the Bengal renaissance than better-known literary figures.

B. C. Chakravarty, *Ravindranath Tagore: His Mind and Art* (New Delhi, 1970).
Robert Crane and Bradford Spengenberg (eds), *Language and Society in Modern India* (New Delhi, 1981).
Ashok Mitra, *Four Painters* (New Delhi, 1965).

ROBERT J. YOUNG

Islamic world

Until the nineteenth century poetry held pride of place in the Islamic world, and poets of the classical style enjoyed the patronage of the wealthy as well as considerable social power. All of that did not end with the modern era, but the arts, particularly the artistic production of the urban literati, were profoundly altered by the sweeping changes that overtook national life generally. Chief among them was the impact of the West, including the spread of nationalism. Whether by outright occupation (as in India, Africa, central Asia and Indonesia), by gunboat diplomacy (as in the Mediterranean) or by means of its ubiquitous merchants and missionaries, the West became an unavoidable fact of life for most Muslim peoples.

The influence of Western power and culture produced a variety of creative responses, including the incorporation of anticolonialist themes into Islamic poetry and prose. More generally, 'the West' aroused new concerns that produced a new consciousness far removed from the messages and structures of classical Islamic literature. The latter were now displaced, although they had in any case seen their best days centuries earlier; more recent authors had largely been content to imitate the classics. Western literature and the arts, whether or not attached to a colonial presence, stimulated writers, and to a lesser extent artists, to 'reinvent' the creative production of Islamic societies. Some efforts, notably in architecture, resulted in the wholesale adoption or imitation of Western styles. In Istanbul, the capital of the Ottoman Empire, baroque excess became the new vogue in palace architecture and interior design. The ruling families of Iran, Egypt and India similarly indulged themselves with new palaces, fountains and offices that combined, often unhappily, Vienna with Delhi or Cairo.

Uncritical imitation characterized literary efforts as well, but this was a temporary state of affairs as Muslim intellectuals, long cut off from non-Islamic sources, embraced the new forms and ideas that now flowed across their borders. Translations of eighteenth-century French and British writings were especially popular in Istanbul and Cairo, often as much for their politics as for their art. Along with the wave of translations, Turks, Persians, Arabs and Indians were introduced to plays and novels, new genres that were soon assimilated into the national repertoire. Islamic literatures were thus to a great extent 'Westernized' by contact with the literary output of the West. But over the long term Islamic literatures can be said to have been nationalized, revived within indigenous traditions. Spurred by Western literature and literary methods, Muslim intellectuals searched within their own cultures for what was native and lasting. Writers and thinkers delved into their national pasts, beyond the hardened categories of classical tradition, in the quest for an authentic national voice. They studied living folk tradition, previously ignored by the makers of 'high culture', and sought out story-tellers and balladeers as living bearers of that authentic voice. By the end of the century a new generation of writers had broken through the strictures of traditional urban literature by combining contemporary themes of nation, justice and patriotism with newly widened vocabularies and patterns of expression. Perhaps the major achievement of the new spirit of experimentation was the breakdown of the barriers that had for so long divided urban and court-centred literature from oral and non-elite language and forms. Although differences still remained, by the end of the century one could speak with some authority of a common literary idiom.

In the Ottoman Empire and Egypt, where there had formerly been one official 'newspaper' (a calendar of government business), dozens of newspapers, scholarly journals and popular magazines now accommodated the rush to read and be read. Heavy censorship by the Ottoman sultans and the Iranian shahs and elsewhere by European colonial authorities muffled the politics of the new periodicals, but authors employed every literary subterfuge to baffle the censors. In any case, thanks to increased mobility and training in a variety of languages, even the most radical thinkers could find a haven out of the reach of their government. Indeed one of the main stimuli to creativity was the constant stream of political refugees from state to state: central Asians and Iranians to Istanbul, Arabs and Turks to Paris and Geneva, North Africans to Damascus and Cairo. In the twentieth century, with the establishment of nation-states in the Islamic world, nineteenth-century literature has been studied less for its own sake than for signs of the presence or absence of Turkish, Arab or Iranian national feeling. More recently, however, as historians have tried to understand the internal dynamics of Islamic societies, they have directed attention to the internal cultural dimensions of the new Islamic literature. However, it remains to be seen how many of the nineteenth-century pioneers will find durable reputations based on aesthetic judgements rather than on their politics.

P. M. Holt, A. K. S. Lambton and B. Lewis (eds), *The Cambridge History of Islam*, vol. 2 (Cambridge, 1977).

MADELINE C. ZILFI

Latin America

Between 1810 and 1830 most of Latin America broke free from three centuries of colonial rule by Spain and Portugal, following the Enlightenment and the great revolutions of 1776 in North America and 1789 in Europe. In literary and artistic terms the colonial period is associated above all with the baroque, which took on its own peculiar forms in the New World setting and has remained an essential ingredient of Latin American artistic identity to this day. However, the late eighteenth century saw the adoption in both literature and architecture of a broadly neoclassical style consonant with the declining prestige of Spain and Portugal and the rising prestige of all things French. French influence remained strong throughout the nineteenth century: indeed, it was because of that influence that this part of America became known, during this period, as 'Latin'.

Although the neoclassical tradition accompanied the early emancipation struggles, the European romantic movement had taken root in South America long before the wars with Spain were over, and romanticism would dominate the rest of the century. Its inherent rebelliousness and its regionalist impulse were well attuned to the spirit of the age in those youthful republics setting out in search of a new national and continental identity. This had to be accomplished without the aid of national theatres, for drama was an art that failed to flourish in the region.

In poetry the outstanding names of the early independence era were Andrés Bello (Venezuela, 1781–1865), author of a celebrated *Allocution to Poetry* (1823), José Joaquín Olmedo (Ecuador, 1780–1847), with his *Song to Bolívar* (1825), and the Brazilians Antônio Gonçalves Dias (1823–64) and Antônio de Castro Alves (1847–71). All of them looked anew at the landscapes of the newly liberated continent and the different cultural and ethnic groups which inhabited it. However, the single most interesting poetic phenomenon of the century was probably the gauchesque movement in Argentina and Uruguay. Its outstanding exponent was José Hernández (1834–86), who created the Argentine national epic *Martín Fierro* (1872) about a gaucho cowboy and rebel. By the century's end Spanish American poets were embarked on a radical new movement called 'modernismo', whose leading lights were the incomparable Rubén Darío (Nicaragua, 1867–1916) and the Cuban freedom fighter José Martí (1853–95). This was the first literary current from the New World to reverse the historical process by influencing Spain, the colonial motherland.

Spain had in fact violently discouraged the writing of prose fiction in its American colonies and had also prohibited imaginative works about their native inhabitants, the 'Indians'. Not surprisingly, then, novels appeared at the same time as the revolt against Spain – the first, *The Itching Parrot* (1816) by the Mexican José Joaquín Fernández de Lizardi (1776–1827), ironically enough, in the Spanish picaresque style. Later narrative landmarks included the first major dictator novels: the documentary *Facundo* (1845) by the Argentinian Domingo Faustino Sarmiento (1811–88), which also inaugurated the great Latin American theme of the frontier between civilization and barbarism; and *Amalia* (1851), by José Mármol (Argentina, 1817–71), which condemned the tyrant Juan Manuel de Rosas. These were followed by *María* (1867), a weepy romantic work by the Colombian Jorge Isaacs (1837–95); the ironic *Peruvian Traditions* of Ricardo Palma (1833–1919), set in the colonial period; and *Birds without a Nest* (1889), a novel condemning the exploitation of the Indians by a pioneering woman novelist, Clorinda Matto de Turner (Peru, 1854–1909). But the greatest novelist of the century, and perhaps the only Latin American writer of unmistakable world rank during the century of independence was the brilliant Brazilian mulatto Machado de Assis (1839–1908), author of works such as *Epitaph of a Small Winner* (1881) and *Dom Casmurro* (1899). In view of Latin America's remarkable contribution to world fiction in the twentieth century, it seems appropriate to end our survey with him.

G. Martin, 'The Literature, Music and Art of Latin America from Independence to *c.*1870', in L. Bethell (ed.), *The Cambridge History of Latin America*, vol. 3: *From Independence to c.1870* (Cambridge, 1985), pp. 797–839.
—— , 'The Literature, Music and Art of Latin America 1870–1930', ibid., vol. 4: *c.1870 to 1930* (Cambridge, 1986), pp. 443–526.

GERALD MARTIN

Western

See DECORATIVE ARTS; MUSIC; NOVEL; PAINTING; POETRY; SCULPTURE; THEATRE AND PERFORMING ARTS.

Arya Samaj   A militant Hindu organization, Arya Samaj was founded by Swami Dayananda (1824–83) in 1874 to defend Hinduism against Western influences and to end abuses such as female infanticide and idolatry which made HINDUISM vulnerable to attack. Preaching a message of reform based on a return to Vedic traditions, the organization became deeply identified with Hindu nationalism and advocated a return to Hinduism by Muslim and Christian converts, large numbers of whom had left degraded levels of the Hindu caste (varna) structure. Creation of congregational forms of worship, which emphazized egalitarian values, and the creation of reconversion rites proved to be successful in reaching many of these individuals although often at the cost of conflict between Hindu and Muslim or Sikh communities. In the Punjab it played a significant role in creating tensions between Muslims and Hindus in the last decades of the nineteenth century.

J. T. Jordens, *Dayananda Saraswati: His Life and Ideas* (Bombay, 1978).

ROBERT J. YOUNG

Ashanti [Asante]   The Ashanti are Akan-speakers (Akan is a member of the Twi (Kwa) language cluster) from the west African hinterland of present-day Ghana and the Ivory Coast. Prior to the late-nineteenth-century Scramble for Africa, they developed a large hegemonical confederation, or grouping of chiefdoms, recognizing the paramountcy of the asantehene, or ruler of the Asante peoples, with Kumasi as their capital. The state was founded by Osei Tutu (*d* 1712) in the late seventeenth century; later military conquests extended its power over smaller polities, eventually creating a hegemonical range extending north–south from the coast to the savannah. By the nineteenth century, when it reached its apogee – gaining control of the rich Akan gold-fields, together with important trade routes – the Ashanti became important gold and slave producers. The state sold war captives to the ATLANTIC SLAVE TRADE (illegal after 1815), but was never heavily dependent on the trade for revenues, however. War captives not exchanged on Atlantic marts were sold into African domestic slavery (*see* SLAVERY (AFRICA)). Likewise, gold not stored for religious/ritual purposes was sold extensively on both domestic and foreign markets. While large gold-production sectors were worked by slave labour, some gold mines were owned by the asantehene, others by tax-paying Akan chiefs.

It was thus a rich state, with large foreign exchange reserves (gold and slaves). Nineteenth-century constitutional reforms rationalized and centralized its administration, including the appointment and promotion of government officials on a merit basis. In the wake of nineteenth-century military reforms, including the stockpiling of Western arms (*see* SEGU BAMANA; ETHIOPIA) – combined with growing British mercantile interests – the stage was set for a series of Ashanti–British wars (1823–31, 1863–74). Refusing to accept a British protectorate (1890), on 20 January 1897 the asantehene was deposed by a British expeditionary force, which proclaimed a protectorate over the region on 16 August 1897 (*see* PREMPEH I).

Ivor Wilks, *Asante in the Nineteenth Century* (Cambridge 1975).

B. MARIE PERINBAM

assimilation, French policies of   Although inspired by the revolutionary decrees of 1792, French policies of assimilation did not take shape until the Second Republic (1848–52), when assimilationist policies were developed for French colonies. Based on the assumption that all men were legally equal 'without distinction of colour', French assimilation policies, however, assumed the superiority of European cultures, especially the French, and the inferiority of most non-European cultures. The expectation, therefore, was that in narrowing the cultural gap Africans could be transformed into 'black Frenchmen' by Gallicizing their political institutions, economic practices and educational systems. Full implementation of these controversial and contradictory policies, however, foundered for the most part on opposition to the extension of French citizenship and civil rights (including voting rights) to peoples whose presence would have altered the face of metropolitan political institutions. The Senegal colony and ALGERIA were about the only territories where assimilation was seriously applied, although several individuals, including the former Senegalese president Léopold Senghor (*b* 1906), successfully 'narrowed the gap' by becoming *évolués*, or those assimilating into French culture and civilization.

B. MARIE PERINBAM

Aston, Louise (*b* 26 November 1814; *d* 21 December 1871)   German poet, novelist, journalist and political radical. She was one of the first generation of professional women writers. Her first volume of poems appeared in 1846. Her literary writings, such as 'Lied einer schlesischen Weberin' (Song of a Silesian Woman Weaver), often addressed political themes. Aston rejected marriage and bourgeois morality; she smoked cigars, wore men's clothes and denounced religion. Exiled from Berlin for her radical views, she returned to fight on the barricades during the 1848 revolution and then joined the Berlin Freischaar expedition against Denmark in Schleswig-Holstein. She also founded a revolutionary newspaper, *Der Freischarler* (The Insurgent), which published seven issues in November and December 1848. Although she was far more radical than her contemporary Louise OTTO-PETERS, they agreed on the need for women to be economically self-sustaining.

GAIL SAVAGE

Ausgleich   *see* COMPROMISE OF 1867.

Austerlitz, Battle of (2 December 1805)   Known as the 'Battle of the Three Emperors', the Battle of Austerlitz shattered the Third Coalition and finally put an end to the Holy Roman Empire. After forcing the main Austrian army to surrender at Ulm, Napoleon BONAPARTE occupied Vienna and advanced into present-day Moravia to confront Francis I of Austria and Alexander I of Russia who had assembled an army of

85,000 men. Somewhat outnumbered, Napoleon enticed the allies into attacking his right wing, and then, using forces that he had hitherto concealed, attacked the forces thus deployed in the flank, splitting the Austro-Russian army in two in the process. Desperate allied counter-attacks proved of no avail, and their troops were driven from the field, having suffered some 27,000 casualties. Completely beaten, Austria was forced to sue for peace on the most unfavourable of terms, losing large quantities of territory in Germany and Italy.

                                                             CHARLES ESDAILE

Australia When James Cook (1728–79) sighted the east coast of Australia in 1770 and claimed it for the British crown under the name of New South Wales, he followed in the wake of Dutch discoverers who had charted parts of the west and south-east in the seventeenth century. Ensuing navigation, especially by Matthew Flinders (1774–1814), revealed that the island continent was 3 million square miles in extent with a coastline of 12,500 miles. The Aboriginal people, numbering about 750,000 in 1788, had already inhabited the continent for at least 50,000 years. Divided into roughly 800 bands, they spoke over 260 languages with numerous dialects. Living as hunters and gatherers in moderate comfort and peace, they had a highly developed Stone Age culture and a deep and diverse knowledge of the land and its resources.

After the War of Independence Britain could no longer transport convicts to its former American territories, and in 1788 the first whites arrived at Sydney to found a penal settlement for the refuse of Britain's overflowing prisons. White civilization was principally founded on the forced labour of the 160,000 convicts who were transported to the Australian colonies from 1788 to 1868. They were one-eighth female and one-third Irish and the vast majority became stable members of society on gaining their freedom. South Australia prided itself in being free from the taint of convictism but western Australia was forced to recognize that its failing economy demanded convict labour by 1850. Transportation ceased to the eastern colonies in the 1840s and 1850s when it became clear that further economic, social and political developments depended on free immigration.

After whaling, sealing and fishing, the settlers turned to the breeding and development of the merino sheep. Pastoralism, with an easily transportable product and a constant demand in Britain for fine wool, shaped an industry that became the basis of the economy. No recognition had been given to the prior occupation of Australia by the Aborigines, and the insatiable demand for pastoral land caused their decimation, the loss of many of their languages and much of their culture. Slaughter and disease also took their toll. They were exterminated in Tasmania (Van Diemen's Land) and reduced to a remnant in the south of the continent but remained more numerous in the centre and northern half.

Free immigration started principally in the 1830s and increased rapidly during and after the GOLD RUSHES of the 1850s when Australia ceased to be a mere sheepwalk. A measure of responsible government was granted by the crown: Australia became the world's largest exporter of gold and the diversity in population changed the nature of the old penal society. (*See also* BUSHRANGERS.) Industry expanded, centred upon Sydney and Melbourne, inland towns mushroomed, railways linked the bush to the city and militant trade unions helped to make Australia 'the working man's paradise'. The matrix of a white society was laid down, based firmly on the British model in politics, education, the Christian religion and the general mores of the people. Republicanism and nationalism, expressed vigorously by the national weekly the *Bulletin* and in some local literature, remained largely muted with loyalty to crown and empire being the principal motif. White racism was practised initially against the Aborigines but then extended to the Chinese on the gold-fields and Pacific labour on the Queensland cane-fields. A society almost totally homogeneous in colour, language, dress, food and outlook was rapidly shaped, although the Gaelic Irish retained some distinctive qualities.

The depression and drought of the 1890s culminated in the foundation of the AUSTRALIAN LABOR PARTY in 1893, based on the need for worker solidarity and political representation. By 1900 the white population was about 3 million, and varying tariff barriers and the lack of a united defence force fuelled moves towards federation of the colonies into a commonwealth in 1901. Lacking a national capital, the federal parliament sat in Melbourne until its transfer to Canberra in 1927. One of its first acts was to legislate the exclusion of non-whites in what became known as the White Australia Policy, based on racist, cultural and economic motives. Federation served to strengthen the bonds with the crown and the second Boer War saw 16,000 Australians enlisting to fight under banners reading 'For Queen and Country' and 'The Empire Right or Wrong'. Australia's post-colonial period had begun.

Manning Clark, *A History of Australia*, 6 vols (Melbourne, 1962–87).
John Molony, *History of Australia* (Melbourne, 1987).

JOHN MOLONY

Australian Labor Party Among the oldest parties of organized labour in the world, the Australian Labor Party (ALP) grew from the trade unions which, after the dislocation caused by the GOLD RUSHES, had reshaped and become intercolonial bodies. In Victoria the EIGHT-HOUR DAY was won in 1856 but its application was not widespread initially. Lacking political representation, partly because of the non-payment of parliamentary members, and hardened in resolve by the defeats suffered by the workers in their struggle against organized capital in the Great Strikes of 1890 and 1891, unionists saw the need for solidarity. The Trades and Labor Council of New South Wales was a strong and well-organized body and from it the ALP had its origins. It had immediate electoral success in New South Wales and held the balance of power in several parliaments.

Pragmatic and reluctant to espouse theory, the party remained free of radicalism and held as its primary purpose the civilizing of capitalism by concentrating on wages, conditions of work and the provision of progressive social benefits. To some, Australia thus became known as a 'social laboratory'. On a more general level, the party was quick to play a vital role in the movement which resulted in the acceptance of federation in 1901 and the formulation of the White Australia Policy by the first federal government. The ALP drew support from rural and urban areas and the majority of Catholics voted for it. State branches were formed in all the colonies and the 'first Labor government in the world' was the Queensland branch of the party in 1899 but it was short-lived. By 1901 the federal party was well established under the leadership of J. C. Watson (1867–1941) who became prime minister in 1904. The ALP remains Australia's oldest political party.

Bede Nairn, *Civilising Capitalism* (Melbourne, 1989).

JOHN MOLONY

Austro-Hungarian Empire *see* HABSBURG EMPIRE.

Austro-Prussian War (1866) War broke out between Austria and Prussia following the defeat of Denmark in 1864 by the two powers and the victors' inability to agree on a redistribution of power in the Germanies. Austria, the dominant power in the GERMAN CONFEDERATION, refused to yield to BISMARCK'S demand that PRUSSIA be granted a greater voice in German affairs and be recognized as the dominant power in northern Germany. Bismarck was willing to go to war to challenge Austrian hegemony in Germany.

The Austrians, underestimating Bismarck's skills and relying on the support of the lesser German states, refused to make meaningful concessions. When Bismarck began negotiations with the Italians (promising them Venetia if they joined Prussia in a war with Austria), Austria turned to Napoleon III of France. The Austrians told the French emperor that if Italy would agree to stay neutral in an Austro-Prussian war they would cede Venetia to Italy. The Italians refused Austria's offer, Bismarck spurned a last-minute attempt to resolve the conflict peacefully and war between Prussia and Austria broke out on 14 June.

The war lasted only six weeks and ended with a decisive Austrian defeat at Sadowa. Under the terms of the preliminary Peace of

Nikolsburg (26 July), Hanover, electoral Hesse, Nassau and the city of Frankfurt were incorporated into Prussia. The German Confederation was abolished, and Germany was divided along the River Main. The states north of the river formed the North German Confederation under Prussian leadership, and those south of the Main – Bavaria, Württemberg and Baden – remained independent and were forced to join a secret military alliance with Prussia against France. Austria lost Venetia to Italy, and its influence in Germany was ended; however, in a show of magnanimity designed to ensure good relations between Prussia and Austria in the future, Bismarck did not force Austria to pay an indemnity or to cede other territory to Prussia. These provisions were incorporated into the final Treaty of Prague, which was signed by the two powers on 23 August 1866.

O. Pflanze, *Bismarck and the Development of Germany*, vol. 1 (Princeton, NJ, 1990).

GEORGE O. KENT

Ayacucho, Battle of (9 December 1824)   The last major battle of the Spanish American wars of independence, Ayacucho secured the emancipation of PERU. At the beginning of 1824 the royalist forces of Viceroy José de la Serna (1770–1831) still controlled much of the country. However, in April Simón BOLÍVAR, who had assembled a 'patriot' army consisting principally of Colombians in the northern city of Trujillo, moved his forces into the highlands, and on 6 August he defeated General Canterac (1787–1836) in a cavalry skirmish at Junín. The royalist army, still intact, withdrew southwards, and while Bolívar returned to Lima his lieutenant, Antonio José de Sucre (1793–1830), manœuvred for position with La Serna and Canterac. They met on 9 December 1824 at Ayacucho, almost 380 miles from Lima. While the royalists possessed a numerical advantage, better artillery and a stronger position, their initial attack was repulsed by Sucre's forces. La Serna was wounded and captured, and the Spanish surrender agreed the same day.

RORY MILLER

B

Babbage, Charles (*b* Teignmouth, 26 December 1792; *d* London, 18 October 1871) English mathematician and inventor. One of the first philosophers of industrialization, he is best known today for his efforts to build a digital computer. Born into a wealthy family, he entered Cambridge University in 1810 and distinguished himself in mathematics. He became a fellow of the Royal Society in 1816, but believed it was a useless institution and did much to promote alternatives, such as the British Association for the Advancement of Science, which he help found in 1831. His book, *The Economy of Manufactures and Machinery*, published in 1832, was an influential study of the basic principles behind new industrial technologies of the time – one of the first studies of the organization of production. As early as 1822, Babbage wrote about the possibilities of making machines perform complex calculations, and he spent the latter half of his long life designing and trying to build very complex devices to do mathematics 'by steam'. His 'difference engine' and 'analytical engine' incorporated important ideas, later applied in the design of digital computers in the twentieth century, but were too complicated and expensive to succeed in his time.

ROBERT FRIEDEL

bacteriology *see* DISEASE, THEORIES OF.

Bahadur Shah II (*b* Delhi, ?1768; *d* Rangoon, 7 November 1862) Ruler of India (1837–58). He came to a throne whose authority was confined to the palace complex (Red Fort) at Delhi where he existed on an allowance provided by the English East India Company. Only the unexpected arrival of the Meerut mutineers on 11 May 1857 (*see* INDIAN MUTINY) thrust this reclusive poet-emperor, ruler over a shadow state, into history. Unable to resist their demands and the pressures from royal princes led by Mirza Mughal (*d* 1857), he eventually assented to act as figurehead for a resurgent Mughal Empire, a move which fated him to be the last Mughal emperor.

When the British took Delhi in September 1857, the princes were slaughtered for their complicity, the population was expelled from the city and Bahadur Shah was taken prisoner. A trial followed, with a decision to exile the emperor and surviving members of the royal family to Rangoon.

Percival Spear, *Twilight of the Mughals* (Karachi, 1973).

ROBERT J. YOUNG

Bailén, Battle of (19 July 1808) At the beginning of the PENINSULAR WAR a force of 20,000 French troops under General Pierre Dupont (1765–1840) was dispatched from Madrid to secure Andalucía. After getting as far as Cordoba, which he stormed amid scenes of the greatest brutality, Dupont became increasingly alarmed at his isolation and decided to retreat. The march was mishandled, however, half of Dupont's troops, together with the general himself, being cut off by a force of Spanish regulars which had seized the town of Bailén. A series of attempts to break through in baking heat having been repulsed, Dupont was forced to capitulate with his entire army. Such an event was naturally an immense blow to Napoleon's prestige, resistance to the French being greatly encouraged both in Spain and the rest of Europe. Yet Bailén was in fact a fluke, its chief practical effect being to lull the Spaniards into a disastrous sense of over-confidence.

CHARLES ESDAILE

Bakunin, Mikhail Aleksandrovich (*b* Novotorzhskii, 18 May 1814; *d* Berne, 19 June 1876) Russian anarchist. Of noble birth and well educated, he devoted his life after a brief army career to revolutionary activity. He actively participated in the 1848 revolutions in Europe (*see* REVOLUTIONS OF 1848). Arrested and sentenced to death, he was extradited to Russia, imprisoned and then exiled to Siberia, whence he escaped, via Japan and America to western Europe. He joined the FIRST INTERNATIONAL in 1868, but fell out with Marx and led the anarchist wing, opposing state socialism and warning of the dangers of despotism. He was expelled in 1872. A tireless yet strangely ineffective revolutionary leader, he left no systematic expression of his views. The clearest is in *Reaction in Germany* (1842) – where he coined the anarchist slogan 'The passion for destruction is also a creative one' – and in his journal the *People's Cause,* published in Geneva.

See also ANARCHISM.

G. P. Maximoff (ed.), *The Political Philosophy of Bakunin* (Glencoe, Ill., 1953).

A. V. KNOWLES

balance of power The phrase 'balance of power' is often used in international politics to define a 'just equilibrium between nations as shall prevent any one of them being in a position to dominate the rest'. Although it was known in ancient history, the concept of a balance of power among nations was refined and expanded by Grotius (1583–1645) and others in the seventeenth century. In the early nineteenth century the phrase was used to describe the system established by the CONGRESS OF VIENNA. The territorial settlement achieved by the congress was meant to prevent any further aggression by France, to forestall one-power domination in Europe and to achieve an equitable balance among the major European powers that would preserve the peace. The balance of power – Great Britain and France on the one hand, and Austria, Prussia and Russia on the other – played an important part in resolving the crisis that followed Belgian independence in 1830, but broke down prior to the Crimean War.

Examples of attempts to invoke the balance-of-power principle during the latter part of the nineteenth century include the MEDITERRANEAN AGREEMENTS of 1887, in which Great Britain, Italy and Austria-Hungary opposed Russia and France, and, shortly after the turn of the century, when the TRIPLE ALLIANCE of Germany, Austria-Hungary and Italy was balanced by the Triple Entente of Great Britain, France and Russia. The breakdown of this balance led to the outbreak of the First World War. Thus, for long periods of the nineteenth century, maintaining a balance of power among the European states acted to prevent a general war.

E. V. Gulick, *Europe's Classical Balance of Power* (New York, 1967).

GEORGE O. KENT

ballot, secret While elections remained confined to very limited numbers of voters in small communities, it seemed natural and simple for the act of voting to be a public one. Traditional assumptions began to be questioned seriously only when the size of the electorate was significantly increased or when a major upheaval led to the drafting of a new constitution. Thus in France the first experiments with the secret ballot began in the 1790s and the system became the general rule during the first half of the nineteenth century. Australia adopted the ballot in 1856. But many liberal, parliamentary states refused to regard the reform as self-evidently desirable. Britain, for example, did not introduce it until 1872 and Denmark as late as 1901. Even in the United States the ballot was no more than semi-secret in the nineteenth century. The parties there printed their own ballot-papers listing all the candidates for office. The voter took one, which he was free to amend, and dropped it into the ballot-box. Not until the 1890s was the production and control of ballot-papers generally taken over by the public authorities and the process of voting made secret.

The unspoken argument for traditional open voting was that it seemed calculated to maintain the influence of landowners and others over the electors. There was a widespread fear about the consequences if the lower classes were left an entirely free choice. Secondly, it was suggested that the secret ballot would effectively disenfranchise illiterate voters, though in practice such men were not likely to be eligible anyway. Thirdly, a strong school of thought from the late eighteenth century onwards held that elections should be designed to foster public spiritedness among the citizenry. In Britain even a reformist Liberal like John Stuart MILL argued that voters were under an obligation to take account of the public interest, not simply personal advantage, and that other citizens were entitled to be aware of actions which affected them. By contrast, the ballot appeared calculated to maximize the extent of private, and by implication corrupt, influences. Finally, the ballot was condemned by association with French subversiveness and the allegedly Catholic penchant for underhandedness and secrecy. It was widely denounced as 'evasive', 'shabby', 'inconsistent with the manly spirit' and 'degrading to Englishmen'.

However, in Britain the ballot found advocates among the late-eighteenth-century parliamentary reformers, and was the subject of a number of petitions in 1830–1. At this time the radicals' chief claim was that it was a necessary means of curtailing the excessive influence of the aristocracy. However, the cabinet dropped the proposal from the scheme that became law in 1832 in order to make it more acceptable to parliament. After 1832 disillusionment with the effects of the Great Reform Act stimulated radical interest in the ballot, for they believed that reform had strengthened the existing hold of the aristocracy (*see* PARLIAMENTARY REFORM). It was also taken up in the late 1830s and 1840s by the Chartists and enshrined as one of the six points of their famous charter (*see* CHARTISM). Francis PLACE was one of those who regarded the ballot as of central importance. However, several leading Chartists remained unconvinced. To some extent, association with Chartist demands served to undermine parliamentary support for the ballot and the issue lost momentum during the mid nineteenth century.

It was revived by the passage of the Second Reform Act in 1867. The enfranchisement of working-class voters had the effect, at the 1868 election, of increasing expenditure and bribery. It was also widely conceded that the urban workers were often vulnerable to intimidation and undue influence by employers; this reinforced the existing claims that tenant farmers in rural Wales and Ireland suffered eviction for opposing the views of Conservative landlords. In this situation the traditional arguments against the ballot rapidly lost their force at least in the Liberal ranks. The Liberal leader, W. E. GLADSTONE, changed his view abruptly in 1869. After appointing a select committee which inquired especially into Australian experience with the ballot, Gladstone introduced a bill in 1870. This was twice rejected by the Conservative majority in the House of Lords but the threat of a dissolution forced them to back down and the ballot was enacted in 1872.

Some historians have suggested that the effects were not very great, partly because voters were reluctant to believe that the ballot could really be secret from landlords, agents and priests. In Ireland the initial breakthrough by the Home Rulers predated the ballot as did the shift to Liberalism in Wales. However, the ballot almost certainly accelerated the trend and facilitated the anti-Conservative revolt in the English counties when the labourers won the vote in 1884. Contemporaries agreed that the ballot had the immediate effect of making elections quieter and less boisterous; fewer police and troops were required. Carried out in the relative privacy of a booth, voting ceased to be the public social occasion it had traditionally been. This greatly promoted the participation of women, who had been granted a municipal vote in 1869 but often felt deterred by the rough, masculine ambience of the hustings.

See also FRANCHISE REFORM, WOMEN'S SUFFRAGE.

B. L. Kinzer, 'The Un-Englishness of the Secret Ballot', *Albion*, 10 (1978), 237–56.
C. O'Leary, *The Elimination of Corrupt Practices in British Elections 1868–1911* (Oxford, 1962).

MARTIN PUGH

Bamaku   *see* SEGU BAMANA.

bank holidays   At the beginning of the nineteenth century the Bank of England closed for business on forty-four days in a year, but the pressures of a rapidly industrializing society reduced these bank holidays to four a year by 1834. Later in the century a growing demand for more leisure time was reflected in the passing through parliament of a Bank Holiday Act in 1871, and a Holidays Extension Act four years later. The Act of 1871 added Boxing Day (New Year's Day in Scotland), Easter Monday, Whit Monday and the first Monday in August to the existing holidays of Good Friday, Christmas Day, May (*see* MAY DAY) and November. Perhaps most significant was the institution of the first Monday in August as a holiday as an entirely secular consideration: it was not, like most other holidays, associated with religious festivals.

J. M. GOLBY

banking   Businesses engaged in financial intermediation, banks seek deposits from those in surplus on the one hand and lend to those in deficit on the other. They are distinguished from other kinds of financial institution because their liabilities, whether notes or deposits, function as money, being transferable as payment in the settlement of debts. The nineteenth century was an important period in banking history, particularly with respect to developments in the economic organization of the banking firm and the banking industry. There was also the emergence of CENTRAL BANKING. Three broad phases of banking development may be distinguished.

The first was a continuation of previously existing trends, with the private bank as the predominant type. Private banks were often firms that had originally engaged in some other trade or profession while practising banking as a subsidiary activity. The partners accepted deposits and used their own capital as a basis for issuing notes, making loans and discounting bills of exchange. Their liability for debts was unlimited. In England there was little banking outside London prior to 1750 but as industrialization proceeded country banking grew rapidly. Much of the new industry was self-financed and the banker's role was to provide working capital by way of short-term credits. Elsewhere in Europe and in the United States bankers similarly participated only to a limited degree in the finance of industry, though in France the Paris *haute banques* did for a time provide long-term finance for certain industries. Financing operations on a wholly different scale were undertaken by those private banks that provided or procured state loans. Two of these, Barings (with Hope & Company) and Rothschilds, successively held the position of leading financier to governments.

The second phase was marked by the spread of joint-stock banking. On the continent of Europe it began after the mid-century, stimulated by the coming of the railways, which brought to prominence sectors of industry that had greater financing demands than could be met by the run of existing institutions. In England it began earlier, under a somewhat different impulse. The perceived vulnerability of private banks to financial crises led to a lifting, in 1826 and 1833, of the legal limit on the number of partners that could comprise a banking firm. The early 'joint-stock' banking co-partnerships differed little, however, from their predecessors and became a force capable of dominating English banking only after 1862 when they could be formed as private limited-liability companies.

With the rise of joint-stock banking in England came the development of deposit banking and the relative decline of note issues. This was due not only to the 1844 restrictions on the right to issue notes but also to the popularity of the cheque. Joint-stock deposit banks of the English type were founded on the Continent but they were not the norm. Far more influential was the example of the French Crédit Mobilier, founded in 1852, which combined deposit banking with the provision of long-term credit, the issue of shares and direct investment in industry. In Germany, for example, all joint-stock banks eventually became 'universal' banks; in France, by contrast, the experiment was short-lived. Universal banking did not develop in England, where banks eschewed long-term commitments. In the United States note-issuing joint-stock banks existed from the beginning. Initially they were governed by the laws of their home state, a circumstance which kept their operations localized as compared to those of private banks but left them no less prey to imprudent behaviour. In 1863–4 the federal government sought to achieve monetary order by providing model banking regulations, together with incentives for banks to become 'national banks' rather than 'state banks'. The outcome was a stable currency but a want of flexibility in banking practice.

The third phase was the bank-concentration movement, which radically altered the shape of banking systems in the last twenty to thirty years of the century. The movement was most marked in England, where waves of amalgamations produced a system dominated by a few big banks with nationwide networks of branches. In Germany, too, mergers played the major part, while in France banks achieved national significance principally by branching. Concentration in Japanese banking was an integral part of the form of economic concentration peculiar to Japan: zaibatsu, the hierarchical arrangements of firms controlled by family dynasties.

Karl Born, *International Banking in the Nineteenth and Twentieth Centuries* (London, 1983).
Charles Kindleberger, *A Financial History of Western Europe* (London, 1984).
GORDON FLETCHER

Bardo, Treaty of (1881)   At the CONGRESS OF BERLIN Bismarck and Lord Salisbury gave their approval to France to establish a protectorate over the north African country TUNISIA, although both France and Italy had economic interests in that region. After the congress the French government hesitated to take action, but when a Tunisian delegation went to Palermo to pay its respects to the king of Italy French public opinion was aroused. The French government used a raid by Kroumir tribesmen into neighbouring Algeria as an excuse to send a punitive expedition into Tunisia, forcing the bey to sign the Treaty of Bardo. The treaty established a French protectorate over Tunisia. Bismarck brushed aside Italy's protests over France's high-handedness, and French rule over the area continued until the Second World War.

A. J. P. Taylor, *The Struggle for the Mastery in Europe 1848–1918* (Oxford, 1954).
GEORGE O. KENT

Baring Crisis (1890)   The major financial crash of the late nineteenth century, the Baring Crisis occurred in 1890 when the European mania for investment in Latin America collapsed. Problems first became evident in 1889 with the failures of de Lesseps's PANAMA CANAL scheme and the Comptoir National d'Escompte's attempt to corner world copper supplies. The deepening financial crisis in ARGENTINA and URUGUAY then made it impossible for the leading London merchant bank of Baring Brothers to meet its liabilities. Barings had been seriously mismanaged, not least in attempting to monopolize an important but speculative concession in Buenos Aires. It appealed for help to the Bank of England whose governor, with the support of other leading merchant banks and the British government, mounted a rescue operation. This saved the City of London from collapse and permitted the reconstruction of Barings, aided particularly by the Argentine government's willingness to adopt deflationary policies and to reschedule the country's debts.

RORY MILLER

Barton, Clara (*b* Oxford, Massachusetts, 25 December 1821; *d* Washington, DC, 12 April 1912)   Founder of the American Red Cross. Before the American Civil War she was employed at the United States patent office (1854–61). With the outbreak of the war in 1861, she organized volunteers to aid the sick and wounded on the field and in hospitals, where her efforts at Antietam and Fredericksburg were particularly notable. At the end of the war President Lincoln commissioned her to locate and identify prisoners and dead buried in unmarked graves. She went to Europe in 1869, where she participated in relief efforts during the Franco-Prussian War and worked with the International Committee of the Red Cross. The United States Senate ratified the Geneva Convention in 1882, forming the American Association of the Red Cross with Barton as its president. After broadening the organization's responsibilities to include wider domestic and international relief efforts, she served again with distinction during the Spanish-American War. She resigned from the Red Cross in 1904.

KEVIN MURPHY

baseball   Though popularly believed to have been invented by Abner Doubleday (1819–93) in Cooperstown, New York, baseball evolved from the English game of rounders. Organized play in the United States dates from the early 1840s and the first modern rules were written in 1845. The sport became professional in 1868 when the Cincinnati Redstockings began signing players to seasonal contracts. Baseball became irrevocably commercial when the National League was formed in 1876. Team-owners were entrepreneurs whose often cut-throat management mirrored the competitive business environment of the GILDED AGE. The reserve clause in players' contracts, not successfully challenged until the 1970s, forced players to stay with one franchise for life, and blacklisting and fining players to preserve owner autonomy was not uncommon. Closely linked to the rise of large metropolises and a more distinct urban culture, baseball appealed to the new middle class and provided spectators with a means to identify with their home towns.

KEVIN MURPHY

Battenberg, Alexander (*b* Verona, 5 April 1857; *d* Graz, 17 November 1893) First prince of Bulgaria (1879–86). The son of Prince Alexander von Hesse (1823–88) and nephew of the Russian emperor, Alexander II, he served with the Russian troops in 1877 against the Ottomans. Elected prince of autonomous BULGARIA by the great national assembly in Tǐrnovo, Alexander dissolved the national assembly in 1880 and suspended the constitution which he considered too liberal in 1881. Russia intervened to restore the constitution in 1883. The unification of Bulgaria and eastern Rumelia (6 September 1885) and the following war with Serbia effected an open conflict with Russia, but won him immense domestic support. Unification was recognized by the powers in 1886 but a pro-Russian officers' coup forced Alexander to abdicate in September 1886, after failing to win Russian backing. Later he was a general in the Austrian army.

Egon Corti, *Alexander von Battenberg* (London, 1954).

MARIA TODOROVA

Bebel, August (*b* Cologne, 22 February 1840; *d* Bad Passugg, Switzerland, 13 August 1913) German socialist leader. Born into an extremely poor family of a Prussian non-commissioned officer, he was brought up by his widowed mother and became a skilled turner after years of wandering as a journeyman. He settled in Leipzig, was elected chairman of the local Workers' Educational Association and later of all the German associations. Moving to the Left, he opposed the Prussian war against Austria of 1866. Under his guidance the Social Democratic Workers' Party was founded at Eisenach in 1869 (*see* EISENACH CONGRESS), in opposition to the German Workers' Association founded by Ferdinand Lassalle which favoured German unification by Prussia. But in 1875 the two parties united, with a programme sharply criticized by Marx. In spite of severe persecution and Bismarck's law against the socialists (1878) (*see* ANTI-SOCIALIST LAW), the united party grew quickly. After years of underground work it was legalized in 1890 and became the strongest German party, polling 3 million votes in 1903 and 4,250,000 in 1912. Until his death, Bebel, who was often imprisoned, kept the party on a steady, radical course of opposition to German armaments and colonial policy, but without any visible success. He was the 'Counter-Kaiser' but had no power.

F. L. Carsten, *Bebel und die Organisation der Massen* [Bebel and the Organization of the Masses] (Berlin, 1991).

F. L. CARSTEN

Beeton, Isabella Mary Mayson (*b* London, 14 March 1836; *d* 6 February 1865) Writer on cookery and other household matters. Educated at Heidelberg, she began writing on domestic topics after her marriage in 1856 to Samuel Beeton (1831–77), an enterprising publisher of illustrated magazines and special-interest publications. Projected by Sam and compiled by Isabella, Beeton's *Book of Household Management*, their most successful venture in the expanding part-work market, introduced a new style of cookery writing emphasizing simplicity, economy and nutrition. Published in volume form in 1861 as a comprehensive manual, it enjoyed an appeal across the classes: a social guide for new members of the middle classes, it was equally indispensable for entrants to domestic service. Following the birth of her fourth child, Isabella died of puerperal fever at the age of 29, a crippling emotional and financial blow from which Sam was not fully to recover.

JOHN BELCHEM

Belgian Congo *see* INDEPENDENT CONGO STATE.

Belgium Known as the Austrian Netherlands in the eighteenth century, Belgium was incorporated into the kingdom of the Netherlands at the CONGRESS OF VIENNA in 1815. The Belgians were predominantly Catholic and spoke Walloon, a French dialect, while the inhabitants of Holland spoke Dutch and were predominantly Protestant. In time, the Belgians came to resent the overbearing attitude of the Dutch and, when a revolution broke out in Paris in July 1830, the Belgians took the opportunity to rise in revolt against the Dutch. Fighting broke out in Brussels between workers and troops in September and the Belgians proclaimed their independence on 4 October 1830.

A month later, at the suggestion of Britain, a conference of the major European powers was called in London to discuss the implication of these developments. Britain was sympathetic to Belgian claims for independence but was even more interested in restricting French influence in the region and preventing a major war. A strong and nationalistic minority in France wanted the government to annex Belgium, but King Louis-Philippe resisted these demands and acknowledged Britain's concerns. Both powers persuaded Russia (which was distracted by a Polish revolt), Prussia and Austria to follow their lead and to disregard the principle of legitimacy. Although the conference recognized the independence of Belgium, it was not until 19 April 1839 that the Netherlands recognized Belgian independence in the

Twenty-four Articles. In article 7 of the agreement all the powers recognized Belgian independence and its perpetual neutrality; this article was later to play an important role in the outbreak of the First World War.

F. R. Bridge and R. Bullen, *The Great Powers and the European State System 1815–1914* (New York, 1980).

GEORGE O. KENT

Bell, Alexander Graham (*b* Edinburgh, 3 March 1847; *d* Baddeck, Nova Scotia, 2 August 1922)   Scots-born American inventor. He is known chiefly as the inventor of the telephone, but is perhaps more significant as the founder of the corporation which marketed it and made it available in many countries. He was a Scot who began experiments in telegraphy in Elgin in 1865. He migrated to Quebec in 1870 and subsequently settled in the United States. His early experiments were undertaken partly as an attempt to communicate with the deaf. He discovered a means of transmitting speech in 1876, which was patented and demonstrated at the Philadelphia Centennial Exposition of that year. In 1877 he applied Thomas EDISON's carbon transmitter to his telephone, and the following year bought the rights to the transmitter invented by Emile Berliner (1851–1929). In 1877 he also established the Bell Telephone Corporation, which by 1900 was the largest corporation in the United States.

See also TELEGRAPHY AND TELEPHONY.

R. V. Bruce, *Bell: Alexander Graham Bell and the Conquest of Solitude* (London, 1973).

BARRIE TRINDER

belle époque   The history of nineteenth-century France, punctuated by periods of deep psychological depression at the inability to resolve a sense of national identity and equality after the Revolution, invited a counter-response in displays of extravagant and probably expiatory public gaiety. The myth of the *belle époque* was one such reaction. The Great Exposition of 1878, itself engendered by intellectual and social attitudes sketched by the Enlightenment, acted as catalyst to a precarious new self-confidence. The succeeding twenty years or so acted as proving-ground for the expression of a range of different political, social and artistic ideas. 'Bohemian' attitudes, ironically, were seen as an essentially French expression of individuality and critical independence within an evolving society where festivity and frivolity might be a part of the new norm. The ephemeral and precarious nature of this new idealism survived neither the DREYFUS Affair nor the storm clouds gathering in Europe, while the seeds of its own destruction were already clear in the work of Toulouse-Lautrec (1864–1901).

M. G. CARROLL

Bello, Muhammad *see* MUHAMMAD BELLO.

Benedetti, Vincent, Count (*b* Bastia, Corsica, 29 April 1817; *d* Paris, 28 March 1900) French diplomat. He is best known for his role in the episode of the Hohenzollern candidature to the Spanish throne. In June 1869, when the Spanish Cortes offered Prince Leopold (1835–1905), a member of the Catholic branch of the Hohenzollern family, the Spanish throne, the French government, alarmed at the prospect of a Hohenzollern monarch on the throne of Spain, instructed Benedetti, its ambassador to Prussia, to persuade King William to intervene and to forbid Leopold to accept the offer. Following his instructions, Benedetti met with the king at Bad Ems in July 1870, but the meetings were unsuccessful and Bismarck publicized the ambassador's failure in the famous EMS DISPATCH. Benedetti's memoirs present a favourable version of the events at Bad Ems but Bismarck's subsequent disclosures about some of Benedetti's earlier diplomatic manœuvres permanently tarnished the ambassador's reputation.

W. A. Fletcher, *The Mission of Vincent Benedetti to Berlin 1864–70* (The Hague, 1965).

GEORGE O. KENT

Benthamism *see* UTILITARIANISM.

Berlin, Conference of (1884–1885) The conference was called by Bismarck to promote an 'open door' policy in central Africa and to settle the competing claims of the European powers in the Congo region and other regions of Africa. Africa was becoming the site of potential conflict between the European powers. The basin of the River Congo was the subject of considerable territorial competition between Great Britain, France, Belgium and Portugal who were concluding treaties with various indigenous tribes and with each other. King Leopold (1835–1909) of the Belgians had acquired large parts of the area under the cover of the International Association of the Congo (*see* INDEPENDENT CONGO STATE), while Germany and Britain were in dispute over various parts of east Africa and the Cameroons in west Africa.

After lengthy negotiations, the conference produced an agreement that allowed free trade and free navigation in the area of the Congo and Niger Rivers and laid down the conditions under which the powers could establish protectorates in the region. Despite allegations to the contrary, the conference did not initiate the SCRAMBLE FOR AFRICA, which in truth was already in full swing, but rather attempted to regulate future territorial settlements. The agreements reached did not last, however; the tariff policies of Belgium, France and Germany soon invalidated the treaty's free-trade and navigation provisions. But it did allow the Europeans to compete for territory in Africa without coming to war.

S. E. Crowe, *The Berlin West African Conference* (London, 1942).
Thomas Pakenham, *The Scramble for Africa* (New York, 1991).

GEORGE O. KENT

Berlin, Congress of (July 1878)   A diplomatic gathering of the European powers after the defeat of Turkey by Russia in the war of 1877–8, the Congress of Berlin was convened because the major European powers believed that Russia had gained too much by the TREATY OF SAN STEFANO. With Bismarck in the role of 'honest broker', the congress revised the terms of the Treaty of San Stefano, addressed the power vacuum created by the defeat of the Ottoman Empire, and came to terms with the emergence of nationalism among the Balkan peoples. The major accomplishments of the congress were the division of BULGARIA into three parts, permission for Austria-Hungary to occupy BOSNIA-HERCEGOVINA and to garrison the Sanjak of Novi-Bazar and the recognition of the independence of Serbia, Montenegro and Romania. The territorial boundaries of Romania were established at the expense of Russia, and Great Britain (in a secret agreement with Turkey) occupied Cyprus. France and Italy were given a free hand in Tunisia and Albania. The sultan was encouraged to institute reforms in his European possessions.

The congress was a severe blow to Russia and, for practical purposes, ended the THREE EMPERORS' LEAGUE of 1873. The great achievement of the congress was to prevent a major war between Russia and the other powers, and it did preserve the peace for a generation. But many of its provisions played a major role in the origins of the First World War. Thus Austria's occupation of Bosnia and Hercegovina was a major source of tension in the Balkans and a cause of the assassination of Archduke Franz Ferdinand (1863–1914) in 1914.

W. N. Medlicott, *The Congress of Berlin and After* (London, 1963).
R. Melvislle and H.-J. Schroeder, *Der Berliner Kongress von 1878* (Munich, 1982).

GEORGE O. KENT

Bernstein, Eduard (*b* Berlin, 6 January 1850; *d* Berlin, 18 December 1932)   Socialist leader. The son of a Jewish engine-driver, he had to leave school early. He became a bank clerk and joined the Social Democratic Workers' Party in 1872. During the period when the party was illegal, he edited its weekly journal, *Sozialdemokrat*, from Zurich and London. There he came under the influence of Fabians and English socialists and wrote *The Preconditions of Socialism* (1899), to revise the party's Marxist programme. Returning to Germany in 1901, he became a Reichstag deputy and leader of the party's 'revisionist' right wing, in opposition to Bebel and other leaders. During the First World War he adopted an antiwar attitude and finally joined the Independent Social Democratic Party (1917). After the revolution of November 1918 he briefly held ministerial office, then rejoined the SPD (*see* SOCIAL DEMOCRATIC PARTY (GERMANY)) and left the Independent Social Democratic Party, which drifted to the Left. Bernstein was convinced that Germany was responsible for causing the world war and favoured the reunification of the two social democratic parties; he remained a Reichstag deputy until 1928. He wrote an important work on *Socialism and Democracy in the Great English Revolution* and many other books and pamphlets. His influence on the development of the SPD after 1945 was strong.

F. L. Carsten, *Eduard Bernstein* (Munich, 1993).

F. L. CARSTEN

Bessemer, Henry (*b* Charlton, Hertfordshire, 13 January 1813; *d* London, 15 March 1898)   English inventor. He is celebrated for the Bessemer process for steel-making, widely used until the 1970s. An inventor whose innovations brought changes in many branches of manufacturing, he acquired skills from his father who operated a type foundry at Charlton in Hertfordshire. As a young man he invented machines for embossing plush and rolling sugar cane. In 1856 he developed mild steel, which combined the qualities of wrought iron and cast iron, which could be made in bulk. After molten cast iron had been poured into a vessel called a converter, air was blown through it causing an exothermic reaction as carbon and other elements were oxidized. In 1858 Bessemer established a steelworks in Sheffield. His process initially worked only with iron from non-phosphoric ores, and it was the work of Sidney Gilchrist Thomas (1850–85) in the 1880s which enabled it to be used with iron from phosphoric ores. (*See* IRON AND STEEL.)

Sir Henry Bessemer, *Sir Henry Bessemer, FRS: An Autobiography* (London, 1905).

BARRIE TRINDER

bicycle   One of the representative examples of nineteenth-century consumer durable items was the bicycle. The first recognizable bicycle was made in Paris in 1816, but it was a clumsy machine propelled by pushing feet along the ground. Kirkpatrick Macmillan (1813–78) of Dumfriesshire developed the first self-propelled bicycle in 1839 which moved by a series of rods and levers. A more practical machine, known as the 'bone-shaker' was produced by Pierre and Ernest Michaux in 1861 in Paris and was adapted by John Starley (1831–81), a Coventry

engineer, into the famous 'penny farthing' in 1870, with pedals
attached directly to the front wheel.

Races and exhibition tours began to be held by the late 1860s, but
bicycles remained largely novelty items because they were not easily
driven. They were heavy – sometimes as much as 160 pounds – often
without brakes, had solid RUBBER tyres and wheels of different size.
The real breakthrough in bicycle design came in 1874 when H. J.
Lawson developed the first machine driven by a continuous chain with
a pedal sprocket between two wheels of equal size. This made cycling
a safer and easier activity and the industry moved out of the small
engineering workshop to factory production. Further improvements,
such as the invention of a pneumatic tyre in 1888, and more efficient
wheel design, established the basic design of the bicycle for the next
eighty years.

The social consequences of the bicycle were particularly important
for the working and middle classes. It provided a relatively cheap form
of transportation which allowed greater separation between home and
place of work, and freed people to range more widely in their leisure
time. Cycling clubs were an important aspect of the youth culture of
the late nineteenth century.

David Rubenstein, 'Cycling in the 1890s', *Victorian Studies*, 21(1) (1977), 47–
71.
John Woodforde, *The Story of the Bicycle* (London, 1970).

RICHARD PRICE

bill on London During the last quarter of the nineteenth century bills
of exchange drawn on banks in London and payable in sterling became the principal means of financing world trade. Bills were a traditional method of providing short-term credit. A buyer or importer of
goods was granted time to resell his goods before payment was due;
while the seller or exporter could obtain his money immediately by
selling the bill in the London discount market at a price fractionally
below face value. The cost of discounting was reduced if the bill bore
the name of a recognized bank. British merchant banks engaged in
international trade began to earn a commission income by guaranteeing or 'accepting' the bills of firms unknown in London. From this
they developed the acceptance credit, a facility under which traders
could draw bills directly on London banks which would then accept
them and arrange for their discount.

GORDON FLETCHER

bimetallism In a bimetallic monetary system the value of the currency unit is legally defined in terms of two metals, usually gold and
silver, in a fixed ratio. The metals are accepted for coinage at the fixed
prices, and gold and silver coins circulate as legal tender. Advocates

claimed that bimetallism would promote greater price stability as compared to a monometallic standard. In the nineteenth century the system was employed by the United States and some European countries but its rejection by Britain, the leading industrial and trading nation, precluded achievement of the universal, managed system recommended by theorists. The main weakness of bimetallism, as it was operated, was that divergence of the world-market price of gold or silver from the mint price would, by Gresham's Law, encourage export of the higher-valued metal, leaving the currency monometallic in practice. By the century's end, gold had triumphed as the international standard (*see* GOLD STANDARD).

GORDON FLETCHER

birth control   As far as historians and demographers can tell, appliance methods of birth control were not widely used in the nineteenth century. The rubber condom and the Dutch cap became available in Europe towards the end of the century, but they were not widely adopted as means of limiting fertility until after the First World War, largely because they were relatively expensive and their distribution was limited. However, other methods were increasingly used from the third quarter of the century onwards, but considerably earlier in France and among certain elite social groups. The 'safe period' was little understood at this time and often misused. Reduced coital frequency and complete sexual abstinence for lengthy periods were also likely to have become common under certain circumstances. The practice of induced ABORTION, while not strictly a form of birth control, is said by some historians to have increased towards the end of the century.

There is still very little knowledge about the forms of birth control available and especially the extent to which they were used by whom, where, when and under what circumstances. What is certain is that the second half of the nineteenth century was characterized by an increasing desire among populations of European origin to limit their fertility, and that the new vital statistics on births, marriages and deaths demonstrate clearly that marital fertility was coming to be widely and effectively controlled. Instead of having seven or eight children, women would have three or four, but the means by which this change was brought about remain far more obscure than the causes of the social transformation of which it was an important manifestation.

Angus McLaren, *Reproductive Rituals* (London, 1984).

R. I. WOODS

Bismarck, Otto von (*b* Schönhausen, Prussia, 1 April 1815; *d* Friedrichruh, near Hamburg, 30 July 1898)   Prusso-German statesman. A member of the Prussian *Junker* nobility, he first came to prominence in 1847 as an arch-conservative member of the Prussian diet. As a

Prussian delegate to the Frankfurt diet of the GERMAN CONFEDERATION (1851–9), he became convinced of the incompatibility of Prussian and Austrian interests in Germany. After sitting out the liberal 'New Era' in Prussia as ambassador to St Petersburg (1859–62), he was appointed minister-president of Prussia in September 1862 at the height of a constitutional conflict between the government and the liberal parliament. Governing unconstitutionally, he forced through army reforms; yet came to win the support of the majority of liberals through his foreign-policy initiatives. Wars with Denmark (1864) and Austria and the south German states (1866) led to the creation of the NORTH GERMAN CONFEDERATION; war with France (1870–1) to that of the German Empire. As imperial chancellor, Bismarck relied until 1878–9 on the support of the liberals; thereafter, on shifting and unstable coalitions. A diplomatic genius, his foreign policy after 1871 was directed to securing the *status quo* through the isolation of France. Mounting tensions with Emperor WILLIAM II led to his resignation in March 1890.

See also ANTI-SOCIALIST LAW.

L. Gall, *Bismarck: The White Revolutionary*, 2 vols (London, 1986).

S. J. SALTER

Blanc, Louis (*b* Madrid, 29 October 1811; *d* Cannes, 12 December 1882) French socialist theoretician, historian and politician. After a number of career starts, he became a journalist for *Le National* and *Le Bon Sens* in the 1830s. He also wrote *Histoire de la Révolution*, one of the first attempts to rehabilitate Robespierre. His most important book was *L'Organisation du travail* (1839), which proposed the establishment of workers' productive co-operatives with the state providing start-up capital, to be repaid by profits which in turn would fund social insurance and finance new co-operatives.

A member of the provisional government of 1848, he presided over the controversial Luxemburg Commission, a forum for projects to revamp society. He fled to London to escape trial for inciting the JUNE DAYS and there wrote *Histoire de la Révolution de 1848*. He was elected to the chamber of deputies in February 1871, voted against the cession of Alsace-Lorraine to the Germans, demanded clemency for the Communards and called for the democratization of the constitution of 1875.

L. Loubere, *Louis Blanc: His Life and his Contribution to the Rise of French Jacobin-Socialism* (Evanston, Ill., 1961).

DONALD SUTHERLAND

Blanqui, Louis Auguste (*b* Puget-Théniers, 1 February 1805; *d* Paris, 1 January 1881) Outstanding French revolutionary, committed to establishing a 'proletarian' social order. He embodied both the political tradition of militant bourgeois republicanism and the new social concerns of artisan-led plebeian protest. At 17 he joined the clandestine Charbonnerie and fought against the Bourbon monarchy in 1830, but after the Lyons silk-weavers' uprising (1834) he rejected the 'mutualist' tactics of Buonarroti and the secret societies (see CARBONARI). A communist, he looked to a 'professional' minority of the proletariat – organized in disciplined, conspiratorial, insurrectionist detachments, such as his 'Society of the Seasons' – to seize state power directly, to which end he led the 1848 invasion of the Paris Assembly. The term 'dictatorship of the proletariat' is of Blanquist origin. A lifelong revolutionary, accorded critical praise by Marx, he spent a total of thirty-three years in prison, his last sentence for membership of the Paris Commune.

Samuel Bernstein, *Auguste Blanqui and the Art of Insurrection* (London, 1971).

TONY BARLEY

Blood River, Battle of (16 December 1838) A force of 470 voortrekkers under Andries PRETORIUS defeated some 3,000 Zulus under DINGANE. In part an act of revenge for Dingane's earlier attack on the voortrekkers, the battle facilitated the establishment of Natalia (see NATAL) but conflict between the Zulus and Europeans continued for many years. The victory at Blood River was marked by the voortrekkers as the Day of the Covenant (or Vow) because of the promise made to God on the eve of battle, to keep the day holy if they were victorious. To mark that victory, the Church of the Vow was built in Pietermaritzburg, Natalia's capital.

SIMON KATZENELLENBOGEN

Blyden, Edward Wilmot (*b* St Thomas, West Indies, 3 August 1832; *d* Freetown, Sierre Leone, 7 February 1912) Leading pan-African nationalist. Arriving in 1850 in the United States for theological training, he left shortly thereafter, repelled by that country's slavery and prevailing racial policies. Migrating to LIBERIA, he served as secretary of state from 1864 to 1866. He was Liberia's ambassador to Great Britain (1877–8), and later president of Liberia College (1880–4). During the 1860s and 1880s, he served the SIERRE LEONE colonial government. Gifted and learned, Blyden produced a far greater impact on his own and subsequent generations in his intellectual pursuits than in his political activism (in 1885 he unsuccessfully ran for the Liberian state presidency). He spoke and wrote extensively on the theory and practice of pan-African nationalism. Favouring Islam over Christianity as the ideological basis for African development, he laid the groundwork for succeeding generations, not least Marcus Garvey

(1887–1940), W. E. B. Dubois (1868–1963), Léopold Senghor (*b* 1906) and Aimé Césaire (*b* 1913).

Hollis R. Lynch, *Edward Wilmot Blyden, Pan-Negro Patriot* (Oxford, 1970).

B. MARIE PERINBAM

Boer Wars   *see* ANGLO-BOER WARS.

Bolívar, Simón (*b* Caracas, 24 July 1783; *d* Santa Marta, 17 December 1830)   Venezuelan revolutionary leader. He was known as 'The Liberator' for his leading role in the Spanish American independence movements. He was born into a wealthy Venezuelan creole family. Well educated and travelled, he came to the fore in the Caracas junta of 1810. Following the defeat of the First Republic in VENEZUELA, he assembled a small guerrilla force and recaptured Caracas in August 1813, after which he was granted supreme power. Divisions within Venezuelan society, however, made the revolution unsustainable and in June 1814 Bolívar withdrew first to Cartagena and then Jamaica and Haiti.

Re-entering Venezuela two years later, he made his base in the Orinoco delta and persuaded the *caudillos* of the plains to co-operate with him. Instead of striking directly at Caracas, he led his forces across the Andes into COLOMBIA where in August 1819 he defeated the royalists at Boyacá and took Bogotá. Victory at Carabobo (*see* BATTLE OF CARABOBO) in 1821 liberated Venezuela, and Bolívar's forces then moved southwards into Ecuador. In July 1822 he met SAN MARTIN at Guayaquil and was asked to lend his army to the liberation of PERU. This was achieved with Sucre's (1793–1830) victory at Ayacucho (*see* BATTLE OF AYACUCHO) and his subsequent campaign in upper Peru (BOLIVIA) in 1824–5.

For a time Bolívar was dictator of Peru and then, from 1828, of Colombia, but in all the countries he liberated the centrifugal forces of *caudillismo* caused internal conflicts, not helped by Bolívar's belief, despite his personal liberalism, that America needed strong paternalistic government. Attempts to create a supranational state to control regional and ethnic conflicts, and to apply his quasi-monarchical Bolivian constitution of 1826 elsewhere, all failed. He died in 1830 on his way into exile, his disillusion evident in comments made shortly before: 'America is ungovernable.' 'Those who serve the revolution plough the sea.' 'The only thing to do in America is emigrate.'

John Lynch, *The Spanish American Revolutions, 1808–1826* (New York, 1986).

RORY MILLER

Bolivia   The republic of Bolivia was created in 1825 when the Spaniards were ejected from Upper Peru. As an independent state Bolivia faced enormous difficulties. Government revenues depended on the head tax on the majority 'Indian' population, and it lacked capital to redevelop mining. Communications were difficult and regional conflicts acute. After the presidency (1829–39) of Andrés Santa Cruz (1792–1865) (*see* PERU) Bolivia became renowned for its frequent violent changes of government. Mining began to revive in the 1860s, and, with government revenues increasing, President Melgarejo (1820–71; president, 1864–71) abolished the Indian communities' rights to hold land. After the WAR OF THE PACIFIC (1879–83) silver exports rose to a peak. However, their decline in the 1890s, together with the economic changes resulting from railway construction, undermined the mining elite's power. In 1899–1900 a violent civil war brought the victory of the liberals, the defeat of the last major indigenous revolt and the conclusive shift of power to La Paz.

Herbert S. Klein, *Bolivia: The Evolution of a Multi-ethnic Society* (New York, 1991).

RORY MILLER

Bonaparte, Josephine [Marie Joséphine Rose Tascher de la Pagerie] (*b* Martinique, 23 June 1763; *d* Malmaison, France, 29 May 1814) Empress of France. She married first the vicomte de Beauharnais (1760–94), who was later executed in the Terror, and Napoleon BONAPARTE in 1796. Despite her scandalous life while he was away on campaign, he always retained a great affection for her. He divorced her in 1809 because she could not bear him an heir but they remained in contact until her death. Her son by her first marriage, Eugène (1781–1824), became viceroy of Italy during the empire; her daughter, Hortense (1783–1837), married Louis Bonaparte (1778–1846) and was queen of Holland (1806–10).

H. Cole, *Josephine* (New York, 1962).

DONALD SUTHERLAND

Bonaparte, Lucien (*b* Ajaccio, Corsica, 21 May 1775; *d* Viterbo, Italy, 29 June 1840)   Younger brother of Napoleon. He fled to France with Corsican nationalists at his heels in the 1790s, and made a living as an army contractor. Elected to the Council of Five Hundred or legislature in 1798, he associated himself with the Jacobins, denouncing corruption and press censorship. As president of the Five Hundred in November 1799, he supported his brother's coup by vouching for Napoleon's love of liberty and by rallying the troops. As minister of the interior, he oversaw the plebiscite on the constitution of the Year VIII (1800) which helped consolidate the dictatorship, and published vastly inflated and fraudulent figures on the vote. Historians believed the deceit until the 1970s. He broke with Napoleon over his marriage, retired to Baltimore, supported Napoleon in the Hundred Days and finally retired to Italy.

DONALD SUTHERLAND

Bonaparte, Napoleon (*b* Ajaccio, Corsica, 15 August 1769; *d* St Helena, 5 May 1821) Emperor of France. Born in Corsica, he became an officer in France in 1785. He was closely associated with the Jacobins and so fell from government favour after the Terror despite his successful campaign at Toulon in 1793. His career restarted after he suppressed a royalist uprising in Paris in October 1795 with the famous 'whiff of grapeshot'. He received the command of the small and miserable army of Italy in 1796 but his brilliance and personal bravery drove the Austrians from most of Italy and ended the war of the First Coalition against France (1792–7). His campaign against the British in Egypt in 1798 was a failure, however, and he returned home the next year to suppress the constitution of the Year III (1795), becoming First Consul.

By a skilful use of victory abroad and profiting from royalist conspiracies against him at home, he became dictator by 1802 and crowned himself emperor in 1804. While successfully negotiating peace with the British and Austrians, he instituted the system of local government by which France is still governed; the CODE NAPOLEON; a CONCORDAT with the church which undercut royalist opposition; major reforms in education for the elite; the Legion of Honour; and, in 1808, a new form of nobility.

War resumed in 1804–5, and he won a series of spectacular victories, beginning with Austerlitz (*see* BATTLE OF AUSTERLITZ) (1805) and ending with Friedland (1807). These victories established his grand empire from Spain to the Baltic. But the European peace he arranged with Alexander I of Russia at Tilsit (1807) deteriorated (*see* TREATY OF TILSIT). The CONTINENTAL SYSTEM failed to bring the British to terms, and the invasion of Spain (1808) and the disastrously executed invasion of Russia (1812) weakened the empire fatally. In 1813 Austria and Prussia joined Britain and Russia against him and, convinced the situation was hopeless, he abdicated at the urging of NEY and retired to Elba in 1814. Louis XVIII was restored but had little popularity among the army and the people. In the following year Napoleon escaped from Elba and reconquered his empire without firing a shot. The Hundred Days ended with his defeat at the BATTLE OF WATERLOO (18 June 1815) and he was exiled to St Helena.

For all his extraordinary charisma, personal qualities and creativity, Napoleon's reign was a disaster for France. Proportionately, more men were killed in his wars than in the First World War; economic growth stagnated for a generation; the regime did not reconcile Frenchmen from the civil wars of the Revolution as he claimed; and it was based on a narrow and self-seeking elite which did its best to entrench the privileges of wealth.

F. Markham, *Napoleon* (New York, 1964).

DONALD SUTHERLAND

Borodino, Battle of (7 September 1812) After nearly a decade of uneasy and deteriorating relations between France and Russia, Napoleon BONAPARTE decided to settle matters by armed intervention. On 23–24 June 1812 a force of 510,000 troops crossed into Russia. Initially, Napoleon's armies were largely unopposed, but at the onset of the autumn, ALEXANDER I, encouraged by his generals and the strength of public opinion, decided to halt the advance. On 7 September some 260,000 troops engaged on a front of less than 3 miles near the village of Borodino to the west of Moscow. When the Russians finally withdrew in the late evening, over 90,000 men lay dead. Seriously weakened, the French advanced into a deserted Moscow. Borodino was by no means one of the decisive battles of history, but it was the first serious military set-back Napoleon had experienced, and the battle has entered the mythology of Russian history.

Christopher Duffy, *Borodino* (London, 1972).

A. V. KNOWLES

Bosnia-Hercegovina After a short existence as independent principalities in the fourteenth century, the regions of Bosnia and Hercegovina in the Western Balkans were incorporated in the Ottoman Empire, in 1463 and 1482 respectively. Mass conversions to Islam and its intermediate position between Catholic Croatia and Orthodox Serbia accounted for the complex religious and ethnic structure of the region. During the decentralization of the Ottoman Empire in the eighteenth century Bosnia was ruled by big semi-independent landlords, and their conservative opposition against the Europeanizing reforms was suppressed only in the middle of the nineteenth century. There were numerous peasant revolts in 1834, 1852–3, 1857–8, 1861–2 and 1875; the latter assumed the character of a national independence struggle and precipitated the EASTERN QUESTION of 1875–8. The CONGRESS OF BERLIN assigned Bosnia-Hercegovina (nominally Ottoman provinces) to Austro-Hungarian occupation. The provinces were annexed by Austria-Hungary in 1908, and after 1918, as part of SERBIA, entered the Yugoslav kingdom.

Robert Donia, *Islam under the Double Eagle* (Boulder, Colo., 1981).

MARIA TODOROVA

Bosporus *see* STRAITS QUESTION.

Botha, Louis (*b* Greytown, Natal, 27 September 1862; *d* Pretoria, 27 August 1919)   First prime minister of the Union of SOUTH AFRICA (1910–19). A soldier, political moderate and Boer nationalist, possessed of a talent for negotiation and toughness, he first came to national attention in the 1890s in his support of the UITLANDERS' rights (mainly British immigrants) to political enfranchisement, despite opposition from the Transvaal's president Kruger. Later champioing the AFRIKANERS' cause during the second Anglo-Boer War (1899–1902), Botha was among those advocating the compromise peace of Vereeniging (May 1902). In 1907 he became the Transvaal's first prime minister. Participating later in the National Convention (1908–9) responsible for shaping the nationalist protocols that created the Union of South Africa (1910), Botha became the union's first prime minister. During the First World War he supported the British, even in the face of an armed Boer uprising, suppressed in 1915.

Monica Wilson and Leonard Thompson (eds), *The Oxford History of South Africa*, 2 vols (Oxford, 1969–71).

B. MARIE PERINBAM

Boulanger, Georges (*b* Rennes, France, 29 April 1837; *d* Brussels, 30 September 1891)   French general and adventurer. He became minister of war for eighteen months in Freycinet's (1818–1923) cabinet in 1886 and gained great popularity for his bellicosity against Germany and for some minor reforms within the army. His forcible retirement from the army in 1888 for leaving his post without permission opened the way for a political career. He was elected in several *départements* as well as for Paris. Although his most visible supporters were prominent radicals and revolutionaries, in fact he was increasingly financed behind the scenes by royalists and he became their instrument in an attempt to overthrow the republic. The government prosecuted him but he fled to Brussels and London. His popularity waned with the publication of his secret dealings with royalists, and he committed suicide on the grave of his mistress in Brussels.

W. Irvine, *The Boulanger Affair Reconsidered: Royalism, Boulangism and the Origins of the Radical Right in France* (New York, 1989).

DONALD SUTHERLAND

bourgeoisie   *see* MIDDLE CLASSES.

Boxer Rising   An example of primitive xenophobia, the Boxer Rising surfaced in northern China in the later 1890s. The Boxers were members of the Society of Righteous and Harmonious Fists, and practised a form of callisthenics which they believed made them immune to gunfire. In response to deteriorating social conditions, they began sporadic attacks on the most visible of the foreigners, Christian missionaries, in Shantung in 1898. The Boxers were originally enemies of the Ch'ing but the empress dowager, Tz'U-HSI, and Prince TUAN engineered a court–Boxer alliance in 1899. In June 1900 Tz'u-hsi unleashed the Boxers against the foreign enclaves in Peking and Tientsin and declared war on the foreigners. Some 250 foreigners outside Peking and large numbers of Chinese Christians were killed. In Peking seventy-six foreigners died in the siege of the legations. An international relief expedition came to the aid of the foreign enclaves in Tientsin and Peking in July and August. Tz'u-hsi and the court fled to Sian, remaining there for a year. Peking was looted by foreign troops, the Summer Palace being razed to the ground, and for six months there were reprisal campaigns in many north China cities. LI HUNG-CHANG, who had not recognized the declaration of war, led the negotiations which led to the imposition of the Boxer Protocol (1901). The failure of the foreign powers to agree among themselves saved China from dismemberment but a huge indemnity of $333 million to be paid over forty years was imposed. The imperial examinations were suspended in forty-five cities and a number of leading officials were executed. The Boxer Rising was a further humiliating defeat for the Ch'ing dynasty.

Joseph W. Esherick, *The Origins of the Boxer Uprising* (Berkeley, Calif., 1987).
Victor C. Purcell, *The Boxer Uprising* (Cambridge, 1963).

JOHN DAVIES

Boyer, Jean Pierre (*b* Port-au-Prince, 1776; *d* Paris, 9 July 1850) Haitian general in the war against the French. He succeeded Alexandre Pétion (1770–1818) as president of HAITI in 1818. Initially he controlled only the south, but after Henri CHRISTOPHE's death in 1820 he reunited the country. In 1822, fearing a French invasion from the east, Haitian forces liberated Santo Domingo from Spanish rule (it remained united with Haiti until 1844). Boyer ruled through military officers who effectively administered the island's *départements*, but problems mounted. Black peasants resented attempts to force them to work on estates and to eradicate voodoo. Exports fell sharply as plantation agriculture collapsed; taxes to pay the French indemnity were resisted, especially in the east; and inflation increased rapidly. In Port-au-Prince and Les Cayes dissident members of the mulatto elite began to demand political liberalization. A revolt against Boyer commenced in Les Cayes in January 1843 and spread through the south. Boyer left Port-au-Prince for exile in March.

RORY MILLER

Bradlaugh, Charles (*b* London, 26 September 1833; *d* London, 30 January 1891) Republican, freethinker and birth-control advocate.

The son of a Hoxton solicitor's clerk, he was early influenced by the secularism of Richard Carlile (1790–1843). He contributed frequently to the radical newspaper the *National Reformer*, and was often persecuted for his beliefs. When he was elected member of parliament for Northampton in 1880, Bradlaugh as an atheist refused to swear an oath of office and was excluded several times from the Commons. An opponent of the monarchy and imperial expansion as well as of socialism and state regulation of wages and hours of labour, he was linked with the radical wing of the Liberal Party, and rarely deviated from an adherence to *laissez-faire*. He actively supported Irish Home Rule and the improvement of conditions in India, but was best known for his REPUBLICANISM, his views on land reform (he urged the confiscation of unused land) and his hostility to established religion.

GREGORY CLAEYS

Brazil   In 1800 Portuguese settlement in Brazil was concentrated in the north-east, the central coast around Rio de Janeiro and the old gold-mining region of Minas Gerais. The population was small: just over 3 million, one-third of whom were slaves. It produced a range of exports for European markets, principally cotton, sugar, tobacco, cacao and coffee.

In 1808 the Portuguese court escaped Napoleon's invasion by fleeing to Brazil on British warships, and Dom João (1767–1826), the prince regent, opened Brazil's trade to foreigners. Having made Brazil equal in status with Portugal in 1815, he resisted Portuguese attempts to force him to return until 1821. The following year, in order to maintain Bragança control, Dom Pedro, his son, declared Brazil's independence (*see* PEDRO I). To protect the autonomy of the Brazilian empire, British mediation with Portugal was essential, but the price was a renewal of the commercial privileges Dom João had granted them and a Brazilian commitment to end the slave trade. Pedro's behaviour antagonized both elite and popular groups and he abdicated in 1831. The succession of provincial rebellions which followed did not cease until 1845.

Nevertheless, for much of PEDRO II's reign Brazil enjoyed political stability, with a professional bureaucracy acting as brokers between Rio and the provincial landowners. Astute use of the emperor's constitutional power to dismiss ministries, dissolve parliament and convoke new elections helped to control political conflicts. Economic growth was remarkable. Coffee exports, principally from Rio de Janeiro but later from São Paulo, outpaced all others, increasing from 1 million bags annually in the 1830s to almost 3 million in the 1860s and nearly 6 million in the 1880s. The needs of the planters meant that the ATLANTIC SLAVE TRADE continued unofficially until 1850, when it was terminated under British pressure. Thereafter the coffee-growing regions purchased slaves from the north-east, exacerbating the relative decline of those provinces. A modern commercial and transport infrastructure centred on Rio and São Paulo developed, due partly to an influx of foreign investment.

The problems of the PARAGUAYAN WAR provoked new criticisms of the imperial system and the social order. In 1870 the Republican Party was formed, and in 1871 the Law of Free Birth passed, undermining the institution of slavery. After 1885 a revived abolitionist movement based in the cities helped numerous slaves to flee the plantations. Parliament abolished slavery in May 1888, making no provisions either for compensation or for the freed slaves. Eighteen months later Pedro II was overthrown in a military coup led by Marshal DEODORO DA FONSECA.

A decade of economic and political turmoil followed. An economic boom turned into an inflationary spiral and culminated in Brazil's acceptance of strict conditions for the rescheduling of its foreign debt in 1898. The military governments of 1889–94 faced revolts from the navy and from Rio Grande do Sul. They were eventually forced out of office by provincial elites led by São Paulo and Minas Gerais, and a decentralized federal republic was established.

Leslie Bethell (ed.), *Brazil: Empire and Republic, 1822–1930* (Cambridge, 1989).
Emilia Viotti da Costa, *The Brazilian Empire: Myths and Histories* (Chicago, 1985).

RORY MILLER

Bright, John (*b* Rochdale, 16 November 1811; *d* Rochdale, 27 March 1889) English radical Liberal politician. Co-founder with Richard COBDEN and leader of the ANTI-CORN LAW LEAGUE and spokesperson for the Manchester School of economic and social policy, he was member of parliament for Durham (1843–7), Manchester (1847–57) and Birmingham (1857–89). Bright's free-trade economic views, cautious support for franchise extension, anti-aristocratic politics and opposition to aggressive foreign policies were combined with a patriarchal opposition to women's rights, a paternal relationship with his employees and opposition to trade unions and social reform. He opposed factory reform because it interfered with the free working of the labour market. Bright thus represented in particularly sharp form the variant of mid-Victorian radicalism that argued for peace abroad and free markets at home. He served in several cabinet posts, and ended his political career in opposition to Irish Home Rule.

Keith Robbins, *John Bright* (London, 1979).

RICHARD PRICE

British North America Act (1867)   Establishing the Confederation of
CANADA, the British North America Act united the provinces of upper
and lower Canada with Nova Scotia, New Brunswick and Prince
Edward Island (which joined in 1873) and allowed for the entrance of
western and northern territories. Confederation was seen as a way of
protecting the provinces against possible United States expansionism,
preserving the western territories for Canadian (mainly Ontario)
development, strengthening the British connection and allowing for
particularist interests such as the French-Canadians. Opposition came
mainly from the Maritime Provinces (which feared that confederation
would economically benefit upper Canada) and to a lesser extent from
the French speakers of lower Canada. The Quebec Conference in 1864
resolved these differences. The language and legal rights of the French
were protected and the Maritime Provinces were guaranteed the east-
erly extension of the Grand Trunk Railway and granted certain tariff
privileges.

Confederation was modelled on the British constitution, with a
cabinet system of government and a strong central legislative to avoid
the centrifugal tendencies of the federal system of the United States.

RICHARD PRICE

British South Africa Company   In 1889 the British South Africa
Company was formed to exploit gold and other resources in central
Africa (the Rhodesias) and, under a British government charter, to
administer the territory. This enabled the British government to maintain imperial interests in the area at virtually no cost. Based initially
on a concession from LOBENGULA secured by Charles Rudd (1844–1916)
and Cecil RHODES, the company also involved other interested groups.
Exaggerated expectations of gold and other mineral reserves, early 'get
rich quick' financing policies, as well as the high costs of subjugating
Africans (such as the Ndebele Rising (*see* MASHONALAND AND NDEBELE
RISINGS)), essential railway construction and administration generally
meant that the company paid no dividends for thirty-five years. Company administration laid the foundations of white minority rule which
lasted for ninety years.

J. S. Galbraith *Crown and Charter: The Early Days of the British South Africa
Company* (Berkeley, Calif., 1974).

SIMON KATZENELLENBOGEN

Brooke, Sir James (*b* Benares, India, 1803; *d* Burrator, Devonshire,
1868)   English soldier who acted as British agent in northern Borneo.
To counter piracy against British trade, centred on Singapore, and to
provide coaling stations *en route* to China, Britain looked to northern
Borneo. In 1841 Brooke was appointed rajah after helping to suppress

a local rebellion in Sarawak in 1839. He aimed to extirpate piracy and to introduce British law and order; he eventually achieved both. To suppress piracy he had to draw on the support of the Royal Navy. Meanwhile, the attempt to provide firm administration led him into a series of territorial gains at the expense of his nominal overlord, the sultan of Brunei. Brooke, behaving rather like an English country squire, ran Sarawak in a paternalist, non-exploitative fashion. Head-hunting was eliminated. He encouraged Chinese immigration but continued to support the traditional method of peasant farming in his territory.

JOHN DAVIES

Brougham, Henry Peter, first Baron Brougham and Vaux (*b* Edinburgh, 19 September 1778; *d* Cannes, France, 7 May 1868) Talented and self-confident British lawyer and Whig politician. Distrusted by the party magnates, he first came to notice through the *Edinburgh Review*. By co-ordinating extraparliamentary pressure with the efforts of the parliamentary opposition, he engineered the withdrawal of the ORDERS IN COUNCIL and the removal of income tax, campaigns which demonstrated the power of public opinion in the unreformed system. As Caroline's (1768–1821) 'attorney-general', he relished the public limelight in defending the queen against divorce proceedings. Appointed lord chancellor by Grey in 1830, he supported the Reform Bill in the Lords before introducing a substantial programme of legal reform. Throughout his career he was prominent in educational reform, promoting mechanics' institutes, the Society for the Diffusion of Useful Knowledge, the University of London, as well as state grants for national education. His talents and achievements notwithstanding, he is best remembered for the carriage named after him.

JOHN BELCHEM

Brown, John (*b* Torrington, Connecticut, 9 May 1800; *d* Charles Town, Virginia, 2 December 1859) American antislavery activist. He grew up in Ohio and engaged unsuccessfully in various trades in New York. Believing himself to be God's chosen instrument against the evil of slavery, he moved to Kansas where in May 1856, with six followers, he murdered five innocent pro-slavery men with swords, in retaliation for the sacking of Lawrence, Kansas. This attack, one of many in 'Bleeding Kansas' in the late 1850s, drew widespread attention and contributed significantly to sectional tensions. On 16 October 1859 Brown and twenty followers seized the United States arsenal at Harpers Ferry in western Virginia as a base from which to trigger a slave rebellion. The raid failed and Brown was quickly captured and executed, but when it became public that Brown had the backing of some prominent northern abolitionists, southern passions were inflamed.

Northern intellectuals such as Ralph Waldo Emerson praised Brown as a martyr in the cause of freedom.

See also ABOLITIONISM.

KEVIN MURPHY

Brunel, Isambard Kingdom (*b* Portsmouth, 9 April 1806; *d* London, 15 September 1859) English engineer. One of the most flamboyant and versatile engineers of Victorian England, he trained as an engineer working for his famous father, Marc Isambard Brunel (1769–1849), on the Thames River tunnel (completed 1843). His first important appointment was as engineer of the Clifton Suspension Bridge at Bristol, which was not finished until 1860. His appointment as engineer to the Bristol docks in 1831 established him as an important marine engineer, while his work on the Great Western Railway, beginning in 1833, extended his reputation to ambitious railway engineering. He was perhaps most famous for his ships, including the *Great Western* (1837), the largest wooden ship afloat; the *Great Britain* (1843), an iron ship pioneering screw propulsion; and the *Great Eastern* (finished 1858), an enormous vessel most notable for its role in laying the Atlantic cable in 1866. This last ambitious effort strained Brunel's health, contributing to his relatively early death.

See also ENGINEERING.

ROBERT FRIEDEL

Bryan, William Jennings (*b* Salem, Illinois, 19 March 1860; *d* Dayton, Tennessee, 26 July 1925) American politician and presidential candidate, the 'Boy Orator of the Platte'. He moved to Lincoln, Nebraska in his youth where he become active in the Democratic Party. During two terms in Congress (1891–5) he spoke out in favour of the coinage of free silver to increase the money supply to aid economically troubled farmers. As presidential candidate in 1896 he appealed to many rural elements associated with populism. He delivered his eloquent 'Cross of Gold' speech at the Democratic convention of 1896, but was soundly defeated in the electoral college by William McKinley, who was supported by powerful eastern business interests. After the Spanish-American War (1898) Bryan ran for president again in 1900, criticizing the Republican Party for its imperialist policies, but public approval of improving economic conditions and growing American strength abroad robbed him of support. After a third unsuccessful bid for the presidency in 1908, he served as Woodrow Wilson's (1856–1924) secretary of state.

KEVIN MURPHY

building societies By the 1870s these specialized FRIENDLY SOCIETIES financed around one in seven of all new houses built in Britain. Their clientele were tradesmen and the better-paid working classes – the same social groups that had started the earliest societies 125 years before. As a mass movement building societies took off in the 1840s. Henceforth most societies operated as savings banks as well as lenders of mortgages. Many also functioned as housing developers, notably 'freehold land' societies which were closely linked to the radical politics of the 1840s (*see* CHARTISM, especially the Land Plan). The present-day Abbey National Building Society began as an adjunct to popular Liberalism and became one of Victorian Britain's largest urban developers.

Societies also had close links with co-operation, Nonconformity and temperance, but also with financial speculation. The movement, which relied heavily on the spirit of voluntarism and SELF-HELP for its success, was dogged by financial scandal (notably the crash in 1892 of the massive Liberator Society, which led to a strict Regulating Act in 1894). In addition, numerous small societies operated outside government registration (first introduced in 1834), usually because their methods involved some form of lottery to determine a member's eligibility for a mortgage. Yet by 1900 building societies had evolved into a powerful force in the British financial market, the means by which the thrift of hundreds of thousands of working people was converted into the capital required to house tens of thousands in homes of their own. Building societies were virtually unknown elsewhere in Europe, but emerged in the United States during the 1830s, in Canada, Australia and New Zealand in the 1840s and shortly afterwards in Natal.

E. J. Cleary, *The Building Society Movement* (London, 1965).

MALCOLM CHASE

Bulgaria Part of the Ottoman Empire since 1393, the Balkan state of Bulgaria lost its nobility throughout five centuries of Ottoman rule, and emerged in the nineteenth century as an egalitarian peasant society with a growing urban middle class. Modern Bulgarian nationalism began with a cultural revival at the end of the eighteenth century which centred around education (and saw the creation of a network of secular schools teaching in modern Bulgarian) and the church question. The Bulgarians were under the jurisdiction of the Constantinople patriarchate as members of the Orthodox Rum millet, and the decades-long struggle for emancipation from the hegemony of the Greek clergy ended with the recognition by the Ottoman Porte of an autonomous church, the Bulgarian exarchate (1870), and of a separate Bulgarian millet.

By the 1860s and 1870s an organized revolutionary movement for political independent had gained strength. The atrocities following the suppression of the April uprising (1876) precipitated the Russo-Turkish war (1877–8) and a shift of European public opinion in favour of Bulgarian independence. The TREATY OF SAN STEFANO (3 March 1878) created a large Bulgaria following the borders of the Bulgarian exarchate (thus including the majority of the Bulgarians). Great-power opposition to the creation of a large Balkan state under Russian influence revoked the terms of the treaty and the CONGRESS OF BERLIN (1878) divided Bulgaria in three: an autonomous Bulgarian principality under Ottoman suzerainty; the autonomous province of Eastern Rumelia under the sultan; while MACEDONIA was given back to the Porte. The Bulgarian principality was ruled by Alexander BATTENBERG (1879–86) under whom the unification with Eastern Rumelia was accomplished (1885). During FERDINAND I's rule (1887–1918) political life vacillated between conservative and liberal cabinets, between a pro-Russian and pro-Western orientation, and saw the emergence of the future influential agrarian and socialist movements, but was dominated by the Macedonian question and the Bulgarian irredenta.

Richard Crampton, *A Short History of Bulgaria* (Cambridge, 1987).

MARIA TODOROVA

Bund Officially, the General Jewish Workers' League in Lithuania, Poland and Russia, the Bund was founded in 1897 as the Jewish socialist party in the Russian Empire. It was characterized by the use of YIDDISH to communicate with the Jewish proletariat; the principle of autonomism, that Jewish workers should defend their own interests within Russia; and the idea of *Doykeyt* ('hereness'), which was a particularist form of secular Jewish nationalism, stressing the specifically eastern European Jewish community in contrast to the Zionist concept of a world-wide Jewish nation (*see* JEWS AND JUDAISM). Originating in Vilnius, the movement constantly oscillated between its embrace of Jewish secular national means, and its desire for universal socialist goals. This tension was never completely resolved, and was symbolized by its position as an autonomous body within the Russian Social Democratic Party. The Bund's membership of around 30,000 by 1903–5 made it a very significant part of the Russian socialist movement.

STEVEN BELLER

Buonarroti, Filippo Michele (*b* Pisa, 1761; *d* Paris 1837) Italian-born political revolutionary. A veteran of the French Revolution and Babeuf's (1760–97) communistic plot against the Directory (1796), he was in exile in Geneva and Brussels until his return to France in 1830, but maintained the revolutionary continuity of Jacobinism. His *Conspiration pour l'égalité dite Babeuf* (History of Babeuf's 'Conspiracy of Equals', 1828) became known as the 'Bible of Revolutionaries', educating a new generation of European leftists and influencing Blanqui and Marx.

It was translated into English by the Chartist leader Bronterre O'Brien (1804–64). Founding secret, conspiratorial cells to infiltrate and manipulate the liberal opposition groups, Buonarroti's 'mutualist' strategy sought to transform society by stages – from constitutional monarchy to liberal, then radical, bourgeois rule, and thence to communism. His 'sublime perfect masters' adopted Masonic hierarchies and rituals. Elements of the CARBONARI conspiracies (1821) were led by Buonarroti's followers, and his agents later formed a leftist faction in the Society of the Rights of Man (France, 1832).

E. J. Hobsbawm, *Primitive Rebels* (Manchester, 1959).

TONY BARLEY

Burton, Sir **Richard Francis** (*b* Torquay, Devon, 19 March 1821; *d* Trieste, Italy, 20 October 1890) British explorer, consular officer, author and linguist, in the nineteenth-century European romantic tradition. Born of a soldier father and well-to-do mother near St Albans, England, he had a desultory education, including five terms at Oxford, where his greatest proficiencies were swordsmanship and languages. Joining the Indian army (1842), he enhanced his knowledge of Indian languages, and gained 'anthropological' insights into Indian cultures, later the subject of several volumes. Subsequent publications followed a perilous journey (1851–3) when, disguised as a pilgrim, he visited the Muslim holy city of Mecca. By 1854 Burton was surveying the Somali coast with J. H. Speke (1827–64). They later searched for the Nile sources, becoming the first Europeans to reach Lake Tanganyika. It was on this mission that, disguised as a Muslim merchant, he visited the forbidden city of Harar in Ethiopia. Appointed British consul at Fernando Po (1861–5), Burton travelled throughout west Africa. Several of his books on Muslim and African cultures are now considered minor classics.

Edward Rice, *Captain Sir Richard Francis Burton* (New York, 1990).

B. MARIE PERINBAM

bushrangers Convicts who escaped into the bush in Australia and lived by robbery were called bushrangers as early as 1805. Mostly young, unmarried and without prospects, they were a type of social bandit. They acquired a deep knowledge of the topography of the region, were sometimes helped by locals who had themselves been convicts and, being often of considerable daring, were able to escape detention for long periods. Van Diemen's Land (Tasmania) was notorious for bushrangers in the early period, the best known being Michael Howe (1787–1818) and Martin Cash (1808–77). In the late 1820s on the mainland, John Donahue (?1806–30) was lionized in a ballad entitled 'Bold Jack Donaghue'. Singing it in public houses was made illegal. Bushranging had become such a disruptive force by 1830 that New South Wales enacted the death penalty for offenders.

The GOLD RUSHES proved a bonanza for bushranging and Frank Gardiner (1830–?1903), Ben Hall (1837–65) and John Gilbert (?1842–65) became household names. The last of the bushrangers was Ned Kelly (1855–80), whose life passed into legend throughout Australia. Born in Victoria of an Irish convict father and Irish mother, Kelly reacted to police brutality and persecution of his family. He took to the high country of north-eastern Victoria in 1878 with three companions. He was responsible for the killing of three armed policemen sent into the bush to kill him. Outlawed, he and his mates held up banks in Victoria and New South Wales but committed no other acts of violence. Surrounded by police at Glenrowan in July 1880, Kelly was captured and the others killed. He was hanged on 11 November. His legendary loyalty, courtesy, courage and initiative combined with his desire to found a republic of the north-east to give him a lasting place in Australian folklore, balladry, literature and painting.

John Molony, *Ned Kelly* (Melbourne, 1989).

JOHN MOLONY

business cycles *see* TRADE CYCLES.

Butler, Josephine (*b* Millfield Hill, Glendale, Northumberland, 13 April 1828; *d* Wooler, Northumberland, 30 December 1906)   English campaigner for the repeal of the CONTAGIOUS DISEASES ACTS. This legislation endeavoured to control the spread of venereal disease by permitting the forcible detention, medical inspection and treatment of women reputed to be prostitutes. The daughter of an enlightened Northumberland landowner, Josephine Grey inherited a family tradition of concern for individual rights, the abolition of slavery and Evangelical religiosity. She married George Butler, an academic and clergyman, in 1852. Grief over the death of her only daughter in 1864 led her to charitable work among prostitutes. She assumed the leadership of the Ladies' National Association in 1869, creating a coalition of middle-class and working-class women to resist the operation of the Contagious Diseases legislation. In 1886 the acts were repealed. Butler's courageous focus on the sexual exploitation of women by men transformed nineteenth-century discussion of the woman question.

GAIL SAVAGE

Byron, George Gordon, sixth Baron (*b* London, 22 January 1788; *d* Missolonghi, Greece, 19 April 1824)   British romantic poet who captured the imagination of educated Europe with his early poetry. In such poems as *Childe Harold's Pilgrimage* (1812–18) and the poetic drama *Manfred* (1817), the Byronic hero appeared, in Macaulay's words, as 'a man proud, moody, cynical, with defiance on his brow, and misery in his heart, a scorner of his kind, implacable in revenge, yet capable of deep and strong affection'. His later poetry, especially *Don Juan* (1819), transformed the influence of his admired eighteenth-century poetic model, Pope (1688–1744), to produce an extraordinary epic, by turns lyrical, cynical, romantic, comic and melancholy. His later life was spent in self-imposed exile in Switzerland and Italy, partly to escape the whiff of scandal that attached to his name in England. He sealed his reputation, and his embracing of liberal politics, by dying of a fever in Greece, while campaigning for the cause of Greek independence from Turkish rule.

SIMON DENTITH

C

Cabet, Etienne (*b* Dijon, 1 January 1798; *d* Saint Louis, 8 November 1856)   French communist theoretician. He was a successful barrister who participated in the revolution of 1830. A supporter of left-wing causes – he was sacked as attorney-general of Corsica in 1832 for supporting the Polish insurrection and was prosecuted unsuccessfully for allegedly insulting Louis-Philippe – he developed his communist ideas in the 1830s. The aim was to replace capitalist production with workers' co-operatives. The ideas themselves were fairly crudely worked out but Cabet became the most popular socialist pundit of his day, in part because of his novel *Voyage en Icarie* (1840), and partly because his ideas struck a cord among distressed artisans, many of whom were being undercut by the advance of ready-to-wear manufacturing methods in the textile trades and ruthless management of the labour force in the construction trades. Despairing of receiving support from the elites of France, he moved to the United States in 1847 and established utopian communities in Texas and Illinois. He died after many acrimonious quarrels with his followers.

See also UTOPIANISM.

C. Johnson, *Utopian Communism in France: Cabet and the Icarians* (Ithaca, NY, 1974).

DONALD SUTHERLAND

Calhoun, John Caldwell (*b* Abbeville District, South Carolina, 18 March, 1782; *d* Washington, DC, 31 March 1850)   Southern statesman and philosopher. Although he began his congressional career as a Warhawk who supported the creation of a national bank and a protective tariff, much of Calhoun's life became devoted to the rights of the south. In 1828 he wrote the *South Carolina Exposition and Protest* which proposed nullification (*see* NULLIFICATION CRISIS) as an alternative to secession. Resigning from the vice-presidency in 1832, he led efforts in South Carolina to nullify the Tariffs of 1828 and 1832. Returned to the Senate, he continued to defend the south, insisting that Congress could not limit the spread of slavery in the federal territories because this violated southern property rights. Just before his death, he also spoke against the COMPROMISE OF 1850. After his death supporters published his *Discourse on the Constitution*, in which he proposed a dual presidency (one northern, one southern) designed to protect the south's minority position.

See also MANIFEST DESTINY.

John Niven, *John C. Calhoun and the Price of Union* (Baton Rouge, La., 1988).
                                                    ALICE E. REAGAN

Canada   Originally inhabited by various aboriginal bands and groupings, then subsequently 'settled' by Europeans, Canada did not exist as a country until late in the nineteenth century. Control of the country, which stretched from the Atlantic to the Pacific and north from the Great Lakes to the northern reaches of Hudson Bay and the fur-trade frontier, lay tentatively with Great Britain, which had defeated France in North America. With the BRITISH NORTH AMERICA ACT of 1867 four newly created provinces (Ontario, Quebec, Nova Scotia and New Brunswick) joined in confederation, the better to resist the United States, develop economically and subordinate francophones and Canadian hinterlands to powerful centralized financial and political interests. Other provinces and northern territories joined the pact in later years. Once a colonial outpost serving the mercantilist aims of a British Empire in need of its staple resources (fish, fur, timber and wheat), Canada had become an independent and economically developing state.

On the periphery, resource extraction still predominated, but along the Great Lakes corridor of southern Ontario to Montreal the post-1850 years saw a diversified industrialization. By the 1880s railways linked the west and east coasts as politicians drafted a National Policy (1879) that rested on the new transportation network and promised immigrant settlement of the western interior and tariff protection for Canadian manufacturing. Yet Canada's population remained sparse, reaching only 5.33 million by 1900, compared to a United States population of 75 million. The long-standing mutual distrust of French and English continued, erupting in the 1885 uprising in the far west led by the Métis Louis Riel (1844–85). Unable to count on the fading powers of the once strong British connection, internally set against itself, Canada had left behind its colonial status by 1900 but had still to chart a truly successful path to nationhood and independence.

R. Louis Gentilcore (ed.), *Historical Atlas of Canada, vol. 2: The Nineteenth Century* (Toronto, 1993).

W. L. Morton, *The Kingdom of Canada: A General History from Earliest Times* (Toronto, 1970).

                                                          BRYAN D. PALMER

canals Used since ancient times for water supply and irrigation needs, canals were developed in Europe for commercial purposes in the twelfth century. The major technological innovation was the pound lock invented by the Dutch in the fourteenth century. By the seventeenth century a network of canals linked the major river systems in France, the Low Countries and Germany.

In the nineteenth century canals were an essential ancillary to industrial development. They dramatically reduced the cost of moving goods and raw materials and, until their displacement by the railway, provided the transportation network for moving raw materials and finished goods. This was particularly true in Britain and the United States where the canal era lasted from *c.*1760 to the mid nineteenth century. The Bridgewater Canal, opened in 1761 to move coal to the growing Manchester market, was the first canal specifically designed to meet industrial needs and its success stimulated a boom in canal construction. It was followed in Britain by the Grand Trunk Canal, which provided a cross-England link between the Trent and Mersey; the Grand Junction Canal linking London with the Midlands, which stimulated industrial development in the Birmingham area; and the Caledonian Ship Canal which underpinned the industrial development of lowland Scotland.

Until 1800 there were only about 100 miles of canals in the United States, but by the end of the century a dense network of 4,000 miles existed. The canal was the key to opening the interior of the country beyond the Allegheny Mountains, the great breakthrough being the construction of the 360 mile Erie Canal between 1817 and 1825 which linked the Hudson valley with the Great Lakes and allowed access between the midwestern prairies and the east coast ports. This was followed by the Champlain Canal (opened in 1823), the Susquehanna–Ohio canal linking Philadelphia and Pittsburg (opened in 1839) and the Illinois–Michigan canal which linked the Great Lakes with the Mississippi river system and thence into the Gulf of Mexico. At the same time a series of canals in Canada connected the Great Lakes together.

The close association between canals and industrial development was continued in Europe, particularly in Belgium, France and parts of Germany. In central Europe the political divisions impeded canal development, but one notable achievement was the linking of the Rhine, Maine and Danube Rivers by the Ludwig Canal in 1840.

The coming of the railways spelled the end of the canal era, although this was less true in Europe than in Britain and America. In

Europe the economies of canal transportation were competitive with the railways. The great river systems formed a densely interlocked transportation network and the terrain allowed easier canal construction with fewer locks. But elsewhere the economics of rail transportation gave railway companies a large advantage. Railways allowed a speedier and more flexible movement of goods with longer uninterrupted hauls and, therefore, much lower unit costs. In order to compete with the railways, canal companies needed to sink large capital resources in improvements which were uncertain to provide profitable returns. By the 1830s the canal era in Britain and America was drawing to a close and few new canals were built after that date. In Britain and the United States rate wars launched by the railways forced the sale or closure of one-third to one-half of canal companies in the 1830s and 1840s and the effective monopolization of industrial transportation by the railways.

The nineteenth century, however, also saw the construction of some of the most famous international canals, particularly the Kiel and Suez and planning for the PANAMA CANAL. These were major engineering feats and all had strategic and military as well as commercial implications. In the 1880s a small canal between Kiel and the Eider Lakes was widened, straightened and deepened to allow easy passage of German warships from the Baltic to the North Sea. The Suez Canal, built by Ferdinand de LESSEPS between 1859 and 1869, allowed easy passage from Europe to the Far East and was particularly important for Britain's access to its Indian empire. The Suez Canal was acquired by the British in 1874. De Lesseps also conceived the Panama Canal, but construction was impeded by physical and political difficulties and was not begun until the United States had secured exclusive rights to operate and construct the canal in 1906.

C. I. Savage, *An Economic History of Transport* (London, 1961).
Ronald E. Shaw, *Canals for a Nation: The Canal Era in the United States 1790–1860* (Lexington, Ky., 1990).

RICHARD PRICE

Canning, George (*b* London, 11 April 1779; *d* Chiswick, 8 August 1827). A talented politician, a Whig until the French Revolution, who carried Pittite policies forward into liberal Toryism. Throughout his career he was hindered by the envy and distrust of less gifted colleagues. His first period as foreign secretary (1807–9) ended in a quarrel (and duel) with Castlereagh, but on the latter's suicide in 1822 Canning returned to the office. Adroit at public relations, he projected a 'liberal' change of direction: in fact, he merely accelerated the process of detachment from the CONGRESS SYSTEM, recognizing that it was in Britain's interest not to police the world but to trade as widely as

possible. When Liverpool died in 1827 Canning was the popular choice
to succeed to the premiership, but his accession was delayed by complex negotiation, protracted by distrust and concern at his support for
Catholic emancipation. When the 'ultra' Tories refused to serve,
Lansdowne (1780–1863) and other Whigs joined the ministry, but this
was not to be a new alignment. On Canning's death a few months
later, the 'confusion of parties' returned.

JOHN BELCHEM

Cape Colony A British colony at the southernmost tip of Africa,
Cape Colony was occupied by Britain in 1795. Control was assumed
by the Batavian Republic from 1803 until 1806, when it reverted to
British rule. It was formally ceded to Britain in 1814 as part of the
Napoleonic war settlement. By the time responsible-government status
was granted in 1872, it had become the base of Britain's presence in
southern Africa and a major defence point for her position in the
Indian Ocean. The growing British population increasingly dominated
the earlier Dutch settlers (*see* AFRIKANERS), some of whom showed their
resentment by the GREAT TREK. Subsequently, considerable political co-
operation between the two groups became possible.

The 1867 discovery of diamonds at Kimberley added a new element
to a primarily agrarian economy, stimulating the building of railways and the influx of European capital. From the 1880s the Cape's
economic dominance was challenged by the Transvaal. It became a
province of the Union of SOUTH AFRICA in 1910, with Cape Town the
legislative capital.

SIMON KATZENELLENBOGEN

Cape-Xhosa War (1877–1878) The Cape-Xhosa War was the ninth
and last of a series of wars on the eastern frontier of the CAPE COLONY.
Pressure on the land had caused some conflict between groups of
Africans but the wars were primarily between Africans and Europeans. The Xhosa were one of the southern Nguni groups occupying
the area between Natal and the Cape. They had borne the brunt of
European penetration, losing large areas of fertile land, but had not
given up without a struggle. The result was the completion of the process
of extending British authority in the Ciskei and Transkei areas. These
conflicts were known (pejoratively) as the Kaffir Wars; they are now
sometimes referred to as the Cape Frontier or simply Frontier Wars.

SIMON KATZENELLENBOGEN

capitalism The word 'capitalism' has acquired various meanings in
its extended use by economists, sociologists and historians. At its most
general, capitalism is understood to be a system that makes use of and
accumulates capital as a factor of production. In this sense capitalism

in one form or another can be seen to have existed for many centuries. The term is, however, usually used with greater historical and cultural specificity and in relation to a much more precise set of meanings, mainly derived from MARX. Marx first employed the term extensively and analytically, seeing capitalism as a distinct economic system arising from the sixteenth century in England and reaching the stage of industrial capitalism from the late eighteenth century. He argued that capitalism would spread around the globe but that it was destined to be superseded by higher forms of economic and social organization based upon communistic ownership and control of the means of production and a more equitable distribution of the benefits of industrial society.

Marx associated capitalism with a host of specific economic, social and cultural characteristics which have remained important in the use of the term in the social sciences ever since. He stressed the spread of production for exchange rather than for subsistence use; the growth of 'free' wage labour (free from coercive feudal obligations and from proprietorial rights to land); the increasing ownership and control of the means of production by employers; the endorsement of private individual, alienable, property rights at the expense of custodial or communal rights; and the increasing prominence of the profit motive in economic behaviour. The most important aspect of his view of capitalism was that its rise was synonymous with the rise of the bourgeoisie to economic and political power. Thus the triumph of capitalism which came about with the growth of industrial capitalism in the nineteenth century was not just the triumph of an economic system but also of a whole social, cultural and political system (mode of production) based on new wealth and a new hegemonic elite. With industrialization came the further proletarianization of labour, greater division of labour, the innovation of powered machinery and factories and a consequent loss of control by workers over the pace and nature of the production process. At the same time, the greater centralization of work and homogenization of labour increased the growth of collective class identity and oppositional consciousness which would in the longer term weaken the system. The hallmark of industrial capitalism for Marx was the increasing use of industrial or fixed capital in place of merchant or circulating capital which resulted in a new form of profit generation predicated upon the full subsumption of labour by capital. Marx saw an inherent tendency for the rate of profit to decline as capitalism progressed, as capital accumulation deepened and as the opportunities for profitable employment of capital dried up. Thus capitalism was destined to fail in the long term.

The influence of Marx's writings on what we understand by the term 'capitalism' has been paramount but also important have been the works of Werner Sombart (1868–1941), who stressed the rationality of the new system; and Max Weber (1864–1920) who emphasized the rise of the capitalist ethic of thrift and industriousness, acquisition and profit-making which he associated with the rise of Protestant Nonconformity in Europe following the Renaissance. V. I. Lenin (1870–1924) initiated a continuing strand within the historiography which sees imperialism – as it developed from the late nineteenth century – inevitably resulting from the insatiable search of advanced capitalist countries for new sources of raw materials and new markets. Thus the political and economic domination of the Third by the First World is seen not only as a legacy of the nineteenth century but also as the inevitable outcome of the unequal world trading system which capitalism spawns.

Joseph Schumpeter (1883–1950) developed Marx's ideas about the increasing importance of businessmen in the social structure and of the business ethic in determining the nature of society, arguing that advanced capitalism would fail partly because of the separation of ownership from the control of enterprise. Twentieth-century developments have also resulted in the use of the term 'monopoly capitalism' to denote the rather different political, social and international circumstances which are associated with the rise of large conglomerates and of multinational firms, and the notion of state capitalism to describe societies which have major state ownership while still maintaining the capitalist conditions of centralized ownership of the means of production, a system of wage labour and the social and economic inequities which go with these.

See also FACTORIES, PROTO-INDUSTRIALIZATION, TRADE CYCLES, WORKING CLASSES.

M. Dobb, *Studies in the Development of Capitalism* (London, 1947).
R. Hilton, *The Transition from Feudalism to Capitalism* (London, 1978).
K. Marx, *Capital*, vol. 1 (Harmondsworth, 1976).
M. Weber, *The Protestant Ethic and the Spirit of Capitalism* (London, 1958).
                                                                    PAT HUDSON

Caprivi, Georg Leo, count von (*b* Berlin, 24 February 1831; *d* Skyren, near Frankfurt an der Oder, 6 February 1899)   German general and statesman, appointed minister-president of Prussia and chancellor of the German Empire in March 1890. He supported a state economic policy favouring industrial and commercial development, and his chancellorship witnessed the conclusion of a number of bilateral treaties providing for mutual reduction of tariff barriers. His trade policies aroused the antagonism of conservative agrarian interests (*see* AGRARIAN LEAGUE), while his failure to secure the passage of educational legislation, which would have increased the influence of the churches, lost him the support of the CENTRE PARTY. Having surrendered control of

Prussia in March 1892, he was vulnerable to intrigues among Prussian ministers. Growing differences with Emperor WILLIAM II and mounting conservative opposition led to his resignation as chancellor in October 1894.

J. A. Nichols *Germany after Bismarck: The Caprivi Era 1890–1894* (Cambridge, Mass. 1958).

S. J. SALTER

Captain Swing The 1830 revolt of the underemployed and pauperized agricultural workers, centred in the corn-growing southern and eastern counties of England, was named for their mythical leader, Captain Swing. The larger background to the revolt was the market-driven transformation of rural society that saw agricultural labourers stripped of customary rights and denied the securities once provided by a paternalistic social order. The revolt took various forms in different counties but included widespread machine-breaking (*see also* LUDDITES) and arson as well as attacks on local elites for failing to discharge traditional paternalist obligations. The government crushed the revolt with military force, later imprisoning or transporting 1,100 individuals. While the uprising succeeded in delaying the introduction of threshing-machines, of greater consequence was the impetus it gave to the debate on Poor Law reform (*see* NEW POOR LAW).

Eric Hobsbawm and George Rude, *Captain Swing: A Social History of the Great English Agricultural Uprising* (London, 1968).

RICHARD J. SODERLUND

Carabobo, Battle of (24 June 1821) The final confrontation in Simon BOLIVAR's campaign to liberate VENEZUELA from Spanish rule, the Battle of Carabobo took place on 24 June 1821. At the end of 1820 Bolívar, already in control of Bogotá and Colombia, had agreed a six-month armistice with the royalist leader, General Morillo (1778–1838), who subsequently retired to Europe. The patriots used the truce to rearm and broke it after two months by seizing the port of Maracaibo. Apart from a small diversionary force making for Caracas, they then converged on the Aragua valley outside Valencia where Bolívar, in combination with forces led by the two principal Venezuelan *caudillos*, Santiago Mariño (1788–1854) and José Antonio Páez (1790–1873), defeated the Spaniards. Five days later Bolívar entered Caracas. Success at Carabobo permitted the patriots to move southwards to engage the remaining royalist forces in the central Andes (*see* BATTLE OF AYACUCHO, SAN MARTIN), even though pockets of resistance remained in Venezuela.

RORY MILLER

Carbonari   The most important of the numerous secret societies that opposed the post-Napoleonic reaction in Italy, the Carbonari owed its origins to underground opposition to the Napoleonic empire, taking its name – 'the charcoal-burners' – from an occupation typical of the peasant insurgents who conducted a guerrilla war against the French in Calabria in the period 1806–11. Originally founded to oppose Napoleonic rule in Naples, the Carbonari at first worked for the return of the Bourbons, but after 1815 its support for constitutionalism and national independence led it into conflict with not only the Neapolitan regime but also those of the rest of Italy. It was, however, neither republican nor anti-Catholic, though it did oppose the temporal power of the church.

Under the leadership of Filippo BUONARROTI, it evolved a complex organization of local cells and an elaborate ritual which resembled that of the Freemasons (although otherwise the two movements had little connection with one another). Membership of the movement was largely centred on students, army officers and the professions, but it was also able to develop strong popular links, d'Azeglio (1798–1866) later claiming that it recruited 'the extremist scum of the lower people'. What is certainly true is that its support was widespread, membership reaching a peak of possibly 300,000. Aiming at violent revolution, the Carbonari launched a long series of risings, of which the most successful were those that took place in Naples in 1820 and in Piedmont in 1821. However, in both cases, success was obtained only because of the widespread involvement of army officers, and in neither was it permanent. With the movement under heavy police pressure, support gradually fell away, the cause now being taken up by Mazzini's (1805–72) Young Italy.

Stuart Woolf, *A History of Italy, 1700–1860: The Social Constraints of Political Change* (London, 1979).

CHARLES ESDAILE

Carlist Wars (1833–1840, 1848, 1870–1876)   So-called after successive pretenders to the Spanish throne, the Carlist Wars, of which there were three separate ones, were initially precipitated by traditionalist dissatisfaction with the pragmatic FERDINAND VII, and the exclusion of his ultra-conservative brother Don Carlos (1788–1855) from the succession to the throne in favour of the infant Isabella II (1830–1904). However, Carlism was the fruit of far more than loyalty to one particular branch of the royal family or even to extreme Catholicism. In the first half of the nineteenth century Spain was already experiencing a slow process of social and economic change based on the rise of capitalism in both agriculture and industry. For many areas that were already poor – upland Aragon, Catalonia and Valencia – this spelled further decline, while for the few regions farmed by a prosperous peasantry – the Basque country and Navarre – it threatened the traditions that had hitherto guaranteed stability. For both groups, the loyalists' liberalism, with its association with modernization, centralization and new economic practices, was a natural enemy, just as the church was a natural ally.

As banditry and the guerrillas of the PENINSULAR WAR provided a tradition of armed resistance, the Carlist leaders therefore found a ready audience, but their ability to challenge the loyalists was limited. In the east and south Carlism was restricted to guerrilla warfare that was able to achieve very little in military terms, while the more solid base provided by Navarre and the Basque country could not arm or equip the armies that it turned out. Increasingly deprived of the support of the rural poor, who turned to anarchism, Carlism therefore disappeared as a military force until revived by the Civil War of 1936–9.

Martin Blinkhorn, *Carlism and Crisis in Spain, 1931–1939* (Cambridge, 1975).

CHARLES ESDAILE

Carlsbad Decrees After preliminary discussions between Prince METTERNICH and Frederick-William III of Prussia, a series of repressive measures were agreed by representatives of ten German states under Metternich's presidency at Carlsbad (Karlovy Vary) in August 1819. They were subsequently passed by a meeting of the full German diet at Frankfurt in September, without opposition. The decrees extended state surveillance and control over the education system, the press and political activity. The incident which ostensibly provoked the measures was the murder, by a radical theology student, Karl Sand, of the reactionary journalist and playwright August von Kotzebue (1761– 1819). The murder provoked widespread public revulsion against radicalism, and enabled Metternich to persuade the other German states of the necessity of urgent action against nationalist agitation by student corporations (*Burschenschaften*) in the universities.

The first decree provided for surveillance of the universities and the removal of subversive teaching staff. A second decree established rigorous press censorship throughout Germany. The decrees also provided for a federal office to deal with political subversion in any of the member states. Beyond this, however, the decrees constituted a starting-point for a revision of the German constitution of 1815 with the aim of eliminating all progressive influences. The following year the German states agreed to a series of acts which effectively transformed the political character of the GERMAN CONFEDERATION, recasting it as an agent of conservatism which had the power to intervene, if necessary, against radical reform within individual states. Metternich thus acquired powerful institutional means to thwart the progressive aspirations of south German constitutionalists and Prussian reformers alike, and the prospects for political change in Germany were stifled for a generation.

TIMOTHY KIRK

Carlyle, Thomas (*b* Ecclefechan, Dumfriesshire, 4 December 1795; *d* London, 4 February 1881)   Scottish historian, biographer and political and philosophical writer who brought the virtues and predilections of his Scottish peasant childhood to his long literary life in London. His historical writing, on *The French Revolution* (1837), *Oliver Cromwell* (1845) and *Frederick the Great* (1858–65), provided a heroic and moralized account of the historical process. His other writings ranged from spiritual autobiography to political pamphleteering. The force and earnestness of his writing lent him a prophetic status in the eyes of many of his contemporaries from the 1840s onwards, especially in addressing what he termed the CONDITION-OF-ENGLAND QUESTION. He was especially opposed to *laissez-faire* beliefs in matters of social and economic life, and attempted a secular restatement of the religion of his childhood in heroic terms fit for the nineteenth century. In later life his belief in the heroic qualities of leadership, and his distrust of democracy, led him to adopt increasingly authoritarian attitudes.

SIMON DENTITH

Carnegie, Andrew (*b* Dunfermline, 25 November 1835; *d* Lenox, Massachusetts, 11 August 1919)   Scots-born American industrialist and philanthropist. The son of a Scottish handweaver, he travelled at 13 with his family to Allegheny, Pennsylvania where he rose from bobbin boy to telegrapher and then, in 1853, to the personal secretary of Thomas Scott (1823–81), later president of the Pennsylvania Railroad. Wise – although by modern standards improper – investments enabled Carnegie to leave the railroad business and embark upon bridge-building and iron-making and, by 1882, the steel industry. Expressing his philosophy in books and articles such as *The Gospel of Wealth* (1889), he defended the accumulation of wealth in Darwinian terms, reflecting the writings of Herbert Spencer. Believing that surplus wealth should be distributed for the public good – in building universities, libraries, hospitals, parks and churches – he gave out hundreds of millions of dollars in his later years.

Harold C. Livesay, *Andrew Carnegie and the Rise of Big Business* (Boston, 1975).

JOHN MARTIN

Carol I [Karl Hohenzollern] (*b* Sigmaringen, 20 April 1839; *d* Sinaia, 10 October 1914)   Prince (1866–81) and king (1881–1914) of ROMANIA.

Scion of the Hohenzollerns-Sigmaringen, he became a Prussian army officer. After Cuza's abdication he was offered the throne and elected overwhelmingly by a plebiscite in 1866. His rule gained wide popularity and rapid recognition. He organized the army on the Prussian model, and in the Russo-Turkish war of 1877–8 had joint command of the Romanian and Russian forces. The TREATY OF SAN STEFANO (1878) gave Romania full independence from the Ottoman Porte, and the country was proclaimed a kingdom in 1881. In the domestic sphere Carol supported the protectionist policies of the liberals aimed at encouraging industry. In 1883 he concluded a secret defensive alliance with Germany and the Habsburgs which was renewed five times but could not be implemented in 1914 against the pro-Entente orientation of the cabinet.

MARIA TODOROVA

carpetbaggers During RECONSTRUCTION (1863–77) white southerners developed the word 'carpetbaggers' as a term of derision to describe northern-born white Republicans who relocated in the south after the American Civil War. Southerners claimed that these supposed political adventurers came south to punish and pillage the region, carrying all their belongings in their carpetbag. In the legend of reconstruction developed during the late nineteenth and early twentieth centuries carpetbaggers were to blame for all the ills suffered by the south during this period. According to southern whites, they were especially responsible for the supposedly 'uppity' behaviour of the AFRICAN-AMERICANS during this period. They insisted that black suffrage and office-holding was a plot designed by carpetbaggers and their Republican masters in Congress to humiliate the defeated south. 'Carpetbag rule' became synonymous with the lurid legend of reconstruction that dominated both popular and scholarly accounts of the era until the late 1950s.

In reality, most carpetbaggers were young men looking for new economic opportunities in the post-war south. They included former soldiers, religious missionaries and entrepreneurs. Some served with the FREEDMEN'S BUREAU, assisting African-Americans in the transition to freedom. Others pioneered the citrus industry in Florida. Their reputation came about because of their political involvement, and southerners labelled them as interfering outsiders who turned African-Americans against their natural allies, their former masters. As the leaders of the new REPUBLICAN PARTY in many southern states, they filled many local, state and national offices formerly dominated by ex-Confederates. Most carpetbaggers were honest, but an important minority became involved in real corruption. In Alabama, Florida, North Carolina and Georgia they participated in railroad-stock speculation and fraud. In other states they bribed legislators to pass laws to benefit their economic enterprises. To most southerners, however, their biggest crime was assisting African-Americans.

Richard N. Current, *Those Terrible Carpetbaggers* (New York, 1988).

ALICE E. REAGAN

Castlereagh, Robert Stewart, Viscount (*b* Mountstewart, County Down, 18 June 1769; *d* North Cray, Kent, 12 August 1822) Prominent Tory politician who enjoyed greater success and respect in foreign policy than in home affairs. As chief secretary for Ireland (1799–1801) he played a prominent part in effecting the Act of Union (*see* IRISH ACT OF UNION) but it was in foreign affairs that he found his metier, although his experience at the war office (1805, 1807–9) did not augur well, terminating in a duel with Canning. Appointed foreign secretary by Liverpool in 1812, he achieved considerable success: having remade the grand alliance, he kept the allies together long enough to defeat Napoleon; thereafter, he sought to preserve a peaceful balance, a 'concert of Europe' in which territorial integrity would be respected – and Britain's commercial dominance safeguarded – by diplomatic conference. However, he became increasingly disillusioned with the CONGRESS SYSTEM as the eastern powers sought to apply the autocratic and interventionist principles of the HOLY ALLIANCE. He began to collapse under the pressure of overwork, aggravated by the hostility he incurred as leader of the House of Commons, upholding the repressive domestic policies of the post-war years. Cold and austere, he took his own life in 1822 to avoid a sexual scandal.

JOHN BELCHEM

casual labour Throughout the nineteenth century casual labour was a widespread phenomenon of the British as of all other economies. Since the income from it was less secure, it featured prominently in Charles Booth's (1840–1916) study of London poverty (1889, 1891). Furthermore, the casual methods of hiring labour, for example at the docks, attracted surplus labourers into an already overstocked labour market. To Booth and later to William Beveridge (1879–1963) it seemed preferable to distribute work more frequently over a smaller body of men and force the rest to look elsewhere, a process described as 'decasualization'. They argued that casual labour bred casual habits, unfitting men for regular work and discouraging foresight. Casual labour was thus disapproved of for economic and moral reasons. The 1890s saw limited attempts at decasualization in certain London docks, but it was not until after 1911 that the state attempted to encourage decasualization.

G. Phillips and N. Whiteside, *Casual Labour* (Oxford, 1985).

E. P. HENNOCK

Catholic emancipation The exclusion of Roman Catholics from the House of Commons was ended only in 1829, after prolonged debate in England and Ireland. Catholics had been subjected to penal laws as a threat to the state in the seventeenth century, and, although they had subsequently been given a measure of relief, at the opening of the nineteenth century the parliamentary oath still prevented them from sitting as members of parliament. William Pitt (1759–1806) tried to end the archaic arrangement at the time of the union with Ireland in 1800–1, only to find that George III (1738–1820) refused to consider what he saw as an infringement of his coronation oath to uphold the Protestant constitution. Over the next quarter-century the Catholic communities of England and Ireland were divided about how far they should be willing to offer 'securities' for good behaviour, in particular a state veto over episcopal appointments, with English Catholics usually more ready than the Irish to make concessions, and laity usually more ready than the clergy. In 1821 and again in 1825 controversial Emancipation Bills actually passed the Commons, only to be defeated by Protestant constitutionalists in the Lords. In 1828 the repeal of the TEST AND CORPORATION ACTS created a precedent for religious toleration, and then Daniel O'CONNELL, the radical leader of the Catholic Association in Ireland, was returned in a by-election for County Clare but unable to take his seat. With Ireland apparently on the brink of civil war, the duke of Wellington's government decided to propose emancipation and, after convincing an extremely reluctant George IV, carried it in April 1829. The measure gave Roman Catholics a new sense of unity and confidence, but also contributed to a resurgence of anti-Catholicism.

Wendy Hinde, *Catholic Emancipation: A Shake to Men's Minds* (Oxford, 1992).

D. W. BEBBINGTON

Catholicism The Roman Catholic Church was persecuted in France after the Revolution but was restored by the CONCORDAT with Napoleon of 1801. The dissolution of the Holy Roman Empire in 1806 ended the shadow of universal Catholic monarchy, while the suppression of the remaining German prince-bishoprics and abbeys in 1803 set a pattern for the anticlerical plunder of religious endowments in Portugal from 1834, in Spain from 1835 and in Mexico from 1857. Napoleon absorbed Rome into his empire and imprisoned PIUS VII from 1809 to 1814, but the diplomatic genius of Cardinal Consalvi (1757–1824) at the Congress of Vienna in 1815 achieved the restoration of the Papal States. The mounting challenge of Italian nationalism to papal rule in central Italy cast Popes LEO XII and GREGORY XVI in the conservative role favoured by the restored Bourbons of France, Spain and Naples, and by Austria, Russia and Prussia. Rome was sustained by ULTRAMONTANISM in both the conservative form of Count Joseph de Maistre (1754–1821), and the liberalism of Félicité de LAMENNAIS who favoured an infallible pope as the guarantor of political liberty. As it was, the brief flirtation of Pope PIUS IX with political liberalism ended in the Roman revolution of 1848. Pius lost most of his dominions to the kingdom of Italy in 1861 and Rome itself in 1870, and in the 'Syllabus errorum' (Syllabus of Errors, 1864) he attacked 'progress, liberalism and modern civilization' root and branch. During his pontificate the church suffered persecution in Russia and from political instability in Spain and Spanish America; in the 1870s it confronted Bismarck's KULTURKAMPF in the new German Empire, while from the 1880s, there was a new wave of anticlericalism in France. Against this anticlericalism, ultramontane devotionalism produced the rallying to Rome declared in the decrees of the First Vatican Council (1869–70) defining the pope's infallibility in faith and morals and his universal jurisdiction over the whole church.

There were many English and German intellectual and literary converts to Catholicism dismayed by the divisions of Protestantism, and there were new Marian apparitions, pilgrimages and shrines, most notably Lourdes (1858), and an enormous growth both in Catholic religious institutions devoted to teaching, nursing and charity and in orders of women religious. CATHOLIC EMANCIPATION in the United Kingdom (1829) heralded a vast expansion of the church throughout the British Empire, especially by Irish immigration, which also created a huge new church in the United States. The church was strengthened in Belgium by the union of liberals and Catholics in 1830 to reject Dutch rule; in Holland, where the hierarchy was restored in 1853; and in Germany by the Centre Party after 1871, while the second half of the century saw a renaissance in Catholic missionary enterprise especially in the areas of French colonization and influence in Africa and Asia. The church defined its attitudes to the challenges of democracy, socialism and trades unionism in the encyclical letters of Pope LEO XIII.

See also PAPACY.

James McCaffrey, *History of the Catholic Church in the Nineteenth Century (1789–1908)*, 2 vols (Dublin, 1910).

SHERIDAN GILLEY

Cato Street Conspiracy Following the imposition of the SIX ACTS, the 'revolutionary party' attempted to murder members of the cabinet while they were dining with Lord Harrowby (1762–1847) in February 1820. Arthur Thistlewood (1770–1820), leader of the conspiracy, reverted to secret activity in the aftermath of PETERLOO. Having hoped for an escalation of mass agitation, Thistlewood was outraged when Henry HUNT abandoned the mass platform to seek redress in parliament and the courts. As public excitement waned, Thistlewood turned to traditional conspiracy, planning a sensational coup in London to provoke a general rising. Entrapped by government agents, he and his co-conspirators were enticed to a loft in Cato Street, where the police nearly bungled the arrests. These events, which seem to have cut across incipient provincial plans for insurrection on 1 April, served to confirm the government in its new repressive powers. Thistlewood and four conspirators were hanged, while five others were transported for life.

JOHN BELCHEM

Cavaignac, Louis Eugène (*b* Paris, 15 October 1802; *d* near Le Mans, 28 October 1857) French general and head of state. The son of a regicide in the Revolution, he combined a military career with membership in the secret societies in the Restoration. He fought almost continuously in Algeria from 1832 to 1848, becoming minister of war in the provisional government of 1848 where he planned the defence of the government against an insurrection. The Constituent Assembly gave him full powers to suppress the JUNE DAYS and after his victory made him 'head of the executive power'. Under his *de facto* presidency, thousands of rebels were deported and several newspapers of both Right and Left were suppressed. His popularity waned as his one-time monarchist allies deserted him, so that he received a derisory 1.5 million votes in the presidential elections of December 1848 against Louis Napoleon. He refused to take an oath to the imperial constitution of 1852.

F. A. de Luna, *The French Republic under Cavaignac, 1848* (Princeton, NJ, 1969).

DONALD SUTHERLAND

Cavour, Count Camillo Benso di (*b* Turin, Piedmont, 1 August 1810; *d* Turin, Italy, 6 June 1861) Prime minister and foreign minister of Sardinia-Piedmont and Italy. Through his newpaper *Il Risorgimento*, and as a member of parliament, he supported constitutional reform and the revolts of 1848. Their failure caused him to reject those who believed that 'Italy can do it by herself', and to involve Piedmont in the Crimean War to gain French and British support. At the Congress of Paris (*see* TREATY OF PARIS) he achieved no concrete results but laid the basis for Italy's future great-power status. He conspired with Napoleon III at Plombières in 1858 to wage war against Austria for Italian unification. In 1859 Cavour orchestrated the plebiscites which brought the northern Italian duchies into union with Piedmont. Controversy exists over his knowledge of GARIBALDI's expedition in 1860.

Denis Mack-Smith, *Cavour* (London, 1985).

LAWRENCE P. ADAMCZYK

cell theory   Cell theory is founded upon the idea that all organisms are aggregates of structural and functional units (cells), each containing an organ (nucleus) and acting as the site of metabolism. The central tenets of cell theory were first proposed in 1838 and 1839 by Matthias Schleiden (1804–81) and Theoder Schwann (1810–82), two German biologists and microscopists. Although an initial idea, that all cells were formed via a process similar to chemical precipitation, was proved false, the view that the cell was the functional and formative basis of life was widely accepted in biology by 1860. The first significant application of cellular theory was the concept of cellular pathology, argued for by Rudolf Virchow (1821–1902) in *Cellular-pathologie* (1858). By 1900 cell theory had led to an understanding of the nervous system, respiratory processes and many aspects of animal and plant structure.

William Coleman, *Biology in the Nineteenth Century* (Cambridge, 1971).

STEVE AMANN

census   The nineteenth century represented a period of rapid development in the history of census-taking. Earlier enumerations throughout the world had largely been based on parochial records or household registers and formed the substance of the military, tax and labour obligations that shaped later censuses. The statistical zeal that characterized the nineteenth century ensured that censuses became more comprehensive in both scope and coverage. From rudimentary headcounts in the early years, by the end of the century they included questions beyond those of age, sex, marital status and birthplace and encapsulated a wide range of social variables such as occupation, housing, religion and education. Newly independent nations in the Americas often used a census (although often incomplete and unreliable) to provide the basis for fresh administrative structures, while other colonial regions replicated the censuses of Europe, with additional questions reflecting local circumstances.

GRAHAM MOONEY

Central American Federation   One of several attempts to form regional federations in Spanish America after independence was the Central American Federation. Initially, the Central American states joined Iturbide's empire in MEXICO but in 1823 they seceded to form the United Provinces of Central America. The federation's history was one of almost constant conflict – between liberals and conservatives, federalists and centralists, the five provinces, different cities in the same province and individual *caudillos*. The bloody civil war of 1826–9 ended in a liberal victory, the presidency of Francisco Morazán (1792–1842) and, in 1834, the move of the capital from Guatemala to San Salvador. The liberals alienated many with their attacks on the church, the Hispanic judicial system, their land policy and their taxation and tariff measures. In 1838 Rafael Carrera (1814–65) led a popular revolt in Guatemala, and Honduras, Nicaragua and Costa Rica all seceded. By the time Carrera defeated Morazán at Guatemala City in March 1840 the federation was dead.

R. L. Woodward, *Central America: A Nation Divided* (New York, 1985).

RORY MILLER

central banking   A central bank is the principal banking institution of a country, having responsibility for the implementation of monetary policy and for the support and regulation of the banking system. Of existing central banks, the first to be founded was the Swedish Riksbank (1668), followed by the Bank of England (1694). In the nineteenth century almost a score came into being, including those of the majority of European countries and Japan. Important experiments also took place in the United States.

Central banks were originally known as banks of issue or national banks and were established by government, in either public or private ownership, for limited purposes such as the provision of loans to the state or reform of the note issue. Only gradually did they take on a full central-banking role. In doing so many modelled themselves on the Bank of England, the prototype central bank. By 1800 the Bank of England was, in practice, acting as banker and lender of last resort to the British banking system, although the obligation was not finally acknowledged until after 1870. The technical problem lay first in determining the size of the gold reserve that would allow the Bank to maintain the convertibility of its notes under the gold standard while meeting demands from the banks for accommodation in a crisis. When this issue was settled by the Bank Charter Act of 1844 in favour of an automatic rule rather than discretionary variation, the emphasis shifted to the means of limiting the level of demand from the banks and hence to the control of bank credit. The solution followed the Bagehot principle that the Bank should lend freely against acceptable security but at a rate of interest set sufficiently high to achieve financial stability.

See also BANKING.

Charles Goodhart, *The Evolution of Central Banks* (London, 1988).

GORDON FLETCHER

Centre Party   The Centre Party was established in 1870 as a political party committed to representing the interests of Roman Catholics, who formed slightly more than one-third of the population of the GERMAN EMPIRE, founded in 1871. Under its leader, Ludwig Windthorst (1812–91), the party rapidly mobilized the Catholic electorate against the anticlerical policies pursued by Bismarck, with liberal support, during the 1870s (see KULTURKAMPF). From 1874 onwards, it consistently won around a quarter of all seats in the Reichstag and, underpinned by a dense network of Catholic associational organizations, also enjoyed strong representation in the parliaments of most of the states of the empire. By the 1890s the imperial government was dependent on its support for the passage of legislation; and its apparent opportunism and skill in extracting from the government concessions to its constituency attracted much criticism. Never simply the political wing of the Catholic Church in Germany, the Centre tended (reflecting its disproportionately rural and small-town electoral constituency) to align with conservatives on questions of social and economic policy, yet was often critical of imperial governments on fiscal and military issues.

D. Blackbourn, *Class, Religion and Local Politics in Wilhelmine Germany* (New Haven, Conn., 1980).

E. L. Evans, *The German Center Party, 1870–1933* (Carbondale, Ill., 1981).

S. J. SALTER

Cetshwayo (*b* c.1825; *d* Eshowe, South Africa, February, 1884) Last independent Zulu chief to challenge seriously Boer and British rule in South Africa. Born into the distinguished lineage of SHAKA, he succeeded in 1872 to the Zulu state with a military potential, but mired in domestic factionalism (see ZULUS). Having consolidated his hold on the internal instruments of state power – including military resources which he reorganized and strengthened – Cetshwayo, relying on British support, aimed to contain Afrikaner encroachments from the Transvaal into the Natal regions. His plans were, however, aborted in April 1877 by Theophilus Shepstone (1815–93), the British Natal administrator who unexpectedly annexed the Transvaal (held until 1881). Subsequently fending off a British attack by Lord Frederic Chelmsford (1827–1905), Cetshwayo defeated the British at Isandhlwana (1879). Succumbing to a counter-attack under General Garnet WOLSELEY, he was defeated, deposed and imprisoned. He returned briefly to power as a British client-chief, but his expected domestic coalition support never came, foundering on a resurgence of lineage factionalism. Forced to flee, he died, possibly at an assassin's hand.

Monica Wilson and Leonard Thompson (eds), *The Oxford History of South Africa*, 2 vols (Oxford, 1969–71).

B. MARIE PERINBAM

Chamberlain, Joseph (*b* London, 8 July 1836; *d* London, 2 July 1914) British Unionist politician. He made his fortune as a screw manufacturer and was able to retire from business in 1874 to devote himself to politics and public service. Having established his reputation as a reforming mayor of Birmingham (1873–5), pioneering policies of 'gas-and-water socialism', he entered parliament as a Liberal in 1876, where he emerged as an advanced radical and even republican. President of the board of trade (1880–5) and president of the local government board (1886) under Gladstone, he resigned in opposition to the policy of Irish HOME RULE. He became a staunch imperialist and served as colonial secretary in Unionist governments (1895–1903), playing a prominent role in the Boer War. He opposed British isolation and championed imperial union. He resigned in 1903 to promote tariff reform but, after a stroke in 1906, left active politics.

Richard Jay, *Joseph Chamberlain: A Political Study* (Oxford, 1981).

DAVID DUTTON

Chang Chih-tung [Zhang Zidong] (*b* 1837; *d* 1909) Distinguished scholar-official. He produced the 'ti-yung' formula – 'Chinese learning for essence, Western learning for practical development'. His career reached its climax in his governor-generalship of Hunan and Hupeh. With LI HUNG-CHANG, he was among the most effective of the provincial reformers. He pressed for the building with foreign funds of the north-south, Peking to Hankow, railway and developed China's first great iron-and-steel complex in east Hupeh. But as the 'ti-yung' formula indicated, there was an ambivalence in his approach to reform. He continued to stress the essential values of Confucianism, winning the support of the empress dowager, Tz'u-hsi, by his insistence on gradual reform. In 1898 he was a strong opponent of K'ang Yu-wei (1858–1927) and the radical reformers but during the BOXER RISING in 1900 he was among those governors who refused to commit their provincially raised armies against the foreign powers.

JOHN DAVIES

charity *see* PHILANTHROPY.

Charles X (*b* Versailles, 9 October 1757; *d* Friuli, 6 November 1836) King of France (1824–30). Born Charles Philippe, comte d'Artois, he was the youngest brother of Louis XVI (1754–93). He developed a passion for gambling, hunting and mistresses and played an altogether destructive role in the early Revolution. He tried to form conspiracies inside France based on sectarian hatreds for Protestants and to persuade the foreign powers to intervene. In 1795 he persuaded the British to let him tag along on an expedition designed to land arms to royalist insurgents in western France but, fortunately for him, weather prevented a landing. He became leader of the Ultraroyalist faction during the Restoration. During his coronation in 1825 he even used the 'King's Touch', a medieval practice in which it was believed that French (and English) kings could cure scrofula. His 'Four Ordinances' of July 1830, dissolving the recently elected assembly, limiting the vote to big landowners and restricting the press, provoked a revolution against the Bourbons. He abdicated in August and died of cholera in 1836. He was the last French king to die in a public ceremony.

V. Beach, *Charles X of France: His Life and Times* (Boulder, Colo., 1971).

DONALD SUTHERLAND

Chartism   A mass movement for democratic rights which flourished throughout England, Wales and Scotland (1838 – *c*.1850), Chartism took its name from the 'People's Charter'. Published in May 1838 by the London Working Men's Association, the document was drawn up by the cabinetmaker William LOVETT and was also signed by several Liberal members of parliament. The charter's famous six points were universal male adult suffrage, vote by secret ballot, the abolition of property qualifications for members of parliament, the payment of members of parliament, equal electoral districts and annual parliaments. The Chartist programme was simple and hardly new, but around it converged a sustained and complex popular movement.

In the wake of the 1832 Reform Act, which extended the franchise predominantly to the urban middle class, there was widespread radical feeling that the majority of people had been politically betrayed. There was also intense opposition to the harshness of the 1834 Poor Law Amendment Act. Chartism harnessed such resentments, building on a well-established tradition of popular democratic politics. The *Northern Star* newspaper (1837–52) was vitally important to unifying Chartism into a national movement. It was founded by Feargus O'CONNOR, charismatic orator and former Irish member of parliament who became Chartism's most influential leader. Chartism was distinguished by its large scale, its national character and its predominately working-class support. It made no formal demands for female suffrage, although many Chartists favoured votes for unmarried women and widows, on the assumption that such women would not be represented by a male household head (*see* WOMEN'S SUFFRAGE). Many women took an active, but generally subordinate, role in the movement. Chartism was strong in major cities such as London, Manchester, Leeds, Birmingham and Glasgow, but the movement took deepest root in smaller, more socially homogeneous manufacturing communities.

Early Chartism (1838–9) focused on mobilizing a national petition to Parliament. The petition, first proposed by the Birmingham Political Union, also demanded universal male suffrage, and was brought together with the charter at a mass meeting in August 1838. At huge demonstrations, sometimes reaching estimated attendances of 100,000 to 200,000, Chartists elected members to a general convention which met in London to superintend the petition's presentation, and sought to devise a strategy to attain Chartist goals following the rejection of their demands. In 1842, and again in 1848, Chartists launched massive petitioning campaigns. The largest petition, that of 1842, collected over 3 million signatures.

Chartism's primary strategy was to bring overwhelming pressure to bear on government, to force change through open constitutional means. There was, however, often an implied threat of violence, as the popular slogan 'Peaceably if we can, forcibly if we must' suggested. Chartists occasionally moved beyond constitutional agitation. Abortive insurrections occurred in 1839–40 and 1848. In the summer of 1842 activists transformed a series of industrial strikes into a general strike demanding that the charter be made law. In 1839–40, 1842 and 1848 the movement saw arrests and the imprisonment of many local and national leaders. At various times Chartists were offered and rejected alliances with middle-class reform associations, most notably with Joseph Sturge's (1793–1859) Complete Suffrage Union. Chartists differed on the merits of these overtures. In general, however, Chartism experienced hostility from most middle-class people. Chartists favoured the repeal of the Act of Union with Ireland, although until 1848 an alliance with Irish nationalists proved elusive.

The two most striking innovations of the 1840s were the formation of the National Charter Association, often regarded as the world's first working-class political party, and the Chartist Land Plan, which settled urban workers on small plots of land. Local branches of the National Charter Association often sustained a rich 'movement culture', including their own Sunday schools, chapels, discussion groups, soirees and co-operative stores. As a practical venture the Land Plan failed, but its wide support reflected urban workers' desire for some form of economic independence. Behind the demand for universal suffrage lay a moral critique of the social values that were becoming dominant under industrial capitalism, and an implicit social programme centring on demands such as the regulation of working hours in factories and minimum-wage standards. There were leaders such as Ernest Jones (1819–69) and George Julian Harney (1817–97) who sought to link Chartism's democratic political demands to socialist goals. Following the defeat of 1848, Chartism fragmented, although the movement maintained a national presence into the early 1850s.

See also RADICALISM, WORKING CLASSES.

James Epstein and Dorothy Thompson (eds), *The Chartist Experience* (London, 1982).

David Jones, *Chartism and the Chartists* (London, 1975).
Dorothy Thompson, *The Chartists* (London, 1984).

JAMES EPSTEIN

Chase, Salmon Portland (*b* Cornish, New Hampshire, 13 January 1808; *d* New York, 7 May 1873)   American jurist and statesman. Following his father's death when Chase was 9, he went to live with his uncle, Philander Chase (1775–1852), an Episcopal bishop, who instilled in him sobriety, puritanical morality and self-righteousness. He was admitted to the Bar at 21 and settled in Cincinnati, Ohio. There he became active in the abolitionist movement and earned the nickname of the 'Attorney-General for Runaway Negroes'. He enthusiastically joined the newly formed Republican Party, won the governorship of Ohio in 1855 and had strong presidential ambitions. When Abraham Lincoln was elected president in 1860, he made Chase his secretary of the treasury. Lincoln accepted Chase's resignation after three years in office, and, despite severe reservations, nominated him in 1864 for chief justice of the supreme court, where he served through the turbulent years of Reconstruction.

JOHN MARTIN

Chateaubriand, François René, vicomte de (*b* Saint Malo, 4 September 1768; *d* Paris, July 1848)   French author and politician. Born to an old but modest family of Breton nobility, he spent the Revolution touring the United States, and in the counter-revolutionary armies, which he claimed ruined his health. Like many royalists, he returned to France to serve Napoleon, but resigned in 1804. Ambassador and foreign minister under the Restoration, his career was sabotaged by the Ultraroyalists. None the less, he refused to serve the July Monarchy.

Le Génie du christianisme, René and *Mémoires d'outre-tombe* are his best-known works. The first was a comparison of the French Revolution with revolutions in antiquity and with seventeenth-century England. The second laid bare the soul of a romantic young man, while the *Mémoires* were a combination of history and autobiography, a sardonic juxtaposition of the self (especially himself) in relation to the grand sweep of events.

P. Barberis, *Chateaubriand: une réaction au monde moderne* (Paris, 1976).
DONALD SUTHERLAND

chemical industry   The heavy-chemical industry – involving the production of inorganic acids, alkalis and bleaching materials – came into being in the nineteenth century. Chemical manufacture was not an industrial leader in this period: IRON AND STEEL, textiles (*see* TEXTILE

INDUSTRIES) and ENGINEERING were the giant sectors, with the chemical trades as the handmaids supplying fertilizers, explosives, acids, soaps, dyes and lubricants to these various dominant trades. Nevertheless, so close was the chemical industry's connection with these other spheres of activity that the demand for its products has itself been described as an index of industrialization. Moreover, from the 1880s a new era of scientific research marked the start of a much more important role for chemicals in the world economy which has continued to the present day. Not surprisingly, throughout this period growth was heavily concentrated in Europe, with first Britain and then Germany holding commercial and technical primacy.

Britain had established itself as the world leader in heavy chemicals by 1870. At the heart of the industry was alkali ('soda ash') – a vital material for the development of the soap, paper and glass industries. Alkali was used for bleaching powders in textiles, and also in the food industry, where it was an ingredient in baking powders and fizzy drinks. For most of the nineteenth century the alkali industry depended upon the Leblanc process, first pioneered in France during the Revolution and then successfully applied on a larger commercial scale in Britain. The greatest period of expansion of the Leblanc process was between 1850 and 1870: total tonnage of alkali in Britain has been estimated at 334,000 in 1866 and 585,000 in 1878. Such was Britain's dominance of the world industry at this time that about half of this total was exported. The alkali industry was based in three districts: Glasgow, Tyneside, and Lancashire and Cheshire. The latter was the most important centre, with a focus around Widnes, a reflection of its advantages of cheap, good-quality salt, limestone and coal, and access to the major port of Liverpool.

Aside from alakali, sulphuric acid and other chemicals were also made in substantial tonnages. So too were fertilizers, with Britain again among the leaders, though processing usually involved no more than the simple compounding of imported guano or the far more important Chilean nitrates.

In the 1870s the world's chemical industry was convulsed by the more efficient ammonia-soda process, the work of two Belgian brothers, Alfred and Ernest Solvay (1838–1922). In 1873 Brunner, Mond & Company (one of the forerunners of Imperial Chemical Industries) began manufacture under licence at Northwich, Cheshire: by introducing the new soda-making process, Brunner, Mond took 90 per cent of the British alkali trade. But Britain was slow to capitalize on the Solvay process and its industry remained heavily tied to the primitive Leblanc technology. The chemical industry therefore began to transfer to more dynamic, less conservative economies in Europe and further afield in America and Russia.

Britain's technology-lag during the transition into a new era in the chemical industry was most marked in dyestuffs. Before the 1850s dyes were made from plants, but in 1856 a British chemist, W. H. Perkin (1838–1907), synthesized mauve from aniline and launched the world's first synthetic-dye business. Between 1856 and 1859 the modern dye industry came into existence and seemed destined to be another British success story. Britain, after all, had the world's largest textile industry, Perkin's technical breakthrough and supplies of coal, coal gas and tar. But Germany's superior system of technical education underlined the importance of research and development. Through its advanced research laboratories, staffed with academically trained scientists, the large-scale, highly concentrated German chemical industry overtook all rivals.

Although Britain still dominated the traditional heavy-chemical sector, its alkali industry was in decline by the end of the century, with exports falling from £2.6 million in 1890 to £1.4 million in 1900. Germany had meanwhile become the leader in the new organic industry: German laboratories made the innovations that launched major new growth areas in plastics and pharmaceuticals in the twentieth century.

See also CHEMISTRY.

L. F. Haber, *The Chemical Industry during the Nineteenth Century* (Oxford, 1958).
William J. Reader, *Imperial Chemical Industries: A History*, 2 vols (Oxford, 1970–5).

GEOFFREY TWEEDALE

chemistry During the first half of the nineteenth century interest centred on atomic theory and the problems of determining atomic weights, while the second half saw the development of organic chemistry. Initially, chemists were interested in theories of chemical affinity, the forces that held elements together as compounds and the characteristic proportions of chemical combinations. Following Antoine Lavoisier (1743–94), Joseph Proust (1754–1826) demonstrated in 1805 that properly purified compounds were in constant composition, establishing the 'law of definite proportions'. In 1808 John Dalton (*see* GAS) expressed the modern form of the 'atomic hypothesis', that there were indivisible elementary units of matter. By 1860 more than eighty such elements had been characterized. In 1869 Dmitri Mendeleyev (1834–1907) provided a sound classification system for these elements via his periodic table, and established the law of periodicity. He argued that, since compounds consisted of some whole number of atoms, the weight of a molecule of one compound would differ from that of another by a multiple of the weights of the constitutive atoms; he arranged the elements accordingly.

Friedrich Wöhler's (1800–82) synthesis of urea in 1828 was the first synthesis of an organic compound from inorganic material and the best evidence against vitalism. Edward Frankland (1825–99) developed the idea of valence in 1849, recognizing that atoms and groups of atoms had a characteristic capacity for combination that could be expressed as a small whole number. In 1843 August Hoffmann (*b* 1818) demonstrated that molecules in coal tar had dyeing properties, leading Will Perkin (1838–1907) to produce a synthetic dye from benzene in 1851. Friedrich Kekulé (1829–96) demonstrated in 1858 the significance of valence for organic compounds, showing that the intervalence of carbon was such that carbon atoms could combine together to form chains, and proposing the oscillatory ring structure (1865) for aromatic compounds, such as benzene. The notion of 'carbon chains' led, especially in Germany, to elucidation of the structures of molecules associated with living organisms and the development of industrial chemistry (*see* CHEMICAL INDUSTRY).

Alexander Findlay, *A Hundred Years of Chemistry* (London, 1965).
Sir Harold Hartley, *Studies in the History of Chemistry* (Oxford, 1971).

STEVE AMANN

Cherokee Unlike their Muskogean neighbours, the Creek, Choctaw and Chickasaw, the Cherokee (inhabiting parts of what is now Tennessee, Georgia and North and South Carolina) were Iroquoian, and linguistically closer to tribes further north. Perceiving colonial frontiersmen as a greater threat than Britain, the Cherokee allied themselves with the English during the American Revolution. In the nineteenth century they attempted accommodation to combat white encroachment. Led by 'mixed-blood' chiefs like John Ross (1790–1866), the tribe centralized its government and wrote a legal code and constitution in July 1827. Like that of the United States, the Cherokee constitution established three branches of government (legislative, executive and judicial) and claimed complete sovereignty over all national (Cherokee) land. By the 1820s Cherokees had adopted the outward trappings of white culture: individual farmsteads, sawmills, gristmills, blacksmith shops, schools, an alphabet and a newspaper (the Cherokee *Phoenix*), and slavery, with over 1,300 African-Americans held in captivity.

Prodded by the federal government to 'remove' themselves west across the Mississippi River and by states like Georgia to submit to state law and sovereignty, some Cherokees voluntarily migrated to the 'Indian country' in future Oklahoma. Although a few Cherokee chiefs signed treaties for removal in 1832 and 1835 and migrated, the majority of the tribe stayed behind. Rounding up the eastern Cherokee in 1838, the army marched them west in what became known as the

'Trail of Tears'. Of the 15,000 who marched west 4,000 died on the trail. Out west the Cherokee recreated the relative prosperity of their eastern existence. Although they tried to remain neutral during the Civil War, they entered into a treaty with the Confederacy which after the Union victory cost them large land cessions in post-war treaties.

Duane H. King (ed.), *The Cherokee Indian Nation: A Troubled History* (Knoxville, Tenn., 1979).

JOHN MARTIN

Chicago School   In architectural history the principles of the Chicago School signify the fusion of discrete phenomena – skyscraper design and the City Beautiful movement. Chicago witnessed the origination of skyscrapers. Representative structures included the Home Insurance Company Building (1883–5), the first true skyscraper, by William Le Baron Jenney (1832–1907), Auditorium Theater and Hotel Building (1887–9) by Denkmar Adler (1844–1900) and Louis Sullivan (1856–1924) and Reliance Building (1894–5) by Daniel Burnham (1846–1912). Characteristically, skyscrapers combined iron frameworks (later steel skeletons) and self-bearing (later suspended) masonry or brickwork exteriors, their unprecedented exploitation of metal permitting previously impossible expanses of fenestration. The Chicago World's Columbian Exposition (1893), especially Burnham's Court of Honor, signalled respect for classical styling and a willingness to respect general, exterior regulating features, for example the painting of all constituent buildings white. The hybrid legacy for later architecture embraced the concepts 'white-city', 'highrise', 'new classicism', 'city beautiful', all of which informed the work of Frank Lloyd Wright (1867–1959).

See also ARCHITECTURE.

DAVID THISTLEWOOD

child-labour laws   State legislation was eventually passed in most of the developed industrial world to restrict the hours of work or monitor the conditions of children in mines and factories. Conventional historical wisdom regarding the 'cataclysmic' impact of the factory system on child labour has recently been challenged by an argument for continuity between rural and industrial labour among children, particularly regarding age of entry and hours of work. The initial decades of factory life were, none the less, a harsh experience for those children working long hours outside the home, often suffering abuse and harsh treatment from adult overseers.

Factory legislation affecting English women and children is commonly identified with the seventh earl of SHAFTESBURY, a prominent Evangelical Protestant and Tory member of parliament who, as Lord

Ashley, campaigned for reforms limiting factory working hours by parliamentary statute. As leader of the 'ten-hours movement', he helped achieve the Factory Act of 1833, preventing the employment of children under 9 in textile mills, while between the ages of 9 and 13 they were supposed to work a maximum forty-eight-hour week and to attend school for two hours each day. Ashley's COAL MINES ACT of 1842, mutilated in the House of Lords, prohibited underground employment of women and girls, and of boys under 10. The restriction of the hours of work of children between 10 and 13 in mines was abandoned. In 1847 a TEN HOURS ACT was finally steered through parliament by John Fielden (1784–1849), limiting the factory working week of women and young people under 18 to fifty-eight hours, of which no more than ten might be worked in any one day.

One of the most glaring abuses of the labour of English women and children was the agricultural 'gang labour' system prevalent in East Anglia and the Midlands, as was made clear from evidence to the 1843 Commission on Children's Employment. Children were employed by gang leaders to work for large farmers pulling turnips or potatoes but their wages were often short-changed by the unscrupulous subcontractors. A special parliamentary commission of inquiry into these practices led to the 1867 Gangs Act which prohibited the employment of children under 8 in gangs. The 1876 Education Act, making it illegal to employ children under 10 in agricultural work, dealt a further blow to 'gangs' as regards children. The system is still in use to recruit unemployed adults from northern cities for farm work.

As a result of the Factory and Workshop Acts (see FACTORY ACTS) of 1867 and the impact of state EDUCATION from the 1870s onwards, the supply of full-time juvenile labour became chiefly concentrated in the adolescent age range 13 to 19. This has been explained, in rather crude economic terms, as conveniently removing large numbers of unskilled child workers from a flooded labour market. Yet child labour in Britain did not end with Factory and Mine Acts or the introduction of compulsory education, as is often erroneously assumed. 'Half-time' work, for example, meant the employment of children on alternate days or half a day spent at the textile mill and the rest in the classroom. The inability of children to concentrate on their school lessons after a morning's hard work in the mills was constantly stressed in parliamentary reports. These partial-exemption children were prevalent in Belfast and the northern worsted-manufacturing towns of Halifax, Bradford, Blackburn and Bolton until the early 1920s. The labour of children 'part-time', both before and after school hours, and on Saturdays, was also widely prevalent, just as it is today. Boys ran errands, sold newspapers or delivered milk, and girls made matchboxes, looked after younger children or performed various unpaid domestic tasks.

In France a handful of isolated activists succeeded in passing the Child Labour Law of 1841, fixing the minimum age at which children might be employed in factories at 8 years and also limiting their hours of work. Since the more reactionary employers could easily avoid proper inspection, it was not until 1874 that more radical and effective French legislation was passed. A Prussian decree of 1839 forbade the employment of children under 9 in mines, ironworks and factories, also limiting the labour of those under 16 to ten hours. In Russia it was not until 1892 that an edict was issued ending the employment of children under 12 and restricting the hours worked by those aged 12 to 15 to eight a day.

See also LABOUR LEGISLATION.

Colin Heywood, *Childhood in Nineteenth-Century France: Work, Health, and Education among the 'Classes Populaires'* (Cambridge, 1988).
Oliver MacDonagh, *Early Victorian Government, 1830–1870* (London, 1977).

JOHN SPRINGHALL

children's literature   In the course of the nineteenth century revolutionary changes in PRINTING technology, the removal of paper taxes and declining paper costs made possible the widening dissemination of print. Publishers discovered that the market for children's books and periodicals in both Britain and America was exceeded only by that for religious literature. (At the 1861 census over 45 per cent of the population of England and Wales were under 20 years of age.) Hence the appearance of many classic British works for children, such as Captain Marryat's *Mr Midshipman Easy* (1834), Thomas Hughes's *Tom Brown's Schooldays* (1857), R. M. Ballantyne's *The Coral Island* (1858), Lewis Carroll's *Alice's Adventures in Wonderland* (1865) and Robert Louis Stevenson's *Treasure Island* (1883), evidence both of a more indulgent attitude towards the young and of an expanding population of literate children craving information and entertainment. The boys' adventure story author George Alfred Henty (1832–1902), with popular titles such as *The Dash for Khartoum* (1892), celebrated public-school manliness and imperialism. The girls' story began to establish itself as a popular British genre from the 1880s with the arrival of the hugely prolific L. T. Meade (1854–1914), who virtually created the girls' boarding-school story, and Evelyn Everett-Green (1856–1932), many of whose 'wholesome' titles were offered as reward books by schools and churches.

In America a whole genre of family stories was inspired by Louisa May Alcott's *Little Women* (1868), while Mark Twain's *The Adventures of Tom Sawyer* (1876) and its sequel, the brilliant *Adventures of Huckleberry Finn* (1884), offer a comic and nostalgic account of boyhood. German children's literature, like English and American, was largely dominated by mediocre sentimental and religious novels about poor children. Exceptions were the brothers Grimm (Jacob, 1785–1863; Wilhelm, 1786–1859), who published their collections of German folk-tales and fairy-stories from 1812 onwards. After Grimm, the most memorable nineteenth-century German children's book was Heinrich Hoffmann's *Struwwelpeter* (1845), a grotesquely morbid collection of cautionary tales. In the 1870s Karl May (1842–1912) began to write his extremely popular series of German Westerns set in America, many featuring 'Old Shatterhand', an American pioneer of German descent. The French publisher Hachette issued a number of books for children from mid-century in the Bibliothèque Rose series. French writers, following Sir Walter Scott's (1771–1832) example, wrote historical novels popular with children, such as those of Alexandre Dumas the elder (1802–83), author of *The Three Musketeers* (1844) and *The Count of Monte Christo* (1844–5). Jules Verne (1828–1905) did not write his books with children in mind but titles such as *Twenty Thousand Leagues under the Seas* (1870) immediately became popular with younger readers; many first appeared in translation in the pages of English juvenile magazines, such as the Religious Tract Society's manly *Boy's Own Paper* (1879–1967).

Humphrey Carpenter and Mari Prichard, *The Oxford Companion to Children's Literature* (Oxford, 1984).
John Rowe Townsend (1965), *Written for Children*, revised edn (London, 1974).
                                                            JOHN SPRINGHALL

Chile During the final years of the Spanish Empire Chile formed an autonomous captaincy-general. The emancipation struggle began in 1810 with the proclamation of a junta in Santiago, but it was not until 1818, with SAN MARTIN's victory at Maipo (*see* BATTLE OF MAIPO), that independence was secured. After the abdication of Bernardo O'HIGGINS as supreme director in 1823, there followed seven years of political uncertainty before the liberals were defeated at the Battle of Lircay. This permitted Diego PORTALES, the leading conservative politician, to introduce an authoritarian and centralist regime.

Nineteenth-century Chile became renowned for its political stability, rare in Latin America. This was due principally to the country's small size (most of the population lived in the central valley – Chile did not control either the Atacama Desert or the area south of Concepción until after 1880), its ethnic homogeneity, the openness of the land-owning elite and the country's economic success. Soon after independence Chile began to export minerals, becoming the largest copper producer in the world, and later grain and flour. Rebellions in 1851 and 1859 were quickly suppressed.

Chile's economic success and institutional stability were both coming under strain when the WAR OF THE PACIFIC broke out in 1879, but the capture of Bolivian and Peruvian territory gave it a world monopoly of nitrates and saved the economy, even though British and German firms quickly came to dominate the industry. The revenues from nitrate exports also increased the power of the executive, reversing the shift of authority towards congress which had begun in the 1860s. The outcome was the bitter civil war of 1891, at the end of which President Balmaceda committed suicide. Thereafter Chile entered the era of the 'parliamentary republic', during which the influence of the landowning elite, which controlled congress and hence access to nitrate revenues, reached a peak.

Brian Loveman, *Chile: The Legacy of Hispanic Capitalism* (Oxford, 1988).

RORY MILLER

China   At the beginning of the nineteenth century China was virtually closed to foreign contact. Foreigners were able to trade with China only through Canton and under the terms of the restrictive Canton system. More vigorous prosecution of the OPIUM TRADE led to the first Anglo-Chinese War (see ANGLO-CHINESE WARS), following which the TREATY OF NANKING forced China to open five TREATY PORTS. Other powers followed Britain's example, imposing a network of treaties, linked by the most-favoured-nation clause, known as the unequal-treaty system.

The CH'ING DYNASTY was also threatened by internal rebellion. Three great rebellions, the Taiping (see TAIPING REBELLION), the Nien (see NIEN REBELLION) and the Muslim rebellions, wracked China from the mid-1850s to the mid-1860s. The moribund dynasty was able to suppress these only with the help of new provincial armies led by TSENG KUO-FAN and LI HUNG-CHANG, but at the cost of increasing provincial autonomy. In the 1860s the dynasty launched a limited Self-strengthening Movement, which attempted to adapt the technology of the West without sacrificing China's 'essence'. Only limited gains were made, however, the programme's failure being clearly demonstrated by China's humiliating defeat in the SINO-JAPANESE WAR. This defeat and the increasing likelihood of China's dismemberment at the hands of the foreign powers gave increasing impetus to the the reform movement led by K'ang Yu-wei (1858–1927). It gained the support of Emperor Kuang Hsu, who initiated the Hundred Days Reform, an attempt to modernize China from above. Snuffed out by Tz'u-hsi's coup, however, it was quickly followed by the xenophobic BOXER RISING, which ended disastrously for China. The Boxer Protocol (1901) imposed heavy reparations on China. As the nineteenth century closed China was also threatened by the embryonic revolutionary movement of Sun Yat-sen (1866–1925).

Jonathan D. Spence, *The Search for Modern China* (New York, 1990).

JOHN DAVIES

Ch'ing dynasty (1644–1911) The Ch'ing, or Manchu, dynasty was the last dynasty of imperial CHINA. It was founded after the conquest of China on the collapse of the Ming dynasty in the seventeenth century. By the nineteenth century the Manchus had completely adopted Han (Chinese) culture and were indistinguishable from the Chinese, despite claims to the contrary by Chinese revolutionaries at the end of the century. However, even by the beginning of the century the dynasty was in serious decline. Its hold on China was further weakened by sustained pressure from the West. The dynasty suffered a series of defeats in the Opium War against Britain and was forced to allow first Britain and then other Western powers commercial privileges in China. Internal rebellions (Taiping, Nien and Muslim) further shook the dynasty.

From the 1860s the dynasty was effectively dominated by TZ'U-HSI, the empress dowager. From the 1860s to the 1890s the dynasty attempted a limited modernization of China, the SELF-STRENGTHENING MOVEMENT. This, however, failed to arrest the decline, as was illustrated by its humiliating defeat at the hands of Japan in the Sino-Japanese War (1894–5). A further sign of the dynasty's increasing weakness was the extraction by a number of foreign powers of extensive concession areas in 1897–8. In 1898 the emperor KUANG HSU sponsored the HUNDRED DAYS REFORM, which was ended by Tz'u-hsi's coup. The BOXER RISING, supported by Tz'u-hsi and conservative court princes, was a last xenophobic attempt to save the dynasty. Defeated by the foreign powers and challenged by revolutionary groups, the dynasty introduced moderate reforms in the first decade of the twentieth century but these failed to prevent its collapse in 1911.

Immanuel C. Y. Hsu, *The Rise of Modern China*, fourth edn (Oxford, 1990).
Jonathan D. Spence, *The Search for Modern China* (New York, 1990).

JOHN DAVIES

cholera A disease spread by the faecal–oral route which results in diarrhoea, dehydration and (in about half of untreated cases) death, cholera is endemic in certain parts of India, and a number of factors led to its extension in a series of world-wide pandemics in the nineteenth century. First, the population dislocation caused by Britain's wars in India both exposed mobile soldiers to the disease and drove many Indians sick with the disease out of the homelands. Secondly, the dramatic improvements in transportation enabled ships to carry cases from port to port without an onboard epidemic working itself through to its deadly climax. Thirdly, the sanitary conditions in many

European and American cities allowed the spread of this exotic visitor either through the water supply or within homes ill-served with the basics of personal hygiene.

Moving out of the Ganges delta around 1817, the first pandemic reached Europe in the early 1830s. The disease was certainly a shocking one. Death frequently came quite quickly. The dehydration produced painful cramps as well as a bluish tinge around the body's extremities. The disease became an important element in working-class anxiety for two reasons. First, debates in Europe about the burden of the poor (fuelled by the doctrine of MALTHUSIANISM) raised the suspicion that the rich (or some other figure of suspicion such as the Jews) were spreading a poison among the poor to reduce their numbers. Secondly, at least in Britain, the poor were reluctant to be taken to cholera hospitals since they felt sure they were merely wanted as cadavers for the experiments of anatomy students (*see* ANATOMY ACT). This class fear produced cholera riots in many countries as the poor reacted with alarm to the cholera measures visited upon them by the rich. These riots were especially severe in Russia.

As the disease made repeated visits (in the late 1840s, mid-1850s and mid-1860s), the initial panic subsided a little. In the early epidemics most countries declared a day of fasting and prayer to atone for the sins which the authorities believed had caused God to send this terrible scourge. But in the 1850s and 1860s this explicit plea for divine mercy was submerged beneath more secular policies of sanitary reform. The earliest sanitary measures taken against cholera recalled the quarantines and *cordons sanitaires* imposed against the plague but, with the enthusiastic support of those commercial interests directly hurt by interruptions to trade, public-health activists increasingly directed the attention of governments to those preventable causes which were thought to encourage the spread of the disease. Decomposing filth littered the cities of Europe and North America, and heaps, pools, sewers and rivers became the focus of a clean-up campaign. The cholera was taken to be emblematic of the evils that befell the badly run city.

Yet the connection between cholera and PUBLIC HEALTH reform was not simple or direct. These sanitary evils were relatively permanent nuisances whereas cholera was an occasional visitor. The sanitary engineering works required to clean up the city were very expensive and required long-term planning and financing to be successful. Furthermore, as more was learned about the disease, its specific character meant that it served increasingly poorly as an example of the public-health problem as a whole. While Edwin Chadwick (1800–90), the English Poor Law and public-health reformer, saw cholera as a direct product of decomposing filth, a miasma, John Snow (1813–58) showed with map and anecdotal evidence that there was probably a specific agent involved which was often spread through water. In particular, Snow claimed that an outbreak in the Soho area of London was effectively halted when he had the handle of the Broad Street pump removed. (*See* THEORIES OF DISEASE.)

Microscopic analysis of drinking-water revealed that a wide variety of tiny creatures were entering people's bodies along with their water. These sorts of analyses reduced people's confidence in their drinking-water and became an important element in debates about water purity. However, it was not until Robert Koch (1843–1910), the great German biologist, managed to isolate and culture the organism in 1884, that the cholera bacillus (*Vibrio cholerae*) was sighted. Now, in the age of the microbe, cholera could be seen in drinking-water. Yet this did not prevent the last significant European outbreak, that of Hamburg in 1892, when unfiltered water took the disease from the emigrants passing through the city on their way to North America and spread it among the poor. As the plague had been in earlier times, cholera became for a while an all-pervasive metaphor for the shocking state of urban industrial civilization.

Michael Durey, *The Return of the Plague: British Society and the Cholera 1831–2* (Dublin, 1979).
Robert Pollitzer, *Cholera* (Geneva, 1959).

GERRY KEARNS

Christian socialism A diverse creed, Christian socialism was negative towards *laissez-faire* capitalism and in favour of a society based on CO-OPERATION. A group including J. M. Ludlow (1821–1911) and led by F. D. Maurice (1805–72) met between 1848 and 1854 for Bible study and promoted producers' associations in London. Through them Ludlow wanted to reorganize society on a Christian basis. By contrast, Maurice aimed to awaken the church to its social obligations by theological teaching. In 1877 Stewart Headlam (1847–1924) founded the Guild of St Matthew. He revered Maurice, but was more sacramental and statist. In reaction, the Christian Social Union was set up in 1889, led by B. F. Westcott (1825–1901), to study social questions. It was liberal catholic, vague, but influential among the church leadership. Only in 1906 was a group founded (the Church Socialist League) which was committed to the common ownership of the means of production. All these groups were Anglican. Nonconformist and Catholic imitations also appeared. Cardinal MANNING, while not calling himself a Christian socialist, supported the cause of the poor, including the agricultural workers and the striking dockers in 1889.

In France, Buchez (1796–1865) advocated a new social order based on the formation of democratic profit-sharing producers' co-operatives, while FOURIER, a non-Christian, influenced many Catholics with his principle of universal harmony. Léon Harmel (1829–1915) promoted co-partnership by workers, starting with his spinning-factory. In Germany, Bishop von Ketteler of Mainz (1811–77) criticized *laissez-faire* capitalism in defence of the weak and pressed for the formation of co-operatives financed by Christians. Pope LEO XIII drew on many of these Catholic insights in composing his 'Rerum novarum' (1891), a workers' charter critical of both capitalism and state socialism.

Peter d'A. Jones, *The Christian Socialist Revival, 1877–1914* (Princeton, NJ, 1968).
Edward Norman, *The Victorian Christian Socialists* (Cambridge, 1987).
Alec R. Vidler, *A Century of Social Catholicism 1820–1920* (London, 1964).

ALAN M. SUGGATE

Christmas During the nineteenth century Christmas became increasingly popular as a festival. The writings of Charles Dickens and Washington Irving (1783–1859) did much to popularize Christmas as a secular festival, especially among the middling ranks of society. Not only did the celebrations of Christmas expand but the nature of the celebrations altered. Alongside the age-old Christmas traditions of merrymaking, feasting and charity, the Victorians put a special emphasis on Christmas as a time for the family in general and children in particular. Many of the elements which went to make up the late-nineteenth-century Christmas drew on customs from various parts of the world. The Christmas tree from Germany, crackers from France and Christmas cards from Britain all became popular items in the celebrations. But perhaps the most important development was the standardization, in the second half of the century, of the physical appearance of Father Christmas or Santa Claus based on the illustrations by Thomas Nast (1840–1902) in the United States.

J. M. Golby and A. W. Purdue, *The Making of the Modern Christmas* (London, 1986).

J. M. GOLBY

Christophe, Henri (*b* ?Grenada, 6 October 1767, *d* Milot 8 October 1820) Ruler of the northern part of HAITI (1807–20). A black from the British West Indies, he initially fought in Saint Domingue for the British but later became a leading general in the movement for Haitian independence. In contrast to Alexandre Pétion (1770–1818) in the south, Christophe preserved the plantation system, with the former slaves working for wages, thus maintaining exports and government revenues. He also avoided international entanglements, refusing to help the emancipation movements in Spanish America and slaves elsewhere in the Caribbean. In 1811 he turned his regime into a kingdom and instituted an elaborate ceremonial at his palace at Sans Souci.

However, opposition to his absolutism, in particular to the plantation system and the labour drafts for public works, increased. His illness in 1820 encouraged conspiracies against him and he committed suicide shortly before a crowd set fire to Sans Souci.

RORY MILLER

Churchill, Randolph Henry Spencer (*b* London, 13 February 1849; *d* London, 24 January 1895) Controversial British Conservative politician. The third son of the seventh duke of Malborough, he became a member of parliament in 1874. He emerged in the so-called 'Fourth Party' as a forthright critic of the Conservative leadership in the years after Disraeli's death and became known as the leading exponent of a policy of progressive Conservatism known as 'Tory Democracy' which was designed to attract the expanding working-class electorate. He was secretary of state for India (1885–6) and became chancellor of the exchequer in 1886, but resigned after only six months in the latter post in protest against defence expenditure. Only 37 years of age, his career was effectively over, and he declined progressively into general paralysis caused by syphilis. He was the father of Sir Winston Churchill (1874–1965).

R. F. Foster, *Lord Randolph Churchill: A Political Life* (Oxford, 1981).

DAVID DUTTON

Civil War, American (1861–1865) The American Civil War began after many years of sectional controversy. By 1860 the north and south had evolved into two very different cultures, the northern one a rapidly developing industrial section that included large cities and a growing number of European immigrants, while the south remained a rural, agricultural society, whose main labour force was chattel slaves. Accustomed to control of the national government, southerners reacted to the victory of the antislavery Abraham LINCOLN in the presidential election of 1860 with a resolve to leave the union. Led by South Carolina, always the centre of secession sentiment, the lower south seceded during the winter of 1860–1 to form the CONFEDERATE STATES OF AMERICA, selecting Jefferson DAVIS from Mississippi as its president. The upper south joined the Confederacy in the spring, when Lincoln called for troops from the states after the South Carolina attack on Fort Sumter (12 April).

Both sides quickly organized their armies after Sumter and prepared to fight with largely green citizen soldiers. Military professionals in the north, expecting a quick victory, planned to use traditional Napoleonic tactics to defeat the south. The Battle of First Bull Run, however, proved that these tactics failed with green troops and rifled small arms. The northern army broke and ran back toward Washington, leaving the southern troops overconfident of their chance for ultimate victory.

Lincoln brought in General George B. McClellan (1826–85), 'the young Napoleon', to reorganize and train the demoralized northern army. Although McClellan proved to be a master at improving morale, it soon became apparent that he was reluctant to use his army. Prodded by Lincoln, he launched the Peninsular Campaign (spring 1862) in an effort to capture the Confederate capital at Richmond. Although the army came within 10 miles of Richmond, McClellan quickly withdrew when the new Confederate commander Robert E. LEE attacked his superior forces. Lincoln continued to suffer frustration in the east throughout the summer of 1862. Not until Antietam (17 September) did the eastern army manage even a draw with the daring Lee. Lincoln used the Antietam draw, which forced Lee to halt his invasion of the north, to issue the preliminary EMANCIPATION PROCLAMATION. This document promised to emancipate southern slaves on 1 January 1863.

If Lincoln experienced frustrations in the east in 1862, in the west Union generals achieved more success. Victories at Forts Henry and Donelson, as well as Shiloh, brought Ulysses S. GRANT to Lincoln's attention. After these successes, Grant focused his attention on Vicksburg, and after several attempts to take the Confederate citadel at Vicksburg, he settled down to a siege of the city (May–July 1863). On 4 July the Confederates in Vicksburg surrendered, putting the Mississippi Valley in Union hands. After further triumphs by Grant at Chattanooga in November, Lincoln put him in charge of the northern war effort.

In the east during 1863, the Union forces finally overcame Lee's Army of Northern Virginia at Gettysburg (1–3 July). This battle destroyed Lee's offensive potential and put the Confederacy on the defensive for the rest of the war (see BATTLE OF GETTYSBURG). Despite the devastating losses in 1863, and growing disaffection at home with Confederate policies that weighed unfairly on non-slave-holders, Confederates still offered stiff resistance to the north during 1864. Grant's invasion of northern Virginia bogged down into a siege of Petersburg, the rail link to Richmond. This accomplished his goal, however, because Grant intended to force Lee to defend Richmond to limit his other options. In the deep south, after a long campaign to capture the southern industrial centre of Atlanta (spring–summer 1864), General William T. SHERMAN launched his devastating 'March through Georgia', attacking civilian morale and destroying all in his path. Waging 'total war' on the south, Sherman arrived at Savannah in early December.

In early spring 1865 Sherman started north, causing more damage in South Carolina, intending to join Grant in Virginia. Conscious of the eastern army's morale, Grant continued to press matters at

Petersburg, slowly encircling the city, tearing up railroads as he went. When a desperate Confederate attack on Fort Stedman (25 March) failed, Grant launched a counter-attack that finally broke Lee's line. By then Grant had over 130,000 men, but Lee had only 35,000. After his lines broke, Lee informed Confederate president Jefferson Davis that Richmond must be abandoned. Davis wanted to fight a guerilla war from the southern mountains, but Lee refused. He and his troops fled to Appomattox court-house, about 125 miles west of Richmond, before Grant's troops cut off their escape. On 9 April Lee surrendered to Grant at the McLean House in Appomattox court-house. Other Confederate forces soon surrendered, and the war ended. Over 600,000 Americans had perished, more than in any other American conflict.

Shelby Foote, *The Civil War: A Narrative*, 3 vols (New York, 1958–74).
James M. McPherson, *Battle Cry of Freedom* (New York, 1988).
David M. Potter, *The Impending Crisis, 1848–1861* (New York, 1975).

ALICE E. REAGAN

Cixi *see* Tz'u-hsi.

Clapham Sect The group of philanthropists and politicians who acted with William WILBERFORCE in the early nineteenth century was known as the Clapham Sect. The phrase, though not coined until 1844, aptly evokes the group's largely religious motivation, its tight-knit quality and the residence of most of its members in and around Clapham, then a dormitory village for the City of London about 5 miles away in the Surrey countryside. The group consisted of bankers, business-men and civil servants who enjoyed close social relations and several of whose families intermarried. Many were attracted by the Evangeli-cal ministry of John Venn (1759–1813), rector of Clapham from 1792, and among the most prominent was Henry Thornton (1760–1815), a banker and member of parliament for Southwark, who achieved fame as the author of the monetarist *Enquiry into the Nature and Effects of the Paper Credit of Great Britain* (1802). Nearly all were Evan-gelical Anglicans and supporters of William Pitt (1759–1806), but William Smith (1756–1835) was a Unitarian Dissenter and Foxite Whig. In the House of Commons the Claphamites favoured firm measures to enforce public order, but they were most notable for their unremitting hostility to the slave trade. The group was responsible for the tactics that led to the abolition of the trade in 1807. Its members ensured that, when the charter of the East India Company was renewed in 1813, Christian missionaries were permitted to enter India. Thornton was first treasurer of the Church Missionary Society (from 1799) and of the British and Foreign Bible Society (from 1804). Members of the group supported London hospitals, Sunday Schools and early efforts to spread popular education by the monitorial system. Their views were propagated through the *Christian Observer*, founded in 1802 and edited by Zachary Macaulay (1768–1838), father of Lord Macaulay. *See* EVANGELICALISM.

E. M. Howse, *Saints in Politics: The 'Clapham Sect' and the Growth of Freedom* (London, 1953).

D. W. BEBBINGTON

class The term 'class' was introduced by early-nineteenth-century contemporaries to describe the basis of social organization. The adoption of the language of class, which superseded the traditional discourse of estates and orders, was driven by industrialization, a process that fractured the older social order. Karl MARX offered a compelling definition of class in capitalist society, an analysis which stressed power, property relationships and an individual's role within the mode of production. While the advent of industrialization subjected Europe to broadly similar forces of change, class structures developed variously in different nations.

The aristocracy, Europe's traditional rulers, proved resilient in the face of sharp socio-economic change (*see* ARISTOCRACIES). The closed aristocracies east of the Elbe, for example, although lacking the sharp entrepreneurial instincts of Britain's nobility, responded forcefully to the end of manorialism, converting their large estates to market agriculture. Throughout Europe the aristocracy remained the wealthiest class for most of the nineteenth century and a bulwark of conservative politics. The agricultural depression, which began around 1875, and the concurrent extension of suffrage rights to the unpropertied, signalled the commencement of the aristocracy's relative decline. While aristocratic identity remained formidable, especially in eastern Europe, the close of the century saw the emergence of a new heterogeneous business elite in much of central and western Europe.

With the exception of Britain, peasants comprised a majority of the European population until 1870. The character of the peasantry shifted substantially over the century. In general, however, the landowning peasants of the Netherlands, France, northern Italy and western Germany proved able at pursuing commercial opportunity. In contrast, the peasants of southern and eastern Europe remained impoverished tenants or landless labourers. Politics came late to peasants. English agricultural labourers organized in trade unions in the 1870s, the first to do so. Only in the 1890s did the staggeringly poor peasants of Andalusia and southern Italy prove receptive to socialism.

Although the rise of the MIDDLE CLASSES to political power and economic prominence is a central theme of nineteenth-century history, differences existed in the pattern and pace of bourgeois development.

In France the devastation of the aristocracy in the revolutionary era allowed the bourgeoisie to secure domination over French political and economic life by 1830. During the second quarter of the century the bourgeoisie also made great, although less decisive, gains in Italy, western Germany and Great Britain. In contrast, east of the Elbe the middle class remained much less developed. The failed revolutions of 1848 ensured the survival of aristocratic governments. But aristocracies were forced to coexist with an increasingly demanding bourgeoisie. The realignment of class power was evidenced by the gains of free-market CAPITALISM and the general adoption of representative government. Ideologically liberal, the bourgeoisie emerged as the hegemonic class by 1875. Thereafter, however, the always-variegated class fragmented further, as genteel capitalists intermarried with landed wealth and embraced conservative politics. Tenuously tied to those above them, the lower middle class experienced substantial growth late in the century. Unlike the case of Britain, however, the ultraconservative *mittlestand* of Germany and France assumed distinct political importance.

The nineteenth century also saw the emergence of a great urban working class (*see* WORKING CLASSES). Artisans dominated the working class in the early decades of the century, with London, Paris and Vienna as especially important centres of craft production. Notably active in radical politics, French and British artisans pursued the establishment of co-operative forms of production as an alternative to the unrestricted competition of capitalism. By mid-century, almost half the adult population of Britain laboured in manufacturing, a proportion that would change little by the century's close. In contrast, only a third of the mid-century Belgian population and 25 per cent of the French population worked in manufacturing. Although industrialization widened throughout Europe after 1850, the working class remained a minority. By 1900, only the Belgian and German working class accounted for more than 40 per cent of the adult population.

After the collapse of CHARTISM, the collective action of British workers was restricted to the workplace. The SKILLED WORKERS organized in trade unions were loyal supporters of the Liberal Party. The last decade of the century, however, did see socialism make tentative inroads. Trade socialism remained a vibrant tradition among skilled French workers, although after 1880 Marxism also gained followers among the factory proletariat. Nevertheless, most French workers remained outside the socialist and labour movement. Alone among European socialist parties, the German Social Democratic Party (SPD) was able to mobilize the great majority of the working class under the banner of Marxism.

Eric Hobsbawm, *The Age of Capital, 1848–1875* (London, 1975).

RICHARD J. SODERLUND

Clay, Henry (*b* Hanover county, Virginia, 12 April 1777; *d* Washington, DC, 29 June 1852) American politican. An early proponent of a strong national government and economy, he began his congressional career as a Warhawk, urging President James Madison towards war with Britain in 1812. After serving as a delegate to the peace talks in Ghent (1814), Clay returned to Congress to propose his American System, which called for an activist state that promoted the creation of a national, interdependent economy through the establishment of a national bank, protective tariff and a network of internal improvements. This plan became the basis of the ideology of the WHIG PARTY, created in 1834 to oppose Andrew Jackson. Throughout his career Clay also endeavoured to promote sectional harmony. He proved instrumental in the passage of three compromises, the MISSOURI COMPROMISE (1820), the Compromise Tariff (1833) and the COMPROMISE OF 1850, all of which were intended to ameliorate sectional tensions and which earned Clay the nickname 'the Great Compromiser'.

Robert V. Remini, *Henry Clay: Statesman for the Union* (New York, 1991).
ALICE E. REAGAN

Clemenceau, Georges (*b* Mouilleron-en-Pareds, 28 September 1841; *d* Paris, 24 November 1929) French politician. From a family of doctors, he became a doctor himself. During the Second Empire he was imprisoned for his writings and his republican activity. He taught French in the United States from 1865 to 1869, and married one of his students. Appointed mayor of the eighteenth *arrondissement* of Paris after the fall of the empire, he voted as a deputy against the annexation of Alsace-Lorraine by Germany and tried to play a conciliatory role during the Paris Commune. He opened the columns of his newspaper, *L'Aurore,* to Zola's famous letter 'J'accuse' during the DREYFUS case.

His tenure as prime minister between 1906 and 1909 is best known for the repression of strikes. During his second tenure in 1917 he chose Foch (1851–1929) to turn back the German advance. He negotiated the Treaty of Versailles for France but a parliamentary cabal forced him to resign in 1919. He was the author of many books: his collected journalism takes up twelve volumes. He is buried facing east to Germany and standing up to face God.

D. Watson, *Georges Clemenceau: A Political Biography* (London, 1974).
DONALD SUTHERLAND

clerks Clerical work was one of the fastest-growing occupational groups in the late nineteenth century. In Britain the number of clerks rose from 91,000 in 1861 to about 390,000 in 1891, and this increase was paralleled in western Europe and the United States. This expansion was due to the growing bureaucratization of both private and public sectors of society in the period. The trend towards systematization of production in heavy industry created greater demand for white-collar personnel – as much as 40 per cent of clerical occupations were in manufacturing industry by the turn of the century. The growing complexity of the world economy stimulated the expansion of BANKING, insurance and commerce. A further influence to be found in all industrial nations was the expanding function and reach of local and central governments.

The social structure of clerical work underwent sharp changes during this period. Entry-level opportunities for employment increased, but the expansion of the labour market lessened job security and placed a downward pressure on wages and conditions. At the same time, the division of labour sharpened the internal specialization of clerical work and opportunities for mobility were reduced. New technologies such as the TYPEWRITER threatened deskilling. Women began to enter what had been an entirely male preserve, and after 1891 became the fastest growing sector of the labour market.

Clerical labour was thus subject to the pressures of proletarianization, but the reaction varied in different countries. In western Europe there was a greater tendency to organize politically, usually in conjunction with other members of the lower middle class. In Britain they remained politically quiescent, but became more insistent on their status differentiation from the working class.

Gregory Anderson, *Victorian Clerks* (Manchester, 1976).

RICHARD PRICE

Cleveland, Stephen Grover (*b* Caldwell, New Jersey, 18 March 1837; *d* Princeton, New Jersey, 24 June 1908)   President of the United States (1885–9, 1893–7). A former assistant district attorney and sheriff, he was elected Democratic mayor of Buffalo in 1881 and governor of New York in 1882. His dedication to reform placed him at odds with TAMMANY HALL, the potent New York City Democratic machine. Partly to woo the MUGWUMPS (disaffected Republicans), the Democrats successfully ran Cleveland in 1884 for president. Defeated by Benjamin Harrison after four years of fighting graft, fiscal waste and the Republican Party's tariff policy, Cleveland returned to his law practice. Elected again in 1892, he became the first president to serve two non-consecutive terms. Following Cleveland's inauguration in early 1893, the country slid into a severe economic depression. Unjustly blamed for the depression, the Democrats lost the presidency in 1896 and, historians argue, suffered a blow they did not recover from until the 1930s.

JOHN MARTIN

coal In earlier times coal had been used by industry – in lime-burning, brewing, glass-making and dyeing, for example – but in the eighteenth century new discoveries and inventions (the steam engine and the application of coal as a fuel in iron-smelting) paved the way for spectacular growth. Thus, just as water power had helped launch the INDUSTRIAL REVOLUTION, so it was coal which sustained and carried forward the process of world industrialization. As the principal extractive industry in the nineteenth century, coal occupied a unique place in the world economy between agriculture and industry. Not only was it a major industry in its own right, but in the industrial nations it was the major source of energy and a key provider for leading industries.

The power and heat supplied to industry by coal increased rapidly in the second half of the nineteenth century. By about 1870 steam coal had passed water power in importance as a source of industrial energy and by this time, too, coal had become the most important metallurgical fuel, a vital raw material for the BESSEMER and SIEMENS steel-making processes. In general, coal supplanted wood as fuel and was used in increasing amounts to manufacture gas for domestic uses for rapidly urbanizing populations. One of its most significant uses was in the railway locomotive, so linking coal with one of the major forces in nineteenth-century industrialization (*see* RAILWAYS).

As the first industrial nation, Britain led the world in coal production for the much of the nineteenth century; it was also the greatest coal-exporting nation. In 1800 most of the coal produced in Britain was used by the domestic consumer for heating; by 1830, however, industrial had already overtaken domestic consumption and by 1870 the latter amounted to less than 18 per cent. Annual coal production in Britain rose from about 11 million tons in 1800 to over 200 million tons in 1900. By 1911 the number of miners in Britain was over a million (more than in any other activity except farming), making them the largest homogeneous group of industrial workers, and coal was second to none in the value it added to the country's output. Nearly two-thirds of coal entering world trade was mined in Britain. Britain's strong performance was related to its fast start, the location and abundance of coal (with about ten producing regions, of which south Wales and the north-east were the most important), an efficient transport system with low-cost freight charges and, above all, demand.

Economically, the nineteenth-century picture in coal was mostly one of steady expansion and prosperity, with prices hardly rising relative to other commodities. This did not depend on any technological revolution: the world's coal in the nineteenth century continued to be mined by muscle power and pick and shovel even in 1900. For most of the century, there were few advances in the technology of coal-cutting, but 'access technology' did improve. From the early nineteenth century there were improvements in methods of laying out workings (with long-wall methods of working substituted for the older pillar-and-stall techniques), more efficient pumps, the substitution of cast iron for wooden tubs, mechanical ventilation fans, better underground transportation, steam-powered winding mechanisms and the safety lamp for increased illumination. These allowed coal to be reached and worked in safer conditions and at greater depths. They also led to an improvement in the quality of coal. After the 1870s the increasing professionalization and education of mining engineers also began making an impact. The influence of these incremental improvements in increasing coal production has often been underestimated. Mechanization occurred mainly after 1900, first in the United States, where electricity and compressed air allowed the use of devices for cutting and undercutting and for hauling.

By the late nineteenth century Britain faced increasing competition from the United States and Germany, where coal-mining was expanding faster. By 1900 Britain had lost its leadership position to America, which raised twice the volume of coal of the British industry.

In 1900 coal virtually monopolized the energy-supply situation. Available statistics are incomplete and unreliable, but it has been estimated that by 1880 coal provided about 97 per cent of a total world energy supply of about 319 million tons of coal equivalent. In 1900, despite the rise of oil and natural gas, the proportion was still 94 per cent out of a total of some 778 million tons.

B. R. Mitchell, *The Economic Development of the British Coal Industry* (Cambridge, 1984).

GEOFFREY TWEEDALE

Coal Mines Act (1842)   The first act to regulate a specific category of workers, the Coal Mines Act excluded female labour and boys under 10 from underground work in mines. Commonly seen as one of the great examples of Victorian humanitarian factory reform, it followed the exposure of appalling working conditions by the Royal Commission on the Employment of Children in the Mines. Although the act established an inspectorate, it should not be seen as presaging the twentieth-century welfare state but more as an intervention by the state to create a gendered labour market and moralize working-class society. Mining was defined as unsuitable for women because its conditions discouraged the virtues of domesticity and morality that women were supposed to uphold. The inspectors were more missionaries combating an uncivilized working-class culture than bureaucrats of a disinterested state. Like most factory legislation, this act was as much about stimulating moral reform among the working class as about mitigating the harshness of capitalism.

See also CHILD-LABOUR LAWS, LABOUR LEGISLATION.

RICHARD PRICE

Cobbett, William (*b* Farnham, Surrey, 9 March 1763; *d* Ash, Surrey, 18 June 1835)　English writer, journalist and activist, best known as a reformer. A humble rural lad, he achieved fame and transient fortune through the power of his brilliant and vitriolic pen, first deployed in defence of the British establishment. Scandal and incompetence during the Napoleonic wars, however, converted him to radicalism. His *Political Register*, established in 1802, relentlessly exposed the workings of 'the Thing', the war-inflated *rentier* culture of political corruption and financial plunder which imposed an intolerable tax burden on the poor. Through a variety of pioneering cheap publications, Cobbett, 'the poor man's friend', educated the masses in the fundamental need for parliamentary reform, while giving vent to his manifold prejudices, many of which had a nostalgic, pre-industrial and Tory tinge (see, for example, his famous *Rural Rides*, 1830). Outside of publishing, he was less successful, even in his beloved farming and as member of parliament for Oldham (1833–5).

George Spater, *William Cobbett: The Poor Man's Friend*, 2 vols (Cambridge, 1982).

JOHN BELCHEM

Cobden, Richard (*b* Midhurst, Kent, 3 June 1804; *d* London, 2 April 1865)　Leading spokesperson in mid-nineteenth-century Britain for free trade, laissez-faire and internationalism. Member of parliament for Stockport (1841–7), the West Riding (1847–57) and then for Rochdale (from 1859), he was a founder and leading strategist of the ANTI-CORN LAW LEAGUE (1838–46) and various other less successful public pressure groups in the period. Cobden represented a utilitarian definition of freedom as absence of all restraint. He opposed equally the Corn Laws and trade unions as restricting the free movement of goods and persons. Although he is always regarded as anti-imperialist, his opposition to the aggressive foreign policy of Lord Palmerston rested on an 'imperialism of free trade' which ensured British dominance of world trade by virtue of its manufacturing and commercial supremacy (*see* ANGLO-FRENCH COMMERCIAL TREATY).

Nicholas Edsall, *Richard Cobden, Independent Radical* (Cambridge, Mass., 1986).

RICHARD PRICE

Code Napoléon　Also known as the *Code Civil*, the Code Napoléon was the system of contract and property law introduced under the Consulate (1799–1804) and is still the basis of French civil law. The collapse of the institutions which before 1789 had governed legal relations – church, regional courts, provinces, guilds – made the redaction of a national civil code a necessity. Throughout the Revolution, various committees of the various assemblies had worked on it but it was Napoleon BONAPARTE who forced the jurists to complete their work.

The code dealt mainly with the acquisition, transmission and protection of property between and among generations. Although a woman's property rights were curtailed, the property she brought to a marriage was protected by contract against her husband and against her heirs. Equal division among heirs was generally required and no will had the right completely to exclude any legitimate child from an estate by will or gift. Tenants had few rights against landlords other than what was specified in a lease. The Napoleonic Code has formed the basis of the codes of many Latin American countries, and of Louisiana and Quebec.

R. Holtman, *The Napoleonic Revolution* (Philadelphia, 1967).

DONALD SUTHERLAND

coffee An evergreen tree or large bush (genus *Coffea* of the *Rubiacea* family), coffee has two main species, Arabica and Robusta. Coffee grows best at about 5,000 feet in well-watered tropical regions. The berries are picked, cleaned and dried to reveal beans which, after roasting and blending, produce the popular beverage. Consumed in Europe from the 1600s and subsequently globally, coffee probably originated in the Middle East or Ethiopia. The Dutch spread cultivation to the East and the Guianas while the French successfully introduced it in Haiti. After 1850 Brazil and later Colombia dominated world production. Coffee became one of the world's most valuble commodities in the nineteenth century and the main export earner for several producing countries. This, and plantation production (Brazil used slave labour until the 1880s), associated coffee cultivation with issues like dependence and neocolonialism.

C. F. Marshall, *The World Coffee Trade* (Cambridge, 1983).

ROBERT G. GREENHILL

Colombia Named New Granada until 1863, the Republic of Colombia formed part of the Federation of Gran Colombia before 1829 (*see* BOLIVAR). Sparsely populated, and divided by formidable geographical obstacles, Colombia played little part in the world economy during the nineteenth century. Nevertheless, it was one of the few Latin American countries to develop mass parties. The conservatives tended to be more Catholic and centralist and had their strongholds in older, ethnically differentiated colonial regions, but from the 1850s the liberals held power, despite major civil wars in 1859–62 and 1876–7. Apart from introducing an overtly federal constitution giving sovereignty to individual states, they ended slavery, separated the church and state, encouraged press freedom and instituted direct popular elections and universal male suffrage (rigging the elections none the less). Their hegemony was ended in 1885–6 by a dissident liberal, Rafael Núñez (1825–94), who took power with conservative support and reversed many of these measures. Conservative dominance endured for fifty years, although their exclusionary measures against the liberals provoked a long and sanguinary civil war in 1899, the so-called 'War of the Thousand Days'.

RORY MILLER

Combination Acts (1799–1800) The Combination Acts were acts of parliament which treated trade-union action to regulate conditions of employment as criminal conspiracy. Previous combination acts had been confined to specific trades; these applied to all workers. Their role in inhibiting trade-unionism has been a matter of debate. Their real significance lies in the way they abandoned the protection of labour conditions and statutory wage regulation of earlier acts and signified a commitment by the state to uphold free-market relations. By criminalizing labour action, they allowed the law to be used by employers as a class instrument. The acts made prosecution cheaper and substituted summary jurisdiction for jury trial. In 1824 they were repealed, but in 1825 the law was tightened again and until 1875 trade-union action remained liable to criminal prosecution.

John V. Orth, *Combination and Conspiracy: A Legal History of Trade Unionism 1721–1906* (Oxford, 1991).

RICHARD PRICE

Commune of Paris *see* PARIS COMMUNE.

Communist Manifesto (1848) A watershed document written by Karl MARX in the 'year of revolutions', the *Communist Manifesto* established 'Marxism' as a distinctive revolutionary tendency within communism. The political programme of the LEAGUE OF THE COMMUNISTS, it announced the modern form of revolutionary organization – a democratic, centralized, internationalist workers' party grounded in the materialist theory of scientific socialism. The utopian and idealist aims, 'putschist' tactics and quasi-Masonic practices of the CARBONARI, BLANQUI's groups and traditional communist organizations were all eschewed.

On the premise that 'The history of all hitherto existing society is the history of class struggles', the manifesto analysed the interrelated development of the two great classes of the modern industrial and commercial world: the bourgeoisie, erstwhile revolutionary victors over feudalism, owners of the means of production and exchange; and the proletariat, exploited wage-slaves of industrial capitalism. Under communist leadership, the organized proletariat would fulfil its historic mission, capturing the state, overthrowing 'all existing social conditions', leading to a classless society in which the state would wither away. Along with these predictions, the manifesto advocated the abolition of bourgeois property, women's liberation from social and domestic prostitution and the transcendence of national antagonisms.

The German original of the manifesto, which utilized parts of ENGELS's draft, *Principles of Communism* (1847), was published anonymously in London, bearing the Communist League watchword: 'Workers of All Countries, Unite!' It soon appeared in six other European languages, the first English version (1850) in the Chartist journal the *Red Republican*. Russian and North American versions followed in 1869 and 1871, by which time the manifesto was attaining widespread influence. Marx and Engels upheld its general tenor throughout their later careers.

TONY BARLEY

communitarianism *see* OWENITES.

Compromise of 1850 In January 1850 Senator Henry CLAY introduced eight resolutions in an attempt to resolve sectional conflict over the extension of slavery into new territory of the United States. When the resulting omnibus bill foundered, Senator Stephen A. Douglas (1813–61) of Illinois broke the bill into five separate ones, calculating that although everyone objected to the omnibus bill, a shifting majority would back each separate one. The strategy worked. California entered the union as a free state. New Mexico became a territory and its boundary with Texas was finalized. The Utah territory was created and, as with New Mexico, the slavery issue was left to 'popular sovereignty'. Congress enacted a stronger FUGITIVE SLAVE ACT. An embarrassment to the federal government, the slave trade (but not slavery itself) in the District of Columbia was abolished. Far from easing sectional tensions, however, the compromise inflamed them.

See also MISSOURI COMPROMISE.

JOHN MARTIN

Compromise of 1867 Also known as the *Ausgleich*, the Compromise of 1867 was the agreement between FRANCIS JOSEPH I and the Hungarian leadership, which turned the HABSBURG EMPIRE into the dual monarchy of Austria-Hungary. Negotiations were conducted between 1865 and February 1867, with ANDRASSY and DEÁK leading the Hungarians. It was ratified by the Hungarian parliament in May 1867, and approved by the Austrian Reichsrat in December. Under the compromise, only three ministries remained common to the Hungarian and

'Austrian' halves of the empire: foreign affairs, defence and joint finances (to pay for the previous two). These common ministers reported annually to the separate meetings of the delegations from the respective parliaments, but were responsible to the emperor alone. There was also a customs union and a sharing of accounts, the terms of which were negotiated at ten-yearly intervals. The compromise has been seen as resulting in Magyar control over Habsburg affairs.

STEVEN BELLER

Comte, Auguste *see* POSITIVISM.

Concordat (1802) The treaty Napoleon BONAPARTE signed with the PAPACY in 1802 which governed church–state relations until 1906 was known as the Concordat. The papacy was the initial loser. Rome had to accept the revolutionary reforms in clerical matters, including the abolition of tithes, the sale of church property and the suppression of many dioceses. By the accompanying Organic Articles, the power of the papacy over appointments and the publication of bulls was much reduced. In the longer term, the church flourished. Clerics who had been persecuted during the Revolution returned to their former places, and the church re-established itself as a major provider of poor relief and education. In the longer term, the Concordat may have weakened the church. There were innumerable unedifying conflicts with local officials over the century regarding precedence while the close association of parish priests with LEGITIMISTS alienated republicans. Clerical influence over women undermined men's authority in the family. The Concordat was unilaterally abrogated in 1906 following the DREYFUS Affair in the vain hope that this would weaken the church fatally.

T. Zeldin (ed.), *Conflicts in French Society* (London, 1970).

DONALD SUTHERLAND

concordats, papal *see* PAPACY.

Condition-of-England Question The phrase 'Condition-of-England Question' was coined by CARLYLE in his essay *Chartism* (1839), by analogy with other important political 'questions'. Carlyle sought to bring the widespread destitution and misery of mid-nineteenth-century England to the centre of political attention. For Carlyle, the extremes of poverty, the comparatively new phenomenon of industrial unemployment and independent working-class political expression in CHARTISM, were all symptomatic of a widespread breakdown of the organic bonds which, in his view, ought to bind the separate members of a society.

But elsewhere in England in the 1840s, and in subsequent

historiography, the term 'Condition of England Question' has taken on a wider meaning. It has come to denote the more widespread sense of crisis about social relations which dominated the 1840s, focusing particularly on the recurrent misery of the new working class created by industrial capitalism. This sense of crisis found expression in a variety of political, social and literary ways. Thus the romantic and backward-looking conservatism of Young England was in part a response to the Condition-of-England Question, as were innumerable middle-class religious and domestic missions to the destitute poor. The sense of crisis found literary expression in a series of 'Condition of England' novels, including Benjamin Disraeli's *Sybil* (1845), Charles Kingsley's *Yeast* (1848) and *Alton Locke* (1850), Elizabeth Gaskell's *Mary Barton* (1848) and Charles Dickens's *Bleak House* (1852–3) and *Hard Times* (1854). Though all these novels had their own distinctive emphases, as did the many other lesser-known novels of the 1840s on similar topics, at the heart of all of them was a vivid and dramatic account of working-class poverty, verging on starvation, designed to inform their middle-class readers and to elicit a sympathetic response.

Thomas Carlyle, 'Chartism', in *Essays* (London, 1839).
Louis Cazamian, *The Social Novel in England 1830–1850* (London, 1973).
SIMON DENTITH

Confederate States of America In 1860–1 a bloc of southern slave-owning states seceded from the North American union, and proclaimed itself an independent nation, the Confederate States of America, initiating the AMERICAN CIVIL WAR. The election of Republican president Abraham Lincoln, who pledged to preserve the union and to restrict slavery's expansion, had prompted the long-threatened separation. South Carolina's state convention announced secession in December 1860. Mississippi, Florida, Alabama, Georgia, Louisiana and Texas swiftly followed. In February 1861 the Confederate congress at Montgomery, Alabama adopted a constitution and appointed Jefferson DAVIS president. Insurrection began on 12 April with the barrage against Fort Sumter. Virginia, Arkansas, North Carolina and Tennessee seceded, before holding referenda. Slave-holders in the 'border states' also favoured separation.

Many arguments were advanced in justification: northern protectionist tariffs, threats to the southern cotton monopoly, incompatibilities of 'national character', the constitutional priority of individual 'states' rights' and abolitionist 'interference'. The fundamental struggle, however, centred on the dominion either of the capitalist wage-labour system prevalent in the industrial north, or of southern plantation-based slave labour which the Confederacy sought to preserve and extend. Vice-President Stephens's (1812–83) 'cornerstone' speech in

Savannah (1861) insisted that the new government was founded upon 'the great truth that the negro is not equal to the white man; that slavery . . . is his natural and moral condition'.

Confederate attempts to secure European recognition and intervention foundered, particularly after Lincoln's Emancipation Proclamation transformed the war into one of abolition, and the increase in Federal battlefield successes after Gettysburg. The absence of southern political parties, coupled with poor white discontent over rich planters' military exemption contributed to the Confederacy's demise. General Robert E. LEE surrendered in April 1865. Davis's cabinet fled the capital, Richmond; he and its remnants were captured near Irwinville, Georgia in May.

James M. McPherson, *Battle Cry of Freedom* (Oxford, 1988).

TONY BARLEY

Congo Free State *see* INDEPENDENT CONGO STATE.

Congress of Paris *see* PARIS, TREATY OF.

Congress System The alliance system established after the defeat of Napoleon to provide collective security between the European powers, the Congress System has been seen as a precursor to twentieth-century attempts at international diplomatic co-operation. The system was established by METTERNICH of Austria-Hungary, CASTLEREAGH of Great Britain and HARDENBERG of Prussia. Its legal basis was established by the Quadruple Alliance Treaty of 1815 which specified that the allies 'were to renew their meetings at fixed periods . . . for the purpose of consulting upon their common interests'.

In 1818 a congress at Aix-la-Chapelle dealt with the withdrawal of the allied armies from France and admitted the latter as a full member of the alliance. From this point the Congress System became a weapon of the conservative monarchies of Europe to comb out revolutionary republicanism. Succeeding congresses were held at Troppau in 1820 and Laibach in 1821 to address the problem of revolutions in Spain and Italy. Metternich urged that the system take concerted action against revolutionary movements wherever they occurred, but the British refused to agree.

At the Congress of Verona in 1822 the question of allied intervention in the Spanish and Greek revolutions was strongly opposed by Britain, and Metternich, caught between his desire to maintain friendly relations with Britain and his inclination to suppress revolutionary movements, was unable to devise a common policy or maintain allied unity. The following year marked the demise of the Congress System when French troops unilaterally invaded Spain to defeat the republicans and restore the monarchy.

See also BALANCE OF POWER, CONGRESS OF VIENNA.

R. Bridge, 'Allied Diplomacy in Peacetime: The Failure of the Congress System 1815–1823', in Alan Sked (ed.), *Europe's Balance of Power 1815–1848* (New York, 1979), pp. 34–53.

GEORGE O. KENT

conscription   As standing armies of professional soldiers emerged in the seventeenth century, various systems of conscription came into force in Europe. The obligation to serve was never universal, however: rulers preferred to safeguard the more 'productive' classes of society for the task of wealth creation; the clergy and the nobility were protected by their status; and entire provinces were exempted by virtue of traditional rights. Generally the result of some form of ballot, conscription was therefore restricted to the agricultural poor. Deeply hostile to such methods on the grounds that armies so raised were sinks of iniquity and the tools of despotism, thinkers such as Rousseau (1712–78) argued that all soldiers should be citizens and all citizens soldiers, from which emerged the concept of the 'nation in arms'.

In 1793 it seemed that theory had become reality, for, surrounded by internal and external enemies, the Jacobins declared all Frenchmen liable for military service. The example was copied elsewhere, especially in Prussia, but after 1815 there was a reaction in favour of armies of long-service professionals raised by very limited systems of selective conscription. Only in Prussia were matters different. Here all men were conscripted, serving in the regular army for three years before passing into a general reserve that could be mobilized in time of war. Assisted by a highly efficient general staff and the immense resources and technological advances afforded by the industrial revolution, this 'new model' army swept all before it in the wars of German unification. As a result, short-service, universal conscription was thereafter quickly adopted by almost every country in Europe, and with it not only new media for social and political conditioning, but also a need for massive social and educational reform.

See also WARFARE.

John Gooch, *Armies in Europe* (London, 1980).

CHARLES ESDAILE

conservatism   Prior to 1789 there was little in the way of a recognized conservative ideology. To be conservative in the eighteenth century was to be normal, to partake willingly in the existing political order and to accept its limitations. Even those who criticized and caricatured that order, like the *philosophes*, sought merely to reform it. Few besides Rousseau (1712–78) envisioned a new principle of order and legitimacy, and few were prepared to follow him in vesting authority in the popular will. The very notion of the 'people' or the 'public' was sharply restricted before 1789, so political discourse was not much concerned with the effort to frame a popular argument in defence of established authority. The defenders of the old regime could thus rely on inertia and deference or make do with vague appeals to order, tradition or, for the devout or gullible, divine right.

All that would change with the French Revolution, which launched not merely a political but also an intellectual challenge to the old order. Inevitably, then, the first really compelling arguments for conservatism arose as critiques of the Revolution. The most famous was Edmund Burke's (1729–97) *Reflections on the Revolution in France* (1790). What made Burke's criticism so successful, aside from the quality of his writing, was his ability to make privilege appear rational. Supporters of the revolution had profited greatly from the broadly diffused Enlightenment sense that human affairs ought to be ordered on rational principles and that it was irrational to accord privileges to groups and individuals on the principle of birth. Burke turned that argument around and claimed that revolutionary efforts to restructure politics and society simultaneously overrated the intelligence and rationality of the present generation and ignored the fact that existing arrangements embodied the intelligence of many previous generations. Revolution was thus not rational, but arrogant, short-sighted and wilfully insensitive to the achievements of our ancestors and the claims of our descendants.

Burke's was a compelling argument which became more convincing as the revolution progressed through the Terror to the dictatorship of Napoleon. It was successful also because it went beyond a mere defence of monarchy, established church and aristocratic privilege. Subsequent efforts to define a workable conservative ideology were not quite so successful, however, precisely because they insisted on defending privilege on irrational grounds. In France, for instance, de Maistre (1753–1821), Chateaubriand and de Bonald (1754–1840) elaborated more fundamentally counter-revolutionary arguments stressing loyalty to the monarch, the state, the church and the pope. These Continental reactionaries, rather than the more moderate Burke, provided the inspiration for the effort, supervised by the Austrian METTERNICH, to restore 'legitimate' monarchies and to suppress revolution after the defeat of Napoleon. The collapse of Metternich's system in 1848 proved the limited appeal of such thinking and made clear the need for a more popular argument for conservative politics.

That need would be filled in part by ROMANTICISM. Although the romantics were as often democrats and republicans as they were conservatives, the romantic sensibility was more congenial to a conservative vision of the social order. The romantic critique of Enlightenment rationalism, its concern for organic connection between the classes in society, its nostalgia for the past and its hostility to Mammon and modern industry could more easily be harnessed to a right-wing programme than to a politics of reform. This affinity was clearest in England in the writings of Wordsworth (1770–1850) and, especially, Coleridge (1772–1834) but was also visible in Germany. It should not be surprising, therefore, that a respectable, if not yet exactly popular, conservatism emerged first in Britain, prompting Daniel O'CONNELL to complain in 1832 of the novel usage: 'Conservative – that is the fashionable term, the new-fangled phrase now used in Polite Society to designate the Tory ascendancy.' Even in Britain, the creation of a modern Conservative Party was a more drawn-out process, but at least there the rhetoric was in place by mid-century. (*See* TORYISM.)

Continental conservatives, however, refused to give up their monarchist and aristocratic allegiances and to adopt a more populist appeal. They continued to defend monarchy and church, and to resist democracy. What in the end moved them toward winning mass support were three factors essentially beyond their control. The first was the depression of 1873–96 (*see* GREAT DEPRESSION), which forced conservative elites into political action to secure protective agricultural tariffs and in order to pre-empt independent mobilization by peasants. The depression also served to move peasants decisively to the Right, arraying them behind their former masters and against markets, modernity and, as they often saw it, the pernicious influence of the Jews. The second was the growth of democracy, which pushed all parties and interests to compete electorally. The third was the rise of socialism and working class. Liberalism was bad, but socialism was unmitigated evil and prompted frantic efforts on the Right to regroup, realign and refashion their appeals to counter the threat from the workers and the Left.

Conservatives in different countries responded to the threats and crises of the late nineteenth century in different ways and with varying degrees of success. Ideologically, they began to appeal more to NATIONALISM and imperialist sentiment and in some cases made use of popular anti-Semitism. Everywhere, however, they recast their arguments so as to make socialism rather than liberalism into the main enemy, and for that they were rewarded with an infusion of support from sections of the MIDDLE CLASSES which might earlier have been considered 'liberal' and given their votes to 'liberal' parties. By the First World War, the fundamental cleavage of modern democratic politics – between a broad-based coalition of conservative forces commited to strong, but limited government and a not-so-broad alliance of workers, alienated intellectuals and various other disaffected groups around a socialist or social-democratic party – was beginning to be visible. It would take two world wars for that arrangement to become normal and for the participants to learn how to maintain order and stability in a polity seemingly designed to preclude consensus and compromise. It would require, among other things, that the defensive and backward-looking conservatism of the nineteenth century be replaced by a truly democratic conservatism.

Edmund Burke (1790), *Reflections on the Revolution in France* (Harmondsworth, 1982).
Russell Kirk, *The Conservative Mind* (Chicago, 1986).
John Weiss, *Conservatism in Europe 1770–1945* (London, 1977).

JAMES E. CRONIN

Contagious Diseases Acts (1864, 1866, 1869) Three acts of parliament in England permitted, in certain garrison and naval towns, the inspection of women whom the police labelled common prostitutes. Women thus examined and found to be suffering from gonorrhoea or syphilis could be detained in a venereal-disease ward (or lock hospital) for up to nine months. The intention of the acts was to reduce the level of VENEREAL DISEASE in the armed services where, by the 1860s, the cases treated each year amounted to almost one-third of the total number of soldiers serving, while in the navy the figure was about one-eighth.

The regulation of prostitution by the state was well established in many European cities, including Paris, and there were many medical reformers who wanted the Contagious Diseases Acts extended to the civilian population of British cities. Yet many thought that the acts seemed to condone PROSTITUTION. Others argued that the state had no business subsidizing the treatment of venereal diseases. The strongest and most effective attack on the acts came from women who objected to the double standard of inspecting and even detaining the women while subjecting their male clients to no restrictions at all. Women were also angry that the acts were a blatant example of male interference with women's bodies.

When the earliest pressure group for repeal was formed (in December 1869) it excluded women from the first meeting at which this 'delicate' subject was discussed. Josephine BUTLER led the Ladies' National Association which rapidly became the leading organ of repeal. It documented the brutalizing effects of the regulation on the prostitutes and was largely responsible for the repeal of the acts in 1886. However, these feminists championed a purely domestic vision of female sexuality, and after the repeal of the acts the movement's energies went into various 'purity' crusades.

Judith R. Walkowitz, *Prostitution and Victorian Society: Women, Class and the State* (Cambridge, 1980).

GERRY KEARNS

Continental System Napoleon's attempt to strangle British trade, the Continental System was based on decrees made at Berlin (21

November 1806) and Milan (17 December 1807) forbidding French merchants as well as allies and neutrals from trading with Britain. The British retaliated with the ORDERS IN COUNCIL, which imposed a counter-blockade on France and its allies. The resulting economic warfare caused great hardship to both countries. The pound was temporarily weakened and French commerce all along the Atlantic and Mediterranean coasts was down to near-zero by 1812. Although some French industries like cotton and regions like the Rhine valley may have benefited, overall, French industry suffered a serious set-back. Politically, British treatment of neutral shipping provoked war with America in 1812 (*see* WAR OF 1812), and Russia's failure to accept the continental system was one of the reasons Napoleon invaded in 1812.

E. Heckscher, *The Continental System: An Economic Interpretation* (Oxford, 1922).

DONALD SUTHERLAND

contraception *see* BIRTH CONTROL.

co-operation The idea that society should be organized around cooperative and collaborative principles, co-operation developed in response to the economic changes of the early nineteenth century when the social effects of the modern trade cycle (*see* TRADE CYCLES) were manifested for the first time. The initial aim of co-operation was to reorder the economy and human existence along more rational lines, and this gave the early years of the movement – until *c.*1860 – a millennial and utopian character (*see* UTOPIAN SOCIALISM). It developed first and most completely in Britain where Robert OWEN was its most famous exponent, but in France Charles FOURIER and SAINT-SIMON developed similar kinds of proposals as Owen's for establishing co-operative communities where men and women could live harmoniously.

Co-operators believed that the enormous productive capacities created by the industrial revolution invalidated the concern of classical political economy with scarcity of resources. If the economy was organized around co-operative principles, a fairer distribution of goods would be achieved and a more stable pattern of output attained. Co-operation was seen as morally superior to competition as well as economically more coherent. Competition tended to drive down wages and prices, deprive working people of the full value of their labour and cause unemployment and economic distress. But this was at odds with man's new ability to harness the productive capacities of nature which, properly organized, laid the material foundations to inspire a new era of harmony and happiness between men and women. These arguments appealed particularly to urban handicraft workers, like the

Lyon silk-workers in France or the London tailors and shoemakers, whose exposure to increasingly competitive markets was undermining traditionals methods and standards of work. In Britain between c.1829 and 1832 these kinds of workers responded to Owenite theories of co-operation (not all of which were approved by Owen himself) in a vast expansion of union organization.

Various efforts were made to create islands of co-operation within the sea of competitive capitalism. It was believed that these practical demonstrations of the superiority of co-operation would incrementally establish the 'new moral world'. In Britain labour exchanges were established in the early 1830s where goods could be exchanged on the basis of the labour they contained. In the United States ambitious attempts were made to establish communitarian settlements, the best known of which was New Harmony in Indiana which lasted from 1825 to 1829 (*see* UTOPIAS). Co-operative workshops were established in Paris during the revolutions of 1848, and co-operative ideals characterized early German working-class organizations like the Labour Brotherhood. But by the late 1840s these attempts had failed or been crushed.

More successful were the co-operative retail stores that formed the heart of the movement after 1860. Early attempts to establish co-operative stores in London and Brighton in the 1820s were intended to be fund-raising precursors of the new co-operative commonwealth. These all disappeared by the early 1830s. The modern co-operative movement dates from 1844 with the establishment of a retail store by a group of Owenite co-operators (still with millennial dreams, however) in Rochdale. By 1862 there were 400 such stores in Britain and by 1891 over 1,300 with 1 million members. But these stores – which consumers joined and then received a dividend on their purchases as members – had moved entirely away from the early dreams of remaking society, although the co-operative movement continued to be involved in labour politics.

Co-operation was limited entirely to the developed world. In Britain, Sweden and Finland consumer co-operatives dominated the movement; elsewhere producer co-operatives tended to be more common. In Germany, for example, co-operation was associated most closely with those who wished to preserve older social structures that rested on the small independent producers. Thus, handicraft workers banded together to form co-operatives that raised credit and supplied raw materials. In the United States the retail co-operative store was entirely unknown, and co-operation (as in Denmark) found its most fertile soil in the agricultural co-operatives of European immigrant farmers in the Midwest who joined together to process and market their products.

G. D. H. Cole, *A History of Socialist Thought 1789–1850* (London, 1953).

J. F. C. Harrison, *Robert Owen and the Owenites in Britain and America* (London, 1969).

RICHARD PRICE

copyright, Literary Copyright protection was slowly extended to authors only in the nineteenth century, although British law was more highly developed than that of most other countries. British authors claimed perpetual protection for their published writings, a futile demand based on common-law precedents: in fact, statutory provision was made for them, with protection extended to twenty-eight years by an act of 1814, forty-two years by an act of 1842, and in 1911 for fifty years beyond their lifetime. In 1887 Britain adhered to the Berne Convention, which established reciprocal international copyright protections. Throughout the century foreign authors were allowed to establish copyright claims and, at least in theory, the piracy of published works from abroad was punishable by law.

This legal structure gave a reasonable protection to writers in Britain and guaranteed the stability of the publishing trade, unlike the United States where authors received a minimal protection of twenty-eight years from federal law, with additional safeguards from state copyright acts. Non-American writers had no copyright protection. As a result, piracy and the uncompensated reprinting of cheap editions of books written by foreign, principally British, authors became a growth industry in the United States during the second half of the century. Agitation rocked the publishing community for a generation after the Civil War until an International Copyright Act was passed in 1891, applying copyright law equally to American and foreign authors.

JOEL H. WIENER

Corn Laws The repeal of the Corn Laws, which regulated the trade in barley, wheat, oats and rye, in 1846 was taken to symbolize the triumph of FREE TRADE. Although the laws dated back to the fifteenth century, the law of 1815 – intended to ease the transition from a wartime to a peacetime economy – made them one of the key political issues of the early nineteenth century. The importation of wheat was prohibited until it reached 80 shillings per bushel. The law worked badly: farmers found that it did not guarantee steady prices; political economists tended to regard it as a perversion of free trade; and radicals saw it as reflecting the undue political power and privilege of the landed elite.

The issue of the Corn Laws was less one of economic doctrine than of politics, although their supposed contribution to high wages underlay the opposition of many manufacturers. The laws were a political metaphor for a wide-ranging debate about the role of the agricultural interest in the society, the proper functions of government and what principles should drive economic policy. These issues cut across party lines. Many Whigs supported the laws until 1845, whereas influential Tories, like Peel, supported freer trade from the mid-1820s.

The Corn Laws came to be associated in the public mind with economic distress, and it was the crisis of 1838–9 that occasioned the formation of the ANTI-CORN LAW LEAGUE, and the IRISH FAMINE of 1845–6 that provided the opportunity for Peel to introduce repeal. By the mid-1840s, political support for the laws was confined to the farming interest. The success of British farming in the mid nineteenth century seemed to justify the arguments of the repealers, although it was more likely due to broader world economic conditions.

S. Fairlie, 'The Nineteenth-Century Corn Law Reconsidered', *Economic History Review*, 18 (1965), 562–75.

RICHARD PRICE

cotton   *see* COTTON FAMINE; TEXTILE INDUSTRIES.

cotton famine (1861–1864)   The slump in Lancashire's textile mills during the American Civil War is known more accurately as 'the Cotton Panic'. Unemployment and short-time in Britain's largest industry peaked in 1862, affecting three-quarters of the labour force of 500,000. The panic was generally attributed to the Federal blockade of rebel ports: the south sought to starve Europe of cotton to compel Britain – which imported 80 per cent of its raw cotton from the southern states – to recognize its independence. However, the industry was already caught in a crisis of demand, not supply, many speculators making their fortunes through stockpiling. Despite their suffering, British workers refused to back 'the Slave Power'. Voluntary relief schemes were introduced and imports of Indian cotton increased as American supplies dwindled.

W. O. Henderson, *The Lancashire Cotton Famine* (Manchester, 1934).

TONY BARLEY

cricket   The game of cricket was well established in Britain at the start of the nineteenth century, especially in the south of the country. The Marylebone Cricket Club was founded in 1787 and its aristocratic membership gradually took over the codification of the game. Roundarm bowling was legalized in 1835 and overarm bowling in 1864. Cricket was a game played by all classes and, especially in the first half of the century, a great deal of money was gambled on matches. A professional all-England eleven toured the country in the 1840s and attracted large crowds. The enthusiasm for cricket was such that whenever Englishmen went abroad they took the game with them. Cricket was introduced into most parts of the British Empire: India in the eighteenth century and Australia, New Zealand, the West Indies, South Africa and Ceylon (Sri Lanka) in the nineteenth. The first Australian interstate cricket match took place in 1856, and in 1861–2 a professional English cricket team toured Australia. In the second half of the century the game became increasingly respectable. The County Cricket championship was started in 1873 and in the same decade bookmakers were prevented from setting up stalls in Lord's.

J. M. GOLBY

Crimean War (1853–1856)   Allying France, Great Britain, the Ottoman Empire and, after 1855, Sardinia against Russia, the Crimean War was ostensibly caused by a dispute between the Roman Catholic and Greek Orthodox clergies over access to the Holy Places in Palestine, which masked a general fear of Russian expansion toward the Mediterranean and the Middle East. In addition, each of the allies had specific reasons for wanting to check Russia. France wanted to nullify the settlement of the CONGRESS OF VIENNA and looked upon Russia as the major obstacle to achieving this aim. Britain was anxious to keep Russia out of the Mediterranean, and British public opinion was also vehemently anti-Russian. The Ottoman Empire, which had fought Russia almost continuously for two centuries, was determined to use the troubles in the Holy Land to settle the score against its old enemy.

The events leading up to the war began in 1852, when the sultan made concessions to France, which considered itself the protector of the Roman Catholic Church in the Holy Land. Russia, representing the Greek Orthodox Church, objected to these concessions on the grounds that they were an insult to Russian honour and accorded too much prestige to France. It made extensive counter-demands on Turkey, which the allies interpreted as a sign that Russia was prepared to go to war. Diplomatic negotiations aimed at averting the war were unsuccessful, although there is some suspicion that the allies secretly hoped that no diplomatic solution would be found.

The war is best remembered for the disastrous charge of the Light Brigade and the work of Florence NIGHTINGALE; it was also the first major conflict to be covered by newspaper correspondents and photographers. Militarily, the Russians were defeated at the Alma River, Balaklava and Inkerman and, despite prolonged resistance, were eventually forced to abandon Sevastopol. Negotiations leading to the TREATY OF PARIS (30 March 1856) were initiated by Napoleon III of France.

Norman Rich, *Why the Crimean War?* (New York, 1985).

GEORGE O. KENT

Crispi, Francesco (*b* Ribéra, Sicily, 4 October 1819; *d* Naples, 12 August 1901)   Italian statesman and prime minister. In his early days he followed MAZZINI and was exiled from Naples in 1849 and from Piedmont in 1853 for republican activity. One of GARIBALDI's Red Shirts and a supporter of republicanism while in parliament, he converted in 1864 to the support the monarchy as the best unifier of Italy. Despite his political career being stunted in 1878 by charges of bigamy, he became prime minister from 1887 to 1891 and 1893 to 1896. Although a member of the Left, Crispi adopted 'transformism' which dominated Italy's politics. His insistence on Italy's spurious claim to great-power status caused him to support the TRIPLE ALLIANCE and to press for an Italian colonial empire. After Italy's defeat at the BATTLE OF ADOWA by the Ethiopians in 1896, he was forced to resign.

LAWRENCE P. ADAMCZYK

Croatia After a brief period of medieval independence, Croatia, a province in the western Balkans, was successively part of Hungary and of the Habsburg Empire (while retaining significant autonomy and its own nobility), and for a period under the Ottomans. It formed part of the Illyrian provinces of Napoleon's empire (1809–13), but after 1814 it was incorporated into the Hungarian crown lands. The harsh Magyarization attempts produced a strong national movement for cultural emancipation. In 1848 Croatia, under Count Josef Jelačić (1801–59), fought the Hungarians and after 1849 became an Austrian crown land. The *Ausgleich* (*see* COMPROMISE OF 1867) handed it back to Hungary. A new wave of Magyarization precipitated the formation of political movements and parties, which sought unification of the southern Slavs, but differed sharply as to the structure of unification. Some argued for Slav unity in one state (Yugoslavism), others for a greater Croatia and others for a loose federation. With the dissolution of Austria-Hungary in 1918 Croatia and Slavonia joined the Yugoslav kingdom.

Francis Eterovich and Christopher Spalatin, *Croatia: Land, People, Culture* (Toronto, 1964–70).

MARIA TODOROVA

Crowther, Samuel Ajayi (*b* Oshogbo, Nigeria, *c.*1808; *d* Lagos, 31 December 1891) Missionary, explorer and first African bishop of the Anglican Church of southern Nigeria. Born in Yorubaland in western Nigeria, and captured (1821) during one of the region's civil wars, he was sold into the Atlantic slave trade. En route to the New World his life was fortuitously changed by the off-shore interception of an anti-slavery British gunboat. Redirecting his slave ship to Freetown, Sierre Leone, Crowther came under the influence of the British Church Missionary Society. On concluding the first part of his formal education, he completed further studies at the Freetown Fourah Bay Institute, thereafter combining missionary work with British-led explorations along the Niger basin. In 1864 he was consecrated bishop of the newly created West African diocese. By the 1880s, however, when the SCRAMBLE FOR AFRICA began to gather momentum, leading British officials stationed in trading communities began to lobby for greater local British control. In the subsequent policy changes Crowther was forced to resign (1890), his agents in particular charged with violating Christian moral values and behaviour.

Jacob F. A. Ajayi, *Christian Missions in Nigeria 1841–1891* (Evanston, Ill., 1969).

B. MARIE PERINBAM

Cuba The history of nineteenth-century Cuba was dominated by the sugar industry and the imperial link with Spain. The revolution in Saint Domingue (*see* HAITI) provided Cuban planters with unexpected opportunities. Further stimuli to the economy came from the liberalization of trade in 1817, the large amount of vacant land in the island and the application of industrial technology to production and transport (Cuba opened the first railway in Latin America in 1838). Although Spain committed itself to ending the slave trade by 1820, in practice slave imports did not cease until the 1860s (*see* ATLANTIC SLAVE TRADE); Chinese immigration then provided an alternative source of labour. By 1860, with an annual output of half a million tons, Cuba was producing about a quarter of the world's sugar.

Cuban society was transformed. In the west large plantations appeared, while the east remained an area of smaller landholdings and poor infrastructure. Population increased from 553,000 (including 199,000 slaves) in 1817 to 1.4 million in 1862. Despite high mortality among the slave population, this figure included 370,000 slaves. Although the fear of social revolution had kept most planters loyal through the Spanish American independence wars, the political problems of nineteenth-century Spain, the growth of commercial links with the United States and antagonism towards Spanish officials and merchants caused many to question the imperial tie. In October 1868 the Ten Years War, the first attempt to secure independence, broke out in the east in response to the imposition of new taxes and Spain's failure to concede greater autonomy. This accelerated the demise of slavery, for the rebels offered freedom to those who fought, while in 1870 the Spanish government passed the Law of Free Birth. After the Peace of Zanjón slavery quickly declined and eventually ended in 1886.

The war destroyed many plantations. Moreover, the early 1880s saw a steep fall in sugar prices, increased taxation and domestic inflation, ruining many landowners. The need to modernize the sugar industry brought an influx of capital from the United States and the consolidation of estates. The crisis also provoked a massive increase in unemployment, banditry and lawlessness. Many Cuban professionals were forced to emigrate, while resentment against Spanish officials and businessmen grew, especially as 250,000 new immigrants arrived from Spain. After the United States substantially increased import tariffs in 1894, causing severe economic disruption in Cuba, political support shifted from the Autonomist Party, which had clearly failed, to the independence advocated by José MARTI and other exiles. Early in 1895 an uprising led by Martí's Cuban Revolutionary Party took hold in the east. Within a year the rebels were fighting in the vicinity of Havana, destroying the plantations of their opponents. Spanish counter-revolutionary measures against the peasantry further impoverished the countryside. However, in April 1898, as the rebels neared victory, the Cuban independence process was irreversibly deformed by the entry of the United States into war with Spain. The peace which concluded the SPANISH-AMERICAN WAR involved no Cuban representatives, and the devastated island ended the century under military occupation by the United States.

Louis A. Pérez, *Cuba: Between Reform and Revolution* (New York, 1988).
Rebecca J. Scott, *Slave Emancipation in Cuba: The Transition to Free Labour* (Princeton, NJ, 1985).

RORY MILLER

Curé d'Ars [Jean-Baptiste Marie Vianney] (*b* Dardilly, near Lyons, 8 May 1786; *d* Ars-en-Dombes, 4 August 1859)   French priest. An army deserter who found it almost impossible to learn his seminary Latin, he became priest of Ars in 1818, where he established an orphanage for destitute girls. His catechetical instructions and extraordinary personal skills as a confessor attracted an enormous following, which kept him confined for up to eighteen hours a day in the confessional. He was beatified in 1905, canonized in 1925 and declared the patron saint of parish priests in 1929.

H. Ghéon, *The Secret of the Curé d'Ars*, trans. F. J. Sheed (London, 1929).
SHERIDAN GILLEY

Custer, George Armstrong (*b* New Rumley, Ohio, 5 December 1839; *d* Little Big Horn, Montana, 25 June 1876)   American cavalry commander. One of the most controversial military figures in history, Custer graduated from the military academy at West Point at the bottom of his class and in the shadow of disciplinary problems. Reckless and flamboyant, he attracted the attention of his superiors and during the Civil War was promoted to major-general. Returned to a captaincy after the war, he took a commision as lieutenant-colonel of the newly created Seventh Cavalry. The discovery of gold in Sioux territory precipitated a rush of miners and eventually military conflict. While tracking the Sioux and Northern Cheyenne tribes in 1876, Custer disobeyed orders and engaged them. He and five companies under his immediate command were wiped out. 'Custer's Last Stand' galvanized public opinion against the 'savages', increased troop movements into native American country and forced the 'sale' of the Sioux lands (*see* SITTING BULL).

JOHN MARTIN

Cuza, Alexandru (*b* Husi, Moldavia, 20 March 1829; *d* Heidelberg, Germany, 15 May 1873)   First prince of ROMANIA. Born into a boyar family, he took part in the 1848 revolution in Moldavia. His double election as hospodar (prince) of Moldavia in January, and of Wallachia in February 1859, linked the principalities in a personal union. In December 1861 the powers recognized the full unification. Under the liberal government of Kogalniceanu (1817–91), Cuza initiated sweeping reforms: secularization of monastery lands (1863); emancipation of serfs and land distribution aimed at creating a class of free peasants (1864); a national system of education with primary and secondary schools and universities in Bucharest and Iaçi; a civil code based on the Code Napoléon; electoral law; centralization of the administration. The strong opposition of the great landlords, and Cuza's political estrangement from both conservatives and liberals, precipitated a conspiracy forcing his abdication in February 1866 and exile to Germany.

Gerald Bobango, *The Emergence of the Romanian National State* (Boulder, Colo., 1979).

MARIA TODOROVA

D

Dalton, John (*b* Eaglesfield, Cumbria, 6 September 1766; *d* Manchester, 27 July 1844) English chemist. One of the great early figures of modern chemistry, he is credited particularly for his promotion of the atomic theory. He was born and raised in a Quaker family of modest means, and educated in Quaker schools. While still in his teens he began teaching mathematics at school in Kendal, where he also first began giving popular lectures on scientific subjects. He moved to Manchester in 1792 and rapidly became active in its growing scientific community. Beginning with work on meteorology, he moved to theoretical speculations about the behaviour of air and gases, and then devised chemical experiments to test his ideas. The result was a series of lectures and publications, largely between 1800 and 1810, which promoted the theory that each element consisted of atoms with specific weights, which could be determined relatively. This laid the foundation for modern atomic theory. When Dalton died in 1844 he was one of England's most honoured scientists.

ROBERT FRIEDEL

Damien, Father [Joseph de Veuster] (*b* Tremeloo, Belgium, 3 January 1840; *d* Molokai, Hawaiian Islands, 15 April 1889) Leper missionary. Professed a member of the Picpus Order of the Sacred Hearts of Jesus and Mary in 1860, he took the name of Damien. He was ordained in Honolulu in 1864 and ministered on Hawaii before going in 1873 to Molokai where he cared for 600 to 800 lepers until his own death from the disease. His character was defended against the Presbyterian C. M. Hyde in a ferocious tract by R. L. Stevenson (1850–94).

J. V. Farrow, *Damien the Leper* (London, 1937).

SHERIDAN GILLEY

Dardanelles   *see* STRAITS QUESTION.

Darwin, Charles Robert (*b* Shrewsbury, 12 February 1809; *d* Down, Kent, 19 April 1882)   English naturalist who developed the theory of EVOLUTION. Committed to the notion that life developed gradually on earth, he began formulating ideas of evolution while serving as ship's naturalist during the voyages of exploration of the HMS *Beagle* (1831–6). He suggested that creatures born with traits better suited to their environment than others of their species would have greater success in sexual competition for mates and that this would insure the perpetuation of advantageous characteristics. Those lacking such characteristics would eventually be replaced. Natural selection thus provided a mechanism for species change over time. (*See* DARWINISM.) He published his ideas in *The Origin of Species* in 1859. His work prompted considerable opposition, especially from theologians.

Peter Bowler, *Charles Darwin: The Man and his Influence (London*, 1990).
BARBARA KAPLAN

Darwinism   The theory of natural selection, which was given its first authoritative statement by Charles DARWIN, remains one of the outstanding scientific achievements of the nineteenth century. In *The Origin of Species* (1859) Darwin argued that the multiple different species of life were not fixed but were subject to modification over time; the mechanism of this change was that of natural selection, by means of which those individuals of a species best adapted to their environment survived to reproduce. Darwin's theory could not have been arrived at without the previous discovery of the immensity of geological time, also a scientific advance of the nineteenth century (*see* GEOLOGY). The theory of evolution, as it has come to be called (though not by Darwin himself), was widely persuasive and had immense implications for human understanding, not least in challenging religious beliefs about creation.

The history of Darwinism, however, has been complicated by the heavy burden of ideology which became associated with the theory. Herbert SPENCER coined the phrase 'the survival of the fittest' to describe the competitive process by which some individuals survived and others did not, apparently sanctifying practices of competitive individualism within the social order. The very term 'evolution' seems to imply progress, as though currently existing species, especially human beings, were the summit of the evolutionary process and not merely the most successful in the current transient environment. These ideological associations of Darwinism were especially active in the late nineteenth century in the form of SOCIAL DARWINISM. This attempted to make a strong analogy between the competitive processes at work in nature within and between species, and competitive processes at work in the social order. The theory thus appeared to lend the sanction of scientific authority to rebarbative social and political policies, including *laissez-faire* economic and social policy, national competition and imperial aggrandizement.

Charles Darwin, *The Origin of Species* (1859).
Greta Jones, *Social Darwinism and English Thought* (Brighton, 1980).

SIMON DENTITH

Davies, Emily (*b* Southampton, 22 April 1830; *d* London, 13 July 1921) Founder of Girton College, Cambridge, who made the advancement of education for women her life's work. The daughter of a clergyman, she had herself suffered acutely from the educational deprivation imposed on middle-class girls. In 1861 she set up a household with her mother in London, a change in personal circumstances which marked the beginning of a productive career. Showing great organizational abilities, Davies assisted the investigation of girls' education conducted by the 1864 Royal Commission on Endowed Schools, successfully campaigned to obtain admission for girls to the local examinations administered by Oxford and Cambridge, published *The Higher Education of Women* (1866) and started organizing a university college for women. Girton College, Cambridge officially opened its doors in 1873. Davies adhered to the equal-rights tradition of feminism, insisting that girls conformed to the same educational standards applied to boys.

Barbara Stephen, *Emily Davies and Girton College* (London, 1927).

GAIL SAVAGE

Davis, Jefferson (*b* Fairview, Kentucky, 3 June 1808; *d* Belvoir, Mississippi, 6 December 1889) President of the Confederate States (1861–5). He graduated from West Point in 1828 and saw action in the Black Hawk War, but left the army in 1835, retiring to his cotton plantation in Mississippi. His political career included service in the House of Representatives, the Senate and as Franklin Pierce's secretary of war from 1853 to 1857. When Pierce left office Davis re-entered the Senate and remained there until Mississippi seceded from the union. From 1861 to 1865 he was president of the CONFEDERATE STATES OF AMERICA. Although he believed in states' rights, Davis was above all committed to the Confederacy. Most historians agree that, while he was a poor administrator, he was beset with insurmountable problems as president. After the war he retired to Beauvoir, his home in Mississippi, where he wrote works like *The Rise and Fall of the Confederate Government* (1881).

JOHN MARTIN

Davis, Thomas Osborne (*b* Mallow, County Cork, 14 October 1814; *d* Dublin, 16 September 1845) Irish nationalist and 'Young Irelander'. The Protestant son of a British army surgeon, he was educated at Trinity College, Dublin and then called to the Bar. A co-founder of the *Nation* (1842), he was impatient with Daniel O'CONNELL's utilitarian nationalism and constitutional methods. Davis preached an Irish cultural identity distinct from that of England but denied the significance of racial and religious divisions in Ireland. His writings, including the famous ballad 'A Nation Once Again', offered all Irish people the vision of an Ireland free from England, although he really wanted to preserve Protestant leadership in Irish politics. More influential upon later generations than among his contemporaries, he was hailed by Arthur Griffith (1872–1922), founder of Sinn Fein, as a 'prophet... whose words and teachings I have tried to translate into practice in politics'.

Richard Davis, *The Young Ireland Movement* (Dublin, 1987).

PATRICK BUCKLAND

Davitt, Michael (*b* Straide, County Mayo, 25 March 1846; *d* Dublin, 31 May 1906) Irish collectivist and secularist. He was brought up in England, where he lost an arm in a factory accident, and worked closely with British socialists. After seven years' imprisonment for his role as organizing secretary of the IRISH REPUBLICAN BROTHERHOOD, he forged links between revolutionary and constitutional nationalism in Ireland. He used the IRISH NATIONAL LAND LEAGUE and PARNELL to exploit the land question and make HOME RULE a mass movement in Ireland, denouncing other agrarian reforms as a Tory plot to thwart nationalism. His advocacy of land nationalization was not understood in Ireland where tenant farmers wanted ownership for themselves. He sat for different Irish constituencies between 1882 and 1899, latterly as an anti-Parnellite, and helped establish the United Irish League (1898). He subsequently devoted himself to travel and journalism, visiting Russia to show sympathy for the revolutionary party.

Theodore Moody, *Davitt and the Irish Revolution, 1846–1882* (Oxford, 1981).

PATRICK BUCKLAND

Deák, Francis [Ferenc] (*b* Söjtör, Hungary, 17 October 1803; *d* Budapest, 29 January 1876) Hungarian statesman. A lawyer, local official and member of the Hungarian diet from 1833, he became a leader of the liberal opposition to the Habsburg administration in 1839. He was a moderate supporter of Louis KOSSUTH, and became justice minister in the 1848 revolutionary government. After the failure of the 1848 revolution, Deák became the leader of the Hungarian cause, basing his case on the principle of legitimacy. He demanded a return to the 1848 constitution, while recognizing the need for an Austro-Hungarian condominium. His moderate form of opposition to Habsburg centralism in the 1850s bore fruit in the 1860s with the weakness of Austria's military and financial position. Deák led the negotiations with the Habsburg regime which led to the COMPROMISE OF 1867. After this triumph of his moderate policies, he retired from public life, but remained a dominant national figure until his death.

STEVEN BELLER

Debs, Eugene Victor (*b* Terre Haute, Indiana, 5 November 1855; *d* Elmhurst, Illinois, 20 October, 1926) Key figure in the American labour movement. He served for thirteen years with the Brotherhood of Locomotive Firemen, where he was appointed national secretary and treasurer at the age of 25. Opposed to trade-union exclusiveness on railroads, he supported industrial unionism and formed the American Railway Union in 1893 to represent all railroad workers. Debs first came to national prominence during the Pullman strike in 1894. The strike was crushed, and Debs jailed. Six months later he emerged an avowed socialist. More concerned with alternatives to capitalism than with working within the capitalist system, he differed sharply from the conservative trade-unionism of his contemporary Samuel GOMPERS. He polled 95,000 votes as a presidential candidate on the Socialist Democratic ticket in 1900. He ran for president three more times on the socialist ticket, the last while in jail in 1920 because of his opposition to the First World War.

KEVIN MURPHY

Decembrists Active in Russia in the aftermath to the Napoleonic wars, the Decembrists consisted of mainly aristocratic army officers. Despite notable differences, they were all agreed on the need for constitutional government and an end to SERFDOM. Their plans varied from mild liberalism to extreme forms of republicanism, and the popular Masonic lodges of which many were members provided fertile ground for unorthodox political thinking. Their proposed *coup d'état* was inspired by the example of the Italian CARBONARI and the German *Tugendbund*. The confusion surrounding the sudden death of ALEXANDER I on 1 December 1825 (hence their name) presented them with an unexpected opportunity, but they were poorly prepared, badly organized and partially defeatist. Largely ignorant of the needs of the mass of the Russian population, they staged a none the less symbolic protest and proved an enduring inspiration to successive generations of Russian revolutionaries.

M. Zetlin, *The Decembrists* (New York, 1958).

A. V. KNOWLES

decorative arts In the nineteenth century the decorative arts initiated and responded to a great many changes in fashion and taste. At the beginning of the century Neoclassicism and Regency were dominant, giving way to a succession of merging and overlapping movements – including Empire Style, Renaissance Revival, Gothic Revival, Elizabethan, Etruscan, Egyptianate, Japonaise, Arts and Crafts and Art Nouveau.

NEOCLASSICISM deployed stylistic characteristics revealed by archaeological discovery, regarding them as meritorious by virtue of their association with a golden age of socio-aesthetic concord. (Western) antiquity was its criterion of taste and, whereas earlier revivalisms had focused on accidentally surviving remnants of former cultures, this movement, especially in its latter stages, sought to discover and reconstruct aspects of antiquity and reclaim them to a modern consciousness. Much of this stylistic reconstruction is now regarded as inaccurate or distorted through decontextualization. However, a principal attribute of the movement is recognized in its moderating of taste in reaction to the rococo – for example as typified in the range of ceramics popularized by Wedgwood & Company, particularly the unglazed stonewares 'basalte', 'rosso antico' and 'jasperware', and in a severely reduced 'architectural' language of decorative motifs (columns and entablatures, urns, ovals discs and so on). Comparable features are found in furniture after Thomas Sheraton (1751–1806) (*Cabinet Dictionary*, 1803; *Cabinet-Maker, Upholsterer and General Artist's Encyclopaedia*, 1805) and Adam-inspired Chippendale, together with a corresponding material sobriety in the use of dark or darkened hardwoods.

Such characteristics were evident also in Regency. This movement initiated stylistic developments that, while centring on the first two decades, were far-reaching in their accommodation of different classical pedigrees (Egyptian, Etruscan, Greek, Roman) and compatible features of the non-classical (Chinese, Oriental) to an eclecticism that was to characterize much of nineteenth-century taste. Highly representative of this tendency was the Grand Service of silver and plate accumulated in Britain by the Prince Regent, especially the many pieces by Paul Storr (1771–1844). In France the (First) Empire style, more or less coeval with Regency, was acknowledged as its direct equivalent and for its role in assimilating Egyptianate motifs to revived classicism stimulated by Napoleon's Egyptian campaigns. Charles Percier (1764–1838) and Pierre-François-Léonard Fontaine (1762–1853) published definitive schemes for furniture and interior decoration in *Recueil de décorations intérieures* (Compendium of Interior Decoration, 1812). Comparable developments in Britain were now distinguished from the post-Sheraton by their use of lighter, native hardwoods.

Classical revivalism encouraged the collection of original antique artefacts and fragments and their deployment in schemes of decoration, as typified in the central court of his own house in London (completed 1812) by John Soane (1753–1837) (John Soane, *Description of the House and Museum, 12 Lincoln's Inn Fields*, 1831). This was a characteristic also of the GOTHIC REVIVAL except that collectors identifying with the latter concentrated on surviving artefacts of the Middle Ages (*see* Soane's Monk's Parlour in the same residence). One of the most influential medieval antiquarian interiors was the home of Walter Scott (1771–1832) at Abbotsford, Roxburghshire (1816–23), by William Atkinson (1773–1839). The most representative of interiors containing only modern artefacts in the Gothic style – furniture, furnishings, metalwork, glass, tiles – was undoubtedly the Houses of Parliament, London (1840–65), by Augustus Welby Northmore Pugin (1812–52). Thousands of examples of 'Gothicized' products, available for use in home decoration, were evident at the Great Exhibition, London (1851), especially in Pugin's Mediaeval Court (Messrs Dickinson, *Comprehensive Pictures of the Mediaeval Court at the Great Exhibition*, 1854).

INTERNATIONAL EXPOSITIONS were important vehicles not only for disseminating taste but also for informing production. For example, at the 1862 London Exhibition Henry Doulton (1820–97) included salt-glazed stoneware as an experimental by-product of his successful sanitary-ware manufacture. Unexpectedly attracting the attention of teachers at the Lambeth School of Art, this prompted the subsequent development of that branch of 'art' or studio pottery in which a craftsperson took responsibility for his or her product from conception to realization. The success of Doulton's art-ware was confirmed at every subsequent international exposition until Chicago (1893) where it received seven of the highest awards. Similarly, Herbert Minton (1793–1858) perfected encaustic tile-making with reference to the medieval floor of the chapter house at Westminster Abbey, but he then extended both the range of designs (geometricization, in pursuit of production economies) and materials (clays of different chromatic burnings) in response to demand arising from exhibition success. It was a characteristic of the decorative arts in this period, then, that exhibitions were occasions for marketing as much as confirmation, and it was a principal paradox that while hand production was gradually displaced, those products succeeded that were tinged with its ethos.

Various nineteenth-century decorative arts were, of course, dependent on, and celebrated, the revival of handicraft. Many did not lend themselves to mass production, and these figured large in the ARTS AND CRAFTS MOVEMENT's panoply as it became a major force from the 1860s, influenced by William MORRIS and John RUSKIN. Hand-crafted production, with medieval associations but gradually accommodating modern practices, was associated in Britain with such artist-designers as John Dando Sedding (1838–91) (metalwork, embroideries, wallpaper), Henry Wilson (1864–1934) (jewellery, metalwork), John Paul Cooper (1869–1933) (jewellery, gold- and silversmithing), Nelson Dawson (1859–1942) (jewellery and silversmithing), Ernest Gimson (1864–1919) (furniture, cabinet-making) and Ernest (1863–1926) and Sidney Barnsley (1865–1926) (furniture, cabinet-making). Comparable figures in America included Gustav Stickley (1857–1942) (furniture, metalwork), Elbert Hubbard (1856–1915) (fine printing and binding) and William L. Price (1861–1916) (pottery, furniture). The contribution of educational establishments should not be neglected: from 1880 the Birmingham School of Art worked to reconstruct repoussé, sgraffito, mosaic, enamelling, glass painting, stone-carving, lapidary work, damascening and wrought ironwork.

Art Nouveau, though in many senses a post-nineteenth-century phenomenon, bore a strong relation to the products of exhibitor-manufacturers of the 1860s and 1870s in the efforts of such as Arthur Lasenby Liberty (1843–1917) to marry fine craftsmanship, commercial production and systematic retailing (Liberty & Company, established 1875). Louis Comfort Tiffany (1848–1933) also anticipated the values of later times when the first year's production of his 'Favrile' glass furnaces at Corona (1894) was acquired by museums.

Susan M. Wright (ed.), *The Decorative Arts of the Victorian Period* (London, 1989).

DAVID THISTLEWOOD

Delagoa Bay At the western edge of the Indian Ocean at Maputo (formerly Lourenço Marques), Mozambique, Delagoa Bay was the finest natural harbour on Africa's east coast. It was a focal point of Anglo-German rivalry in the area and of conflict between the British in the CAPE COLONY and the Boers in the TRANSVAAL who saw the port, held by the Portuguese, as a vital means of access to the coast outside British control. As gold-mining developed in the Transvaal, the right to recruit much-needed labour in Mozambique was conditional on the substantial use of the port and the railway linking it to the mining area.

Simon E. Katzenellenbogen, *South Africa and Southern Mozambique: Labour Railways and Trade in the Making of a Relationship* (Manchester, 1982).

SIMON KATZENELLENBOGEN

Democratic Party The origins of the Democratic Party in the United States may be traced to the opposition to John Quincy ADAMS that formed around Andrew JACKSON following the disputed presidential election of 1824. The demise of the FEDERALIST PARTY left the Democratic-Republican Party as the only national party whose presidential candidates each attracted the support of different sections. In the election none of the four candidates polled the necessary electoral votes to win. Jackson won ninety-nine electoral votes and a plurality of the popular vote, while Adams won eighty-four electoral votes. Henry CLAY, a defeated candidate, threw his support in the House of Representatives behind Adams and became his secretary of state. Charging that this 'corrupt bargain' betrayed the will of the people, anti-administration elements rallied to the charismatic figure of Jackson, and in the election of 1828 he was swept into office by the support of planters and farmers in the south and west and of small entrepreneurs, artisans and factory workers in urban areas.

Jackson's presidency has been the subject of sharp debate among historians, but it is agreed that his new party, the Jacksonian Democrats, ushered in a new party system. Jackson's party was touted by many contemporaries as the party of the 'common man'. The party came into being in a more complex, mobile and expanding society than had existed in the revolutionary era, and Democrats favoured the advances in political democracy that had been made by individual states. On the national level it was committed to limiting the powers of the federal government and allowing the states maximum sovereignty.

Opposition to Jackson coalesced into the WHIG PARTY, but with the exception of two brief and unsuccessful Whig interludes the Democratic Party retained control of the White House until 1860. Until the 1850s the party enjoyed superior national organization, functioning as a vehicle for the resolution of sectional tensions. With the rise of the REPUBLICAN PARTY after the KANSAS-NEBRASKA ACT, the repeal of the MISSOURI COMPROMISE in 1854 and the DRED SCOTT CASE in 1857, the party began to break up along sectional lines, culminating in the nomination of two presidential candidates, Stephen Douglas (1813–61) and John C. Breckinridge (1821–75), in 1860. During the Civil War, northern 'War Democrats' supported Lincoln and those publicly opposed were known as 'Copperheads' (implying treason).

After conservative white southerners, sometimes called Bourbons, regained control of their state governments in the name of white supremacy after reconstruction, the 'solid South', freed from the intervention of outsiders, was a consistent source of Democratic strength. Between 1880 and 1892 no southern or border state gave an electoral vote to a Republican candidate. Democratic principles of states' rights, tariff reduction, administrative economy and limited government had appeal outside the south as well. Resenting prohibition, public school and sabbatarian legislation demanded by the pietistic wing of the Republican Party, Catholics and other ethnic groups in the north gravitated towards the Democrats, and substantial numbers of immigrants were attracted to Democratic machines such as New York City's TAMMANY HALL.

Democratic appeal after the war also rested on a desire for a return to simple solutions to complex problems. To Americans weary of the reconstruction policies of northern Republicans and fearful of rapidly changing social conditions, the solution of governing little and leaving as much as possible to states and localities was reassuring if not always realistic. From the southern base of about 135 electoral votes, the party managed to elect Grover CLEVELAND to the presidency twice (1884, 1888). Cleveland, however, became unpopular within his party for being too closely identified with conservative north-eastern interests.

After the severe depression of 1893, Republicans successfully identified their party with a sound currency and the tariff, and in the congressional elections of 1894 Republicans took control of the House of Representatives, defeating many prominent Democrats and bringing on a major political realignment. The Democratic Party was split once again along sectional lines. This second crisis in the history of the party pitted Cleveland and the north-eastern conservatism he represented against the insurgent southern and western wings of the party associated with populism (*see* POPULISM (UNITED STATES)). The defeat of presidential candidate William Jennings BRYAN in 1896 ushered in a period of Republican dominance.

Paul Kleppner, *The Third Electoral System, 1853–1892: Parties, Voters and Political Cultures* (Chapel Hill, NC, 1979).
Arthur M. Schlesinger Jr, *The Age of Jackson*, abridged edn (New York, 1949).

KEVIN MURPHY

Denmark   *see* SCANDINAVIA.

Deodoro da Fonseca (*b* Alagoas, Brazil, 5 August 1827; *d* Paris 1892)   Marshal of the Brazilian army and veteran of the PARAGUAYAN WAR. His prestige was such that republican conspirators saw him as an essential figurehead for the plot to overthrow Emperor PEDRO II in November 1889. Deodoro, however, was reluctant to break his allegiance to the monarchy. He seems to have acted out of frustration with the intransigence of the prime minister, Ouro Prêto (1836–1912), who had exacerbated the serious discontent that existed within the army over issues like discipline, pay and promotions. Deodoro held the presidency for two years. Autocratic and monarchist in temperament, he was unable to reconcile the heterogeneous elements in the republican coalition, which ranged from opportunistic former monarchists to military radicals. In November 1891 he resigned in favour of Marshal Floriano Peixoto (1839–95), his vice-president and the leader of the 'Jacobin' faction.

RORY MILLER

department stores   The term 'department store' originated in the United States and referred to a large shop selling a wide variety of consumer goods on different floors or in different sections. In France Aristide Boucicaut (1810–77), the father of modern merchandizing, expanded the celebrated Bon Marché shop in Paris into the largest retail enterprise in the world. The extension of retailing was a central theme in the nineteenth century's social and economic history, and was as relevant to the development of modern society as the industrial revolution which had preceded it. Accordingly, the pioneers of large-scale retailing, like 'Universal Provider' William Whiteley in London and Marshall Field in Chicago, although less well-known than great inventors and businessmen, have done much to mould the forms of modern society, advancing the spectacularization of the commodity and making it loom even larger in cultural and political life.

Michael B. Miller, *The Bon Marché: Bourgeois Culture and the Department Store, 1869–1920* (London, 1981).

JOHN SPRINGHALL

Deroin, Jeanne Françoise (*b* Paris, 1805; *d* London, 1894)   French socialist and feminist. A teacher by profession, she was friends with most of the leading socialist writers of the day and, like many of them, believed that Christ was a superior secular philosopher because of his humanitarianism. During the 1848 revolution she founded the Club de l'Emancipation des Femmes (Club for the Emancipation of Women) which demanded full equality for men and women. She helped found a general association of working-class co-operatives in late 1849, but this was dissolved the next year and she was sentenced to six months in prison. She had to flee to England in 1852 following the establishment of the Second Empire. She never returned to France but remained an active writer until the 1860s.

C. Moses, *French Feminism in the Nineteenth Century* (Albany, NY, 1984).

DONALD SUTHERLAND

Díaz, Porfirio (*b* Oaxaca, Mexico, 15 September 1830; *d* Paris, 2 July 1915)   Soldier and president of Mexico (1876–80, 1884–1911). He came to prominence in MEXICO due to his military leadership in the struggle against MAXIMILIAN. In 1871–2 he led an unsuccessful revolt against the re-election of JUAREZ as president, but a similar rebellion in 1876 against Sebastián Lerdo (1825–89) gained more support and he won power. For many historians Díaz was the architect of modern Mexico. He established internal order through his control of state governors, local political chiefs and the army. Liberal economic policies brought a massive influx of foreign investment and a rapid increase in mineral and agricultural exports: between 1876 and 1900 economic growth averaged 8 per cent annually. This was achieved, however, at high social cost. The rural poor lost their lands, while the swelling population of the cities saw little improvement in living conditions. Political, social and economic pressures combined to force Díaz out of office in the revolution of 1910.

RORY MILLER

Dickens, Charles (*b* Portsmouth, 7 February 1812; *d* Gad's Hill, 9 June 1870) English novelist and journalist. One of the outstanding figures of the nineteenth century, he enjoyed a massive popularity not only in Britain, but also in America and, in translation, in Europe. He became famous in the 1830s with comic novels such as *Pickwick Papers* (1836–7) and the powerful criminal and sentimental story *Oliver Twist* (1837–8). For the next thirty years he produced a stream of increasingly serious and ambitious works of fiction, maintaining a popular readership for novels which sought to embrace the extraordinary variety of nineteenth-century life. In addition, he conducted two popular journals, *Household Words* and *All the Year Round*, which published, in addition to fiction by Dickens himself and by other writers, campaigning and educational journalism. Dickens's writing provided enduringly popular images of his own day, so that the ways in which we now understand nineteenth-century life continue to be shaped by figures and images drawn from *Oliver Twist*, *A Christmas Carol* (1843), *David Copperfield* (1849–50), and his other great novels.

SIMON DENTITH

Dingane (*b* Natal, *c*.1795; *d* Natal, 15 March 1840) Zulu king, half-brother of SHAKA. With another half-brother, he plotted again Shaka, surprising and stabbing him to death in September 1828. The change from Shaka's militarism and cruelty was generally welcomed by many ZULUS and European traders, but Dingane himself was often cruel, though perhaps not as ruthless. He was somewhat vacillating and uncertain as to how to respond to traders and missionaries whom he feared could be precursors of more formal European control. He initially accepted a group of voortrekkers (*see* GREAT TREK) on condition that they recover some stolen cattle, but when they did so he massacred the party. After his defeat at the BATTLE OF BLOOD RIVER, he sought to regain stature by attacking Swaziland, but was weakened by MPANDE's defection. He fled northwards and was killed, probably with the support of, although not by, the Swazi king.

SIMON KATZENELLENBOGEN

disease, theories of There were three areas where theories of disease were important. The first was in medical science where attempts were made to explain sickness and propose cures. Secondly, there was the lay understanding of being unwell and the things patients did for themselves which might or might not have included seeking professional help. Thirdly, there was the area of public health, where governments tried to define their responsibilities and the strategies they could adopt to mitigate the social dislocation and suffering which disease occasioned. In all these areas understanding and practice were guided by various theories of disease.

Over time there were changes in the way disease was understood, at least by the medical profession, but many conflicting theoretical frameworks were entertained by scientists and their public. Some saw disease as a punishment or trial sent by God to teach Job-like acceptance or to give rise to sustained reflection which might lead to repentance. Yet even the Old Testament contained a series of regulations on personal and public hygiene which justified a more active approach. Hippocrates codified Greek knowledge about the importance of aspect, drainage and weather in explaining the natural origins of some diseases. Galen systematized the medical knowledge of the Roman world but focused more on the internal causes of sickness than on the external threats to health. In particular, he identified an imbalance in the body's humours or fluids (phlegm, choler, black choler and blood) as the root cause of illness and argued that people's life-styles produced these imbalances. The sorts of potions Galen mixed to counter humoral imbalance remained a mainstay of both lay and professional treatments of disease.

In the 1880s bacteriology transformed the medical understanding of disease, building on the work of Louis PASTEUR. Before this, two developments dramatically refined the traditions of Hippocrates and Galen. Justus Liebig (1803–73) pioneered the study of organic chemistry and, in particular, studied the process of fermentation of yeast which seemed to show how organic decomposition could produce the sort of activity which could explain how filth generated disease (the miasmatic theory). This tradition was enhanced by developments in microscopy which raised the possibility of actually seeing the minute particles which were undergoing change in fermentation. It was with his demonstration that fermentation was not spontaneous but involved the presence of specific micro-organisms that Pasteur launched the bacteriological revolution.

The second important research tradition looked at the internal economy of the body. In 1792 Luigi Galvani (1737–98) demonstrated a connection between muscular activity and the provision of an electric charge. This changed the medical understanding of the internal balances of the body and electrical predisposing causes of disease, be they in the body or in the atmosphere, were sought.

Yeasts, funguses, atmospheric electricity – these and other topics dominated the medical debates about the causes of disease, while humours, specifics and daily regimens reigned supreme in lay medicine. There was inevitably a great deal of interaction between these ways of looking at disease, since the lay population was the main market for medical science and DOCTORS relied pre-eminently on patients' accounts of their own sicknesses in divining causes and administering cures.

The two approaches also overlapped in the official field of developing PUBLIC HEALTH policies. Here theories of disease were very closely tied to questions about state medical practice. In fact, the official medical knowledge was a great simplification of professional medical writings. In the case of epidemic disease, scholarly complexity was reduced to the question of the contagiousness of disease since the necessity of quarantine was the major practical issue which needed to be resolved. We may say that the mid nineteenth century was the high point of anticontagionist understandings of disease and that bacteriology encouraged a more nuanced approach to this issue. In the case of smallpox, official medicine had to cope with the advisability of VACCINATION and revaccination and the effectiveness of this preventive measure was accepted much earlier in many other European countries than in Britain. With many diseases, the claim that the predisposing causes were partly moral in character led to attempts to regulate the lives of the poor to make them less of a threat to the rich; these sorts of considerations dominated debates about the causes of VENEREAL DISEASE.

See also MEDICINE.

Roy Porter and Dorothy Porter, *In Sickness and in Health: The British Experience 1650–1850* (London, 1988).
Harry Wain, *A History of Preventive Medicine* (Springfield Ill., 1970).

GERRY KEARNS

disestablishment The separation of church and state had been upheld in the abstract by certain divines in NONCONFORMITY during the eighteenth century, but first impinged on practical politics in Britain as a result of debate surrounding the constitutional revolution of 1828–32. In particular, CATHOLIC EMANCIPATION provoked Presbyterian Dissenters in Scotland into arguing that disestablishment was the only ultimate safeguard against Catholic power-seeking. During the 1830s the Scottish Dissenters, called Voluntaries because they advocated free choice in religion, resisted appeals by the Church of Scotland for state assistance with church extension. In 1833–4 there was an upsurge of calls for disestablishment by Nonconformists in England, prompted by the sense that they would remain second-class citizens so long as Anglicanism was the national religion. They were also inspired by the example of the United States, where in 1833 the last relic of establishment was swept away in Massachusetts. Increasingly, Nonconformists imbibed Scottish Voluntaryism, contending that any public support for religion was contrary to the Christian gospel. In 1844 Edward Miall (1809–81), the editor of the weekly *Nonconformist*, founded the British Anti-State Church Association to campaign for disestablishment. From 1853, when it changed its name to the Liberation Society, the organization broadened its strategy to oppose other dissenting grievances such as church rates. Drawing on the enthusiasm of Congregational and Baptist ministers, it gained its greatest support in the small towns of the south and east of England. During the 1860s and 1870s it enjoyed a higher income than the Liberal Party.

In Ireland the existence of an established Anglican body, technically since 1801 the United Church of England and Ireland, constituted a standing grievance to the Roman Catholic majority of the population. W. E. GLADSTONE, originally a resolute defender of the established church in Ireland as well as England, eventually determined that, in order to conciliate the Catholics, disestablishment should be conceded. As Liberal leader he fought the 1868 general election on the issue and steered an Irish Disestablishment Bill through the Commons in the following year. Vehement opposition, spearheaded by the Church Institution created in 1859, was taken up by the Conservative majority in the House of Lords. Skilfully mustering Whig support, the Conservatives engineered a constitutional confrontation on the question before, in the end, a generous financial settlement was arranged for the Church of Ireland. Disestablishment took place in Ireland on 1 January 1871. Later in the year, hoping to benefit from the momentum of the issue, Miall proposed an English disestablishment motion, but drew little support. Although the question came to the fore during the 1885 general election, the disestablishment of the Church of England never gained the backing of most Liberal members of parliament, let alone the House of Commons.

In Scotland the United Presbyterians, the inheritors of the Dissenting tradition, continued to advocate the Voluntary principle in the later nineteenth century. The Free Church of Scotland, originally accepting establishmentarianism, believed that the abolition of patronage in 1874 gave an unfair advantage to the Church of Scotland and so a majority began to agitate for Scottish disestablishment. There was pressure for the issue to become Liberal policy, and eventually, in 1889, Gladstone declared in its favour. By 1895, however, the Free Church was turning to reunion discussions, and so its zeal for disestablishment cooled. Although the subject was the central question of Scottish politics for two decades, disestablishment was never to be carried in Scotland. In Wales the issue achieved even greater salience from the 1860s onwards. There Nonconformity claimed four-fifths of the church-goers, so that the Church of England, English-speaking and supported by the Anglicized gentry, seemed an 'alien church'. From the late 1880s the agitation for Welsh disestablishment was severed from the broader Liberation Society campaign and became the focus of national feeling in the principality. With the return of a Liberal government in 1892, debate quickened. The Church Defence Institution (as the Church Institution had become in 1871) rallied resistance, and the Conservatives showed the strength of their hostility by dividing the Commons against the first reading of the preliminary (but abortive) Welsh Church Suspensory Bill in 1893. In each of the following two sessions a Welsh Disestablishment Bill was considered by the Commons but failed for want of time. It was not until 1914 that Welsh disestablishment was to be carried and not until 1920 that it was enacted.

P. M. H. Bell, *Disestablishment in Ireland and Wales* (London, 1969).
W. H. Mackintosh, *Disestablishment and Liberation: The Movement for the Separation of the Anglican Church from State Control* (London, 1972).

D. W. BEBBINGTON

Disraeli, Benjamin first earl of Beaconsfield (*b* London, 21 December 1804; *d* London, 19 April 1881) British statesman, pre-eminent Conservative leader of the nineteenth century and Gladstone's great rival. Before entering parliament in 1837 he had a moderately successful literary career. He achieved political and literary prominence in the mid-1840s when he led the attack on Peel over repeal of the Corn Laws and with the publication of his best novels (*Tancred, Coningsby* and *Sybil*). Out of office until 1867 (apart from two short-lived governments), he seized the issue of PARLIAMENTARY REFORM to rehabilitate the Conservative party from its antireform reputation.

He became prime minister in 1868 and between 1874 and 1880, when his ministry was marked by major social reforms in housing, factory and trade-union law and by an aggressive foreign policy in South Africa and on the EASTERN QUESTION. He arranged the purchase of the Suez Canal for Britain in 1875.

Disraeli's political beliefs defy easy definition. Although he is conventionally regarded as an opportunist, it is more helpful to see him as a 'Tory democrat', who believed that the task of the Conservative Party was to revitalize the paternal connection between the lower and the landed classes. Thus his evocation of the monarchy and imperialism were designed to attach nationalism to the Conservative Party and his support for social reforms in the 1870s demonstrated that progress was no monopoly of Liberals. In these respects, Disraeli established the predominant themes of Conservative Party politics for the next hundred years (*see* TORYISM).

Robert Blake, *Disraeli* (London, 1966).
Richard Davis, *Disraeli* (Boston, 1976).

RICHARD PRICE

Dissenters *see* NONCONFORMITY.

divorce   As an institution, divorce took its modern form during the nineteenth century. The French Revolution provided the impetus for the first stage in the modern transformation of divorce. A very liberal divorce law implemented by the revolutionary regime in 1792 permitted divorce by mutual consent as well as divorce actions on numerous grounds including incompatibility. In a dramatic response, thousands of estranged couples took advantage of the opportunity to end their marriages. This radical experiment proved short-lived, and the French enacted a conservative revision of this statute under the CODE NAPOLEON (1804), eliminating divorce by mutual consent and reducing the number of grounds for divorce to three (adultery, cruelty, conviction of a serious crime). With the 1816 restoration of the monarchy, the French abolished divorce altogether. Although the expanding French Empire had spread these innovations throughout Europe, this influence too proved fleeting as divorce, tainted by the French association and incompatible with regional traditions, failed to take hold in areas such as Italy.

The middle of the century saw a more permanent change as statutes enacting secular divorce took effect in England in 1857, in Prussia in 1875 and in France in 1884. Despite some variation, these legal changes all took as a point of departure the concept of marital fault and sought to protect the innocent spouse from the transgressions of the guilty spouse. What constituted acceptable grounds for divorce varied, but adultery always served to justify divorce. Of other commonly accepted grounds for divorce, cruelty proved especially malleable, subject as it was to judicial interpretation. Spousal abuse met with less tolerance during the period and, in some jurisdictions, notably the United States, the concept of mental cruelty gained legal recognition.

The reform of divorce law exhibited a number of other general trends. First, secular courts took over the responsibility of regulating marriage and divorce from other institutions such as church courts and legislative bodies. In addition, statute law increasingly expressed principles of equity rather than religious doctrine. As a result, wives as well as husbands, and couples of modest means as well as the well-to-do, could avail themselves of divorce.

The rapid rate of increase in the number of divorcing couples as a consequence of these legal changes took on threatening dimensions to contemporaries. The number of divorces in France tripled between 1885 and 1910. The English divorce court, the most conservative in Europe, granted only 588 divorce petitions in 1910, but that represented a fivefold increase from 1867. In light of the trajectory of these trends, the pressure for enlightened reform of the law gave way to consternation at the apparent fragility of the marital bond, which produced a late-nineteenth-century reaction against divorce.

In the debate over divorce the United States became the pre-eminent example of the divorcing society. Although the patchwork of divorce statutes among the different states makes generalization difficult, the liberalizing trends in statute and decision could be seen in most regions, with New York and South Carolina standing out as restrictive exceptions. The ease with which couples could obtain divorce in some states, and the consequent increase in divorce, reached a greater magnitude here than other Western countries. In 1910 American courts granted 83,045 divorces, four times more than the total number of divorces in all the countries of Europe combined.

The issue of divorce was a natural concomitant to the nineteenth-century discussion of the family. Those who perceived the traditional family structure to be oppressive, such as the utopian socialists (*see* UTOPIAN SOCIALISM), looked to divorce as a necessary stage in the development of more egalitarian relationships between men and women. The actual implementation of divorce legislation owed little to this point of view, however. Rather, legislators sought to buttress the traditional family by permitting the innocent spouse to leave a marital relationship that did not conform to the standards of fidelity and civility expected of traditional family life. These standards actually became higher and more exacting during the nineteenth century as a consequence of the pervasive influence of the ideology of domesticity. At the end of the period, eugenic concerns expressed themselves in the arguments for insanity as a grounds for divorce. The increase in the number of divorces, however, appeared to contemporaries as an unintended and disturbing result of legal reform. This motivated a conservative reaction against divorce which in turn marked a hiatus in further liberalization of divorce laws until the middle of the twentieth century.

Roderick Phillips, *Putting Asunder: A History of Divorce in Western Society* (Cambridge, 1988).

GAIL SAVAGE

Dock Strike (1889) One of the most important strikes in British labour history, the Dock Strike of 1889 highlighted the dynamics of the NEW UNIONISM. Triggered by a dispute over PIECE-WORK payment, the strike initially involved only the unorganized ranks of the miserably paid and casually employed dock workers (*see* CASUAL LABOUR). It gained new momentum, however, when other sections of the normally segmented dockland workforce, including 'aristocratic' stevedores and lightermen, went out. By 22 August the dockland work stoppage was complete, with 100,000 men idle. The dockers demanded an increase in wages, an end to sweating and exploitative hiring practices. A notable feature of the strike was the vital assistance which the dockers' leader, Ben Tillett (1860–1943), received from socialist trade-union activists, including Tom Mann (1856–1941) and John Burns (1858–1943) of the Engineers' Union and Will Thorne of the Gas Workers' Union.

Facing fierce resistance from the employers, the strike committee distributed strike benefits and organized pickets to keep out blackleg labour. The most dramatic aspect of the strike was the daily processions of the dockers, thousands strong, through the streets of the City of London. Despite their severe hardships, the men carried out the processions in a peaceful and disciplined manner, securing considerable financial support from a sympathetic public. With the strike at its nadir, a huge grant from Australian trade-unionists saved the dockers from defeat. Pressurized by Cardinal MANNING, the recalcitrant employers finally agreed to negotiate and in mid-September granted the strikers' main demands, including the 'dockers' tanner'. The strike represented a great victory for the dockers, facilitating the formation of a large general union and dramatizing the larger trend of trade-union organization among the unskilled and semi-skilled (*see* GENERAL UNIONISM).

John Lovell, *Stevedores and Dockers: A Study of Trade Unionism in the Port of London 1870–1914* (London, 1969).

RICHARD J. SODERLUND

doctors   During the first half of the nineteenth century the stature and influence of doctors throughout most of Europe was shaped largely by the wider social changes identified with the French Revolution of 1789. Previously, the patient had been the dominant partner in the doctor–patient relationship, and possessed control over the treatment given. The system had largely been determined by patronage, with the patient selecting the physician on the basis of qualities not necessarily associated with medical proficiency: social status, elegance and integrity often held sway over technical skill. However, in the late eighteenth and early nineteenth centuries strong centralized control of health-care and welfare facilities, through the provision of a state system of hospitals, engendered the period now recognized as 'hospital' or 'clinical' medicine. A doctor's select coterie of affluent clientele was replaced by a mass of patients, mostly the poorer classes who could not afford private attendance. A constant stream of new patients sustained a stock of research material and literally provided bodies for autopsies in the medical schools. Thus the power relationship between patient and doctor was radically transformed. Through examination rather than observation, diagnosis rather then prognosis and the replacement of therapy with pathology, the sick person became a set of malfunctioning organs: less of a person and more of an object. The physician was now the dominant partner in the relationship. This imbalance was further exacerbated by the removal of medical knowledge and experimentation from the clinic into the laboratory, identifiable most obviously in Prussia from the middle decades of the century. Medicine became an applied science, characterized by a wide social distance between the patient and doctor. Two career structures developed under this system, which differentiated between the researcher and the practitioner. Because research tended to dominate laboratory resources, those working in this field became a professional and scientific elite to whom the state would readily turn for advice when allocating medical funding. This enabled the research community to promote their vested interests over other areas of medicine.

In Britain, however, the new institutional and interpersonal structures appearing on the Continent did not eradicate strict divisions within the profession itself. Though a gross over-simplification, the demarcation lines between physician (professional), surgeon (craftsman) and apothecary (tradesman) existed for much of the century and prevented medicine from wielding the wider social power it now enjoys. The Apothecaries Act of 1815 differentiated between general practitioners and mere druggists, but represented only a lukewarm attempt at regulation and licensing. The Medical Reform Act of 1858 did unite the profession under the General Medical Council, and although nominal tripartite divisions were maintained for the benefit of the surgeons and physicians, in practical terms they were now meaningless. It became illegal for those not on a register of all legal practitioners to represent themselves as general practitioners, although healing by non-registered doctors was not outlawed. The evolution of the European model that incorporated systematic clinical training, the close co-ordination of hospitals and medical schools, professional specialization and the influence of research on teaching and practice served to attract large numbers from the unregulated American medical profession. A variety of sectarian colleges specializing in homoeopathic, eclectic and botanic medicine proliferated in the United States, but the basic problem was that most medical practitioners had little or no formal preparation. As a result, between the years 1875 and 1914, approximately 15,000 American physicians studied abroad. They returned to lobby for an improved position for the American medical profession, but not until the formation of the National Confederation of State Examining and Licensing Boards in 1891 was a strengthened teaching programme promoted. At the turn of the century, standards were beginning to rise, the numbers in the medical profession were reduced and the public image and efficiency were consequently enhanced.

The medical profession, it has been argued, played a backstage role in the development of the public-health movement in the nineteenth century, since sanitary reform was preventive rather than curative, an agenda which placed civil engineers above doctors. However, practitioners did much to investigate the determinants of disease and were instrumental in informing debates over THEORIES OF DISEASE, and at the grass-roots level they were well placed to take up state-created positions in a new medical police.

See also MEDICINE, PUBLIC HEALTH.

N. D. Jewson, 'The Disappearance of the Sick-Man from Medical Cosmology, 1770–1870', *Sociology*, 10 (1976), 225–44.

GRAHAM MOONEY

domesticity   Industrialization and the increasing primacy of wage labour in the nineteenth century dictated the geographical separation of remunerated and household labour. This had the effect of defining a male public sphere as distinct from a female private sphere of the home which provided a sheltered place of emotional nurture and moral sustenance. The contemporary view of the essential differences between men and women served to explain and justify this division of labour by GENDER.

The defining features of domesticity as a way of life and as an ideology developed first among the MIDDLE CLASSES. Increasing prosperity allowed middle-class men to support their families without recourse to the earnings of their wives or daughters. This style of domestic life became increasingly idealized and normative, stimulating a lively market for advice books such as Sarah Stickney Ellis's (c.1800–72) *Women of England* (1838), Isabella BEETON's *Book of Household Management* (1861) and Catherine Beecher's (1800–78) *Treatise on Domestic Economy* (1858). The ideology of domesticity lent the middle class a measure of moral authority which augmented their increasing political power. The aristocratic elite found itself discredited by the moral laxness associated with its way of life. Working-class families contended with economic realities that often precluded conformity with this ideal, although respectable working-class families aspired to it where possible.

The logic of domesticity justified the exclusion of women from the workforce and the denial to women of political rights as unsuitable for their nature and for their proper role. The moral authority attributed to women also gave them pride in their domestic accomplishments. In addition, this stance could justify improved education for women to enable them to carry out their moral and maternal duties. The variety of positions derived from the ideology of domesticity underline the ubiquity, plasticity and power of the concept.

Leonore Davidoff and Catherine Hall, *Family Fortunes: Men and Women of the English Middle Class* (London, 1987).

Bonnie G. Smith, *Ladies of the Leisure Class: The Bourgeoises of Northern France in the Nineteenth Century* (Princeton, NJ, 1981).

GAIL SAVAGE

domestic servants   Domestic service should be seen as an important residual form of the institution of household service which was common in western Europe, and the areas of the world dominated by this region, from at least the early modern period up to the twentieth century. Under this institution young men and women lived and worked in the households of non-relatives for a period before they married and set up their own homes, this relationship being based on a formal contract of employment for a set length of time.

In predominantly rural economies this institution was mainly associated with agricultural work, that is servitude in husbandry. With the process of industrialization and urbanization from the eighteenth century onwards there was a concomitant dissociation of productive activities and the home. The latter came to be the sphere into which middle-class men could retire from the rigours of business life, and from which productive activities and men who were not family members were excluded. Servitude survived in an increasingly feminine form to provide personal services to the family. The life-cycle and migrant nature of earlier forms of servitude was preserved, however, the majority of domestic servants being young, unmarried women from the countryside. In the New World there was also a racial component, with poor African-American or native-American women forming a vital element of the servant population.

Domestic service so constituted was an institution of major economic and social importance. During the process of URBANIZATION and industrialization domestic service was one of the most important forms of paid employment for women. In France in 1866, for example, domestic servants comprised 29 per cent of all occupied women. Comparable figures can be quoted for the United States in the late nineteenth century. In England and Wales the decennial censuses of the mid-Victorian period showed well over a million women so employed, over 40 per cent of the female workforce. Similarly, in modern developing countries such as Peru domestic servants represented as much as a quarter of all working women. Service was thus seen as providing a means by which countrywomen were integrated both physically and socially into urban life. It was indeed suggested at the time that the skills learned in middle-class households enabled servants to make advantageous marriages.

More recently, historians have also argued that for the middle, and upper classes servants were a vital component of that 'paraphernalia of gentility' which marked them off from the rest of society. Freedom from household chores for women of these classes was seen as the prerequisite for the cultivation of those feminine domestic virtues which were assumed to be the basis of the high Victorian 'home' (*see* DOMESTICITY). Servants provided leisure, comfort and a barrier to the outside world. The extent to which the ability of middle-class families to dispose of the labour of other social groups in this manner represented a shift towards greater inequalities in the distribution of wealth has been little explored.

In this light, much emphasis has been given to the vast servant retinues of aristocratic and wealthy employers, where specialization of function led to the proliferation of types of servant and the establishment of strict social hierarchies 'below stairs'. In practice, however, service was a much more socially widespread phenomena, and a large number of servants worked alone in quite modest households. At one extreme, young women might work in the homes of farmers or shopkeepers, where some productive activities were still carried on, undertaking some retailing and agricultural tasks as well as waiting on the family. Minding the shop or helping in cheese-making alternated with cooking, cleaning and nursing children. Domestic service in this form shaded off imperceptibly into the vast world of charwomen and casual cleaners who supplemented or replaced the work of live-in servants in many homes. At the other extreme, one might find households employing the full panoply of butlers, chefs, cooks, housemaids, footmen, gardeners and so on, which were so lovingly described in the pages of such publications as Mrs BEETON's *Book of Household Management*. At the apogee of the servant-owning classes, the hundreds of servants in aristocratic mansions were communities in their own right which had important economic and social effects on the surrounding rural areas.

In many societies a stigma was attached to domestic service as a lowly occupation fit only for country bumpkins. In material terms, however, it was in most cases better remunerated than the sorts of work which women with few skills could expect to earn in the countryside. When one included free board and lodging, it was even comparable with some of the best-paid jobs for women in the Victorian cities. The aversion to service, especially among urban-born women, seems to have sprung more from the implied loss of freedom associated with servitude than from pecuniary considerations alone.

As industrial societies matured and became more urbanized, domestic service declined in importance, a process that was under way in Britain in the late nineteenth century. Various reasons, both in terms of supply and demand, have been put forward for this. On the demand side, it has been argued that rising middle-class expectations, unmatched by increasing real income, led to the squeezing out of expenditure on servants. Others see the rise of labour-saving gadgets as undermining the need for intrusive domestics. Such arguments, however, do not seem to square with contemporary perceptions of a problematic lack of suitable servants, the late-nineteenth- and early-twentieth-century 'servant problem'. Perhaps more attention should be paid to the supply-side arguments, in which new employments for women in offices and shops attracted urban women away from what was perceived as servile and degrading work. This in part might be seen as yet another wave of productive work leaving the household, as family shops were replaced by large-scale commercial outlets.

Edward Higgs, *Domestic Servants and Households in Rochdale, 1851–1871* (New York, 1986).

David M. Katzman, *Seven Days a Week: Women and Domestic Service in Industrialising America* (London, 1981).

Teresa McBride, *The Domestic Revolution* (London, 1976).

Daniel E. Sutherland, *Americans and their Servants: Domestic Service in the United States from 1800 to 1920* (London, 1981).

EDWARD HIGGS

Dost Mohammed (*b* Afghanistan, 1793; *d* Herat, 9 June 1863) Ruler of AFGHANISTAN (1826–39, 1842–63). He seized power in central Afghanistan in 1826, following it up with a successful foray into areas south of Afghanistan where he dealt a crushing defeat to the Sikhs at Jamrad in 1836. However, he was deposed by Shah Shuja (1780–1842), who was supported by an expeditionary force provided by the English East India Company. Dost Mohammed returned in 1842 at the invitation of the British who had reconsidered their policies as a result of the assassination of Shah Shuja and the disastrous consequences of the first Afghan War (1839–42). Loss of an entire army, heavy expenses and realization that control over Afghanistan was impossible led the British to withdraw, leaving the restored monarch to consolidate control. Having accepted the Tripartite Agreement of 1838 which acknowledged the loss of territory south of Afghanistan, Dost Mohammed was left to rule independently within Afghanistan.

N. D. Ahmed, *The Survival of Afghanistan* (Lahore, 1979).

ROBERT J. YOUNG

Douglass, Frederick (*b* Tuckahoe, Maryland, ? February 1817; *d* Washington, DC, 20 February 1895) Prominent African-American spokesperson. He escaped from slavery in 1838 and settled in New Bedford, Massachusetts. Recruited by the Massachusetts Anti-slavery Society in 1841, he became a powerful voice of ABOLITIONISM. A gifted speaker and an imposing presence, Douglass toured widely, gradually broadening his subject-matter from descriptions of his own experiences in bondage to criticism of the extension of slavery and the church's timidity on the issue. He added to his stature by publishing his widely read classic autobiography, *Narrative of the Life of Frederick Douglass*, in 1845. To earn money to buy his freedom he lectured in England and Ireland, and founded the antislavery weekly North Star (1847–64) when he returned. During the Civil War Douglass helped to organize two African-American regiments. Later he served as marshal of the District of Columbia and as US consul-general to Haiti (1889–91).

KEVIN MURPHY

drama　*see* THEATRE AND PERFORMING ARTS.

Dred Scott Case (1848–1857)　In 1834 Dred Scott (?1795–1858), an African-American slave, was taken by his owner to the free state of Illinois and from there to the Wisconsin Territory where the MISSOURI COMPROMISE had 'forever prohibited' slavery. Later Scott was brought back to Missouri, a slave state. When his owner died, Scott sued in Missouri state courts for his freedom, arguing that his residence in free territory (Illinois) made him free. The case was appealed to the supreme court, where Chief Justice Roger Taney (1777–1864) ruled that Scott was not a citizen and could not sue in a federal court, and further that the Missouri Compromise was unconstitutional, since it violated the fifth amendment of the constitution by depriving citizens of property without due process. The decision increased sectional tension by reinforcing northern fears of a 'slave power conspiracy' to dominate the national government.

KEVIN MURPHY

Dreikaiserbund　*see* THREE EMPERORS' LEAGUE.

Dreyfus, Alfred (*b* Mulhouse, 19 October 1859; *d* Paris, 12 July 1935)　French victim of ANTI-SEMITISM. He was an artillery captain serving on the general staff when the French counter-espionage service discovered a list of documents in the German embassy which suggested that someone was handing over secret artillery information to the Germans. Suspicion fell on Dreyfus because he was a Jew and because of his military expertise. Tried in secret, he was sentenced to Devil's Island in 1894. His brother and influential friends secured evidence that another officer was the spy and began a campaign to have him exonerated (1840–1902) which included the publication of Zola's Famous letter *J'accuse*. The country divided into 'Dreyfusards', who believed a grave injustice had been done to an innocent man, and 'anti-Dreyfusards', who believed that the honour of the army must be protected at all costs. The Dreyfusard compaign was ineffective, however, until Major H. J. Henry (1846–98) admitted he had faked a document to make Dreyfus appear guilty. Henry then killed himself.

None the less, a military court in Rennes found Dreyfus guilty 'with extenuating circumstances', but granted him an amnesty. Not until 1906 did a civilian appeals court finally reverse the verdict. Dreyfus served in the First World War and died in obscurity. Many Dreyfusards considered the 'Affair' to be the finest moment in their lives.

J.-D. Denis, *The Affair: The Case of Alfred Dreyfus* (New York, 1986).

DONALD SUTHERLAND

drugs Narcotic drugs became a prominent feature of nineteenth-century life. While opium had been used for medicinal purposes for hundreds of years in China and India, it had been a relatively minor part of Western medicine. However, in nineteenth-century Europe and North America, opium assumed an important role both in the pharmacopoeia of orthodox medicine and as an ingredient in patent medicines and in over-the-counter chemists' remedies. Opium was particularly popular in the form of laudanum – tincture of opium – which was taken orally, and was effective as an analgesic, a febrifuge and a specific for gastro-intestinal distress. Both in Britain and North America opium was regularly given to children as a 'quietener', and was occasionally used as an intoxicant. Because of its popularity and its high toxicity, it figured prominently in both suicides and accidental poisonings.

When Alexander Wood (1817–84) developed the hypodermic syringe in 1858, it became possible to administer narcotic drugs much more efficiently through subcutaneous injection. Physicians often prescribed morphine, the alkaloid of opium and ten times as powerful, for relief of pain, with little appreciation of its addictive effects. From the 1860s to the 1880s, hundreds of thousands of patients, often elderly and female, became morphine addicts.

During the nineteenth century a number of people began to use narcotic drugs for recreational purposes. Chinese smokers discovered the pleasures of the opium pipe due to the large-scale importation of the drug by the English East India Company. By the 1830s an estimated 4 per cent of the population of China regularly smoked opium (*see* OPIUM TRADE). From China the habit of opium-smoking migrated to the West, where it was adopted most notably by certain artists and writers. But in Europe and North America, most recreational drug-users preferred to get high through sniffing or injecting alkaloid drugs such as cocaine, morphine and, later, heroin. By the end of the nineteenth century recreational drug use persisted among socially marginal groups and had become stigmatized as deviant behaviour.

Terry M. Parssinen, *Secret Passions, Secret Remedies: Narcotic Drugs in British Society, 1820–1920* (Philadelphia, 1983).

TERRY PARSSINEN

Druse A religious minority of the Ottoman Empire, the Druse were concentrated in the province of Syria (modern Syria, Lebanon and Israel). Although deriving from Shi'ite roots, they rejected fundamental Islamic doctrines, for which they substituted, among other things, belief in the incarnation of the Fatimid caliph al-Hakim (reigned 996–1021). Since theirs was a closed, initiatory faith and they were regarded as heretics by Muslims, they tended to live isolated from the dominant population. Over the centuries, however, the Druse were frequently a party to alliances with either Christians or Muslims.

In the nineteenth century, as the Ottoman grip on Syria slackened and Syria was drawn into the world economy, competition for its resources increased. The shifting coalitions of the early nineteenth century gave way to firmer alignments as the British increasingly supported Druse claims, the French backed the Maronites and the Ottomans tried to fend off both. Violent encounters between the Druse and Maronites in the 1840s culminated in 1858–60 in a conflict that engulfed Lebanon. Although the conflict had arisen from socio-economic issues within each community as well as between them, hostilities reduced to sectarianism as Druse forces attacked Maronite settlements. In Damascus local Christians were massacred by mobs of Druse, Bedouin and Damascene Muslims. The 1860 massacres led to separate administrative status, under Ottoman rule, for the largely Maronite enclave of Mount Lebanon. Druse unrest recurred in the 1870s and 1890s under pressure from the more prosperous Maronites, but they were unable to obtain similar protection.

Kemal S. Salibi, *The Modern History of Lebanon* (New York, 1965).

MADELINE C. ZILFI

Dual Alliance (7 October 1879) In the aftermath of the CONGRESS OF BERLIN, the Dual Alliance agreement was signed by Germany and Austria-Hungary on 7 October 1879. Russian nationalists blamed Bismarck for their 'diplomatic defeat' at the congress and recriminations on both sides had further exacerbated German-Russian relations. Ever fearful that Russia would lead an anti-German alliance, Bismarck decided to conclude an alliance with Austria. As the dominant partner in the alliance, Bismarck was able to restrain Austria's aggressive designs in the Balkans (which would have provoked Russia) and, at the same time, to assure Russia of Germany's peaceful intentions in that region. The major clauses of the Dual Alliance provided for military assistance if either power were attacked by Russia and neutrality if either were attacked by another power (such as France). The alliance, originally concluded for five years, was renewed regularly and lasted until 1918.

O. Pflanze, *Bismarck and the Development of Germany*, vol. 2 (Princeton, NJ, 1990).

GEORGE O. KENT

duelling The word 'duel', from the archaic Latin *duellum* (war), was used in medieval times to refer to judicial combats and was in the early modern period reinterpreted to mean conflict between two men over affairs of honour. The new duelling was formulated and elaborated in sixteenth-century Italy, then quickly taken up in France, whose soldiers saw regular campaigns in Italy, and from there by stages it spread over Europe. The practice was often frowned on, but more readily tolerated as it gradually took on a refined and elitist character. An elaborate etiquette was upheld by 'seconds' who had ceased to take part in the fray alongside their principals. Duelling was most prevalent among the officer corps in European countries where aristocratic values were under pressure from an encroaching democratization.

One of the more infamous pistol duels occurred in the United States where, in 1804, the vice-president, Aaron Burr (1756–1836), shot and mortally wounded Alexander Hamilton (1757–1804), one of the founding fathers of the republic. Britain's foreign secretary George Canning had an encounter in 1809 on Putney Heath with the war minister Castlereagh. Canning was wounded at the second shot and both resigned. The outspoken Irish leader Daniel O'Connell fatally wounded Captain D'Esterre in a duel in 1815, and in the summer of the same year was challenged by Robert Peel, chief secretary for Ireland, to a duel abroad, which police were in time to prevent. In 1829 the 60-year-old duke of Wellington, then British premier, fought a duel with the earl of Winchilsea (1791–1858) over the duke's conversion to Catholic emancipation, but both men fired wide.

Duelling lingered on in Britain down to the middle of the nineteenth century, boredom and daily frictions making it a common occurrence in overseas garrisons. This male custom persisted on the Continent until the slaughter of the First World War made the shedding of blood over petty private quarrels superfluous.

Victor Kiernan, *The Duel in European History: Honour and the Reign of Aristocracy* (Oxford, 1988).

JOHN SPRINGHALL

Duruy, Jean Victor (*b* Paris, 11 September 1811; *d* Paris, 25 November 1894) French historian and minister. While history professor at the Collège Henri IV in Paris, he published numerous books and articles on Roman history. Seconded as an official to the ministry of education, he was named minister in 1863, despite his well-known opposition to Napoleon III and much to his astonishment. He presided over a huge expansion of the school system, the creation of adult classes and scholarly libraries, the improvement of teacher-training, special training-schools for those destined to a non-academic or official career, the spread of education for girls, and the creation of research institutes at the University of Paris. With the fall of the empire in 1870, he resumed his historical writing on the Roman Empire and published an influential general history of France.

S. Horvath-Peterson, *Victor Duruy and French Education: Liberal Reform in the Second Empire* (Baton Rouge, La., 1984).

DONALD SUTHERLAND

E

---◆◆---

Eastern Question   The central issues underlying the Eastern Question, one of the leading issues of international relations in the nineteenth century, were control of the Dardanelles (*see* STRAITS QUESTION) and territorial competition in the Balkans. Both were brought to the fore by the domestic as well as military decline of the Ottoman Empire from the sixteenth century onwards. The continuing struggle among the powers to weaken and replace the empire was increasingly attended by the rising nationalism of the Greeks and southern Slavs, their desire for independence from Turkish rule and religious strife between Christians and Muslims living in the region.

The Eastern Question first became a major issue under Catherine the Great (1729–96), when Russia was able to force the Turks in the Treaty of Kutchuk Kainarji (1774) to cede the northern shore of the Black Sea to Russia and to grant Russia the right to intervene on behalf of the Christians living in the Ottoman Empire. From this time forward, the Balkan Slavs had looked to Russia as their liberator, and the Russian government not only encouraged this but manœuvered to reinstate the patriarch of the Orthodox Church in Constantinople. Russian economic expansion had also led to a large increase in foreign trade, and these goods had to pass through the Dardanelles, which made the security of the Straits essential to the economic well-being of Russia.

Throughout the nineteenth century diplomatic crises, revolts and wars testified to the inability of the powers to devise a lasting settlement to the Eastern Question. These included the revolts on the Peleponnese, in Wallachia and in Moldavia in 1821; the war of 1828–9 between Russia and Turkey; the Egyptian crisis of 1832–3; the CRIMEAN WAR of 1853–6; the revolts in Bosnia-Hercegovina, Serbia and Montenegro in 1875–6; the Russo-Turkish war of 1877–8; the various crises over Bulgaria, Bosnia and Hercegovina between 1878 and 1908 and, finally, the two Balkan wars of 1912–13. It was only after the First World War, the defeat of the Ottoman Empire and the Treaty of Lausanne (1923) that the Eastern Question finally ceased to be a factor in European politics.

M. S. Anderson, *The Eastern Question, 1774–1923* (New York, 1966).

GEORGE O. KENT

East India Company, English *see* GOVERNMENT OF INDIA ACT.

Eddy, Mary Baker (*b* Bow, New Hampshire, 16 July 1821; *d* Concord, New Hampshire, 3 December 1910) American founder of the Christian Science Church. She had long suffered from complex health problems when she sought treatment from a faith healer who was popular throughout New England. His successful restoration of her mental equilibrium inspired her to formulate what she called Christian Science, which held that disease was caused by the mind alone. In 1875 she published a textbook, *Science and Health*, and in 1879 she formed the Church of Christ, Scientist, in Boston. Widely popular, she sent out 'healers' who carried her message throughout the country and to Europe. By 1910 her adherents numbered over 100,000 and her estate was worth over $2 million. She administered church affairs from retirement in Concord, New Hampshire until her death. Eddy's was among the most notable of numerous sects springing up in the United States in the late nineteenth century.

KEVIN MURPHY

Edison, Thomas Alva (*b* Milan, Ohio, 11 February 1847; *d* West Orange, New Jersey, 27 October 1931) The most prolific electrical inventor in history. Raised in modest circumstances, the scantily educated Edison became a travelling telegraph operator at 14. His early twenties were spent in New York City, where he attracted attention from capitalists for improvements in equipment that printed stock prices and telegraph circuits. With the money he thus earned, he built a laboratory in Menlo Park, New Jersey in 1876, and proceeded to turn out astonishing inventions: the phonograph (1877), the carbon telephone transmitter (1878), the incandescent electric light (1879) and the generators, conductors and regulators that became the basis for electrical light and power systems. In 1886 he constructed a new laboratory at West Orange, New Jersey, pioneered the organized pursuit of invention and contributed to such technologies as motion pictures, radiography, storage batteries and sound-recording.

ROBERT FRIEDEL

education National education systems in Europe, in so far as they existed at the end of the eighteenth century, owed their foundation and support mainly to the church. Roman Catholics, through their elementary schools, secondary schools and universities, aimed to perpetuate their governing elite. Protestants aimed to provide elementary education for all, with secondary and university education for male students able to profit from them. For girls, opportunities opened up in the early Renaissance period had disappeared; even at the elementary level the educational facilities available to them were poor.

Industrial revolutions transformed education throughout the world. In Great Britain the labour needs of the first industrial society stimulated interest in the education of children, the future workforce. At New Lanark, Robert OWEN experimented with the education of 3- to 12-year-olds; his permanent contribution proved to be the idea of the infant school, publicized by Samuel Wilderspin (c.1792–1866) through the London Infant School Society (1824). In Germany, Friedrich Froebel (1782–1852) began a longer-lasting movement with the kindergarten, a psychological training of little children through play and occupation.

State intervention, often resisted by the church, was to be the main feature of nineteenth-century education. Austria, with the General Schools Regulations of 1774, placed primary education under state control, followed by Prussia in 1794. Revolutionary France, in 1795, laid down that there should be a primary school in every canton. Industrialization made the state's role appear indispensable. Even Belgium, which had broken away from the United Netherlands in 1830 on the very issue of centrally directed education legislation found itself, by the 1840s, obliged to introduce it for economic reasons.

In securing compulsory elementary education, Germany was preeminent. Saxony introduced legislation in 1769; Prussia, having in theory adopted compulsion under Frederick the Great's (1712–86) General Regulations of 1763, bent itself to the task of establishing it following the defeat at Jena in 1806. By the time the British Cross Commission investigated compulsion in 1886 it had been adopted (in theory) in Austria, Bavaria, Denmark, France, Hungary, Italy, Japan, Spain, Sweden, Switzerland, the United Kingdom and Württemberg, though in the United States it had still not been adopted in seventeen states. By now elementary education was free throughout western Europe except in Austrian Silesia, Bohemia, Hungary, Moravia, Saxony, Spain and Portugal; Great Britain passed a free-education act five years later. In North America it was free in all thirty-seven states of the United States and in Nova Scotia, Prince Edward Island, New Brunswick, Ontario and British Columbia. Education was also free in New Zealand and Queensland, Australia.

Elementary education for all eventually involved the training of teachers. In the early nineteenth century the monitorial method of instructing classes, popularized by Andrew Bell (1753–1832) and Joseph Lancaster (1778–1838) won support for its cheapness and apparent effectiveness in dealing with large numbers of pupils. But Johann Heinrich Pestalozzi (1746–1827), who had inaugurated a system of training at Yverdon, Switzerland, between 1805 and 1825, set a pattern which was to be adopted in neighbouring countries. Prussia, establishing 'normal schools' under its Law of 1819, laid down that the principal aim of such schools was 'to form men, sound both in body and mind, and to imbue the pupils with the sentiment of religion, and with that zeal and love for the duties of a schoolmaster which is so closely allied with religion'. In France *écoles normales* for the training of male and female elementary-school teachers were set up in each *département* from 1833. The first American 'normal school', based on the Prussian model, was set up at Lexington in 1839, half its costs being met by a local manufacturer. In England, where the stereotype of a teacher was that of a person inefficient, illiterate and good for nothing, teacher-training was introduced in the 1840s for both men and women. Evidence assembled by the Newcastle Commission (1858) confirmed its value.

Despite efforts to establish institutions with modern and scientific curricula in England and Scotland in the eighteenth century, post-elementary schools at the beginning of the nineteenth century tended to be classically based. These schools found keen defenders. In France Fourcroy's (1755–1809) Law of 1802, establishing secondary schools as a local-government responsibility, laid out a new curriculum based on French, Geography, History and Mathematics as well as Latin, but in 1809 further legislation restored the preponderance of the classics. In Prussia Wilhelm von Humboldt (1763–1835) laid the foundations of a national system of humanistic education in 1809–10 and introduced into the 'gymnasium' (a term deployed from 1812) the cult of Latin and Greek. Responding to public demand for a secondary school offering technical instruction, the Prussian government recognized the *Realschule* (originally a practically based secondary school founded by Johann Hecker (1707–68) in Berlin in 1747) in 1819, but, reacting to the abusive epithet *Nutzlichheitskramschule* (utilitarian crammer school), its curricula yielded to the gymnasium model as the century progressed. In England new modern schools emerged in the post-Waterloo (1815) period but the fashion set by Thomas Arnold (1795–1842) at Rugby for boarding-schools with a revived classical curriculum proved overwhelmingly attractive for parents. Only in Switzerland was a modern secondary school, the *Industrieschule*, taken up unreservedly.

Later in the century compulsory elementary education provided incentives for growing numbers of poor but able boys to develop their talents; in the United States the Kalamazoo (Michigan) case of 1874, establishing that secondary education constituted part of the common school system and could be paid for by public taxation, provided a precedent that, as the Bryce Commission (1894–5) discovered, was being acted on in Austria, Belgium, France, Germany, Norway, Sweden and Switzerland. Training for secondary schoolmasters was by no means as widely taken up as it was for their elementary counterparts. In England a university degree was, for most of the nineteenth century, taken to be a teaching qualification; in Prussia, by contrast, rules were laid down in 1831 for a postgraduate course consisting either of a probationary year, under instruction, in a school or of attendance for three years at a pedagogical seminary.

By the mid nineteenth century leaders in the movement to reform and extend girls' education had become active. In England Frances Mary Buss (1827–94) and Dorothea Beale (1831–1906) both headmistresses, the former of a day school, the latter of a boarding-school, successfully pressed the claims of girls to share in the historic endowments previously reserved for secondary boys' schools at the Schools Inquiry Commission of 1864–7. The subsequent Endowed Schools Act (1869) permitted many academic high schools for girls to be established. The Girls' Public Day School Company (later Trust), founded in 1872, used the device of a limited-liability company to establish girls' schools: by 1893 it controlled thirty-six. In France an Association for Girls' Secondary Courses was formed in 1867 and a law of 1880 provided secondary schools for girls, the first *lycée* opening in Montpellier in 1881. In Germany it was not until the 1890s that the state laid down a curriculum for higher girls' schools, and girls were prepared for the *Abitur*, the university entrance examination. The first public high school in the United States (Worcester, Massachusetts, 1824) began the process of making secondary education available to girls as well as boys.

Post-elementary or continuation schools for pupils unable to gain entry to secondary schools were already being set up towards the end of the eighteenth century in Bavaria, Prussia and Saxony. German states continued to lead the way. In Saxony, Sunday Schools were taken over to provide practice and additional instruction in reading, writing and arithmetic. Saxony's School Law of 1835 urged the addition of instruction in the practice of the constitution and in industrial innovation and sought to make attendance compulsory. The German Imperial Law of 1891 obliged employers to guarantee the attendance of all male workers under the age of 18; thereafter the ethos of continuation schools was established through the influence of Georg Kerschensteiner (1854–1932), the Bavarian inspector of schools, who believed that the schools should carry out the double task of promoting national prosperity and providing young people with a humanistic education. The Cross Commission reported in 1888 that although few continuation schools had been provided in English-speaking territories they were being created on the German model throughout western Europe, and that they were already compulsory in Austria, Hungary and parts of Switzerland.

The commission condemned the narrowness of the evening-school curriculum in Great Britain. These schools – known everywhere as 'night schools' – had first been set up by the government in 1851, but under the 1862 Revised Code they were restricted to elementary education. The commission's findings, however, led in the 1890s to grants being made available for a wider range of subjects and for students over the age of 21. This led to a sixfold increase in attendances by 1902; as late as 1898, however, over half the students were taking the 'three Rs', showing that help was still needed. Indeed, all industrialized countries had to cope with the problem of undereducated artisans in the late nineteenth century. Although in many parts of Europe, notably Sweden, Finland and Great Britain, the majority of the population could probably read by 1800, mass writing literacy was not achieved until about 1900.

Britain's provision of technical education lagged well behind that of its European and American competitors. The Samuelson Commission (1881–4), set up to investigate the situation, found superior technical education in France, Germany, Belgium, Switzerland, Austria and the United States. Its extremely wide-ranging reports provided an excellent picture of current technical education in the European and North American continents. Features of the European systems included evening courses linked to local industries, including both theoretical and practical subjects (as in the Belgian *Ecoles Industrielles*); half-time and full-time study (in the Prussian Bochum mining-school); and evening and Sunday schools financed by central and local government (in Saxony). In the early 1880s the only institution in England which could match German and Belgian facilities was the Oldham School of Science and Art. The Technical Instruction Act of 1889 was merely permissive; nevertheless, it provided the impetus for new, locally supported technical institutions and classes, often using the premises of former mechanics' institutes.

Apart from evening schools and technical education, the nineteenth century saw the founding and development of numerous adult-education institutions in Europe and the United States. In the latter the lyceums were notable in the first half of the century; in Great Britain the Adult School Movement, providing literacy teaching for men and women, developed from a school in Bristol in 1812, and MECHANICS' INSTITUTES arrived at a higher academic level. From the 1850s Working Men's Colleges, based on principles of CHRISTIAN SOCIALISM and on the belief in the importance of liberal, as opposed to technical, education for the working man, spread out from London. In both Britain and the

United States University Extension began to take university education to a wider public. In Britain its formal roots were in lectures given in 1867 by a young Cambridge don, James Stuart (1843–1913), to organizations of middle-class women and working men. In 1873 Cambridge set up a syndicate for local lectures followed by London (1876) and Oxford (1878). From the mid-1880s the United States deployed the same model of university lectures given off-campus. Their initial success faded; in England, while extension lectures were of great importance to the higher education of women and to the development of new UNIVERSITIES, they generally failed to reach working men.

Organized correspondence education also began in the 1880s; in the United States a 'correspondence university' was established in 1883, and in 1892 the University of Chicago opened a correspondence department, soon copied by other universities. In Europe the Netherlands was one of several countries where correspondence education developed significantly in the 1890s. Much adult education and learning in the nineteenth century also took place in informal groups, popular movements and voluntary organizations, linked to and inspired by the political, social, scientific and technological changes of the period.

Royal Commission on Technical Instruction (Samuelson), *Second Report* (London, 1884).

Royal Commission on the Elementary Education Acts (Cross), *Final Report* (London, 1888).

Royal Commission on Secondary Education (Bryce), *Report*, vol. 5 (London, 1895).

UNESCO, *World Survey of Education, vol. 2: Primary Education* (Paris, 1958); vol. 3: *Secondary Education* (Paris, 1961).

ROBIN BETTS AND SYLVIA HARROP

Egypt Like most of the Arabic-speaking Middle East, Egypt began the nineteenth century as a province of the Ottoman Empire. Although Ottoman sovereignty lasted until the First World War, the country's real rulers between 1807 and 1882 were members of the dynasty established by MUHAMMAD ALI, the Ottoman viceroy credited with setting Egypt on the path of modernization and national independence. When Muhammad Ali came to power in the aftermath of the Napoleonic expedition, Egypt was a neglected land rich in grain but even richer in promise. To consolidate his position, he reorganized the military, and land and tax systems, until he had achieved the kind of control that the Ottomans had only dreamed of. He constructed factories, irrigation systems, roads, canals and schools and expanded cash-crop production. In the 1830s his powerful army was twice prevented from overtaking the Ottoman Empire by the intervention of Europe. Egypt none the less became autonomous and its governorship, later the office of khedive, hereditary in Muhammad Ali's line. His son Sa'id Pasha

(1822–63) and grandson ISMAIL PASHA undertook further projects, including the Suez Canal, opened in 1869.

By 1881 Egypt was badly in debt and its economy disordered. When URABI PASHA's revolt threatened to overturn the regime, Britain invaded in 1882 and effectively ruled until after the First World War. The British made major contributions in the field of public health, administration and public works, but their racial arrogance and colonization through local and imported minorities helped to focus the nationalist sentiments that Urabi's revolt had ignited.

Arthur Goldschmidt Jr, *Modern Egypt: The Formation of a Nation-State* (Boulder, Colo., 1988).

MADELINE C. ZILFI

eight-hour day   The demand for a legislated eight-hour working day was a common theme of most labour movements in the late nineteenth century. It had first been raised in Britain (where it drew on the legend of King Alfred's division of the day into three parts of eight hours) in 1833 by the followers of Robert Owen as part of the hours agitation of that period (*see* OWENITES). In the 1860s it was included in the programme of the FIRST INTERNATIONAL; it was the major issue at the inaugural congress of the SECOND INTERNATIONAL in 1889; and the origins of MAY DAY lay in the proposal of the American Federation of Labor for simultaneous demonstrations in support of eight hours.

The emergence of the eight-hour-day issue during the 1880s in all industrialized countries reflected three major influences. First, the impact of the GREAT DEPRESSION (1873–96) which saw a general intensification of labour, increased unemployment and breaches in the restrictions on working hours that many skilled workers had secured in the late 1860s and early 1870s. Secondly, the emergence of socialist-influenced economic and political theories which argued that universal hour-restrictions would help eliminate economic fluctuations, stabilize wages, control the tendencies to overwork and increase economic efficiency through encouraging mechanization and technical change. These arguments were familiar to labour and had lain at the root of earlier efforts to control working hours, but through the writings of people like Sidney WEBB in Britain and George Gunton in the United States they now entered more fully into the discourse of parliamentary politics. The Parti Ouvrier Française of Jules Guesde began to introduce eight-hour-day bills in the French chamber in 1880. And, thirdly, the expansion of recreational opportunities in the late nineteenth century led to the demand for a sharper division between work and leisure time. In addition, as in early shorter-hours movements, it was argued that the quality of family life would improve under an eight-hour regime.

But in all industrialized countries organized labour was ambivalent about the demand for a legislated eight-hour day. The opposition rested on a variety of arguments. Craft workers were ideologically suspicious of state-sponsored interference in hours of work, believing that a reduction in hours should be secured by labour's own efforts. In Britain, for example, the TRADES UNION CONGRESS resisted attempts to support the eight-hour day until 1890. Some unskilled workers feared it would mean a reduction of wages. Other workers – like the British cotton unions – feared it would give the competitive advantage to textile industries in countries like India. And, indeed, it was recognized that a legislated eight-hour day could work only on an international scale. In France syndicalists opposed it because of its statist implications.

After an initial spurt of international co-operation and enthusiasm, however, the movement collapsed under the weight of employer opposition and the economic downturn of the 1890s. Although the British and French governments introduced the eight-hour day in their establishments in the 1890s, the initiative returned to individual unions like the British blast-furnacemen and the engineers whose strikes in the 1890s over the eight-hour day were unsuccessful. Some individual trades, like the British coal-miners, secured the eight-hour working day in the early 1900s, but it did not become a recognized international standard for the work day until after the First World War, and even then its spread was interrupted by the depression of the interwar years.

Gary Cross, *A Quest for Time: The Reduction of Work in Britain and France 1840–1940* (Berkeley, Calif., 1989).

RICHARD PRICE

Eisenach Congress (7–9 August 1869)   In June 1863 the League of German Workers' Associations (VDAV) was formed in reaction to the ALL-GERMAN WORKERS' ASSOCIATION (ADAV). With the Prussian victory over Austria in 1866 and the formation of the North German Confederation, the VDAV came to oppose Prussian domination. Elections on a wide franchise for the Reichstag of the North German Confederation, as well as increasing strike activity and trade-unionism, encouraged the VDAV to stress its class character. This led to the Eisenach Congress. Two hundred and sixty-three delegates representing some 155,000 workers, drawn from both the VDAV and dissidents from the ADAV, founded the Social Democratic Workers' Party (SDAP). Its programme stressed the principle of a 'free people's state' above all else. Its socio-economic principles were derived from Marx and the International Working Men's Association (IWMA) (*see* FIRST INTERNATIONAL). The SDAP affiliated to the IWMA. Under its 'immediate demands' the SDAP called for parliamentary democracy, referenda to propose laws and censure government and the replacement of standing armies with people's militias. Reforms in education, censorship, rights of organization and taxation were demanded. Apart from labour-protection measures, the only specifically 'class' demand was state funding for producer co-operatives. The party also formed an umbrella organization for trade unions.

The SDAP established its own newspaper, *Der Volksstaat*. The annual congress was made the sovereign body. The running of affairs was given to an elected, collective leadership under the supervision of a control commission, contrasting with the autocratic ADAV. The SDAP struggled through the Franco-Prussian war, and then economic downturn and political harassment. In the Reichstag elections of 1871 and 1874 it received 39,000 and 171,000 votes respectively. In 1875 it merged with the ADAV.

Helga Grebing, *The History of the German Labour Movement* (Leamington Spa, 1985).
Gary Steenson, *'Not One Man! Not One Penny!' German Social Democracy, 1863–1914* (Pittsburgh, 1981).

JOHN BREUILLY

electoral systems During the nineteenth century the trend towards a wider franchise and the development of governments dependent on elected assemblies focused attention increasingly on methods of election. It became clear that the type of system adopted could exert a powerful influence over the substance of policy and the legitimacy of the regime. In the early and mid nineteenth century Western countries largely used territorial constituencies returning one or two members in which those elected were required to win either a simple or relative majority (known as a 'plurality' in the United States), or an absolute majority of votes. However, the results of these systems proved to be so unfair between parties and so erratic in operation that discussion about alternatives steadily developed. In the 1850s methods of achieving proportional results were advocated simultaneously by Thomas Hare (1806–91) in Britain and Professor Carl Andrae in Denmark. Their ideas were subsequently refined, notably by the Belgian Victor D'Hondt whose system came to be widely applied in twentieth-century Europe. By 1900 a few states had already abandoned majority systems for proportional representation (PR), and most did so shortly before the First World War or in 1919–20. In the context of this long-term trend, Britain, the United States and France stood out as eccentric in their attachment to non-proportional systems.

Single-member constituencies were used in Germany, Italy, Denmark, Sweden and, in effect, the United States and the Netherlands where elections were staggered. Multimember seats with the block vote (that is two votes per elector in a two-member seat) prevailed in Britain, Belgium, Norway, Switzerland and Italy (from 1882). Since the block vote exaggerated the unrepresentativeness of the system, it was modified by the limited vote in Britain during 1867–84 where in some three-member constituencies electors cast only two votes; this was expected to give representation to minorities. The simple majority was sufficient in Britain, the United States, Denmark and Sweden. But several states perceived the inadequacies of simple majorities early on and required the winning candidate to obtain an absolute majority at a second ballot (Belgium, the Netherlands, Italy, Germany) or even a third (Switzerland). France distinguished itself by changing its system nine times between 1817 and 1889. These included repeated switches from single- to multimember seats and between the simple majority and the second-ballot system. Such blatant attempts at electoral engineering designed to maintain governments in office frequently failed.

Disillusionment with existing electoral systems is attributable to several factors. Experience showed that even the second ballot failed to prevent the unfair and erratic results of majority voting. In societies recently emerging from authoritarian to parliamentary regimes it was regarded as desirable to avoid the destabilizing effects of highly biased or exaggerated representation. The greater continuity and stability of proportional systems was also seen as helpful in promoting the development of better-organized and more cohesive political parties. Countries characterized by serious cultural divisions saw PR as having a moderating and unifying effect. In some states the move towards PR was part of a compromise over franchise reform in that conservatives saw it as a safeguard against socialism. The German Social Democrats committed themselves to PR at the Erfurt Conference in 1891. In Denmark the single-transferable-vote system of PR first began to be used in 1855 for federal council elections, and was extended to the upper chamber, though not the lower, in 1866 to help protect the landowners. In Belgium a campaign for PR was under way by the 1860s, fuelled by the prolonged dominance of Catholic interests. The rise of the socialist party and the start of universal suffrage in 1894 aroused Catholic fears that the socialists might win a majority on a minority of the votes. In 1899 Belgium introduced a party-list system using the D'Hondt Rule. The criticism that PR led to the multiplication of parties has virtually no basis in fact. In Denmark, Belgium, the Netherlands, Sweden, Austria, Switzerland, Italy, France and Germany a multiparty system preceded the introduction of PR by many years and was in no sense caused by it.

Both Britain and the United States remained committed to simple-majority systems of election. To some extent, this was because discussion about the fairness of representation concentrated on the territorial aspect. Americans thought it important to represent each regional community and its attached interests rather than parties. British reformers were concerned to correct the over-representation of the south at the expense of industrial centres. Not until the 1880s was PR considered. But the party leaders saw it as strengthening the role of rebels and undermining party discipline. The adoption of single-member seats in 1885 was believed to be fairer to minorities. In particular, the Conservative Party expected to benefit from the change, as indeed it did.

See also FRANCHISE REFORM, PARLIAMENTARY REFORM.

Andrew M. Carstairs, *A Short History of Electoral Systems in Western Europe* (London, 1980).

MARTIN PUGH

electricity and electrical industry   Electrical phenomena had attracted the attention of European thinkers since the seventeenth century, but the use of electricity, first as an aid to communication, then for lighting and finally as a means of transmitting power, did not occur until the nineteenth century. It marked a significant change in the relationship between science and ENGINEERING. Hitherto, engineers had been mainly responsible for the major industrial advances, using only rule of thumb and often working in isolation: now it was the turn of the scientists, working in many countries, whose theories and laboratories were to launch the electrical industry and a new branch of engineering.

Static-electricity generators were devised in the eighteenth century, but it was only with Volta's (1745–1827) invention of the Voltaic pile in 1800 that a steady source of current became available. More delicate and complicated experiments were now possible, including work on electromagnetism. The earliest attempts to develop an electrical communication system grew directly out of research in electromagnetic theory. The French scientist André Marie AMPÈRE relied on the Danish scientist Hans Oersted's (1777–1851) discovery of the relationship between electricity and magnetism to suggest the possibility of electrical communication by means of a needle moved by the opening and closing of a circuit. Germany was involved in later development work, but the first commercial system was established in the Britain in 1837 by Charles Wheatstone (1802–75) and William Cooke (1806–79). Soon afterwards, Samuel B. Morse (1791–1872) developed his famous system of dots and dashes (the Morse code) between 1837 and 1835. In the United States printing telegraphs were introduced by Morse's rivals, while in Britain dial and automatic systems were developed. Later the telegraph was superseded by the telephone, which provided a revolutionary service: conversation at a distance. The principal innovation was the work of Alexander Graham BELL, who registered an American patent in 1876. (*See* TELEGRAPHY AND TELEPHONY.)

Meanwhile, by 1831 Michael FARADAY provided the basis for electricity generation by devising and developing systems of electromagnetic induction. But it was not until 1870 that the true ancestor of the modern dynamo appeared in Paris, the invention of the Belgian engineer Théophile Gramme (1826–1901). With improvements made jointly by the Swiss engineer Emil Burgin and Colonel R. B. Crompton (1845–1940), the Gramme machine was developed in England into the Crompton dynamo which, together with the somewhat similar generator developed by the brothers William (1823–83) and Werner (1816–92) Siemens, supplied current to most of the early installations in Britain.

The generation of electricity began to have an enormous impact on everyday life with the development of electric light. By the 1870s inventors had begun to tackle a problem that many experts regarded as insoluble: the subdividing of electric current and leading it into incandescent lamps. By 1878, however, the incandescent light bulb (using a carbon filament in an evacuated glass tube) had been invented by the American Thomas EDISON and the Englishman Joseph Swan (1828–1914). A significant event was the opening in 1882 of the central station at Pearl Street, New York, which launched commercial domestic lighting in America. Several installations also followed in London, which culminated in the lighting of the law courts – the largest installation of its kind in the world at the time of its completion in 1883. The demand for generators, meters, light bulbs and plugs saw the rise of the large electrical firms, such as Ferranti and the General Electric Company (GEC) in Britain, Westinghouse in America and Siemens-Halske in Germany (*see* SIEMENS).

A controllable supply of electricity also offered many commercial opportunities, not only within the industry, but also in such processes as silver-plating. The production of aluminium by an electrolytic process after the 1880s also highlighted the crucial role of electricity in triggering developments in other industries. It was followed by successful attmpts to melt steel, so launching an eventual competitor to the Siemens and Bessemer processes. Finally, the possibilities of electric traction were soon recognized, leading to the development of urban tramways and underground railways in the late nineteenth century.

Theoretically, electrical engineering may be said to have emerged in 1864 when the Scottish physicist and mathematician James Clerk Maxwell (1831–79) summarized the basic laws of electricity in mathematical form and predicted that radiation of electromagnetic energy would occur in a form that later became known as radio waves. By the last decade of the nineteenth century, Maxwell's theories and the work of Heinrich Hertz (1857–94) in Germany were the basis of experimental radio communications, which were a prelude to the foundation of the electronics industry of the twentieth century.

Brian Bowers, *A History of Electric Light and Power* (London, 1982).
P. Dunsheath, *A History of Electrical Engineering* (London, 1962).

GEOFFREY TWEEDALE

El Hadj Omar *see* 'UMAR IBN SA'ID TAL.

Emancipation Proclamation (1 January 1863) With the Emancipation Proclamation President Abraham LINCOLN freed those slaves still held in Confederate hands as of 1 January 1863. However, the proclamation failed to free any slaves in the border states (Maryland, Kentucky, Missouri, Delaware) or in areas already recaptured by Union troops (Louisiana, Tennessee, Virginia); basically, Lincoln freed those slaves outside of his power. He justified the proclamation as a military necessity, and hoped to use it to discourage European interference in the war. The ploy worked, because the radicals in the British parliament, led by John Bright, welcomed the proclamation and used their influence to stop Tory efforts to side with the south.

Lincoln issued the proclamation only after much thought. He hated slavery, but also shared the prejudices of most white Americans about AFRICAN-AMERICANS. Concerned that the impact of freeing nearly 4 million slaves, with few skills and no education might seriously disrupt American society, Lincoln favoured a gradual approach to emancipation. He hoped to establish a period of apprenticeship, lasting as long as twenty-five years, during which blacks might gain an education and more job skills. He also wanted to compensate slave-owners for their property, and favoured a scheme to return the freed slaves to Africa. His experiment with a compensation plan in Delaware, however, failed when slave-owners demanded too much money. To make matters worse for Lincoln, African-American leaders such as Frederick DOUGLASS angrily rejected the idea of colonization, insisting that American blacks were American citizens.

At the same time, Congress and the Union army took small steps against slavery. In 1861 Congress passed the first of two Confiscation Acts, providing for the confiscation of all slaves used by the Confederate military. In May 1861 General Benjamin Butler (1818–93), a Massachusetts politician and lawyer turned soldier, declared all slaves who came within his lines 'contrabands' of war, and refused to return them to their owners. If the south claimed to be out of the union, reasoned Butler, the FUGITIVE SLAVE ACT (1850) no longer applied. The following year, Congress also outlawed slavery in Washington, DC and in the federal territories. It also passed a second Confiscation Act which set up a legal mechanism to deprive southerners of their slaves. At the same time, radical Republican congressmen and senators who supported abolition, such as Charles Sumner (1811–74) of Massachusetts, kept up constant pressure on the president to act against slavery.

By the summer of 1862, realizing that compensated emancipation had little chance of passage, Lincoln decided to issue an emancipation proclamation. He produced the document in June, presenting it to his cabinet. Although the cabinet approved it, the secretary of state, William SEWARD, advised Lincoln to wait for a major Union victory in the east. Lincoln agreed because he believed that the proclamation might make the north look desperate, and waited until 22 September, after the Battle of Antietam (17 September) to issue the proclamation. The preliminary document offered the south one last chance to return to the union with slavery intact. If any state returned by 1 January 1863, it could keep its slaves, but after 1 January slaves in areas still in rebellion were free.

African-Americans in the north greeted the proclamation with great joy. Many individuals, black and white, questioned its real worth, however, insisting that it failed to go far enough. Lincoln himself feared that the proclamation might be overturned by the southern-dominated supreme court once the war ended. After his re-election in 1864, Lincoln and the Republican-dominated Congress, created the thirteenth amendment which finally abolished slavery. Sent to the states for ratification in early 1865, it passed enough states by December to become a part of the United States constitution.

In the south slaves received word of the proclamation through their underground network. Many left their masters to seek family members traded away, to find the Union army or simply see what freedom was really like. Other slaves agreed to stay with their former owners, but insisted on wages. They often refused to put up with white whims and tantrums any more. Ex-owners complained that their supposedly loyal 'people' seemed to forget their place, as ex-slaves talked back to them. Approximately 140,000 ex-slaves took advantage of the proclamation to volunteer for the Union army. Organized in separate black units with white officers, they demonstrated to doubting whites that they were fighters. They also served as powerful role models in the African-American community.

See also AMERICAN CIVIL WAR, FREEDMEN'S BUREAU, SLAVERY (UNITED STATES).

Mary Frances Berry, *Military Necessity and Civil Rights Policy: Black Citizenship and the Constitution, 1861–1868* (Port Washington, Wisc., 1977).
John Hope Franklin, *The Emancipation Proclamation, 1863* (Garden City, NJ, 1963).
Louis Gerteis, *From Contraband to Freedman: Federal Policy toward Southern Blacks, 1861–1865* (Westport, Conn., 1975).

ALICE E. REAGAN

Embargo Act (1807) Believing war to be a policy of last resort, President Thomas JEFFERSON and James Madison, his secretary of state, urged Congress to prohibit trade with Europe in response to British and French violations of American neutrality during the Napoleonic wars. British impressment of American sailors especially galled the United States. The *Essex* decision, British ORDERS IN COUNCIL, (*see also* CONTINENTAL SYSTEM), the Berlin Decree and finally, in 1807, the Chesapeake Affair aroused American anger, and in December 1807 Congress passed the Embargo Act. All American ships were prohibited from sailing for foreign ports. Because trade was so profitable, violations were common and enforcement lax. Although it hurt some British manufacturers, the embargo helped British shipping by removing American competition. In early 1809, with the economy in shambles (exports fell from $108 million in 1806 to $22 million in 1808), Congress repealed the Embargo Act and replaced it with the equally ineffective Nonintercourse Act.

JOHN MARTIN

Emerson, Ralph Waldo (*b* Boston, 25 May 1803; *d* Concord, Massachusetts, 27 April 1882)   American poet and essayist. He was one of the most important intellectual figures of his time, influencing a generation of American ante-bellum reformers. He briefly taught in a school and in 1829 became minister of the Second Unitarian Church in Boston. After resigning and travelling to Europe, he came into contact with English romanticism, transcendentalism and German idealism. On returning to the United States, he began a career as a lecturer, and his lyceum appearances drew large audiences. His essays of the 1830s, 'Nature', 'The American Scholar' and 'Divinity School Address', among others, are clues to his somewhat unsystematic philosophy. He was associated with the American transcendentalists and briefly edited their publication the *Dial*. Rejecting empiricism and arguing that intuition was the path to ultimate truth, Emerson encouraged individuals to look to themselves and to nature for knowledge and called for a distinctly American culture free of European influence.

KEVIN MURPHY

Emmet, Robert (*b* Dublin, 1778; *d* Dublin, 20 September 1803) United Irishman, committed to the establishment of a non-sectarian Irish republic. His education at Trinity College, Dublin and his career prospects were cut short by membership of the United Irish Society. He was in France during the 1798 rising and returning to Ireland in 1802, planned a rising to take Ireland out of the United Kingdom without French aid. Impressively bedecked in a white and green general's uniform, he was supremely ready for the rising, which attracted no widespread support, as he led a hundred undisciplined followers to attack Dublin Castle on 23 July 1803. The concluding words of his speech from the dock secured him a prominent place in Irish nationalist mythology: 'When my country takes its place among the nations of the earth, then, and not till then, let my epitaph be written.' He was hanged.

Raymond Postgate, *Robert Emmet* (London, 1931).

PATRICK BUCKLAND

empire   *see* IMPERIALISM.

Employer's Liability Act (1880)   The first legislative measure in Britain which granted workmen or their families the right to compensation from employers for injuries suffered at work came in 1880 with the Employers' Liability Act. Since the 1837 case of *Priestley* v. *Fowler*, workplace-liability law had been governed, much to the employers' advantage, by the doctrine of common employment. That doctrine freed an employer from liability for accidents if the injury which an employee suffered was caused by a fellow employee, including managers and supervisors 'in common employment' with the injured party. The law thus effectively relieved employers of the obligation to provide safe work conditions and compelled trade unions to assume responsibility for injured members, an enormous financial burden which they could ill afford.

With broad trade-union backing, and especially strong support from miners and railway workers, Alexander McDonald (1821–81) introduced a bill to reform the law in 1876. The powerful railway companies succeeded in initially blocking reform. The bill's advocates resubmitted it, however, after an 1876 select committee on employers' liability recommended the abolition of the defence of common employment in certain cases. The Liberal government finally steered a compromise measure through parliament in 1880.

The act did indeed significantly narrow the defence of common employment. Nevertheless, from the trade-unionists' perspective, the law remained weak and unsatisfactory. The 1880 Act, for example, did not apply to entire categories of employment or kinds of accidents. Even more objectionable, the act allowed workmen to contract out, a procedure which led to the proliferation of employer-sponsored mutual-insurance schemes, further reducing ties between unions and their members. Eventually, however, the omissions were redressed by statutes of 1897 and 1906 which extended coverage to several million workers.

See also MASTER AND SERVANT LAW.

David G. Hanes, *The First British Workmen's Compensation Act, 1897* (New Haven, Conn., 1968).

RICHARD J. SODERLUND

Ems Dispatch The French ambassador BENEDETTI met WILLIAM I, king of Prussia, on 13 July 1870 at Bad Ems, a German spa town, to discuss the candidature of Prince Leopold von Hohenzollern-Sigmaringen for the Spanish throne, vacant since the revolution of 1868. Leopold, who belonged to a Catholic branch of the Prussian ruling-house, had been offered and had accepted the throne in June. William had supported his claim reluctantly, BISMARCK more enthusiastically. When the news became public, the beleaguered French government, supported by the other great powers, urged Spain to allow Leopold to withdraw, and he did so. At Bad Ems Benedetti asked William to confirm that the candidature had been withdrawn, which he did. William refused, however, to give the ambassador an assurance that the Hohenzollern candidature would never be renewed. The exchange was restrained and courteous, and William recorded it in a telegram which he then sent to Bismarck in Berlin, suggesting that the minister-president might publish the ambassador's second request if he considered it politic. (The demand for an assurance of non-renewal of the candidature might be construed as an attempt by France to humiliate Prussia.) Bismarck edited the telegram in a way which gave a distorted impression of the atmosphere of the interview: the effect of the shortened text was to suggest that there had been an exchange of insults between the ambassador and the king. He then released the amended text to the press. It created a furore in both Berlin and Paris, and was instrumental in preparing public opinion in both countries for the ensuing FRANCO-PRUSSIAN WAR.

TIMOTHY KIRK

enclosure The gathering together of the scattered strips and commons of open-field farming into compact holdings, or enclosure (by hedges, fences or walls), permitted greater farming efficiency. In England the process began in the late fifteenth century, but its pace varied considerably over time and between regions. Although at least three-fifths of the open-field acreage had been enclosed before the 1760s, the greatest single surge occurred between 1793 and 1815, coinciding with the leap in food prices during the wars against France. Even after 1815 some open-field parishes (mainly in the south Midlands) survived, but enclosure was effectively complete by mid-century.

Few issues in English history have been as controversial. Enclosure lay at the heart of England's agricultural (and thus general economic) achievement, while it epitomized the dilemmas of trading off social equity against economic growth. Open-field systems were not incapable of improved yields, as their critics (including many historians) have suggested. The gross gains in productivity brought by enclosure were arguably exaggerated and certainly distributed unevenly. Smallholders did not disappear at enclosure – indeed, in the late eighteenth century their number increased – but they were rewarded with holdings of marginal utility. Their considerable collective contribution to agricultural output declined, and they found it difficult to compete against technically progressive larger farmers. Even the latter, however, saw increasing amounts of their gross income swallowed up in rent to landlords. Enclosure also made large sections of rural society vulnerable to pauperization. Seasonal unemployment increased, and opportunities for women's and children's employment diminished. Landless labourers' customary access to grazing or firewood, central to augmenting low incomes, was extinguished. Against a background of declining real wages and stricter measures against POACHING, the loss was felt acutely.

See AGRICULTURE.

R. C. Allen, *Enclosure and the Yeoman* (Oxford, 1992).
J. D. Chambers and G. E. Mingay, *The Agricultural Revolution, 1750–1880* (London, 1966).
K. D. M. Snell, *Annals of the Labouring Poor* (Cambridge, 1985).

MALCOLM CHASE

energy At the beginning of the nineteenth century most interest in what would now be called energy was focused on the idea of radiant heat. Experiments by a variety of scientists, particularly William Hershel (1738–1822) and James Forbes (1809–68) had suggested that heat had properties similar to light and should therefore be explained by the same theories. Until about 1820, physicists accepted the particle theory of light, and so assumed that heat was formed of individual particles.

The first major advance in the study of energy was the recognition of heat as a form of energy instead of a substance that passed from one body to another. Among those chiefly responsible for this were Count Rumford (1750–1814) and Sir Humphry Davy (1778–1829). Rumford, while engaged in boring cannons for the Bavarian government, noted that the mechanical work in rotating the boring-tool was producing heat without limit. He concluded that this heat must be the result of the transmission of motion and that heat was a form of motion. Davy performed similar experiments involving rubbing blocks of ice together in a vacuum. The heat generated melted the ice, leading Davy to conclude that the heat was transferred to the ice in the form of vibrations of the corpuscles – molecules – that made up every body. This laid the foundation for the kinetic theory of heat, in which the heat of a body was associated with the energy of its molecules.

Sadi Carnot's (1796–1832) *Reflections on the Motive Power of Heat* (1824), the first detailed essay on the theory of heat, considered the theoretical limitations in producing motion from heat. Carnot's conclusion was that the motion of a steam engine was caused by the transportation of heat from a warm body to a cold body, thus re-establishing equilibrium. He believed that the quantity of heat was conserved, that it flowed like water from one object to another.

In 1849 James Joule (1818–89) determined that heat could be transformed into mechanical work by means of engines. He showed that the amount of heat produced by friction was proportional to the force expended and also discovered specific relationships between mechanical force – in terms of weights falling from a height – and heat. The study of forces led to the concept of work: when a force moved a body on which it acted, it did work on that object. Joule determined that, although human effort could be made easier by the use of machines, no machine could do more work than the energy that was put into it. He defined energy as the ability to do work and showed that in any transformation of heat into mechanical energy each unit of heat had a constant mechanical equivalent. Energy had different forms and could change from one form to another; however, in all these transformations, there was neither gain nor loss of energy. These paved the way for the discovery of the principle of conservation of energy, first stated by Helmholtz (1821–94) in 1847 as the conservation of 'force', but reformulated in terms of energy by Julius Robert von Mayer (1814–78), and known as the First Law of Thermodynamics.

Rudolf Clausius (1822–88) discovered the Second Law of Thermodynamics by reconciling the results of Carnot and Joule on the conservation of heat during work and the subsequent transfer of heat to a cooler body. He concentrated not on what was conserved, but on the transfer of heat to mechanical work. In 1854 Clausius realized that, although energy was always conserved, it became increasingly unavailable due to the increase of a property he called 'entropy', a measure of randomness in the system. Josiah Willard Gibbs (1839–1903) extended the understanding of thermodynamics to include energy and entropy in a generalized manner which could account for multicomponent systems, introducing the concepts of chemical potential and free energy. All forms of energy could be completely transformed into heat, while heat could only be converted into other forms of energy when it flowed to a cooler object. Scientists, therefore, became persuaded that energy was conserved and that heat, mechanical motion, electricity, magnetism and chemical bonding energies were all interconvertible.

Stephen Brush, *The Kind of Motion We Call Heat* (Amsterdam, 1976).
P. M. Harman, *Energy, Force, and Matter* (Cambridge, 1982).

STEVE AMANN

Engels, Friedrich (*b* Barmen, 28 November 1820; *d* London, 5 August 1895)   German socialist. The son of a wealthy cotton manufacturer, he co-edited with MARX *Rheinische Zeitung* (later *Neue Rheinische Zeitung*). He moved to Paris with Marx in 1843 at the beginning of a lifelong friendship. He collaborated with Marx on the COMMUNIST

MANIFESTO (1847), wrote *The Condition of the Working Class in England* (1845) and actively participated in the German Revolution of 1848. From 1849 he lived in England, first in Manchester as a partner in the family cotton firm and later in London, and continued to co-operate closely with Marx (whom he supported financially). He was to become the political mentor of the nascent German Social Democratic Party. His London house became the centre of socialist intellectual activities, which included the provision of good food and wine. His books, *The German Peasants War*, the *Anti-Dühring* and *The Origins of the Family, Private Property and the State*, were to instruct generations of Continental socialists. After Marx's death he edited the later volumes of *Capital* and other Marx manuscripts. He was more open-minded and worldly than his old friend, and was widely known as 'the general' for his intimate knowledge of military affairs.

See also MARXISM.

Gustav Mayer, *Friedrich Engels*, 2 vols (Frankfurt, 1975).

F. L. CARSTEN

engineering As an industry and a profession, engineering was a product of the process of industrialization which it did so much to stimulate. The demand for major constructional works such as canals, roads, bridges and dams in the eighteenth century created a continuing need for industries that could manufacture the desired equipment and for the men with the skill to design and build the latest technologies. Thus grew up the first branch of specialization, the 'civil' engineers, who founded their own engineering society – the world's first – in London in 1818.

As the leading industrial nation, Britain supplied the impetus to engineering developments in the early nineteenth century. The civil engineers – the great railway-, canal- and bridge-builders, such as Isambard Kingdom BRUNEL, Robert Stephenson (1803–59) and Joseph Locke (1805–60) – were the first to achieve prominence. But engineering soon began widening beyond the 'civils' to another increasingly important group, the mechanical engineers, who were concerned with engine-making and machine-making. The artisans, millwrights and instrument-makers of the late eighteenth century were the first such engineers, but after 1815 the provision of motive power and machinery for the textile, coal and iron industries, and the building of railway locomotives and marine engines, launched a major spurt of growth. The invention of the steam engine – based on the earlier achievements of Savery (*c*.1650–1715), Newcomen (1663–1729) and Watt (1736–1819) – was crucial, providing both the driving force for mechanization itself and also for machine-making. Developments were also linked to the growth in heavy iron (then later steel) founding and forging, which were themselves to be major employers of engineers.

In the early nineteenth century the enginering and machine-tool industry emerged in London and Manchester, with the latter soon becoming dominant. Firms such as Nasmyth's and Whitworth's became outstanding makers of mass-produced and standardized machine tools. Sir Joseph Whitworth (1803–87), for example, achieved fame for the accuracy of his machine tools and his standardization of screw threads. Later, in the north-east of England the massive growth of the coal and iron industries, together with railway- and early steamship-building, brought about a considerable development of heavy engineering. The firm of W. G. Armstrong of Elswick, founded in 1847, was perhaps the most famous. In that year, the growing importance of the profession was marked when the mechanical engineers founded their own institute in Birmingham.

Engineering had, it seemed, secured Britain's position as the 'workshop of the world' by the time the Great Exhibition was staged in 1851. Even the building, Joseph Paxton's (1801–65) Crystal Palace, was another wonder of Victorian engineering. But Britain's leadership did not go undisputed. The United States was already busy improving imported technologies: for example, it had already produced pioneers in high-pressure steam design such as Oliver Evans (1755–1819) and George Corliss (1817–88). The growth of American engineering before 1850 was almost as spectacular as that of the British, as its industrialists seized labour-saving technologies with alacrity. In a host of manufactures (such as clocks, guns, sewing-machines and woodworking tools) American engineers pushed ahead with the development of standardized mass-production techniques to supersede older handicraft methods. The so-called American System of Manufactures allowed the United States to challenge Britain in many sectors of the engineering trades in the final quarter of the nineteenth century.

By then engineering had come of age. It was now a world-wide calling, as other nations such as Germany, France and Japan entered the industrial arena. An engineer could find employment laying a transatlantic cable, designing a steamship, building an American railroad, a Victorian city sewer, a Bessemer steelworks, a colonial dam or constructing an electrical generator. No longer the preserve of the 'civils', it had become a highly professionalized career with a host of specialities. The CHEMICAL INDUSTRY (where the term 'chemical engineer' was in use by the end of the nineteenth century), IRON AND STEEL, telegraphy, electricity (which had its own institution in London after 1871) and mining all offered scope for the engineer (see TELEGRAPHY AND TELEPHONY, ELECTRICITY AND ELECTRICAL INDUSTRY). By the end of the nineteenth century there were inter alia also official bodies for marine, gas, municipal, heating and ventilating, water, sanitary, concrete and foundry engineers. As James Nasmyth remarked, these were 'glorious times for the Engineers'.

R. A. Buchanan, *The Engineers: A History of the Engineering Profession in Britain, 1750–1914* (London, 1989).

Richard S. Kirby et al., *Engineering in History* (New York, 1956).

A. E. Musson, 'The Engineering Industry', in Roy Church (ed.), *The Dynamics of Victorian Business: Problems and Perspectives to the 1870s* (London, 1980), pp. 87–106.

GEOFFREY TWEEDALE

Ethiopia The mythical heritage of Ethiopia dates back to the early first millennium BC, to the alleged union of the Hebrew king Solomon and the queen of Sheba whose mythical son, Menelik I, is said to have founded the Solomonic dynasty. Chronicles in the Amharic script, dating from the thirteenth to the twentieth century, allegedly record the re-emergence of this dynasty some time after the decline of the Christian state of Axum, an ancient Abyssinian monarchy about which we know little. (The alternative name for Ethiopia, 'Abyssinia', has fallen into desuetude since the end of the Second World War. Possibly a corruption of 'Habasha', it referred more specifically to the northern Axumite region of the Abyssinian, now the Ethiopian, Highlands. It was also a general term for the early Christian highlanders.)

After more than a century of relative isolation, internal disorder and dynastic decline, the emperor TEWODORUS II came to power in 1855. He laid the foundations for a modern nineteenth-century state by establishing internal unity, rationalizing the state administrative system and professionalizing its servants, including salaried, merit appointments. Pursuing some of these policies, MENELIK II embarked on what some historians call a 'secondary empire', or an internal African imperialism coinciding in some instances with the European SCRAMBLE FOR AFRICA. It was in the process of building this 'secondary empire' that Menelik defeated the Italians at the BATTLE OF ADOWA (1896).

B. MARIE PERINBAM

Eto Shinpei (*b* Saga, 1834; *d* Saga, 1874) Japanese samurai who participated in the MEIJI RESTORATION. A native of the domain of Hizen, he was an unusual member of the remarkable group of talented young men from samurai families, mainly in the domains of Choshu, Satsuma and Tosa, who engineered the downfall of the Tokugawa shogunate, after its failure to repel the attempts of the Western powers to open up Japan. He became a member of the Meiji government after the restoration, but broke with the ruling oligarchy in the 1870s. On return to his native domain, he served as a rallying-point for samurai discontented at their loss of feudal privileges, eventually leading them in an unsuccessful rebellion. He was executed in 1874.

JOHN DAVIES

eugenics The 'science' of the production of good human offspring, eugenics was an important component of public debate in early-twentieth-century Europe and North America, and informed policies on immigration and the sterilization of the unfit. The roots of this movement lay in late-nineteenth-century Britain and developed in Social Darwinist circles (*see* SOCIAL DARWINISM).

The term was coined in 1883 by Francis Galton (1822–1911), explorer, statistician, scientist of independent means and cousin of Charles Darwin. Galton argued that selective breeding would enable the human race to improve itself. Satisfied that it could be statistically demonstrated that intelligence ran in families, he railed against birth control among the middle classes since this would deprive Britain of its finest children and allow the national stock to be diluted by the fertile lower classes.

Karl Pearson (1857–1936) refined Galton's statistical approach and brought positivist, socialist and imperialist concerns to the new field of eugenics. Believing initially that the excessive reproduction of the unfit resulted from capitalism's need for cheap immigrant labour, Pearson moved on to blame the liberal state for so ameliorating the keen survival of the fittest that defectives were swamping the nation. Eugenics became the scientific basis for a sweeping attack on reformism and in particular the whole idea of environmentalism. Nature rather than nurture was in control since the truly important controls on intelligence and health were conveyed from generation to generation through heredity.

Daniel J. Kevles, *In the Name of Eugenics: Genetics and the Uses of Human Heredity* (New York, 1985).

GERRY KEARNS

Eugénie de Montijo (*b* Granada, 5 May 1826; *d* Madrid, 11 July 1920) Empress of France. From a family of Spanish grandees, she married NAPOLEON III in 1853 out of ambition and to satisfy his desire to marry into a distinguished family. She took a great interest in charity work, but her influence on the Mexican expedition, papal rights in Rome and the issues which brought about the Franco-Prussian War was disastrous. After the fall of the empire she fled to England with the help of her dentist. Following the death of her son at the hands of Zulus in South Africa (1879), she became a world traveller. During the First World War she established a hospital for the wounded at Farnborough, England. She was routinely seen riding her bicycle through the streets of Paris in her nineties.

N. Barker, *Distaff Diplomacy: The Empress Eugénie and the Foreign Policy of the Second Empire* (Austin, Tex., 1967).

DONALD SUTHERLAND

Eureka Stockade On 3 December 1854 at the Eureka lead in Ballarat, Australia, British forces and Victorian police attacked a flimsy barricade held by gold-diggers. About thirty diggers died, many were wounded and there were six military deaths. The diggers were protesting their lack of political rights, their inability to take up land, the brutal administration of the fields and the obligation to pay for a licence to seek gold. Charles Hotham's (1806–55) government was determined 'to crush the democratic agitation at one blow'. Melbourne juries, however, refused to convict thirteen diggers on a charge of high treason. Reform was rapidly pushed through with the granting of democratic rights, the abolition of the licence and unlocking of the land. Eureka was seen as the birthplace of Australian democracy, and the Southern Cross flag, under which the diggers swore to stand by each other, became a potent symbol. Eureka ranks with the Anzacs and Ned Kelly in Australian folklore.

See also GOLD RUSHES.

John Molony, *Eureka* (Melbourne, 1984).

JOHN MOLONY

Evangelicalism The prevailing form of popular Protestantism in Britain, Evangelicalism had four main characteristics. It held that conversion was the essential beginning of the Christian life, though Evangelicals differed among themselves about whether conversion must be sudden or might be gradual. It showed great respect for the Bible, which was treated as the supreme authority for matters of faith and conduct. While accepting the whole range of orthodox doctrines, it laid particular emphasis on the cross of Christ as the means by which sins were forgiven. And it was unusually activist, expecting adherents to be diligent in evangelism and good works. Believers with these characteristics were to be found in all the orthodox Protestant denominations. In the Church of England the number of Evangelical clergy rose from about 500 in 1800 to about 6,500 in 1853, though falling away thereafter. The peak of their influence came in the late 1850s when six bishops were appointed from their ranks and an Evangelical, J. B. Sumner (1780–1862), was archbishop of Canterbury. The chief party badge was support for the Church Missionary Society. Evangelicalism permeated the NONCONFORMITY of England and Wales even more thoroughly, dominating the Congregationalists and Baptists and constituting the whole of METHODISM. In Scotland many Evangelicals led by Thomas Chalmers (1780–1847) left the established church in the Disruption of 1843 to form the Free Church, but Evangelicalism soon regained the ascendancy in the Church of Scotland and shaped most of the other Protestant denominations. Evangelicals dominated Irish Protestantism, gained some influence in Continental Europe, proliferated in America and made an impact on many other lands through foreign missions.

In the early years of the century Evangelical thought, moulded by the Enlightenment, maintained an optimistic confidence in the ways of Providence. There was widespread acceptance of post-millennialism, the belief that the spread of the gospel would bring about a millennium of peace and plenty before the second advent of Christ, and, although most Evangelicals remained Calvinists, they taught a moderate version of their creed. There was a corresponding pragmatism, fostered among Anglicans by Charles Simeon (1759–1836) of Cambridge, that encouraged interdenominational co-operation. From the 1820s, however, there was a more pessimistic mood of which Edward Irving (1792–1834) was the herald. Irving decried pragmatism and publicized the pre-millennial doctrine that Christ would return in person before the millennium. The fresh teaching, associated with a novel form of biblical literalism, was spread by the (so-called Plymouth) Brethren and by authoritative figures in the Church of England, but had little influence over Nonconformity.

Meanwhile Evangelicals set about reforming the country. The campaign for the abolition of the slave trade was steered to success in 1807 by the CLAPHAM SECT led by William WILBERFORCE. In the middle decades of the century Lord SHAFTESBURY promoted Factory Acts, public-health measures and much else. A plethora of voluntary societies for evangelism and PHILANTHROPY, Protestant propaganda and sabbath observance, held their annual 'May Meetings' at the Exeter Hall in London. District visiting, inspired by Chalmers, gave rise to city missions. Bibles, tracts and other literature were distributed in abundance. Sunday schools, often staffed by working-class teachers, drew in most of the working-class population in childhood. The domestic ideal of the family gathered for prayer around the open Bible, though often associated with the middle classes, was upheld far more widely. Evangelicalism fostered the notion that women should remain in the home to care for children, but also encouraged them to active philanthropy. The movement did much to shape 'Victorian values'.

Although often undermined by the rivalry of church and chapel, interdenominational co-operation continued in the Evangelical Alliance founded in 1846, a revival movement between 1859 and the mid-1860s and support for the visiting American evangelists Moody (1837–99) and Sankey (1840–1908) in 1873–5. Thereafter there sprang up a number of organizations teaching holiness by faith, of which the SALVATION ARMY made the greatest impact on the working classes. More influential on the middle classes was the version of holiness taught at the annual Keswick Conventions from 1875. Although Darwinian evolution and higher criticism of the Bible were assimilated painlessly by many Evangelicals, neglect of central doctrines did provoke the eminent Baptist preacher C. H. Spurgeon (1834–92) into protest in the Downgrade Controversy of 1887–8. Some Anglicans opposed the spread of ritualism through the Church Association, founded in 1865, while Nonconformists increasingly adopted a social gospel in which TEM-PERANCE loomed large.

D. W. Bebbington, *Evangelicalism in Modern Britain: A History from the 1730s to the 1980s* (London, 1989).

D. W. BEBBINGTON

evolution The theory of evolution was developed during the nine-teenth century as a scientifically tenable explanation of the organic diversity and adaptedness observed in the world. It argued that organ-isms then living were the descendants of quite different ancestral forms, and that the changes which had taken place served to maintain or increase the adaptedness of a biological species to its environment. Charles DARWIN and Russell Wallace (1823–1913) arrived independ-ently at theories of evolution and published preliminary essays in 1858, although Darwin had priority, having completed a preliminary draft of an account in 1844; Darwin further elaborated his theory in *The Origin of Species* (1859).

The idea of evolution has ancient forerunners. In ancient Greece Parmenides thought that observed changes were only sensory illusions, Heraclitus believed that everything was in constant flux and Anaximander surmised that man had arisen from fish-like ancestors. In the eighteenth century Charles Linnaeus (1707–78) argued that all organisms, even inanimate objects, constituted a single uninterrupted 'great chain of being', beginning with minerals and rocks, and pro-gressing through increasingly complex forms to man at the top of the hierarchy.

Lamarck's (1744–1829) *Philosophie zoologique* (Philosophy of Zoology, 1809) postulated the first modern evolutionary view of the origin of organisms. He accepted a 'chain of being', adding that all life had a drive for perfection which led organisms to evolve to higher states on the chain, a mechanism called orthogenesis. He assumed that strengths and weaknesses acquired during the lifetime of an individual were heritable by its progeny. The strongest critic of Lamarck's theory, Georges Cuvier (1769–1832), used dissection to compare the struc-ture, size, position and relative importance of various parts of an animal to those in other animals and argued that there was not one chain but many phyla of organisms. William Wells, Edward Blyth (1810–73), Patrick Matthew (1871–1930) and Robert Chambers (1802–71) also anticipated various aspects of Darwinian evolution. Some of the scientists who influenced Darwin and paved the way for the acceptance of his ideas include William Whewell (1794–1866), William Buckland (1784–1856), Baden-Powell (1857–1941), John Herschel (1792–1871) and Charles Lyell (1797–1875) (*see* GEOLOGY), and Richard Owen (1804–92).

What distinguished Darwin's theory from its predecessors and convinced the scientific community was that the theory of natural selection explained how evolution occurred. Darwin realized that very gradual organic evolution based on minute changes could account for the diversity in nature; there was no need for sudden major changes to explain adaptation to a new climate. These 'successful' characteristics arose and were passed on to successive generations through inheritance. The reasoning can be summarized as follows: (1) all living species produce more offspring than can survive; (2) individuals of a species are not genetically identical, and some are more fit to survive and reproduce in certain environments than others; (3) the succeeding generations will contain relatively more progeny of the fitter ancestors than of the less fit, and the average fitness will therefore increase.

In *The Origin* Darwin only hinted that the human species had evolved from non-human ancestors. However, the point was made forcefully by Herbert Spencer, Thomas Huxley and Ernst Haeckel (1834–1919), laying the groundwork for Darwin's *The Descent of Man* (1871), where he introduced sexual selection as another mechanism for evolution. Individuals of the same species, particularly males, competed for mates; those who were most attractive were likely to have more progeny. Thus the hereditary traits of the winners in this competition were passed on to the offspring and were more prevalent in the next generation.

The works of Darwin raised an intellectual storm among churchmen, conservative thinkers (*see* SOCIAL DARWINISM) and some biologists. The familiar term 'survival of the fittest', commonly attributed to Darwin, was actually introduced by Herbert Spencer and frequently misapplied to social rather than zoological groups. By 1875 the British biological community as a whole was certainly in favour of the majority of Darwin's views, although natural selection was not seen as an adequate mechanism to explain the transmission of hereditary traits. The accepted view of heredity was that the blood of the parents mixed or fused to form the blood of the offspring, but if this were true sexual reproduction would rapidly erode and eventually destroy the genetic variability that was the driving force behind evolution. This difficulty was not removed until the rediscovery in 1900 of Gregor MENDEL's work (1867), which showed that heredity was transmitted by independent segregating hereditary units that became known as genes.

Michael Ruse, *The Darwinian Revolution* (Chicago, 1979).

STEVE AMANN

exploration By 1800 exploration of the oceans and coastlines of the globe had made great strides. Thanks to scientific navigators like Cook (1728–79), the eighteenth century had seen vast improvements in the mapping of the Pacific and Australasia. Detailed investigation by Europeans of the interiors of most continents was left to nineteenth-century explorers, stimulated by the prospects of trade, by missionary ambitions and (generally later) by colonial claims.

Africa provided the most spectacular expeditions. On successive journeys from the 1850s to the 1870s the Scottish missionary-explorer David LIVINGSTONE traced the Zambezi, discovered the Victoria Falls and investigated the complex drainage system between Lake Nyasa and Lake Tanganyika. But it was the quest for the source of the Nile that truly captured the imagination. Success finally fell to John Speke (1827–64), who, on an east African expedition with Richard Burton in 1857, travelled on alone, discovered Lake Victoria and convinced himself that this was the source of the Nile. Burton did not believe him, but Speke was able to convince the world after a further trip in 1862.

The exploration of Australia advanced at around the same time. In 1830 Charles Sturt (1795–1869) discovered the Darling River, and discredited the widely held theory that the centre of the continent was a vast inland sea. In 1840–1 Edward Eyre (1815–1901) traced the southern desert regions while Robert Burke (1820–61) and William Wills (1834–61) shortly after made the first traverse of the continent from south to north.

North America was crossed from east to west for the first time by the Americans Meriwether Lewis (1774–1809) and William Clark (1770–1838) in 1806 (*see* LEWIS AND CLARK EXPEDITION). Notable attempts were still being made to find a navigable north-west passage from the Atlantic to the Pacific. These resulted in failure but, nevertheless, stimulated polar exploration. The Norwegian Fridtjof Nansen (1861–1930) got close to the North Pole in 1893; the American Robert Peary (1856–1920), succeeded in 1909. The Norwegian Roald Amundsen (1872–1928) made it to the South Pole in 1911. By that time, global exploration had become part of the international imperial rivalry leading inexorably to the First World War.

J. N. Baker, *A History of Geographical Discovery and Exploration* (London, 1933).

ROY PORTER

explosives The importance of explosives lies in their use as the means of propelling projectiles from guns, in mines and quarries and in civil engineering. Gunpowder, also called black power, a finely ground mixture of saltpetre, sulphur and charcoal, was the only form of explosive generally available until the 1860s. Gun-cotton was demonstrated in England in the 1840s, but a factory established to manufacture it at Faversham was destroyed by an explosion. Manufacture on a large scale was revived in 1872 at Waltham Abbey where other British military propellants were developed, notably cordite, first manufactured in 1891.

The development of other new forms of explosives was due principally to Alfred Bernhard Nobel (1833–96), a Swede who spent most of his youth in Russia. From 1859 he experimented with nitroglycerine which had first been prepared by the Italian Ascanio Sobrero (1812–88) in 1846. Nitroglycerine was unstable, until 1866 when Nobel combined it with kieselguhr to make dynamite, a name which was applied to other explosives made from nitroglycerine. The previous year he had invented a detonator, using mercury fulminate, and in the 1870s and 1880s he developed blasting gelatine, and Ballistite, a 'smokeless powder' which could be used for military purposes. In the 1860s he founded a corporation which established factories in many countries, of which only that at Hurum, Norway is preserved in its original condition. The construction of the Hoosac Tunnel, Massachusetts, completed in 1876, was one of the first major civil-engineering projects in which explosives were extensively employed.

E. Bergengren, *Alfred Nobel: The Man and his Work*, trans. A. Blair (London, 1962).

Sir Gilbert T. Morgan and David Doig Pratt, *British Chemical Industry: Its Rise and Development* (London, 1938).

BARRIE TRINDER

F

Fabian Society A leading intellectual circle and powerful force for progressive reform and gradualist socialism in late-nineteenth-century Britain, the Fabian Society was founded in London in 1884. It took its name from the cautious Roman general who vanquished Hannibal with decisively timed attacks. The society established its own distinct ideological character only after Fabian founders were joined by a number of middle-class intellectuals, including Annie Besant (1847–1933), Sidney Olivier (1859–1943), Graham Wallas (1858–1932) and, most notably, George Bernard Shaw (1856–1950) and Sidney WEBB. Rejecting the revolutionary tenets of Marxism, the Fabians advocated a collectivist reconstruction of society consistent with the principles of the liberal-utilitarian tradition. They first outlined their comprehensive vision of evolutionary change in *Fabian Essays*, published in 1889. Citing recent developments like the extension of democracy and the progress of 'gas and water municipal socialism', Fabian writers contended that increased state intervention successfully redressed both the injustice and inefficiency of capitalism.

Viewing themselves as a new class of professional experts who were capable of devising solutions to the ills of modern society, the Fabians also adopted the tactics of permeation. Holding positions of responsibility in existing political parties and administrative bodies, they sought to educate the public and, more crucially, to influence the influential. From its London base the society implemented this elitist strategy, helping to forge a Radical–Liberal alliance in the London county council in the 1890s.

As a consequence of its middle-class composition and technocratic orientation, the society had a strained relationship with the larger labour movement. Yet, while it was a reluctant participant in the 1893 establishment of the INDEPENDENT LABOUR PARTY, the society was a primary sponsor of the Labour Representation Committee in 1900. Its greatest contribution, however, derived from its educational endeavours and broad intellectual influence.

Norman and Jeanne MacKenzie, *The Fabians* (New York, 1977).

RICHARD J. SODERLUND

factories The growth of factory production was associated with a stage in the industrialization process of advanced economies when large-scale water- or steam-powered technologies were adopted which necessitated centralized rather than dispersed production. Factories, however, pre-dated such innovations, notable examples being found in the early modern silk industries of western Europe and in urban WORKHOUSES in Britain, where the poor were put to work in a regulated fashion in large establishments. Factory production was advantageous where expensive raw materials were involved and/or where labour needed careful regulation to ensure the quality or quantity of goods produced. There is thus some debate about the causes of the initial growth and spread of factories between those who see technology as the determining factor and those who argue that the expansion of factory production was the outcome of the increasingly competitive market society of the eighteenth and nineteenth centuries which placed pressure on entrepreneurs to take greater control of the production process.

The gathering of workers under one roof enabled greater division and specialization of labour, closer supervision and greater intensity of effort. There was resistance to factory employment in the early nineteenth century as people associated factories with workhouses, slavery, loss of independence and loss of control over the pace and nature of work. Women and children (with little tradition of manufacturing for the market as independent agents and no tradition of organized resistance to employers) were thus important as early factory workers. Women remain a major component of the non-supervisory factory workforce. Marx stressed that the centralization of work (together with the homogenization of labour which technological progress inevitably brought) would lead to the growth of collective resistance and class consciousness. Factories, however, created new skill and supervisory hierarchies within the workforce almost as fast as older ones were destroyed. Divisions based on gender, age and 'skill', together with the promotion of company identity through welfare schemes and recreational provision, have been more prominent features of factory employment since the later nineteenth century than industrial conflict. Despite this, the symbol of the factory has had a central place in informing the socialist critique of capitalism.

Early on factory work involved long hours and arduous conditions in an unregulated environment. By the mid nineteenth century factory-reform movements in western Europe and government legislation worked to improve some of the worst excesses of factory regimes. Child labour was gradually excluded and the hours and conditions of female work were regulated. (*See* CHILD-LABOUR LAWS, FACTORY ACTS.)

Factories in the late nineteenth and twentieth centuries have been associated with the imposition of complex supervisory hierarchies and the rise of forms of scientific management designed to maximize the output of relatively homogeneous, mass-produced goods such as textiles, processed foods, domestic white goods and cars. The most notable set of ideas concerning the management of large subdivided and de-skilled workforces is associated with the American F. W. TAYLOR, whose scheme concentrated on the division of labour and on tight control of the labour process with no place for job security or paternalistic provision in the employment relationship (Taylorism). The introduction of conveyer-belt organization and technologies, and a stress on payment by results, associated notably with Henry Ford (1863–1947) (and subsequently referred to as Fordism), have been dominant features of factories in the twentieth century as have various other control and payment systems, notably the Bedaux system. Also prominent in a limited number of larger factory concerns have been complex schemes of paternalistic welfare and recreational provision, for example Lever Brothers and Cadbury's in Britain, and Krupps in Germany. In Japan factories took root in a different culture, where the family and nationalism were of crucial importance. Japanese factories have been closely associated with forms of corporate paternalism, identity and loyalty unknown in the West. Japanese factory-management systems involve job security, flexibility of job boundaries, small-group collective co-operation and internal labour markets.

R. P. Dore, *British Factory – Japanese Factory* (London, 1973).
C. R. Littler, *The Development of the Labour Process in Capitalist Societies* (London, 1982).
S. Marglin, 'What Do Bosses Do?', *Review of Radical Political Economy*, 6 (1974), 60–112.
S. Pollard, *The Genesis of Modern Management* (Harmondsworth, 1968).

PAT HUDSON

Factory Acts A body of legislation which regulated the working conditions in FACTORIES, particularly in the TEXTILE INDUSTRIES. The initial impetus for factory regulation came from late-eighteenth-century humanitarians disturbed by the harsh treatment of children in the spinning-mills of the cotton industry. Early factory reformers remained preoccupied with the cotton industry, in part because of its predominance in Britain's industrial expansion. However, representatives of the landed classes, threatened by industrialization, were also eager to challenge the misdeeds of manufacturers.

The earliest legislation, sponsored by the elder Sir Robert Peel (1750–1830), sought to limit children working in cotton mills to twelve hours per day. However, neither the Act of 1802, which concerned pauper apprentices, nor the 1819 Act, which pertained to 'free' child labour, included enforcement provisions. Subsequent statutes passed in 1825 and 1829 outlined additional restrictions on child labour in cotton mills. But these acts had limited impact since they, too, failed to stipulate enforcement procedures.

By 1830 the issue of factory reform emerged as a principal point of conflict between capital and labour. Driven by the agitation of the working-class Short Time Movement, particularly strong in the textile districts of the North, Earl GREY's Whig government took up the issue of factory reform in 1832. Evidence gathered by an 1832 select committee constituted a stark indictment of the factory system, detailing the prevalence of overwork, ill-health and deformity among factory children. The resulting piece of legislation, the landmark Factory Act of 1833, sought to address the aroused moral concerns of the nation, establishing the state's right to intervene in private economic matters to protect those who could not protect themselves. The act prohibited children under 9 from working in textile mills and restricted those aged 9 to 13 to eight hours of work per day. It also mandated modest schooling for mill children. Of even greater consequence, the act established an enforcement apparatus, with four appointed factory inspectors empowered to prosecute and fine offenders in their respective districts.

Although a striking innovation in social policy, the act was written in the language of conventional political economy, reflecting the powerful influence of organized manufacturers and Benthamite intellectuals like Chadwick (1801–90) (*see* UTILITARIANISM). Thwarting the Short Time Movement and its proposed Ten Hours Bill, the act rejected any regulation of adult labour as an infringement of economic freedom outside the proper function of the state. Moreover, since the act caused many manufacturers to adopt the relay system of employing children, it effectively lengthened the work-day of numerous adult mill-workers to fourteen or sixteen hours.

The factory movement never regained the intensity of 1830–3. Nevertheless, the champion of the Short Time Movement, Lord Ashley (the future earl of SHAFTESBURY), continued to push the passage of a Ten Hours Bill and other reform measures in parliament. An 1842 inquiry on the employment of children in mines documented shocking abuses and led to Ashley's 1842 Act prohibiting children under 10 and women from underground mine labour (*see* COAL MINES ACT). An Act of 1844 further shortened the work-day of mill children to a maximum of seven hours and strengthened the mandatory provision of schooling for 'half-timers'. More importantly, the act also placed women textile workers in the class of protected persons, restricting their hours of work to twelve a day and sixty-nine per week.

Factory reformers almost gained their ultimate objective with the Act of 1847, which established the ten-and-a-half-hour day (*see* TEN HOURS ACT). Sponsored by John Fielden (1784–1849), a radical manufacturer from Todmorden, the act represented a fundamental breach of political economy and softening of liberalism. This altered stance towards state intervention signalled a new willingness on the part of segments of the manufacturing middle class to compromise with the demands of the working class, an important step in the con-struction of social and political stability, Amending Acts of 1850 and 1853 closed the loopholes used by a minority of manufacturers to evade the intention of the 1847 Act.

The factory movement vanished after 1850 but parliament, still prodded by Shaftesbury, extended regulation beyond the textile industries. Two Acts of 1867, covering premises with more than fifty employees, as well as small shops, placed the children, young people and women employed in glassworks, metal-working, paper, pottery and lace manufacture, as well as other industries, under state regulation. The Tory-sponsored Act of 1874 finally achieved the ten-hour day for women and young persons, although men remained outside the protection of the law. Thereafter, the coming of the Great Depression (1873–96) forestalled the possibility of additional factory legislation.

See also CHILD-LABOUR LAWS, LABOUR LEGISLATION.

Derek Fraser, *The Evolution of the British Welfare State* (London, 1973).
Ursula Henriques, *Before the Welfare State* (London, 1979).

RICHARD J. SODERLUND

Faraday, Michael (*b* Newington, Surrey, 22 September 1791; *d* Hampton Court, Middlesex, 25 August 1867) English scientist, a key figure in the development of an understanding of electricity. Born into a very poor family, he was educated largely through his reading as a bookbinder's apprentice. Public lectures and discussion groups in London supplemented his reading and brought him to the Royal Institution. Faraday became Humphry Davy's (1778–1829) assistant in 1813, and spent the rest of his working life in the instititition. He became proficient in performing chemical and electrical experiments and, under the influence of his Nonconformist church and a faith in the interconnectedness of nature, he pursued important ideas about the relationships among electricity, magnetism, chemical action and light. His greatest contributions were the discovery of electromagnetic induction (the principle behind dynamos and transformers) in 1831, and his field theory developed in the 1840s. His popular lectures were instrumental in raising the status of science among the Victorian upper classes.

See also ELECTRICITY AND ELECTRICAL INDUSTRY.

ROBERT FRIEDEL

Fashoda Crisis (1898) During the latter part of the Scramble for Africa the Fashoda Crisis brought Britain and France close to war. The French were bitter at the continued British occupation of EGYPT (from 1882), believing that their role as the preponderant European influence in Egypt had been usurped. The prestige of both nations was at stake. While the French general J. B. Marchand (1863–1934) raced from Gabon to Fashoda on the White Nile in order to block the British occupation of Egypt, the British general KITCHENER hurried up the Nile to prevent Marchand from occupying the southern Sudan. They met at Fashoda, and it is said that Kitchener, in his forceful style, persuaded Marchand that the scramble was hardly worth the fight. As Europe held its breath in the belief that France and Britain were on the brink of war, as an apocryphal story goes, Marchand's messenger newly arrived at the Kitchener camp relayed the word that champagne on the house was available. Subsequent diplomatic negotiations resolved tense Anglo-French colonial (and other) disagreements, culminating eventually in the 1904 Anglo-French Entente.

David L. Lewis, *The Race to Fashoda* (New York, 1987).

B. MARIE PERINBAM

Fath Ali Shah (*b* 1771; *d* Isfahan, 20 October 1834) Second Qajar ruler of Persia. He succeeded to the throne in 1797 on the death of his uncle Aqa Mohammed, founder of the dynasty that ruled PERSIA until 1925. Although the Qajars represented tribal nomadism, Fath Ali's indulgence of urban elements, particularly Persia's hierarchy of Shi'ite mullahs, won support for his centralizing efforts. None the less, Persia remained prey to tribal factionalism and European incursions, both of which were aggravated by Fath Ali's inability to establish a modern standing army to replace his tribal soldiery. With Russia's acquisition of Georgia in 1813, Fath Ali turned increasingly to the British, with mixed results. Brief campaigns against the Ottomans and the Afghans in 1813 were disruptive and costly, but both were overshadowed by the disastrous war with Russia that erupted in 1826. Russia gained Erivan and Nakhichevan as well as extraterritorial rights for Russians resident in Iran. Fath Ali was succeeded by his grandson Mohammed Mirza (1742–97).

Peter Avery, *Modern Iran* (New York, 1967).

MADELINE C. ZILFI

Fawcett, Millicent Garrett (*b* Aldeburgh, 11 June 1847; *d* London, 5 August 1920)   Most prominent leader of the constitutional women's suffrage movement in England. The younger sister of Elizabeth Garrett ANDERSON, Millicent Garrett married Henry Fawcett (1833–84), Liberal member of parliament and Cambridge professor of political economy, in 1867. Her husband's constant companion and secretary because of his blindness, Fawcett soon gained public recognition in her own right as an expert in political economy. Widowed in 1884, she subsequently focused her energies on women's issues, especially suffrage. A lifelong Liberal, she epitomized the equal-rights tradition of feminism. She was president of the National Union of Women's Suffrage Societies from 1890 until 1918. Her skills as a political organizer during the long struggle for WOMEN'S SUFFRAGE made an incalculable contribution to the ultimate success of the movement.

Ray Strachey, *Millicent Garrett Fawcett* (London, 1931).

GAIL SAVAGE

Federalist Party   Organized during the first term of President George Washington (1732–99), the Federalist Party comprised men who favoured a strong federal union. Though the framers of the United States constitution had not foreseen the formation of political parties, the first party system grew out of the political divisions in Washington's cabinet, taking shape as the Federalists under Alexander Hamilton (1757–1804) and the Democratic-Republicans under Thomas JEFFERSON. Hamilton's conservative policies as Washington's secretary of the treasury were designed to encourage commercial and industrial expansion and to benefit well-established merchants and large landowners in the north. In foreign affairs, Federalists were pro-British. The antiparty bias of the age was clearly demonstrated by the Alien and Sedition Laws of 1798, designed to restrict Republican criticism of Federalist policies.

The party permanently lost control of the White House when Jefferson was elected president in 1800 but retained a base in New England from which it continued to function. The last Federalist candidate for president, Rufus King (1755–1827), received only thirty-four electoral votes in 1816, though as a minority party the Federalists continued to elect candidates to Congress until 1825.

During the War of 1812, elements of the Federalist Party gathered in Hartford, Connecticut to discuss measures to protect New England shipping interests and increase Federalist control in a period of Republican domination. The convention's resolutions nearly coincided with the Andrew JACKSON's victory at New Orleans, however, and the party's prestige was severely damaged.

The Federalist Party flourished before the decline of deferential politics

and the changes in state constitutions that removed property requirements for voting, and some historians have suggested that the Federalists and Democratic-Republicans were not true parties in that they
lacked the grass-roots organization that came to characterize the second party system of the Jacksonian era.

Shaw Livermore Jr, *The Twilight of Federalism: The Disintegration of the
Federalist Party, 1815–30* (Princeton, NJ, 1962).

KEVIN MURPHY

feminism   The term 'feminism' entered the English language from
France during the 1890s. Disagreement about its meaning attended the
earliest formulations of the concept. What properly defines feminism
or qualifies an individual as a feminist remains problematic even today. Keeping in mind the qualifying caveats implied by the cacophony
of divergent opinion, recognizably feminist individuals, ideas and organizations appear to exhibit two central characteristics. First, the
belief that women, although fully human, have suffered systematic
social, political and economic disadvantages appears to be an essential
component of a feminist perspective. Secondly, this point of view in
turn justifies and animates political activism to correct the inequities
of women's lives.

Such activism and the ideological apparatus to justify it developed
during the course of the nineteenth century, antedating the emergence
of feminist terminology by a hundred years. Mary Wollstonecraft's
(1759–97) *Vindication of the Rights of Woman* (1792) served as a
foundation document for modern feminism, employing the seventeenth-
and eighteenth-century rhetoric of political rights, which had been
explicitly restricted to men, on behalf of the claims of women.
Wollstonecraft's thinking provided the impetus for the equal rights or
individualist tradition of feminism that strove to obtain for women the
same political and legal rights enjoyed by men. Later elaborated by
John Stuart MILL and Harriet TAYLOR in *The Subjection of Women*
(1869), this became the prominent tradition in the Anglo-American
world, justifying the campaigns to secure for women the vote, equal
access to education and employment and protection for married wom-
en's property (*see* MARRIED WOMEN'S PROPERTY ACT). This stance denied
either the existence or the significance of any essential differences in
the nature of men and women and thereby challenged the ideology of
DOMESTICITY that characterized popular thinking about the position of
men and women in society.

The reverence for motherhood and the belief in the special moral
nature of women also provided inspiration for feminist ideas and
movements. Educational opportunity for women could be defended on
the grounds of the need to prepare women for motherhood, for example, and women's suffrage could be understood as necessary to raise

the moral standard of political life. This point of view, termed 'relational feminism', formed an important theme in all discussions of the woman question during the nineteenth century, and became the prominent form of feminism in Continental Europe. Ellen Key (1849–1926), a Swedish writer and activist, developed a systematic statement of this point of view, stressing the distinctiveness of women's essential nature, which she identified with the capacity for motherhood.

Another important variant of nineteenth-century feminism developed in conjunction with socialism. The position of women was a key component of the UTOPIAN SOCIALISM associated with Robert Owen and Charles Fourier, signifying the extent of progress achieved by civilization. The radical reordering of society envisioned by these thinkers required the development of a new type of family life that would free women from the tyranny of traditional family life. Accordingly, adherents of this point of view advocated DIVORCE, BIRTH CONTROL and sexual equality in order to achieve these ends. Flora TRISTAN in France and Anna Wheeler (1785–1848), who coauthored *Appeal of One-Half of the Human Race* (1825) with William Thompson (1785–1833), were examples of feminists inspired by this tradition.

The scientific socialism developed by Karl MARX and Friedrich ENGELS also recognized the oppression of women under capitalism and within the bourgeois family. August BEBEL, a leading German socialist, put the socialist case for feminism in *Woman and Socialism* (1879), and Engels elaborated a Marxist critique of the family in his *Origin of the Family, Private Property and the State* (1884). Nevertheless, socialist movements during the late nineteenth century subordinated questions of gender exploitation to questions of class exploitation. Friction between feminist organizations inspired by the equal-rights tradition, dominated by middle-class women not always sympathetic to issues relevant to working-class life and working-class organizations led by men such as Pierre-Joseph PROUDHON, imbued with patriarchal notions of the proper division of labour within the family, continually obstructed attempts to integrate the two movements. Socialist feminism thus had little influence on either socialist politics or feminist politics, although it did generate much important thinking on the woman question.

See also GENDER, PATRIARCHY, WOMEN'S SUFFRAGE.

Karen Offen, 'Defining Feminism: A Comparative Historical Approach', *Signs*, 14 (1988), 119–57.

Jane Rendall, *The Origins of Modern Feminism: Women in Britain, France, and the United States, 1780–1860* (Chicago, 1985).

GAIL SAVAGE

Fenians *see* IRISH REPUBLICAN BROTHERHOOD.

Ferdinand I (*b* Vienna, 26 February 1861; *d* Coburg, 10 September 1948) Prince and king of Bulgaria (1887–1918). Elected ruler of autonomous BULGARIA after Alexander BATTENBERG's abdication, he was dominated in his politics by his powerful prime minister, STAMBOLOV. Ferdinand managed to secure great-power recognition only after he dismissed Stambolov (1894) and re-established relations with Russia (1896). In his internal policy he encouraged domestic industry, railroad communications and strong personal rule. His active foreign policy was dominated by the Macedonian question. Using Austria-Hungary's annexation of Bosnia-Hercegovina, Ferdinand proclaimed Bulgaria's full independence on 5 October 1908 and was crowned king. The victorious first Balkan War (1912–13) between Bulgaria, Serbia, Greece and Montenegro against the Ottomans was followed by the defeat of Bulgaria in the second Balkan war (1913). Plunging a weary country into the First World War on the side of the central powers, Ferdinand abdicated after Bulgaria's military defeat.

Stephen Constant, *Foxy Ferdinand, Tsar of Bulgaria* (New York, 1980).

MARIA TODOROVA

Ferdinand VII (*b* El Escorial, 14 October 1784; *d* Madrid, 29 September 1833) King of Spain. The eldest son of Charles IV (1788–1808), he was bitterly at odds with his parents, and especially with the royal favourite GODOY. Placed on the throne by a military coup in March 1808, he was promptly deposed by the French, and spent the years 1808–14 in prison. Revered as *el rey deseado*, as soon as he was released, he presided over the termination of the liberal reforms of the PENINSULAR WAR by means of another military coup in May 1814. The army soon became dissatisfied with his rule, however, the result being the restitution of constitutionalism in the revolution of 1820. Three years later French intervention again crushed the liberals. Ferdinand was never the clerical obscurantist of legend, but rather followed a balanced internal policy which recalled the enlightened absolutism of the eighteenth century.

CHARLES ESDAILE

Ferry, Jules (*b* Saint Dié, 15 April 1832; *d* Paris, 17 March 1893) French politician. He was active in electoral and journalistic opposition to the empire, for which he was prosecuted several times. He was one of those proclaiming the fall of the Second Empire in September 1871, but his role in rationing the food supply of Paris during the siege made him greatly unpopular. He was minister of education from 1879 to 1884 and, although conservative on everything else (against amnesty for the Communards, freedom of association and divorce), he was a fierce anticlerical and broke the clerical monopoly on education. As prime minister in 1880, he prescribed physical and military training in schools, dissolved 300 teaching orders and later passed the law which bears his name, requiring free, primary and obligatory education for children. He did much to expand the French colonial empire.

F. Furet and J. Ozouf, *Reading and Writing: Literacy in France from Calvin to Jules Ferry* (Cambridge, 1982).

DONALD SUTHERLAND

Feuerbach, Ludwig Andreas (*b* Landshut, Bavaria, 28 July 1804; *d* Rechenberg, near Nuremberg, Bavaria, 13 September 1872)   Young Hegelian philosopher and critical theologian. Uncovering the contradictions in HEGEL's philosophy and recasting it on materialist foundations ('Thought is a product of being, not being of thought'), Feuerbach gave rise to the Left Hegelian movement, of which Marx and Engels were the outstanding representatives. He evolved a naturalistic humanism based on physiology and anthropology and on the view of philosophy as an attempt to grasp the world in its totality as a purely natural order. The physical and the psychological in man form an indissoluble whole, whence his dictum 'Man is what he eats'. In his most influential work, *Das Wesen des Christentums* (1841) – translated as *The Essence of Christianity* by George Eliot (1819–80) in 1854 – he proclaims that man, not God, is the 'true ens realissimum', and reduces theology and religion to a branch of anthropology. Religion is 'the dream of the human mind': alienated man, projecting his own thwarted but potentially infinite capacities on to an objectified deity, then proceeds to love and becomes enslaved by his own construction. Liberation consists in his coming to understand his self-deception and in taking possession of his fate in this, the only world there is, directing his love to his fellow humans, not to God. Apart from Feuerbach's impact on Marx and Engels, all subsequent serious criticism of religion is indebted to him, and he influenced thinkers as various as Freud (1856–1939), Durkheim (1858–1917), Heidegger (1889–1976), Sartre, (1905–80), Ernst Bloch (1885–1977) and Karl Barth (1886–1968).

S. Hook, *From Hegel to Marx* (New York, 1936).

ROGER HAUSHEER

Fichte, Johann Gottlieb (*b* Rammenau, Oberlausitz, 19 May 1762; *d* Berlin, 27 January 1814)   German Idealist philosopher. Developing beyond Kant (1724–1804), who had shown that the most general features constitutive of our world – space, time, causality – are the forms imposed on experience by our minds, Fichte, in his *Wissenschaftslehre* (Doctrine of Knowledge, 1794), asserted that everything, including even the material of experience itself, is created by the human subject: the absolute self-positing ego also posits the non-ego, or world of external objects, as a field for infinite ethical action. Fichte is thus the first thinker in the history of Western thought to state explicitly the primacy of will over intellect, of creation over discovery. At a stroke he sweeps aside the static objective structures erected by two millennia of rationalist Western metaphysics and replaces them with a vision of the cosmos as a vast arena for the open-ended, dynamic process of man's infinite striving towards an unattainable ideal goal, namely total self-realization. This contains the seed of all subsequent German philosophies of the will down to Schopenhauer (1788–1860), Nietzsche and beyond. Of especial contemporary interest was Fichte's *Reden an die deutsche Nation* (Speeches to the German Nation, 1814) which is the first explicit formulation of the doctrine of nationalism which spread through much of Europe in the second half of the nineteenth century and has become a world-wide phenomenon today. He is a clear precursor of voluntarist currents of thought like existentialism, and has been claimed as an intellectual ancestor alike by Marxists and by Fascists and National-Socialists.

ROGER HAUSHEER

Fillmore, Millard (*b* Locke, New York, 7 January 1800; *d* Buffalo, New York, 8 March 1874)   President of the United States (1850–3). He practised law in Buffalo and, as leader of the Whig Party, served two terms in the House of Representatives. With Henry CLAY's support he was elected vice president in 1848 on the Whig ticket. Fillmore became the thirteenth president of the United States when Zachary Taylor died on 9 July 1850. He signed the COMPROMISE OF 1850 and enforced its fugitive-slave provisions. He approved the Perry mission to Japan, opening that country to Western commerce. He steadfastly refused to take a position on the divisive issue of slavery and was not re-elected. Though he ran for president as a Know-Nothing candidate in 1856, his political career effectively ended when he left the presidency. Some historians have viewed him as typical of the 'blundering generation' whose lack of leadership and indecision led to the Civil War.

KEVIN MURPHY

Finland   *see* SCANDINAVIA.

First International (1864–1876)   The first attempt to organize international co-operation between European working-class organizations, the First International (also known as the International Working Men's Association) was founded in 1864 following the 1863 Polish national uprising. It included both British liberal trade-unionists and radical Continental socialists. It soon came under the influence of MARX and ENGELS who initially encouraged it to focus on issues such as the treatment of Fenian prisoners and international action against strikebreakers. By the late 1860s, however, it had become more openly socialist and in 1868 it adopted a programme of collectivization. The PARIS COMMUNE in 1871 intensified the debate between the supporters of BAKUNIN and those of Marx over whether the working class should seek political power or not. This struggle climaxed at the Hague Conference of 1872, at which Bakunin and his supporters were expelled. The headquarters were also moved from London to New York, which effectively ended its influence on European working-class movements.

Henryk Katz, *The Emancipation of Labor: A History of the First International* (Westport, Conn., 1992).

RICHARD PRICE

football The game of football was originally played with few rules, the only common factors being that a ball was involved and the games were invariably rough. The codification and organization of the game of association football took place largely within the British public schools during the 1850s and 1860s. In 1863 the Football Association, composed mainly of southern clubs, was formed. Increasing numbers of working men took up the game, forming clubs often attached to pubs, churches and chapels. By 1882 there was one set of accepted rules for the whole of Great Britain, and by the end of the century the game was the most popular spectator sport in the country. The money coming into the game was spent on building new grounds, often in central urban sites, and for paying an increasing number of professional players.

The game spread from Britain to various parts of the world. British sailors introduced football to the Brazilians in the 1870s and British businessmen to the Austrians at about the same time. By the end of the century most European countries were playing football as developed in Britain but there were few football leagues and virtually no professional players.

T. Mason, *Association Football and English Society 1863–1915* (Brighton, 1981).

J. M. GOLBY

Fouché, Joseph (*b* Le Pellerin, near Nantes, 21 May 1759; *d* Trieste, 25 December 1820) French Jacobin revolutionary and minister of police. He taught for the Oratorians before 1789 and became president of the Jacobin Club of Nantes during the Revolution. Elected to the National Convention, he distinguished himself by his dechristianization campaign in which he attempted to remove all symbols of Christianity, and by his ruthless repression in Lyons. He ran foul of Robespierre (having ordered the slogan 'Death is an Eternal Sleep' to be posted before all cemeteries) for his atheism and subsequently played a major role in ending the Terror. He lived by operating gambling casinos in Italy until he became Napoleon's minister of police on two occasions. He was particularly adept at rooting out royalist conspiracies. He played a major role in the domestic intrigues which brought the master down but was exiled as a regicide in 1816. The archdechristianizer is buried in the cathedral at Trieste.

H. Cole, *Fouché: The Unprincipled Patriot* (New York, 1971).

DONALD SUTHERLAND

Fourier, Charles (*b* Besançon, 7 April 1772; *d* Paris, 10 October 1837) French socialist theoretician. His fortune was utterly ruined during the French Revolution, but while rebuilding it in Lyons he undertook a study of the theory of passions whose purpose was to discover social laws. One of the most important axioms of this study was that poverty threatened the happiness of all. He founded 'phalansteries', or agricultural colonies with supporting workshops which were designed to be centres of communitarian production. One of these still exists north of Paris as a museum. The governments of the empire and the Restoration ignored him, and the rich upon whom he placed great hopes disdained him. As he became more desperate for attention, he made increasingly outlandish claims such as being able to melt the polar ice caps and turn the ocean to lemonade. He developed an enormous following in the 1820s and 1830s.

See also UTOPIANISM, UTOPIAS.

J. Beecher, *Charles Fourier: The Visionary and his World* (Berkeley, Calif., 1986).

DONALD SUTHERLAND

France The major paradox of French history in the nineteenth century was the instability of its political institutions and the stability of its society. Population grew slowly, migration to the cities was fairly moderate, living and health standards grew comparatively well and literacy boomed. Thanks to Napoleon BONAPARTE's post-revolutionary settlement, the elite was well entrenched in its wealth and privileges and the distribution of wealth remained largely unperturbed. There was also a broad consensus among the elite that parliamentary government of some sort was essential – the authoritarian phase of NAPOLEON III's Second Empire was the exception that proved the rule. Unfortunately, the elite was divided over its loyalties to the three ruling houses (LEGITIMISTS, Orleanists and Bonapartists) and determined to prevent, by force if necessary (*see* JUNE DAYS, PARIS COMMUNE), the establishment of a popular democracy based on small property until the THIRD REPUBLIC.

DONALD SUTHERLAND

franchise reform During the first half of the nineteenth century virtually all Western societies restricted the franchise to a small minority of their population. This was effected typically by some form of property qualification or a means test reflecting ownership of land or payment of taxes. In addition, a variety of age limitations were imposed: 30 years in Denmark (1848), 23 in the Netherlands (1850) and 25 in Italy (1861), Belgium (1893) and Norway (1897). A number of states also employed both negative and positive educational tests. Literacy was required in Italy and the United States, while in Belgium and Britain electors could obtain extra votes for higher educational qualifications. Finally, the female sex was generally excluded, although a few women did exercise the vote in Britain and the United States in the late eighteenth century. Legal bans were introduced by the United States in 1807 and Britain in 1832.

The major franchise extensions frequently went hand in hand with significant constitutional developments involving either the overthrow of traditional autocratic regimes or the creation of new national states. In such circumstances franchise reform was seen as a necessary expedient for fostering a degree of legitimacy and stability in the new state. France advanced from a means-tested qualification in 1789 to universal male suffrage in 1848. Italy granted male suffrage in 1861, qualified by age, literacy and property restrictions, which confined the electorate to under 2 per cent of the population. In 1867 the new North German Confederation enjoyed universal male suffrage, as did the imperial German parliament in 1871, but the electoral system was weighted so as to minimize the practical effect.

Growing pressure for reform invariably reflected the expansion of an urban population increasingly critical of the political control exercised by the landed and clerical, especially Catholic, interests. By the 1860s liberal parties commonly occupied the leading role in this movement. Yet liberals often felt inhibited by their middle-class base and hesitated to mobilize mass support because of fears about the consequences of universal suffrage. By the 1880s, however, the emergence of social democratic and socialist organizations strengthened the reformers' position. Several more states – Belgium in 1893, Norway in 1897 – achieved something close to universal male suffrage. None the less, most countries failed to make the change until shortly before the First World War or just afterwards.

In spite of their reputation as liberal, representative states, Britain and the United States severely restricted participation in elections during the nineteenth century. To some extent this was because in both countries parliamentary authority was so firmly established that the size of the electorate seemed less important than elsewhere. A succession of reforms bills in 1832, 1867 and 1884 still left only 12 per cent of the population enfranchised in Britain by 1886. From its foundation it had been intended that the United States would be governed by men of property, though the original constitution left each state to determine voting qualifications. Consequently, only New Hampshire, Pennsylvania and Georgia enfranchised men without property qualifications. The pressure for democratization came from the frontier states where there was much less of a social elite. None of the new states that joined the union after the original thirteen used property qualifications, and by 1859 such restrictions had been abandoned everywhere. In 1868 the fourteenth amendment to the Constitution opened the franchise to male citizens aged 21, and prohibited discrimination on grounds of race and colour. However, in practice the black population continued to be largely excluded from the electorate by means of educational, literacy and tax-paying requirements.

From the 1860s onwards campaigns for the enfranchisement of women developed, especially in Britain and the United States. In the latter country the realization in the aftermath of the Civil War that blacks were to be given voting rights had a stimulating effect on feminists. By the end of the century an organized women's movement had spread, particularly in the Anglo-Saxon, Protestant societies of northern Europe, Scandinavia, North America and the British colonies. It was in the frontier territories, where a sparse population made it desirable to attract females both as wives and as workers, that the first successes came. Wyoming enfranchised women in 1869, followed by six other states by 1896; New Zealand did so in 1893 and Australia in 1902. (*See* WOMEN'S SUFFRAGE.)

See also ELECTORAL SYSTEMS, PARLIAMENTARY REFORM.

Bruce A. Campbell, *The American Electorate* (New York, 1979).
Andrew M. Carstairs, *A Short History of Electoral Systems in Western Europe* (London, 1980).

MARTIN PUGH

Francia, José Gaspar Rodríguez de (*b* Asunción, 6 January 1766; *d* Asunción, 20 September 1840) Dictator of Paraguay. The son of a creole military officer, he studied theology but then practised law. An official of the Asunción *cabildo* (municipal council), he became an indispensable figure in the movement to secure autonomy from Spain and Buenos Aires, and in October 1814 was granted absolute powers as supreme dictator. To preserve independence, Francia isolated PARAGUAY from the turmoil of the River Plate (*see* ARGENTINA), imprisoned foreigners who ventured into Paraguay, repressed and despoiled the creole elite, especially after a suspected conspiracy against him in 1820, reorganized the army and brought all state affairs under his personal control. Foreign trade was severely restricted, stimulating domestic production to fill Paraguayans' needs for foodstuffs and basic manufactures. Social inequalities were reduced, the Guaraní language promoted and the concept of a Paraguayan nation defended, in contrast to the turmoil beyond its borders.

RORY MILLER

Francis II (*b* Florence, 12 February 1768; *d* Vienna, 2 March 1835)   As Francis II, last Holy Roman Emperor of the Germans (1792–1806); as Francis I, first emperor of Austria (1804–35). He became Holy Roman Emperor in 1792. His early reign was dominated by war with revolutionary and then Napoleonic France. A series of military calamities and ever more humiliating treaties ensued. One result was the substituting of the title 'emperor of Austria' (1804) for that of Holy Roman Emperor (he abdicated in 1806); another was a marriage alliance with Napoleon in 1810. From this low point, under the guidance of METTERNICH, Francis presided over Austria's resurgence as a member of the triumphant anti-Napoleonic coalition and the leading power, with England, in the post-1815 international system. The experience of revolution led Francis to a very conservative attitude to government after 1815. His refusal to reform Austria's governmental system and repression of liberal opposition have been seen as partly responsible for subsequent Austrian backwardness.

STEVEN BELLER

Francis Joseph I (*b* Vienna, 18 August 1830; *d* Vienna, 21 November 1916)   Emperor of Austria (1848–1916), king of Hungary (1867–1916). Made emperor on 2 December 1848, in the aftermath of the 1848 revolution, the young Francis Joseph set about preserving the HABSBURG EMPIRE and the dynasty's position therein. This remained his goal throughout his long reign, although the strategies thereto changed radically over time, from neo-absolutism (1850s), to liberal dualism (1866–79), conservative quasi-federalism (1879–92) and even universal suffrage in 1906. Known for his bureaucratic diligence, he ruled as well as reigned. He stood by the COMPROMISE OF 1867 with the Hungarians, but doggedly kept control over those sectors essential to Habsburg power: the army and foreign policy. By his death in 1916 he had become the symbol of continuity and unity in Austria-Hungary, but his policies have also been blamed for the ultimate collapse of that state.

Jean-Paul Bled, *Franz Joseph*, trans. Teresa Bridgeman (Cambridge, Mass., 1992).

STEVEN BELLER

Franco-Prussian War (1870–1871)   In the struggle between France and Prussia for diplomatic dominance in Europe, Bismarck provoked France into a war that he believed would lead to the UNIFICATION OF GERMANY under Prussian leadership. Napoleon III declared war on 19

July 1870 in the mistaken expectation that the south German states would join France in resisting Prussian hegemony. The efficient mobilization of the German armies and their superior organizational methods allowed them to outmanœuvre the French. Within six weeks the French suffered two decisive defeats at Metz and Sedan, in western France, where Napoleon III was captured. In Paris (*see* PARIS COMMUNE) the THIRD REPUBLIC was declared and resistance continued until January 1871. On 18 January 1871 William I was declared emperor of Germany. By the Treaty of Frankfurt, France surrendered ALSACE-LORRAINE and paid heavy indemnities to Germany. Thus opened a period of growing diplomatic tension in Europe which culminated in the First World War.

RICHARD PRICE

Franco-Russian Alliance The agreement signed between France and Russia on 4 January 1894, the Franco-Russian Alliance provided for mutual assistance and aid in the event that either was attacked by a member of the TRIPLE ALLIANCE. The agreement included a military convention that had been signed in 1892. The alliance came about because Germany failed to renew the REINSURANCE TREATY which Bismarck had signed with Russia. Germany and Russia had been drifting apart diplomatically during the final years of Bismarck's chancellorship. Germany's refusal to extend much needed financial loans to Russia forced the latter to turn to Paris for assistance. France, still smarting from the defeat inflicted on it by Germany in the Franco-Prussian War and the loss of Alsace-Lorraine to Germany, welcomed Russia's advances and granted it extensive credits.

A further bond between the two partners was their mutual fear of Great Britain. France had clashed repeatedly with Britain in Africa and south-east Asia; Britain had confronted Russia in Afghanistan and the Far East. And in the early 1890s there were rumours that Britain was about to join the Triple Alliance between Germany, Austria-Hungary and Italy. In addition, Tsar Alexander III hated Germany and its kaiser, William II, and believed that war with Germany was inevitable; he had worked for an alliance with France since about 1890. Thus military, economic and personal considerations combined to encourage this alliance, which lasted until 1917.

George Kennan, *The Fateful Alliance* (New York, 1984).

GEORGE O. KENT

Frankfurt Parliament (1848–1849) Elections to the Frankfurt Parliament, or the German National Assembly (GNA), took place throughout the German lands in April–May 1848. The assembly convened in mid-May at Frankfurt am Main. Its principal purpose was to draw up and implement a constitution for a German nation-state. In the spring of 1848 the GNA established a provisional government headed by the Austrian archduke Johann (1782–1859). During the summer of 1848 much time was spent drawing up the section of the constitution concerned with 'basic rights'. The GNA demonstrated pronounced liberal tendencies as it abolished privileges and sought to entrench individual freedom in political, social, economic and religious spheres, though this was not always popular. The major problems, however, concerned the boundaries of the nation-state, its form of government and the relationship between it, Austria and Prussia. The GNA generally took the boundaries of the GERMAN CONFEDERATION as those of the new state, although there were problems in relation to Danish parts of Schleswig, Polish parts of eastern Prussia and Czech parts of Austria. Institutionally, the GNA came down in favour of hereditary, constitutional monarchy. Finally, a majority of the GNA voted to offer the crown to the king of Prussia, with the final constitution also incorporating many democratic elements. By then, however, the GNA had lost much popular support; the counter-revolution was well advanced; many deputies disagreed with the decisions; the revived Habsburg government opposed the proposed constitution. Finally, the king of Prussia rejected the offer of the crown. A rump of the GNA moved to Stuttgart. There were some radical and popular actions in support of the new constitution in parts of Germany. These were soon repressed. The GNA was finally dissolved on 18 June 1849.

Frank Eyck, *The Frankfurt Parliament 1848–1849* (London, 1968).
James Sheehan, *German History 1770–1866* (Oxford, 1989).

JOHN BREUILLY

Frederick-William III (*b* Potsdam, 3 August 1770; *d* Berlin, 7 June 1840)   King of Prussia (1797–1840). Succeeding his father, Frederick-William II (1744–97) as king of Prussia in 1797, he inherited a situation of political and military decline which had become evident after the death of Frederick II ('the Great') in 1786. While his modest habits and exemplary family life were considered admirable, his passivity and hesitancy in times of crisis attracted criticism. Only under the immediate impact of the Prussian defeat by Napoleon in 1806 did the king accept proposals from STEIN, HARDENBERG and others to undertake major reforms of the state and economy. Finally persuaded to launch a war of liberation against Napoleon, he addressed a patriotic appeal – 'To my People' – to the Prussian nation (1813). Following Napoleon's defeat and Prussia's gains at the CONGRESS OF VIENNA, Frederick-William III brought the era of reform to an end and ensured that Prussia became a pillar of the post-Napoleonic Restoration.

ELIZABETH HARVEY

Frederick-William IV (*b* Berlin, 15 October 1795; *d* Potsdam, 2 January 1861) King of Prussia (1840–61). On becoming king in 1840, he was welcomed by liberal reformers. Hopes of a new era were disappointed when he turned out to be fundamentally conservative, attached to a romanticized idea of the German nation but opposed to modern liberal constitutionalism. During the REVOLUTIONS OF 1848, he initially embraced his new role as constitutional monarch and advocate of the German national cause. However, he soon turned against the revolution, dissolving the Prussian constituent assembly in December 1848. In March 1849 he rejected the offer by the FRANKFURT PARLIAMENT of the title of emperor of a united Germany (excluding Austria). This triggered the collapse of the Frankfurt Parliament and ended liberal hopes of bringing about German unity by constitutional means. The final years of his reign in Prussia were characterized by reaction, repression and censorship. In 1857, due to his illness and diminishing mental capacity, his brother WILLIAM I took over as regent.

ELIZABETH HARVEY

Freedmen's Bureau (1865–1872) As early as 1863 a presidential commission chaired by Samuel Gridley Howe (1801–76) recommended the creation of a government agency to assist freed American slaves in their transition to an independent life, but until 1865 it could not be agreed where to locate the bureau within the government bureaucracy. On 3 March 1865 Congress established the Freedmen's Bureau, placing it in the war department, with a life of one year. The bureau received no funds at the time. President Abraham Lincoln appointed General Oliver O. Howard (1830–1909) as the bureau's commissioner. Howard appointed ten assistant commissioners to carry out the bureau's mission in the southern states. Approximately 900 individuals, many of them ex-soldiers, served with the bureau at some point in its history.

The bureau took on many tasks during its career. From the beginning it passed out rations to destitute AFRICAN-AMERICANS and southern white refugees. Thousands of whites received food or clothing from the bureau, although most of the 21 million rations doled out by the agency went to the freedmen. Despite white complaints that freedmen used the rations from the bureau as an excuse not to work, the agency helped only those in extreme need. The organization established 100 hospitals for the freedmen. Over 4,000 schools, staffed often by northern missionaries or already literate African-Americans, offered both primary and secondary education to southern blacks under the bureau's auspices. The agency also helped the freedmen find jobs and negotiate fair contracts. In addition, it supervised about 800,000 acres of abandoned or confiscated land, settling a small number of freedmen on this land, before President Andrew JOHNSON returned most of it to its former owners in mid-1865.

With the passage of laws that sought to render the freedmen second-class citizens in most southern states, Congress decided in 1866 to extend the life of the Freedmen's Bureau for two years and increase its power to protect ex-slaves. But President Johnson, a southerner with little sympathy for the freedmen, vetoed the new law, insisting that it was unconstitutional and wasteful. Congress overrode Johnson's veto in July 1866. The new law directed the bureau to establish courts to hear discrimination cases involving freedmen, as well as cases dealing with contractual disputes between landowners and their labourers. In 1868 Congress again extended the bureau for one year, but after 1869 the agency gradually faded. By 1872 other government organizations took on the bureau's functions.

The bureau proved popular among the freedmen, but southern white opinion was more critical. White landowners resented the bureau's interference between them and their labourers, especially when they found themselves in bureau courts. They believed that they alone knew what was best for their former slaves, and insisted that bureau activities only soured southern race relations. Some southern whites even insisted that this was the bureau's true purpose. Since many of the bureau agents were also Republicans, who worked for the agency by day and for the Republican Party by night, southern whites also saw the organization as a partisan one. Thus, bureau agents received threats from the Ku Klux Klan, and bureau schools were burned in some areas. Even the female school teachers, often religious missionaries, faced hostility from recalcitrant southern whites determined to maintain white supremacy.

Most bureau agents genuinely sought to help the freedmen and the destitute in the post-war south. Some individual agents, however, misused funds or engaged in other corrupt activities. In some areas African-Americans also complained of socially conservative agents who sided with landowners at the freedmen's expense. The Georgia assistant commissioner, Davis Tilson (1830–95), was notorious in this matter, often agreeing to low-wage contracts designed by the landowners. He removed agents such as Captain John Emory Bryant (1836–1900), a future Republican leader, whom he viewed as too sympathetic to the Georgia freedmen.

The Freedmen's Bureau produced a mixed record, for although it helped establish black schools and hospitals, it failed in its mission to establish a system of truly free labour in the south. At the same time, it represented the first social-welfare agency ever established by the federal government. Despite its insistence on its vital mission, Congress provided very few funds for its operation. Commissioner Howard and his subordinates received only about $18 million in four years.

Approximately half the money went into rations, and only about $500,000 towards schools. Despite southern white criticism, however, the agency helped many starving southerners of both races and provided African-Americans with services the southern states often failed to provide even for its white citizens.

See also RECONSTRUCTION.

George R. Bentley, *A History of the Freedmen's Bureau* (New York, 1970).
Ira Berlin et al., *Freedom: A Documentary History of Emancipation, 1861–1868* (Cambridge, 1983).
William S. McFeely, *Yankee Stepfather: General O. O. Howard and the Freedmen* (New York, 1970).

ALICE E. REAGAN

Free-soil Party (1847–1848)   While the MISSOURI COMPROMISE was thought to have settled the issue of which territories would be free or slave, the Freesoil Party grew out of a dispute over the status of territory acquired from Mexico in the Mexican–American War. In 1846 David Wilmot (1814–68), a Pennsylvania congressman, attached a proviso to an appropriations bill for the war which would have barred the institution of slavery in any territories gained from that conflict. The proviso was struck down, but it raised the issue of whether or not slavery would be allowed to expand as the United States grew geographically.

Galvanized by Wilmot's proviso, the Freesoil Party consisted of members of the former LIBERTY PARTY, 'Conscience' Whigs and New York 'Barnburners' who left the Democratic Party rather than tolerate a pro-slavery position. Formally organized with the slogan 'Free soil, free speech, free labor and free men', the party nominated Martin VAN BUREN for president in 1848, who polled 10 per cent of the popular vote. The three elements of the party were fundamentally incompatible, however, and after the 'settlement' of the issue of slavery in the territories by the COMPROMISE OF 1850, support of the Freesoil Party dwindled. In 1854 it was absorbed into the REPUBLICAN PARTY.

The appearance of Freesoilers as a third party demonstrated the inability of the expanding republic's existing political structure to deal with the political, social and economic issues raised by the institution of slavery. Distinct from abolitionists, who held that slavery was a moral evil, Freesoilers sought to avoid economic competition with plantation slavery and often were indifferent to the plight of African-Americans in bondage.

T. C. Smith, *The Liberty and Freesoil Parties* (New York, 1967).

KEVIN MURPHY

free trade   During the eighteenth century the British Empire was a vast free-trade system protected by statutes like the NAVIGATION ACTS and monopolies like the East India Company designed to retain all trade in British hands. This system, known as mercantilism, came under increasing theoretical attack in the eighteenth century, most notably by Adam Smith (1723–90). Smith argued that mercantilism distorted economic development in the interests of politically powerful groups able to secure protection. The results were that consumers paid artificially high prices and resources were allocated inefficiently. A free market would allow natural competition to keep prices at their lowest possible level and ensure the best allocation of productive resources. Although Smith recognized the need for exceptions to a complete free-trade economic system, free trade quickly found acceptance among political economists and after 1820 appealed to those politicians contemplating how best to handle the vast expansion of Britain's productive capacities.

Free trade was, in general terms, the policy favoured by those who believed Britain's economic policy should be directed towards exploiting the greatly increasing world market; protectionists tended to favour concentrating on developing the home market (*see* PROTECTIONISM). But free trade remained only an economic theory until after the Napoleonic wars, when economic and political conditions began to demonstrate to business groups the restraints of mercantilism. Thus Lancashire cotton exports to India grew enormously after the removal of the East India Company's monopoly in 1813, but the China market remained under the Company's control until 1834. In addition, the expanding cotton industry increasingly chafed under the import duties on raw cotton from the United States.

A further factor increasing support for free trade was the growing awareness of the untapped market potential outside of the formal empire. But mercantalist restrictions impeded the exploitation of these markets. The raw materials and primary products that these countries could exchange for British manufactured goods were excluded by the high tariffs designed to protect native British goods or products of the empire. In its turn this restricted the growth of British trade because foreign countries needed to sell their primary products in the British market in order to purchase British manufacturing products. It was for this reason that political support for free trade came to rest on the manufacturing interest as a whole and the CORN LAWS came to symbolize the worst effects of the protectionist system.

Free trade had many supporters within the political establishment from the 1820s, but it did not become practical politics until the 1840s when the Royal Commission on Import Duties (1841) reported strongly in favour of free trade as an answer to the trade depression of the late 1830s, and the ANTI-CORN LAW LEAGUE organized middle-class opinion around the issue. The administration of Sir Robert PEEL (1841–6) gradually introduced free trade, reducing the number of dutiable items from over 1,100 to forty-eight. But the caution that accompanied this fiscal revolution should be noted. The success of free trade in stimulating economic expansion was not assured, and tariff duties produced 43 per cent of government revenue. Thus Peel reintroduced the income tax to compensate for the loss of customs revenue. But British industry was poised to take full advantage of free trade, and over the next ten years British exports increased as much as they had over the previous forty years. Imports also increased. Ironically, food prices, which had been the centrepiece of the Anti-Corn Law League's arguments, did not fall.

The appeal of free trade was integral to the dominant position Britain occupied in world trade during the mid nineteenth century. As a theory of resource allocation, it argued that the market should determine what countries could most efficiently produce, thus promising a complementarity to the world economy which some ideologues such as Richard COBDEN believed would guarantee world peace. But free trade was blatantly imperialistic; in many cases, such as China (*see* ANGLO-CHINESE WARS), it was intruded only by force of arms. Followed to its logical conclusion, free trade would have maintained Britain as the workshop of the world, supplying manufactured goods and receiving primary products. Britain, then, was the only country to be firmly committed to free trade throughout the nineteenth century, although for a brief moment in the 1860s it did look as though other countries were following its lead (*see* ANGLO-FRENCH COMMERCIAL TREATY).

Barry Gordon, *Economic Doctrine and Tory Liberalism* (London, 1979).
Norman McCord, *Free Trade* (Newton Abbot, 1976).
Barry Turner, *Free Trade and Protectionism* (London, 1971).

                                                                RICHARD PRICE

Freud, Sigmund *see* PSYCHOLOGY.

Frick, Henry Clay (*b* West Overton, Pennsylvania, 19 December, 1849; *d* New York, 2 December 1919)   American industrialist and philanthropist. He established himself in the coke industry at the age of 21. After Carnegie Brothers gained the controlling interest in Frick Coke, Frick became an integral part of the Carnegie steel organization. A proponent of vertical integration, he convinced a reluctant Andrew CARNEGIE to buy a railroad as well as an iron mine in the newly opened Mesabi Range. While Carnegie was in Scotland in 1892, Frick became embroiled in a labour dispute which led to the Homestead Strike. Frick brought in a force of Pinkerton detectives to protect the plant, only to see them beaten off by the strikers. During the strike, he also survived an assassination attempt by anarchist Alexander Berkman (1870–1936). The strike ended when the strikers' funds ran out, and Frick reopened with non-union workers. His collection of Old Masters became the basis for the Frick Collection in New York.

George Harvey, *Henry Clay Frick, the Man* (New York, 1928).

ALICE E. REAGAN

friendly societies The means of securing, through regular small subscriptions, sickness benefits and/or a decent funeral (thus avoiding the indignity of an unmarked pauper's grave), friendly societies were of two main types. The older, examples of which can be traced back to the mid-eighteenth century, were autonomous local 'box clubs' (often attached to a public house, place of work or worship). The second type originated in the 1830s, partly in reaction to the NEW POOR LAW, when national 'affiliated orders' emerged, with a strong emphasis on sociable branch life and ritual and titles to match, for example Independent Order of Oddfellows, Ancient Order of Foresters. British emigration carried these orders to North America and the empire.

In the earlier part of the century it was often difficult to distinguish between friendly societies and trade unions, and the latter usually continued to provide welfare benefits. An 1834 Act gave friendly societies unequivocal legal recognition long before this was forthcoming for other institutions of the labour movement. None the less, many smaller societies never registered. Accurate membership figures are therefore impossible to calculate, but by 1872 the total number of societies probably exceeded 32,000, with some 4 million members. By 1888 around 80 per cent of adult British males belonged to a society, compared to no more than 10 per cent who were trade-unionists. Membership was densest in the industrial Midlands and north, but by no means confined to industrial workers or to men. Towards the end of the century a new type of society, the 'collecting' society, emerged. These were strictly commercial organizations, which employed an agent on commission to collect subscriptions and administer benefits, and made no social requirements of members: they catered especially for the growing need to provide for pensions in old age (*see* OLD-AGE PENSIONS). Unlike the voluntary societies, they expanded rather than contracted as a result of welfare reforms of the early 1900s.

See also BUILDING SOCIETIES, POOR RELIEF.

P. H. J. H. Godsen, *The Friendly Societies in England, 1815–1875* (Manchester, 1961).
——, *Self-help: Voluntary Associations in Nineteenth-Century Britain* (London, 1973).

MALCOLM CHASE

Fry, Elizabeth Gurney (*b* Earlham, Norfolk, 21 May 1780; *d* Ramsgate, Kent, 12 October 1845) English prison reformer. The 'Angel of the

Prisons', Elizabeth Fry, a Quaker matron with nine children, began her campaign for prison reform after visiting Newgate in 1816, at the height of public concern over the post-war crime wave. While seeking to retrieve souls from eternal damnation, she laboured hard to improve welfare in prisons through the provision of schools and visitors, a mission which soon extended to personal inspection of female convict ships. The success of her efforts, which recognized prisoners as individuals capable of self-respect and rehabilitation, was to force a change in attitudes in prison systems across Europe. An indefatigable philanthropist, she established night shelters for the homeless, district visiting-societies for the poor and libraries for coastguard stations, while also promoting nursing reform and women's education.

JOHN BELCHEM

Fuad Pasha, Keçecizade Mehmed (*b* Istanbul, 1815; *d* Nice, 12 February 1869) Ottoman reformer, foreign minister and grand vizier. Although he was the son of an Islamic judge, he was among the first generation of Ottomans to receive a secular education. His training and intelligence gained him the favour of the reformer MUSTAFA RESHID PASHA. In August 1852 Fuad became foreign minister while Ali Pasha (1744–1822), another protégé of Reshid, became grand vizier. Although the younger men were often at odds with their mentor, the three controlled Ottoman affairs during the reigns of Abdulmejid (1839–56) and Abdulaziz (1856–76). Appointed foreign minister again in 1855, Fuad was instrumental in the promulgation of the imperial decree which granted equal rights to non-Muslims. Along with brief tenures as foreign minister between 1858 and 1861, he served as a special envoy to Syria in the aftermath of the DRUSE–Maronite disturbances. As grand vizier from November 1861 to January 1863, and June 1863 to June 1866, Fuad was responsible for a number of reforms, but the period was dominated by financial crisis and nationalist rebellions. After a brief stint as foreign minister in 1867, he retired to Nice, where he died.

Bernard Lewis, *The Emergence of Modern Turkey* (Oxford, 1968).

MADELINE C. ZILFI

Fugitive Slave Act (1850) One of the five acts of the COMPROMISE OF 1850, the Fugitive Slave Act allowed slave-catchers to hunt escaped slaves in northern states and in the territories. It was an attempt to strengthen the existing law on escaped slaves. Once captured, suspected runaway slaves were not entitled to a jury trial. Rather, slave-catchers brought them before specially appointed commissioners who received $10 if the captured person was certified a slave and only $5 if certification was denied. The law also required citizens to help federal marshals with enforcement. Anyone who interfered with the prosecution of the law could be fined $1,000 and imprisoned up to six months. There was no limit on the time that could elapse before an escaped slave could be captured.

Although slave-catchers (labelled 'kidnappers' in the north) caught one escaped slave nineteen years after he found freedom in the north, the law was generally ineffective. In the first six years of the law's existence, probably fewer than 200 slaves were returned to slave-owners – a fraction of the number of slaves who passed through the 'underground railroad' to freedom in the north and Canada. The Fugitive Slave Act served to intensify and widen the antislavery impulse in the north. One of the law's most adamant opponents, Frederick DOUGLASS (himself an escaped slave), said that 'the only way to make the Fugitive Slave Law a dead letter is to make a half dozen or more dead kidnappers'.

Stanley W. Campbell, *Slave Catchers: Enforcement of the Fugitive Slave Law, 1850–1860* (Chapel Hill, NC, 1968).

JOHN MARTIN

G

Gaelic Revival Spearheaded by the Gaelic Athletic Association (GAA) and the Gaelic League, the Gaelic Revival sought to preserve Ireland's Gaelic heritage and counter the dominance of British culture in the late nineteenth century. The GAA was founded in 1884 by Michael Cusack (1847–1906) to preserve and cultivate 'our National Pastimes'. Members were banned from supporting non-Irish games, particularly cricket. Serving members of the crown forces were excluded. Gaining huge popularity in the countryside, it partly achieved its vision of an Ireland 'dotted all over with miniature armies of hurlers, bowlers, jumpers, weight-throwers, merry dancers and joyous singers'. The town-based Gaelic League, formed in 1893, was dedicated to the 'de-Anglicization of Ireland' through the revival and preservation of Irish as a spoken language and the development of a modern literature in Irish. Its founder, Douglas Hyde (1860–1949), a Protestant, wanted a forum for all sections of political and religious opinion to meet for a common cultural purpose, creating a new Ireland, in which Catholics ceased 'crawling to social position' and Protestants took a real interest in Ireland's wrongs. With burgeoning branches, a newspaper (*Claideamdh Solius*), an annual festival of Irish culture (an tOireachtas) and travelling teachers, the league was poised to secure for Irish a place in the school curriculum.

The GAA was explicitly anti-English, while the league was avowedly non-political. By demonstrating Ireland's cultural distinctiveness, both underpinned the demand for self-government. They also deepened divisions in Ireland by equating Ireland and Irishness with rural and Catholic values and excluding Protestants and 'West Britons'. The GAA soon became a vehicle for the IRISH REPUBLICAN BROTHERHOOD, although not until 1915 did the league resolve that its primary aim was Ireland's political independence.

John Hutchinson, *The Dynamics of Cultural Nationalism: The Gaelic Revival and the Creation of the Irish Nation State* (London, 1987).

PATRICK BUCKLAND

Gambetta, Léon (*b* Cahors, 2 April 1838; *d* Ville d'Avray, 31 December 1882)   French republican politician. He was a relatively obscure barrister until a brilliant speech against the Second Empire in a political trial in 1868 brought him to national attention. He was elected to Paris-Belleville and Marseilles in 1869 and became a minister in the Government of National Defence following the overthrow of the Second Empire. Escaping the siege of Paris in a balloon in October 1870, he became virtual head of government. He organized new levies to replace the defeated imperial army and, despite the defeat of his armies, wanted to continue the war against Prussia. Throughout the 1870s he struggled for the democratic republic, denouncing government by priests, and demanding separation of church and state, income tax and the freedom to form unions. His only government (1881) lasted only seventy-four days, however, because of the jealousy of other republican politicians. He died the following year of complications following a shooting accident.

J. P. T. Bury, *Gambetta and the Making of the Third Republic* (London, 1973).

DONALD SUTHERLAND

Garfield, James Abram (*b* near Orange, Ohio, 19 November 1831; *d* Elberon, New Jersey, 19 September 1881)   President of the United States (1881). An antislavery Ohioan, Garfield helped form the 42nd Ohio Volunteer Infantry at the outbreak of the Civil War and by 1863 had been promoted to major-general. He resigned in that year and was elected to the House of Representatives as a Republican, where he served until 1880. Although tainted by scandals, such as the Crédit Mobilier, he remained independent from the 'Stalwart' (supporters of Ulysses S. Grant) and 'Half Breed' (supporters of James G. Blaine (1830–93)) factions of the REPUBLICAN PARTY. When the Republican nominating-convention of 1880 became deadlocked, Garfield became a compromise candidate on the thirty-sixth ballot. With Chester A. ARTHUR as his running mate, Garfield took the presidency but a deranged office-seeker, Charles Guiteau (1841–82), shot him in the back just months later, on 2 July 1881.

JOHN MARTIN

Garibaldi, Giuseppe (*b* 4 July 1807, Nice; *d* 2 June 1882, Caprera, Sardinia)   Italian revolutionary republican and soldier. A member of MAZZINI's Young Italy, Garibaldi was forced into exile in 1834. Escaping to South America, he won fame as a soldier, especially in Uruguay. After his return to Italy, Garibaldi's reputation grew because of his defence of the short-lived Roman republic. Upon returning from a second exile in the United States, he was given a command during the Austrian War of 1859. In May 1860 he embarked on his famous conquest of Sicily and Naples with his army of 1,000 republican 'Red Shirts'. He quickly defeated the Neapolitans and surprisingly surrendered his conquest to VICTOR EMMANUEL II to form the kingdom of Italy. In 1862 and 1867 he led two unsuccessful attempts to conquer Rome and fought for Italy against Austria in 1866.

Jasper Ridley, *Garibaldi* (New York, 1974).

LAWRENCE P. ADAMCZYK

Garrison, William Lloyd (*b* Newburyport, Massachusetts, 10 December 1805; *d* New York, 24 May, 1879)   One of the most notable and influential of American ante-bellum advocates of ABOLITIONISM. He founded and edited the Massachusetts newspaper the *Liberator*, whose first issue in 1831 stated unequivocally that 'I am in earnest, I will not equivocate, and I WILL BE HEARD.' Rigid and uncompromising, Garrison would not tolerate the use of political aid or force in his quest for the unconditional and immediate abolition of slavery, relying wholly on moral suasion and the powerful, inflammatory language of his paper. In 1854 he publicly burned a copy of the American constitution, and on another occasion called it 'a covenant with death, an agreement with hell' because it permitted slavery. He was imprisoned for libel and frequently risked personal danger in his public appearances. Disliked in the north and reviled in the south, his brand of agitation heightened sectional tensions which led to the Civil War.

KEVIN MURPHY

gas   The study of gases and the development of kinetic theory and statistical mechanics led to an understanding of the external manifestations of energy, such as heat and temperature, and the internal structure of matter itself. In 1808 John DALTON proposed the law of partial pressures – that the pressure exerted by each gas in a mixture was independent of the other gases, and that the total pressure of a mixture was equal to the sum of the individual pressures. Dalton's atomic theory assumed that gases were composed of small indivisible atoms, that all atoms of a particular element were alike in mass and all other properties and that the various types of atoms combined to form compounds. In the same year Joseph Gay-Lussac (1778–1850) reported that when gases reacted under identical conditions of temperature and pressure, the volumes involved were always in the ratio of small whole numbers, suggesting that equal volumes of gases must contain equal numbers of atoms. In 1811 Amedeo Avogadro (1776–1856), however, postulated that equal volumes of gases contained the same number of molecules (at the same temperature and pressure).

Rudolf Clausius's (1822–88) *On the Kind of Motion We Call Heat* (1857) was the first analysis of the dynamics of gas-particle motion, including a calculation of the 'mean free path' of a gas molecule. James Clerk Maxwell (1831–79) showed in 1859 that the mean energy of a gas molecule in a mixture of gases was independent of mass. This led to the kinetic theory which explained the behaviour of gases by assuming that any gas was 'ideal': composed of identical molecules that were far apart compared to their size, affect each other only upon collision. Ludwig Boltzmann (1844–1906) investigated the relationship between the temperature and energy of gas molecules, laying the foundation for statistical mechanics; he theoretically demonstrated in 1883 a law of black-body radiation which had been found experimentally by Josef Stefan (1835–93).

Stephen Brush, *The Kind of Motion We Call Heat* (Amsterdam, 1976).

STEVE AMANN

gender The concept of gender – the social organization of the relationship between males and females, masculinity and femininity – is particularly useful because it allows for an analytic distinction between biological sex and the myriad of meanings assigned to each sex in different cultural and historical contexts. Although many dictionaries define gender strictly as a grammatical classification, its meaning has expanded since the late 1970s, especially among European and North American scholars. The notion of gender is rooted in Simone de Beauvoir's assertion that 'one is not born a woman' (*The Second Sex*, 1949). Feminist scholars began to develop and expand on de Beauvoir's insight, exploring how the subordination of women is created and reproduced. While the English language differentiates between sex and gender, not all languages make that distinction and these questions have not always translated easily into other languages and national historical projects. Gender, however, has become an exceedingly important analytic concept and numerous historical studies have been devoted to understanding gender and its relationship to other historical problems.

Historians argue that gender is a primary way of describing and legitimating relations of power. Citizenship, and the social and political power it conferred, was defined as distinctly masculine in the nineteenth century. Politicians frequently compared the state to a well-ordered family and opposed WOMEN'S SUFFRAGE because it would disrupt the natural order of both the state and the family. Similarly, most Christian denominations long excluded women from the priesthood because women's subordination to men was believed to be central to the right ordering of family, church and state as it mirrored men's humility before God. Hence, gender is central to an understanding both of the lives of historical women and men and of the distinctions between masculinity and femininity that are used to explicate and upohold systems of classification and social order.

Historians have argued that while biological difference is, at the anatomical level, self-evident, its social significance is not. During the nineteenth century, for example, the ideal of DOMESTICITY dominated Anglo-American discussions of femininity. Devoted to children and home, moral and sensitive to the needs of others, the ideal woman lived in the 'private' realm while man occupied the 'public' realm of business and politics. Nineteenth-century social commentators extolled these distinctions as natural and inevitable, yet it is clear that this ideal was particular to the nineteenth-century middle class. Not only was this notion of femininity and masculinity different from earlier conceptions of gender but working-class women were considered especially qualified for many kinds of arduous, waged, public labour.

Historians have also examined how masculinity and femininity were formed in relation to other social distinctions. For example, in the ante-bellum American south, enslaved people were not understood to be masculine and feminine in precisely the same ways as their slave masters. This was made evident in an 1851 speech by Sojourner Truth (1795–1883), a former slave and abolitionist. She responded to a man who objected to women entering the world of work and politics because they were fragile creatures, deserving of special care. Truth described her years of toil in the fields and the loss of her children to the slave markets and asked 'Ar'n't I a woman?' Four years later the Missouri state court provided one answer to Truth's question. A woman named Celia murdered her slave master after enduring his repeated rapes. The defence counsel argued that she acted in self-defence and that state law protected 'any woman' from rape. The court declared that 'any woman' did not refer to slave women and found Celia guilty. 'Womanhood' did not refer to biology, nor did it include everyone who might be designated female. Rather, it was a social classification entwined with ideas about race, class and other social distinctions.

See also FEMINISM, PATRIARCHY.

Evelyn Brooks Higgenbotham, 'African American Women's History and the Metalanguage of Race', *Signs*, 17(2) (1992), 251–74.
Joan Scott, 'Gender: A Useful Category of Historical Analysis', in Joan Scott (ed.), *Gender and the Politics of History* (New York, 1988), pp. 28–50.

PAMELA J. WALKER

General Confederation of French Labour   In September 1895 the General Confederation of French Labour was formed out of a number of unions and industrial federations. On the eve of the First World War it represented about a third of the unionized workforce and was a major force in presenting workers' demands for a reduction in the cost of living, for the EIGHT-HOUR DAY and welfare reform and against the use of troops in strike-breaking. 'Anarcho-syndicalists' (*see* ANARCHISM), who eschewed electoral activity and who believed that the socialist revolution could be provoked through strikes, were also influential within its ranks. Despite talk of a revolutionary general strike should war break out among the European powers, the confederation supported the French government in the First World War and adopted a reformist stance between the wars. Since 1947 it has generally supported the Communist Party.

V. Lorwin, *The French Labor Movement* (Cambridge, Mass., 1954).

DONALD SUTHERLAND

general unionism General unions were trade unions that enrolled all grades and classes of labourers irrespective of trade. They were distinguished from craft unions, which organized only skilled workers by trade, and industrial unions, which organized by industry. They were to be found in most industrial countries during the late nineteenth-century expansion of trade-unionism. The KNIGHTS OF LABOR and the Industrial Workers of the World (in Canada and the United States) and the Australian Workers Union are examples. General unionism had lasting effects only on British trade-union organization.

Although there were some attempts to organize unskilled labourers (*see* UNSKILLED LABOUR) – particularly in the building trades – in the 1870s, the general unions proper emerged from the NEW UNIONISM of the late 1880s which focused on previously unorganized groups. The purpose of the (usually) revolutionary socialists who created the original general unions – such as the Gas-workers and General Labourers' Union, the Dockworkers' union, the National Amalgamated Union of Labour and the Workers' Union – was to organize all possible competitors for the same job and thereby maximize the bargaining power of unskilled workers. In fact, these unions typically emanated from groups – such as stokers in the gasworks – who possessed some degree of skill which gave them a scarcity value in the labour market. In times of trade depression like the 1890s their membership contracted to this core group. Thus, until around the First World War, these unions survived only by behaving more like the exclusive craft unions.

The major general unions of the twentieth century, such as the Transport and General Workers' Union and the General and Municipal Workers' Union, emerged from these organizations in the next phase of trade-union expansion after 1911.

Eric Hobsbawm, 'General Labour Unions in Britain, 1889–1914', in *Labouring Men* (London, 1964), pp. 179–203.

RICHARD PRICE

geology By the nineteenth century the study of the earth's structure and the processes acting on it focused on the time-scale, surface-shaping forces, the construction of maps showing the planet's internal structure and on identifying and classifying deposits. James Hutton's (1726–97) *Theory of the Earth* (1795) gave geology its modern foundation, arguing, first, that sedimentary rocks were laid down in sequence and therefore had a discernable history, and secondly, that the processes acting on the surface today – erosion, volcanism, deposition – had also acted in the past, and such processes would have needed a vast amount of time to give the surface its current structure. Such arguments (known as uniformitarianism) refuted the accepted opinion – 'catastrophism' – that receding flood waters had produced the earth's landscape, and that the earth had been created as recently as 4004 BC. Charles Lyell's (1797–1875) *Principles of Geology* (1830) used examples from throughout the world to support Hutton's views. In 1840 Louis Agassiz (1807–73) argued that glacial forces had helped create the earth's appearance, and that clay and boulders in the mountain valleys of Europe and America had been deposited by retreating glaciers.

In the first two decades of the nineteenth century William Smith (1769–1839) produced a series of geological maps detailing the faunal succession in parts of Great Britain. Each rock unit, he noticed, contained its own distinguishing assemblage of fossils. Geologists could thereby identify rock units by the fossils they contained, allowing stratigraphic classification of time equivalency between rock strata, the formulation of the geological time-scale and the production of geological survey maps. This was of great value in the development of the exploration for economically valuable minerals.

Greene, Mott, *Geology in the Nineteenth Century* (Ithaca, NY, 1982).

STEVE AMANN

George IV (*b* London, 12 August 1762; *d* Windsor, 25 May 1830) Regent (1811–20), king of Great Britain and Ireland (1820–30). A notorious profligate and libertine, George, the eldest son of George III (1738–1820), was unable to reverse the decline in the influence of the crown as patronage diminished. 'Prinny' entered public life in characteristic Hanoverian fashion, patronizing an 'anticourt' to which opposition politicians flocked. On becoming regent, however, he chose not to appoint his erstwhile Whig friends, after which his hostility to reform and indifference to distress caused public offence, compounded by his continuing extravagance and moral laxity. He fell further into disrepute on accession to the throne when he insisted on instigating divorce proceedings against Caroline of Brunswick (1768–1821), whom he had married in 1795, ten years after his secret (and invalid) marriage to the Catholic Mrs Fitzherbert (1756–1837), one of his many mistresses. A lazy and increasingly obese dilettante, he had some artistic taste, best exemplified by his patronage of the architect John Nash (1752–1835).

JOHN BELCHEM

George, Henry (*b* Philadelphia, 2 September 1839; *d* New York, 29 October 1897) American economist and reformer. Born into a religious family of merchants and publishers, he was largely self-educated, and was successively a clerk, sailor, printer and publisher. Struck by rampant land speculation in post-Civil War California, he devoted much of his life to explaining increasing land prices. From his first pamphlet, *Our Land and Land Policy* (1871), George argued that everyone had an equal right to the land, which when owned privately deprived many of the fruits of their labour. Taxes thus ought to fall on land alone. His best-known work, *Progress and Poverty* (1879), contended that all rent ought to be converted into taxation. Its success established the immensely influential 'single tax' movement, whose Land and Labor Clubs were founded throughout the United States, and met with considerable interest in Britain and Australia. He ran several times for office, including the mayoralty of New York.

GREGORY CLAEYS

German Confederation (1815–1866) Established as part of the European security system after Napoleon's defeat, the German Confederation succeeded the Holy Roman Empire, with some thirty-nine states, ranging from the two major ones of PRUSSIA and Austria (*see* HABSBURG EMPIRE) to four small city-states. It included non-German areas and rulers and excluded some German-speaking territories. The confederal diet met in Frankfurt under the presidency of Austria. Plans to establish a confederal army and to harmonize constitutional arrangements failed. Austria and Prussia used the confederation after 1819 to impose political restrictions throughout Germany, and the confederation came to be seen as an obstacle to national and liberal aspirations. There were, however, positive features in the way the confederation allowed independent states to co-ordinate policies and encouraged a national politics within a federated framework. The confederation lapsed during the 1848 revolution, was restored in 1850–1 and collapsed in the face of Austro–Prussian rivalry in 1866.

James Sheehan, *German History 1770–1866* (Oxford, 1989).

JOHN BREUILLY

German National Assembly *see* FRANKFURT PARLIAMENT.

Germany, unification of (1864–1871) When BISMARCK was appointed minister-president of Prussia in September 1862, 'Germany' consisted of thirty-nine states organized in the GERMAN CONFEDERATION and dominated by Austria and Prussia. Until 1848 Prussia had accepted the leading position of Austria. The revolution of 1848 temporarily destroyed the confederation, promoted national feeling and conflict, almost destroyed Austria, aroused Prussian ambitions in northern Germany and revealed the incompatibility of the multinational Habsburg dynasty and the idea of a German nation-state (see REVOLUTIONS OF 1848). An uneasy partnership was resumed by 1852 with the restoration of the confederation and the abandonment of expansionist policies threatened by both states. Prussian population and economic growth was more rapid than in Austria. Through the Customs Union Prussia tied most of the other German states to itself, and also ensured that Austria did not become a member. Industrial growth not only meant economic strength and support from a growing middle class, but also increased state revenue. Furthermore, railway-building and the capacity to mass-produce new weapons meant industrialization had military consequences. Austria was weakened by its policy of neutrality during the Crimean War (1854–6) which antagonized its former Russian ally. It was further damaged by the war of 1859 with France and Piedmont which led to the loss of some Italian possessions and financial crisis, and stimulated German nationalism.

In the early years of the reign of WILLIAM I (Prussian regent 1858; king from 1861), liberal nationalists hoped that Prussia would lead the way in unifying Germany. However, tensions arose over the king's plans for military reform. The appointment of Bismarck as minister-president in the midst of a constitutional conflict between William and the Prussian lower house (Landtag) set back any prospect of cooperation between the government and the national movement. Bismarck was hostile to the national movement. His major foreign-policy concern was to create a clear sphere of influence for Prussia in north and central Germany. His chance came in 1864 with conflict between Germany and Denmark over the status of the duchies of Schleswig and Holstein (see SCHLESWIG-HOLSTEIN QUESTION). Austria and Prussia acted independently of both the confederation and the national movement, finally waging war with Denmark and occupying the duchies.

In the period of rising tension between Austria and Prussia after 1864 both states sought to attract support from other states and the national movement, but Prussia in particular had little success. When war did break out in 1866 the confederation and most individual German states supported Austria, and the national movement was paralysed. The swift Prussian victory was followed by a generous peace settlement with Austria to ensure a rapid end to the war before any international complications could arise. Bismarck sought to bring much of the national movement over to him by offering reconciliation over the Prussian constitutional crisis, establishing the NORTH GERMAN

CONFEDERATION, and pursuing through the confederation economic reforms based on liberal principles. However, Austria cherished hopes of reversing the decisions of 1866–7; France was hostile because of resentment at not making any profit out of the Austro-Prussian conflict; and opinion in the German states south of the River Main remained resolutely anti-Prussian.

Bismarck's motives over the Hohenzollern candidacy for the Spanish throne, the issue which led to war with France, remain a matter of debate, but it is undeniable that victory over France solved these three problems (*see* FRANCO-PRUSSIAN WAR). The south German states were bound by a military alliance to enter the war on the Prussia's side. Austria did not feel strong enough to risk renewed defeat. Nationalism was reinforced by anti-French feeling. Defeat of France increased anti-German feeling but removed, for the foreseeable future, any chance of acting on it. This time Prussia did not seek a rapid end to the war after the initial military victory at Sedan. The war dragged on, Alsace and Lorraine were annexed, and a large indemnity imposed on France. The south German states were incorporated into the German Empire, which was declared at Versailles in January 1871.

It was a federalist constitution, conceding many powers to the individual states. There was an uneasy balance between imperial and state, especially Prussian, institutions; and traditional institutions such as the Prussian and other surviving state monarchies and new institutions such as the German emperorship and the imperial and state parliaments. Within this complex constitutional structure Bismarck occupied a pivotal position and was to dominate the affairs of the new German state for the next twenty years.

William Carr, *The Origins of the Wars of German Unification* (London, 1991).
Otto Pflanze, *Bismarck and the Development of Modern Germany, vol. 1: The Period of Unification, 1815–1871* (Princeton, NJ, 1990).

JOHN BREUILLY

Geronimo (*b* Chihuahua, Mexico, *c*.1829; *d* Fort Sill, Oklahoma, 17 February 1909)   Leader of part of the Chiracahua Apache tribe. He was the last native American to surrender formally to the United States. Although his name was Goyakla, 'One who Yawns', the American press called him Geronimo (Spanish for Jerome). Living in the northern parts of the Mexican states of Chihuahua and Sonora, the Chiracahua occasionally ranged into south-eastern Arizona and south-western New Mexico. Although the United States forced them on to a reservation in 1877, Geronimo's band fled several times and either surrendered or were recaptured. Before his final capture, he led a band of fewer than fifty men and women who eluded and harassed forty-two companies of American infantry and cavalry and 4,000 Mexican soldiers. In the years following his surrender in 1886 Geronimo appeared at Wild West shows and public occasions, like the St Louis World's Fair in 1904.

JOHN MARTIN

Gettysburg, Battle of (1–3 July 1863)   During the AMERICAN CIVIL WAR the Confederate army of northern Virginia, commanded by General Robert E. LEE, invaded Pennsylvania hoping to find supplies and attract the support of the European powers. After Lee's army encountered scouts from the Union army of the Potomac, commanded by General George Meade (1815–72), north of Gettysburg, Confederates drove the smaller Union forces back to Cemetery Ridge. On the second day Lee attempted flanking actions at both ends of the Union line, but could not drive them from their superior position. Both sides suffered massive casualties, but Lee elected to continue the offensive on the third day. He called for a frontal assault (Pickett's Charge) on the Union centre which failed. This represented the first major Union victory in the east and, coupled with the surrender of Vicksburg (4 July), served as a major turning-point for the Union. After Gettysburg Lee's army never regained offensive momentum.

Bruce Catton, *Gettysburg: The Final Fury* (Garden City, NJ, 1974).

ALICE E. REAGAN

Ghent, Treaty of (24 December 1814)   The WAR OF 1812 between the United States and Great Britain, in which neither side achieved a clear-cut victory, ended with the Treaty of Ghent. The treaty confirmed the *status quo ante bellum* and set up three joint commissions to establish the United States–Canadian boundary from the mouth of the St Croix River to the Lake of the Woods. It did not address several of the major causes of the war: British maritime rights (the search of neutral ships and the Royal Navy's impressment at sea of British-born American sailors), British disregard for the United States' 3 mile limit and problems with several native-American tribes. Most of these issues were subsequently addressed in negotiations between the United States and Britain.

GEORGE O. KENT

Gilbert, William Schwenk (*b* London, 18 November 1836; *d* Harrow, 29 May 1911) and **Sullivan, Arthur** (*b* London, 13 May 1842; *d* London, 22 November 1900)   Authors of the most famous British comic operas of the nineteenth century. Their speciality was satirizing political, social and cultural movements. Gilbert was a playwright turned librettist, Sullivan a serious composer with a gift for devising popular melodies that perfectly complemented the parodies of Gilbert's verses. Their collaboration began in 1870, but their real success came after 1877 when Richard D'Oyly Carte (1844–1901) began to produce their operas and built the Savoy Theatre to stage them. *HMS Pinafore* (1878) was followed by *The Pirates of Penzance* (1879), *Patience* (1881), *Princess Ida* (1884), *The Mikado* (1885), *Ruddigore* (1887), *The Yeomen of the Guard* (1888) and *The Gondoliers* (1889). Their partnership was never easy, however. Sullivan hankered to compose more serious work, and their collaboration ceased in 1890, although they worked together again on two unsuccessful productions in the late 1890s.

RICHARD PRICE

Gilded Age The period in United States history from the end of the Civil War (1861–5) to the presidency of Theodore Roosevelt was christened 'the Gilded Age' by the novelists Mark Twain (1835–1910) and Charles Dudley Warner (1829–1900) in their satirical narrative of greed and corruption, *The Gilded Age* (1873). Lifting episodes from the daily papers, they exposed and condemned what they saw as the spirit of their age: the apotheosis of money. Every chapter teemed with characters on the make, including self-deceived and scheming speculators; legislators buying and selling votes; women ruined by seducers and seducers, in their turn, ruined by their vengeful victims.

Journalists' headlines often seemed to confirm this representation of the late nineteenth century. The period saw political machines dominate urban politics (see, for example, TAMMANY HALL); electioneers registered so many accusations of corruption during the presidential election of 1876 that some writers dubbed the eventual winner 'Ruther*fraud* B. Hayes'. Shortly before that controversy, a real-life sex scandal rocked New York City, involving a prominent clergyman. The notorious affair strengthened the voice of free-love advocates, who denounced marriage itself as just another of America's crass economic relationships.

While corruption and money-grubbing surely existed, the outrage in headlines and editorials revealed, at the same time, that most Americans continued to value honest labour. Indeed, one of the exciting dramas of the Gilded Age was a struggle over who would control that work and who would benefit from it. As much as the late nineteenth century represented the emergence of sleazy politicians and greedy businessmen, it also embodied an important transitional phase of American history in which various groups energetically organized to create a new society.

Business and industrial enterprises led this organizational flurry. Many grew so large in the last decades of the nineteenth century that they were able to control entire portions of the market in various goods or services. These enterprises, which included John D. ROCKEFELLER's oil enterprise, Andrew CARNEGIE's steel empire, and J. P. MORGAN's finance industries, drew the far-flung United States together, pulled power out of the hands of local elites and concentrated it instead in the hands of a few corporate giants.

Americans outside the corporate leadership sensed a loss of control over their lives and organized to wrest power away from the corporate moguls. These initiatives drew millions of Americans into voluntary associations. The KNIGHTS OF LABOR, for instance, claimed over 700,000 members by 1886. More than a million rural Americans joined local granges in the 1870s. Over the next decade organizers drew 5 million members into the farmers' alliance movement. Evangelical women organized the WOMEN'S CHRISTIAN TEMPERANCE UNION (WCTU). During the 1880s an older organization, the American Social Science Association, gave birth to more specialized professional organizations like the American Historical Association, the American Economics Association and the American Statistics Association.

Each of these organizations, in its way, sought to shape a new future for the United States. The Knights of Labor, farmers' alliances and sometimes the WCTU offered a co-operative alternative to the corporate organization of the United States. These groups hoped and worked for an economy in which labourers together owned and operated their industries and in which the federal government – representing the national community – owned or regulated the industries that affected the entire country. (These included especially the railroads, telegraphs and the finance industry.) During the 1890s this cooperative alternative to corporate domination found political expression in the People's Party, or populism (see POPULISM (UNITED STATES)).

Social scientists, lawyers, social workers, nurses and doctors offered a professional and bureaucratic alternative to corporate control. Instead of leaving decisions in the hands of businessmen, professionals suggested that because they were disinterested and expert they should make the big decisions affecting community life, and they lobbied hard to convince non-professionals to accept their authority.

Although the battles among these alternatives were not entirely over by the end of the nineteenth century, the outlines of the future were clear. The organization of the American economy would subordinate wage labour within increasingly large and centralized industrial enterprises while professional elites and workers would shift in and out of alliances that continually renegotiated limits on the power of corporate managers.

Lawrence Goodwyn, *Democratic Promise: The Populist Moment in America* (New York, 1976).
Herbert G. Gutman, *Work, Culture and Society in Industrializing America* (New York, 1976).
Robert H. Wiebe, *The Search for Order, 1877–1920* (New York, 1967).

ROBYN MUNCY

Giolitti, Giovanni (*b* Mondovì, Piedmont, 27 October 1842; *d* Cavour, Italy, 17 July 1928)   Five times prime minister of Italy and seven times interior minister. A civil servant for twenty years, he was first elected to parliament in 1882. His first government, from May 1892 until November 1893, was dominated by the Banco Romana scandal involving high government officials. Giolitti is best known for his skilful manipulation of the fluid Italian party structure, known as transformism, and his ability 'to make elections' through traditional, undemocratic methods of controlling them. A moderate leftist with no strong convictions, he was willing to implement socialist programmes in order to decrease the socialist-party threat to his position. The period from 1901 to 1914 is known as the Giolittian era for, although he was not always prime minister, his influence on policy during these years was constant.

LAWRENCE P. ADAMCZYK

Gladstone, William Ewart (*b* Liverpool, 29 December 1809; *d* Hawarden, Flintshire, 19 May 1898)   Pre-eminent Liberal leader of the nineteenth century, prime minister (1868–74, 1880–5, 1886, 1892–4). His parents were Scottish; his father was a Liverpool merchant who owned plantations in the West Indies and encouraged free enquiry among his children. Gladstone began in the world of trade and commerce, encountered the traditional elite and intellectual life at Eton and Oxford and when he married Catherine Glynne (1812–1900) in 1839 he joined the landed gentry. In conjunction with his complex personality, these experiences help to explain his politics. He was a man of contradictions: impulsive but cautious; romantic and practical; capable of tortured logic, yet full of passion; an Evangelical who was doctrinally high church and sympathetic to Catholicism; of scholarly temperament and talent, yet a brilliant parliamentary and political tactician; freethinking and disputatious, but grounded in seemingly rigid religious conviction. Gladstone directed these traits into enormously creative channels by his faith that religion could bring order to society and his commitment to individual emancipation. For him, the task of politics was to realize these possibilities. Once Gladstone was convinced that a certain political measure would encourage political, social, economic and intellectual liberty, he pursued it with vigour and moral passion. This led to seemingly sudden political shifts – most notably his 'conversion' to Irish HOME RULE in 1885 – which opened him to the charge of hypocritical priggishness.

His political practice combined a deep attachment to traditional social order and a commitment to liberating reforms which increased with age. He began life as a Conservative member of parliament sitting for a rotten borough; under the influence of Peel and following his experience as chancellor of the exchequer in the 1850s, he attached himself to the WHIGS, to become the leading spokesperson of middle-class LIBERALISM by the mid-1860s. He was a leading opponent of aggressive foreign policies (most famously expressed in his Midlothian campaign of 1879–80) and a proponent of cautious expansion of the franchise. His support of Irish Home Rule from 1885 split the Liberal Party, but placed Ireland at the centre of the political agenda for the next forty years.

E. J. Feuchtwanger, *Gladstone* (London, 1975).

RICHARD PRICE

Gneisenau, August Wilhelm Anton, Count Neithardt von (*b* Schilda, Saxony, 27 October 1760; *d* Posen, 23 August 1831)   Prussian military leader. He gained his reputation as a military commander during the war against Napoleon in 1806–7. Following Prussia's defeat, he emerged as a leading member of the group of reformers which included STEIN and HARDENBERG, and was appointed by King Frederick-William III in 1807 to the military reform commission. Gneisenau and other army reformers (Scharnhorst (1755–1813), Boyen (1771–1848)) succeeded in curbing the aristocratic monopoly of the officer corps, reorganizing officer-training and reforming army disciplinary procedures; however, they failed to push through universal conscription, which they saw as the precondition for a genuinely national army. After withdrawing from military duties between 1809 and 1812 and undertaking diplomatic activity aimed at promoting a war of liberation, Gneisenau returned to active service and played a prominent role as a commander of Prussian forces in the campaigns against Napoleon (1813–15). After 1815 he remained in the army, but was increasingly marginalized politically.

ELIZABETH HARVEY

Godoy, Manuel de (*b* Badajoz, 12 May 1767; *d* Paris, 4 October 1851)   Spanish statesman. As royal favourite and supposed lover of the queen, he has received much of the blame for Spain's weakness in the Revolutionary and Napoleonic period. However, although his background was relatively humble and his rise to power as secretary of state and generalissimo extraordinarily rapid, much of the abuse is unfounded. A convinced reformer, Godoy attempted to continue with the enlightened policies of Charles III (1759–88), while rebuilding the Spanish army under cover of an alliance with France. Discredited by economic and military misfortunes, and his own personal failings, however, he was shunned by progressive opinion, while simultaneously earning the hostility of the church, the army, the lower classes, the aristocracy and the future Ferdinand VII. He was eventually toppled in a military coup when Napoleon intervened in Spain in 1808. Escaping abroad, he lived the rest of his life in exile.

CHARLES ESDAILE

Goethe, Johann Wolfgang von (*b* Frankfurt am Main, 28 August 1749; *d* Weimar, 22 March 1832)   German writer. Born the son of a lawyer, he studied in Strasburg, where he became involved with Gottfried Herder (1744–1803) and the pre-romantic school of German writing known as *Sturm und Drang*. In 1774 he published the popular epistolary novel *Die Leiden des jungen Werthers* (The Sorrows of Young Werther), whose hero's suicide was imitated by young romantics across Europe. In 1776 Goethe was appointed a privy councillor in Weimar, where he spent much of the rest of his life, and where he later formed the close creative friendship with Friedrich Schiller (1759–1805), which lasted until the death of the latter. It was during this period that Goethe completed the novel *Wilhelm Meisters Lehrjahre* (Wilhelm Meister's Apprenticeship, 1795–6), wrote *Hermann und Dorothea* (1797) and resumed work on *Faust* (1808–32). Virtually all of Schiller's best work was also written during these years. The work of the two came to constitute a 'Weimar classicism' which represented the golden age of German literature for nineteenth-century Germans, and established the reputations of Goethe and Schiller as Germany's greatest national writers.

TIMOTHY KIRK

gold rushes   The nineteenth century saw an unprecedented rise in gold production because of the chance discoveries made of the metal, especially in California and AUSTRALIA. Thousands of men virtually rushed from place to place when they heard of new strikes. They rapidly plundered the surface and subsurface deposits and rushed on again. Shanty towns mushroomed overnight and, in most cases, as quickly disappeared when the readily discoverable gold petered out. Fortunes were made by a few. The rest endured hardship and made little. Prices climbed for food and transport, labour became scarce in other sectors, wages were raised fivefold, and in California, which had been very recently purchased by the United States from Mexico, much lawlessness prevailed. The first strike took place there in January 1848 when the population was 15,000. Diggers arrived from all over the world in 1849, hence the term 'forty-niners', and the population rose to 269,000. In the years 1848–56, 800 tons of gold were produced.

Gold was discovered in Australia in 1851. Men returned from California, bringing the methods acquired there with them. In the 'golden decade' of the 1850s Victoria experienced continuous rushes at places such as Ballarat and Bendigo and over 1,000 tons of gold were produced, amounting to 40 per cent of the world's total. The population rose from 80,000 to half a million, including 40,000 Chinese. There were further discoveries on the Yukon (1896), Alaska (1898) and Witwatersrand in South Africa (1883). Johannesburg was built on gold. The Golden Mile at Kalgoorlie in Western Australia was opened in 1892–3. Russia, especially eastern Siberia, continued to produce large quantities of gold but it was the Californian and Australian discoveries that had a profound effect on world markets for gold.

Geoffrey Blainey, *The Rush that Never Ended* (Melbourne, 1963).

JOHN MOLONY

gold standard   The use of gold as a country's monetary standard is known as the gold standard. The currency unit is defined in terms of a fixed weight of gold; paper currency should be convertible into gold coin on demand, and the free export of gold be permitted. By 1900 such a system had become monetary orthodoxy. Britain had restricted the use of silver in 1774, and a full gold standard was in force there from 1821. Elsewhere a silver standard was widely employed, though France and the United States officially operated a bimetallic standard. The disadvantage of BIMETALLISM was its dependence on an unchanging world price ratio for the two metals: any increase in the world price of one would result in its disappearance from circulation. Until mid-century there were few problems, but subsequent gold discoveries disrupted bimetallic regimes.

Germany led the way to the general adoption of gold in 1871, and the falling price of silver resulting from German sales and new discoveries resulted in its general abandonment as a monetary standard. By 1880 France, the Netherlands, Belgium, the Scandinavian countries, Switzerland and *de facto* the United States were on gold. With fixed gold parities, currencies were in effect participating in an international financial system of fixed exchange rates, which Russia, Japan, Austria-Hungary, India and some Latin American countries had joined by 1900. This, and the dynamic nature of world trade in the late nineteenth century, implied for later generations that the gold standard was an effective mechanism for financial stability and smooth balance-of-payments adjustment. In fact, the way in which the gold standard secured adjustment, the nature of central-bank discretion in its operation, the importance to it of sterling and its true contribution to the growth of the international economy remain controversial issues.

Barry Eichengreen (ed.), *The Gold Standard in Theory and History* (New York, 1985).

HENRY FINCH

Gompers, Samuel (*b* London, 27 January 1850; *d* San Antonio, Texas, 13 December 1924)   American labour leader. Born of Dutch Jewish working-class parents, Gompers as a youth joined the New York Cigarmakers' Union and later became its president (1874–81). He played the key role in organizing the AMERICAN FEDERATION OF LABOR (1886) of which he remained president, except for one year (1895), until his death. Committed to keeping unionism separate from politics and opposed to 'socialistic' theories, he stressed practical demands in wages and hours. He sought to limit AFL membership to workers organized on strictly occupational lines and used salaried organizers and a labour press to keep the ranks of workers solid. As the KNIGHTS OF LABOR waned, his vision of labour's place in American society was vindicated, and he became the acknowledged leader of the American labour movement. During the First World War he was labour's spokesman for national unity.

Samuel Gompers, *Seventy Years of Life and Labor*, 2 vols (New York, 1943).
KEVIN MURPHY

Gordon, Charles George (*b* Woolwich, 28 January 1833; *d* Khartoum, 26 January 1885) English general and administrator. Known as 'Chinese Gordon' because of his role in repressing the Taiping Rebellion in China in the early 1860s, he served in the Egyptian khedive Ismail's administration in the SUDAN (1872–9), as one of a series of British administrators in Egyptian service, and was later governor-general of the Sudan (1877–80). While in the Sudan he sought to suppress domestic slavery and the 'Arab' slave trade, angering Muslim dealers who for generations had profited from this commerce. Together with Samuel Baker (1821–93), he unsuccessfully sought to extend Egyptian control over Uganda. Considering service in the Belgian king's (Leopold II) Congo Free State, Gordon was later appointed commander of the British forces in the Cape Colony. He is best remembered for the unsuccessful relief of British forces at Khartoum (1884–5), under siege by the Sudanese Mahdi MUHAMMAD 'AHMAD IBN 'ABDALLAH, founder of a shortlived Muslim state (1881–98). With the city's capture in 1885, Gordon was killed.

B. MARIE PERINBAM

Gore, Catherine (*b* East Retford, Nottinghamshire, 1799; *d* Linwood, Lynhurst, Hampshire, 29 January 1861) Popular and prolific English novelist of the Silver Fork school. She published approximately seventy novels between 1824 and 1862. Although they are not of great literary merit, Gore's novels astutely documented her social world, portraying the metamorphosis of Regency brilliance and frivolity into Victorian moralistic serious-mindedness. Gore contributed to the development of the novel by linking the romances of the early years of the century to the realistic domestic fiction of later decades. Focusing on life among the fashionable elite, she celebrated the domestic virtues. Her more interesting novels include *Cecil; or, The Adventures of a Coxcomb* (1841), which gave a detailed and critical portrait of a Regency dandy and his world, and *Mrs Armytage; or, Female Domination* (1836), generally considered her best novel, which delivered a warning about the dangers of allowing a woman too much freedom and power.

Vineta Colby, *Yesterday's Woman: Domestic Realism in the English Novel* (Princeton, NJ, 1974).

GAIL SAVAGE

Gothic Revival This style of architecture was perfected in the nineteenth century. Its most significant manifestations were British, their referent styles ('Early English', 'Decorated' and 'Perpendicular') defined by Thomas Rickman (1776–1841) in his *Attempt to Discriminate the Styles in English Architecture* (1819). Precedents included the romantic fashion of 'gothicizing' great houses, exemplified in the restyling (1750–94) of Strawberry Hill, Twickenham by Horace Walpole (1717–97). Characteristic features included asymmetrical planning, long galleries, pointed arches, medieval towers and elaborate traceries.

Eighty per cent of churches resulting from the Church Building Act (1818) were Gothic for economic (no costly porticoes or pediments) as much as ideological reasons. Augustus Welby Northmore Pugin (1812–52) augmented pragmatic with ethical justification in his publications *Contrasts* (1836) and *Apology for Contrasts* (1837), proposing readoption of medieval social values, associating the condition of architecture with the quality of religious observance and requiring an overt display of Christian symbolism in architecture as a means of moral witness. Adoption of the Gothicized designs of Pugin and Charles Barry (1795–1860) to rebuild the Houses of Parliament (1840–65) confirmed it as an endemic national idiom. British respect for the scholarly expertise of Eugène Emmanuel Viollet-le-Duc (1814–79) acknowledged French claims to cultural origins. George Gilbert Scott (1811–78), a prolific architect in Gothic, modernized the antiquarian position in his book *Remarks on Secular and Domestic Architecture. Present and Future* (1857), in which he stressed the idiom's descent from masonic (non-scholastic) craft practices, and condoned the abandonment of archaic details for sounder practicalities. Among the finest manifestations of the resulting architectural aesthetic were Scott's St Pancras Hotel, London (1868–74), the Church of All Saints, London (1859) by William Butterfield (1814–1900) and Manchester Town Hall (1868–77) by Alfred Waterhouse (1830–1905).

See also ARCHITECTURE.

Kenneth Clark (1928), *The Gothic Revival*, revised edn (London, 1962).

DAVID THISTLEWOOD

Government of India Act (1853) Mounting concern over the English East India Company's administration in INDIA led to the Government of India Act in 1853. It was simply the latest in a series of efforts by parliament to limit patronage and to create a more effective and quali-fied administration in India. The last renewal of the Company's char-ter, in 1833, had precipitated profound questioning of the need for the East India Company to continue in its present role. Parliamentary opinion, deeply influenced by the so-called Manchester Radicals, went beyond questions of reform and limitations of political patronage to favour merit and even suggest that the charter should not be renewed.

By taking steps to reform, the Government of India Act was in-tended to weaken opposition to charter renewal. Under the aegis of Sir Charles Wood (1800–85), the Act of 1853 contained modest pro-posals for reform in the civil service, military, high courts and Indian councils.

R. J. Moore, *Sir Charles Wood's Indian Policy* (Manchester, 1966)

ROBERT J. YOUNG

Grant, Ulysses Simpson (*b* Point Pleasant, Ohio, 27 April 1822; *d* Mount McGregor, New York, 23 July 1885) Civil War general and eighteenth president of the United States. A graduate of West Point (1843), he served with distinction during the Mexican-American War (1846–8). When the AMERICAN CIVIL WAR began in 1861 he volun-teered to work as a recruiting officer. During 1862 he emerged as the leading general in the western theatre, with victories at Forts Henry and Donelson, and at Shiloh. His reputation rose further in 1863 with his masterly capture of the Confederate citadel of Vicksburg and his victory at Chattanooga. Brought east by Lincoln to take command of the entire war effort in early 1864, he laid siege to Petersburg until it fell in April 1865. He then accepted the surrender of Robert E. Lee's army of northern Virginia on 9 April. Seen by Americans as one of the primary heroes of the Civil War, Grant was elected president in 1868, serving two terms. These were marred by scandals and nepotism which greatly tarnished his image.

William S. McFeely, *Grant: A Biography* (New York, 1981).

ALICE E. REAGAN

Great Britain The Roman invader Julius Caesar first named the is-land 'Britain' in the mistaken belief that his predecessors, the Belgic invaders of Britain, were Britanni. The more grandiose-sounding 'Great Britain' is a multinational state which, at various stages and in various combinations, has collectively embraced Wales, Scotland, England and Ireland. Union between England and Wales was achieved by a series of parliamentary acts in the sixteenth century. The union of England and Scotland was affected by the succession in 1603 of James VI of Scotland to the English throne as James I. An official act establishing an 'incorporating' union was not passed until 1707, when Scotland lost its own parliament in exchange for representation in Westminster. The union of Great Britain and Ireland was enacted in 1800. The Irish parliament was abolished and, in the following year, the United Kingdom of Great Britain and Ireland was established (*see* IRISH ACT OF UNION). The present United Kingdom of Great Britain and Northern Ireland took form in 1921 with the partition of Ireland.

JOHN SPRINGHALL

Great Depression (1873–1896)   The term 'Great Depression' refers to a roughly twenty-year period characterized by contemporaries – especially the upper and middle classes and landowning groups – as a time of 'depression of prices, a depression of interest, a depression of profits'. As with most populist sentiments, these doubts and complaints about an economic malaise appear to have been based more on feeling than on objective analysis.

Some evidence for a depression in Britain can certainly be found in this period. Checks to money wages may have been one source of discontent in this period, with gains to real wages coming from falling prices rather than wage increases. It was also a period of increasing bitterness in labour relations, with employers attempting to keep up prices against a rapidly unionizing labour force. Certainly, in agriculture falling prices meant lower profits and rents for the landowners and decreasing employment opportunities for farm-workers. Since the farming interests tended to be the most articulate groups in society, they ensured that the concept of a depression received maximum publicity.

On the other hand, economic historians have long been aware that other sectors of the economy did not demonstrate any particularly pronounced evidence of depression. The rate of population growth slackened after about 1880, but this trend continued until about 1911 and the twenty years between 1875 and 1895 were in no way unique. The percentage share of the national product and labour force going into agriculture also declined, though again this was part of a long-term structural trend in the economy, by no means confined to these 'depression' years. National income also rose in the second half of the nineteenth century, faster than before 1850, and faster than population. Real wages were also rising in the same period, with the years between 1873 and 1896 being unexceptional, except that the rise came from falling prices rather than rising wages. The same is true of the data for unemployment, industrial output and productivity, which show few distinguishing characteristics for these years.

But the Great Depression may not entirely be a myth. The data relating to Britain's international trading position – the value of foreign trade, the balance of trade and payments and capital flows – do show some significant trends for the depression years. Export values of the early 1870s, for example, were not surpassed until the second half of the 1890s. The decline in the rate of growth in the volume of exports is also marked. In the case of cotton goods, export values (in current prices) of 1872 were not equalled again until 1904, with 1895 as a low point. With such a high proportion of output in certain industries such as cotton destined for exports, this could have led to manufacturers having less profit for investment. Capital exports also fell away at the start of the Great Depression, though they recovered before 1890 to hit a new peak.

It is clear that the Great Depression defies a single unitary explanation. Historians, aware of this, have tended in recent years to relate contemporary sentiments about depression to larger questions about Britain's industrial performance in the late nineteenth century, especially in comparison with its industrial rivals, such as Germany and the United States. There has been careful evaluation of Britain's growth rates, ouput and productivity and also of its alleged 'entrepreneurial failure' – the weakness of its enterprise culture, the poor quality of scientific education, the low rates of investment in key industries and the tardiness in exploiting new technologies. But this has not resolved the reason for Britain's loss of industrial leadership. Such investigations have necessarily looked at long-term trends in the economy and have related the Great Depression to more general nineteenth-century developments. This has tended to diminish the significance of the term, though the fact that certain nineteenth-century commentators were convinced of the existence of a Great Depression and the fact that historians have found major gaps in performance between Britain and its competitors will ensure the term's survival.

Peter Mathias, *The First Industrial Nation: An Economic History of Britain 1700–1914*, second edn (London, 1983).
S. B. Saul, *The Myth of the Great Depression, 1873–1896* (London, 1969).

GEOFFREY TWEEDALE

Great Exhibition *see* INTERNATIONAL EXPOSITIONS.

Great Trek (1834–1848) Pressure on land was a major stimulus to the Great Trek, as the Boers moved beyond the frontiers of the CAPE COLONY in order to occupy land in the interior outside of British jurisdiction. Antagonism to British authority also played a part, although this point has been exaggerated by later Afrikaner nationalists. Preliminary reconnaissance led to the organized movement of about 15,000 people referred to as 'voortrekkers'. Trek leaders tended to be highly individualistic and argumentative. A number of fairly small republics were later absorbed into larger ones. The Republic of Natalia was formed in 1839, after the withdrawal of British troops from Port Natal. The British annexed NATAL in 1843, leading to the Boers' withdrawal (*see* ORANGE FREE STATE). Boers also moved into the territory north of the Vaal River (*see* TRANSVAAL) but the unified South African republic was established there only in 1864.

SIMON KATZENELLENBOGEN

Greece A province of the Ottoman Empire at the beginning of the nineteenth century, Greece won its independence in 1832 following a long struggle for emancipation, the origins of which may be found in the intellectual revival that took place among educated Greeks in the late eighteenth century. Much encouraged by the French Revolution and the Serbian revolt of 1804, Greek exiles in Russia formed a secret society known as the Philiki Etairia, which helped provoke a national revolt in 1821. The military backbone was provided by the *klephts* – bandit gangs which had been resisting Ottoman authority for centuries. At first the response of the powers was lukewarm or even hostile, but liberal opinion everywhere was much excited, the Greeks therefore receiving the support of many foreign volunteers. Moreover, the Turks were held in check (though with growing difficulty), and practical considerations soon began to persuade Britain, France and Russia to take a more favourable line. Full independence was eventually obtained with their assistance.

Greece now became a kingdom under Otto of Bavaria, (1832–62), but emancipation was accompanied by many problems, including poverty, backwardness, truncated frontiers, factionalism and financial chaos. A constitution was granted in 1844, but this made little difference, and the increasingly unpopular Otto was dethroned by a rising in 1862. He was replaced by the Danish George I (1863–1913) and Greece became a 'crowned democracy'; but until the end of the century its politics remained a byword for corruption and intrigue, being further disrupted by tension between modernizers and conservatives. At the same time, Greece remained poor and backward, and was in consequence, in spite of Ottoman decline, unable to redeem its irredentist ambitions until 1913, when the Balkan Wars established its present frontiers.

Richard Clogg, *A Short History of Modern Greece* (Cambridge, 1979).

CHARLES ESDAILE

Greenback Party Supported mainly by economically troubled farmers in the west and south of the United States who were heavily in debt after the panic of 1873, the Greenback Party was formed in 1874 to expand the currency. Greenback paper notes were first issued in 1862 to meet the expenses of the Civil War, and by 1865 some $400 million were still outstanding. Farmers wanted more greenbacks added to circulation to spur inflation, but when Ulysses S. Grant vetoed the inflation bill passed by Congress in 1874, the Greenback Party was formed.

The Resumption Act of 1875 provided that the treasury would redeem greenbacks in gold by 1879, thereby reducing the number of greenbacks in circulation. This measure contracted the currency and its value appreciated, the two things farmers and debtors most feared. Greenbackers advocated repeal of this act, arguing that resumption would further depress prices. They were further outraged at a proposal to redeem war bonds purchased with inflated currency during the war with more valuable currency later.

In 1876 the party nominated Peter Cooper (1791–1883) for president, who polled 81,000 votes. The rural base of the party was later supplemented by some embittered labour organizations to form the Greenback-Labor Party. Strengthened by this urban support, the party polled over 1 million votes in the congressional elections of 1878 and elected fourteen representatives to Congress. President Rutherford B. Hayes (1822–93) resisted all opposition, however, and resumption was accomplished, rendering the party moribund by 1880.

Pressure to increase the money supply did not vanish. Farmers turned in the 1880s and 1890s to the free coinage of silver to solve their economic problems and found new political expression of their discontent in populism (*see* POPULISM (UNITED STATES)).

Irwin Unger, *The Greenback Era: A Social and Political History of American Finance, 1865–1879* (Princeton, NJ, 1964).

KEVIN MURPHY

Gregory XVI [Bartolomeo Alberto Cappellari] (*b* Belluno, Venetian Republic, 18 September 1765; *d* Rome, 1 June 1846)   Pope (1831–46). Of noble family, he was professed a monk of the Camaldolese congregation in 1783, taking the name of Mauro. He was ordained in 1787 and became abbot of San Gregorio in 1805. In 1826 he became cardinal prefect of the Congregation for the Propagation of the Faith, and his election as pope in 1831 signalled the triumph of the intransigently conservative *zelanti* party. Austria was called in to repress two nationalist risings in the Papal States in 1831, and afterwards Gregory opposed both Gioberti's (1801–52) moderate Catholic programme for a federated Italy headed by the pope and the anticlerical MAZZINI's vision of a united Italy arising from the ashes of the papal Temporal Power. Further revolts were suppressed in 1843 and 1845. Gregory defended the church against persecution in Spain, Portugal and Russia, but condemned the Polish rebellion of 1830–1 against Russia, and the liberal Catholicism of Hugues-Félicité de LAMENNAIS in his encyclicals 'Mirari vos' in 1832 and 'Singulari nos' in 1834. He would not allow railway building in the Papal States. His unremitting opposition to Italian political aspirations left an impossible legacy to his successors.

A. Fliche and V. Martin (eds), *Histoire de l'Église*, vol. 20: *La crise révolutionnaire 1789–1846*, by Jean Leflon (Paris, 1949), bk. 3, pp. 426–516.

SHERIDAN GILLEY

Grey, Charles, second Earl (*b* Fallodon, Northumberland, 13 March 1764; *d* 17 July 1845)   English statesman. A Foxite Whig, out of office for twenty-three years after serving as foreign secretary (1806–7), he was invited to form a ministry in 1830, by which time public demand for PARLIAMENTARY REFORM was irresistible. A self-confessed aristocrat 'both by position and by nature', Grey wisely calculated that the best way to conserve the traditional political order was to promote a thorough, once-and-for-all, measure of reform, the details of which he entrusted to his radical colleagues. Having persevered with the Reform Bill throughout a lengthy constitutional crisis, Grey took the opportunity to retire to his beloved Northumberland in 1834 when his cabinet divided over Irish affairs.

JOHN BELCHEM

Guadalupe Hidalgo, Treaty of (1848)   Signed in February 1848 between the United States government and the Mexican administration of General José Joaquín Herrera (1792–1854), the Treaty of Guadalupe Hidalgo ended the MEXICAN-AMERICAN WAR. In return for a payment of $15 million and the United States government's agreement to pay claims against Mexico valued at $3.25 million, Herrera recognized the independence of Texas and sold California, New Mexico and the vast area between them to the United States. After ratification by the Senate the United States withdrew its troops from Mexico in July 1848. Within a year gold had been discovered in California.

A few years later, in 1853, the poverty-stricken Mexican government, now headed by Santa Anna, ceded further territory to the United States. In the so-called Gadsden Purchase the United States paid $10 million for the Mesilla Valley, in what is now southern New Mexico and Arizona.

RORY MILLER

Guesde, Jules [Matthieu Basile] (*b* Paris, 12 November 1845; *d* Saint-Mandé, 28 July 1922)   French left-wing politician. He began as a radical republican journalist, but became a socialist during the Paris Commune and founded in 1877 the first Marxist socialist periodical in France, *L'Égalité*. In 1880, accompanied by Paul Lafargue (1842–1911), Marx's son-in-law, he visited London to consult with Marx and Engels about the programme and constitution of the new party he was engaged in creating. The resulting documents were adopted at the second congress of the party in 1880, but divisions soon arose and one section, led by Paul Brousse (1854–1912) who opposed the doctrine of revolutionary socialism, created a rival party whose members became known as the 'Possibilists'. In 1882 Guesde formed the Parti Ouvrier Français in close association with the national federation of trade unions. A prolific writer and notable orator, Guesde was elected to the chamber of deputies in 1893, where he remained until 1921, and had a prominent role in the SECOND INTERNATIONAL. Although he generally opposed participation by socialists in bourgeois governments, on the outbreak of war in 1914 he, like the great majority of socialist leaders, supported the war, declaring that German imperialism had to be destroyed. He was a government minister in 1914–16.

Val R. Lorwin, *The French Labour Movement* (Cambridge, Mass., 1954). Alexandre Zévaès, *Jules Guesde* (Paris, 1929).

TOM BOTTOMORE

Guizot, François Pierre Guillaume (*b* Nîmes, 4 October 1787; *d* Val-Richer, 12 October 1874)   French historian, politician and Protestant leader. His father was guillotined as a counter-revolutionary. Guizot combined the position of history professor with various official and political positions. He became minister of education under Louis-Philippe and passed the law which required every commune in France to establish a primary school and provided government financial support for them. Guizot believed that moralizing the masses would inoculate them from revolutionary intentions. He symbolized the 'bourgeois' nature of the July Monarchy, as epitomized by his famous aphorism 'Enrich yourself by saving and work'. Prime minister in 1847, he was forced to resign after street disturbances in Paris in February 1848 and fled to London. He translated Gibbon (1737–94) and published histories of representative government and the English Civil War. Throughout his life he devoted himself to promoting Protestant organizations.

Douglas Johnson, *Guizot: Aspects of French History, 1787–1874* (Westport, Conn., 1974).

DONALD SUTHERLAND

H

Habsburg Empire   Also known as Austria, the Habsburg Monarchy and, after 1867, Austria-Hungary or the Dual Monarchy, the Habsburg Empire, with its capital in Vienna, occupied most of central Europe. It comprised the Austrian hereditary lands (present-day Austria and Slovenia), the Bohemian crown lands (Bohemia, Moravia and Austrian Silesia), Galicia (southern Poland), the Bukovina (now in the Ukraine/Romania) and Hungary (including Transylvania (now in Romania), Slovakia and Croatia-Slavonia). During the course of the century it also lost valuable territories in northern Italy, and gained Bosnia-Hercegovina. The Habsburg Empire had a population of around 21 million in 1789 (excluding Lombardy), and 45.4 million in 1900 (excluding Bosnia-Hercegovina). In terms of economic development, the western provinces were on a par with other Western economies, but the eastern provinces, especially Galicia, were severely underdeveloped.

The empire's main characteristic, and its main problem in an age of nationalism, was that it was a dynastic agglomeration, with a population composed of many nationalities, some 'historic' (dominant) such as the Germans, Hungarians, Poles and Italians, and some not, such as the Romanians and the Slav nationalities: Czechs, Slovaks, Slovenes, Croats, Serbs and Ruthenes. In addition, there were the empire's Jews, whose situation resisted national classification. The history of the Habsburg Empire in the nineteenth century can be seen as centred on the struggle to keep this multinational state together, while at the same time preserving the great-power status of the Habsburg dynasty, which the state was intended to support.

At the beginning of the century, under the rule of Francis I (see FRANCIS II), the empire suffered a series of humiliating military and diplomatic defeats by Napoleon. Then, under the guidance of METTERNICH, as a member of the successful anti-French coalition, it emerged from the CONGRESS OF VIENNA as the main power-broker in Continental Europe, with most of its territories and prestige restored, and the leading position in Germany and Italy. At home and abroad the imperial regime came to be seen as the leader of reaction, trying to keep revolution (liberalism) from the door. The REVOLUTIONS OF 1848, with the Hungarian Kossuth leading the way, threatened the existence of the empire, but the efforts of loyal generals, such as RADETZKY and WINDISCHGRÄTZ, and the falling out of the revolutionaries along class and national lines, rescued the imperial heritage for the new emperor, FRANCIS JOSEPH I.

An attempt in the 1850s to rule by a system of neo-absolutist centralism ended in financial crisis, defeat by France in northern Italy in 1859 and the loss of Lombardy. There followed a turn to liberal constitutionalism, and then reconciliation with the Hungarian leadership. The competition with Prussia over control of Germany led to defeat in the AUSTRO-PRUSSIAN WAR in 1866, which effectively excluded Habsburg influence in German affairs, and also led to the loss of Venetia. The conflict with the Hungarians was settled by the COMPROMISE OF 1867, and a liberal constitution was introduced into the Austrian half of the empire, although the name 'Austria' was not allowed officially by the terms of the compromise.

What emerged from the events of 1866–7 was an empire split into two semi-independent states held together by the emperor, his court, common armed forces, a common foreign policy, a common currency and a customs union, but with no common cabinet as such, and strongly divergent constitutions and political constellations. In Austria, or Cisleithania (after the River Leitha, along which the Austrian–Hungarian border ran) a long period of political dominance by German liberals was replaced in the 1880s by a conservative-clerical-Slav coalition, Taaffe's (1833–95) 'Iron Ring'. German fear of threats to their hegemonial position eventually led to the Badeni Crisis of 1897 over the language question in the Bohemian crown lands. By 1900 the Austrian Reichsrat was paralysed by the German–Czech conflict, with government functioning through the bureaucracy.

In Hungary (Transleithania) the Hungarian regime pursued ruthlessly pro-Magyar policies (although Magyars constituted only half of the population), including the attempted Magyarization of the other nationalities, with the acquiescence of Francis Joseph. As emperor, however, Francis Joseph doggedly refused any Hungarian challenges to his control over the army. This was to lead to a prolonged crisis from 1903. By 1900 the Habsburg Empire was still intact, but its nationality problems and its dualism were already proving very troublesome, especially when it came to adequate financing of its armed forces, the ultimate guarantee of its status as a great power and indeed its continued existence.

Alan Sked, *The Decline and Fall of the Habsburg Empire* (London, 1989).
A. J. P. Taylor, *The Habsburg Monarchy 1809–1918* (London, 1949).

STEVEN BELLER

Hague Conferences (1899, 1907) The first Hague Conference, convened by NICHOLAS II of Russia, was held between 18 May and 29 July 1899. Russia proposed a general European disarmament or arms limitation, and urged the powers to revise the laws and customs of warfare. It was widely known that the tsar's proposals were motivated less by ideals than by his government's financial difficulties and its inability to keep up with the armament race of the major European powers. Although twenty-six states were represented at the conference, most delegates distrusted the Russian plan and the conference accomplished little. However, two lasting achievements were the signing of a convention for the peaceful settlement of international disputes and the establishment of a permanent court of arbitration. A definition of the laws of warfare was also agreed on.

The second peace conference, also convened by Nicholas II, was attended by forty-four states and lasted from 15 June to 18 October 1907. President Theodore Roosevelt of the United States had first proposed such a conference in October 1904, but it was postponed because of the Russo-Japanese war. At the second conference British attempts to achieve some armaments limitations were defeated by many of the powers led by Germany. However, the delegates succeeded in passing several conventions dealing with arbitration, the collection of debts, the rights and obligations of neutrals and the rules of land and sea warfare. The international treaties that resulted from these two conferences were known as the Hague Convention.

Carnegie Endowment for International Peace, *The Proceedings of the Hague Peace Conference*, 5 vols (New York, 1920–1).

GEORGE O. KENT

Haiti The state of Haiti had its origins in the slave revolt which began in the French colony of Saint Domingue in 1791. Independence was proclaimed in 1804 by Jean Jacques Dessalines (*c.*1758–1806), a former slave who led the resistance to Napoleon's forces after the deportation of Toussaint l'Ouverture (1746–1803). Dessalines was assassinated in 1806 and the country split into two (*see* Henri CHRISTOPHE), until Jean Pierre BOYER reunited it in 1820. Haiti faced many problems. Although France recognized independence, in return for a 150 million franc indemnity in 1825, Haiti's leaders found it necessary, on several occasions, to intervene in eastern Hispaniola to counter the threat of invasion. The land policies instituted early in the century resulted in the ruin of the plantations and the creation of a subsistence peasantry. Tensions between blacks and mulattos also exacerbated the divisions. Yet the instability of Haiti should not be overdrawn: presidents tended to retain office, with the support of urban mulattos, for lengthy periods, although they often exercised little control over semi-autonomous military leaders in the countryside.

D. Nicholls, *From Dessalines to Duvalier: Race, Colour and National Independence in Haiti* (Cambridge, 1979).

RORY MILLER

handloom weavers The largest manufacturing occupation during the early decades of the nineteenth century, handloom weaving employed as many as 500,000 people in all branches of the textile industry by 1830. Its tragic decline and degradation after 1820 exemplified the human cost of the INDUSTRIAL REVOLUTION. The late-eighteenth-century mechanization of cotton- and worsted-spinning fuelled a rapid expansion of handloom weaving in the traditional PUTTING-OUT SYSTEM of production. The intense demand for weavers initially insured high wages of 25 shillings or more per week, making the last decade of the eighteenth century the handloom weavers' golden age. While the weavers in most textile sectors abandoned apprenticeship restrictions, they continued to operate within a customary work culture. Often combining wage labour with smallholdings, handloom weavers possessed their own distinct patterns of work and leisure and exercised control over their pace of work.

Towards the close of the Napoleonic wars, however, the market for weavers' labour reached saturation point, signalling the commencement of their decline. Notwithstanding brief spells of relative prosperity, handloom weavers were reduced to earnings of 5 shillings or less per week by the early 1830s and faced chronic unemployment. The handloom weavers responded to the crisis of their trade by petitioning parliament for statutory intervention and the restoration of paternalist practices such as the fixing of wage rates by magistrates. Despite sympathetic parliamentary inquiries, however, British governments rejected the weavers' demands for a minimum wage and the regulation of competition. When manufacturers introduced power looms on a wide scale around 1830 it both accelerated the weavers' decline and sealed their fate. Thousands of handloom weavers continued to eke out a miserable existence until the disappearance of the trade in the 1850s.

See also TEXTILE INDUSTRIES.

E. P. Thompson, *The Making of the English Working Class* (New York, 1966), pp. 269–313.

RICHARD J. SODERLUND

Hardenberg Karl August, prince von (*b* Essenrode, 31 May 1750; *d* Genoa, 26 November 1822) Prussian statesman. His reforming career in Prussia began as administrator of Ansbach-Bayreuth. After the defeat by the French in October 1806 Hardenberg advised FREDERICK-WILLIAM III to continue resistance. Dismissed on Napoleon's insistence in 1807, Hardenberg returned in 1810 to the new office of state chancellor. He continued with economic reforms and tried to rationalize Prussian administration, also convening public assemblies in his search for support. Hardenberg was handicapped by financial crisis, internal opposition, especially from nobles, and the distractions of foreign policy and war. He framed Prussian policy at the CONGRESS OF VIENNA, but his internal reform programme began to lose momentum with the king's refusal to grant a constitution and renewed repressive legislation. He survived by compromising, something which has helped to sustain his reputation as a courtier figure lacking in conviction. When he died in 1822 the office of state chancellor died with him.

James Sheehan, *German History 1770–1866* (Oxford, 1989).

JOHN BREUILLY

Hardie, James Keir (*b* Legbrannock, Lanarkshire, 15 August 1856; *d* Cumnock, Lanarkshire, 26 September 1915)   Scottish socialist leader and principal architect of the coalition that became the LABOUR PARTY. The illegitimate son of a poor farm servant, he learned the hardships of working-class life at first hand, labouring as a collier up to the age of 23. After serving as a miners' union leader and journalist, Hardie converted to gradualist, non-violent socialism and emerged as a leader of the NEW UNIONISM. One of the independent labour candidates elected to parliament in 1892, he played a major role in creating the INDE-PENDENT LABOUR PARTY the following year. His tireless labour for the advance of the working class came to fruition with the formation of the Labour Representation Committee in 1900. Renowned for his passionate moral fervour and deeply held religious convictions, he gave the early socialist movement much of its ethical basis.

Kenneth Morgan, *Keir Hardie* (Oxford, 1967).

RICHARD J. SODERLUND

Harmsworth, Alfred, first Viscount Northcliffe (*b* near Dublin, 15 July 1865; *d* London, 14 August 1922)   Irish press magnate who was largely responsible for the revolution in popular journalism in Britain. He was largely self-educated and trained as a freelance journalist. In 1888 he founded *Answers*, a successful melange of anecdotes, puns and paragraphs of information which copied the formula pioneered in George Newnes's (1851–1910) *Tit-Bits*. Six years later Harmsworth purchased the London *Evening News* and transformed it into a leading journal of crime and popular news. He then founded two of Britain's greatest newspapers: the halfpenny *Daily Mail* (1896), which described itself as 'the busy man's journal' because of its policy of condensing the news; and the *Daily Mirror* (1903), the first successful pictorial morning tabloid newspaper in the world. Together these newspapers prefigured nearly all of the characteristics of the modern mass press and influenced newspapers everywhere. Harmsworth, who was ennobled in 1905, subsequently bought the *Observer* and *The Times*, and with his brother Harold, Viscount Rothermere (1868–1940), became the proprietor of the largest publishing company in the world. During the First World War he served as director of propaganda. He contributed little to the intellectual growth of journalism but helped to bring about immense changes by giving expression to the tastes of ordinary readers.

See also NEWSPAPERS.

Reginald Pound and Geoffrey Harmsworth, *Northcliffe* (London, 1959).

JOEL H. WIENER

Harrison, Benjamin (*b* North Bend, Ohio, 20 August 1833; *d* Indianapolis, 13 March 1901) President of the United States (1889–93) The grandson of William Henry HARRISON, he was a lawyer and ardent member of the Republican Party. During the Civil War he led the 70th Indiana infantry as a colonel and, briefly, brigadier general. Following the war, he returned to Indiana politics and ran unsuccessfully for governor. A strong supporter of civil-service reform and intensely interested in Indian affairs, Harrison was nominated in 1888 for president as Indiana's favourite-son candidate and won, receiving less popular but more electoral votes than his Democratic opponent, Grover Cleveland. Popular dissatisfaction with the MCKINLEY Tariff passed under Harrison led to his defeat for re-election in 1892. He returned to Indiana, resumed his law practice and, because of his legal acumen, was chosen by Venezuela in 1898 as chief counsel in boundary-dispute negotiations with Great Britain.

JOHN MARTIN

Harrison, William Henry (*b* Berkeley Plantation, Virginia, 9 February 1773; *d* Washington, DC, 4 April 1841) President of the United States (1841). Although born in tidewater Virginia, he is more famous for his western exploits. In 1791 the army sent him west and in 1800 he was appointed governor of the Indiana Territory. In 1811 he led the territorial militia against the Shawnee Indians under TECUMSEH and Tenskwatawa (?1768–?1834), and fought them to a draw at Tippecanoe. The whites claimed victory and Harrison became a hero. Promoted to the rank of brigadier general during the WAR OF 1812, he led the victorious American forces against the British and native-American Indians at the Battle of the Thames. His popularity and fame as an Indian fighter led to the Whig nomination for president in

1840. Although the slogan 'Tippecanoe and Tyler too!' helped him win, Harrison became ill at his rainy, cold inauguration and died less than a month later.

JOHN MARTIN

Hatch Act (1887) Named for Representative William Hatch (1833–96) of Missouri who sponsored the bill in Congress, the Hatch Act represented an attempt by the federal government to promote agricultural research in the United States. During the late nineteenth century American farmers demanded effective fertilizers. In Connecticut (1875) and North Carolina (1877) state experiment stations already existed, which performed analysis of fertilizers sent in by farmers. During the early 1870s, inspired by efforts by German and English scientists, American researchers began to lobby for federal funds to assist further such state efforts. A bill proposed in 1884 failed when it placed control of the research with the United States department of agriculture, not the land-grant colleges where researchers believed the money belonged. Hatch introduced his bill in 1886, providing for $15,000 a year for each state research effort. The bill was passed the following year, creating the agricultural research stations now known as the Agricultural Research Service.

Margaret Rossiter, *The Emergence of Agricultural Science: Justis Liebig and the Americans* (New Haven, Conn., 1975).

ALICE E. REAGAN

Hausa Traders, farmers and mostly urban dwellers, the Hausa are Chadic-speakers (a subgroup of Afro-Asiatic languages), found mainly in northern Nigeria and Niger. The early history of the people remains obscure, although the oral and written literatures suggest a fusion between the Hausa and Fulani (Fulfulde-speakers) identities since about the fifteenth century, when the latter began migrating into Hausaland from various western Sudanese political economies. Both oral and locally written literatures (the latter in classical Arabic) dating from the fifteenth and sixteenth centuries also testify to the emergence of Islamized, urbanized and literate civil and military elites. These elites formed the core of the seven early Hausa states that are estimated to have existed.

By the nineteenth century, as traders and producers of consumer goods and manufactures, most Hausa states were rich, some even powerful. Hausa trading networks extended over all Nigeria and beyond, into large sections of present-day Cameroon, Benin, Togo and Ghana. As itinerant traders, they carried their Muslim faith with them, but in the early nineteenth century this 'mixed' with the doctrines and practices of indigenous and pre-Islamic religious beliefs. Viewing this mixing from a Meccan perspective, and finding it offensive, Islamized religious elites initiated important reform movements. Led by UTHMAN DAN FODIO, descendant of one of the Islamized Fulani (or Fulbe) lineages migrating into northern Nigeria in the mid fifteenth century, the reforms culminated in the Sokoto caliphate being established around 1812. In the early twentieth century the caliphate, incorporating thirty-eight emirates administered by an imam (Muslim cleric), fell to the British, although eastern Nigeria was not 'pacified' until about 1918.

Mahdi Adamu, *The Hausa Factor in West African History* (Zaira, 1978).
Murray Last, 'Reform in West Africa: The *Jihad* Movements of the Nineteenth Century', in J. F. J. Ajayi and Michael Crowder (eds), *History of West Africa*, second edn, vol. 2 (New York, 1985), pp. 1–29.

B. MARIE PERINBAM

Haussman, Georges Eugène (*b* Paris, 29 March 1809; *d* Paris, 11 January 1891) French official. A trained lawyer, he entered the prefectoral service under Louis-Philippe, supported Louis Napoleon's coup and was appointed prefect of the Seine in 1853. He is best known for his reconstruction of Paris, the construction of long and wide avenues and boulevards to facilitate traffic (and control crowds, if his enemies are to be believed), the improvement of the Bois de Vincennes and the Bois de Boulogne around Paris, the circular railway around the city and the construction of the massive sewer system. The title 'baron' was a personal affectation since he was never ennobled. He was very unpopular for his improvised financing of his improvements, their enormous costs and his brusque manner. Napoleon III sacrificed him in a bid for popularity in 1870. He sat as a Bonapartist deputy from Corsica under the Third Republic from 1877 to 1881.

D. Pinkney *Napoleon III and the Rebuilding of Paris* (Princeton, NJ, 1958).

DONALD SUTHERLAND

Hay, John (*b* Salem, Indiana, 8 October 1838; *d* Newbury, New Hampshire, 1 July 1905) American statesman. He attended Brown University, and later served as private secretary to Abraham Lincoln during the Civil War. After a period as a journalist, he was appointed assistant secretary of state under Rutherford B. Hayes (1879–81), and from 1898 until his death served as secretary of state. Under William McKinley he shaped foreign policy and was responsible for the Open Door policy in China (1899) (*see* OPEN DOOR DOCTRINE). Writing to Theodore Roosevelt about the Spanish-American War, Hay said, 'it has been a splendid little war; begun with the highest motives, carried out with magnificent intelligence and spirit.' He negotiated the Hay-Pauncefote treaty in 1901 which gave the United States exclusive rights to build the Panama Canal. In addition to his public career, Hay was a novelist and poet and collaborated with John G. Nicolay

(1832–1901) to write the ten-volume *Abraham Lincoln: A History*, published in 1890.

KEVIN MURPHY

Haymarket Massacre (4 May 1886)   On 3 May 1886 a strike for an eight-hour working day in Chicago's Haymarket Square degenerated into a mêlée, and police curbed it, killing and wounding several demonstrators. The next day, at a meeting called to protest the 'massacre', an unidentified person threw a bomb, and in the ensuing panic seven policemen were killed and over fifty injured. A jury convicted eight anarchists, and Judge Joseph E. Gary (1821–1906), suggesting that those who had incited the riot were equally guilty of murder, sentenced seven to death and one to prison. Of the seven condemned, four were hanged, one committed suicide and the sentences of two were commuted to life imprisonment. In 1893 the reform-minded judge John P. Altgeld (1847–1902) charged a miscarriage of justice and pardoned the three who were still alive. For this and for his opposition to Grover Cleveland's intervention during the Pullman strike in 1892, he was vilified and not returned to office.

In 1886 over 600,000 workers were unemployed due to strikes, shut-downs or lockouts, and the Haymarket Affair was only one of the more notable in a series of violent responses to industrialization and the wage system. Yet the violence was not often unprovoked. Companies used their resources to hire guards and detectives to break strikes, and occasionally state and federal authorities intervened on their behalf. Because of such incidents, the courts became more repressive, the police more brutal and gradually public sympathy for the plight of urban workers dwindled, delaying many specific goals, such as the EIGHT-HOUR DAY, for a generation.

Henry David, *The Haymarket Affair* (New York, 1936).

KEVIN MURPHY

Hearst, William Randolph (*b* San Francisco, 29 April 1863; *d* Beverly Hills, California, 14 August 1951)   American newspaper publisher. After attending Harvard (1882–5), he began his career in the newspaper business as manager of the *San Francisco Examiner*, owned by his father. In 1895 he bought the *New York Journal* and engaged Joseph Pulitzer's (1847–1911) *The World* in a circulation battle. In the rush for subscribers both men debased accurate journalistic style by employing the techniques of 'yellow journalism'. The most newsworthy subject of the time was the Cuban Civil War and the possibility of a Spanish-American War. Both sides sent a corps of artists and reporters to furnish the American public with details of Spanish atrocities against rebel forces. Hearst exploited the situation to the fullest and greatly increased the circulation of his paper, winning the battle with Pulitzer and going on to build a publishing empire which eventually included motion-picture and radio companies. He was flamboyant and dictatorial, his sensationalism matched by his business acumen.

See also NEWSPAPERS.

KEVIN MURPHY

Hegel, Georg Wilhelm Friedrich (*b* Stuttgart, 27 August 1770; *d* Berlin, 14 November 1831)   German Idealist philosopher. He was probably the first philosopher to conceive of the whole of reality as a single historical process, the subject of which is *Geist* – or Spirit – of which finite human beings, and also peoples and civilizations, are at once the bearers and emanations. Philosophy is the story of the way in which *Geist*, initially alienated from itself, proceeds by dialectical steps embodied in historical stages – thesis giving rise to antithesis, the clash of these producing a higher synthesis, and the latter becoming in turn a new thesis, and so on indefinitely – towards its ultimate goal, namely total self-realization and oneness with itself, which Hegel variously terms 'absolute knowledge' and 'absolute freedom' (which for him were identical). This dark metaphysics, according to which humans attain true freedom only by conforming to the laws of the rational, organic state, which embodies absolute freedom, gives rise to a potentially oppressive doctrine of liberty which is opposed to that of classical Anglo-Saxon liberal thinkers like J. S. Mill. MARX was deeply influenced by Hegel, especially by his *Philosophy of Right*, (1821). Other important works by Hegel are *The Phenomenology of Mind* (1807) and *The Philosophy of History* (1830–1).

Much of the history of philosophy since Hegel is the story of the development of, and not least reactions against, his principal theses, from Kierkegaard to the existentialists. And his influence on the subsequent development of historiography, sociology, anthropology, aesthetics, theology and political thought has been immense. Above all, his practical political impact on the modern world has been great, chiefly through the part his ideas played in German nationalism and through his vastly influential disciple Karl Marx.

ROGER HAUSHEER

Heine, Heinrich (*b* Düsseldorf, 13 December 1797; *d* Paris, 17 February 1856)   German writer. He was born into a middle-class Jewish family in the Rhineland, where his childhood experience of the French occupation was a formative influence. He later studied law, and at the same time frequented the literary salons of Berlin. He started to publish poetry as a young man in the 1820s and established his reputation with *Das Buch der Lieder* (1827). After the 1830 Revolution he emigrated to Paris, where he spent much of the rest of his life. Heine was a controversial figure in Germany. His witty, satirical writing was considered cynical and subversive by the authorities and Metternich identified him as a member of the 'Young Germany' school of revolutionary writers whose work was banned by the federal diet in 1835. He published explicitly revolutionary poems in *Vorwärts* under the editorship of Karl Marx, but his unpopularity in Germany probably arose as much from the assertive cosmopolitanism of his style as from his politics.

TIMOTHY KIRK

Helvetic Republic Established by France on 5 February 1798, following Napoleon's victories in Italy (1796–7) and sporadic republican revolts in Switzerland, the Helvetic Republic excluded Neuchâtel, Geneva, the bishopric of Basle, the Valtelline and Mulhouse. Its godfathers were Frédéric Laharpe (1754–1838) and Peter Ochs (1752–1821). The republic was composed of twenty-three cantons loosely tied together by a government comprising an elected assembly, a senate and a directory. Many Swiss were dissatisfied with the new republic, and this led to riots which eventually caused the French government to attempt a number of changes, such as the Constitution of Malmaison of May 1801. After the defeat of Napoleon, the original frontiers of Switzerland were restored by the CONGRESS OF VIENNA and a new federal pact restored the old institutions.

E. Bonjour, *A Short History of Switzerland* (Oxford, 1952).

GEORGE O. KENT

Herzen, Alexander Ivanovich (*b* Moscow, 25 March 1812; *d* Paris, 9 January 1870) Russian political thinker. The illegitimate son of a nobleman, he became interested in social and political problems at Moscow University. This led to his arrest and exile to the provinces in 1834. In 1847 he obtained permission to emigrate. He witnessed the events of the 1848 revolutions, in which he was largely disappointed and which he described in *From the Other Shore* (1850), and settled in London in 1852. Five years later he began publishing his influential journal the *Bell*, in which he pursued a serious criticism of Russia's social order. He had a unique vision of Russia's socialist future based on the peasant commune as an independent, self-governing institution. One of the founders of Russian populism (*see* POPULISM (RUSSIA)), he opposed violent revolution and always upheld the value of the individual.

E. D. J. Acton, *Alexander Herzen and the Role of the Intellectual Revolutionary* (Cambridge, 1979).

A. V. KNOWLES

Herzl, Theodor (*b* Budapest, 2 May 1860; *d* Edlach, Austria, 3 July 1904) Journalist and Jewish statesman. He moved with his parents to Vienna in 1878, where he became a prominent journalist and play-wright. Initially convinced by the liberal view which equated true Jewish emancipation with assimilation, Herzl came to view the latter as impossible, made so by the resurgence of ANTI-SEMITISM, especially in Vienna and Paris (from which he reported in 1891–5). Thus he was led to write *Der Judenstaat* (The Jewish State) in 1895, which pleaded for Jewish emancipation through the realization of an independent state. Herzl subsequently launched a one-man campaign, which became the movement of political Zionism, when he joined forces with pre-existing Zionist groups. Although his own efforts to realize a Jewish state in Palestine were unsuccessful, Herzl can be regarded as laying the foundations for the subsequent state of Israel.

Steven Beller, *Herzl* (London, 1991).

STEVEN BELLER

Hinduism A religious tradition with antecedents perhaps reaching back as far as the third millennium BC, Hinduism has ever been open to new influences. Lacking a clearly defined body of theology and beliefs and subject to wide regional variations, it has traditionally met the challenge of newly arrived and competing theologies by assimilat-ing their most appealing aspects rather than by total rejection. Thus the arrival of Western influences and Christian missionary efforts elic-ited a dynamic response which transformed modern Hinduism. The initial catalyst for the transformation was Christian missionary efforts and the interrelated development of modern educational structures. Fort William College, established by the English East India Company in the eighteenth century, deeply influenced by the Baptist Mission at Serampore, and distinguished and dedicated individuals such as William Carey (1761–1834), had an immediate impact on the elite groups which passed through it. Expansion of Christian mission schools after 1813 had an equally significant impact on the lower levels of Hindu society.

Leaders such as RAM MOHAN ROY emerged by the second decade of the nineteenth century to challenge corrupt practices and call for a 'Hindu reformation'. In a series of publications that continued until his death (1834), he openly espoused a Christian ethic, encouraged a work-ing relationship with missionary elements for social reforms and at-tacked abuses such as widow-burning (suttee), infanticide and child marriage as un-Hindu in origin. He and the organization he founded in 1828 (Brahma Samaj) fostered a return to a Hinduism largely cen-tred on the Upanishads and the *Bhagavadgita* which he translated into and interpreted in vernacular Bengali. Indeed, his selection of a core of thirteen Upanishads, which exhibited a monotheistic influence, and emphasis on the *Bhagavadgita* gave Hinduism a common core which became a popularly accepted standard as the century progressed. Thus he has been called the father of modern Hinduism as well as of modern India. The Brahmo Samaj organization gradually moved beyond the confines of Bengal and, by 1867, it was actively involved in spreading the Hindu reformation.

In mid-century the deep inroads of Western learning, the erosion of traditional society under the impact of a rapidly expanding communications and transportation network and the emotionally charged spectre of mass Christian conversions in the lower levels of Hindu society engendered a Hindu backlash which saw a parting of the ways between Christian missionaries and Hindu reformers. Many of the emerging Hindu reform movements of the second half of the century turned their backs on Western influences and sought to defend Hinduism against the onslaught of the Christian West. It was a theme which evolved into Hindu nationalism and was employed by individuals as dissimilar as the politician TILAK in the agitations of the 1890s and Swami Dayananda (see ARYA SAMAJ).

The rising tide of Hindu nationalism produced the Arya Samaj (1874), which actively embarked on efforts to create a Hindu INDIA, generate missionary activities among the vulnerable lower jati (subcastes), hitherto deemed untouchable, and sponsor the return of those who had converted to Christianity, Sikhism or Islam to escape the oppression of 'untouchable' status. The organization actively attacked practices such as idolatry, female infanticide and untouchability as un-Hindu foreign influences. While preaching a return to 'pure' Hinduism, it created popular new forms of congregational worship – remarkably like those of the despised Christian Evangelicals – and emphasized a devotional approach (bhakti) that no longer required costly and elaborate rituals or the services of brahman priests.

Simultaneously, a less aggressive and equally popular movement emerged in Bengal which further defined modern Hinduism. Centred around a Bengali holy man, Ramakrishna, (1836–86), who believed that a series of revelations had shown him that the major world religions each held universal truths, the movement had a deep impact. Swami Vivekananda (1863–1902) transformed the movement into the Ramakrishna Mission, an altruistic charitable organization which embodied the finest principals of service to society and generated a network of hospitals and charitable institutions, organized along Western lines and often parallel to Christian missionary institutions. It also marked the beginning of a Hinduism which appealed to the West. Indeed, Vivekananda's brilliant discourse on Hinduism at the parliament of religions in Chicago (1893) marked a radical departure from the traditional isolation of Hinduism and the ability of Hinduism to adapt to change.

Ainslie Embree. *The Hindu Tradition* (New York, 1966).
K. M. Sen, *Hinduism* (New York, 1961).
Jadish Sharma (ed.), *Individuals and Ideas in Modern India* (Calcutta, 1982).

ROBERT J. YOUNG

Hodgskin, Thomas (*b* Chatham, Kent, 12 December 1787; *d* Feltham, Middlesex, 21 August 1869) English writer and the first political economist to provide an economic justification for trade-unionism. His writings, particularly *Labour Defended against the Claims of Capital* (1825), emphasized labour as the source of all value and the expropriation of this wealth by capitalists as labourers were separated from the means of production. His theories derived from Ricardian economics (*see* David RICARDO), but turned them against capitalists and in favour of labour. He attacked Bentham (1748–1832) for placing too much emphasis on government, which he saw as inherently coercive. His theories reflected the concerns of popular politics of the period in their focus on the corrupting forces of capitalism and government. He influenced Marx, but was not anticapitalist and believed in small producers competing freely in an economic and social world undistorted by powerful economic or governmental interests.

Elie Halevy, *Thomas Hodgskin*, trans. A. J. Taylor (London, 1956).

RICHARD PRICE

Holy Alliance A document ostensibly based on Christian principles, the Holy Alliance was signed on 26 September 1815 by all European rulers except the pope, the sultan and the king of England. It reflected ALEXANDER I of Russia's wish for a loose international alliance based on religious ideals. The alliance is believed to have been inspired by the visions of the baroness von Krüdener (1764–1824), a spiritual adviser to the tsar, and by his readings of the abbé de Saint Pierre (1737–1814), an eighteenth-century cleric.

The alliance should not be confused with the Quadruple Alliance of 20 November 1815 between Great Britain, Austria, Russia and Prussia.

M. Bourquin, *Histoire de la Sainte Alliance* (Geneva, 1954).

GEORGE O. KENT

Home Rule Since 1800 there had been various attempts to repeal the IRISH ACT OF UNION by the re-establishment of an Irish parliament with limited powers of self-government for Ireland within the British Empire, by constitutionalists such as O'CONNELL and revolutionaries such as Robert EMMETT (1803), the Young Irelanders (1848) and the Fenians (1867) (*see* IRISH REPUBLICAN BROTHERHOOD). However, a sustained, popular movement for Home Rule arose only after the formation of

Isaac Butt's (1813–79) Home Government Association in 1870, a conservative group alarmed both by Gladstone's reforms of land and church and by the plight of imprisoned Fenians. After winning the support of the Roman Catholic hierarchy, disappointed with the English connection after Gladstone's refusal to endow the Catholic University of Ireland, the association broadened its platform and became in 1873 the Home Rule League, taking the popular side on such issues as land reform and denominational education. Its unexpected success in the 1874 general election led to the formation of the Irish Parliamentary Party, which dominated Irish politics for the next forty years. The Land League (*see* IRISH NATIONAL LAND LEAGUE) crisis of 1879 turned the Home Rule movement into a Catholic and democratic movement, while the formation of the Irish National League in 1882 confirmed the ascendancy of constitutional nationalism, complete with a comprehensive constituency organization under central control.

The Home Rule movement became a powerful force because of the ascendancy of the better-off tenant farmers in post-famine Ireland, the collapse of agricultural prices in the late 1870s and the brilliant leadership of Michael DAVITT and PARNELL. Republicans were prepared to wait for their independent Ireland and co-operate in the meantime in 'the grand coalition' of Parnellism – the hybrid of Fenianism, the church, constitutionalists and agrarian radicals which Parnell directed towards winning Home Rule. The coalition was vague on what Home Rule entailed, but its preoccupations were summed up in 1885 by William Walsh (1841–1921), the Roman Catholic archbishop of Dublin: 'Politics now simply mean food and clothes and decent houses for Irishmen and women at home ... the three great corporal works of mercy ... the protection of the weak against the strong, and the soil of Ireland for the Irish race rather than for a select gang of strangers and spoilers.' It had little time for mainly Protestant Irish Unionists (*see* IRISH UNIONISM), who opposed Home Rule. Only when desperately searching for allies after the split did Parnell acknowledge that 'until the religious prejudices of the minority are conciliated ... Ireland can never enjoy perfect freedom, Ireland can never be united'.

Parnellites swept the electoral board in Ireland outside north-east Ulster and Trinity College, Dublin, finally prompting Gladstone to introduce on 8 April 1886 his First Home Rule Bill. Gladstone's experience with Ireland during his last ministry had been a rancorous one. His government had imprisoned Parnell and other leaders as part of its far-reaching measures of coercion to suppress agrarian terror, while Home Rulers had railed against the 'cruel wrongs' being perpetrated on Ireland. Home Rule seemed the only way of restoring the normal rule of law in Ireland. There was to be an Irish legislature and an executive responsible to it and a seemingly endless list of matters excluded from its jurisdiction, including peace and war, defence and colonial affairs, customs and excise, trade and navigation, the post office and coinage. Accepted by Parnell as a temporary measure, the bill failed in the Commons by 343 votes to 311. Its slightly more generous successor, the Second Home Rule Bill, was defeated in the Lords in 1893.

The bills failed because of the opposition of Irish Protestants and Unionists, north and south, and the imperialism of the Conservative and Unionist Party in Britain. An additional obstacle after 1890 was the vicious split in the Home Rule movement following the O'Shea divorce. The majority of the Irish Parliamentary Party preferred to jettison Parnell rather than lose the Liberal alliance. They were supported by the Roman Catholic Church in Ireland and the majority of people in the countryside, thus destroying Parnell's hybrid movement.

The vituperative recrimination between Parnellites and anti-Parnellites, and the Unionist policy of killing Home Rule by kindness, with more Land Acts and cash for the west of Ireland, confused Home Rule politics. They were revitalized only by the resumption of land agitation in the west, this time against graziers and ranchers. William O'Brien's (1852–1928) United Irish League, founded in 1898, provided the instrument that led to the reuniting of the Home Rule movement under John REDMOND in 1900.

Paul Bew, *C. S. Parnell* (Dublin, 1980).
D. G. Boyce, *Nationalism in Ireland* (London, 1982).

PATRICK BUCKLAND

homesteaders In the seventy years after 1862 'homesteaders' received patent to nearly 250 million acres of free public land in the United States, helping to slow the trend towards farm tenancy. Beginning in the 1780s, the United States passed legislation to sell off western lands to gain revenue and to encourage the settlement of the west by independent yeomen farmers. Although the Federalists doubled the price of public land in the 1790s, Thomas Jefferson and the Democratic Republicans reduced the price and minimum purchase size in 1804. By 1860 a growing movement of eastern working men was pressing for free land, asserting that western land was worthless without the improvements of their labour: clearing, ploughing, fencing and the building of homes. Pro-slavery sourtherners who wanted to rein in the growth of the west pressurized Buchanan to veto a Homestead Act in 1860. With the secession of the southern states in 1861, however, northern and western Republicans in Congress passed the Homestead Act on 27 May 1862. The act enabled citizens (or intended citizens) over 21 years of age and head of a household to select up to 160 acres of unclaimed public land. After five years of residence, homesteaders could receive title to the land if they had made certain improvements and paid a modest registration fee. The homesteader could receive title any time after six months of residence, by paying $1.25 per acre, the price of public land. A later amendment allowed veterans to count Civil War service towards the five-year-residence requirement. Although land speculators found loopholes in the law that allowed them to accumulate large tracts of homestead land, the Homestead Act enabled over a million farmers to gain title to western lands.

Paul W. Gates, *History of Public Land Law Development* (Washington, DC, 1968).

JOHN MARTIN

homosexuality (male) The concept of homosexuality originated in the nineteenth century. Before then religious, ethical and judicial considerations focused on sodomy, a word that was used to refer to the entire range of sexual activities between men. Only later did sexologists begin to consider the subjects of same-sex desire as a distinct kind of person. By the end of the century two main theories were current: the third-sex theory, which maintained that the homosexual was an individual with the body of a man and the soul of a woman; and the inversion model, according to which same-sex object-choice was a congenital anomaly with no necessary relation to gender inversion. Sexologists like Havelock Ellis (1859–1939) advocated decriminalizing sexual relations between men, and homosexuals like John Addington Symonds (1840–93), who collaborated with Ellis in writing *Sexual Inversion* (1896), Edward Carpenter (1844–1929) and, earlier in Germany, Karl Ulrichs (1825–95) were eager to establish the understanding of homosexuality on a scientific basis.

None the less, at the end of the century homosexuals were in some ways worse off than sodomites had been at the start. In France and other countries under the influence of the CODE NAPOLEON of 1810, voluntary sexual acts between men had been decriminalized. The marquis de Sade (1740–1814) had argued, in libertine philosophic vein, that 'it makes absolutely no difference whether one enjoys a girl or a boy . . . No inclinations or tastes can exist in us save the ones we have from Nature.' Jeremy Bentham (1748–1832) wrote at length, between 1774 and 1824, on the need for legal reform and the utility of sex between men as a way of avoiding the dangers of overpopulation. Such views could not be published openly, but they surfaced obliquely and were to be found expressed in pornographic material during periods of reform and utopian hope during the remainder of the century. However, the very different view of sexologists like Sigmund Freud (1856–1939) at the end of the century that homosexuality was a form of arrested development proved far more influential.

Despite the views of sexologists and criminologists in favour of decriminlizing sexual activities between men, legislative repression increased after 1870. In 1885 the Labouchère Amendment, under which

Oscar Wilde (1854–1900) was successfully prosecuted a decade later, became law. In Germany homosexual acts were criminalized after provisions within Prussian law were extended to the entire country following the unification of Germany in 1871. Sexual scandals involving highly placed persons followed in England in 1889–90 and in Germany in 1902 and 1906.

Homosexual scandals at the end of the century reflected a crisis within male elites. The weakened positions of Britain and France and rivalry with Germany increased tensions within elite groups and provoked a need to find scapegoats. Elite men passed most of their lives within all-male institutions such as schools, clubs, universities, the military service, parliamentary bodies and the church. These institutions promoted intimate male bonding – and the devaluation of women – at the same time as society was placing a higher value than ever before on the importance of marriage and respectability. By the 1890s, when the emancipation of women, the vote for working men, the growth of a radical press, and the development of labour and socialist politics put privileged men on the defensive, a significant number of homosexual men had begun to reject the double bind. Politically and personally, it became more difficult to sustain the compromise of a double life which included both marriage and covert sex with men, usually of a lower class. Some men abandoned such relationships, or declined to marry and instead formed affective, sexual and cultural alliances with other like-minded men. In England this development was so marked between 1890 and 1894 that it is reasonable to speak of a homosexual renaissance in the arts during those years. The contemporaneous emergence of homosexuality as an explicit topic in sexology encouraged men attracted to other men to define their identities in relation to that choice. Even attempts such as the Wilde trials to suppress homosexual culture, though effective, paradoxically encouraged counter-efforts such as the founding of the Scientific Humanitarian Committee by Magnus Hirschfeld (1868–1935) in Germany in 1898.

The study of desire between men in the nineteenth century can take one of five directions. One is that of vernacular history, which began with studies of trial records and continues apace in attempts to recover the lost history of sexual networks and subcultures in cities such as London and New York and in all-male institutions. Another is to trace the developing medical discourse, which led from the forensic science of Johann Müller and Ambroise Tardieu, with its emphasis on bodily signs of perversion, to the views of the sexologists discussed above. Another is to trace the efforts made to comprehend desire between males by using ancient Greek models, either the pedagogical model of Athenian pederasty, associated with Socrates, and familiar to boys from their study of the classics at school and university, or the model of Spartan pederasty, military in character, and a prominent focus of attention for scholars who were both nationalists (especially German) and philologists. Spartan pederasty demonstrated the utility of sexual desire between men in sacrificial service to the nation-state. Yet another direction is the displacement of fascination with male–male sexual relations to Oriental locales, as though such interests were the special province of southern or eastern races and climates. This tendency is evident in Goethe's (1749–1832) *West-Easterly Divan*, in the essay on pederasty that Richard Burton appended to his translation of the *Arabian Nights* in the 1880s and in Pierre Loti's (1850–1923) journals of life in the Near East.

The arts, especially poetry, provided the space in which questions about desire between men could be most easily addressed. In France the third-sex theory was first represented in *Mademoiselle de Maupin* (1835), a scandalous and witty novel by a young aesthete named Théophile Gautier (1811–72). Besides being a pioneer sexologist and campaigner for legal reform, Karl Maria Kertbeny (1824–82), the German-Hungarian who invented the term 'homosexuality' was also a translator and a friend of Charles Baudelaire (1821–67). In England poets like Alfred Tennyson (1809–92) and Gerard Manley Hopkins (1844–89) attempted to validate male intimacy within models which preserved the traditional primacy of marriage or endorsed celibacy within a life dedicated to God. In the United States Walt Whitman (1819–91) theorized sexual and emotional ties between men; in *Leaves of Grass* (1855) he affirmed the love of comrades in a democratic and egalitarian national epic which likewise validated the body and an active sexual desire on the part of women. While a genteel tradition of ardent but celibate homoerotic poetry, dubbed 'Uranian', continued in England well into the twentieth century, Whitman's radicalism made a remarkable impact on cultural attitudes towards male love in England and on the Continent.

See also LESBIANISM.

Richard Bellamora, *Masculine Desire: The Sexual Politics of Victorian Aestheticism* (Chapel Hill, N.C., 1990).
Michel Foucault, *The History of Sexuality, vol. 1* (New York, 1980).
Robert K. Martin, *The Homosexual Tradition in American Poetry* (Austin, Tex., 1979).
George L. Mosse, *Nationalism and Sexuality* (Madison, Wisc., 1985).
Eve Kosofsky Sedgwick, *Between Men* (New York, 1985).
Jeffrey Weeks, *Sexuality and its Discontents* (London, 1985).

RICHARD DELLAMORA

Hong Kong During the first Anglo-Chinese War (1839–41) (*see* ANGLO-CHINESE WARS) the British community retreated from Canton to the island of Hong Kong off the south China coast, which was about 30 square miles in area and largely uninhabited. It was separated from the mainland peninsula of Kowloon by what was discovered to be one of the most splendid natural harbours in the world. At the end of the war Hong Kong was ceded to Britain by the TREATY OF NANKING, and began its development as a major entrepôt for Britain in the Far East. In 1860, after the second Anglo-Chinese War (1857–8), the peninsula of Kowloon was ceded to Britain in the Convention of Peking. In 1898, during the foreign scramble for concessions in China, Britain forced China to lease to it for ninety-nine years the New Territories north of Kowloon, thereby significantly increasing the British territory on the mainland.

JOHN DAVIES

Horton, James Africanus Beale (*b* Gloucester, Sierra Leone, 1 June 1835; *d* Freetown, Sierra Leone, 15 October 1883) Prominent creole African nationalist and 'anthropologist' who, as early as the 1860s, argued for the adoption of Western-style political institutions for an independent Africa. He was educated at missionary schools in Sierra Leone, later training as a doctor at King's College, London, and Edinburgh University (1853–9). Serving as an army physician, he eventually headed the British Gold Coast army medical services, retiring at the rank of lieutenant-general. He was ideologically committed to the Western model of change, favouring the adoption of not only Western institutions, science and technology into African socio-political systems, but also Western education and values, including Christianity. Horton's 'modernizing' ideas and work were compatible with the prevailing nineteenth-century imperial mind-set, but were in conflict with those of his contemporary Edward W. BLYDEN, who favoured the promotion of a distinct African identity. Horton's extensive works included political treatises and technical works on medicine, climate and geography.

Christopher Fyfe, *Africanus Horton, 1835–1883* (New York, 1972).

B. MARIE PERINBAM

housing *see* SOCIAL HOUSING.

Humboldt, Alexander von, Baron (*b* Berlin, 14 September 1769; *d* Berlin, 6 May 1859) German explorer, geographer and scientist. Although not regarded by his widowed mother as the intellectual equal of his elder brother Karl Wilhelm von HUMBOLDT, Alexander was to distinguish himself in a number of fields, including physical geography, systematic meteorology, geology, mineralogy and mining technology. He is best known as an explorer (most notably of Central and South America) and as a disseminator of scientific knowledge. A thorough empiricist, forever experimenting, measuring and recording, he was one of the last great figures of the Enlightenment, drawn towards

Paris for much of his intellectual life. An indefatigable man of science, his last major work, *Kosmos* (4 vols, 1845–62) endeavoured to provide a popular audience with a comprehensive physical panorama of the universe. His parlous finances compelled him to seek political employment, where he was to be handicapped by his liberal reputation and support of the revolutions of 1848. He died in poverty in his Berlin apartment, mortgaged to his valet.

JOHN BELCHEM

Humboldt, Karl Wilhelm von (*b* Potsdam, 22 June 1767; *d* Tegel, Berlin, 8 April 1835)   German humanist, statesman, philologist and philosopher of language. From 1819, having sought in vain to achieve a constitutional monarchy for Prussia in the post-Napoleonic settlement, he devoted his life to scholarship and thought. A friend of Gœthe (1749–1832) and Schiller (1759–1805), he was a chief proponent of the idea of 'Humanität' in the era of German Idealism. The Hellenic world, representing ideally an organic diversity in unity, was held up as a model to the torn modern world. The individual is everything and the final goal was 'the highest and most proportional development of his powers to a complete and consistent whole'. He became a critic of the narrowly analytic and rationalistic categories of the Enlightenment, and his views on politics, humane learning, art, and above all language – he emphasizes imaginative empathy and a faculty of divination, supported by exact scholarship – contributed to the revolution in human self-understanding which runs from Hamann (1730–88) and Herder (1744–1803) through the German romantics and historicists to Dilthey (1833–1911) Windelband (1848–1915) and Meinecke (1862–1954). In his *Ideas towards an Attempt to Determine the Limits of State Action*, which directly influenced J. S. Mill's *On Liberty*, he advocated a minimal state and maximum freedom in education and religion. He prized diversity and variety beyond all things. Involved in founding the University of Berlin in 1811, and creating by his educational reforms the idea of the 'humanistisches Gymnasium', Humboldt helped to shape the German system of education for well over a century.

Marianne Cowan (ed.), *Humanist without Portfolio: An Anthology* (Detroit, 1963).

ROGER HAUSHEER

Hundred Days Reform   The emperor KUANG HSU announced a series of reforms in 1898. The leading figure in the Hundred Days Reform was the young scholar K'ang Yu-wei (1858–1927), who provided a philosophical justification from within Confucianism for radical reform. He disputed the authenticity of the classical texts which had supported Confucian orthodoxy from the time of the Sung dynasty and claimed that Confucius himself had favoured reform. He and his disciple Liang Ch'i-ch'ao (1873–1921) also adopted SOCIAL DARWINISM, which extended the principle of the 'survival of the fittest' to the struggle between nations. They argued that those nations, such as Meiji Japan, that adopted reform would survive. In 1898, when China was threatened with dismemberment at the hands of the foreign powers, K'ang advised Kuang Hsu that if China were to survive as an independent nation it must sweep away the old institutions, including the imperial-examination system, which had made it weak in the face of foreign aggression. Kuang Hsu responded enthusiastically to K'ang's memorials (petitions to the emperor), and between June and September 1898 issued a series of reform edicts which created a coherent reform programme in the areas of education, government administration and industry.

In the reformed examination system the eight-legged essay, an excessively formalized exercise at the heart of the old system, was to be abolished and greater emphasis given to questions of practical government. A university, offering Chinese and Western learning was to be established at Peking and some of the old academies were to be converted into modern schools. Mining, industrial management and railway engineering were to be studied in vocational schools. Local officials were to co-ordinate commercial, agricultural and industrial reforms, and new ministries in Peking would supervise the development of a modern economy. For the first time China was to have an annual budget prepared by the ministry of revenues. The armed forces were to be modernized and strengthened. A new fleet of modern warships was to be built or bought, and army training was to be based on Western models. To make these programmes effective, the imperial bureaucracy was to be reorganized and simplified, sinecures abolished and younger reformist officials, such as K'ang and Liang, brought into the imperial service.

The reforms met with strenuous opposition from conservative officials and members of the imperial court, who saw them as damaging to China's future and destructive of its true essence. Many provincial authorities also disregarded the emperor's orders for reform, believing that real power in China lay not with him but with TZ'U-HSI. Kuang Hsu mistakenly believed that Tz'u-his would support the reform programme. She, however, saw reform as an attempt to wrest power from her and threw in her lot with the conservatives, winning the support of the imperial army commander, Jung-lu (d 1903) and later that of his subordinate Yuan Shih-kai (1859–1916), the commander of the northern (Peiyang) army, the most modern army in China, and thought to be sympathetic to reform. With their support, Tz'u-hsi staged a coup in September. Kuang Hsu made one last attempt to save his programme by appealing to ministers in the capital and the provinces to publicize the reforms. He ordered Yuan to march on Peking and arrest Tz'u-hsi. His appeal to his ministers went unheeded and Yuan did not march. Kuang Hsu was placed under palace arrest where he remained for the rest of his life. K'ang Yu-wei and Liang Ch'i-ch'ao escaped to Japan but a number of reformers were arrested and executed. Most of the reforms were reversed, the eight-legged essay and many government sinecures being restored, but the University of Peking and a number of the modernized academies were allowed to continue in modified form.

The attempt to reform China from above, in the fashion of the MEIJI RESTORATION in Japan, had failed. The major causes of the failure were the lack of experience of the reformers and the determination of the empress dowager, supported by the court conservatives, to cling to power. The imperial court led by Tz'u-hsi began to encourage antiforeign feeling (see BOXER RISING), but an increasing number of young Chinese people began to argue that reform from above would never succeed and that the only way to save China was through a violent revolutionary overthrow of the Manchus.

Immanuel C. Y. Hsu, *The Rise of Modern China*, fourth edn (Oxford, 1990).
Luke S. K. Kwang, *A Mosaic of the Hundred Days* (Cambridge, Mass., 1984).
JOHN DAVIES

Hung Hsiu-ch'uan [Hong Xiuquan] (*b* Kwantung, 1814; *d* Nanking, 1864) Taiping leader. Born of Hakka parents, he showed scholastic promise and entered the civil-service examinations at Canton, but failed four times. There he met Christian missionaries and after his third examination failure claimed to have experienced visions. After his fourth failure in 1843 a rereading of missionary tracts convinced him that the old man of his visions was God the father, that Christ was his elder brother and that he was God's younger son. He baptized himself and began to make converts to his Society of God-Worshippers. In 1844 he moved to Kwangsi, gaining support among the Hakkas which provided the base for the TAIPING REBELLION. Hung declared himself 'Heavenly King of the Kingdom of Heavenly Peace' (1853), ruling from Nanking. The Taipings were wracked by dissension in the mid-1850s. Hung resigned power to his brothers and sank into an orgy of pleasure. As Nanking fell to TSENG KUO-FAN's army in 1864, Hung committed suicide.

JOHN DAVIES

Hunt, Henry (*b* Upavon, Wiltshire, 6 November 1773; *d* Alresford, Hampshire, 13 February 1835) Leader of the popular radical movement in Britain after 1815, called 'Orator Hunt'. A gentleman farmer, he converted to RADICALISM during the Napoleonic wars. By appealing to the myth of English libertarian history, his populist rhetoric broke through the restraints of traditional extraparliamentary politics. He encouraged the people to seek their democratic rights in open constitutional manner, 'peaceably if we can, forcibly if we must'. A continuum of moral and physical force, this strategy of intimidation dominated radical agitation until CHARTISM collapsed. The star attraction at the ill-fated PETERLOO meeting, Hunt received thirty months' imprisonment. He lost popularity (and his seat for Preston) for opposing the Reform Bill of 1832, a democratic stand later applauded by the Chartists.

John Belchem, *'Orator' Hunt: Henry Hunt and English Working-Class Radicalism* (Oxford, 1985).

JOHN BELCHEM

hunting By 1800 fox-hunting was a fashionable and fast-growing sport, replacing deer- and hare-hunting as the most popular country sport pursuit in Britain. Hunting involved most of the rural community, and although as the century progressed it tended to become increasingly the preserve of the wealthy, it did much to unite rural societies. Country gentlemen formed the majority of regular huntsmen but small farmers also hunted. The sport became more organized, and hunting 'countries' or territories were divided up between regular hunts. The costs of hunting were high and were often borne by local aristocratic families. However, by the 1830s the maintenance of a fashionable pack cost between £4,000 and £5,000 per annum and it was becoming customary for hunts to be supported by subscriptions. Whereas in 1810 there were only twenty-four subscription packs, by 1850 there were over a hundred. The subscription system ensured that the master of the hunt received an annual income which included the cost of the upkeep of the pack and the payment of the hunt servants. An important duty of the master was that of maintaining good relations with those over whose land the hunt took place. Despite the damage inflicted by hunts, there was relatively little opposition to fox-hunting from local landowners, although towards the end of the century farmers hit by the agricultural depression demanded heavier compensation for damages to their property.

A fashionable social life accompanied hunting which consisted of hunt balls and dinners. Growing numbers of women took up the sport from the 1850s, as did newly wealthy industrialists. The money these men contributed to the sport did much to sustain it in parts of the country after the agricultural depression of the 1870s.

See also ANIMAL SPORTS AND CRUELTY.

R. Carr, *English Foxhunting* (London, 1976).

J. M. GOLBY

Huxley, Thomas Henry (*b* Ealing, Middlesex, 4 May 1825; *d* Eastbourne, Sussex, 29 June 1895) English scientist, educationalist and controversialist. He combined scientific work in biology with more wide-ranging defences of science as a way of thought and as an appropriate basis for education. His controversial skills were formidable, and in defence of the theory of EVOLUTION they earned him the soubriquet of 'Darwin's bulldog'. He coined the term 'agnostic' to describe his pervasive scepticism in matters of religion, where an attitude of doubt was as appropriate as in all other areas of knowledge. In later years he resisted attempts by other enthusiasts of evolutionary theory to draw analogies from the natural world as guides to social and economic policy. He also wrote and acted widely in support of scientific education.

SIMON DENTITH

hydrotherapy The medical treatment of hydrotherapy involves the external application of water to mobilize stiff joints or strengthen weak muscles. The patient is immersed in a large bath or tank of water, and the affected limbs are exercised. The treatment gained popularity in the nineteenth century with the redevelopment of spas. These were found throughout Europe, based on spring waters, which were prescribed as tonics because of their mineral contents. Many of the spas developed baths so that the patients could absorb the beneficial properties of the waters through their skin. Exercises for patients suffering from wasting diseases were introduced as part of a general 'cure'. Hydrotherapy developed from the spa movement through the pioneering work of Priessnitz (1790–1851), a German physician who rejected treatment with drugs, purges and bleeding in favour of cleansing the body with water. His techniques included inducing sweating after hot and cold baths and drinking at least twelve glasses of water a day.

SALLY SHEARD

I

Iceland *see* SCANDINAVIA.

imperialism The word 'imperialism' embraces a general tendency by one society to acquire, control or exercise power over another and, from 1870, the organized rule of overseas colonial possessions by representatives from an imperial, predominantly European, centre. Late-nineteenth-century imperialism hence refers to fundamental shifts in the relationship between advanced, industrial Western states and technologically backward non-Western societies. The process of formal political occupation by colonial powers in Africa, the Near East, southeast Asia and the Pacific has been termed the 'new imperialism' by historians, to distinguish it from previous informal empires of trade or of large-scale white settlement. These distinctions are important because a great many disagreements about 'imperialism' are due to inappropriate definitions of, and choices of evidence about, this contentious and amorphous topic.

Before the 1880s there was very little colonial rivalry because much of Continental Europe had more urgent tasks of national unification and the acquisitive British promoted the myth of FREE TRADE internationalism. Continental Europe's new interest in colonial adventures brought it into direct competition with Britain. Thus the occupation of Egypt by Britain under Gladstone's Liberal government in 1882, essential for control of the naval route through the Suez Canal to India, Britain's principal possession, led an embittered France to retaliate by annexations in north-west Africa and a jealous Germany to follow suit (1884–5) in both east and west Africa, primarily for diplomatic ends. The CONFERENCE OF BERLIN (1885) attempted to lay down internationally agreed rules for the partition of Africa and was a clear sign of Bismarckian Germany's sudden emergence, together with King Leopold

(1835–1909) of Belgium's Congo Free State, as a significant player in the territorial expansion of Europe overseas (*see* SCRAMBLE FOR AFRICA).

CHINA remained by far the greatest, if also the most illusory, of all the colonial prizes to be won in the 1890s. The crumbling Ch'ing dynasty lost a war with Japan over Korea (1894–5) and this was followed by the European 'battle' for economic concessions, centred on China, which rose to a height in 1898 with demands for trading 'spheres of influence'. Increasing international tension also arose in the 1890s between Britain and Russia over attempts to gain influence in Persia, as well as between Britain, Russia and Germany over railway activities in the Ottoman Empire. In the Pacific north Borneo, most of New Guinea and the Cook Islands came under the British flag in the 1880s, and the southern Solomon Islands in 1893. A convention of 1886 between Britain and Germany demarcated their respective 'spheres of influence' in the rest of the western Pacific.

Imperialism, as the name given to the forces or motives which lay behind colonial expansion, acquired a new and more negative connotation in the early twentieth century when it was related in varying ways by Lenin (1870–1924) and others to a particular stage of development in capitalist economies requiring external investment, as well as sources of raw materials and new markets. Non-Marxists have argued that colonialism, imperialism and the expansion of capitalism were not necessarily synonymous. In any case, the classic theories of 'economic imperialism' were basically unconcerned with colonial expansion in the 1880s and 1890s. Marxist theorists were not historians intent on explaining the 'scramble' for African colonies, but political activists predicting the future behaviour of expanding capitalism in the world economy – thus it is useless to belabour them for their alleged failure to 'fit the facts' of late-nineteenth-century imperialism.

It is also difficult to link such fashionable racial ideologies as SOCIAL DARWINISM in any precise way with the onset of imperialism. Social Darwinism asserted the rightful duty of the 'superior' white races to dominate and exploit the 'inferior' coloured races, as well as encouraging conflict between European nations, as a part of the biological 'struggle' between species towards evolutionary 'progress'. Significantly, Rudyard Kipling's (1865–1936) poem 'The White Man's Burden' (1899) was dedicated to making the United States aware of its 'civilizing mission', following conquest of the Philippine Islands from Spain. Racial views, such as social Darwinism, were made more respectable during the period of colonial annexations by the application of developing pseudo-scientific theories to what are now regarded as empirically false concepts of a measurable scale of human evolution (*see* THEORIES OF RACE).

Norman Etherington, *Theories of Imperialism: War, Conquest and Capital* (London, 1984).

R. Koebner and H. D. Schmidt, *Imperialism: The Story and Significance of a Political Word, 1840–1960* (Cambridge, 1964).

JOHN SPRINGHALL

impressionism and post-impressionism Among the first art movements to be celebrated for their 'modernist' origination of techniques in rejection of academic practices were impressionism and post-impressionism. After the 1863 exhibition at the Salon des Refusés, Paris, Edouard Manet (1832–83), and especially his painting *Déjeuner sur l'herbe* (Lunch on the Grass, 1863), became the focus for an informal association of artists keen to break with pictorial and technical conventions. These included Camille Pissarro (1830–1903), Edgar Degas (1834–1917), Alfred Sisley (1839–99), Claude Monet (1840–1926), Frédéric Bazille (1841–70), Berthe Morisot (1841–95), Pierre Auguste Renoir (1841–1919) and Mary Cassatt (1845–1926). Among their objectives was to respond to contemporary life with an 'honest' vision, to evoke in their paintings perceptual sensations experienced in the presence of their subject-matter.

This 'new realism' required techniques for capturing transient, usually outdoor, appearances (hence rapid brushwork) and an extended palette capable of recording intense brightness besides colours discernible in shadows. Representative images include Pissarro's *Hoarfrost: The Old Road to Ennery, Pontoise* (1873) and Monet's *Impression: Mist* (originally *Impression: Sunrise*) (1872). Intentionally hostile criticism of the latter in 1874 succeeded only in brilliantly characterizing the movement as 'impressionist'. Pissarro's and Monet's refuge in London during the Franco-Prussian War (1870–1) provided contact with the work of English precursors John Constable (1776–1837) and Joseph Mallord William Turner (1775–1851). Spontaneous renditions of what was to be seen in nature (Constable) and of what might be felt in nature's presence (Turner), the French artists' devotion to commonplace subject-matter and their interest in the documentary potential of photography were among the numerous shaping influences of impressionism.

Such interests help distinguish impressionists from post-impressionists. The latter were not an association (even in the informal sense of impressionism), but were retrospectively identified by the English art theorist Roger Fry (1866–1934) as having made use of, as well as significant individual departures from, impressionist advances in pursuit of individual objectives. They included Paul Cézanne (1839–1906), Paul Gauguin (1848–1903), Vincent Van Gogh (1853–90), Georges Seurat (1859–91), Paul Signac (1863–1935), Henri de Toulouse-Lautrec (1864–1901), Pierre Bonnard (1867–1947) and Edouard Vuillard (1868–1940). Their characteristic achievements included the palpable representation of a structural reality discernible in nature, as in Cézanne's many paintings of Montagne Sainte-Victoire executed after c.1885, besides the highly charged emotional expressions of Van Gogh, typified in *The Church at Auvers* (1890). Seurat sought a specifically modern science of pictorial composition (colours divided into chromatic constituents and combined on the canvas in minute 'pointillist' formations), resulting in monumental compositions such as *Sunday on the Grande-Jatte 1884* (1884–6). In contrast, Bonnard and Vuillard provided 'intimiste' glimpses of suburban life. At yet another extreme was Gauguin, whose quest for a primitive symbolism led to self-imposed exile in the south Pacific, a legacy of images such as *Where Do We Come from? What Are We? Where Are We Going?* (1897) and – in the wish to create synthetic images embodying appearances, emotions and feelings – one of the great aesthetic preoccupations of the following century.

David Bomford et al., *Art in the Making: Studies in Impressionism* (London, 1990).

Robert Rosenblum and H. W. Janson, *Art of the Nineteenth Century* (London, 1984).

Richard Shone, *The Post-impressionists* (London, 1979).

DAVID THISTLEWOOD

Independent Congo State   The personal fiefdom of King Leopold II (1835–1909) of the Belgians, the Independent Congo State was effectively created by the CONFERENCE OF BERLIN (1884–5) as a neutral buffer between the European powers competing in Africa. Having decided that Belgium should have a colony, whether the Belgians wanted one or not, Leopold first tried to purchase the Philippines, then manipulated international interest in expanding 'legitimate' trade in Africa to secure support for his eventual acquisition of some 905,567 square miles of land in the heart of Africa which he ruled absolutely. He shrewdly and unscrupulously secured great-power acquiescence to the establishment of monopoly trading. With British financial support, a railway was built linking the navigable portions of the Congo, Kasai and Oubangi Rivers to the Atlantic Ocean. As Leopold wanted rapid, substantial profit, he focused on exploiting easily available resources that required relatively little capital investment. State agents, paid on commission, used torture and mutilation to maximize rubber and ivory collection by Africans. Tinged with commercial rivalry, reports of these abuses by British vice-consul Roger Casement (1864–1916) led to the formation of the Congo Reform Association, which ultimately generated sufficient international pressure to force Belgium to annex the Congo in 1908.

Leopold's interest in the mineral-rich Katanga (Shaba) region was stirred in 1890 when Cecil RHODES threatened to include it in BRITISH SOUTH AFRICA COMPANY territory. When a Congo State expedition secured Leopold's claim, a Belgian geologist advised against attempting to exploit the region's great copper wealth on the grounds that the required investment would be too great. Some of the huge profits from exploiting Congo State resources went to Belgium as buildings, broad avenues and parks. A large part went to Leopold himself. None went back to Africans.

Neal Ascherson, *The King Incorporated: Leopold II in the Age of Trusts* (London, 1963).
Ruth Slade, *King Leopold's Congo* (London, 1962).

SIMON KATZENELLENBOGEN

Independent Labour Party   Founded in 1893, the Independent Labour Party (ILP) was the first socialist political party to attain a national presence in Britain. The party's formation highlighted the growing influence of socialism in the labour movement and marked the shifting contours of working-class political consciousness. Although it achieved only minor electoral success in its own right, the ILP's leaders took a central role in forging the Labour Representation Committee in 1900, a crucial breakthrough in the establishment of labour as an independent political estate in British society.

The impetus of independent working-class politics emerged in the late 1880s from the conflict between the Lib-Labs of the TRADES UNION CONGRESS and the younger socialist new unionists. Rejecting the old guards' cautious political reformism and commitment to the Liberal values of individualism and self-help, socialist activists pursued militant confrontation at the workplace and argued for more extensive regulation of working conditions by the state. After securing significant influence in major trade unions, the socialists initiated a movement to construct a new politics along class lines.

The entry of socialists into local-level politics laid the groundwork for the creation of the ILP. A coalition of Bradford trade-unionists and socialists founded the immediate parent of the ILP, the Bradford Labour Union, in the aftermath of a divisive 1891 strike. Thereafter, labour activists, similarly committed to the goal of independent working-class politics, founded local labour parties in Manchester, Newcastle and several other cities. The election to parliament of three independent labour candidates in the 1892 general election further galvanized the movement, prompting the decision to hold a conference for the purpose of uniting the rapidly multiplying local bodies into a national party of labour.

The conference, held at Bradford on 13–14 January 1893, drew 120 delegates from local labour parties, branches of the SOCIAL DEMOCRATIC FEDERATION and FABIAN SOCIETY, as well as a handful of trade unions. A number of socialist veterans attended, including Edward Aveling (1849–98), Ben Tillett (1860–1943), George Bernard Shaw (1856–1950), Robert Blatchford (1851–1943) and Keir HARDIE. In recognition of the movement's origins in local labour groups, and with an eye towards gaining the allegiance of non-socialist trade unions, participants avoided mention of socialism in naming the new party, opting instead for the inclusive, 'independent labour'. Nevertheless, the party adopted socialism as its ultimate goal, albeit a decidedly non-doctrinaire socialism. Drawing on the rich tradition of British social criticism and inspired by the morality nurtured in Nonconformist chapels, the founders of the ILP articulated a political ethos that can best be termed ethical socialism. At the same time, having embraced the election of independent labour men to parliament as their highest priority, ILP founders also outlined a pragmatic reform programme for labour consistent with nineteenth-century RADICALISM.

Despite a weak organizational structure, meagre financial support and only marginal trade-union backing, the ILP emerged as the largest socialist body in Britain within a year of its formation, with several hundred branches and 20,000 members. Pursuing vigorous action in local politics, the party gained the election of many municipal officials. However, the ILP met bitter disappointment in the 1895 general election, losing every parliamentary race it entered, including that of Keir Hardie, its popular leader. Greatly humbled, ILP strategists determined that future success depended on drawing more substantial support from the trade unions.

Towards that end, the ILP undertook construction of a broader labour alliance. With decisive consequences for future British politics, those efforts coincided with a concerted employers' offensive against the trade unions and a series of legal decisions which undermined trade-union status (*see* TAFF VALE). Gravely threatened, several unions came to see the cause of independent political representation as crucial to their very survival. After 1895 ILP policies also increasingly converged with reformist tendencies within the Liberal Party which allowed a rapprochement with Liberal trade-unionists on many issues. In February 1900, on receiving the endorsement of the Trades Union Congress, a national conference of socialists and trade-unionists met in London to take up the issue of permanent independent labour representation in parliament. Skilfully managed by ILP leaders, Hardie and Ramsay MacDonald (1866–1937), the conference gave birth to the Labour Representation Committee, a body which represented the socialist societies and trade unions and supported independent labour candidates for parliament. Thereafter, while retaining its socialist outlook, the ILP increasingly adopted pragmatic tactics in order to consolidate the political alliance with the trade unions. After 1906 the ILP survived as a notable component of the LABOUR PARTY, shaping the new organization's political orientation.

David Howell, *British Workers and the Independent Labour Party, 1888–190*
    (Manchester, 1983).

Keith Laybourn and Jack Reynolds, *Liberalism and the Rise of Labour, 1890–1918* (London, 1984).

RICHARD J. SODERLUND

India At the beginning of the nineteenth century India was a subcontinent in flux. The days of the Mughal Empire had long since passed and most of the succeeding indigenous states had succumbed to British influence or were in decline. With the exception of the MARATHA- and Sikh- (*see* SIKHS) based states centred respectively at Poona and Lahore, there was little to impede the unrelenting expansion of the English East India Company's sphere of influence. By 1805 the surviving claimants to Mughal authority were little more than pensioners of the Company, and British hegemony was established virtually throughout the entire subcontinent. From that point until the final destruction of Maratha power in 1818, expansion proceeded with relatively little conflict.

The rising significance of India in British foreign policy was obvious as the century progressed. A policy on India evolved which assumed the necessity to block rival European powers' land access to India while consolidating control over areas already absorbed. This involved an ongoing concern with 'Frontier Policy' in the north-west regions as British political control penetrated ever more north-westerly in the early decades of the century. Concern with Napoleonic France's approach to India was superseded by fears of Persia's and eventually Russia's penetration as the century progressed. Periodic set-backs to British authority – such as the first Afghan War (1837–42) – occurred but had little long-term effect on British expansion. Indeed, no sooner was the Afghan War concluded than the British annexed Sind. Before the decade was over, the Punjab was also absorbed (1849). These acquisitions seemed to many British people merely the inevitable consolidation of control over much of the Indo-Gangetic region and a preface to the final integration of all of India from Calcutta to Karachi under British rule. In an age when utilitarian concepts of progress held sway, it was a grand design which needed only a few additional annexations to complete. Governor General Lord Dalhousie (1812–60) was the architect to complete it. Having initiated the so-called 'Doctrine of Lapse', which denied dynasties the traditional right to adopt an heir if there was no natural heir, he acquired the missing link, the kingdom of Oudh, which controlled the upper Ganges Valley.

However, Lord Dalhousie's unrelenting pressure on the indigenous states, compounded by the widespread destabilization of newly annexed territories triggered a backlash, the Sepoy Mutiny of 1857 (*see* INDIAN MUTINY), which constituted a watershed in nineteenth-century Indian history. The mutiny was speedily put down with a minimum of difficulty and considerable support from Indian military units brought in from the Punjab. The insurrection had remained localized and largely without direction. More important than the insurrection itself was its aftermath: the crown took possession of the East India Company's responsibilities in the subcontinent; the Indian army was reconstructed along lines that were to persist for a century; and both civil and military services recruited more capable individuals to oversee the efficient administration of India within the British Empire. (*see* GOVERNMENT OF INDIA ACT) Moreover, the Indian public, clearly aware of the crown's resolve to play a dominant role on the subcontinent, fell behind British authority as never before while clamouring for a larger role as loyal subjects of the empire.

Between 1858 and 1885 the subcontinent not only experienced an unprecedented period of economic growth – best mirrored in the rise of the great metropolitan centres of Calcutta, Madras and Bombay and in a general increase in population – but also took significant steps in the direction of a nationally integrated economy, a comprehensive communications and transportation network and a common system of English-language education, up to university level, which created the underpinnings of modern India. It also saw the emergence of a significant body of Anglicized and educated Indians who aspired to serve in the imperial bureaucracy.

In 1885, as a result of the Ilbert Bill, which attempted to place Europeans under the jurisdiction of Indian judges, there was a vicious white backlash which suggested to Indians that they needed to organize to support their interests. The result was the formation of the INDIAN NATIONAL CONGRESS, which gradually evolved as a sounding-board for Indian opinion and by the end of the century constituted critical opposition at times. Additionally – most notably in the Bombay-Poona region – there were signs of growing opposition to British policy although as yet little opposition to British rule. At the end of the century Britain remained securely in control of the subcontinent, loyally supported by the vast majority of India's population who took pride in being part of the British Empire. However, the seeds of a nationalist movement, which would soon question British authority, had been sown.

See also HINDUISM.

Percieval Griffiths, *Modern India* (Delhi, 1962).
Philip Woodruff, *The Men who Ruled India*, 2 vols (London, 1954).

ROBERT J. YOUNG

Indian Mutiny (1857–1858)   Also known as the Sepoy Mutiny, the Indian Mutiny represented the most serious threat to British authority in nineteenth-century India. It was the end-result of a protracted period of British expansion in the upper Ganges Valley in the 1840s during the administration (1848–56) of Lord Dalhousie (1812–60).

Several venerable states, including the kingdom of Oudh, disappeared under the unrelenting 'Doctrine of Lapse', a policy which declared the English East India Company heir in the event of there being no natural heir, replacing the time-honoured tradition that allowed rulers to adopt heirs.

The mutiny centred in the heartland of ancient Oudh and was largely limited to the area, which had been destabilized by Company annexation. The end of Oudh's royal line saw the demise of traditional patterns of landholding and tenure in military and civil services as well as royal patronage of traditional religious and educational institutions.

The mutiny was triggered by the insensitive British demand that Hindu and Muslim sepoys utilize a new cartridge greased in animal tallow, which was defiling to Hindus and Muslims. Troops which refused were harshly punished or imprisoned. Finally, in Meerut in June 1857, an attempt to free Indian prisoners by their fellows evolved into an insurrection which spread rapidly up and down the Ganges Valley but remained regional. British troops, supported by sepoys drawn from other regions in India, most notably the Sikhs, counter-attacked and suppressed the revolt with relative ease. Although the mutineers had initially proclaimed the restoration of Mughal authority, there were few signs of organized resistance beyond the local level.

The most immediate impact of the mutiny was a retreat from the 'Doctrine of Lapse', the replacement of the rule of the English East India Company by that of the British government and a thorough reform of military and civil services (*see* GOVERNMENT OF INDIA ACT).

George MacMunn, *The Indian Mutiny in Perspective* (London, 1931).

ROBERT J. YOUNG

Indian National Congress In a speech to Calcutta University graduates in 1883, a retired British civil-service officer, A. O. Hume (1829–1912), called on them to form an organization to regenerate and unify INDIA. The idea found an immediate response among the highly Anglicized Indian elites who were deeply influenced by both the Brahmo Samaj movement and the agitation for Home Rule in Ireland. An additional impetus to action was the overt racism manifested in the recent rejection of the Ilbert Bill, which would have allowed Indian judges to preside over trials of Europeans.

A meeting was called in 1885 which reflected the concerns of the Indian elite and some sympathetic British supporters. From this time, up to 1897, the voice of the Indian National Congress was an English voice since all discussions, minutes and so on were in English. Eminently conservative in origin, the organization moved away only slowly from its original mission to become a political entity. Agitation surrounding the activities of TILAK in the 1890s, his imprisonment in 1897 and Lord Curzon's (1859–1927) partition of Bengal in 1905 nudged the conservative leadership aside and provided for more aggressive militant leadership, under which the Indian National Congress began to build a broader base, to speak in terms of eventual independence and to advocate Indian nationalism. Under the influence of individuals such as Lala Rajpat Rai (1865–1928) and Tilak, the tactics later identified with the independence movement, such as the boycott, hartal (strike) and mass demonstrations, emerged. The Indian National Congress had become the dominant popular voice for nationalist sentiment and remained so until independence in 1947. Thereafter, it continued as the dominant political party in an independent, partitioned India.

Girija Mookerjee, *The History of Indian National Congress* (Delhi, 1974).

ROBERT J. YOUNG

indirect rule   The term 'indirect rule' referred to the various types of colonial rule in Africa which governed through indigenous chiefs and local institutions. In some instances indirect rule also included recognition of African rights in land, in others rights over local budgets and in others the non-intervention of Christian missionaries and educators in African local affairs, customs and religions. Indirect rule was most favoured where limited revenue restricted the expensive employment of European officials in direct administration.

Indirect rule has often, mistakenly, been associated exclusively with Frederik J. Lugard (1858–1945) in Uganda, where he served the Imperial East Africa Company (1889–92), and in northern Nigeria where, as a servant of the Royal Niger Company and later as governor of Nigeria (1912–19), he was involved in the SCRAMBLE FOR AFRICA. Indirect rule was, however, widely used throughout Africa, not only by the British but also by the French who, without adopting the terminology, introduced different types of indirect rule throughout many of their African territories, including Morocco and ALGERIA. As may well be imagined, it did not always preserve indigenous institutions in their pristine forms, not that this was possible or even desirable, given the forces of change. Instead, in a number of instances newly created types of local institutions of governance (some of which maintained a fiction of being 'traditional') were established at one time or other throughout the colonial era, in the name of indirect rule.

Robert O. Collins (ed.), *Western African History* (New York, 1990), pp. 228–38.
Michael Crowder and Obaro Ikime (eds), *West African Chiefs* (New York, 1970).

B. MARIE PERINBAM

individualism   Though it draws on intellectual and social roots that go back at least to the Renaissance and the Reformation, the word 'individualism' was a nineteenth-century coinage which summed up some characteristic nineteenth-century preoccupations. The significance of the term is complicated by the different meanings attached to it by different writers, by the varying (indeed contrary) valuations attached to it in different national cultures and by its being used to denote both actual behaviour and varying kinds of ethical and economic beliefs.

At root, individualism as a term presupposes a way of conceiving society as made up of discrete individuals. Therefore, even at this basic level of description, it was unappealing to both conservatives and socialists in the nineteenth century for whom the social order or the social good must be the starting-point. In so far as individualism further implied that the pursuit of individual interest was ethically and economically desirable, it can be seen that its challenge and appeal varied widely in different contexts of argument. Thus in France individualism generally appeared negatively as meaning a state of social atomism and absence of positive social ideals. In German social thought individualism took on more positive overtones, alluding to the element of distinctive individuality apparently threatened by the levelling out of the modern world. In England and still more in the United States, however, individualism took on positive connotations of quite a different kind, given the greater importance of classical liberal ideas in these countries. In the United States, above all, individualism came to appear, in the course of the century, as the distinctive American virtue and the basis of America's social and economic success. Indeed, for some writers, individualism became the ethical aspect of SOCIAL DARWINISM, since the pursuit of individual interest at the expense of the less capable apparently guaranteed the survival of the fittest.

Steven Lukes, *Individualism* (Oxford, 1973).

SIMON DENTITH

industrial revolution   The term 'industrial revolution' (coined by Arnold Toynbee (1852–83) in lectures published posthumously in 1884, though it was apparently also used in France in the early nineteenth century as a conscious parallel to the French Revolution) refers to the economic, technological, social and structural changes that occurred between about 1780 and 1840 in Britain. These changes then spread in unequal fashion to Continental Europe and a few countries overseas, so that within a couple of generations the nature of the world's economy and society was transformed. Before then, craft technology was dominant, depending on hand-tools, simple machines, individual skills and small-workshop or domestic production. After its impact, powered special-purpose machines, skilled technicians (*see* SKILLED WORKERS) and FACTORIES became part of the economy. The volume and diversity of goods increased (though there was also increasing standardization), while costs fell and incomes (especially of the middle and wealthier classes) increased.

A number of factors contributed to the rise of modern large-scale industrial CAPITALISM in Britain: adequate supplies of capital, raw materials and labour; and access to suitable home and overseas markets. In the late eighteenth century wealth was accumulating in Britain. Overseas trade, especially with the colonies, was profitable, allowing income to be diverted into mining and manufactures. The Bank of England, the London financial houses, the country banks and the various exchanges provided the financial framework for the expansion of private enterprise. In raw materials Britain had adequate supplies of coal and iron (even if bar iron for steel had to be imported from Sweden), which were conveniently located near ports. Growth industries, such as woollen and leather goods, could rely on ample supplies of domestic raw materials. The growing population (in the nineteenth century it increased from 16 million to over 40 million) provided both the labour force for the new factories and an expanding home demand for manufactures. The expansion of British AGRICULTURE provided additional raw materials to certain industries as well as the extra food needed for a growing population. High wages in the towns led to an exodus from the countryside, which created the labour force for the new urban factories. Britain's favourable geographic location on world trade routes and its efficient mercantile marine gave the country relatively easy access to foreign markets. Finally, a host of incremental improvements abetted the cost-reducing impact of new technology: for example, organizational changes, from the diffusion of the factory to the establishment of better property rights, and the creation of technical societies to complement the traditionally famous inventiveness of British artisans and engineers in the key industries – iron production, the steam engine, textile production and precision machine work.

Since much of the data for these developments is sketchy, some historians have doubted the accuracy of the term 'revolution', with its connotations of a steam-powered, factory-based machine age. They have located revolutions in earlier times, such as the seventeenth century; or have pointed out that the term is over-dramatic, especially since growth was relatively slow-paced (British gross national product grew at only about 2 to 3 per cent in the late eighteenth and early nineteenth centuries). They have also highlighted how traditional and unmechanized most British industry was, even by the 1840s. Nor did the growth of manufacturing sweep over the entire face of Britain. However, the term has retained its general importance to describe the first industrialization of a national economy in the world. Of significance was the critical lead that had been established by key areas of British technology over its foreign rivals. By the early nineteenth century this had precipitated the first transfers of British technology across the Atlantic and to Europe. The way in which the United States imported and then adapted British textile technology for its own use by the 1830s is an example.

The classical period of the industrial revolution was over by the 1840s, but the scale and extent of the changes could be seen in the later development of the British and world economy. For example, British national income was growing most rapidly in the second half of the nineteenth century, with marked increases in the standard of living. Manufactures, mining and building increased their share of the national output, while the numbers involved in agriculture fell. By then late starters, such as the United States, had embraced technological change even more readily and successfully than Britain. Among other nations that industrialized after 1860 were Germany, Japan, Austria, Hungary, Italy, Sweden and Russia. By 1900 these countries had emulated and sometimes surpassed the British model, adding new science-based industries such as electrical engineering (*see* ELECTRICITY AND ELECTRICAL INDUSTRY) and chemicals (*see* CHEMICAL INDUSTRY) to the traditional engines of the industrial revolution – COAL, cotton (*see* TEXTILE INDUSTRIES), ENGINEERING and IRON AND STEEL.

See also PROTO-INDUSTRIALIZATION.

Pat Hudson, *Britain's Industrial Revolution* (London, 1992).
D. McCloskey and R. Floud (eds), *The Cambridge Economic History of Britain since 1700, vol. 1: 1700–1860* (Cambridge, 1981).
Peter Mathias, *The First Industrial Nation: An Economic History of Britain 1700–1914*, second edn (London, 1983).

GEOFFREY TWEEDALE

infant mortality   By convention, infant mortality – the death of live born babies before they reach their first birthday – is expressed as an annual rate: the number of infant deaths in a year per thousand live births occurring in the same year. Infant mortality rates remained high throughout the nineteenth century. Where environmental circumstances were particularly favourable and babies were breast-fed and generally well cared for, rates of 80 to 100 could be expected, but in the worst excesses of urban poverty, rates in excess of 300 were more likely. Even in rural areas where infants were not routinely breast-fed, perhaps half of all live born children would not reach their fifth birthday. There were also clear differences in infant mortality between social-class groups, and children born to unmarried mothers were particularly at risk. During the late nineteenth century national levels of infant mortality, which averaged between 150 and 200, began a secular decline in many parts of western and northern Europe, to be followed in succeeding decades by other populations of European origin. The causes of the timing of this decline in infant mortality are still not fully understood, but they seem to be broadly linked with the coincidental decline in marital fertility; the drive for mass education, and the important effects that had for the role and training of young women; the improvement of urban living conditions, especially the sanitary environment; and developments in obstetric, ante- and post-natal care (*see* OBSTETRICS).

R. I. Woods, P. A. Watterson and J. H. Woodward, 'The Causes of Rapid Infant Mortality Decline in England and Wales, 1861–1921', parts 1 and 2, *Population Studies*, 42 (1988), 343–66; 43 (1989), 113–32.

R. I. WOODS

international expositions   Sited in national or regional capitals, international expositions were occasions for expressing cultural and political identity to a world audience, and for energizing trade through advertisement of national achievements in arts and science, fashion and innovation, agriculture, education, industry and technology, manufacturing and, often, imperial expansion. Capitals also hosted similar exhibitions of other nations, their hierarchies conveyed by the size and lavishness of pavilions and their conventionalized location within exposition complexes. Catalogues of their exhibits provide snapshots of cultural values objectified in works of art, design and invention. Their permanent reports inform the study of diplomatic relations, international competition and, because they emphasized technical and cultural progress, contemporary architecture and city-planning. The most important (attendances of over 5 million) were: London (1851, 1862, 1886); Paris (1855, 1867, 1878, 1889, 1900); Vienna (1873); Philadelphia (1876); Glasgow (1888); Chicago (1893) (*see* CHICAGO SCHOOL); Brussels (1897).

John Allwood, *The Great Exhibitions* (London, 1977).

DAVID THISTLEWOOD

International Working Men's Association   *see* FIRST INTERNATIONAL.

Iran   *see* PERSIA.

Ireland   *see* HOME RULE; IRISH FAMINE; IRISH REPUBLICAN BROTHERHOOD; IRISH UNIONISM.

Irish famine (1845–1851)   The 'Great Famine' in Ireland, the last great subsistence crisis in western Europe, was caused by the successive failure of Ireland's staple food, the potato, and the failure of government and other agencies to provide adequate relief. When an unknown fungus attacked the potato, a partial failure in 1845 was followed by a total failure in 1846, and famine reached its height in the winter of 1846–7. Private charities, notably the Quakers, provided relief and the British government imported maize, established soup kitchens and devised public works to enable people to earn money to buy food. The export of food from Ireland was not prohibited, although a temporary ban in 1846–7, while foreign supplies were being obtained, would probably have saved lives. One million people died from disease or starvation, the brunt of starvation falling more severely on young children owing to their exacting dietary requirements. A further million migrated, mainly to the United States, sometimes in 'coffin ships'. The Great Famine differed from previous Irish famines owing to the unusual severity of the crop failures by nineteenth-century standards and the long-term impact on the Irish rural economy. The change from an arable to pastoral economy may have been triggered by the depression following the ending of the French wars, but the prolongation of the blight and the loss of 2 million people, particularly among the labourers and cottiers, made the famine a real watershed in the development of Irish society. The famine burns on in Irish nationalist thinking as the most telling indictment of British rule under the union.

Mary E. Daly, *The Famine in Ireland* (Dublin, 1986).

PATRICK BUCKLAND

Irish Question   *see* HOME RULE.

Irish Republican Brotherhood   Originally the Irish Revolutionary Brotherhood, the Irish Republican Brotherhood was founded in Dublin on 17 March 1858 by James Stephens (1825–1901), a Young Irelander wounded in the 1848 Rising, and influenced by French radical ideas. An American auxiliary movement founded simultaneously gave the name 'Fenians' to the whole organization. They were prompted by disgust at the corruption and ineptitude of Irish representatives at Westminster and the prospect of the collapse of British power in face of mutiny in India and rising tension with France. The aim was to overthrow, 'Soon or Never', the British state and create an Irish republic. Besides Stephens's disputes with the American wing, there was tension between the brotherhood's roles as a secret society bound by a solemn oath of allegiance to 'the Irish Republic now virtually established' and as a social club providing leisure activities for its members – clerks, publicans, shopkeepers, shoemakers, tailors, building-workers and soldiers. The Fenians were also denounced by the Roman Catholic hierarchy (although they had supporters among the lower clergy), and were pursued by the government. Despite Stephens's replacement as head organizer by Thomas Kelly (1833–1908), an American Civil War veteran, the eventual rising in March 1867 was poorly planned and easily suppressed. The execution of the 'Manchester Martyrs' saved the Fenians from ridicule. After 1873 the brotherhood decided to support movements working for Irish self-government, a policy which, though temporarily abandoned in 1877, enabled members to work with PARNELL and infiltrate other organizations, notably the Gaelic Athletic Association (*see* GAELIC REVIVAL). A slow recovery from eclipse in the 1890s began with the prominent part the brotherhood played in the 1798 centenary celebrations, but an influx of young blood, especially from Belfast, was needed for the brotherhood to be able to capitalize on the failures of the Home Rule movement.

Léon Ó Broin, *Revolutionary Underground: The Story of the Irish Republican Brotherhood, 1858–1924* (Dublin, 1976).

PATRICK BUCKLAND

Irish Unionism   A movement of opposition to Irish HOME RULE, Irish Unionism comprised largely Irish Protestants who were two-thirds of Ulster's population and a tenth of that of the other three provinces. Irish Unionists wanted to maintain the Union. Arguing that Ireland had prospered from the British connection, they refused to be forced to give up the conditions of their success in return for a restored Irish parliament dominated by unsavoury elements who would destroy Ireland's prosperity and the Protestant ascendancy. After initial attempts in 1885–6 to present a united front, Unionists in Ulster and elsewhere went separate ways. The southern Unionists worked through the Irish Loyal and Patriotic Union and, after 1891, the Irish Unionist Alliance. Scattered and isolated among the Catholic and nationalist community, they concentrated on campaigning against Home Rule in parliament and among the British electorate, emphasizing the 'new communism' of the Land League (*see* IRISH NATIONAL LAND LEAGUE) and the empire's benefits to Ireland. The more compact and confident Ulster Unionists organized through the Ulster Loyalist Anti-Repeal Union and the Ulster Convention. They emphasized the religious objections to Home Rule, raising the spectre of 'Rome Rule'. Besides fighting elections in Ireland and campaigning in Britain, they were prepared to resist Home Rule by force of arms if necessary, using the slogan 'Ulster will fight, and Ulster will be right'. The combined efforts of Irish Unionists helped to defeat the first two Home Rule Bills, although southern Unionists' patient work behind the scenes was eclipsed by the spectacular demonstrations of Ulster Unionists. Ulster Unionist separateness reflected the distinctive regional development of Ulster, separated from the rest of Ireland by Scottish settlement, Evangelical Protestantism and industrial development. North-east Ulster had more in common with Merseyside and Clydeside than with the rest of Ireland.

See also IRISH ACT OF UNION.

Patrick Buckland, *Irish Unionism, 1885–1923: A Documentary History* (Belfast, 1973).

PATRICK BUCKLAND

iron and steel The iron and steel industry was transformed in both scale and technique in the nineteenth century. Innovations in the manufacture of iron and steel and in the fabrication of products from the metals altered the organization of the industry and its capacity for large-scale production. Likewise, the rise of important technologies like steam engines, railroads (*see* RAILWAYS), iron shipbuilding and iron-frame construction increased the demand for iron and steel and made the materials even more central to the technological order.

Novel techniques for iron production from the eighteenth century, such as the use of coke rather than charcoal as fuel, became more widely significant in the first half of the nineteenth century, when steam power was applied to assist the blast in coke furnaces, thus enabling even larger furnaces to be fired while reducing unit costs. The use of large, often steam-powered, machines for fabricating iron through rolling, slitting and drawing further increased demand for the material while reducing the cost of finished products.

The production of steel was, before the late eighteenth century, a difficult craft. In the mid eighteenth century the use of reverberatory furnaces to produce the high heats to melt steel gave some hint of how useful the material might be if it could be produced more cheaply. In 1856 Henry BESSEMER announced a new process for making steel from pig-iron, using a device for blowing air through the molten iron. A similar process was patented in the United States by William Kelly (1811–88). With the contributions of others to increase the quality of the steel produced, their process provided the first source of inexpensive steel. This steel possessed a superior combination of workability, strength and durability over traditional wrought iron.

Even more important than Bessemer steel was that produced by the open-hearth process, which utilized scrap iron and low-grade fuels to make an even more economical product. Later in the century the British experimenters, Percy Gilchrist (1851–1935) and Sidney Thomas (1850–85) devised the means for using cheaper, phosphorous-rich ores in the open-hearth process, thus opening the door for the expansion of the industry in places like Germany and the United States, which rapidly overtook Great Britain as leading producers.

W. K. V. Gale, *Iron and Steel* (London, 1969).

ROBERT FRIEDEL

Islam The official religion of the OTTOMAN EMPIRE, PERSIA and parts of India, Islam was also the faith of millions in China, Indonesia, central Asia and Africa. Although there was a continuing tradition of reform among Muslim peoples prior to the rise of the European empires, the inability of Islamic states to fend off European encroachment was a powerful catalyst for change after the middle of the eighteenth century.

In response to the challenges of the nineteenth century, the Ottoman

Empire, still the largest and most powerful Islamic state in the world, and the autonomous Ottoman province of EGYPT introduced reforms which reduced the role of Islam in public life and deprived the ulema of their traditional monopoly over education and justice. Since religious courts and schools remained, however, the nineteenth century saw the emergence of two antagonistic sets of institutions, elites and constituencies. Inasmuch as secularization was government-imposed, Western in form and, for obvious reasons, popular with religious minorities, the Muslim population increasingly faulted their government, especially when the reforms did not prevent further European and Russian conquests of Muslim territory. In the Middle East the contradiction between Europe as modern model and Europe as brutal colonizer weakened the forces of political liberalism and secularism. Indeed, resistance movements against European domination often targeted domestic groups whose embracing of Western culture appeared to abet Europe's imperial goals. Frequently the government itself was seen as Europe's agent, as in Egypt at the time of the Urabi Pasha revolt (see AHMAD URABI PASHA) and Persia under the Qajars.

Islamic revivalism directed at the moral rejuvenation of state and society was as old as Islam itself. Western imperialism and the intrusive modernization of indigenous regimes, however, provided a riveting new focus for popular religious leaders. Some of these founded new organizations, others transformed venerable brotherhoods by the force of their personalities. All were concerned to fuse anti-foreign or anti-government resistance with a summons to salvationary purification, restoration of the holy law or Messianic deliverance.

A significant number of movements emanated from the tribes of the Arab and African deserts. Even before Europe became a factor, the WAHHABIS of northern Arabia challenged their Ottoman sovereigns and contemporary Islam by waging a war of purification against practices that had arisen after the Prophet Muhammad's era. Although Wahhabi violence against fellow Muslims was condemned outside the peninsula, the movement's radical reformism enjoyed a wide audience. Just as Wahhabism had drawn inspiration from ideas current among thinkers elsewhere in the Islamic world, the pilgrimage to Mecca (hajj) and the international nature of Islamic coteries further disseminated revivalist theology.

SIDI MUHAMMAD IBN ALI AL-SANUSI in Libya favoured peaceful methods to convince Muslims to renew their faith through membership in desert-based communities bound by worship and labour. As part of the Ottoman Empire, Libya benefited from modernization projects, and relations between the regime and the Sanusi lodges were relatively amicable. Later in the nineteenth century the sultans' claims to the caliphate, and hence to spiritual authority over all Muslims, was upheld in Sanusi circles.

In Algeria, where European penetration was early and direct, the Qadiriya under ABD AL-QADIR rallied anticolonial resistance while promoting the austere values of primordial Islam. Abd al-Qadir's organization of desert tribesmen into hierarchized units of militant initiates blended the traditional Sufi system of deference to a sheikh-master with newer reformist elements.

The Mahdist movement (*see* MAHDISM) in the Sudan presented another variation of neo-Sufi activism. The Sudan's increasing subjection to the aggressive modernization of Egyptian rule provoked a violent reaction against the Turkish-speaking elite who dominated the Egyptian administration. MUHAMMAD 'AHMAD IBN 'ABDALLAH, an ascetic Sufi sheikh, declared himself to be the Mahdi, the promised deliverer, and mobilized his tribal followers to expel the Egyptians in 1881. As with other such risings, the Mahdists' motives were as diverse as the groups that were attracted to their banner, but the movement's chief attraction was the charismatic person of the Mahdi himself.

Desert tribesmen were only the most militant of the popular groups operating in the century. Religious orders representing older traditions as well as neo-Sufism were active throughout the urban centres of the Islamic world. Mosques and religious colleges also continued to draw their audiences, and teachers brought back new ideas from their travels to Mecca and other centres. Perhaps the most striking characteristic of Islam in the nineteenth century, however, was its regionalism. However much cross-pollination occurred, and however much Islamic ritual conveyed the sense of confessional unity, in the end Islam manifested itself differently according to local conditions.

The summons to the jihad, or holy war, occurred with some frequency in the least populated and most peripheral areas of the Islamic world but it had little appeal beyond the groups that had invoked it. Europeans, however, tended to view Islam and Muslims as all of a piece. Thus during the First World War the Entente powers feared that a call to holy war would result in a universal revolt of Muslims everywhere. When the Ottoman sultan did, in fact, declare the war a jihad, the response was anything but universal.

Ira Lapidus, *A History of Islamic Societies* (Cambridge, 1988).
Malise Ruthven, *Islam in the World* (Oxford, 1984).
John Voll, *Islam: Continuity and Change in the Modern World* (Boulder, Colo., 1982).

MADELINE C. ZILFI

Ismail Pasha (*b* Cairo, 30 December 1830; *d* Istanbul, 6 March 1895)   Khedive of EGYPT (1863–79). The son of Ibrahim Pasha (1789–1848) and grandson of MUHAMMAD ALI, founder of the Egyptian dynasty, he succeeded his uncle Sa'id Pasha (1822–63) in 1863 after studying in Europe and serving in the government of his suzerain, the

Ottoman sultan. His experience enabled him to secure greater independence from the Ottomans while maintaining cordial relations. He was a man of imagination and daring who was in many respects the second 'founder of modern Egypt'. His ambitions for a prosperous and powerful Egypt, however, exceeded Egypt's resources and his own talents. Although his accomplishments included the Suez Canal, networks of schools, railways and roads and numerous other reforms and innovations, his extravagance set in motion a spiral of national indebtedness, European meddling and domestic turmoil that led to his deposition in 1879 and to the British occupation of Egypt in 1882. He was succeeded by his son Muhammad Tawfiq (see TAWFIQ PASHA).

P. J. Vatikiotis, *The History of Egypt from Muhammad Ali to Mubarak* (Baltimore, 1986).

MADELINE C. ZILFI

Itagaki Taisuke (*b* Tosa, 1837; *d* 1919) Japanese samurai. He was an important member of the remarkable group of talented young men, mainly from the domains of Choshu, Satsuma and Tosa, who engineered the downfall of the Tokugawa shogunate and the MEIJI RESTORATION. Having served in the Meiji government, he broke with the ruling oligarchy in the 1870s to become one of the founding fathers of Japanese party politics, leading the liberal party. Following a partial reconciliation with his former colleagues in the oligarchy in the 1890s, he held a number of government posts up to 1900.

JOHN DAVIES

Italy Until 1861, when a united Kingdom of Italy was proclaimed, 'Italy' was merely a geographic expression. Napoleon destroyed the *ancien régime* in Italy, reorganized its political boundaries and brought the ideas of liberty, equality and fraternity to the Italians. While the CONGRESS OF VIENNA (1815) tried to restore the old order by returning the pope to his estates, the Bourbons to Naples and the Savoys to Piedmont, it also established Austria's predominant influence in Italy by allowing the Habsburgs to annex Lombardy and Venetia, and Habsburg collaterals to govern the duchies of Tuscany, Parma and Modena. In doing so the congress dashed the hopes of Italian liberals who, believing in the ideas Napoleon introduced, wished for a united Italy. This Risorgimento, a resurgence of Italian nationalism and a desire for a restoration of the greatness that Italy had known in ancient and Renaissance days, would be the driving force towards unification. The failure of revolts in Naples (1820), Piedmont (1821), Modena, Parma and the Papal States (1831) inspired MAZZINI to found Young Italy. Moderate liberals saw Mazzini as too radical and considered more appealing a confederation of Italian states under the presidency of the pope.

The revolts of 1848 (*see* REVOLUTIONS OF 1848) attempted to rid Italy of Austrian domination and force the rulers of Naples, Tuscany, Piedmont and the Papal States to grant constitutions. Charles Albert (1798–1849), king of Sardinia-Piedmont, was convinced that declaring war on Austria could save the revolution for the monarchical forces and protect his regime from republicans. Defeated by the Austrian general Radetzky at the Battles of Custozza and Novara near Milan, Charles Albert was forced to abdicate in favour of his son VICTOR EMMANUEL II. The revolts set up republics in Rome, Venice and Florence, but with the support of the French the pope returned to Rome, the Austrians restored the dukes of central Italy and the revolutionary movement was suppressed. The one achievement, the Piedmontese constitution of 1848, which would later become the basis for the constitution of united Italy, seemed the only hope for reformers.

Italian unity was finally achieved through the work of the Piedmontese prime minister, Count CAVOUR. Manipulating Austria into declaring war, France and Piedmont were able to repel Austrians at the BATTLES OF MAGENTA AND SOLFERINO. The truce of Villafranca (1859) ceded Lombardy to Piedmont and was supposed to restore the deposed central Italian dukes to their thrones but it never occurred, the duchies voting instead for union with Piedmont. In exchange for French help, Piedmont ceded to Napoleon III both Nice and Savoy. GARIBALDI's expedition to Sicily and Naples defeated the Bourbon king and Garibaldi surrendered his conquests to Victor Emmanuel II. When the Kingdom of Italy was proclaimed in 1861 it was a unitary state created through conquest, not a federated state created through diplomacy and was, therefore, dominated by the more developed, prosperous and populated north. Only Latium (the area around Rome) and Venetia were not included in the new kingdom.

Allied with Bismarck in the Seven Weeks War, Italy, despite its defeat by Austria, secured the cession of Venetia. During the FRANCO-PRUSSIAN WAR, Napoleon was forced to withdraw the garrison which had been protecting Rome since 1849 and the Italian army marched in and annexed the city, completing the unification of Italy. Despoiling the pope of his temporal estates created a tense relationship between the Italian government and the PAPACY over this 'Roman Question', which was one of the standard features of Italian foreign policy in the second half of the century.

Italian parliamentary politics shifted in the so-called 'Revolution of 1876', when the Left finally succeeded in securing a parliamentary majority. The policy of 'transformism' adopted by Agostino Depretis after 1876 continued the fluid party structure by co-opting members of the Right into ministries of the Left and maintaining the Left in power but creating an amorphous and ill-defined policy. Fearing French aggression after the loss of Tunis as well as over the Roman Question,

Depretis allied Italy to Germany and Austria in the TRIPLE ALLIANCE (1882). This alliance, however, was on shaky ground because Italian irredentists pushed for the annexation of Trentino and Trieste, which belonged to Austria. Despite being included among the great powers, Italy could never quite measure up to that image and its initial attempt to secure an empire in Africa ended in disaster at the BATTLE OF ADOWA in 1896.

Frank Coppa, *Dictionary of Modern Italian History* (London, 1985).
Denis Mack Smith, *Italy and its Monarchy* (London, 1989).

LAWRENCE P. ADAMCZYK

Ito Hirobumi (*b* Choshu, 1841; *d* Korea, 1909)   Japanese samurai who rose to high office after the MEIJI RESTORATION. A prominent member of the remarkable group of talented young men from samurai families, mainly based in the domains of the Choshu, Satsuma and Tosa, who engineered the downfall of the Tokugawa shogunate, he became one of the most important figures in the tightly knit oligarchy which dominated Japanese politics from the Meiji Restoration into the twentieth century. As well as holding high government office, he was one of the architects of the Meiji Constitution of 1889. He was later appointed to a lesser post, resident-general in Korea, where he met an untimely death at the hand of an assassin.

JOHN DAVIES

Iturbide, Agustín de (*b* Valladolid, Spain, 27 September 1783; *d* Padilla, 19 July 1824)   Soldier and Emperor Agustín I of MEXICO. The son of Spanish immigrants, he became a royalist military officer during the Mexican insurgency after 1810. In February 1821 he rejected viceregal authority and made an agreement with Vicente Guerrero (1782–1831), the guerrilla leader he had been fighting, to call for independence under a constitutional monarchy. Although he obtained the surrender of the Spanish viceroy, Iturbide began to lose control of Mexico after the election of congress early in 1822. To salvage his position, he orchestrated demonstrations to have himself acclaimed as emperor. An extravagant coronation took place in July, but his government faced serious fiscal problems and increasing discontent. Although he closed congress, the army turned against him, supporting SANTA ANNA's call to rebellion. Itúrbide abdicated in March 1823, but returned from Europe in July 1824 under the misapprehension that Mexicans would welcome him. He was executed a few days later.

RORY MILLER

J

Jackson, Andrew (*b* Waxhaw Settlement, South Carolina, 15 March 1767; *d* Nashville, Tennessee, 8 June 1845) President of the United States (1829–37). Half-heartedly studying law before heading west in 1788, he became a planter and major-general of the Tennessee militia. In the War of 1812 Jackson led the successful defence of New Orleans. Running for president as a national hero in 1824, he lost when the election was put to the House of Representatives and Henry Clay threw his support to John Quincy Adams. Calling this a 'corrupt bargain' and running under the banner of the new DEMOCRATIC PARTY, Jackson swept the election in 1828 and served two terms which were fraught with controversy. Although the historiography of Jackson's presidency is contradictory, historians agree that both the office of president and party organization grew stronger during the Jacksonian era.

Richard Latner, *The Presidency of Andrew Jackson: White House Politics, 1829–1837* (Athens, Ga., 1979).

JOHN MARTIN

Jackson, Thomas Jonathan ['Stonewall Jackson'] (*b* Clarksburg, Virginia, 21 January 1824; *d* Guiney's Station, Virginia, 10 May 1863) A leading Confederate general in the American Civil War. He graduated from the United States Military Academy in 1846, served in the Mexican War and taught mathematics at the Virginia Military Institute (1851–61). He acquired his sobriquet at the first Battle of Bull Run (1861) because of the steadfastness of his brigade. His campaigns in the Shenandoah Valley (1862), where he out-manœuvred and defeated vastly superior Union forces, were a study in deception, mobility and offensive striking power. He then joined the army of northern Virginia under Robert E. LEE and participated with distinction at Antietam and Fredericksburg. At Chancellorsville in May 1863 he was fatally wounded by his own men while reconnoitring between the lines. He was noted for his personal eccentricities as much as for his tactical and strategic acumen. A devout Calvinist, beloved by his soldiers and feared by his enemies, Jackson was Lee's ablest lieutenant.

KEVIN MURPHY

Jack the Ripper Nickname supplied in grisly letters to the press by a notorious, but so far unidentified, serial killer whose bloody disembowellings of London East End prostitutes in the autumn of 1888 inaugurated the modern sex crime. The definitive Ripper killings, of Mary Ann Nichols, Annie Chapman, Catherine Eddowes, Elizabeth Stride and Mary Kelly, all took place within a short distance of each other in poverty-stricken Whitechapel. Proposed suspects have ranged from the barrister Montague Druitt (1857–88) to the poisoner George Chapman (1865–1903), from the queen's physician Sir William Gull (1816–90) to the painter Walter Sickert (1860–1942). The closeness of Whitechapel to the City of London, and the presence locally of Toynbee Hall university settlement, has led many 'Ripperologists' to propose an upper-class, even royal, murderer. The more likely probability that Jack was an anonymous sex killer of low self-esteem is less appealing to the sensation-seeking public.

Donald Rumbelow, *The Complete Jack the Ripper*, revised edn (Harmondsworth, 1988).

JOHN SPRINGHALL

Jameson Raid (1895) An abortive and covert military operation against the TRANSVAAL republic, by about 500 Rhodesian police and volunteers, the Jameson Raid was led by Leander Starr Jameson (1853–1917), a doctor in the service of Cecil RHODES's British South Africa Company in Matabeleland (Southern Rhodesia). Connived at by Rhodes, who had vastly overestimated the region's mineral resources, the invading forces from the Bechuanaland Protectorate (now Botswana) expected their covert military operation to coincide with a planned Uitlander uprising in Johannesburg. No such uprising came, and with the invaders' easy defeat, the planned overthrow of the KRUGER government foundered. So did Rhodes's scheme to weaken the Boer government by coercing Kruger into enfranchising the UITLANDERS, which would have weakened Boer political power. The raid's failure destroyed Rhodes's political career, further embittering Anglo-Boer relations.

Leonard M. Thompson, 'Great Britain and the Afrikaner Republics 1870–1899', in M. Wilson and L. M. Thompson, *History of South Africa*, vol. 2 (Oxford, 1971), pp. 289–324.

B. MARIE PERINBAM

Japan A feudal society at the beginning of the nineteenth century, ruled by the Tokugawa shogunate, Japan was opened up to Western trade by the American Commodore Perry (1794–1858). In 1854 the shogunate was forced to open Shimoda and Hakodate to American trade. This submission to Western pressure led to revolt against the shogunate by samurai from Satsuma, Choshu and Tosa. The outcome was the overthrow of the shogunate and the restoration of the emperor (*see* MEIJI RESTORATION), in fact a revolution. Determined that Japan would never again be humiliated, the Meiji government modernized the nation, using the West as model. Feudalism was swept away, and reforms covering finance, industry, agriculture, the armed forces, education, transport, the legal system and the constitution (the Meiji Constitution, 1890) were introduced. In the 1890s Japan emerged on the world scene as the first modernized Asian state with the defeat of China in the SINO-JAPANESE WAR.

JOHN DAVIES

Jaurès, Jean (*b* Castres, 3 September 1859; *d* Paris, 31 July 1914) French socialist politician and historian. He grew up on a farm and graduated first in his class from the prestigious Ecole Normale Supérieure. He became a socialist after his election to the Chamber of Deputies in 1885. Strongly influenced by Marx, his socialism was not so much dogmatic as humane and eclectic. Although he believed in the class struggle and the inevitability of the collapse of capitalism, he retained the older French socialist tradition of workers' co-operatives, tried to form broad alliances with students, workers and intellectuals and believed socialism could be attained by peaceful methods like universal suffrage. He was a passionate Dreyfusard, much to the disgust of some of his socialist colleagues. His emotional internationalism and hostility to war provoked his assassination by a crazed nationalist in a café in Paris in July 1914. His *Histoire socialiste de la Révolution française* (Socialist History of the French Revolution, 1901–7) is still worth reading.

H. Goldberg, *The Life of Jean Jaurès* (Madison, Wisc., 1962).

DONALD SUTHERLAND

Jefferson, Thomas (*b* Goochland County, Virginia, 13 April 1743; *d* Albemarle County, Virginia, 4 July 1826) President of the United States (1801–9). Virginia's delegate to the Continental Congress in 1776, he authored the Declaration of Independence. As George Washington's (1732–99) Secretary of State, Jefferson discovered his distaste for the policies of Washington's treasury secretary, Alexander Hamilton (1757–1804). By 1800 these differences had grown into opposing political parties: Jefferson's Democratic-Republicans and Hamilton and John Adams's (1735–1826) Federalists. Jefferson won the presidency in what he called the 'Revolution of 1800'. Believing in a strict interpretation of the Constitution and that the future of the republic lay with landholding farmers, he had difficulty reconciling his personal philosophy with the necessities of executive action (*see* EMBARGO ACT, LOUISIANA PURCHASE). Following his second term, Jefferson retired to private life and devoted time to founding and designing the University of Virginia.

Merrill Peterson, *Thomas Jefferson and the New Nation* (New York, 1970).

JOHN MARTIN

Jena, Battle of (14 October 1806)   One of Napoleon BONAPARTE's most dramatic victories, Jena broke the military reputation of the PRUSSIA of the eighteenth century. Provoked beyond reason by the emperor's refusal to recognize its interests, Prussia went to war with France in September 1806, but Napoleon outmanoeuvred its disorganized and badly commanded armies, routing part of them at Jena (though much of the credit in fact belongs to Marshal Davout (1770–1823) who on the same day defeated a much larger force at Auerstadt). There followed a rapid pursuit in which Prussia was completely overrun amid a complete absence of popular resistance. Horrified by what had occurred, not to mention the humiliations imposed on Prussia by the peace settlement, a reformist group headed by STEIN then embarked on a plan of civil and military reform that laid the foundations for the revival of 1813–14, and, ultimately, for the victories of Sadowa in Bohemia (3 July 1866) and Sedan in northern France (1–2 September 1870).

CHARLES ESDAILE

Jews and Judaism   In the nineteenth century the Jews experienced a series of radical transformations: large demographic shifts, a revolution in legal status (with Russia the large exception), high economic and social mobility, religious reform and secularization and the emergence of both ANTI-SEMITISM and Jewish nationalism (Zionism). In the early nineteenth century (*c*.1820) the world Jewish population was around 3,281,000, most of whom (2,730,000) lived in Europe (Russia, 1,600,000; Habsburg Empire, 568,000; Germany, 223,000). By 1900 the world Jewish population had risen to around 10,602,500, with 8,690,000 still in Europe (Russia, 5,190,000; Habsburg Empire, 2,069,000; Germany, 520,000), but with 1,000,000 now in North America, the result largely of mass migration from the oppression and poverty of the Russian Empire.

Western and central European Jewry concerned itself for much of the nineteenth century with the movement for emancipation. In Western countries (France, England, Holland and Italy) the emancipation process was generally swift and unproblematic, leading to a more or less complete assimilation of the relatively small Jewish communities. In central Europe, however, the struggle for full emancipation was much longer (1867 in the Habsburg Empire, 1866–71 in Germany). As a result, the central European version of emancipation, basing itself on the Haskalah (Jewish Enlightenment), came to combine the demand for an end to anti-Jewish discrimination and acceptance of Jews in their host states as full citizens with equal rights, with a conscious effort at the self-improvement of the Jews themselves, in terms of religious practice, economic occupation and moral-cultural attitudes. (The modernization of the Jewish religion in the form of both reform and neo-orthodoxy can be seen as tied to this emancipatory strategy.) This created a specifically Jewish ideology of emancipation, which meant that the very efforts of Jews to integrate into the national communities marked them out as different, generally more liberal and universalist than the political consensus of their host societies. The situation in the Habsburg Empire was greatly complicated in this respect by the various nationality conflicts, in which Jews often found themselves on both sides and the target of both rival groups.

Eastern European Jewry took a different path of development than either its western or central European counterparts. In Galicia (Austrian southern Poland) Jews gained legal equality, but did not modernize along the lines of other Jewish communities in the Habsburg Empire. In Romania the government successfully skirted international requirements to grant Jews equal rights by classifying them as foreigners. In Russia, with the largest Jewish community, the century saw little or no improvement in the legal status of Jews. The regime tried various methods, from forced assimilation to limited liberalization but the end of the century saw Jews still as second-class subjects, confined to the Pale (the former extent of the Polish-Lithuanian kingdom), with some privileged exceptions. There were also, from the 1880s, waves of pogroms (the worst being Kishinev in 1903) which encouraged mass immigration to the West. Given this situation, eastern European Jewry chose largely to modernize within a Jewish framework rather than to integrate with the surrounding societies as Jews to the west were doing. Culturally, the effect was the emergence of a modern YIDDISH and Hebrew literature, a Jewish secular culture; politically, there arose the BUND, a distinct Jewish socialist party in Russia; also, from the 1880s, there emerged Zionism, the movement for a Jewish state, which was to receive political coherence from the Viennese journalist, Theodor HERZL. Zionism was initially poorly received by western and central European Jewry, the bulk of its early support coming from eastern European Jewry.

Economically, the traditional concentration of Jews in finance and commerce meant that some Jews became very wealthy from the triumph of capitalism, and overall Jews outside eastern Europe achieved a relatively high rate of upward social mobility, the exaggerated perception of which is seen to have been a cause of anti-Semitism.

The traditional Jewish emphasis on education, combined with the emancipationist identification of Jews with liberalism, also led to individuals of Jewish religion or descent being very prominent in liberal and socialist politics, and in cultural modernism (for example Karl Marx, Ferdinand Lassalle, Heinrich Heine, Sigmund Freud (1866–1939)). This, added to their large urban presence, led to Jews being identified with modernism and liberalism generally, not just by anti-Semites. The power of this symbolic identification was best exemplified at the end of the century by the DREYFUS Affair.

H. H. Ben-Sasson, *A History of the Jewish People* (Cambridge, Mass., 1976). David Sorkin, *The Transformation of German Jewry* (Oxford, 1987).

                                                                    STEVEN BELLER

jihad *see* ISLAM.

jingoism The word 'jingoism' was a pejorative term for a foreign policy of warlike sentiment or belligerent chauvinism. It derived from the phrase 'By Jingo', either an expression of surprise or an old conjuror's gibberish term, used by the writer G. W. Hunt (1825–77) in a British music-hall song, from whence its bellicose meaning was acquired. G. H. Macdermott performed the song in support of Prime Minister Disraeli's dispatch of a British fleet to the Dardanelles during the 1877–8 Russo-Turkish war:

We don't want to fight, but By Jingo if we do,
We've got the ships, we've got the men, we've got the money too.
We've fought the Bear before, and while we're Britons true,
The Russians shall not have Constantinople.

While 'the Great Macdermott' was on stage Disraeli's private secretary, Monty Corry (1838–1903), supposedly stood in the wings to gauge the song's popularity.

Penny Summerfield, 'Patriotism and Empire: Music-Hall Entertainment, 1870–1914', in John M. MacKenzie (ed.), *Imperialism and Popular Culture* (Manchester, 1986), pp. 17–48.

                                                                    JOHN SPRINGHALL

Johnson, Andrew (*b* Raleigh, North Carolina, 29 December 1808; *d* near Carter's Station, Tennessee, 31 July 1875) President the United States (1865–9). An ardent nationalist, as well as the spokesman for non-slaveholders, he refused to leave his seat in Congress when Tennessee seceded in 1861. After serving as military governor of Tennessee, he became Lincoln's running mate in 1864 to appeal to border-state

Unionists. On Lincoln's assassination he became president. Despite harsh words for southern planter-aristocrats whom he hated, Johnson pursued a RECONSTRUCTION policy that saw many ex-Confederates regain political power. This led to a conflict with the Republican-controlled Congress, which designed a more rigorous plan. When Johnson used his power to impede the enforcement of congressional policy, he was impeached by the House of Representatives. He escaped removal from office by one vote, partly because the Republicans feared a backlash in an election year. Just before his death, he returned to Washington as a senator from Tennessee.

Hans L. Trefousse, *Andrew Johnson: A Biography* (New York, 1989).

ALICE E. REAGAN

Josephine, empress of France *see* BONAPARTE, JOSEPHINE.

Joubert, Piet [Petrus Jacobus] (*b* Prince Albert, Cape Colony, 20 January 1831; *d* Pretoria, 17 March 1900)   Boer politician and military leader. From poor beginnings – his parents had joined the Boer trek to Natal (1837) – he became a considerable landowner, successful law agent and businessman. While most Boers wanted to maintain an agricultural and relatively isolated economy and society, Joubert looked to co-operation with British and other foreign enterprises – several of which he was closely involved with – to promote railways and exploit the mineral and other resources of the Transvaal. Although respected by the Boers as a commandant-general, he was not well trusted, hence his nickname 'Slim (Sly) Piet'. His conciliatory attitude towards the UITLANDERS caused displeasure, as did his short temper. A strong opponent of KRUGER's concession and railway policies, he ran against him unsuccessfully in four presidential elections.

SIMON KATZENELLENBOGEN

Juárez, Benito (*b* Guelatao (Oaxaca), 21 March 1806; *d* Mexico City, 18 July 1872)   President of MEXICO (1858–72). A Zapotec Indian, he qualified in law and was elected to congress in 1846. He served six years as governor of Oaxaca before being exiled by SANTA ANNA. He became secretary of justice in the Reform government of 1855, passing the law which circumscribed the privileges of army and church courts, and then chief justice. In 1858, after the conservatives had ejected the liberals from the capital, he was acclaimed constitutional president. His first electoral victory came in 1861, but Mexico's inability to pay foreign creditors quickly resulted in the French occupation. Juárez led the liberal resistance to MAXIMILIAN, and won new elections in 1867, forming the administration which began the post-war reconstruction of Mexico. However, opposition from liberal rivals to his further re-election was growing. Although he won a close contest in 1871, he faced a rebellion from Porfirio DIAZ before dying in July the following year.

RORY MILLER

July Revolution *see* REVOLUTIONS OF 1830–1832.

June Days The insurrection which broke out in Paris between 23 and 26 June 1848 was ostensibly caused by the dissolution of the national workshops, government-run workhouses designed to alleviate unemployment at a time when unemployment in some trades was over 50 per cent. More generally, working people feared that a largely monarchist Constituent Assembly would undo the gains they had made since the beginning of 1848. Thousands of working people and national guards participated on the barricades but, unlike February 1848, the army remained loyal to the regime and provincial republicans were appalled. Under General CAVAIGNAC, the insurrection was overcome in three days. About 1,500 insurgents were killed, many after the rising; 11,000 were arrested and 4,500 were jailed or deported (one gain of 1848 was the abolition of the death penalty in political cases). Highly organized and sizeable trades in the furniture, building and locomotive works tended to be more rebellious than the dispersed and feminized textile trades.

M. Traugott, *Armies of the Poor* (Princeton, NJ, 1985).

DONALD SUTHERLAND

Junkers The nobles of north-eastern Germany, mainly the Prussian provinces of Brandenburg, Pomerania, West and East Prussia and Mecklenburg, were known as *Junkers* ('young lords'). Many *Junker* families were not rich, their members earning their livelihood in the Prussian state service. Their estates were farmed with the labour services of servile peasants who were tied to the soil, often with their families. In the first half of the nineteenth century the peasants were freed and their services gradually abolished, but the lords were 'compensated' by the cession of large amounts of land, so that their estates grew and became consolidated; they were secured undivided by a complex system of entail.

The *Junkers* dominated the higher posts in the officer corps and the bureaucracy, but this dominion was threatened by the revolution of 1848 (*see* REVOLUTIONS OF 1848). They countered by the formation of a '*Junker* Parliament' and violent opposition, which was ultimately successful, thanks to the Prussian army. In 1847 77 per cent of Prussian officers were noblemen, and in 1860 the figure was 65 per cent. The Prussian cadet school provided for younger sons. Until 1914 many regiments of the guards did not have a single commoner among their officers. Around 1910 eleven of twelve provincial governors were nobles, as were twenty-three of thirty-six *Regierungspräsidenten* (administrators of larger districts), but the true strength of the *Junkers* was based on the *Landrat* (rural councillor) who was by tradition a local nobleman.

With the growth of industry and large towns, many rural labourers moved west or overseas. The chronic shortage of labour was met by the importation of seasonal Polish workers who lived under miserable conditions and were not allowed to settle. When Bismarck in 1872 tried to introduce some self-government in the countryside to assist the *Landrat* he met fierce *Junker* opposition. To overcome it twenty-five new members of the Prussian Herrenhaus (House of Lords) had to be created. Conditions on the large estates remained semi-feudal until 1918. The *Junkers* looked to the royal house of Prussia for protection, not to the new-fangled German Empire, which many detested, and they preserved their power into the twentieth century.

F. L. Carsten, *A History of the Prussian Junkers* (London, 1989).

F. L. CARSTEN

K

────◆────

Kaffir War *see* CAPE-XHOSA WAR.

Kansas-Nebraska Act (1854)   Written by Senator Stephen A. Douglas (1813–61) of Illinois, the Kansas-Nebraska Act separated the unorganized Nebraska Territory into the Kansas and Nebraska territories. Douglas, in his efforts to have Chicago named as the eastern terminus of the transcontinental railroad, saw Nebraska's unorganized status as a roadblock to his plans. By 1854 attempts to create Nebraska had become entangled in the sectional conflict. Douglas proposed that the two new territories be organized under the principle of popular sovereignty, where the people of the area voted to keep or abolish slavery. Southerners, long unhappy with the MISSOURI COMPROMISE restrictions which forbade slavery north of 36°30' parallel, demanded that the act repeal the long-standing compromise. Douglas consented and the bill was passed. Northern anger over this law led to the creation of the REPUBLICAN PARTY. At the same time, many northern Democrats lost their seats in Congress, and the Democratic Party increasingly became the party of southern rights.

James A. Rawley, *Race and Politics: 'Bleeding' Kansas and the Coming of the Civil War* (Philadelphia, 1969).

ALICE E. REAGAN

Karageorge [Karadjordjević]   Kara George Petrovich (*b* Vesevac, 14 November 1762; *d* Radovanje, 25 July 1817) founded the ruling Serbian dynasty, the Karageorge. A peasant and warrior turned wealthy merchant, he led the spontaneous Serbian revolt against Ottoman misrule in 1804 which turned into a war of independence. His legendary courage and military genius, and a favourable international conjuncture, brought initial success to the Serbs. The first Serbian constitution proclaimed Kara George supreme hereditary leader (1808), but following the defeat of the revolt he fled to Austria and Russia. In 1817 he returned to SERBIA to organize a general Balkan uprising but was murdered by his rival Milosh OBRENOVICH. His third son, Alexander (*b* Topola, 11 October 1806; *d* Timisoara, 3 May 1885), became prince of Serbia (1842–58). His reign marked the development of national educational and judicial systems but the struggle for supremacy between the prince and the oligarchic council forced Alexander to abdicate and live in exile in Banat.

Michael Petrovich, *A History of Modern Serbia, 1804–1918* (New York and London, 1976).

MARIA TODOROVA

Kassa Ras   *see* TEWODORUS II.

Kautsky, Karl (*b* Prague, 16 October 1854; *d* Amsterdam, 17 October 1938)   Leading theoretician of the Social Democratic Party (*see* SOCIAL DEMOCRATIC PARTY (GERMANY)) before the First World War. He joined the Austrian Social Democratic Party in 1875 and acted as private secretary to ENGELS in London between 1885 and 1890. Between 1883 and 1917 he was editor of the SPD's newspaper *Die Neue Zeit*. Kautsky played a leading role in the formula.ion of the SPD's 1891 Erfurt programme, which combined a Marxist analysis of contemporary capitalism with a series of immediate demands for political and social reform. A leading figure in the socialist SECOND INTERNATIONAL, he successfully defended the Erfurt programme and the political strategy which lay behind it against both the 'revisionist' critique launched by Eduard BERNSTEIN at the turn of the century and the demands associated with Rosa Luxemburg (1871–1919) for its emendation in a radical direction.

D. Geary *Karl Kautsky* (Manchester, 1986).

S. J. SALTER

Kelly, Ned   *see* BUSHRANGERS.

Kierkegaard, Søren Aabye (*b* Copenhagen, 5 May 1813; *d* Copenhagen, 4 November 1855)   Danish philosopher and writer on theology, whose work represented a decisive break with the philosophical rationalism of HEGEL. In upholding the power of 'existence' against the Hegelian preoccupation with being, Kierkegaard is generally regarded as the founder of modern existentialism, although he never used the term and would not have approved of the secular application of his ideas. Through unconditioned choice, through what Kierkegaard regarded as a 'leap of faith', man could move through the three stages of existence

– aesthetic, ethical and religious – although the act of choice always involved uncertainty, a notion examined in detail in a series of books, including *Either/Or* (1843), *Fear and Trembling* (1843), *The Concept of Dread* (1844) and *Concluding Unscientific Postscript* (1846).

JOHN BELCHEM

Kitchener, Horatio Herbert, first Earl Kitchener of Khartoum (*b* Listowel, Ireland, 24 June 1850; *d* at sea, 5 June 1916)   Irish soldier and statesman. He served in the Middle East and was appointed to command the Egyptian army in 1892. Known particularly for his systematic and thorough organizational methods, his reconquest of the SUDAN from the forces of the Mahdi (*see* MUHAMMAD 'AHMAD IBN 'ABADALLAH) in 1898 led to his appointment as governor-general of the Sudan. He played a leading role in the defeat of the Boers in the Boer War (1899–1902), serving as commander-in-chief from November 1900 and initiating the concentration camps to combat the guerrilla tactics of the Boers. His subsequent career led him to become commander-in-chief in India and proconsul in Egypt and, most importantly, secretary of state for war from June 1914.

Philip Magnus, *Kitchener: Portrait of an Imperialist* (London, 1958).

RICHARD PRICE

Knights of Labor   Formed as a secret order in 1869 at a tailors' meeting in Philadelphia, the Knights of Labor were the most important of the early American labour groups. In 1879, under the leadership of Terence POWDERLY, it was organized nationally as an industrial union with membership open to unskilled workers, African-Americans, immigrants and women, all of whom were excluded from trade unions. Powderly eliminated the secrecy and religious ritual from the organization, but retained the ceremony that appealed to nineteenth-century workers. Boycott campaigns and a successful strike against Jay Gould's (1836–92) Southwestern Railway system in 1885 swelled the Knights' membership approximately sevenfold in less than a year. This rapid growth threatened the national trade unions, who in 1886 formed the AMERICAN FEDERATION OF LABOR, which sought more limited goals and was better organized.

Founded before the factory system was firmly established, the Knights attempted to avert the evils of industrialism through reform. Advocating producer and consumer co-operatives in an effort to create a more harmonious society, they urged worker unity against corporations, banks and railroads. Under Powderly, the ultimate goal of the Knights was to abolish the wage system so that every man could be his own employer. This approach, while attractive in the abstract, did not give the organization sufficient bargaining power with employers and handicapped the Knights.

The HAYMARKET MASSACRE of 1886 dealt a blow to the Knights' prestige, and factional disputes impeded progress towards its goals of equal work for equal pay, the abolition of child labour and the EIGHT-HOUR DAY. Membership dropped rapidly from a peak of 700,000 in 1886, and by 1900 it was practically extinct.

Leon Fink, *Workingmen's Democracy: The Knights of Labor and American Politics* (Urbana, Ill., 1983).

KEVIN MURPHY

Kossuth, Louis [Lajos] (*b* Monok, Hungary, 19 September 1802; *d* Turin, Italy, 20 March 1894)   Leader of the 1848 Hungarian Revolution. From an impoverished Lutheran family of the minor Hungarian gentry, the young Kossuth soon became a prominent liberal nationalist politician and journalist, campaigning for national political and economic freedom. A great orator, his speech of 3 March 1848 at the Hungarian diet sparked the 1848 revolution in Hungary (*see* REVOLUTIONS OF 1848). He became finance minister and effective leader of the subsequent revolutionary government. His aim was Hungarian independence from Austria, at first with a Habsburg king, but after war broke out with the Habsburgs in September 1848 he supported the deposition of the Habsburgs in April 1849. The defeat of the Hungarians in 1849, seen as partly due to Kossuth's harsh policy to the non-Magyar nationalities, led to his exile. Fêted in the West, Kossuth opposed the COMPROMISE OF 1867 and never returned to Hungary.

Istvan Deak, *The Lawful Revolution: Louis Kossuth and the Hungarians, 1848–9* (New York, 1979).

STEVEN BELLER

Kropotkin, Prince Peter Alekseevich (*b* Moscow, 27 November 1842; *d* Dmitrov, 8 February 1921)   Russian anarchist. Born into a wealthy, aristocratic family, he achieved early distinction as a geographer but from the late 1860s devoted himself to political activities which led to his arrest and imprisonment. He escaped to Switzerland, from where he was deported in 1881 for spreading revolutionary propaganda, and settled in England. Rejecting Marx as pseudo-scientific and potentially totalitarian, he was more in sympathy with BAKUNIN while rejecting his violence. He developed a theory of communist ANARCHISM based on the idea of mutual aid; he rejected state power and private property and proposed a federation of all mankind into spontaneously formed, mutually supportive communities. He returned to Russia in 1917, but refused a post in Kerensky's (1881–1970) provisional government. He was as untrusting of Lenin and the Bolsheviks as he had been of the tsars.

Martin A. Miller, *Kropotkin* (Chicago, 1976).

A. V. KNOWLES

Kruger, Stephanus Johannes Paulus [Paul] (*b* ?Bulhoek, Cape Colony, 10 October 1825; *d* Clarens, Switzerland, 14 July 1904) Transvaal political leader. A strong, conservative Calvinist whose family had been part of the early trek from the Cape, he entered TRANSVAAL politics in 1857, to become commandant-general (1863–73), and was involved in the Basuto Wars. As chief negotiator following British annexation of the republic in 1877, he opposed British federation plans and later helped to negotiate the PRETORIA CONVENTION. As president of the Transvaal from 1883, he angered the British by policies to promote economic independence: the granting of various exclusive concessionary rights (for example alcohol and dynamite); and attempts to restrict rail access to the Transvaal from Natal and the Cape. Always approachable by his followers, he was resolute in opposition to British encroachments, but was not averse to serious negotiation. Unable to resolve differences with the British, he planned the Boers' war strategy, but went into exile in 1900.

SIMON KATZENELLENBOGEN

Krupp, Alfred (*b* Essen, 26 April 1812; *d* Essen, 14 July 1887) German industrialist. After the death of his father, he took over the struggling steel firm Fried. Krupp of Essen and became its sole owner in 1848. The firm's spectacular success under Krupp was based both on innovative production techniques, some of which were copied from British and French firms, and on the effective exploitation of markets. From the 1850s onwards the Krupp fortunes were boosted by the demand for steel created by the expansion of the rail network, while Prussian army contracts for cast-steel cannon laid the basis for a long tradition of Krupp arms-manufacturing. In the late nineteenth century the firm developed vertical forms of industrial organization through the acquisition of coal-mines and shipping. The firm's commitment to paternalistic welfare measures for its vast workforce (such as company housing) was matched by its determination to banish free trade unions from the workplace.

ELIZABETH HARVEY

Kuang Hsu [Guangxu] (*b* Peking, 1871; *d* Peking, 1908) Emperor of China (1875–1908). His personal rule began only in 1889; even then ultimate power lay with TZ'U-HSI, the empress dowager. In 1898 Kuang Hsu temporarily shook off her control. In the wake of China's defeat in the Sino-Japanese War and in the face of possible dismemberment by the foreign powers, he responded enthusiastically to the ideas of a group of young reformers led by K'ang Yu-wei (1858–1927). In June 1898 he launched the HUNDRED DAYS REFORM, issuing a series of edicts aimed at the political, constitutional, educational, economic and industrial transformation of China. The reforms were strongly opposed by Tz'u-hsi, who staged a palace coup. K'ang escaped to Japan but other reformers were executed, and the emperor spent the rest of his life under house arrest. He died in 1908, a day before Tz'u-hsi. It seems likely that he was poisoned on her instructions.

JOHN DAVIES

Kulturkampf The term *Kulturkampf* ('struggle of cultures') was coined by the Prussian Left-liberal Virchow (1821–1902), and subsequently adopted by historians, to describe the conflict between the Roman Catholic Church and the Prussian and imperial German governments during the 1870s. The origins of the conflict lay in BISMARCK's doubts about the loyalty of the Catholic population to the newly created German Empire. The drive for secularization (in practice directed solely against the influence of the Catholic Church) began in 1871 with the restriction of the political activities of clergymen. In 1872 the Prussian government claimed exclusive rights to inspect schools, and the Jesuit order was banned from the empire. The Prussian 'May Laws' of 1873 restricted the disciplinary prerogatives of clergymen to the religious sphere and debarred non-German clerics and German clergymen educated abroad from exercising their office. The expatriation law of 1874 empowered the Prussian government to expel clergymen. The year 1875 marked the high point of the *Kulturkampf*, witnessing the dissolution of most religious orders, the withholding of government subsidies to the Catholic Church and the introduction of obligatory civil marriage. Many bishops and priests were imprisoned or expelled. Throughout, the Prussian and imperial governments were supported by the anticlerical National Liberal Party and many Left liberals. Politically, the *Kulturkampf* was a failure, merely strengthening the CENTRE PARTY and consolidating a Catholic political subculture. From 1880 onwards, it was gradually wound down, its legislative basis largely being repealed in 1886.

D. Blackbourn, *Populists and Patricians* (London, 1987).

S. J. SALTER

L

labour legislation   The statutory framework devised to regulate the industrial workforce, labour legislation varied greatly in different European countries depending on legal traditions, the extent and pace of industrialization and the character of political rule. As the first industrial nation, Britain had the earliest body of labour law. Legislation aimed initially at the creation of a free market in labour. Towards that end, statutes of 1824 and 1825 repealed the COMBINATION ACTS (1799–1800) and legalized trade unions. Crucially, labour legislation also fulfilled a disciplinary function, defining virtually all activity undertaken in defence of trade-union demands as a crime, a logical consequence of the incomplete nature of industrialization and inability of employers to impose managerial authority. By 1875 British labour law had undergone fundamental change. As trade unions were integrated into rationalized systems of collective bargaining, statutes of 1871 and 1875 also granted them more secure legal status and the right to conduct peaceful picketing.

Labour was subject to harsher legal treatment on the Continent. French labour legislation proscribed all forms of worker association and punished combination with imprisonment. Only in 1864 did Napoleon III repeal the ban on strikes. The leaders of the THIRD REPUBLIC finally granted legal rights to trade unions in 1884. However, working conditions remained virtually unregulated. In contrast to France, Germany's late industrialization allowed the guild system to survive until the mid nineteenth century. Thereafter, Germany's rapid economic take-off necessitated the provision of a new legal framework for labour relations. The 1869 *Gewerbeordonung* granted workers the right to form trade unions and to conduct strikes, although whole classes of workers remained outside the purview of the law. Opposition to trade unions continued to be formidable, however, and under the 1877 ANTI-SOCIALIST LAW several national unions were repressed. Pursuing a conservative paternalistic strategy, the Bismarckian state sought to wean workers away from socialism with the provision of welfare benefits.

Bob Hepple (ed.), *The Making of Labour Law in Europe: A Comparative Study of Nine Countries up to 1945* (London, 1986).

RICHARD J. SODERLUND

Labour Party Many historians have identified the mass-based National Charter Association (*see* CHARTISM), founded in 1840, as the first working-class political party. However, the 1848 collapse of the Chartist challenge hastened a working-class retreat from politics. While local Chartist associations survived into the 1850s, preserving the heritage of radical working-class political independence, the seeming permanence of liberal capitalism furthered a new alignment of class and political forces. During the mid nineteenth century working-class political leaders generally shunned independent labour politics in favour of an accommodation with liberalism. Under the auspices of the Labour Representation League, a number of 'respectable' working men were allowed to stand for parliament as Liberal candidates, but the parliamentary committee of the TRADES UNION CONGRESS (TUC), the primary exponent of Lib-Labism (as this form of political representation was known), ensured the commitment of the labour movement to an alliance with the Liberal Party.

The emergence of new social forces in British society was signalled by the socialist revival of the 1880s. The SOCIAL DEMOCRATIC FEDERATION introduced Marxism to Britain; other notable organizations included the Socialist League and the FABIAN SOCIETY. Although they never gained a mass following, the socialist societies did inspire a younger generation of trade-union activists to pursue new strategies for working-class advancement. Of great importance for future labour politics was the convergence of emerging socialist currents with changes in workplace experience, in particular the proliferation of semi-skilled occupations. This development acted as a solvent on the sectionalism which characterized the mid-Victorian labour movement, fostering the growth of a distinct working-class identity. The founding of 'new unions' (*see* NEW UNIONISM) by the late 1880s was one expression of the shifting terrain of class and work. The socialist activists who led the new unions were forceful advocates for greater state regulation of working conditions, a position at odds with that of TUC Lib-Lab leaders. Increasingly dissatisfied with TUC adherence to an apparently indifferent Liberal Party, new-unionists opened up a bitter debate within the labour movement. Keir HARDIE's 1888 by-election campaign in mid-Lanark reflected the breach in labour-movement ranks and led to the formation of the Scottish Labour Party.

With the retrenchment of new unions in the early 1890s and the growing awareness of the limits of industrial struggle, British labour activists initiated political campaigns in local elections. Encouraged by the success of three independent labour candidates in the 1892 general election, socialists and trade-unionists formed local labour parties to contest for municipal power. That development culminated with the 1893 founding of a national party of labour, the INDEPENDENT LABOUR PARTY. Although it lent the cause of independent labour politics new force, initial hopes for a major electoral breakthrough were dashed as the party failed to elect a single candidate in the 1895 general election. That failure pointed to the imperative of gaining strong trade-union support.

A broad-based offensive against organized labour, marked by the formation of strong employers' associations and fierce industrial conflicts in coal (1893), cotton (1893), boot- and shoe-manufacturing (1895) and engineering (1897–8) finally compelled trade unions to take up the cause of independent labour political representation. Crucially, the 1890s employers' offensive coincided with a series of legal decisions which gravely undermined the financial status and legality of trade-union activities, particularly picketing. In 1899, driven by the need to safeguard its position and overturn adverse legal decisions, the TUC agreed to hold a national conference with socialists to work towards independent labour representation in parliament.

At the conference, held in London on 27 February 1900, delegates from the socialist societies and several trade unions founded the Labour Representation Committee (LRC), the predecessor of the Labour Party. The establishment of the LRC, dedicated to securing a distinct labour group in parliament, marked a major step in the evolution of labour as a political estate in British society. Constrained by its dependence on the liberal-inclined trade unions and anxious to reach an accommodation with the vastly more powerful Liberal Party, the LRC refrained from advancing a socialist programme. Rather, it adopted a cautious and pragmatic political orientation consistent with labour's radical-liberal tradition, best termed 'labourism'. The 1901 TAFF VALE decision, which shattered trade-union financial security, further strengthened the support of organized labour for the LRC, lending the young organization new political weight. After a significant breakthrough in the 1906 general election, the LRC changed its official name to the Labour Party.

John Belchem, *Class, Party and the Political System in Britain, 1867–1914* (Oxford, 1990).
Henry Pelling, *Origins of the Labour Party* (Oxford, 1965).

RICHARD J. SODERLUND

laissez-faire *see* FREE TRADE.

Lamartine, Alphonse Marie Louis de (*b* Mâcon, 21 October 1790; *d* Paris, 28 February 1869)   French poet, historian and politician. After a short military and diplomatic career, he was elected deputy in 1833. Politically, he began as a romantic legitimist (*see* LEGITIMISTS) and then embraced more and more progressive causes. He was the virtual head of the provisional government of 1848 and, as foreign minister, refused to intervene in foreign revolutions. Trounced in the presidential elections of December 1848, he lost every other election he contested.

He accumulated many debts and had to live from his writing and eventually accept a pension from Napoleon III. He was a prodigious writer. His widely read *Jocelyn* (1836) has 9,000 verses and his *Histoire des Girondins* (History of the Girondins, 1847) comprises 3,000 pages. The latter reflected his preoccupation with great orators and with individuals personifying great movements and institutions. The Revolution was seen as a stage in the implementation of Christian morality on earth. He is little read today.

W. Fortescue, *Alphonse de Lamartine: A Political Biography* (London, 1983).

DONALD SUTHERLAND

Lamennais, Hugues-Félicité Robert de (*b* St Malo, 19 June 1782; *d* Paris, 27 February 1854)   French religious and political writer. He was influenced by his brother Jean Marie Robert de Lamennais (1780–1860), founder of the Brothers of Christian Instruction, with whom he wrote the anti-Napoleonic *Réflexions sur l'état de l'Eglise* (1809). He was ordained in 1816, and published the *Essai sur l'indifférence en matière de religion* (4 vols, 1817–23) which argued for the primacy of primitive revelation, tradition and the *raison générale* or *sens commun* over the individual reason or private judgement. His *De la Religion considérée dans ses rapports avec l'ordre politique et civil* (1825–6) championed the papacy against Gallicanism, while in *Des progrès de la Révolution* (1829) he opposed the French monarchy and the church–state connection in the name of religious liberty. This 'Liberal Catholicism', broadcast in his journal *L'Avenir* from 1830, was condemned by Pope GREGORY XVI in 'Mirari vos' (1832). Lamennais attacked Gregory in the apocalyptic *Paroles d'un croyant* (1834) and was condemned in the Pope's 'Singulari nos' (1834). Lamennais's *Esquisse d'une philosophie* (1840–6) offered a spiritual substitute for Christianity, and he was elected a left-wing deputy in 1848. Despite his personal failure, his democratic and socialist views dominated the political Left, his Liberal Catholic disciples transformed the French church and his ultramontanism triumphed at the First Vatican Council (1869–70).

A. R. Vidler, *Prophecy and Papacy: A Study of Lamennais, the Church and the Revolution* (London, 1954).

SHERIDAN GILLEY

Land League, Irish National   Founded in Dublin on 21 October 1881, with PARNELL as president, the Irish National Land League was modelled on the Land League of Mayo, which had been established the previous August by Michael DAVITT, in a response to the agricultural depression of the late 1870s which threatened eviction for smaller farmers and falling living standards for larger farmers and shopkeepers. Its radical constitution declared that 'the land of Ireland belongs to the people of Ireland, to be held and cultivated for the sustenance of those whom God decreed to the inhabitants thereof'. Some wanted the 'three Fs' (fair rent, free sale and fixity of tenure); others sought to destroy landlordism and establish peasant proprietorship. For three years, ardently supported by Irish America, the league dominated the countryside, preventing evictions and land-grabbing with such techniques as the boycott, while trying to thwart government attempts to suppress the agitation, which included the arrest and unsuccessful trial of Parnell and other leaders in 1880 and their imprisonment in October 1881.

Superficially uniting the Irish countryside, the league ignored the plight of labourers and fostered the interests of larger farmers rather than those of smaller farmers in the west. Gladstone's Land Act of 1881, securing the 'three Fs', suited those who could pay rent but left untouched the problem of tenants with uneconomic holdings. Politically, the Land League destroyed the electoral influence of the landlords and confirmed Parnell's leadership of the HOME RULE movement. Parnell and the government, both equally alarmed at soaring agrarian crime, reached agreement in the 'Kilmainham Treaty' in April 1882 which secured Parnell's release and signalled an end to this phase of the land war. The rightward drift of the land and Home Rule movements was confirmed in the following October by the formation of the National League.

Paul Bew, *Land and the National Question in Ireland, 1858–82* (Dublin, 1978).
PATRICK BUCKLAND

Lassalle, Ferdinand (*b* Breslau, 11 April 1825; *d* Geneva, 31 August 1864)   German social democrat. Having studied philosophy, history and philology at university, he was attracted to radical ideas and participated in democratic movements in the Rhinelands in 1848–9. He served a short prison sentence and never left Germany after 1849. He spent much of the 1850s as legal champion of his patroness, the duchess von Hatzfeldt (1805–81), and writing philosophical and literary works. He corresponded with Marx, whose ideas he used in ways Marx disliked. In 1862 workers in Leipzig asked Lassalle, who had a reputation as a courageous gentleman radical, for guidance in their attempts at national organization. This led to the formation of the ALL-GERMAN WORKERS' ASSOCIATION which Lassalle autocratically led until his death in a duel in August 1864. His flamboyant personality, radical antiliberalism (for example he had secret talks with Bismarck) and positive regard for state-led socialism left an enduring mark on the German labour movement.

Shlomo Na'aman, *Lassalle* (Hanover, 1970).

JOHN BREUILLY

League of the Communists Founded in London in 1847, the League of the Communists was a successor to earlier secret societies. Its members were mainly German artisans living in Switzerland, Paris and London. Its first programme was written by ENGELS, an uneasy combination of Marxism with radical, utopian and conspiratorial ideas. Its second programme was the COMMUNIST MANIFESTO. Published just before the outbreak of revolution, the manifesto had little immediate impact.

The open politics of the revolutionary years marginalized the league, but MARX refounded it in exile. However, many members opposed his economic determinism, preferring republican attempts to foment a second revolution. The league split into factions led by Marx and by August Willich (1810–78) and Karl Schapper (1812–70). Following communist trials in Cologne, Marx formally dissolved the league in late 1852. Its historical significance lay in what it revealed of artisan politics and of the political strategy of Marx.

Dirk Struik, *Birth of the Communist Manifesto* (New York, 1971).

JOHN BREUILLY

Ledru-Rollin, Alexandre Auguste (*b* Paris, 2 February 1807; *d* Fontenay-aux-Roses, 2 December 1874) French politician. He became well known for defending a number of left-wing causes before the Bar in the 1830s. Elected to Le Mans in 1841 as a 'radical', he financed the newspaper *La Réforme* in the 1840s, which expressed a variety of left-wing ideas. A major organizer of the banquet campaign of 1847, which demanded an enlarging of the suffrage, he became minister of the interior in the provisional government following the 1848 Revolution. He ran against Louis Napoleon in the December 1848 presidential elections. A leader of the Montagnards in the Legislative Assembly, he fled to London following the abortive protest against French suppression of the Roman Republic in June 1849. He is generally held to have been an ineffective leader but was constrained by being a democrat in a country that was largely monarchist until the 1870s.

A. Colman, *Ledru-Rollin and the Second French Republic* (New York, 1922).

DONALD SUTHERLAND

Lee, Robert E. (*b* Westmoreland County, Virginia, 19 January 1807; *d* Lexington, Virginia, 12 October 1870) Leading southern general in the AMERICAN CIVIL WAR. Born into a Virginia family with a distinguished record of military service, he graduated from the United States Military Academy in 1829 and served during the Mexican War and as superintendent at West Point. At the beginning of the Civil War, Abraham Lincoln offered him field command of the Union army. Reluctantly, Lee resigned his commission to defend his native state. When Joseph E. Johnston (1807–91) was wounded in June 1862, Lee assumed command of the Confederate army of northern Virginia. His military record over the next three years, with the exception of Gettysburg (1863) (*see* BATTLE OF GETTYSBURG), was one of often surpassing brilliance. Lee conducted the war in the east as one of offensive manœuvre until in the spring of 1864 the preponderant forces of Ulysses S. Grant compelled him to fight defensively. Defeated at Appomattox in 1865, he served as president of Washington College until his death.

KEVIN MURPHY

Legitimists The royalist party loyal to the elder branch of the Bourbons after its overthrow in July 1830 and opposed to the younger branch (or Orleanists), the Legitimists were represented until 1850 by LOUIS-PHILIPPE. When Charles X's grandson the comte de Chambord (1820–83) died childless, most Legitimists switched their allegiance to the Orleanist pretender. The comte de Chambord (who was so lazy he could not tie his own shoelaces) missed several occasions to arrange his own restoration by his refusal to compromise with the Orleanists. His supporters were so sure of his restoration in 1874 that they had his coronation carriage built, but his refusal to accept the tricolour flag dashed the plan. Legitimists had the reputation of being a reactionary party but it is doubtful if many of them wanted a restoration of the old regime. There were many innovative landowners in their ranks and, in electoral terms, it is arguable that they were the largest single party from 1848 to the 1870s.

T. Zeldin, *France, 1848–1945*, vol. 1: *Ambition, Love and Politics* (Oxford, 1973).

DONALD SUTHERLAND

Leipzig, Battle of (16–19 October 1813) The largest battle of the Napoleonic wars, Leipzig is central to the German national myth as the moment when the German people supposedly defeated Napoleon BONAPARTE. In fact, however, the emperor's downfall was brought about by an overwhelming combination of the great powers and their regular armies. After failing to defeat the forces of his Prussian, Russian,

Swedish and Austrian opponents individually, Napoleon was eventually cornered near Leipzig in a highly dangerous position, with his
back to a river. After three days of fighting the immense numerical
superiority of the allies forced him to give way, retreat turning into
rout when a vital bridge was demolished prematurely. French casualties numbered some 68,000 men; most of Napoleon's satellites now
went over to the allies; and revolt broke out in Holland. Favourable
peace terms might have been secured, but the Napoleonic Empire was
finished.

CHARLES ESDAILE

Leo XII [Annibale Francesco Clemente Melchiore Girolamo Nicola
della Genga] (*b* near Spoleto, 22 August 1760; *d* Rome, 10 February
1829) Pope (1823–9). Of a noble family, he became secret chamberlain to Pius VI (1717–99), titular archbishop of Tyre, and nuncio to
Lucerne in 1793, nuncio to Cologne in 1794 and nuncio extraordinary
to the Diet of Ratisbon in 1805. During the imprisonment of PIUS VII
he retired to his abbey of Monticelli; in 1814 he was appointed papal
envoy extraordinary to Louis XVIII and in 1816 cardinal-bishop of
Sinigaglia. His quarrel with the moderate Cardinal Consalvi (1757–
1824) inclined him to the conservative *zelanti* party and, on his election by the conclave of 1823, he abolished lay participation in the
government of the Papal States, restored the Jewish ghetto and banned
the carnival waltzes. Lay unrest was repressed, but survived in the
secret societies of CARBONARI. Leo suffered poor health throughout his
pontificate – he remarked that the cardinals had elected a corpse. His
conservative policies left intractable problems to his successors.

A. Fliche and V. Martin (eds), *Histoire de l'Église*, vol. 20: *La Crise
révolutionnaire 1789–1846*, by Jean Leflon (Paris, 1949), bk. 3, pp. 377–
408.

SHERIDAN GILLEY

Leo XIII [Gioacchino Vincenzo Raffaele Luigi Pecci] (*b* Carpineto, 2
March 1810; *d* Rome, 20 July 1903) Pope (1878–1903). Of a noble
family, he was appointed a domestic prelate to GREGORY XVI in 1837
and became delegate to Benevento (1838) and Perugia (1841) and
nuncio to Brussels (1843). From 1846 to 1878 he was archbishop of
Perugia. He failed as pope in attempts to restore good relations with
anticlerical administrations in Italy and France and with anti-Catholic
Russia. He declared Anglican orders null and void in 1896, but secured the repeal of the May Laws in Germany, while in a series of
encyclical letters, 'Immortale Dei' (1885), 'Praestantissimum' (1888),
'Rerum novarum' (1891) and 'Graves de communi re' (1901), he
expounded the Catholic understanding of the relations between state,
society and church; condemned secular socialism; and defended trade

unions, a just wage and Christian democracy. In 1883 he opened the Vatican archives to historical study. His encyclical 'Aeterni Patris' (1879) led to the revival of the philosophy of St Thomas Aquinas, and 'Providentissimus Deus' (1893) to the creation in 1902 of the Pontifical Biblical Commission. He erected 248 new episcopal or archiepiscopal sees and forty-eight vicariates of prefectures apostolic. A scholar, elegant Latin stylist and diplomat, he restored the stature of the papacy in the second longest pontificate in modern history.

E. Soderini, *Il pontificato di Leone XIII*, 3 vols (Milan, 1932–3); vols 1 and 2, trans. B. B. Carter (London, 1934–5).

SHERIDAN GILLEY

Leopold II, king of Belgium *see* INDEPENDENT CONGO STATE.

lesbianism Questions concerning the definition of lesbianism, as well as the relationships between various discourses about sexuality, ideology and gender, are so profoundly contentious that they make assessing lesbianism as an idea, a sexual practice and a culture of same-sex female desire during the nineteenth century extremely complex. The debate between historians and theorists of male homosexuality over essentialism (the contention that homosexuality is a transhistorical and transcultural phenomenon) and social constructionism (the claim that it is a historically and culturally specific aspect of late-capitalist urban societies) has been largely won by those upholding the latter theory. Lesbian historiographers and theorists remain more divided. On the chief question – did 'lesbians' and 'lesbianism' exist in the nineteenth century – historians differ, depending on whether they stress continuity between past and present definitions, or discontinuity. The former say yes, the latter no.

Those who stress continuity want to define lesbianism more inclusively, if less historically, as something other than a sexual practice of female deviants, outlaws and low life. Wishing to escape the modernist clinical definition of lesbianism as a set of sexual practices performed by women who were not quite women, those who accept the continuity model find a perennial 'lesbian continuum'. All women could potentially by placed on the continuum based on their love for women and their resistance, however slight or temporary, to what the American lesbian poet-theorist Adrienne Rich has termed 'compulsory heterosexuality'. By that Rich means the ideologically and materially enforced insistence that women see themselves entirely as the complements of men and live under male control.

In previous times and places, women whom some experts would in current shorthand consider lesbians lived in situations as varied as the Western European medieval communities of the beguines, Chinese marriage-resisting communities, convents, brothels and in native

American unified households. In the nineteenth century, according to the continuity model, these women-loving women were mainly perceived and perceived themselves as respectable women of delicate, even noble, feelings. They were known as 'romantic friends'. Lillian Faderman has compiled abundant evidence from poems, letters, journals and memoirs of the frequency and passionate intensity with which many middle- and upper-class women in England, Scotland, France, Germany and the United States spent their emotional lives in 'romantic friendships' with other women. The twentieth-century demarcation between heterosexual and lesbian women was unknown and would have been unfathomable, partly because the terms, as well as the technical sexological categories, were not invented until late in the nineteenth century. Only as a result of the popularization of the ideas of the sexologists and doctors, which in this view were part of an antifeminist backlash, were romantic friendships considered pathological and deviant, that is lesbian.

In the earlier part of the century, when women were excluded from higher education, the professions and well-paid work, most women were forced to marry. Because of the Victorian injunction that 'good' women be passionless and the doctrine of the separate spheres, the evidence of feminist historians suggests that they experienced their deepest relationships with other women rather than with men. Among the distinguished women who were involved in such relationships were the French writer George Sand (1804–76) and the American poet Emily Dickinson (1830–86).

Later in the century, when social change fostered by the growth of FEMINISM allowed some women entrance to the public sphere, it became possible for educated women to remain unmarried and to enter the professions. These romantic friends, who were known legally as spinsters, often lived their feminist principles in long-term monogamous relationships termed 'Boston marriages'. Such a relationship was the subject of Henry James's (1843–1916) novel *The Bostonians* (1885). While acknowledging that interpretation of these written documents is difficult, continuity theorists argue that most romantic friends probably did not engage in genital sex, but none the less, because of the depth of their feelings, should be included among what twentieth-century post-Freudians call lesbians.

Other sexual historians and cultural theorists, influenced by the French thinker Michel Foucault (1926–84), believe that properly, that is historically speaking, the category and subcultural community of women we now call lesbian came into existence only towards the end of the nineteenth century, as an outgrowth of and a reaction to capitalism, feminism and the writings of the sexologists. In this view, lesbians arrived later on the world historical scene than did gay men because patriarchal notions such as female asexuality, combined with bourgeois imprisonment within the home, made it impossible for women-loving women to have the self-consciousness and material means necessary to see themselves and be seen by others in terms of a lesbian sexual identity. While female as well as male same-sex sexual relations have always existed, those who argue the discontinuity model mainly regard the nomination 'lesbian' as fitting at most only the last hundred years of Western culture.

Experts taking the latter approach demand a historical model for lesbianism which, because it is more sensitive to race, class and ethnic differences, is also more interested in expanding the notion of the sorts of women who should be studied as lesbians. Through searching nineteenth-century and even earlier police reports as well as legal and medical scandals to find women-loving women who were other than white, bourgeois and generally supportive of the dominant culture, these historians have traced an alternative history and culture of lesbians who, unlike the earlier romantic friends or the later middle- and upper-class 'new woman' professionals, were rebels rather than ladies. These women, many of whom were genitally sexual, frequently supported themselves as prostitutes and transvestites or 'passing women', becoming famous or infamous as pirates, soldiers, doctors, politicians and artists.

While literary theorists may endorse either the continuity or the discontinuity model, it is more likely that they will use the latter and use it to argue that none of the discourses involved in studying lesbianism during this period was in itself simply conducive or hostile to its growth. For example, what Elaine Marks calls the 'Sappho model' of women's same-sex relationships has been inscribed since the ancient Greek poet's time mainly by and for men. During this period it was used by the male French aesthetes and decadents, such as Gautier (1811–72), Balzac (1799–1850) and Baudelaire (1821–67), in poetry and prose, as well as by the bisexual female novelist Colette (1873–1954) for purposes that were sometimes pornographic, apologetic or lyrical, depending not only on genre, but also on how each reader read them, which this group insists is inevitably contradictory and ultimately political.

See also HOMOSEXUALITY (MALE).

George Chauncey Jr, 'From Sexual Inversion to Homosexuality: Medicine and the Changing Conceptualization of Female Deviance', *Salmagundi*, 58–9 (1983), 114–46.

Lillian Faderman, *Surpassing the Love of Men: Romantic Friendship and Love between Women from the Renaissance to the Present* (New York, 1981).

Elaine Marks, 'Lesbian Intertextuality', in *Homosexualities and French Literature* (London, 1979), pp. 353–77.

Adrienne Rich, *Compulsory Heterosexuality and Lesbian Existence* (London, 1981).

Martha Vicinus, 'Sexuality and Power: A Review of Current Work in the History of Sexuality', *Feminist Studies*, 6(1) (1982), 133–56.

KATHLEEN MARTINDALE

Lesseps, Ferdinand, vicomte de (*b* Versailles, 9 November 1805; *d* La Chenaie, 7 December 1894)   French diplomat, builder of the Suez Canal. He entered the consular service in 1825, and while on station in the Middle East was fired with the idea of the Suez Canal. After being forcibly retired from service, he began raising the capital for the canal company. Work began in 1859 and the canal was completed ten years later. Disraeli later bought control of the canal company for Britain. De Lesseps undertook construction of the PANAMA CANAL in 1880 but the company failed in 1888 amid cries of scandal after de Lesseps refused to modify engineering plans.

J. Pudney, *Suez: De Lesseps' Canal* (New York, 1969).

DONALD SUTHERLAND

Lewis and Clark Expedition (1804–1806)   In January 1803 President Thomas Jefferson sought and gained an appropriation from Congress to send an expedition to travel and map the west and to lay the groundwork for the extension of the American fur trade. The following year, Captain Meriwether Lewis (1774–1809) (Jefferson's private secretary) and William Clark (1770–1838) led the expedition to explore the headwaters of the Missouri River and find a way to the Pacific Ocean. The group portaged across the continental divide and descended to the Pacific on the Clearwater, Salmon and Columbia Rivers. Of the numerous encounters with Indians, only one was violent. Twenty-eight months after they left, Lewis and Clark returned, their expedition a success. They had travelled more than 8,000 miles with only one casualty, Sergeant Charles Floyd. The knowledge they provided was invaluable to the opening of the trans-Mississippi west and the expansion of the American fur trade.

JOHN MARTIN

liberalism   With socialism, and especially Marxism, liberalism is one of the two main political tendencies of modern times. It is based on the notion that society should permit the maximum individual freedom compatible with order and regular government. The product of a British tradition of civil liberties and religious toleration in particular – it was first applied as a label to a political party in Spain in 1810 with the British constitutional model in mind – liberalism assumed many forms in the nineteenth century. In general, however, it focused on the importance of the rule of law, the protection of individual rights, the sanctity of the individual conscience and of moral autonomy and the legitimation of the state through popular sovereignty and consent.

Economic liberalism focused more narrowly on the arguments for freedom of trade against public and private monopolies and state interference and regulation of most kinds. Building on the *laissez-faire* ideals of Adam Smith (1723–90) and the physiocrats in particular, nineteenth-century economic liberals like Jean Baptiste Say (1767–1832), David RICARDO, Richard COBDEN and John BRIGHT extolled the virtues of unhindered competition and self-interest, contending that the market left alone was nearly always self-rectifying and tended to the maximum possible volume of commodity production. These arguments gained the greatest influence in Britain, where classical political economy was founded, and in the United States. Elsewhere in Europe various forms of PROTECTIONISM, aiming at tariff barriers to permit native industry to develop, were its principal competitors, along with the centralizing, regulatory systems of common property ownership associated with SOCIALISM.

Philosophically, nineteenth-century liberals were primarily opponents of PATERNALISM, or the idea that the majority of individuals were largely incapable of self-government or of knowing their own true interest, and thus required supervision by more educated and virtuous elites. The most famous statement against this ideal was John Stuart MILL's *On Liberty* (1859), which argued for freedom of opinion and debate, the virtues of individuality and dangers of conformity for social progress generally, and attempted to define a sphere of self-regarding actions with which society should have no right to interfere. (Generally excepted from this plea for liberty was colonial rule over 'backward peoples'.) This notion of liberty was, of course, not unique to the nineteenth century, but Mill, building on the analysis of social conformity presented by de Tocqueville (1805–59) in *De la Démocratie en Amerique* (Democracy in America, 1835–9), believed that in an era of increasing democracy, a greater threat to individual freedom came from conformity than from more traditional forms of political tyranny.

However, other types of liberals, often writing in the idealist tradition, such as T. H. Green (1836–82), contrasted liberty as the absence of external coercion to an ideal of freedom as the ability to fulfil the potential of one's capacities. Here the state, rather than possessing the primarily negative tendency to impinge on individual liberty, could potentially provide conditions to aid individual self-fulfilment, such as education. This more positive ideal accorded with both some romantic and most socialist conceptions of the relationship between state and individual. At the other extreme, claims for individual freedom were taken to imply the need to abolish centralized state power entirely, for example in the anarchist INDIVIDUALISM of the American Josiah Warren (1798–1874), or the more collectivist ANARCHISM of PROUDHON and communist anarchism of BAKUNIN and KROPOTKIN.

Politically, nineteenth-century liberals aimed primarily to extend representative institutions, though without necessarily proposing universal suffrage or, with many republicans, the abolition of the monarchy. Many of the key events of the period, such as the REVOLUTIONS OF 1848, focused on such demands, and drew inspiration from the American and French Revolutions in particular. Similarly, much liberal thought in the period can be understood in terms of an extension of rights, first to all white males, then to women, the enslaved, the labouring classes and the colonized. Many liberals, however, attempted to confine the franchise to those they thought capable of exercising it responsibly. Even J. S. Mill demanded literacy tests and proposed prohibiting those in receipt of state support from voting. Such restrictions were attacked by radicals, for whom universal suffrage was nearly always a key goal. As early as the 1840s, too, liberals were widely attacked by critics, especially socialists, who doubted the ability of free trade to alleviate poverty fundamentally, or the efficacy of an enlarged suffrage to meet the same ends. Various forms of 'New Liberalism' emerged by the end of the century, notably in the writings of John Hobson (1858–1940), which attempted to wed socialist and liberal ideals, and by turning away from the more negative conception of the state did much to found the modern concept of the liberal welfare state. The relative weakness of liberalism in nineteenth-century Continental politics has also been explained by the presence of more powerful paternalist traditions there.

Isaiah Berlin, *Four Essays on Liberty* (London, 1968).
R. D. Cumming, *Human Nature and History: A Study of the Development of Liberal Thought*, 2 vols (Chicago, 1969).
J. S. Mill (1859), *On Liberty* (London, 1859).

GREGORY CLAEYS

Liberia Founded in the 1820s as a home for freed AFRICAN-AMERICANS, partly in imitation of the SIERRA LEONE settlement, Liberia ('land of the free') became an 'independent republic' in 1847. The Americo-Liberian settlers established towns on the coast, notably a capital, Monrovia, but their religion and culture tended to divorce them from the interior peoples and even their coastal neighbours. When they attempted to extend their 'civilizing' influence, minor wars ensued, but the interior peoples largely maintained their way of life. Little economic development occurred, although the Kru coastal people were employed as seamen on European vessels. In the 1870s E. W. BLYDEN, an educationalist, politician and prolific writer, travelled some way into the interior, and later became the 'Father of West African Nationalism'. When 'Partition' occurred, peripheral territories claimed by Liberia were lost to the British and French, yet Liberia, to some extent protected by the United States, never became a European colony.

P. E. H. HAIR

Liberty Party   Among the first of numerous third parties in nineteenth-century American politics, the Liberty Party grew out of a disagreement over the tactics ABOLITIONISM should employ to eradicate slavery. In 1840, at the American Anti-slavery Society meeting, those advocating political action split away from the group led by William Lloyd GARRISON, with his tactics of moral suasion and his support of other less popular reform causes, such as women's rights. With the financial support of Lewis (1788–1873) and Arthur Tappan (1786–1865), James G. Birney (1792–1857) ran for president as the Liberty Party candidate in 1844 and garnered 2.3 per cent of the popular vote and no electoral votes, though his success in splitting the Whig vote helped carry James K. Polk into the White House. The Liberty Party was absorbed into the FREE-SOIL PARTY along with other northern antislavery and abolitionist elements, later forming the radical wing of the Republican Party.

KEVIN MURPHY

libraries and archives   During the nineteenth century libraries and archives were changed by the large-scale entry of government, at various levels, into the provision of services. This arose not merely from a perception of the usefulness of services to government, but because of manifest demand from potential users. Standards of literacy and general education in the United States and several European countries attained levels at which libraries could be seen as valuable rather than ornamental. While in the eighteenth century the great majority of library and archive institutions either relied on some form of endowment by benefactors or were funded by the contributions of users, by 1900 there was a significant sector supported from the receipts of taxation. This more substantial and stable resource-base permitted many new, and some established, library and archive institutions to acquire sizeable collections, to expand the scope of their work with these holdings and, most of all, to plan with confidence for the future. This, in turn, led to considerable advances in technique and the development of library and archive professions.

A few national libraries had been created before the beginning of the century. The French Bibliothèque Nationale was designated soon after the outbreak of revolution in 1789, incorporating the royal collections, dating back to 1595 and earlier, and enriched by the revolutionary confiscations of aristocratic and ecclesiastical libraries. It grew from fewer than a million volumes at the beginning of the nineteenth century to more than 3 million in 1908, and this called for enormous administrative reorganization and a new building in the 1850s. The history of the equivalent British institution, the British Museum Library, which had opened to users in 1759, paralleled this closely, with the gift of royal collections and the purchase of important private collections calling for development on a similar scale. Sir Antonio Panizzi's (1797–1879) period at the library (1831–68) saw the preparation of cataloguing rules and a printed catalogue, enforcement of legal deposit, great expansion of the library's acquisitions and new building, including the magnificent Reading Room. Almost from its foundation in 1800, the Library of Congress, despite set-backs such as destruction by the British army in 1814, functioned as the national library of the United States. Its influence on library practice was enormous, not least through the widespread adoption of its classification scheme by other libraries. The United States was also advanced in creating specialized government libraries. Some of these, such as the Department of State Library and the Department of the Treasury Library (both 1789) predated the century. Major nineteenth-century foundations included the Department of the Navy Library (1820), the Army Medical Library (c.1836) and the Department of Agriculture Library (1862). The century also saw the foundation of many other national libraries, for instance the Russian Imperial Library (1810–11), the Brazilian and Argentinian national libraries (both 1810), the Belgian Royal Library (1837) and the German Imperial Library (1870).

The direct contribution of government also extended to archive service. The French Archives Nationale (1789) can be seen as the first formal recognition that the state had a responsibility to preserve and make its documentary heritage available to citizens. With the Archives Départementales (1796) France completed a national system for its archives which was elaborated during the nineteenth century. In Britain the Public Record Act of 1838 brought together numerous separate accumulations of national records into what was to become the classic example of a centralized system. Archive development elsewhere used French and British concepts and models, which were not usually enshrined in legislation until the twentieth century.

At the beginning of the century France already had a public-library system, the Bibliothèques Municipales, based on the revolutionary confiscations of books and manuscripts. These were, however, more like provincial research libraries than public libraries to serve the whole population for educational, recreational and information purposes. In England and Wales the Public Libraries Act of 1850, although flawed, permitted cities and towns to provide a library service, financed from local taxation, to their inhabitants if they so chose. Many, led by major cities such as Liverpool, Manchester and Birmingham, adopted the act and commenced to explore the ill-defined potential for this type of service. By contrast, in the United States the Boston Public Library (1852) was remarkable for the clarity and foresight with which its founders defined its purposes and functions. The idea of the public library spread and found a particular welcome in the Scandinavian countries before the end of the century.

Although academic institutions in many countries retained much of their semi-private status, their library provision tended to be affected by increasing government concern with educational matters. Great research libraries progressed or emerged in a number of institutions. Harvard University's old-established libraries advanced as swiftly as any, and Cornell University (1868) and the Universities of California (1869) and Chicago (1892), for example, founded important libraries. In Germany the libraries at Göttingen, Heidelberg, Leipzig, Breslau and Strasburg Universities came to reflect the strength of German scientific and scholarly research.

Gradually, the people employed in the new and growing libraries began to conceive of themselves as a profession. In 1876 the American Library Association was founded, followed in 1877 in Britain by the creation of an organization named with insolent baldness, the Library Association. The year 1876 was, quite spectacularly, one in which librarianship took on its modern character. Melvil Dewey (1851–1931) published his *Decimal Classification*; the seminal *Report on Public Libraries in the United States of America* appeared, with Charles Ammi Cutter's (1837–1903) *Rules for a Dictionary Catalog* attached; a professional journal edited by Dewey, the *Library Journal*, began publication; and Dewey founded a company, the Library Bureau, to provide products and services for library use. Dewey also set up the School of Library Service at Columbia University in 1887. Thus in the last quarter of the century the elements which made up the profession had been assembled, and arguably the key feature of twentieth-century library development has been the informed advocacy provided by that profession world-wide.

Anthony Hobson, *Great Libraries* (London, 1970).
Elmer D. Johnson and Michael H. Harris, *History of Libraries in the Western World* (Metuchen, NJ, 1976).
Josephine Smith, *A Chronology of Librarianship* (Metuchen, NJ, 1968).

PAUL STURGES

Liebig, Justus, baron von (*b* Darmstadt, Germany, 12 May 1803; *d* Munich, 18 April 1873) German chemist, one of the founders of modern CHEMISTRY, pioneering in theory, applications and education. Exposed to practical chemistry in his father's shop, the young Liebig quickly showed his precocity, and earned a degree at Erlangen before he was 20. Training in the superior laboratories of Paris inspired him to attempt to establish similar facilities in Germany, which he did at the University of Giessen, beginning in 1824. His laboratory there became a centre of chemical education in the 1830s and 1840s, and provided the model for modern training in the sciences both in Germany and elsewhere. His years at the University of Munich, where he worked after 1851, were devoted largely to public lectures and promoting applications. Liebig's contributions to experimental practice, chemical theory (especially in organic chemistry), practical applications in agriculture and physiology and popularization made him one of the most influential scientists of his time.

ROBERT FRIEDEL

Liebknecht, Wilhelm (*b* Giessen, 29 March 1826; *d* Berlin, 7 August 1900) German social democrat. He studied philosophy, philology and theology at university. Influenced by republicanism and socialism, he was active in the 1848 revolution, especially the uprising of 1849. Exile took him to London and collaboration with Marx. He returned to Germany in 1862, helping establish the ALL-GERMAN WORKERS' ASSOCIATION. He left it in 1865, moving to Leipzig where he worked with BEBEL, opposing Prussian domination in Germany and founding the Social Democratic Workers' party (*see* EISENACH CONGRESS). He and Bebel opposed the Franco-Prussian War, supported the Paris Commune and were imprisoned. He was a socialist deputy in the Reichstag (1867–71, 1874–88). He edited socialist newspapers and helped draft the Gotha (1875) and Erfurt (1891) programmes. He remained active as an intransigent radical democrat and socialist up to his death, although his interest was in maintaining political unity rather than ideological purity in the labour movement.

R. H. Dominick, *Wilhelm Liebknecht and the Founding of the German Social Democratic Party* (Chapel Hill, NC, 1982).

JOHN BREUILLY

Li Hung-chang [Li Hongzhang] (*b* Anhwei, 1823; *d* Peking, 1901) Chinese statesman. He came to prominence during the TAIPING REBELLION when he raised the Huai army which repelled the Taiping attack on Shanghai (1862). From then on he was at the centre of politics in China, occupying prestigious posts and often acting as troubleshooter for the Ch'ing court. Li was the leading advocate of 'self-strengthening' (*see* SELF-STRENGTHENING MOVEMENT). His position as governor-general of Chih-li for twenty-five years enabled him to build up a substantial military and industrial empire in northern China. He also co-ordinated self-strengthening throughout China, being responsible, for example, for the Nanking Arsenal and the Merchants' Steam Navigation Company. Although he saw the need for military strength, he opposed political and social reform. During the BOXER RISING he did much to limit the damage to China by leading a group of provincial governors in refusing to implement the court's declaration of war on the foreign powers.

JOHN DAVIES

Lincoln, Abraham (*b* Hardin County, Kentucky, 12 February 1809; *d* Washington, DC, 15 April 1865) President of the United States (1861–5). He emerged as the leader of the new Republican Party in Illinois during the mid-1850s. From his youth Lincoln hated slavery, considering it immoral. At the same time, like many other northerners, he refused to believe that African-Americans could ever achieve the same level of development as whites. Like many other residents of the north, Lincoln experienced outrage at the passage of the KANSAS-NEBRASKA ACT (1854), and joined the new party. He gained national attention for the first time in 1858 when he ran against the incumbent senator Stephen Douglas (1813–61). Their debates received national press coverage, and many Republicans outside Illinois saw Lincoln as a moderate who promised slavery's 'ultimate extinction', rather than calling for immediate abolition. Chosen as the moderate candidate in 1860 over William Seward, Lincoln won the presidential race with 39 per cent of the popular vote. His election prompted the lower south to leave the union.

Inaugurated in March 1861, Lincoln spent all his career in the White House as a war president (*see* AMERICAN CIVIL WAR). A fast learner who grew with the job, he was also a superb politician with an excellent sense of timing. He fought the war to preserve the union, and freed the slaves in the EMANCIPATION PROCLAMATION out of military necessity. Indeed, he favoured compensated emancipation and the colonization of the ex-slaves in Africa. Often ignoring heavy criticism from the press and more radical elements in his own party, Lincoln won the re-election in 1864, and perceived this as a mandate to carry the Union war effort to victory. Unfortunately, he never had the opportunity to enjoy the north's victory, for he was assassinated by John Wilkes Booth (1839–65), an actor, a week after the war concluded in the east.

James M. McPherson, *Abraham Lincoln and the Second American Revolution* (New York, 1991).
Stephen B. Oates, *With Malice toward None* (New York, 1977).

ALICE E. REAGAN

Lin Tse-hsü [Lin Xexu] (*b* Fukien, 1785; *d* Lli, 1850) Chinese official. A distinguished scholar from a modest background, he achieved China's greatest scholastic honour, membership of the Hanlin Academy. A varied official career took him by 1837 to the governor-generalship of Hunan and Hupei, where he vigorously prosecuted anti-opium measures. However, his experience there, where the problem was one of home-grown opium, did not prepare him for Canton, the centre of the foreign OPIUM TRADE, where he was sent by the Ch'ing court as imperial commissioner in 1839 to enforce the prohibition of the trade. Despite his initial intentions, he came into direct collision with the foreign importers, ordering the surrender of all foreign opium and imprisoning the British merchants in their factories. This precipitated the first Anglo-Chinese War (*see* ANGLO-CHINESE WARS). After the war Lin was sent into internal exile in the far west of China.

A. Waley, *The Opium War through Chinese Eyes* (London, 1958).

JOHN DAVIES

Lister, Joseph, first Baron (*b* Upton, Essex, 5 April 1827; *d* Walmer, Kent, 10 February 1912) English surgeon who invented antiseptic surgery. He received his MD degree from University College London in 1852. As a surgeon at the Glasgow Royal Infirmary, he became concerned over high mortality rates in amputation cases due to subsequent infection, and began experiments in antisepsis. He theorized that infection might be caused by pollen-like dust and developed the technique of spraying carbolic acid (phenol) on the wound during surgery to form an antiseptic barrier. This protected the site from infection and resulted in dramatically lowered mortality. Despite initial resistance from the medical community, his methods were adopted. Lister was raised to the peerage in 1897 and was the first physician to sit in the House of Lords.

Douglas Guthrie, *Lord Lister: His Life and Doctrine* (Edinburgh, 1949).

BARBARA KAPLAN

Liverpool, Robert Banks Jenkinson, second earl of (*b* London, 7 June 1770; *d* London, 4 December 1828) English statesman and prime minister (1812–27). Having entered parliament at the age of 20, he held all three secretaryships of state before succeeding to the premiership in 1812, when other politicians of greater reputation chose not to take the office. Contrary to expectation, the ministry survived: the longest-serving British prime minister of the century, Liverpool remained in office until a stroke forced him to resign in 1827, when confusion returned to parliamentary politics. His success owed much to his tact and judgement in chairing the cabinet and his application of the traditional administrative ethic of service to the crown, but a distinct party alignment became increasingly apparent. With its combination of traditional ministerial goals and Tory objectives, his ministry attracted most of the conflicting parliamentary groups, but as patronage diminished its wider support was mobilized through new forms of party organization, discipline and propaganda. By no means flamboyant, Liverpool supervised a crucial transition in British parliamentary government.

JOHN BELCHEM

Livingstone, David (*b* Blantyre, Lanarkshire, 19 March 1813; *d* Chitambo, central Africa, 1 May 1873) Scottish missionary and explorer. After training in medicine in Scotland, he worked first in Botswana. From the 1850s until his death he made extensive journeys through regions of central Africa previously little known to the outside world. His published accounts, lively and pungent, combined humane and scientific reports of a highly informative order with moral appeals for the development of 'Christianity, Commerce and Civilization' in these regions. For better or worse in different aspects, he focused attention on central Africa, not least by the circumstances of his death there. His views on missionary progress were idiosyncratic, while his formidable and prickly individuality to some extent ruined his later projects – particularly the Zambezi exploration of 1858–64 – and lessened his contemporary reputation. The character and writings of this most influential Christian missionary in Africa in the nineteenth century continue to exercise African historiography.

Tim Jeal, *Livingstone* (London, 1973).
D. Livingstone, *Missionary Travels and Researches in South Africa* (London, 1857).

P. E. H. HAIR

Lloyd, Marie [Matilda Alice Victoria Wood] (*b* London, 12 February 1870; *d* London, 7 October 1922)　Internationally known star of the British MUSIC HALL. From the East End working class, she had a 'narrow escape from becoming a schoolteacher' before her rapid rise as singer-comedienne on the West End stage at the age of 15. Her prime style was of the knowing young woman bent on a good time, signalling her intentions by minute emphases of tone and gesture that beguiled audiences into a delighted complicity. Careless of respectability and famously generous, 'Our Marie' remained a great popular favourite, though the alleged indecency of her performances and the irregularities of her private life led to her exclusion from music hall's first Royal Command performance (1912). One of many famous admirers, T. S. Eliot (1888–1965), praised Lloyd for 'expressing the soul of the people'.

Dan Farson, *Marie Lloyd and Music Hall* (London, 1972).

PETER BAILEY

Lobengula (*b* western Transvaal, *c.*1830; *d* Binga District, Matabeleland, January 1894)　Ndebele king. He succeeded his father, Mzilikazi (*c.*1770–1868) in March 1870, but was not universally accepted. He attempted to limit the entry of Europeans (sometimes quite violently), apart from missionaries (allowing conversion, although he himself did not convert) and some traders, from whose presence he sought personal benefit. This often conflicted with his need to keep his followers happy. After granting a mining concession in 1867, he signed the more significant Grobler treaty of friendship with the Transvaal (1888), then another giving the high comissioner for South Africa a considerable measure of influence and finally the Rudd concession (*see* BRITISH SOUTH AFRICA COMPANY). A punitive raid against the Shona, for many years subjected to and increasingly resentful of Ndebele rule, resulted in attempts by a company expedition to subdue Lobengula's army. The king succeeded in fending them off until his death.

SIMON KATZENELLENBOGEN

Louis XVIII (*b* Versailles, 17 November 1755; *d* Paris, 16 September 1824) King of France (1814–24). The younger brother of Louis XVI (1754–93), he supported the liberals in 1789 to advance his own ambition but fled the country in 1791. As self-appointed regent and later pretender, he declared himself an unreconstructed foe of all the reforms of the Revolution and thus made a restoration impossible. This attitude also continued the civil war within France and opened the way for Napoleon Bonaparte's dictatorship to end it. He ascended the throne after the defeat of Napoleon and accepted the role of a constitutional monarch. As king he played the constitutional game well enough, although the repression he sanctioned following the assassination of his heir, the duc de Berry (1778–1820), did nothing to win the trust of the liberals. As the experience of his brother and successor, CHARLES X, was to show, the regime did not command a broad enough basis of support among the elites.

P. Mansel, *Louis XVIII* (London, 1981).

DONALD SUTHERLAND

Louisiana Purchase (1803) At the end of the French and Indian War (1754–63), Louisiana, with its port of New Orleans and the Mississippi River, passed to Spain. After American independence, United States diplomats obtained Spanish permission to use the port of New Orleans, as well as the Mississippi. When Napoleon secretly bought Louisiana back in 1802, this jeopardized American economic development of the Midwest. President Thomas Jefferson sent James Monroe (1758–1831) to France to buy New Orleans from Napoleon. By the time Monroe arrived, Napoleon had abandoned his his plans to create a new French empire in North America. He stunned Monroe by offering to sell him all of Louisiana for $15 million. Unsure whether the constitution allowed such a large purchase, and fearful what it might mean for a republic, Jefferson decided to accept the offer, proclaiming it as the ideal home for yeomen farmers. The purchase doubled the size of the United States.

Alexander DeConde, *The Affair of Louisiana* (New York, 1976).

ALICE E. REAGAN

Louis Napoleon *see* NAPOLEON III.

Louis-Philippe (*b* Paris, 6 October 1773; *d* Claremont, England, 26 August 1850)   King of France (1830–48). One of a handful of liberal nobles in 1789, he later fled abroad. His father, the duc d'Orléans (1747–93), who was later executed, took the name of Philippe Egalité and, as deputy, voted for the death of his cousin Louis XVI (1754–93). The new duc d'Orléans supported the liberal opposition in the Restoration and was made king in the revolution of July 1830 (*see* REVOLUTIONS OF 1830–1832). Although he tried to steer a middle course between royalist and republican extremes, his own authoritarian temper, the emergence of the cartoon press and his sumptuous living brought him little respect. The monarchy succumbed to a street riot in February 1848 because no one considered the dynasty as anything other than provisional. No French head of state survived more assassination attempts.

T. Howarth, *Citizen-King: The Life of Louis-Philippe, King of the French* (London, 1961).

DONALD SUTHERLAND

Lovett, William (*b* Newlyn, Cornwall, 8 May 1800; *d* London, 8 August 1877)   Leader of the moderate wing of CHARTISM in Britain. A cabinetmaker by trade, he became a leading advocate of radical reform and Owenite co-operation (*see* OWENITES). In 1836 he founded the London Working Men's Association, which promoted contacts among British, American and Continental workers. Two years later he drafted the famous People's Charter, with its six points setting out the basis for a political democracy. Imprisoned for seditious libel in 1839–40, Lovett headed an influential segment of Chartism, primarily supported by London artisans, which espoused self-help, education and temperance reform. He fiercely attacked the 'physical force' Chartists led by Feargus O'CONNOR, whom he accused of favouring violence. These views increasingly lost Lovett popularity among many politically conscious working men and he spent the remainder of his life establishing schools, writing pamphlets and lecturing before small audiences on the virtues of individual effort and personal morality.

Joel H. Wiener *William Lovett* (Manchester, 1989).

JOEL H. WIENER

Luddites   Their name derived from the mythical leader 'General Ludd', the Luddites were bands of English craftsmen involved in machine-breaking and other forms of 'collective bargaining by riot' in the textile and hosiery districts of England between 1811 and 1817. Ludd's name, an essential feature of the secret oaths, threatening letters, arms

raids and machine-breaking which characterized the movement, probably owed its origin to a hapless Leicestershire youth named Ludlam
who had inadvertently smashed a stocking-frame. Whatever its prov-
enance, the name is now frequently misused: 'Luddite' has become a
generic term applied to opponents of technological innovation.

Not necessarily antitechnological, machine-breaking was a familiar
tactic of early trade-unionism, a useful adjunct to peaceable methods
of collective bargaining. In the absence of modern organization, industrial sabotage imposed solidarity on the workforce and prevented
blacklegging. Like other forms of direct-action protest, such 'collective
bargaining by riot' was disciplined and backward-looking. Violence
was used only against those employers who infringed the traditions of
the trade, customs and conventions enshrined in centuries-old paternalistic legislation governing work practices, apprenticeship and payment. Luddism began in this traditional manner, at a time when
constitutional efforts to enforce this obsolescent legislation proved
unavailing. In the interests of *laissez-faire*, parliament chose to repeal
the old paternalistic statutes, leaving workers unprotected against
wartime inflation and adverse changes in the labour process. Occurring at the crisis-point in the abrogation of paternalism, Luddism was
to acquire political dimensions, particularly in the northern districts where there was some co-ordination between machine-breaking
gangs and underground radical groups.

During the distress of 1811–12, the worst crisis of the Napoleonic
wars, General Ludd's 'army of redressers' first displayed their strength
in the east Midlands hosiery district. Here framework-knitters deployed a variety of complementary forms, constitutional and violent,
to protect traditional practices against custom-breaking hosiers who
cut costs, standards and quality by producing inferior stockings or
'cut-ups' by means of 'colting', employing unskilled apprenticed
labour on wide frames. While Gravener Henson (1785–1852), the
Nottingham trade-union leader, continued to seek parliamentary redress, the offending stocking-frames were symbolically smashed. At
first this was the work of crowds, but it was soon to be undertaken
by small specialist groups who struck with precision and were accorded
safe custody by the local community. As Luddism spread into Yorkshire,
industrial sabotage took on a different function, more in line with the
popular understanding of antimachinery Luddite violence. Yorkshire
Luddites looked to the vengeance of 'Enoch', the hammer of destruction, to smash the shearing-frames and finishing-machinery which
threatened the croppers with technological redundancy. Direct action
was the only option in the woollen industry: in 1809 parliament had
repealed all the old statutes regulating the trade in the course of rejecting the Wiltshire shearmen's petition to enforce the centuries-old ban
on gig-mills. Here, too, Luddism was highly organized, but although

links were forged with underground radical groups, there was no region-wide revolutionary network. Secret oaths notwithstanding, discipline proved difficult to impose: as attention shifted from the destruction of machinery to the seizure of arms, ordinary criminals took advantage of the crisis. In Lancashire, where cotton workers had been petitioning in vain for a minimum wage, steam looms were the ostensible target, but Luddism merged with a wider general protest against the hated 'war system'. From the outset, Lancashire Luddism was political in thrust and eclectic in tactics, providing the strongest evidence of an insurrectionary turn to the agitation, particularly in the aftermath of the attacks on factories at Rawfolds and Middleton in April 1812. The revolutionary impulse, however, was not sustained.

Luddism cannot be understood in strictly industrial terms, nor should it be seen as a revolutionary political movement. It is perhaps best characterized as a crucial episode in the politicization of discontent. Workers were quick to draw a political lesson as parliament not only abrogated PATERNALISM but also dispatched large numbers of troops to defend factories. Defeated and disabused, workers in the Luddite counties abandoned traditional collective bargaining by riot in favour of RADICALISM, a programme recommended by Major Cartwright (1740–1824) in his pioneering petitioning tours of the industrial districts. There were minor outbreaks of Luddism in 1814 and in 1816–17, by which time most workers looked to the radical mass platform to secure democratic control of the state and the economy.

John Dinwiddy, 'Luddism and Politics in the Northern Counties', *Social History*, 4 (1979), 33–63.
M. I. Thomis, *The Luddites: Machine-breaking in Regency England* (Newton Abbot, 1970).

JOHN BELCHEM

Ludwig II (*b* Nymphenburg, 25 August 1845; *d* Starnberger See, 13 June 1886) King of Bavaria (1864–86). He succeeded to the throne in 1864 and allied Bavaria with Austria against Prussia in the Seven Weeks War of 1866. After Austria's defeat he chose to ally himself with Bismarck rather than with France, and joined Prussia in the Franco-Prussian War. In 1870, prompted by Bismarck, he led the call for the establishment of a German empire in an address to the German princes. Ludwig was also a patron of the arts and admirer of Wagner (1813–83), whom he was nevertheless compelled by his own government and by public opinion to expel from Munich. He incurred immense debts from the construction of extravagant castles at Linderhof, Herrnchiemsee and Neuschwanstein, and withdrew increasingly from politics and society during the 1880s. Known as 'Ludwig the Mad', he was officially declared insane in June 1886 and drowned himself shortly afterwards in the Starnberger See. His psychiatrist also drowned in an attempt to save him.

TIMOTHY KIRK

Lueger, Karl (*b* Vienna, 24 October 1844; *d* Vienna, 10 March 1910) Founding leader of the Austrian Christian Social Party. A lawyer and municipal politician, he became a figure of national importance in the 1890s. He did so by assembling a motley antiliberal coalition, whose main cohesive force – and appeal to the Viennese electorate – was ANTI-SEMITISM. Partly due to this, Lueger's gaining of the coveted mayoralty of Vienna was delayed for two years by Francis Joseph I's refusal to confirm his election. The imperial authorities eventually conceded in 1897, and Lueger went on to be a very effective and popular mayor of Vienna, instigating large municipalization programmes in the city. He also formed the Christian Social Party into one of the most powerful political parties in the Habsburg Empire. Lueger's successful political use of anti-Semitism remains, however, his chief and most controversial legacy.

John Boyer, *Political Radicalism in Late Imperial Vienna* (Chicago, 1981).

STEVEN BELLER

Luneville, Treaty of (9 February 1801)   Signed by France and Austria following the Battles of Marengo (14 June 1800), in northern Italy, and Hohenlinden (3 December 1800), east of Munich, in which Napoleon defeated the Austrian armies, the Treaty of Luneville specifically reaffirmed the terms laid down in the Treaty of Campo Formio (17 October 1797) – that the Austrians cede the Belgian provinces and the left bank of the Rhine (including the fortress of Mainz) to France – but forced Austria to forgo the compensations stipulated by the earlier treaty. In addition, Austria agreed to cede the grand duchy of Tuscany to Parma, thus relinquishing its influence in Italy and recognizing the Batavian, Helvetian, Cisalpine, and Ligurian Republics. By the Treaty of Luneville Spain also ceded Louisiana to France, which sold it to the United States in 1803 (*see* LOUISIANA PURCHASE).

GEORGE O. KENT

M

Macarthur, Mary (*b* Glasgow, 13 August 1880; *d* 1 January 1921) Trade-union organizer in England. She became involved with the Shop Assistants' Union as a consequence of her connection with her father's business as a draper in Glasgow. In 1903 she left home for London, where she became the secretary of the Women's Trade Union League, embarking on a career as a journalist, speaker and organizer. She founded the National Federation of Women Workers, a general labour union, in 1906, and began publication of the newspaper *Woman Worker* in 1907. She married Will Anderson, a fellow trade-union activist, in 1911. Anderson died during the 1919 influenza epidemic and Macarthur, who never recovered from this personal blow, died of cancer two years later. As a socialist feminist, Mary Macarthur defended protective factory legislation and supported adult suffrage, always insisting on the saliency of class in the struggle for equality.

Mary Agnes Hamilton, *Mary Macarthur: A Biographical Sketch* (London, 1925).

GAIL SAVAGE

Macedonia The strategic location of Macedonia in the central Balkans, its complex history and its mixed population (Bulgarians, Greeks, Turks, Albanians, Serbs, Jews, Armenians and other ethnic groups) presented a major international problem at the time of the Ottoman Empire's disintegration. It was a centre of the Bulgarian cultural revival, but the CONGRESS OF BERLIN returned it to the sultan, giving rise to the notorious Macedonian Question. The 1880s and 1890s saw strong, peaceful Bulgarian and Greek religious and educational penetration and, at the same time, clashes between Bulgarian, Greek and Serbian bands (cheti) which fought the Turks and each other, promoting each country's irredenta. In 1893 the Internal Macedonian Revolutionary

Organization was formed in Salonica, under the leadership of Dame Gruev (1871–1906), Gotse Delchev (1872–1903) and Yane Sandanski (1872–1915), which promoted the idea of an autonomous Macedonia within a Balkan federation.

Duncan Perry, *The Politics of Terror* (Durham, NC, 1988).

MARIA TODOROVA

Mackenzie, William Lyon (*b* Dundee, 12 March 1795; *d* Toronto, 28 August 1861)   Feisty leader of 1830s reform movement in Upper CANADA (now, roughly, the province of Ontario). An editor/publisher, he opposed an appointed aristocratic elite, dubbed 'the Family Compact', emphasizing the need to dissolve the colonial relationship and embrace elective, democratic political institutions responsible to respectable citizens. He gained support among the disgruntled yeomanry and the independent producers of the towns, as well as from disaffected ethnic and national groups. With the possibility of constitutional reform exhausted by 1836, Mackenzie led other reformers towards rebellion. The 1836–7 insurrection was a decisive military defeat for the reform cause. Mackenzie fled to the United States, but returned to Toronto in 1850, spending the last decade of his life isolated and politically marginalized. He died destitute and disillusioned, but he had contributed significantly to the development of Canadian parliamentary democracy which, implemented in part in reforms of the 1840s, came to be mythologized as 'responsible government'.

BRYAN D. PALMER

McKinley, William (*b* Niles, Ohio, 29 January 1843; *d* Buffalo, NY, 14 September 1901)   President of the United States (1897–1901). After serving with distinction during the Civil War, he began a long career as a Republican politician. During his career in Congress (1877–83, 1885–91) he became an authority on tariff legislation. His protectionist McKinley Tariff (1890) set the average tariff rate at 49.5 per cent, the highest to date. The protégé of Republican boss Mark Hanna (1837–1904), McKinley became the party nominee for president in 1896. Supporting the gold standard, his party defeated the free-silver Democrats. As president, McKinley promoted American overseas expansion, annexing Hawaii (1898), and reluctantly declaring war on Spain in the same year. As a consequence of its victory in the SPANISH-AMERICAN WAR, the United States acquired Guam, Puerto Rico and the Philippines, and McKinley won a second term. In September 1901 he was mortally wounded by the anarchist Leon Czolgosz (1873–1901) while visiting the Pan-American Exposition in Buffalo, and died a few days later.

Lewis L. Gould, *The Presidency of William McKinley* (Lawrence, Kan., 1980).

ALICE E. REAGAN

McKinley Tariff *see* MCKINLEY, WILLIAM.

Madison, James (*b* Port Conway, Virginia, 16 March 1751; *d* Orange County, Virginia, 28 June 1836)   Founding father and eventual president of the United States (1809–17). His genius in framing the constitution was his most enduring contribution to the nation. He joined with John Jay (1745–1829) and Alexander Hamilton (1757–1804) in writing essays defending the constitution (later collected as *The Federalist Papers*) and supporting ratification. With Thomas JEFFERSON's election in 1800, Madison returned to national politics as secretary of state and worked closely with Jefferson on the EMBARGO ACT of 1807. European conflict and eventual war with Britain made Madison's two terms as president difficult. His hopes for a rapid victory in the WAR OF 1812 proved unfounded as the British burned Washington, and Madison and his family were forced to flee. On leaving the presidency, he retired from politics. He replaced Jefferson on his death in 1826 as rector of the University of Virginia.

JOHN MARTIN

Mafeking, Siege of   A militarily insignificant event in the Boer War of 1899–1902 (*see* ANGLO-BOER WARS), the Siege of Mafeking propelled to fame Colonel Robert Baden-Powell (1857–1941), founder of the Boy Scouts. The relief of the town on 17 May 1900 sparked celebrated 'mafficking' riots in Britain. Baden-Powell organized the defence of the town against a desultory Boer siege with panache which the press publicized and celebrated as evidence of British pluck and valour amid a series of initial serious military defeats. The devices that Baden-Powell used to maintain morale and deceive the Boers were later drawn on in his manuals of scouting. White inhabitants of the town – among them Cecil Rhodes – continued to live quite well during the siege, but blacks were reduced to eating dogs and other pets.

RICHARD PRICE

Magenta (4 June 1859) **and Solferino, Battles of** (20 June 1859)   The two major battles of the War of 1859 between France and Piedmont with Austria, the Battles of Magenta and Solferino (in northern Italy) were enormous bloodbaths, without truly defeating the Austrians. The Austrians withdrew from Lombardy to the QUADRILATERAL fortresses to defend Venetia. NAPOLEON III, upset at the sight of the carnage of the battles, fearful of further bloodshed with an attack on the Quadrilateral and worried about Prussian troops on the Rhenish border, abandoned the war and signed the Truce of Villafranca, which VICTOR EMMANUEL II accepted but which caused CAVOUR to resign in disagreement. The battles secured the cession of Lombardy, but not Venetia, to Piedmont and set off the revolts in the Italian duchies against their

Habsburg rulers, which led to the unification of Italy. The carnage of the battles inspired the foundation of the Red Cross.

LAWRENCE P. ADAMCZYK

Mahdi, Muhammad Ahmad ibn 'Abdallah al- see MUHAMMAD AHMAD IBN 'ABDALLAH AL-MAHDI.

Mahdism Religious revival within ISLAM occasionally takes the form of acceptance of a Mahdi. The emergence of a Mahdi, MUHAMMAD AHMAD IBN 'ABDALLAH, in the Egyptian SUDAN in the 1880s conflated grievances against the Egyptian administration among sections of the Arab population – largely protests against innovations thought to be non-Islamic or non-traditional. Theoretically, the Mahdist regime aimed to reproduce the ideal world-conquering Islamic polity assumed to have existed in the days of the Prophet Muhammad. In practice, after the death of the Mahdi, the regime of his successor, the Khalifa, while outwardly loyal to its founding ideology, and therefore often repressive in its conservatism and brutal to non-Muslims, increasingly accepted more conventional forms and ceased to be aggressive. On the grounds that it blocked French colonial expansion and 'kept the bed warm' for themselves, the British did not intervene until 1898, when the Mahdist regime was crushed at the BATTLE OF OMDURMAN.

P. E. H. HAIR

Mahmud II (*b* Istanbul, 20 July 1784; *d* Istanbul, 1 July 1839) Ottoman sultan (1808–39). He succeeded to the throne amid violent conflict between reformist supporters and reactionary elements centred on the janissary corps. In 1826, with the aid of his new-style troops, Mahmud had the janissaries encircled at their barracks and slaughtered. His bureaucratic reforms, new technical schools and encouragement of Western ideas set the pattern for the century of secularizing reforms that followed. His efforts to preserve the empire's territory were less successful, as Russian troops advanced into the Caucasus and the Serbian and Greek revolutions permanently inflamed the Balkans. In addition, the Ottoman governor of Egypt, MUHAMMAD ALI, seized control over Egypt and dispatched an army against his sovereign. Mahmud died shortly before the European powers intervened to preserve the Ottoman throne.

Bernard Lewis, *The Emergence of Modern Turkey* (Oxford, 1968).

MADELINE C. ZILFI

Maipo, Battle of (5 April 1818) The last major battle in the campaign for the independence of CHILE from Spanish rule, the Battle of Maipo was said by SAN MARTIN, the victorious general, to have 'decided the fate of South America'. After leading his forces across the

Andes from Argentina, San Martín had already defeated the royalist army at Chacabuco, north of Santiago, on 12 February 1817, giving the patriots control of the Chilean capital. The royalists, under General Osorio (*d* 1819), regrouped near Talcahuano, 180 miles south of Santiago, and then moved back northwards. They inflicted a defeat on San Martín at Cancha Rayada near Talca on 19 March 1818, threatening Santiago once again, but were then themselves routed at Maipo, south of Santiago, on 5 April. The royalists then made their way southwards through Araucanian territory to Valdivia, from where they were ejected in 1820 by Lord Cochrane (1775–1860), though a small Spanish garrison remained on the remote island of Chiloé until 1826.

RORY MILLER

Majuba, Battle of *see* ANGLO-BOER WARS.

malaria A parasitic disease, malaria is normally associated with tropical and subtropical regions. The vector is the female anopheles mosquito. Clinical features include periods of shivering and sweaty fevers. The main effect of the disease is to weaken the patient, thus making the individual more susceptible to other conditions. Endemic in many parts of Africa, Asia and Europe, it centred on swamp land and marshes, which provided breeding-grounds for the mosquito. It spread to the Americas following settlement in the eighteenth century.

There were five main epidemic outbreaks during the nineteenth century, that of 1823–8 being particularly severe. As Europeans in tropical areas were especially at risk, malaria posed an effective barrier to rapid colonization. Traditional treatments included purging, starvation and bleeding until QUININE was found to be an effective remedy. Malaria declined in Europe and North America in the late nineteenth century due to drainage projects, which destroyed the mosquito habitats.

SALLY SHEARD

Malthusianism In 1798 Thomas Robert Malthus (1766–1834) published *An Essay on the Principle of Population*, in which he argued that utopian views on the perfectibility of humanity would flounder on the tendency of population growth to outstrip the increase in the supply of food. In other words, scarcity was a permanent feature of society. Malthus shifted the emphasis in his second edition of the essay (1803) away from the attack on utopianism to a more extensive consideration of those factors which by restricting the number of births (the preventive checks) or by increasing the number of deaths (the positive checks) kept population and food supply in equilibrium. This fuller treatment at least raised the prospect that people could exercise conscious control over the balance between population and resources. Malthus disapproved of contraception and mainly referred to the postponement of marriage, although other writers, notably Francis PLACE, were less coy.

Malthus's principle of population growth expanding to outstrip food supply gave rise to 'Malthusian' arguments about a wide range of social problems. However, they were most directly relevant to contemporary debates about the Poor Law where they were used to support the claim that outdoor relief, or doles, were merely a stimulus to the labouring classes to marry earlier and thus have more children. Given a relatively fixed food supply (the essential starting-point for Malthus's deductions), the principle of population could even be urged in support of a callous indifference to the poor in that their hardship might merely be taken as evidence that they were surplus to the carrying capacity of the country. A number of passages in Malthus's early writings appear to support such a dismal view, and it was largely on this account that his ideas came to be abused so strongly by Karl Marx and other socialists.

In the late nineteenth century the term 'neo-Malthusian' came into vogue to refer to middle-class people practising contraception within marriage (see BIRTH CONTROL). The difference in fertility between the rich and the poor which resulted from family planning among the rich was a matter of great concern to the eugenicists (see EUGENICS).

Donald Winch, *Malthus* (Oxford, 1987).

GERRY KEARNS

mamluks Slave soldiers, especially those of Turkish and Circassian origin, the mamluks achieved control over EGYPT, first as a dynasty from 1250 to 1517 and thereafter as *de facto* governors under Ottoman suzerainty. Napoleon Bonaparte's invasion of Egypt in 1798 temporarily displaced both the Ottomans and their mamluk vassals. After the British and Ottoman expeditionary force expelled the French in 1801, the new Ottoman governor, MUHAMMAD ALI, prevented the mamluks from regaining power. In 1811, on the pretext of making peace, he invited several hundred of their leaders to a banquet and had them slaughtered where they sat. Although the early centuries of mamluk rule had brought about a flowering of Egyptian art and architecture, the later mamluk chiefs were too often brutal and rapacious to be much mourned.

Afaf Lutfi al-Sayyid Marsot, *Egypt in the Reign of Muhammad Ali* (Cambridge, 1984).

MADELINE C. ZILFI

Manchester School *see* FREE TRADE.

Manifest Destiny First used by John L. O'Sullivan, editor of the *Democratic Review* (1845), the phrase 'Manifest Destiny' expressed the view that it was America's divine mission to become a continental nation. It was based on the assumption that American civilization and government were superior. Politicians and ordinary individuals alike claimed that by acquiring a continental empire the United States would bring civilization to the native Americans of the west, as well as the Mexicans.

The first objective of Manifest Destiny was Texas. Many Americans, including political leaders such as Andrew JACKSON, believed that John Quincy Adams had made a mistake when he renounced American claims to Texas in the Adams-Onis Treaty (1819). After Texas declared itself independent from Mexico in 1835, the wealthy Americans living in east Texas requested annexation. Although many Americans favoured the idea, the Jackson administration hesitated, fearing difficulties with Mexico, as well as problems concerning the expansion of slavery. By 1844 the United States had rejected Texan requests for annexation several times, and Texans began to hint that they might form an alliance with abolitionist Great Britain, a prospect that caused anglophobe Andrew Jackson to call for immediate annexation. John C. CALHOUN, the secretary of state, attempted to gain annexation by treaty, but before he submitted the document he wrote a public letter in which he 'twisted the lion's tail', by warning that if abolitionist Britain gained a foothold in Texas it would spell disaster for southern slave-holders. Calhoun thus reopened the issue closed by the MISSOURI COMPROMISE (1820), by tying territorial expansion to slavery. The two issues never separated again before the Civil War. In anger, the Senate voted down the treaty, leaving the Texas issue for the presidential election of 1844.

Oregon also excited American imaginations during the 1840s. Since 1818 the United States and Great Britain had jointly occupied Oregon, but by 1844 Americans wanted all of the territory. The cry became '54° 40' or Fight', as Oregon joined Texas as a political issue.

At first the leading candidates of each party in 1844 tried to avoid the expansion issue. Henry CLAY straddled the issue, insisting that he favoured the acquisition of Texas, but not at the moment. Martin VAN BUREN agreed. The Democratic Party, however, made Manifest Destiny their platform and chose James K. POLK, a dark-horse expansionist, as their candidate. Polk carried the election on this issue. Before he entered the White House, however, Congress annexed Texas by joint resolution. As president, Polk continued to pursue expansionism. He negotiated a treaty with Great Britain which divided Oregon at the forty-ninth parallel. Many in the north-west condemned this as a betrayal of Polk's campaign promise to take all of Oregon. The president also demonstrated an interest in California and New Mexico early during his term. He sent emissaries to Mexico City with an offer to buy the two territories, which was rejected by the Mexican governmen

At the same time, a quarrel began over the Texas–Mexico border. Texans insisted that their boundary was the Rio Grande, but Mexico claimed that Texas ended at the Nueces River. Polk sent an 'army of observation' under General Zachary TAYLOR to the Rio Grande. When Mexican troops supposedly ambushed American soldiers, Congress approved Polk's request for a declaration of war.

The MEXICAN-AMERICAN WAR (1846–8) settled the Texas boundary with Mexico. At the same time, by the TREATY OF GUADALUPE HIDALGO (1848), the United States received the Mexican Cession, including New Mexico, Arizona, Utah, Nevada and California. The acquisition of this new territory reopened the slavery question. During the conflict the Wilmot Proviso, which banned slavery in any territory gained as a result of the Mexican War, had passed the House of Representatives. Southerners reacted with threats of secession. The matter became even more serious after the California gold rush (1848) sent over 80,000 people west in one year. California requested permission in 1849 to enter the union as a free state. At the same time, southerners supported claims by Texas over nearly half of New Mexico. The COMPROMISE OF 1850 admitted California as a free state, but settled the Texas boundary in favour of New Mexico.

During the 1850s Americans, especially southerners looking for more slave territory, cast covetous eyes on Latin America. The government made several attempts to buy Cuba from Spain, because southerners feared the consequences of Cuban emancipation. Spain refused to sell. In addition, American filibusters, usually southerners, attempted to take over Mexico, Nicaragua and Honduras. Southerners wanted to turn this territory into the Empire of the Golden Circle for slavery. Their insistence on the expansion of slavery irritated many northerners, and contributed to sectional difficulties (*see* SLAVERY (UNITED STATES)).

William H. Goetzman, *When the Eagle Screamed: The Romantic Horizon in American Diplomacy, 1800–1860* (New York, 1966).
Frederick Merk, *Manifest Destiny and Mission in American History: A Reinterpretation* (New York, 1963).
Albert K. Weinberg, *Manifest Destiny: A Study of Nationalist Expansion in American History* (Chicago, 1963).

ALICE E. REAGAN

Manilla Bay, Battle of (1 May 1898) In February 1898, two months before the SPANISH-AMERICAN WAR began, assistant secretary of the navy Theodore Roosevelt instructed George Dewey (1837–1917), the commander of the Asiatic squadron, to attack the Spanish fleet in the Philippines in the event of war. When the United States Congress declared war on 20 April, Dewey left his base at Hong Kong and engaged the Spanish fleet with four cruisers and two gunboats, methodically destroying all ten Spanish vessels at the cost of only eight wounded and no American ships lost. The outmoded warships of the Spanish were hopelessly outgunned by the modern steel navy of the United States. This decisive battle resulted in the acquisition of the Philippines and the extension of American interests in the western Pacific and marked the emergence of the United States as a world power.

KEVIN MURPHY

Manning, Henry Edward (*b* London, 15 July 1808; *d* London, 14 January 1892) Cardinal and social reformer. Born into a rich banking family, he underwent an Evangelical conversion on his father's bankruptcy. He was ordained and appointed rector of Lavington, Sussex, in 1833, and made archdeacon of Chichester in 1841. He became a Roman Catholic in 1851, when he was ordained a priest, and in 1857 was appointed provost of Westminster, founding the Oblates of Saint Charles Borromeo to evangelize London. In 1865 he succeeded his mentor WISEMAN as second archbishop of Westminster, and was made cardinal in 1875. He championed the pope's temporal power and crusaded for papal infallibility at the First Vatican Council (1869–70). In the 1870s he became an ardent temperance advocate and defender of trade unions and of the rights of labour, a career he climaxed by resolving the DOCK STRIKE of 1889. A friend of Irish nationalism and a foe of both capitalists and Liberal Catholics, he founded his radical political attitudes in religious dogma. He married Caroline Sargent (*d* 1837) and cherished her memory.

V. A. McClelland, *Cardinal Manning: His Public Life and Influence 1865–1892* (London, 1962).

David Newsome, *The Parting of Friends: A Study of the Wilberforces and Henry Manning* (London, 1966).

SHERIDAN GILLEY

Maori Wars (mainly 1863–1872) More appropriately termed the New Zealand Wars, these North Island conflicts were most disruptive in the 1860s when Maoris resisted erosion of their sovereignty by settlers greedy for land. Two years after central North Island tribes had chosen a Maori king in 1858, fighting erupted in Taranaki and became widespread south of Auckland between 1863 and 1872. Maoris led by chiefs such as Titokowaru (*d* 1888) and Te Kooti (*c.*1830–93) were innovative and effective in the use of *pa* (forts) and earthworks. However, government forces (mainly British troops) numbered 18,000 at their peak and had better logistic supplies and more devastating fire-power. Few died, but subsequent land confiscations and Land Court sales undermined Maori independence and welfare.

See also NEW ZEALAND.

James Belich, *The New Zealand Wars and the Victorian Interpretation of Racial Conflict* (Auckland, 1986).

Keith Sinclair, *Kinds of Peace: Maori People after the Wars, 1870–85* (Auckland, 1991).

MICHAEL C. PUGH

Maratha A population located in western India, the Maratha were once ruled from Poona. They established a reputation as invincible cavalrymen as they moved out of their homeland in the seventeenth and eighteenth centuries to fill the power vacuum left by the decline of Mughal authority. By the end of the seventeenth century, under leaders such as the folk hero Shivaji (1627–80), they had wrested autonomy from the Mughals and begun to establish a parallel state within the Mughal Empire. By the end of the eighteenth century, they had extended their influence northward into the Doab and the Ganges Valley, to the vicinity of Kerala on the Malabar Coast and Mysore and Madras on the Coromandel Coast. Until their power was finally broken (1818) after a series of three Anglo-Maratha Wars, they challenged British authority in the vicinity of Bombay and Madras and thwarted the East India Company's attempts at hegemony in INDIA.

Hari Ram Gupta, *Marathas and Panipat* (Chandigarh, 1961).

ROBERT J. YOUNG

Married Women's Property Act (1857) Together with suffrage (*see* WOMEN'S SUFFRAGE), PROSTITUTION and EDUCATION, the question of a married woman's control over her own property became a primary focus of the women's-rights movement of the nineteenth century. Although different systems of law exhibited important variations, all required that the husband's identity absorb his wife's on their marriage, abrogating her property rights. This legal dictum, known as 'coverture' in English common law, presumed that all women married and that all men lived up to their obligations as husbands. Reality for many women did not conform to this idealized scenario, thus fuelling a movement to change the law which achieved considerable success in England and Wales, and the United States. In an economy that increasingly depended on fluidity of capital and in political systems that equated personhood with property-ownership, the right to own property represented a crucial aspect of attaining equality for women.

In England and Wales 1854 saw the publication of two essays, *English Laws for Women in the Nineteenth Century* by Caroline Norton (1808–77) and *A Brief Summary of the Most Important Laws concerning Women* by Barbara Smith Bodichon (1827–91), which exposed the precarious position of married women. The personal circumstances of Norton, a popular and prominent literary figure who lived at the legal mercy of an abusive and vindictive husband, had been a public scandal for years and served as a vivid illustration of how the law as it stood disadvantaged married women. In 1855 Bodichon organized a committee of like-minded women drawn from an informal feminist group known as the Langham Place Circle to begin working to change the law. The 1857 Divorce Act, which gave divorced and separated women independent control of their property, represented an early, partial success. Further remedy had to wait until later in the century. The Married Women's Property Committee, formed in 1868, campaigned on behalf of further reform, disbanding in 1882 after legislation passed in 1870, 1878 and 1882 gave wives full control over their wages and property.

In enacting this reform, parliament applied the legal standard of equity, which had previously governed the marriage contracts used to protect the property of well-to-do women, to the situation of all married women. This legislation thus represented an instance of the general trend towards equity in English law as well as a milestone in the struggle for women's rights.

In the United States the feminist and abolitionist Sarah Grimke (1792–1873) published *Letters on the Equality of the Sexes* (1837), which attacked the status of married women under common law. Elizabeth Cady STANTON took a particular interest in this issue, and it figured prominently in the 'Declarations of Sentiments' issued by the 1848 SENECA FALLS CONVENTION. Legislators proved more open to implementing this reform than to granting women the vote. Mississippi became the first state to pass a married women's property statute and, by 1865, twenty-nine states had passed such laws.

The confluence of two factors explain the relative success of those pressing for this reform in England and Wales, and the United States. First, the individualist, natural-rights logic behind the demand had widespread appeal, even among men. It could easily appear illogical and inconsistent to restrict the exercise of property rights to men. In addition, economic enterprise required a fluidity of capital that could find itself frustrated by the clumsy expedients taken to protect the property of affluent women when they married. The logic of capitalistic endeavour demanded that wives as well as husbands be legally competent to earn and to spend, to buy and to sell unhampered by either the legal doctrine of coverture or the attempts to circumvent coverture with prenuptial contracts.

In other countries, especially those governed by Roman law, the principle of community property served to provide wives with somewhat more protection of their property than the Anglo-American common law. Wives, nevertheless, did not enjoy an independent legal identity, and feminists across Europe took up this issue. Ellen Key (1849–1926), for instance, thought such legal reform crucial for the creation of a family life based on equity. In France, prominent feminists such as Maria Deraismes (1828–94) and Leon Richer (1824–1911) called for equal rights in marriage, but until Jeanne-Elisabeth Archer Schmahl (1846–1915) formed L'Avant Courviere (The Forerunner) as a single-issue pressure group to work on behalf of legal reform no progress occurred. The first French married women's property act – the *Loi Schmahl* – became law in the early years of the twentieth century.

See also FEMINISM.

Norma Basch, *In the Eyes of the Law: Women, Marriage and Property in Nineteenth-Century New York* (Ithaca, NY, 1982).

Lee Holcolmbe, *Wives and Property: Reform of the Married Women's Property Law in Nineteenth-Century England* (Toronto, 1983).

GAIL SAVAGE

Martí, José (*b* Havana, Cuba, 28 January 1853; *d* Dos Ríos, Cuba, 19 May 1895) Principal ideologist of Cuban independence. Born of Spanish parents, he was revered by Cubans of all persuasions. His criticism of the Spaniards during the Ten Years War led to his exile from CUBA in 1871. He studied at Zaragoza and then travelled in Europe and Central America. Deported from Cuba again in 1878, he moved to New York in 1880 and became prominent not only as a writer and journalist with a growing literary reputation, but also as an organizer of the exile community. In 1892 he formed the Cuban Revolutionary Party to unite separatists around the principles of armed struggle, democracy, social justice and equality. At the same time, he expressed his fears both of military *caudillismo* and of American intervention and annexation of Cuba were the war to be prolonged. Three months after the uprising began in February 1895, Martí was killed in a skirmish with Spanish forces.

RORY MILLER

Martineau, Harriet (*b* Norwich, 12 June 1802; *d* Ambleside, Westmorland, 27 June 1876) English journalist, historian and novelist. She was formed as an intellectual by the Unitarian education she received as a child in Norwich, and by the radical Unitarian milieu of William James Fox (1786–1864). She was the outstanding independent woman intellectual in England in the first half of the nineteenth century, and showed a lifelong commitment to abolitionism and feminism, especially on the question of women's education. She made her name by her popularizing *Illustrations of Political Economy*, showing a mastery of economics not then expected of a woman. She moved from the Unitarianism of her childhood to an antitheological positivism, expressed in her translation and condensation of Comte's *Positive Philosophy* (1853). Her *Autobiography* (1855) provides an unrivalled account of the upbringing of a middle-class girl in a provincial town in the early nineteenth century, as well as descriptions of many leading contemporary intellectuals and writers.

SIMON DENTITH

Marx, Karl (*b* Trier, 5 May 1818; *d* London, 17 March 1883)   Social theorist and the founder of modern socialist thought. He was born into a prosperous family in Rhenish Prussia and studied law, history and philosophy at the University of Berlin, where he was deeply influenced by Hegelian thinkers whose radical politics he adopted. In the 1840s he worked as a newspaper editor and was engaged in socialist politics in Paris and Brussels and – during the revolutions of 1848 – in Cologne. It was as a member of the LEAGUE OF THE COMMUNISTS (a radical association of exiled German working men) that in 1848 he wrote his best-known and most notorious work, the COMMUNIST MANIFESTO. In the summer of that year he moved to London, largely to escape the rising tide of counter-revolutionary repression in Europe, where he remained for the rest of his life.

Marx made a fairly meagre living in London by writing newspaper articles (most notably in the 1850s for the *New York Tribune*), but he also received support from his wealthy friend and collaborator Friedrich ENGELS. Although he continued his political work in London (*see* FIRST INTERNATIONAL), the most important aspect of his life there was the many hours he spent in the Reading Room of the British Museum, reputedly in seat G7. It was during this period that he published his most substantial analyses of the history, politics and economics of capitalist society, *Contribution to a Critique of Political Economy* (1859), *Capital* (vol. 1, 1867) and *The Civil War in France* (1871). Much of his work, however, remained hidden away in obscure publications, untranslated or in manuscript form. This was true of works that later came to be regarded as important, such as his writings on the Revolution of 1848 in France and Louis Napoleon, *Class Struggles in France* and *The Eighteenth Brumaire of Louis Napoleon*. Indeed, some pieces that shed great light on his intellectual development, such as *Economic and Philosophical Manuscripts* of the 1840s and *Grundrisse* of the 1850s, were not disseminated until the 1950s and 1960s. But by the 1880s the growth of organized SOCIALISM secured a wide audience for the works of Marx and the publication and translation of his major works, including the unfinished parts of *Kapital* itself, was organized by Engels.

Marx was a complex thinker whose ideas ranged across economics, philosophy, history and sociology, but perhaps the core of his work was the attempt to provide an all-encompassing framework for understanding the movement and development of history. This integrative purpose was typical of nineteenth-century thought, although it is antithetical to the main intellectual currents of the twentieth century. Marx was the intellectual heir to the eighteenth-century Enlightenment and to German idealism. From the former he took his notion that material conditions were the most important determinants of historical and social developments; from the latter he took his idea that history moved in a dialectical way. He departed from Hegelianism, however, in his materialism and in his emphasis on the class struggle as the essential motor of history.

David McLellan, *Karl Marx: His Life and Thought* (London, 1973).
Allen W. Wood, *Karl Marx* (London, 1981).

RICHARD PRICE

Marxism *see* SOCIALISM.

Mashonaland and Ndebele Risings (1896–1897) A revolt by the people of Matabeleland against BRITISH SOUTH AFRICA COMPANY rule began in March 1896, and was followed in June by a revolt in Mashonaland. Europeans were taken completely by surprise, having been totally unaware of the degree of antagonism towards them and with no real understanding either of Ndebele and Shona culture and history or of the relationship between the two groups. In the absence of a strong leader following the death of LOBENGULA, the Ndebele people tended to look to the priests of the Mwari religious cult to provide a unifying focal point. Cult leaders also played a major role among the Shona. Unwilling or unable to understand the real reasons for the revolt, company administrators saw the priests as the prime instigators of the risings, and executed those whom they considered most important. Some positive changes in white attitudes resulted from the rebellions, but their greatest importance has been as significant examples of primary resistance to colonial rule to which later nationalist movements referred.

T. O. Ranger, *Revolt in Southern Rhodes 1896–7: A Study in African Resistance* (London, 1967).

SIMON KATZENELLENBOGEN

Master and Servant Law A body of penal labour law which served as a major resource for British employers in enforcing industrial discipline, the Master and Servant Law assigned fundamentally unequal status to masters and workers within the employment relationship, a central feature of production relationships in early capitalism. The most important statute, the 1823 Master and Servant Act, imposed criminal penalties on employees, including mandatory terms of imprisonment, for breach of contract. In contrast, employers were liable only for civil damages. Employers in the iron and building trades, cutlery manufacture, mining and domestic industries made wide use of this coercive law, prosecuting workmen for the neglect of work and related offences. Employers also commonly resorted to the law to break strikes. In 1863 the trade-union movement began efforts to reform the law. That initiative eventually gained the passage of the 1875 Employers and Workmen Act, a measure which secured equal status for employees under the law.

See also EMPLOYER'S LIABILITY ACT.

RICHARD J. SODERLUND

Maximilian, Ferdinand-Joseph (*b* Schönbrunn, 6 July 1832; *d* Querétaro, Mexico, 19 June 1867) Habsburg prince whom NAPOLEON III recruited as emperor of MEXICO after the French occupation of the country in 1862–3. Maximilian was promised the support of 20,000 French troops until the end of 1867. He arrived in Mexico in May 1864. While he fell out with the church over his refusal to restore confiscated ecclesiastical property and with conservative landowners over his attempts at social reform, he was unable to persuade JUAREZ and the liberals to accept him, and after the American Civil War ended they were able to acquire arms and recruit mercenaries. Napoleon then began to withdraw his troops because of the European crisis. Forced to rely on the conservatives for an army, Maximilian lost support and surrendered to the liberals in Querétaro in May 1867. In reprisal for French executions of liberal officers, he was condemned to death and shot.

RORY MILLER

May Day The history of May Day as the workers' holiday is inseparable from movements to limit the hours of labour to eight. The most important of these first developed in the United States in 1866. Legislation for eight hours was first achieved in the state of Illinois, with effect from 1 May 1867. Yet legislation was not everywhere achievable, and in the United States and Europe the issue became one of direct action. The American strikes of 1 May 1886, the associated martyrdom of the Chicago anarchists and a decision at the 1888 American Federation of Labor congress had considerable impact in Europe. The 1889 foundation congress of the SECOND INTERNATIONAL resolved to join with the Americans in declaring the 1890 May Day an 'international manifestation' in favour of the EIGHT-HOUR DAY. The subsequent meetings, demonstrations and strikes in May 1890 and 1891, often taking on the character of general strikes, were on a scale never seen before. May Day was launched, henceforth the world over, rich in symbolism and pictorial representation, in the international calendar of labour and communist movements and festivals.

See also BANK HOLIDAYS.

JOHN L. HALSTEAD

Mazzini, Giuseppe (*b* Genoa, 22 June 1805; *d* Pisa, 10 March 1872) Italian patriot and author. Originally a member of the CARBONARI, a secret republican society, he found them too ritualistic and disorganized. Forced into exile in 1831, he returned to Italy sporadically, most notably in 1848 where he helped govern the short-lived Roman Republic. In 1831 he founded 'Young Italy', a movement of broader scope and more popular composition than the Carbonari whose objective was the unification of ITALY as a republic through education of the young coupled with guerilla activity. His ideas spread, forming various chapters of 'Young Europe' across the Continent. In his writings Mazzini promoted the idea of Italy as one 'nation' with common customs, language and history. Thanks to Mazzini, Italy saw itself as a great nation with a sacred mission to promote nationalism.

LAWRENCE P. ADAMCZYK

mechanics' institutes Prominent providers of adult education in the nineteenth century, mechanics' institutes arose from a strong interest in science among all classes which dated back to the eighteenth century. The first institute was established in Glasgow in 1823, rapidly followed by others in major British cities. Most early institutes shared a common aim, to bring the new knowledge in science and technology to the working man. By the 1850s, however, these original aims were largely forsaken. For most working men, the educational level and fees had proved too high. The name 'mechanics' institute', however, covered many different types of institution. Local conditions determined their foundation, the nature of their membership and the types of educational and other facilities offered. This was true both in Britain and elsewhere in the world, where some institutes were founded by British emigrants while others sprang up independently, predominantly in the United States and Australia.

Ian Inkster (ed.), *The Steam Intellect Societies: Essays on Culture, Education and Industry c.1820–1914* (Nottingham, 1985).

SYLVIA HARROP

medicine Remarkable changes were witnessed in medicine during the nineteenth century as the progress of scientific thought, especially up to 1850, became deeply influenced by the intellectual and moral libertarian ideals embodied by the French Revolution. Material and cultural growth, allied to a new sense of realism, overcame the transcendental tendencies of philosophy, religion, dogmatism and mysticism that characterized the natural sciences during earlier periods. In replacing metaphysical approaches, the work of the clinical, and later the laboratory, scientist became the study of natural processes through experimentation and controlled observation. This was influenced particularly by Auguste Comte's (1798–1857) philosophy of Positivism, which sought to consider factuality, based on objective and accurate methods of reasoning.

The French School dominated clinical developments in the early part of the century, largely due to a growth in the provision of hospitals and university research which ushered in an era of symptomatology and diagnosis. The systematic study of tissue (histology), rather than organs, can be traced to Bichat's (1771–1802) *Anatomie généralé*, published in 1801. It was during this period that Laënnec (1781–1826) invented the stethoscope (1819); the foundations for medical statistics were laid by Pierre Louis (1787–1872) through his studies of tuberculosis and typhoid fever published in 1825 and 1829; Brettoneau (1778–1862) definitely established the clinical entity of diphtheria (1826); and Cruveilhier's (1791–1874) work provided early descriptions of sclerosis and muscular atrophy (1829–42). These are but a handful of the many examples.

However, the rapidity of progress in medical science was such that 'clinical medicine' was soon replaced by what came to be known as 'laboratory medicine', dominated by the work of a number of German scientific men. Linked with progress in histology, the efforts of Schleiden (1804–81) in 1838 demonstrated the cell structure of plants and that plant growth was due to an increase in the number of cells, findings also confirmed for animal tissue by Schwann (1810–82) in 1839. Important as this new CELL THEORY was, Schleiden and Schwann's misplaced belief that cell formation was the product of an unorganized cytoblast was rejected by Rudolph Virchow (1821–1902), who formulated the theory of cell pathology whereby cells were reproduced by the division of a nucleus and cytoplasm. That the body became 'a cell-state in which every cell is citizen', where disease was 'a conflict of citizens in this state, brought about by the action of external forces' (*Cellular-pathologie*, 1858), represented a historic break with metaphysical constructions. He argued that pathology should be based rather on the positive investigation of the visible reaction of cells to the causes of disease. On the heels of his discovery came a number of important findings for ailments such as degeneration, inflammation, syphilis and malignant tumours. Great strides were made in the understanding of the cardiovascular system, the digestive tract and endocrine system. All were made possible by a vibrant area of study in Europe and beyond. Eighteen chairs of pathology were founded in Germany, ten in Austria, and nineteen in Italy, while the New York Pathological Society, the oldest of its kind, was founded in 1844.

However, the 'germ theory', formulated by the microbiologists (bacteriology) Pasteur and Koch (1843–1910) in the final quarter of the century, served to deflect attention from cellular pathology and the clinics. The importance of investigation under the microscope was again asserted and the importance of the individual's reaction to disease was reaffirmed. Yet the germ theory also helped to retrieve some Hippocratic concepts. Knowledge of the patient's heredity and environment became vital for proper treatment. General pathology, all but lost at the beginning of the century, took priority over Virchow's local pathology (*see* THEORIES OF DISEASE).

Throughout the whole of the nineteenth century, more than ever before, the progress of medicine was driven by advances in the other sciences, especially physics and chemistry. For example, a number of therapeutic measures such as electrotherapy and orthopaedics were derived either directly or indirectly from physics; while the discovery that organic compounds were subject to ordinary chemical law was vital for understanding the physiology of the metabolism. But the overriding aspect of the nineteenth-century evolution in medicine was the expansion of professional specialisms. The general practitioner of the eighteenth century, well versed in most aspects of medicine, had become all but extinct. Laboratory techniques, employing specific knowledge and methods, served to emphasize this trend. By 1900 newly formed sub-disciplines of paediatrics, otology, larynology, dermatology, syphilology and neurology had emerged to complement the advances in the traditions of anatomy, pathology, physiology, ophthalmology, psychiatry, obstetrics and gynaecology. It has been argued that success in these specialities was at the expense of investigation into the social factors in the origin of disease. Nevertheless, it must be noted that the discoveries of microbiology enabled a greater understanding of the laws governing infectious diseases. Medical innovation, taking on the role of social science rather belatedly, therefore influenced the progression of public-health reform (*see* DOCTORS, PUBLIC HEALTH).

A. Castiglioni *A History of Medicine*, trans. E. B. Krumbhaar second edn, (London, 1958).

GRAHAM MOONEY

Mediterranean Agreements (1887) The first Mediterranean Agreement was concluded on 12 February 1887 between Britain and Italy (later joined by Austria–Hungary and Spain), and had been promoted by Bismarck in an effort to exacerbate Anglo-French difficulties over EGYPT and French–Italian tensions over Libya and tariff matters. Thus the agreement was primarily directed against France and Russia, and provided for the maintenance of the *status quo* in the Mediterranean, Adriatic, Aegean and Black Seas, pledging mutual support in case of intervention by a third party.

The Second Mediterranean Agreement (or 'Near Eastern Entente') was signed on 12 December 1887 by Austria, Italy and Great Britain.

It reaffirmed the *status quo* in the Near East and asserted that the signatories to the agreement would come to the aid of the Ottoman Empire if its independence or rights in Bulgaria or the Straits were threatened. Bismarck, who had been instrumental in the formation of the agreement, refused to sign it. The Second Mediterranean Agreement thus essentially nullified the effect of the REINSURANCE TREATY, which pledged German support for Russia's drive towards the Straits, because it bound Britain, Austria and Italy to oppose such a drive.

A. J. P. Taylor, *The Struggle for the Mastery in Europe 1848–1918* (Oxford, 1954).

GEORGE O. KENT

Meiji Restoration   The origins of the Meiji Restoration – more accurately a revolution, a revolution from above – can be traced to the 1830s. Internal strains in JAPAN were compounded by external pressures from the West, culminating in the visits of the American Commodore Perry (1794–1858) in 1853 and 1854. Despite the opposition of the feudal domains opposed to concessions, the decaying Tokugawa shogunate had to submit to American and other foreign demands that Japan be opened to trade. With these concessions to the West, the shogunate's days were effectively numbered, and after a palace coup in January 1868 a group of anti-Tokugawa court nobles and samurai from the domains of Satsuma and Choshu declared the shogunate to be at an end and its lands confiscated. The government of Japan was to be returned to the emperor. The coup led to a brief civil war but national unity was restored under the young emperor, who took the reign title of Meiji ('enlightened rule'), in the spring of 1869. The restoration of the emperor was the beginning of a long process of radical change.

The emperor's role being largely an honorary one, the effective leaders of Meiji Japan came from the lower strata of the samurai class. They embarked on the modernization of Japan, their programme being summed up in the slogan 'Rich country, strong army'. The new leaders were young, able and flexible. Although initially anti-Western, they quickly saw the the need to abolish the feudal system and the autonomous feudal units which stood in the way of the modernization of the government, economy and army. In 1869 they persuaded the daimyo (leaders) of Satsuma, Choshu, Tosa and Hizen to offer their domains to the emperor. The other daimyo were obliged to follow suit. Two years later the domains were abolished altogether and Japan was divided into ken (prefectures). A more difficult task was that of stripping the samurai of their social, economic and political privileges. The samurai, who comprised 6 per cent of the population, monopolized military power and political leadership and enjoyed hereditary salaries. In 1873, in its most revolutionary act, the Meiji government introduced universal military service, recruited an army of peasants and destroyed the samurai monopoly of military service. The samurai also lost their privileged economic status. In 1876 they were forced to commute their remaining stipends, already cut in 1869, into reduced lump-sum payments. The attack on samurai privileges led to samurai revolts, the most serious in 1877 in Satsuma when the government's peasant army crushed the rebels. The abolition of feudalism cleared away the traditional social and political system, and the Meiji government's political control of Japan was now unchallenged. However, the development of new political institutions, of a new economic and industrial system and of an education system to underpin Japan's independence was a more difficult enterprise.

To avoid dependence on Western capitalism, whose predatory nature they distrusted, the Meiji leaders eschewed foreign loans. They were, however, prepared to use foreign experts in the short term. Their reforms included investment in strategic industries, such as shipbuilding and munitions, as well as in consumer industries, such as cotton-spinning and silk-reeling. A modern currency system was created with the yen as the basic unit, in 1871. Currency reform was supported by the creation of a modern banking system. Developments in communications included the establishment of a modern postal and telegraphic system and the introduction of railways in Japan, the first line being built in 1872. A modern budgetary system, based on a fixed land tax, was accompanied by the recognition of the private ownership of peasant plots. The Meiji leaders saw the need to create an educated public to support a modernized economy. Students were sent abroad to study in the West and Western teachers were brought to Japan. In 1871 a ministry of education was established which embarked on an ambitious programme of universal education. An educational system extending from elementary school to university (Tokyo University was founded in 1877) was eventually established. In the late 1870s the Meiji leaders began to prepare for the drafting of a constitution. A cabinet system of government was introduced in 1885 and the Meiji Constitution was promulgated in 1889 as a gift from the emperor. Thus the Meiji reforms modernized Japan and prepared the way for its emergence as a world power by the end of the nineteenth century.

W. G. Beasley, *The Meiji Restoration* (London, 1973).
E. O. Reischauer, *Japan: The Story of a Nation* (London, 1970).

JOHN DAVIES

Melbourne, William Lamb, second Viscount (*b* London, 15 March 1779; *d* Melbourne House, Derbyshire, 24 November 1848) English statesman, prime minister (1834, 1835–41). A moderate Whig, whose political indolence, graceful manners and easy morals belonged to an earlier age, he failed to revivify the WHIGS after Grey's retirement in 1834. As Grey's home secretary, he had displayed some spirit in crushing the CAPTAIN SWING riots; as prime minister, however, he found it difficult to maintain an effective cabinet. In November 1834 he provided William IV with the opportunity to dismiss the Whigs, only to be recalled to office in April 1835. With the accession of the 'girl-queen' Victoria, he diverted his attention from cabinet to court, serving as mentor and private secretary to the monarch in a relationship of mutual admiration. Victoria's impetuous behaviour in the 'bedchamber crisis' of 1839 forced him to rescind his resignation, leading to two further years of ineffective Whig rule.

JOHN BELCHEM

Mendel, Gregor Johann (*b* Heinzendorf, Austria, 22 July 1822; *d* Brünn, Austria-Hungary, 6 January 1884)   Austrian botanist. An Augustinian monk, he conducted breeding experiments on garden peas in his monastery garden. He discovered basic mathematical laws of inheritance long before the concept of the gene was established. By self-pollinating pea plants and keeping records over several plant generations, Mendel found that certain paired traits retained their identity according to simple, fixed ratios rather than becoming blended over time. He published his findings in 1865 in an obscure scientific journal, but later abandoned his researches. Although his discovery supplied important evidence for DARWINISM, Darwin never knew his work. Mendel's laws of inheritance finally were resurrected by Hugo De Vries (1848–1935) in 1900.

Vitezslav Orel, *Mendel*, tran. Stephen Finn (Oxford, 1984).

BARBARA KAPLAN

Menelik II (*b* Ankobar, Ethiopia, 17 August 1844; *d* Addis Ababa, 12 December 1913)   Emperor of Ethiopia (1889–1913). When TEWODORUS II invaded Shewa in 1855, Menelik, son of the negus, was imprisoned. He escaped in 1865, returning home to declare himself negus. While his rival Yohannes IV reigned, Menelik expanded southwards, defending his territory against Egypt and subsequently taking the imperial throne in 1889. His friendship with Italy led to the 1889 Treaty of Uccialli, which he subsequently repudiated, angered particularly by Italy's claim that it made Ethiopia an Italian protectorate. After his defeat of the Italian forces at the BATTLE OF ADOWA (1893), Ethiopia became more generally accepted internationally as a political force. Caught up in Anglo-French and Egyptian rivalries, Menelik successfully defended Ethiopia against foreign encroachment. He did, however, seek foreign help in his efforts to continue to modernize Ethiopia's economy, education, telecommunications and railways. He suffered a series of strokes in 1906–7, following which his wife and grandson acted as regents until his death.

SIMON KATZENELLENBOGEN

Methodism A form of popular Protestantism, Methodism had been organized by John Wesley (1703–91) as a series of societies within the Church of England, but by the nineteenth century it consisted of a group of autonomous denominations. Methodist religion was the most exuberant version of EVANGELICALISM, delighting in the hymns of Charles Wesley (1707–88) and the distinctive Arminian teaching that, since Christ died for all humanity, anyone could exercise saving faith. Methodists were also unusual in claiming that the believer could reach a state of perfect holiness on earth. Members met in small weekly classes to discuss their spiritual progress, their right to do so being proved by the possession of a prized quarterly ticket. The movement drew strength from the opportunities it provided for laypeople, including women, to become class leaders and conduct cottage prayer meetings. A great majority of Methodist services was taken by unordained local preachers, while the regular ministers, or 'travelling preachers', remained for only two or three years in any given area. Methodism recruited heavily in the skilled working classes and lower middle classes, its emphasis on reading, respectability and self-improvement often opening avenues of upward social mobility. Its appeal was particularly strong in large upland parishes, growing industrial towns and new mining communities where the Church of England was relatively weak. Growth characteristically came in spurts with subsequent declines, but the general trend was for membership to outstrip population increase in the first half of the century and then to fall behind it in the last two decades. Although non-members normally exceeded members among regular chapel-goers, in 1851 attenders were estimated to include 7.7 per cent of the population of England and Wales.

The largest Methodist denomination, the Wesleyans, enjoyed more support than all the others put together. Resentment against the domination of its governing conference by Jabez Bunting (1779–1858), the leading Wesleyan official between about 1814 and 1851, was one of the chief reasons for Methodist fragmentation, but the process had begun earlier. In the 1790s the Methodist New Connexion had split off as a result of a campaign for greater lay rights. The Primitive Methodists, or 'Ranters', were enthusiastic revivalists who could not abide the restraints imposed by the Wesleyan conference. They broke away in 1810 following official condemnation of camp meetings, open-air preaching festivals imported from the United States, and, with a powerful appeal to working people, grew into the second largest Methodist body. The Bible Christians, though largely confined to Devon and Cornwall, were launched as a similar revivalist organization in

1815. Popular resentment against a 'popish' organ installed by wealthy trustees at Brunswick Chapel, Leeds led to the creation of the Protestant Methodists in 1828. Six years later the commencement of regular ministerial training in a theological institution precipitated the secession of the Wesleyan Methodist Association. The last two bodies merged in the 1850s with Wesleyan Reformers protesting against conference authoritarianism to form the United Methodist Free Churches. Always standing apart were the Calvinistic Methodists of Wales who repudiated Arminian doctrine and, by persistent evangelism in the Welsh language, became the strongest denomination in the principality.

During the first two decades of the nineteenth century fears of possible government repression induced Methodists to make frequent protestations of loyalty to crown and constitution. When political radicalism emerged in the ranks, those responsible were instantly expelled. The aversion of the Methodist leadership to radical tendencies was so great that the French historian Elie Halévy judged Methodism to have saved England from revolution – though he underestimated the resilience of the state apparatus. The Wesleyan reputation for conservatism was reinforced by the support of its leaders for the established Church of England in the 1830s and the imposition of a 'no politics' rule on the travelling preachers. Already by the 1841 general election, however, an overwhelming majority of members and ministers took the Liberal side in politics. Anti-Catholicism was a powerful influence on Wesleyan public attitudes because of fears for the welfare of the Irish branch of the movement in a predominantly Roman Catholic land. The extensive Wesleyan Methodist Missionary Society gave supporters a concern with imperial affairs while the strength of American Methodism induced a sense of kinship with the United States. In the later years of the century the various Methodist denominations nurtured many trade-union leaders and the progressive Wesleyan minister Hugh Price Hughes (1847–1902) voiced a commitment to social reform that was to be widespread in Methodism after 1900.

Rupert Davies et al. (ed.), *A History of the Methodist Church in Great Britain*, 4 vols (London, 1965–88), vols 2–4.
David Hempton, *Methodism and Politics in British Society, 1750–1850* (London, 1984).

D. W. BEBBINGTON

Metternich, Clemens, prince von (*b* Kolenz, 15 May 1773; *d* Vienna, 11 June 1859) Austrian statesman. He was born in the Rhineland and fled to Vienna in 1794, where he joined the Austrian diplomatic service. He was posted first to Dresden (1801–3), then to Berlin (1803–6) and finally to Paris (1806–9) before his appointment as Austrian foreign minister (1809). He took Austria into the Fourth Coalition and subsequently presided over the CONGRESS OF VIENNA (1815). He was appointed chancellor of Austria in 1821, but as a foreigner was able to exercise only limited influence over the domestic policy of the Austrian Empire. Metternich was a conservative whose preferred system of government (for Austria and for Europe as a whole) was based on the authority of the monarch backed up by a powerful bureaucracy. His preoccupation as chancellor and as a leading European statesman was the defence of the 1815 settlement against the threat of revolution. He duly sought to eliminate this threat by means of surveillance and censorship, but he also recognized that the pursuit of his conservative aims in the nineteenth century required the reform of institutions. Any aspirations he may have had to reform the administration of the Habsburg monarchy, however, were frustrated by the reluctance of the emperor Francis I (*see* FRANCIS II) to adopt more orderly governmental practices. After 1828 in particular, his influence in domestic politics was reduced by the rise of Count Kolowrath, who became the leading member of the Austrian state council. Kolowrath pressed for reductions in the budgets of the army and police, bodies which Metternich deemed essential to the maintenance of his repressive political system. When revolution broke out in 1848 Metternich immediately became a focus for popular disaffection. He fled to England, returning to Austria the following year to spend the rest of his life in retirement.

A. Palmer, *Metternich* (London, 1972).

TIMOTHY KIRK

Mexican-American War (1846–1848) The war between Mexico and the United States had its origins in the permission granted by Mexico for settlers from the north to colonize Texas in the 1820s, and the subsequent declaration of Texan independence in 1836. In 1844 James K. Polk was elected president of the United States. The following year his proposal to annex Texas passed the Congress, the boundary with Mexico being fixed at the Rio Grande rather than the traditional Nueces River. Polk also invited the Mexicans to sell California and waited for them to provoke war. This occurred in April 1846 with an attack on American troops east of the Rio Grande.

As well as instituting a naval blockade, American forces headed for California and invaded northern Mexico. They permitted SANTA ANNA to return from exile in the hope of his agreement to peace, but after being nominated as president in December 1846 he led an army northwards and fought a stalemate at Buena Vista near Monterrey in February 1847 before returning to the capital. In March American forces devastated Veracruz and marched on Mexico City, which they occupied in September 1847. Santa Anna resigned the presidency and fled into exile, leaving the government of General Herrera (1792–1854) to make peace (*see* TREATY OF GUADALUPE HIDALGO).

RORY MILLER

Mexico The Viceroyalty of New Spain, from which Mexico was formed, stretched from California to the Yucatán, encompassing many different environments: the Indian territories of the northern frontier penetrated in 1800 only by Spanish missions, the densely populated mining and farming areas of the Bajío north of Mexico City and tropical lowlands on the Gulf Coast. The economy and population of Spain's most valuable colony grew rapidly, creating enormous social pressures.

Father Miguel Hidalgo (1753–1811) led Indians and mestizos from the Bajío in rebellion against the viceregal government in 1810. After his defeat the more perceptive Father José María Morelos (1765–1815) continued the insurgency, but Spaniards and wealthy creoles had become alarmed at the threat of social upheaval and supported the counter-revolution directed by General Calleja (1753–1828). Independence in 1821 was essentially a conservative reaction to the liberalization of Spain. ITURBIDE's Plan de Iguala proposed a monarchy, the protection of the church and equal rights for Spaniards and creoles.

Regional differences, ideological conflicts (especially over the form of government and privileges of the church and army), personal ambitions and acute fiscal difficulties made the first thirty years of independence an era of total instability, epitomized by the career of SANTA ANNA. Civil wars and conflicts with Spain, France and the United States (*see* MEXICAN-AMERICAN WAR) impeded continuity in administration and tax collection and wrecked the economy. By 1850 Mexico was effectively dominated by regional caudillos beyond the control of the capital.

In 1855 the Revolution of Ayutla ousted Santa Anna and the conservatives. Two years later the liberals promulgated a new constitution. This precipitated renewed and vicious conflict with the church from which the liberals emerged victorious in 1861. The French invasion and retreat of the JUAREZ government in 1863, however, then provided their opponents with an unexpected opportunity (*see* MAXIMILIAN), at least until Napoleon III withdrew his army in 1867. In fact, foreign intervention permitted Juárez to forge a degree of national unity and finally to discredit the conservatives. After their defeat Juárez and his successor, Sebastián Lerdo de Tejada (1825–89), were able to begin the construction of a more effective state by co-opting or repressing recalcitrant caudillos.

Despite Porfirio DIAZ's successful rebellion in 1876, this process continued. Díaz (president 1876–80, 1884–1911) brought appointments, elections, the army and the police and the award of concessions under his personal control. His policies of 'the carrot or the stick', co-option or repression, were aided by railway construction (around 8,500 miles by 1900) and the rapid economic growth which Mexico enjoyed. Increasing exports (minerals and agricultural products), a developing and more integrated domestic economy (including the expansion of manufacturing and a banking system), growing government revenues and a massive influx of foreign investment brought about a remarkable transformation. But the gains flowed primarily to a small elite and to foreigners; most Mexicans, particularly the Indians and the rural poor, suffered the curtailment of rights to land and political participation, leaving Mexico in 1900, as in 1810, on the edge of a volcano.

Leslie Bethell (ed.), *Mexico since Independence* (Cambridge, 1991).
M. C. Meyer and W. L. Sherman, *The Course of Mexican History* (New York, 1987).

RORY MILLER

middle classes Also known as the bourgeoisie, the middle classes were a variegated socio-economic group based in commerce, finance and manufacturing and including the professions, shopkeepers and (particularly in continental Europe and North America) self-employed artisans. Although socially diffuse, the middle classes exercised increasing economic and political power over the course of the nineteenth century. Prior to 1800 this group was usually referred to as the middling rank or order, a designation of status which placed it between the nobility and commonality. While the older usage lingered on, the term 'middle classes' became increasingly dominant after 1820. The new language of CLASS reflected both a shift in prevalent perceptions and a change in the social order itself.

The ambivalent relationship of the middle classes to Britain's traditional rulers was a central determinant of bourgeois definition and development. Dependent on the aristocracy for patronage, the late-eighteenth-century middle classes were bound to the landed elite in ties of deference. Those relationships of deference were profoundly strained as a result of the Napoleonic wars, conflicts which imposed vastly disproportionate economic burdens on merchants and manufacturers. The enactment of the CORN LAWS in 1815 further galvanized middle-class resentment against aristocratic government, increasingly equated with parasitism and corruption.

An incipient bourgeois consciousness was chiefly manifested by the organization of pressure groups. Aristocratic domination of the state remained the central concern of the politicized middle classes and concerted agitation for melioration culminated in the 1832 Reform Act. That measure marked the entry of a new interest group, principally northern manufacturers, to the political nation. Equally important, it opened the way for municipal reform in 1835, the transfer of power in provincial cities to the rate-paying middle classes. In those surroundings, the proliferation of voluntary societies proved central to the further gestation of bourgeois identity, allowing a divergent class to submerge religious, political and status divisions while extending their influence and strengthening shared ideals.

The early years of Victoria's reign saw the completed articulation of bourgeois ideology and values, both of which dramatically altered British society. Middle-class cultural hegemony was evidenced by the gains of the life-style of respectability among all social strata, with its family-centred social life and insistence on sobriety, frugality, educational attainment, religious observance and sexual propriety. The ascendancy of political economy, after 1850 an unrivalled framework for socio-economic analysis, paralleled the success of bourgeois cultural values. A core of ideas centred on the sovereignty of the market, POLITICAL ECONOMY constituted a universal philosophy of liberty.

Fortified with Evangelical certainty, mid-century middle-class activists registered their political presence by contesting remaining state-mandated restrictions which hindered individual opportunity and market competition. The ANTI-CORN LAW LEAGUE epitomized the crusade-like ethos of the newly confident LIBERALISM. The 1846 repeal of the Corn Laws, that conspicuous bastion of aristocratic monopoly, seemed to presage coming middle-class political ascendancy.

But national power remained elusive as the middle classes found their influence checked by a durable aristocracy, albeit an upper class thoroughly committed to the imperatives of market relationships and virtues of the liberal state. Local politics, especially the urban centres, remained the principal site of bourgeois rule. Given the decentralized nature of the Victorian state, this arrangement placed extensive power in middle-class hands, including local taxation and administration of the Poor Law, criminal law and police. The reform movement of the urban centres illustrated the determination of the middle classes to reconstruct local politics to their own standards, although that process was markedly uneven, a consequence of abiding intraclass divisions. Middle-class rivalries, in fact, dominated urban politics, as the growing ranks of bourgeois Anglican Tories contested Liberal Dissenters and the Victorian 'shopocracy' sought advantage over genteel capitalists. Although dominant, Gladstonian urban radicalism, with its agenda of civil equality, disestablishment and temperance, remained only one current of middle-class political expression.

Bourgeois fragmentation accelerated after 1880 as the expansion of finance capitalism fuelled an explosion of lower-middle-class white-collar occupations. Politically conservative, the drift of this stratum into TORYISM signalled the decline of mid-Victorian liberalism. Concurrently, the protracted process of accommodation and negotiation that had long shaped aristocratic–middle-class relationships culminated in the emergence of a new 'business class' in the upper reaches of society. While powerful class distinctions persisted, the demonstrably pronounced integration of landed, commercial, financial and manufacturing interests indicated that a major restructuring of the British elite had taken place.

Theodore Koditschek, *Class Formation and Urban Industrial Society: Bradford, 1750–1850* (Cambridge, 1990).

R. J. Morris, *Class, Sect and Party: The Making of the British Middle Class: Leeds, 1820–1850* (Manchester, 1990).

RICHARD J. SODERLUND

migration, international The nineteenth century was the age of mass migration. People moved across national boundaries and between continents in larger numbers than ever before. Population flows internationally were particularly marked in the years between 1870 and 1914. Nor was this simply a European phenomenon. Its global character is shown by the fact that in the forty years before 1914 some 4.1 million migrants left India permanently, mainly for Ceylon and Burma, but also for Africa, Mauritius, Fiji and the Caribbean. Five million Chinese migrated to southern Asia, largely the Dutch East Indies and Malaya.

But it was migration from Europe that was the most important, both quantitatively and in terms of economic significance. Some 52 million emigrants left Europe between 1815 and 1930. Their main sources were the United Kingdom (including Ireland) with 18.7 million, Italy with 9.9 million, Germany with 4.8 million and Spain and Portugal with 6.2 million. Their main destinations were the United States, which took 33 million, followed by the Argentine (6.4 million), Canada (5 million), Brazil (4 million) and Australia (3.5 million). Smaller numbers, but carrying wholly disproportionate influence, found niches in Africa and Asia through the European imperial systems. In some countries, such as Algeria or South Africa, the inflows were on a scale sufficient to form white settler societies.

At one level the motivation of these migrants is simple to understand: to achieve a better life for themselves and their families. But it is more difficult to explain the timing and extent of migration, why migrants came more from particular countries or regions of countries than others or how they chose their destinations. Nor is it always easy to comprehend the return flows of migrants to their country of origin. These could be large, as in the case of Italy, or small, as in the case of Ireland.

Causes like famine, economic depression or unemployment play a part in explaining both the extent and the timing of migration. It is no accident, for example, that of the almost 3 million European migrants to the United States in 1845–54, 80 per cent were German or Irish.

These were responding to the mid-century rural crisis in the two countries (*see* IRISH FAMINE). But over the century as a whole, individuals
and families seemed to have been moved not by crisis considerations,
but by calculations involving comparisons of conditions at home and
prospects abroad.

Yet migration was always a selective process. Some people attempted
a new life abroad; others chose to stay at home. Despite the fact that
it must have been in the economic interests of even larger numbers to
leave – income differentials between Europe and the Americas remained wide throughout the century – most opted not to migrate.
There is a further paradox. The most economically advanced countries, and also the most politically liberal, situated in north-western
Europe, also happened to be the most emigration-prone societies. Inhabitants of the poorer regions of southern Europe participated in the
transatlantic traffic in fewer numbers and later in historical time.

Perhaps differential levels of migration are best explained in terms
of 'emigration causing emigration'. Once emigration had started from
a particular country, or from a region within it – for whatever reason
– it made migration easier for later migrants. Earlier emigrants wrote
home praising their adopted land, sent back remittances to pay for the
passages of friends and relatives, arranged employment or housing for
newly arrived migrants and generally eased their passage. This helps
explain the frequently localized nature of emigration whereby whole
localities of, for example, Sicily or Calabria, moved to urban destinations in the United States.

The migration of people from Europe must be seen in conjunction
with the parallel migration of capital. By 1914 some £2,300 million
of European capital had been invested in North America and £1,800
million in Latin America. Together these sums represent a figure equal
to one and a half times the national income of Britain in 1913. Capital
flows enabled the overseas countries to develop their infrastructures,
particularly in the railway systems, more rapidly than they would
otherwise have done. Thus capital provided jobs, and helped open up
the interiors of the new countries. In this way it helped generate exports, particularly agricultural goods, thereby both helping to pay
interest on the borrowed money and cheapening the price of agricultural goods in Europe. This in turn swelled the ranks of migrants, as
small-scale European farmers found it difficult to compete with the
foodstuffs produced in the rich prairies of the United States and Canada,
the pampas of the Argentine or the grazing lands of Australia and
New Zealand. Thus the migration of capital and labour interacted
with each other.

There was no evidence of migration slowing down before the Great
War, rather the reverse. However, by the early twentieth century the
origin of migrants had shifted away from northern and western

Europe to the south and east of the continent. Although temporarily halted during the war, it resumed in the early 1920s. But by this time measures to restrict migration flows were becoming increasingly important. In the United States restrictive immigration legislation was enacted in 1924 and 1927. In totalitarian countries, like Italy, Russia and Hungary, emigration was controlled. But it was the depression of the 1930s that finally stopped the great wave of European migration that had lasted over a century. With falling incomes and high unemployment in the erstwhile recipient countries, the potential benefits to be gained from migration were reduced, and no longer outweighed the dislocation caused by the migrants uprooting themselves from the country of their birth.

Dudley Baines, *Emigration from Europe 1815–1939* (London, 1991).
J. Foreman-Peck, *A History of the World Economy: International Relations since 1850* (Brighton, 1983).

D. S. JOHNSON AND LIAM KENNEDY

Mill, Harriet *see* TAYLOR, HARRIET.

Mill, John Stuart (*b* London, 20 May 1806; *d* Avignon, France, 8 May 1873) English philosopher and economist. The leading liberal intellectual of the nineteenth century, he was inculcated as a child into the principles of political economy and UTILITARIANISM, by his father, James Mill (1773–1836), and by Jeremy Bentham (1748–1832). These profound influences were partially tempered in later life by the romanticism of Wordsworth (1770–1850) and Coleridge (1772–1834), by Auguste Comte's (1798–1857) POSITIVISM and by a commitment to market socialism. Mill produced substantial contributions to philosophy, economics and political theory, insisting on the principles of liberty, free enquiry and inductive reasoning. His radicalism made him a consistent enemy of patriarchal government, both in the state and in the family; in this he was influenced by his wife, Harriet TAYLOR, who contributed to the writing of his most influential work, *On Liberty* (1859), and who also confirmed his feminism, expressed in *The Subjection of Women* (1869). From 1865 to 1868 he was member of parliament for Westminster.

M. St J. Packe, *The Life of John Stuart Mill* (London, 1954).

SIMON DENTITH

Millerand, Alexandre (*b* Paris, 10 February 1859; *d* Versailles, 7 April 1943) French politician and president. A barrister, he made his name defending miners on strike at Décazeville in 1883 and was elected as a socialist to the Chamber of Deputies in 1885. He joined the Waldeck-Rousseau cabinet of republican defence in 1898, which provoked a furious debate among socialists in France and abroad over whether a socialist should join a bourgeois government. Minister on various occasions after 1909, he reorganized state railways and suppressed strikes. He resigned the war ministry in 1915, accused of delay in furnishing heavy artillery. Prime minister in 1920, he applied the Treaty of Versailles and stifled revolutionary strikes. Elected president in 1920, he was forced to resign in 1924 when he tried to make the presidency a more effective office in national politics.

M. Farrar, *Principled Pragmatist: The Political Career of Alexandre Millerand* (New York, 1991).

DONALD SUTHERLAND

Milner, Alfred, first Viscount Milner (*b* Giessen, Germany, 23 March 1854; *d* Sturry Court, Kent, 13 May 1925)   Leading English imperialist administrator and politician. He served in Egypt (1889–92) and as chairman of the board of inland revenue (1892–7) before becoming high commissioner in SOUTH AFRICA. In South Africa he pursued a policy designed to subordinate the Boer republics to British hegemony and from 1898 accepted the likelihood of war to secure this aim. He was responsible for the post-war settlement in South Africa, assisted by a group of young men known as his 'kindergarten'. He retired from public life in 1905, but re-emerged as colonial secretary at the end of the First World War.

V. Halperin, *Lord Milner and the Empire* (London, 1952).

RICHARD PRICE

Mirambo (*d* 1884)   Chief of the Nyamwezi in east Africa. He united various clans, creating a powerful political unit by the 1870s, with his capital at Urambo. By 1880 he controlled the major trade routes to Buganda and to Ujiji on Lake Tanganyika, and generally threatened Arab commercial dominance in much of the region. His strength was based in part on his ability to secure arms, often from Arab traders, and his employment of mercenaries from among the Nguni further south. Sultan Bargash (*c*.1834–88) of Zanzibar, in a rather precarious position with regard to all Europeans, supported Mirambo only until one of Mirambo's client chiefs killed two members of an expedition on behalf of King Leopold II's (1835–1909) INDEPENDENT CONGO STATE. The unity of Mirambo's kingdom did not long survive his death.

SIMON KATZENELLENBOGEN

missionaries   The nineteenth century was an age not merely of unprecedented Western political and economic expansion, but also of the expansion of Christianity from its territorial heartland in European 'Christendom' to Africa, Asia, the Caribbean and the Pacific. South

America was generally seen as part of Catholic Christendom rather than as mission territory. North America, initially a field for Christian missionary activity along the frontier, had itself become by the later nineteenth century a major exporter of missionaries to the non-Western world. Although the term 'missionaries' usually refers to those sent out from the Western churches, much of the work of evangelization was performed by indigenous missionaries or evangelists. Their contribution has left relatively few traces in missionary records, but is receiving increasing attention from historians.

At the opening of the nineteenth century the Roman Catholic Church was in no state or mood for expansion. Rome itself was paralysed, and many of the religious orders that had staffed earlier Catholic missions had been dissolved. The total Catholic missionary force was probably less than 300 in number. In the Protestant churches, however, the missionary awakening had already begun, stimulated by the Evangelical Revival of the eighteenth century, which led to the formation of voluntary societies for the conduct of mission both at home and overseas. The first Evangelical foreign missionary societies were formed in Britain, commencing with the Baptist Missionary Society (1792). The London Missionary Society (1795), Church Missionary Society (1799) and Wesleyan Methodist Missionary Society (1818) followed. The first American foreign-mission organization, the American Board of Commissioners for Foreign Missions, was founded in 1810. Similar societies appeared in Continental Europe, beginning with the Basle Mission (1815).

The Protestant missionary awakening was one influence behind the revival of Catholic missionary endeavour following the re-establishment of the Congregation of the Propagation of the Faith (Propaganda) in 1817; others were the recovery of the Roman Catholic Church itself and the enhanced devotion to the papacy evident in Catholic Europe after 1815. The older missionary orders, such as the Paris Society for Foreign Missions (1663), were revived and grew rapidly. New Catholic agencies were also formed, such as the Society of Missionaries of Africa (the White Fathers), founded by Cardinal Lavigerie (1825–92) in 1868, or, in Britain, St Joseph's Society for Foreign Missions (the Mill Hill Fathers), established by Herbert Vaughan (1832–1903) in 1866. In contrast to the predominant Protestant model, Catholic missionary agencies were not voluntary associations controlled by lay subscribers, but clerical religious orders, controlled from Rome by the Propaganda. By the late Victorian period Roman Catholic missions were again a substantial force, and rivalry with Protestant missionaries (for example in Uganda) was often intense.

During the first half of the century British Protestant missionaries were characteristically drawn from the artisan classes and were relatively poorly educated. The missionary profession carried low social status, and recruits were scarce. From the late 1870s this picture changed. Well-publicized missionary deaths on the field, such as that of David LIVINGSTONE in central Africa in 1873, or the martyrdom of Bishop Patteson (1827–71) in Melanesia in 1871, established the type of the missionary hero firmly in the Victorian romantic imagination. University graduates began to volunteer in large numbers for missionary service, particularly with the Church Missionary Society. Missionary enthusiasm and the broader imperial idealism of late-Victorian Britain increasingly converged, although they never became wholly identified. Parallel trends were observable in Germany during the Bismarck era, and in the United States, where the vision of refashioning the globe through the dissemination of Protestant civilization became an integral part of American national identity.

As a result of these trends, the global Protestant missionary force had grown by the turn of the century to over 18,000. The bulk (70 per cent by 1910) of this force was made up of lay persons. Lay preponderance was a reflection of the growing acceptance since the 1870s of medical missions, and of the increasing dominance in both medical and educational spheres of single women, hitherto excluded from the movement. Approximately half of all Protestant missionaries in 1900 (still the largest single national bloc) were British. The American missionary force was, however, growing more rapidly, and by 1910 would overtake its British counterpart. Both Catholic and Protestant sectors of the missionary movement would continue to expand in the twentieth century.

See also CATHOLICISM, EVANGELICALISM.

W. R. Hutchison, *Errand to the World: American Protestant Thought and Foreign Missions* (Chicago, 1987).
Brian Stanley, *The Bible and the Flag: British Protestant Missionaries and Imperialism in the Nineteenth and Twentieth Centuries* (Leicester, 1990).

BRIAN STANLEY

Missouri Compromise (1820)   In 1819 the territory of Missouri requested permission to enter the union as a slave state. This touched off a year-long heated debate, because northern politicians feared that it would upset the balance between slave and free states in the United States Senate. Led by New York Federalist James Tallmadge (1778–1853), northerners tried to abolish slavery in Missouri. In the end, through the efforts of Jesse Thomas (1777–1853) of Illinois and Henry CLAY of Kentucky, Congress reached a compromise. Missouri joined the union as a slave state, and Maine separated from Massachusetts to become a free state. This action maintained the balance in the Senate. In order to discourage more controversy, Congress also drew an imaginary line at the 36° 30' parallel, and barred slavery above that line in the LOUISIANA PURCHASE. This law effectively removed the issue of slavery in the territories from political debate until the 1840s. By then most Americans viewed it as a sacred pact.

Glover Moore, *The Missouri Controversy, 1819–1821* (Lexington, Ky., 1953).

ALICE E. REAGAN

Molly Maguires (1862–1877) Bleak conditions in north-eastern Pennsylvania's anthracite coal-mines, as well as mine-owners' control of local politicians and judges, led Irish coal-miners to revive the Molly Maguires, a secret society within the Ancient Order of Hibernians. In Ireland the Mollies used extralegal methods in their fight against unjust landlords. In Pennsylvania the secret society used intimidation, arson and murder against the mine-owners. When the miners finally managed to establish a union, and strike in 1875, owners of the Philadelphia and Reading Railroad called in the Pinkerton detectives (*see* PINKERTON DETECTIVE AGENCY). James McParlin (1844–1919), one of the Pinkertons, infiltrated the Molly Maguires, and his testimony to authorities led to the destruction of both the Mollies and the union. After a series of trials, twenty miners were hanged. Public opinion sided with the government and management because of the violence blamed on the Mollies. Many other labour organizations faced similar image problems during the late nineteenth century.

J. Walter Coleman, *The Molly Maguire Riots: Industrial Conflict in the Pennsylvania Coal Region* (New York, 1969).

ALICE E. REAGAN

Moltke, Helmuth Karl, count von (*b* Parchim, Mecklenburg, 26 October 1800; *d* ?Berlin, 24 April 1891) Prussian military leader and strategist. Chief of general staff of the Prussian army from 1857 to 1888, he was an expert on scientific and technological questions and military logistics, and his pioneering use of railways to move troops made him one of the architects of modern warfare. He applied his insights to notable effect in planning the Prussian campaigns of 1864, 1866 and 1870 (*see* UNIFICATION OF GERMANY), and was celebrated for his contribution to the victories of Sadowa (Königgrätz) against Austria (1866) and Sedan against France (1870). Moltke was also notable for his role in transforming the general staff into a major power-base in the Prussian state and later in the German Empire. His desire to prevent politicians placing constraints on the thinking of military strategists was exemplified during the FRANCO-PRUSSIAN WAR of 1870–1, when he clashed with Bismarck and argued, against Bismarck's objections, for a 'war of extermination' against France.

ELIZABETH HARVEY

Monroe Doctrine (1823)   Created by President James Monroe's (1758–1831) secretary of state, John Quincy ADAMS, the Monroe Doctrine became the primary enunciation of American foreign policy during the nineteenth century. Concerned with the status of the former colonies of Spain, which declared their independence during the Napoleonic wars, the United States believed it to be in its best interest to discourage any further European interference in the Western hemisphere. The Americans agreed in their perception of the New World as a haven for democracy, and also saw new markets opening for American goods. In his annual address in December 1823 Monroe proclaimed the new doctrine. In the future, he said, the United States would stay out of the affairs of Europe. At the same time, he warned Europe not to attempt any further colonial ventures in Latin America. This proclamation established the American tradition of isolationism, as well as its often paternal attitude toward Latin America.

Ernest R. May, *The Making of the Monroe Doctrine* (Cambridge, Mass., 1975).

ALICE E. REAGAN

Montenegro   A mountainous region in the western Balkans, Montenegro (Crna Gora, or Black Mountain) was nominally part of the Ottoman Empire from 1499, but enjoyed virtual independence. Since 1697 it had been theocratically ruled by the Orthodox princes-bishops (vladike) of the Njegosh family, and in close foreign political alliance with Russia. During Peter I's (*c*.1747–1830) reign (1782–1830) Montenegro increased its territory in wars against the Turks and Napoleon. Under the rule (1830–51) of Peter II (1813–51), one of the greatest Serbo-Croatian poets, enlightened reforms were introduced. In 1851 Danilo II (1826–60) turned Montenegro into a secularized principality. During the fifty-eight-year long reign (1860–1918) of Nicholas I (1860–1918) Montenegro supported the insurrection of Bosnia-Hercegovina (1875), fought against the Ottoman Empire and by the CONGRESS OF BERLIN (1878) acquired full independence and doubled its territory. Montenegro received a constitutional regime in 1905, became a kingdom in 1910 and joined the Yugoslav kingdom as part of SERBIA (1917).

Christopher Boehm, *Montenegrin Social Organization and Values* (New York, 1983).

MARIA TODOROVA

Morgan, John Pierpont (*b* Hartford, Connecticut, 17 April 1837; *d* Rome, 31 March 1913)   American investment banker. The son of British banker Junius S. Morgan (1813–90), he began his career as his father's agent in the United States. With ties in London and Paris, his firm, Drexel & Morgan (1871), soon became one of the world's leading financial houses. After the failure of rival Jay Cooke (1821–1905) in 1873, Morgan had little American competition. He used his power as an investment banker to promote vertical integration in corporate America, in an effort to make big business more cost-efficient. During the Panic of 1893, he was part of a syndicate that sold gold to the government to prop up American gold reserves. When he sold the bonds he received for the gold at a profit, it only furthered his reputation as a pirate. A noted yatchsman, he also was a benefactor of the Metropolitan Museum of Art in New York.

Ron Chernow, *The House of Morgan: An American Banking Dynasty and the Rise of Modern Finance* (New York, 1990).

ALICE E. REAGAN

Mormons Founded in 1830 in New York state by Joseph Smith (1805–44), the Church of Jesus Christ of the Latter Day Saints, as the Mormon church is officially called, was one of the most important of the new sects issuing from the religious revivalism of the American ante-bellum period. Smith claimed to have received divine revelation from God which he incorporated into the Book of Mormon, an anthology of personal guidance, religious concepts and history which described the native-American Indians as the lost tribes of Israel.

Mormon communities were characterized by a robust economic life, a close-knit social pattern and contempt for other sects, qualities that caused tension with other 'gentile' settlements. Searching for a Zion where they could live peacefully, the Mormons first moved to Kirtland, Ohio, then to Independence, Missouri and then again to Nauvoo, Illinois, where they founded a thriving community of 15,000. A crisis developed in 1843 when Smith claimed to have received another divine revelation, this time justifying polygamy. As a result, the church split, Smith was imprisoned and conflict with non-Mormons turned violent. In June 1844 a mob took Smith from jail and murdered him.

Benefiting immensely from the organizational genius and stern, able leadership of Brigham Young (1801–77), almost the entire Mormon community trekked west from Nauvoo to the isolated Salt Lake basin (1846–7), which Young designated as the new Zion. Using co-operative labour and applying amazing energy to a wasteland, the Mormons transformed the desert into a productive agricultural area. After the Utah Territory was organized, the church remained the dominant political and religious force in the area.

The practice of polygamy, widely reviled in American newspapers, was finally abolished in 1890 as a prerequisite to statehood, and Utah was admitted to the union in 1896.

Wallace Stegner, *The Gathering of Zion: The Story of the Mormon Trail* (New York, 1964).

KEVIN MURPHY

Morrill Act (1862) Sponsored by Representative Justin Morrill (1810–98) of Vermont, the Morrill Act established the American land-grant college system. One of several pieces of Republican economic legislation, it passed Congress and became law only after the southern states seceded from the union. Together with the HOMESTEAD ACT, Morrill Tariff, Pacific Railroad Act and several banking reforms, it formed the 'Second American System', which the Republicans believed would transform the American economy into an industrial power. The act provided a mechanism to use the proceeds from the sale of federal lands to endow at least one college in each state. At these democratic institutions students paid low tuition fees and studied new disciplines, agriculture and the mechanic arts in preparation for practical careers. In addition, in order to overcome the ante-bellum southern advantage in military training, the act provided for instruction in military science and tactics, a programme that later evolved into ROTC (Reserve Officer Training Corps).

William B. Parker, *The Life and Public Service of Justin Smith Morrill* (Boston, 1924).

ALICE E. REAGAN

Morris, William (*b* Walthamstow, near London, 24 March 1834; *d* Hammersmith, near London, 3 October 1896) English poet, artist, designer, writer and revolutionary socialist. Born into a wealthy bourgeois family, he moved from the romantic medievalism of the PRE-RAPHAELITES to political activism and socialism; revolutionary politics dominated the last fifteen years of his life. Prodigiously energetic and inspiring, he had a profound influence on the ARTS AND CRAFTS MOVE-MENT, interior design, printing and English socialism. Partly influenced by John RUSKIN, but also by his later encounter with the writing of Karl MARX, he developed a distinctive social and aesthetic vision, based on an idea of unalienated work which would express the whole range of human powers and enjoyment. His own life exemplified such a vision, through the work of the firm of Morris & Company, and through his writing and political activism, in which a socialist transformation of society was envisaged as reuniting the useful and the beautiful in pleasurable work.

E. P. Thompson, *William Morris: Romantic to Revolutionary* (London, 1955).

SIMON DENTITH

Mpande (*b* Babanango, Natal, 1798; *d* Mahlabathini, Natal, 1872) Zulu king. Mpande was a contemporary of the Zulu king DINGANE, who did not consider him a serious military rival but strongly resented his growing support among the ZULUS. When in 1839 Mpande learned that Dingane was threatening to kill him, he moved into Boer-held territory, where he was recognized as king by both his followers and Andries PRETORIUS. He accepted Boer overlordship not because of weakness, but because he considered resistance futile at the time, and because it freed him to extend his power among the Zulus. His soldierly skills were often belittled – sex, not fighting, is often said to have been his primary interest – but he did maintain the Zulu military organization involving age-banded regiments sufficiently to allow his son CETSHWAYO to use it against the British. Zulu elders named Cetshwayo regent in 1857, the physically and mentally incapacitated Mpande remaining nominal sovereign until his death.

SIMON KATZENELLENBOGEN

Mugwumps   The 'Mugwumps', as their opponents called them, were a reform faction of the REPUBLICAN PARTY in the 1880s. Opposed to the candidacy of James G. Blaine (1830–93) for president in 1884, the Mugwumps rejected the party and voted for the Democratic candidate, Grover CLEVELAND, who won by a small margin. Although 'Mugwump' was actually the Algonquian word for 'great chieftain' (given them by a newspaper in derision), party regulars joked that they had their 'mugs' on one side of the fence and their 'wumps' on the other. Many of the Mugwumps were publishers and editors and had, therefore, more influence than their small numbers might indicate. The Mugwumps encouraged 'good government', even winning some municipal elections and legislative victories. Seeking to ease the corrupt party system's grip on the electorate, they advocated the Australian SECRET BALLOT (then non-existent in the United States), which states began adopting in the early 1890s.

JOHN MARTIN

Muhammad Ahmad ibn 'Abdallah al-Mahdi (*b* northern Sudan, 12 August 1844; *d* 22 June 1885)   Islamic reformer and founder of an Islamic state in the southern Sudan, who proclaimed himself the Mahdi (*see* MAHDISM). Known for his religious zeal and learning, he was a member of a Sufi brotherhood, a mystical religious order. Nurturing grievances against the 'corrupt' Egyptian administration of the Sudan, where religious practices were lax and beliefs mixed with pre-Islamic or indigenous religious teachings, Muhammad withdrew (1879) into isolation and contemplation. Proclaiming himself the Mahdi, or 'divinely guided one', in 1881 (self-proclaimed Mahdi had been appearing throughout north Africa since the tenth century), he launched a jihad, or holy war and founded a religious state by conquest. He came into conflict with the Egyptians and the British, and battle was joined in 1883 at Khartoum, defended by General Charles G. GORDON. In 1885

Khartoum fell and Gordon was killed, leaving Muhammad master of most of the Sudan until his death shortly thereafter. The state survived until 1898.

P. M. Holt, *The Mahdist State in the Sudan 1881–1898*, second edn (Oxford, 1970).

B. MARIE PERINBAM

Muhammad Ali (*b* Kavala, Macedonia, *c.*1770; *d* Alexandria, 2 August 1849)   Albanian officer in the Ottoman army and traditionally regarded as the founder of modern EGYPT. He set in motion Egypt's southward expansion, which by the 1880s had extended into the Sudan, the Great Lakes region, the eastern Congo and the Ethiopian borderlands. Arriving in Egypt with the Ottoman (and British) forces sent to recover Egypt from the MAMLUKS after the Napoleonic invasion (1798), Muhammad seized power in 1811. Establishing a state based primarily on military power, he initiated military reforms relying primarily on French and Italian models. Administrative innovations such as tax and land reforms, together with economic initiatives, including the development of armaments industries, textiles, tanneries and shipbuilding, were established largely to support the army, the mainstay of his power. Muhammad's armies also conquered in the Middle East. Fearful of his growing influence, the European powers forced his withdrawal in 1841. No successor demonstrated the same drive and 'modernizing' skills.

Afar Lufti al-Sayyid Marsot, *Egypt in the Reign of Muhammad Ali* (Cambridge, 1984).

B. MARIE PERINBAM

Muhammad Bello (*b* October/November 1781; *d* 26 October 1837) Sokoto caliph. The son of UTHMAN DAN FODIO, the founder of the Sokoto caliphate in northern NIGERIA, he was born on one of his father's prejihad preaching tours and later, as a child, accompanied his father in such work. Actively engaged in the 1804 hegira, he was the second person then to pay formal homage to Uthman. An intrepid warrior, Muhammad became commander-in-chief of the jihad army in 1808, sealing its success by sacking Alkalawa, the capital of Gobir, and killing its king. Also a principal administrator of the emerging caliphate, the founder of its capital Sokoto and a productive scholar, he was elected 'commander of the faithful' after Uthman's death in 1817. He ruled for twenty years, developing and consolidating the new state, and received the English traveller Clapperton (1788–1827). His descendants still rule the Sokoto caliphate, today the major traditional polity within Nigeria.

D. Murray Last, *The Sokoto Caliphate* (London, 1967).

HUMPHREY J. FISHER

Münchengratz, Treaty of (1833)   Under the terms of the Treaty of Münchengratz, Tsar ALEXANDER I of Russia and Emperor FRANCIS II of Austria agreed to maintain the integrity of the Ottoman Empire and the power of the sultan. A secret article made it clear that the agreement was directed against MUHAMMAD ALI, the hereditary pasha of Egypt, who was in rebellion against the sultan. The two emperors also agreed that their governments would co-operate should any changes occur in the Near East. Prussia subsequently adhered to this agreement, which aroused British and French fears of a second HOLY ALLIANCE.

M. S. Anderson, *The Eastern Question, 1774–1923* (New York, 1966).

GEORGE O. KENT

Murat, Joachim (*b* La Bastide-Fortunière, 25 March 1767; *d* Pizzo, Calabria, 13 October 1815)   French marshal. A volunteer in the cavalry regiments before the Revolution, he later became known for his association with extreme revolutionaries. In October 1795 he commanded Bonaparte's artillery against a royalist uprising in Paris. The next year, he became Bonaparte's aide-de-camp in the first Italian campaign and followed his master to Egypt. In the November 1799 coup he expelled the deputies hostile to Bonaparte's coup. He married Caroline Bonaparte (1782–1839) and in 1809 was made king of Naples. In 1813 he vainly attempted to save his kingdom by negotiating with the allies but was later shot by partisans of the Neapolitan Bourbons. As a soldier he was known for his dashing cavalry charges.

DONALD SUTHERLAND

museums   The prototype of museums was a palace, the Louvre, Paris (1793), the great repository for spoils of Napoleonic conquest and works of art transferring to public ownership in post-revolutionary France. The museum as treasure-house, its private apartments converted to public display, its style deriving from the domestic splendour of an aristocracy, became an irresistible motif. No longer a collection of curiosities, the museum was to become an educational institution, generally in celebration of national heritage and scientific achievement. By the 1830s there were national galleries in most of the major capitals. But the vitality and expansion of local museums should also be noted, particularly in the United States, where Philadelphia, New York and Chicago all had major museums before the formal recognition of the Smithsonian Institution as a national museum in 1881. Other national museums embodied additional values and aspirations. The British Museum new building (1824–47), by Robert Smirke (1781–1867) combined open access with principles of the scholarly retreat and the research collection, typified in the famous Reading Room (1854–7) by Sydney Smirke (1798–1877). It was stylistically related to contemporary German museums – the Glyptothek, Munich (1816–34) by Leo von Klenze (1784–1864), his Pinakothek in the same city (1822–36) and the Altes Museum, Berlin – which identified religious and aesthetic observance within the context of a classical temple motif (*see* NEOCLASSICISM). Klenze's Walhalla, Regensburg (1830–42) outmatched the triumphalism of the Louvre in its fusion of 'Tempel der Kunst' and military celebration.

A romantic alternative to this tendency had been realized in the Dulwich Picture Gallery, London (1811–14) by John Soane (1753–1837). This emphasized the other-worldly by incorporating the mausoleum of its patrons, its architecturally simple but atmospherically powerful environment evoking melodramatic conceptions of an initiation chamber and a tomb of art. When Britain seriously addressed the necessity of housing a national art collection, William Wilkins (1778–1839), architect of the National Gallery, London (1832–8), produced a polite, scholarly building of Renaissance inspiration yet without the dramatic invention of Soane or the cohesive unity achieved by Smirke. Its neighbour, the National Portrait Gallery (1890–5) by Ewan Christian (1814–95), was equally undistinguished except in its restrained use of Arts and Crafts details within a Renaissance context, an eclecticism common towards the century's close. More whole-hearted examples of an Arts and Crafts aesthetic were evident in the Whitechapel Art Gallery, London (1895–1901) by Charles Harrison Townsend (1851–1928), his Horniman Museum (1896–1901) in the same city and the Sezession Palace, Vienna (1898) by Joseph Olbrich (1867–1908). (*See* ARTS AND CRAFTS MOVEMENT.)

The history of museum design is replete with stylistic rivalry, as typified in the otherwise closely related Fitzwilliam Museum, Cambridge (1834–44), a neoclassical design by George Basevi (1794–1845), the Greek-inspired but almost baroque Ashmolean Museum and Taylorian Institute (1841–5) by Charles Cockerell (1788–1863) and the University Museum, Oxford (1855–60) in GOTHIC REVIVAL by Thomas Deane (1792–1871) and Benjamin Woodward (1815–61). Comparable variations occurred in the United States, where the Second Empire French (Renaissance) style of the Corcoran Gallery of Art (first building), Washington, DC (1859–74) by James Renwick Jr (1818–95) gave way to the more restrained, Beaux Arts classicism of its present building (1893–5) by Ernest Flagg (1857–1947), while disregarding the Victorian Gothic affiliations of New York as manifested in the Metropolitan Museum of Art (1874–9) by Calvert Vaux (1824–95).

A tradition originating wholly within the nineteenth century was exemplified in the Great Exhibition of 1851 and its descendants (*see* INTERNATIONAL EXPOSITIONS). Respecting neither romantic nor classical models but expressing the spirit of its technological age, the building popularly known as the Crystal Palace, London (1850–1) by Joseph Paxton (1803–65) embodied an engineering aesthetic considered appropriate for displaying designs and manufactures. Its glazed cast-iron envelope suggesting apparently limitless extension, and its transparency blurring distinctions between interior and exterior environments, it focused attention on exhibition content as never before. It was the antithesis of exhibition building as monument, and gave rise to the practical habit of separating the functional parts of museums, essentially industrial structures of iron (steel) and glass, from their principal elevations which could be dressed in appropriate architectural forms.

Immediate descendants were the community of museums ('Albertopolis') developed for London in permanent consequence of the Great Exhibition. The South Kensington Museum (1859–72) (renamed Victoria and Albert Museum, 1899) begun in Renaissance style by the military engineer Francis Fowke (1823–65), was completed (1899–1909) with a frontage of baroque revival by Aston Webb (1849–1930). The nearby Natural History Museum (1873–81) by Alfred Waterhouse (1830–1905) was nominally Romanesque, though prolifically decorated with figures of animals and prehistoric creatures far removed from the style's official canon. Thus pavilions could masquerade as palaces, temples, tombs or even bestiaries: relieved of structural allegiance to a particular style, late-Victorian museums could splendidly encapsulate the eclecticism of their age.

Jay Cantor, 'Temples of the Arts: Museum Architecture in Nineteenth Century America', *Metropolitan Museum of Art Bulletin*, 28 (1970), 331–54.
Henry-Russell Hitchcock, *Early Museum Architecture* (Hartford, Conn., 1934).
DAVID THISTLEWOOD

music The history of music in the nineteenth century is generally considered as beginning with the Congress of Vienna (1814) and ending with the First World War (1914). The term 'romantic' has been used to describe the music of this era and, even though it is still encountered, most historians now refer more neutrally to 'nineteenth-century music'. The establishment of a 'classic' repertory formed a body of material against which composers during the century measured themselves. Franz Joseph Haydn (1732–1809), Wolfgang Amadeus Mozart (1756–1791) and the early works of Ludwig van Beethoven (1770–1827) were particularly important contributors to this repertory. The musical elements used by these earlier composers formed the basis for nineteenth-century style. Tonality and the eighteenth-century concept of key continued to serve as a primary organizing musical element, but the tendency throughout the century was to explore new tonal relationships and to expand tonal vocabulary. Harmony tended to become richer and more varied, with a higher degree of dissonance whose preparation and resolution became less conventional. Melody grew in importance as an organizational element. The orchestra increased in size and variety with the 'improvement' of existing instruments and the invention of new ones. Mass production and distribution took the piano into millions of homes where it served as the focal point for music-making.

Large-scale musical productions, opera and ballet, were supported in a variety of ways depending on local political and economic conditions. This ranged from the continuation of royal patronage in Saint Petersburg, to bureaucratic control under changing governments in Paris and private enterprise in London. Musicians formed philharmonic societies to promote and perform symphonic music. Chamber music was performed in the salons of nobility, and increasingly in the establishments of music publishers and instrument manufacturers. The formation of choral and singing societies was perhaps the most widespread innovation in organized music-making. These societies engendered new compositions, provided the impetus for major revivals of old music and acted as a means of musical education for large numbers of people.

Beethoven stood at the beginning of the century as the single most powerful figure, whose shadow was cast over the entire period. His early and middle works were easily accepted while his late compositions gained general approval only gradually. These were dubbed 'romantic' for their departure from the established Viennese style, which was called 'classical'. Beethoven's late style included a wider harmonic palette, greater polyphony and an expansive and freer treatment of established forms. The Ninth Symphony (1824) displayed these features plus other new features for this form, such as the linking together of movements thematically and the association of text with the setting of Schiller's 'Ode to Joy' in the finale. Beethoven acted as a source of inspiration and intimidation for the composers who followed, especially those who concentrated on instrumental music.

Gioacchino Rossini (1792–1868) was also a key figure in the early development of nineteenth-century music. His operas gained wide popular acceptance, making him one of the first and few composers to achieve great wealth from his compositions. While the comic operas retain their bright wit and charm to this day, the serious works, noted for their assimilation of the comic tradition, were more influential at the time. A serious opera, *Semiramide* (1823), became a catalogue of Italian operatic forms which served as closely followed models during the first half of the century. The German *Lied* tradition flowered in the early part of the century, with some of the most important contributions by Franz Schubert (1797–1828). His song-cycle *Die Winterreise* (The Winter's Journey, 1828) stands as one of the monuments of this repertory. This tradition continued throughout the period and inspired important song traditions in other countries.

Romanticism in France arrived with the works of Hector Berlioz (1803–69), and in Italy with the operas of Vincenzo Bellini (1801–35) and Gaetano Donizetti (1797–1848). The *Symphonie fantastique* (1830) by Berlioz was linked with a detailed programme which cast it in the romantic mould. The term 'idée fixe', a recurring musical idea with an extramusical association, was most closely associated with this work. The music of Berlioz demonstrated his expertise in orchestration as did his treatise *Grand Traité d'instrumentation et d'orchestration modernes* (1843). He also gave insightful views on contemporary musical life in the music criticism he wrote for various European newspapers which was reproduced throughout the world. This generation of Italians was noted for the melodic content of their music, especially the long expressive melodies of Bellini; the forms remain Rossinian, but the topics reflected romantic literature.

Solo performers of many instruments followed in the footsteps of the violinist Niccolò Paganini (1782–1840), who engendered a movement that revered virtuosity and established the importance of individual interpretation. As a virtuoso pianist, Franz Liszt (1811–86) surpassed Paganini as was seen in his compositions for solo piano, including his *Transcendental Études* (early version, 1839; final version, 1852) and numerous transcriptions of operas and symphonic works. Liszt, a leading member of the so-called New German School, also composed symphonic poems and the 'Faust' and 'Dante' Symphonies (1857). Small poetic pieces developed into an important genre, primarily those for the piano, which became a fixture in most middle-class homes. The nocturnes and preludes of Frédéric Chopin (1810–49) are among the best examples of this music, and *Carnaval* (1834) by Robert Schumann (1810–56) also exemplifies this genre.

Following Beethoven, Schumann and Felix Mendelssohn (1809–47) were among the leading composers of symphonies and choral-orchestral works. Mendelssohn's oratorio *Elijah* (1846), which deeply influenced Protestant church music in England, demonstrated this movement. French grand opera became firmly established with works by the German-born and Italian-trained Giacomo Meyerbeer (1791–1864). His *Les Huguenots* (1836) demonstrated the trade-mark characteristics of this style, which included lavish scenes, dramatic vocal writing and the importance of spectacle. Composers of this genre turned to Eugène Scribe (1791–1861), whose librettos played the drama of individuals against a backdrop of large-scale political and religious strife.

German music during the second half of the nineteenth century was dominated by Richard Wagner (1813–83). His ideas, music and personality combined with his fierce nationalism to create an influence that touched all aspects of musical life. Wagner became known first as a polemicist who described his ideas on music and its future in such writings as *Oper und Drama* (1851, revised 1868). The term 'Gesamt-kunstwerk' summarized his view that all operatic elements, including music, text and stage presentation, must unite for the purpose of musical drama, and that only in this unification could these separate arts achieve the culmination of their intrinsic value. The tetralogy of music dramas, *Der Ring des Nibelungen* (The Ring of The Nibelung, 1876, first complete performance) exemplified these ideas. *Tristan und Isolde* (1865) greatly influenced harmony in the second half of the nineteenth century. By avoiding resolution of dissonance and relying on the pull of tonality to a central key, Wagner illustrated in music the dramatic concept of longing. But many view this score as the beginning of the demise of tonality through the emancipation of dissonance and a high degree of chromaticism, which led ultimately to the atonal music of the early twentieth century. Wagner used leitmotifs as important organizational tools by associating a coherent musical idea with a person, place, thing, concept or any other aspect of the drama. When it recurred, the leitmotif had to remain recognizable, but could be altered or combined with one or more other leitmotifs to create a new dramatic situation.

Giuseppe Verdi (1813–1901) continued the tradition of Italian opera, but reshaped it in a way that brought music and drama into closer alignment. His three operas at mid-century, *Rigoletto* (1851), *Il Trovatore* (1853) and *La Traviata* (1853), still followed Rossinian models but were not as formally rigid, and the moments of dramatic action were more elaborate, with a greater degree of motivic development. Verdi's later operas bore the imprint of his experiences in France and yet retain the overriding importance of melody, an essential Italian characteristic. For example, *Aida* (1871) displayed a great amount of spectacle, a basic ingredient of French grand opera, but it was still clearly an Italian composition. Tito Ricordi, Verdi's publisher, was instrumental in prodding the composer into writing his last two operas, *Otello* (1887) and *Falstaff* (1893), thus demonstrating the increased importance of music publishing in all aspects of musical life. These works had a continuous texture, but moments of dramatic stasis still resembled set-pieces, with the surrounding music functioning as a transition into or out of those moments.

Instrumental music developed, with the introduction of extramusical devices such as programmes and literary titles or associations. Johannes Brahms (1833–97) came to represent a conservative movement which reasserted the value of absolute music. The intellectual framework of this movement was a foil for Wagnerian concepts. Although conservative in name, Brahms used the musical elements of his age and fashioned an approach to sonata and symphonic composition, including a feeling of continuous development, that established him as a master of these forms. His Fourth and final Symphony (1885) was one of the greatest monuments of symphonic literature. The symphony flowered toward the end of the century and produced a repertory that still dominates concert halls, with important contributions from César Franck (1822–90), Anton Bruckner (1824–96), Peter Ilich Tchaikovsky (1840–93), Antonín Dvořák (1841–1904) and many others.

Led by Camille Saint-Saëns (1835–1921), France began to reassert its own musical style around the time of the Franco-Prussian War, and although this provided a new impetus to instrumental music in the 1870s, the French work most remembered from that decade is the opera *Carmen* (1875) by Georges Bizet (1838–75). *Carmen* reflected the changing taste from the spectacle of grand opera to personal drama on a more human scale, and also used exotic, non-traditional elements, in this case Spanish music.

Nationalistic Russian composers also made their mark at this time. The epic quality of their work was seen in the opera *Boris Godunov* (1874) by Modest Mussorgsky (1839–81), and their brilliance in the orchestral piece *Scheherazade* (1888) by Nikolas Rimsky-Korsakov (1844–1908). Remembered as an expert orchestrator, his posthumously published book *Principles of Orchestration* (1913) was the first major treatise on the subject after Berlioz.

By the end of the century composers sought new approaches to their art, but their musical vocabulary remained firmly rooted in nineteenth-century style. In Italy melodrama was heightened in the *verismo* movement, with librettos stressing violent emotions among the working class and a consequent immediacy of musical style. The works of the most important Italian composer of this period, Giacomo Puccini (1858–1924), exhibit many of these characteristics, but his highly complex scores also display other attributes, especially those associated with contemporary music in France. His most popular works are *La Bohème* (1896), *Tosca* (1900) and *Madama Butterfly* (1904).

The French composer Claude Debussy (1862–1918) was a primary figure in the transition from the nineteenth to the twentieth centuries. His aesthetic goals aligned his works with Symbolist poets such as Mallarmé (1842–98) and Verlaine (1844–96), as seen in his orchestral depiction of *L'Après-midi d'un faune* and his opera *Pelléas et Mélisande* (1902), which is a masterpiece of French text-setting. His compositions for piano exhibited a new approach to the instrument and were arguably the most important contribution to that repertory since Chopin. Debussy's music featured non-Western harmonies and the use of non-functional harmony for tonal colour. Notwithstanding the association with literature, his musical techniques led many to compare him with impressionistic painters and he is most closely associated with the term impressionism.

Followers of Wagner at the turn of the century, frequently called post-Wagnerians, included Richard Strauss (1864–1949) whose many symphonic poems demonstrated his mastery of the large late-nine-teenth-century orchestra. His most important modernistic contribu-tions were operas that were adaptations of stage plays, such as *Salome* (1905) and *Elektra* (1909), but his most popular work was the more conservative *Der Rosenkavalier* (1911), based on a traditional libretto. The last great symphonist of the nineteenth century, however, was Gustav Mahler (1860–1911), whose works were noted for their use of vocal and choral forces, for the numerous musical quotations within and between works and for their size and complexity, for example his Eighth Symphony, frequently called the 'Symphony of a Thousand' (1910). The number of performers, however, did not preclude him from writing music of extreme delicacy. This last generation of com-posers expanded tonality to its extremes and explored non-functional harmony. The abandonment of tonality was the single most salient feature defining music at the end of the nineteenth century, and the experiments to replace it marked the beginning of the twentieth century.

Carl Dahlhaus, *Nineteenth-Century Music*, trans. J. Bradford Robinson (Berkeley, Calif., 1989).

Rey M. Longyear, *Nineteenth-Century Romanticism in Music* second edn (Englewood Cliffs, NJ, 1973).

LUKE JENSEN

music hall A popular form of variety entertainment in Britain, music hall grew from a tavern pastime in the early nineteenth century to become the leading form of modern show business by 1900, its rapid rise and commercialization paralleled in the similar institutions of American vaudeville and the French *café chantant*. Thereafter, music hall lost ground to film, radio and, most conclusively, television. As an industry it was dead by the 1950s, though as a distinctive comic style it still survives.

Created by the demands of an expanding urban population in the 1830s and 1840s, the early pub music halls converted their traditional amateur club or neighbourhood sing-songs into regular, professionalized programmes of entertainment, financed by the sale of food and drink. From the mid-century, publican entrepreneurs sought to maximize the new market opportunity by expanding into larger, more elaborate, purpose-built premises with direct charge for admissions. Drink sales remained important to the economy of the new halls, though incurring the hostility of temperance reformers and others who doubted their proprietors' claim to offer improved or RATIONAL RECREATION for the people.

By the first great boom years of the 1860s, music halls outnumbered theatres and were thoroughly commercialized, with big stars on sen-sational salaries, professional songwriters, managers, agents, a specialist press and advertising tie-ins. Heavier capital investment brought the deluxe or variety hall of the 1880s which reproduced the house and stage design of the legitimate theatre and facilitated more spectacular productions. Though it thereby laid further claim to respectability, music hall remained embattled with reformers and licensing authorities over liquor, PROSTITUTION and the alleged indecency of its entertainments. While an undergrowth of small, often still pub-based halls survived, notably in the north of England, rising costs and tougher competition forced out many independent proprietors. By the late century music hall conformed to the general pattern of industrial development in its increasing control by large national and regional combines, whose massive new Empires and Palaces dominated the big city centres and their growing suburbs. Internationally syndicated troupes toured Europe, North America and the white colonies.

As variety entertainment, music hall offered a wide range of acts drawn from folk traditions, fairground, theatre and concert stage, but its most distinctive idiom was the comic song. Commonly an account of some (mis)adventure in everyday life, often romantic, its delivery was much enlivened by the performer's impromptu exchanges with the audience and the use of parody and innuendo. The latter provoked the critics' charge of indecency and led to managerial censorship. Despite these and other controls within the industry, and the increased scale and pretensions of the variety theatre, the great comic stars of the later period, like Marie LLOYD, maintained an active intimacy with their public. Music hall was also frustrated in its bid for respectability by the 1843 Theatres Act which forbade it from staging legitimate drama, though it was later allowed the dramatic interlude or sketch. Increased recruitment from mainstream theatre contributed to the creeping embourgeoisement of the variety profession.

Audiences were predominantly working and lower middle class with a high proportion of single young men and women. The heavy attendance of prostitutes drew in middle-class males on the prowl, but not until the late nineteenth century and the conspicuous improvement of its image and amenities did music hall secure middle-class family patronage. The classic music hall retained much of the informal sociability of the pub, and its promenading and demonstrative crowd provided a show in itself, as well as making its traditional contribution to the chorus. Fixed seating and the reduction of drinking in the auditorium produced a more stabilized and passive audience, and the combines' standardization of entertainment for a national market made music hall a powerful agent in the homogenization of popular taste.

As a prototypical modern entertainment industry, music hall provided an instructive example of the impact of capitalism on POPULAR CULTURE, drawing its product from the self-generating forms of everyday life while packaging and promoting them as a commodity in search of maximum profit. Attacked in its heyday as proof of the degeneracy of modern culture, music hall was later much idealized as traditionally English. In confronting its many myths, modern scholars acknowledge its assertive lower-class character while stressing its aggressive jingoistic patriotism and generally conservative mentality; certainly it was an important, if still not yet fully researched, medium in shaping and reflecting popular values in the nineteenth century.

Peter Bailey (ed.), *Music Hall: The Business of Pleasure* (Milton Keynes, 1986).
J. S. Bratton (ed.), *Music Hall: Performance and Style* (Milton Keynes, 1986).

PETER BAILEY

N

Nanking, Treaty of (1842)   The first Anglo-Chinese War was concluded by the Treaty of Nanking (*see* ANGLO-CHINESE WARS). The first of the 'unequal treaties' between China and foreign powers, it had far-reaching consequences. As well as paying an indemnity, China was forced to open five TREATY PORTS to British subjects where they were free to trade. HONG KONG was ceded in perpetuity to Britain. The restrictive Canton system of trade was swept away, British merchants now being free to trade with whomever they wished under a fixed regular tariff. British citizens would enjoy the right of extraterritoriality. Apart from compensation for opium destroyed in 1839, there was no reference to the drug in the treaty. Nanking was quickly followed by treaties with France and the United States. While the clauses of the treaty were moderate, it did open the way to further demands by foreign powers and was later seen by Chinese nationalists as the beginning of ruthless Western imperialism.

JOHN DAVIES

Napoleon I   *see* BONAPARTE, NAPOLEON.

Napoleon III (*b* Paris, 20 April 1808; *d* Chislehurst, England, 9 January 1873)   Emperor of France. Born Charles Louis Napoleon Bonaparte, the nephew of Napoleon I BONAPARTE, he became the Bonapartist pretender in 1832 on the death of his cousin 'Napoleon II'. He was a thought to be a ridiculous figure. His attempts to repeat the Elba precedent by hoisting the Bonapartist standard at Strasburg (1836) and Boulogne (1840) were fiascos. His chance came with the Revolution of 1848. Monarchists thought they could use him while they tried to patch up their divisions (*see* LEGITIMISTS), so he ran for president in December 1848 with their support. He won by a phenomenal

6 million votes, 70 per cent of the votes cast. He wooed sections of the army into staging a coup in 1851 and the next year a plebiscite ratified the restoration of the empire. Although extraordinarily authoritarian at first, Napoleon III believed he could avoid further revolutions by liberalizing the empire, so that by the Constitution of 1870 France was a quasi-democracy. He was not wrong in this calculation since neither he nor his governments lost a single plebiscite or election between 1848 and 1870. Despite the unprecedented prosperity of the reign, republicans never forgave the coup of 1851 and exploited the disasters of the Franco-Prussian War to overthrow him in September 1870. He died during an operation to remove gallstones.

J. P. T. Bury, *Napoleon III and the Second Empire* (London, 1964).

DONALD SUTHERLAND

Napoleonic Code   *see* CODE NAPOLEON.

Narodniks   *see* POPULISM (RUSSIA).

Natal   Europeans began to move into the British colony of Natal in south-eastern Africa in the late eighteenth and early nineteenth centuries. Two British traders were authorized to set up at Port Natal (Durban) in 1824, and a Cape Colony magistrate was sent there in 1837. The first Boer Republic (Natalia) was established there in 1839 (*see* GREAT TREK) but was annexed to the Cape in 1843. The region's economy was primarily agrarian, sugar and, less successfully, cotton being the major exports. Coal-mining was also important. The port at Durban had difficulty competing with Cape ports and with DELAGOA BAY, relying heavily on its rail link, completed in 1895, with the TRANSVAAL mines.

The most 'British' of the South African territories, the colony was considered relatively insignificant. It became a constituent province of the Union of South Africa in 1910, its relative unimportance indicated by the fact that no centralized government function (legislative, judicial or executive) was based there.

SIMON KATZENELLENBOGEN

national guard   Next to a liberal constitution, a national guard was the single most important objective of the revolutionaries of the period 1815–48, for it was the only means by which newly won liberties could be protected from reaction. At the same time, the propertied classes needed a means of keeping under control the crowds who had actually done most of the fighting (membership was generally restricted by a property qualification). Though the idea can be found in the work of Rousseau (1712–78), practical models were afforded by the

Revolutionary and Napoleonic eras, in the form of the French National Guard of 1789, the civic militia that had guarded the Cortes of Cádiz and the Prussian *Landwehr*. As a military force, however, national guards generally proved of little use, and, with the passing of the 'age of revolutions', they were generally absorbed into the regular forces or transformed into national *gendarmeries*.

CHARLES ESDAILE

nationalism   In its modern form, nationalism – support for ideas and political movements asserting the right of a nation to independence and self–government – is generally traced to the French Revolution and to subsequent reaction outside France against Napoleon's imperialism. During the nineteenth century it played a role of enormous importance, particularly in Europe.

The growth of nationalism depended on the spread of national consciousness, the sense of belonging to a nation. This arose among groups sharing, in various different combinations, a measure of common ground in terms of religion, culture, political history and language. From the late eighteenth century a small number of European intellectuals – historians, poets, philosophers, philologists – helped to develop national consciousness by drawing attention to what was distinctive in the language, traditions, folklore and history of different peoples. The 'romantic nationalists' of the early nineteenth century, of whom the Italian MAZZINI was the most famous, fostered the idea that nationality was the primary source of social identity, more important than allegiance to a dynasty, faith or locality, or membership of an estate or social class. They gloried in the sheer variety among nations, championed the notion that each nation (and especially their own) had an organic life and unique historical mission and developed myths, symbols and a highly charged rhetoric to celebrate the nation.

In most cases the sense of national identity was initially concentrated among an educated and urban minority. It was among this minority that movements campaigning for the political rights of different nations succeeded in mobilizing support. The success of many of these movements, and the rapid increase in the appeal of nationalism, can be understood in terms of three themes on which the assertion of the right of national self-determination played.

The first concerned the untold benefits which the creation of a nation-state, an independent country bringing together and run by and for the members of the nation, promised to deliver. For those who felt themselves to be politically, socially or economically disadvantaged, here was the solution. All the resources of the modern state would be at the disposal of their nation. In every field policy could be designed in the interests of their culture, customs and material well-being. Special status could be given to their language, and with it privileged access to education and to the growing number of posts at the direct or indirect disposal of government. Native producers and entrepreneurs could be protected against foreign competition, regional differences harmonized and the national economy actively developed. The promise of national independence and unification proved particularly attractive among minorities within Europe's multinational empires – those of Russia, Turkey and Austria. The most militant nationalist movement against tsarist rule was that of the Poles, who staged two major uprisings (see POLAND), and by the end of the century nationalist pressure was evident in the Baltic, the Ukraine and the Caucasus. Ottoman authority in the Balkans was eroded by waves of nationalist protest and the empire was forced to cede outright independence to GREECE in 1830 and to ROMANIA, SERBIA and MONTENEGRO in 1878. The Habsburgs were driven from Italy (1859–66), forced to concede internal self-government to the Hungarians (1867), and confronted by mounting nationalist agitation from the other minorities within the empire.

The second key theme of nationalism concerned the rights of the people within the nation-state. The assertion of national sovereignty denied not only the sovereignty of foreign overlords but also the divine right of kings. By extension, nationalism also repudiated the supranational authority of the church, the privileged status of the nobility and the legitimacy of every aspect of the social order not expressly sanctioned by the nation. It was this implicitly democratic dimension of nationalism which lent it such a radical edge in the early nineteenth century. It challenged not only the international order but also the political and social hierarchy. Hence the attraction it exercised over middle- and lower-class urban groups frustrated by the power and privileges of their social superiors. But hence, too, the divisions which affected many nationalist movements, especially in the aftermath of the REVOLUTIONS OF 1848. Relatively affluent and socially conservative nationalists aspired to a nation-state based on constitutional government, civil liberties and equality of opportunity. They took alarm at the much more far-reaching redistribution of power and even property envisaged by their more plebeian and radical allies.

What blunted the social radicalism of nationalism was the third theme on which it played, the need for social discipline and deference if the goal of the nation-state was to be achieved and then defended against foreigners abroad and alien or disloyal elements at home. This was the theme exploited with supreme skill by the century's most important nation-builders, CAVOUR and BISMARCK. They succeeded in projecting the conservative monarchies they served, those of Piedmont and Prussia, as the most effective rallying points for national unification of ITALY (1861) and Germany (1871) (see UNIFICATION OF GERMANY) respectively. In the later nineteenth century it became increasingly common for governments to pursue cultural, foreign and colonial policies deliberately designed to excite nationalist sentiment and rally popular support behind them. Even a government as reactionary as that of the tsars sought to arouse Russian nationalism to supplement traditional loyalty to the monarchy. In Japan bureaucratic elites appealed to nationalism to maintain the social order while undertaking a dramatic programme of modernization to enable the country to withstand political, economic and cultural pressure from Europe's great powers (see MEIJI RESTORATION).

By the end of the century, nationalism was becoming ever more closely identified with the political right in Europe. The foundation of the Second International Working Men's Association (see SECOND INTERNATIONAL) in 1889 symbolized the repudiation of nationalism by much of the socialist Left. But the democratic promise of nationalism was by no means exhausted. Political movements dedicated to the creation of new nation-states would continue to play on it throughout the twentieth century and far beyond the borders of Europe.

Peter Alter, Nationalism (London, 1989).
John Breuilly, Nationalism and the State (Manchester, 1982).
Eric Hobsbawm, Nations and Nationalism: Programme, Myth, Reality (London, 1990).

EDWARD ACTON

National Union of the Working Classes A London-based ultra-radical organization established in 1831, the National Union of the Working Classes (NUWC) attracted Owenite co-operators (see OWENITES), followers of SPENCE, parish radicals, trade-unionists and freethinkers in a move towards a class-based formulation of the radical programme, incorporating 'new' theories and practices, notably general trades-unionism, anticapitalist economics and the language of class. This diverse membership ensured lively debate but precluded united political action during the Reform Bill agitation (see PARLIAMENTARY REFORM), when the NUWC 'stood at ease'. Once the bill was passed, however, the NUWC became confrontational, encouraged by its expatriate Irish members to lead the extraparliamentary protest against the Irish Coercion Act. After the police dispersed the preliminary meeting on Cold Bath Fields in May 1833, the NUWC was forced to abandon militant plans for a national convention to concentrate on workers' political education and press freedom, helping prepare the way for CHARTISM.

JOHN BELCHEM

native Americans see CHEROKEES; GERONIMO; NEZ PERCÉ WAR.

naturalism The meaning of 'naturalism' is now predominantly centred on its use in literary and artistic discourse, but its history before the nineteenth century is relevant both to the meaning of the term and the artistic practices to which it refers. In arguments from at least the seventeenth century, to be a 'naturalist' meant to prefer natural, and therefore not theological, explanations for human behaviour. From the seventeenth century also comes a meaning for 'naturalist' which is almost synonymous with 'scientist', since it alludes to the close and detailed study of nature, especially organic life. This latter meaning of naturalist was a strong one in the nineteenth century and has survived to the present. In the late nineteenth century, however, 'naturalism' came to denote an artistic and especially literary movement, in France, Germany, Britain and the United States. Although much nineteenth-century usage of the term overlapped with REALISM and even with 'impressionism' (see IMPRESSIONISM AND POST-IMPRESSIONISM), it is possible, in retrospect, to distinguish a more precise meaning for 'naturalism'. An artistic practice in novels, drama and to a lesser extent the visual arts, it took as its model the scientific attitude, sought to describe human behaviour in an objective way and took as the sole determinants on that behaviour the heredity and environment that had produced it.

The country in which naturalism was most influential, both as an explicit theory and as a realized artistic practice, was France. This is largely because of the outstanding talent of Emile Zola (1840–1902), whose *Thérèse Raquin* (1867) can be thought of as the first naturalist novel. In his preface to the second edition, Zola defended his novel against charges of immorality by comparing his writing to the activity of a doctor or even a surgeon; his was not to make judgements but to investigate 'a strange physiological case'. Similarly, in the 'experimental novel' *Le Roman expérimental* (1879) the dominant analogy is with science. The naturalist novel was experimental not in the sense of being technically innovative but because it was like an experiment in natural science: a certain set of conditions were established by the novelist, of heredity and environment, and then he would merely observe the results. There were evident flaws in this theory, which ignored the imaginative activity of the novelist, the fictional nature of the novel and the rhetorical weight of its material. But Zola did produce a striking body of novels, including *L'Assommoir* (1877), *Nana* (1880), *Germinal* (1885), *La Terre* (1887) and *La Bete Humaine* (1890), in which human lives were understood in the context of minute description of the particular circumstances that pressed on them, and in the light of their heredity. Moreover, the scientific spirit and some reforming zeal led Zola and other naturalists to pay special consideration to poor social conditions and problematic areas of social life; thus *Germinal* depicted the life of a great mining community, while *Nana* confronted the problem of prostitution.

Partly because of the success of Zola's writing, naturalism was influential on a number of minor novelists in France, and a naturalist phase also marked the writing of Guy de Maupassant (1850–93) and Joris-Karl Huysmans (1848–1907). By the 1890s, however, naturalism was no longer a powerful literary tendency in France. But the prestige of French culture in the late nineteenth century meant that naturalism was influential elsewhere in Europe and America, though later than in France. In England a powerful tradition of realist writing persisted, so that the self-conscious naturalism of Zola had comparatively little impact. The novels of George Gissing (1857–1903) in the 1880s and 1890s shared some of the features of naturalism in their close attention to the often miserable features of ordinary lives, but they lacked the scientific or 'experimental' impulse of French naturalism. Perhaps only George Moore's *Esther Waters* (1894) can fairly be called a naturalist novel; it was a painstaking account of the life of an unmarried mother, given in a way that made no judgement on her but explained her behaviour by attention to the environment which surrounded her.

In Germany and in Scandinavia naturalism found expression more powerfully in the theatre than in the novel. The Norwegian Henrik Ibsen (1828–1906) in a series of mature plays, and the Swede August Strindberg (1849–1912) in his early plays, both achieved remarkable success in using the technical resources of the theatre to show human beings acted on by their environment, in an idiom that might fairly be called naturalist. Their influence, and the wide discussion given to Zola's theories in Germany, contributed to the remarkable success of Gerhart Hauptmann (1862–1946), whose play *The Weavers* (1892) is perhaps the greatest naturalist drama, successfully bringing a social movement to life in powerful and immediate detail. In the United States the influence of Zola was more debatable, but a number of novelists at the end of the century, including Stephen Crane (1871–1900) and Frank Norris (1870–1902) attempted novels in a naturalist idiom that eschewed moralistic commentary and dealt with themes taken from working-class life. Here more than in Europe naturalism remained an important aesthetic tendency well into the twentieth century.

Naturalism was thus a widely influential artistic practice, with an unusually explicit theory, especially in the writings of Zola, to act as explanation and defence of its practice. Its value and importance remain controversial to this day. It was certainly important in taking seriously the lives of people otherwise excluded from art, and treating them in an objective and non-judgemental spirit. The naivety of the theory, in considering writing only as it appeared to reflect a reality beyond itself and not as it might act on that reality, should not obscure the real achievements of the writers in works which often transcended the theory. Its fundamental limitation, however, was perhaps suggested by its very technical success in rendering the actuality of the environments which surrounded the human beings whom naturalism treated. Obscured by this brilliance of surface detail, the underlying determinants of human history were perhaps forgotten.

Lilian R. Furst and Peter N. Skrine, *Naturalism* (London, 1971).

SIMON DENTITH

Navarino, Battle of (20 October 1827)   The last battle of the age of sail and the decisive victory in the war for Greek independence, Navarino was the result of the decision of Britain, France and Russia to impose a mediated settlement on the combatants. Although naval squadrons were dispatched to the Greek coast, the intention was to use peaceful means in the hope that the Turks – the real subject of the mediation – might simply be overawed. However, in the event – to the great embarrassment of the British government in particular – when the allies confronted the much larger Turkish force anchored in Navarino Bay off the western coast of the Peloponnese in the hope of forcing it to withdraw, the Turks refused to submit and opened fire. In the four hours of fighting that followed, they were crushed, losing sixty ships and 8,000 men. The independence of GREECE was now assured.

CHARLES ESDAILE

navies   In the nineteenth century navies were faced with rising costs and technological changes. In 1815 the British fleet of wooden sailing ships enjoyed an unchallengeable supremacy over foreign rivals, a situation unchanged by mid-century despite occasional alarms about the revival of French sea power. Thereafter, the pace of change, from sails to engines fuelled by coal and later oil, and from wood to iron and steel, gathered momentum and was accompanied by the advent of new weapons, including explosive shells and torpedoes. Continuous technical development constituted a permanent challenge to British naval supremacy by threatening to make existing warships obsolete at regular intervals. The threat was exacerbated by the rise of the Japanese and American navies which created threats to the security of British global interests.

C. J. Bartlett (ed.), *Britain Pre-eminent: Studies of British World Influence in the Nineteenth Century* (London, 1969).

A. N. RYAN

Navigation Acts   The earliest Navigation Acts can be traced back to the fourteenth century. From the 1650s they were designed primarily to confer by statute a monopoly of British shipping in the colonial trades, thereby promoting the fiscal interests of government, the prosperity of the shipping industry and the increase, for reasons of both profit and naval power, of the seafaring population. The repeal of the Navigation Acts was associated with a movement in favour of free trade, as opposed to protection, as the key to prosperity. Its principal protagonists in the nineteenth century were David RICARDO, John BRIGHT and Richard COBDEN. The Navigation Acts however did not belong exclusively to the politics of prosperity. Since they were seen traditionally to underpin the prosperity of the shipping industry, they were seen to underpin British naval supremacy. Even Adam Smith (1723–90), the eighteenth-century apostle of free trade, had placed them firmly in the politics of defence. After 1815, however, perspectives changed. Industrial and maritime supremacy seemed to make protective legislation irrelevant to British interests, indeed harmful to them. In his *Statistical Account of the British Empire* (1839) John R. McCulloch argued that the volume of British shipping owed less in the new conditions to protected colonial trades than to unprotected foreign trades. It was because they no longer seemed to serve vital interests that the Navigation Acts were repealed in 1849.

K. Fielden, 'The Rise and Fall of Free Trade', in C. J. Bartlett (ed.), *Britain Pre-eminent: Studies of British World Influence in the Nineteenth Century* (London, 1969), pp. 76–100.

A. N. RYAN

Ndebele Rising *see* MASHONALAND AND NDEBELE RISINGS.

Nelson, Horatio, Viscount Nelson (*b* Burnham Thorpe, Norfolk, 29 September 1758; *d* off Cape Trafalgar, 21 October 1805) British naval officer. He became a national hero in the 1790s through services against France and Spain with the Mediterranean fleet, during which he lost an arm and the sight of an eye. He fought with distinction at the battle of Cape St Vincent (1797) and demolished the Toulon fleet in Aboukir Bay (1798). He reinforced his standing as saviour of the nation by operations against the Danes at Copenhagen (1801). For Nelson, death in the pursuit of glory was not too great a sacrifice. He was struck down on the quarter deck of HMS *Victory* during his triumph over a Franco-Spanish fleet at Trafalgar (*see* BATTLE OF TRAFALGAR).

Tom Pocock, *Horatio Nelson* (London, 1987).

A. N. RYAN

neoclassicism Expressing a complex variety of civic, national, imperial and socio-economic values, ranging (paradoxically) from cultural identification with ancient civilizations to New World emancipation from European regimes, neoclassicism pervaded Western architecture. In so far as it may be separated from classicism – a consistent force in the post-medieval world – neoclassicism may be seen as interposing between archaeological correctness and decorative eclecticism. It shared with the former a dependence on rules of symmetry, proportion and the consistency of classical 'orders'; and it merged with the latter in its admission of motifs of mixed classical descent (Roman, Renaissance, Palladian) and architects' personal interpretations. Representative buildings typifying this aesthetic range include the Altes Museum, Berlin (1822–3) by Karl Friedrich Schinkel (1781–1841); St George's Hall, Liverpool (1838–56) by Harvey Elmes (1814–47) and Charles Cockerell (1788–1863); and *Cumberland Terrace*, London (1826–7) by John Nash (1752–1835).

See also ARCHITECTURE, PAINTING, SCULPTURE.

Robin Middleton and David Watkin, *Neoclassical and Nineteenth Century Architecture* (London, 1987).

DAVID THISTLEWOOD

Newman, John Henry (*b* London, 21 February 1801; *d* Birmingham, 11 August 1890)   Cardinal and theologian. The son of a banker, he underwent an Evangelical conversion at 15. Elected a fellow of Oriel, Oxford in 1822 and appointed Vicar of St Mary's, Oxford in 1828, he inspired in 1833 the OXFORD MOVEMENT to renew the Church of England with the Catholic teachings of the early Christian Fathers. With John Keble (1792–1866), Edward Bouverie Pusey (1800–82) and Richard Hurrell Froude (1803–36), he published the *Tracts for the Times*, which ceased in 1841 when his *Tract 90* raised a storm by reconciling the Thirty-nine Articles with Catholic teaching. He resigned his parish in 1843, and submitted to Rome in 1845, justifying this with the classic *Essay on the Development of Christian Doctrine*. In 1848 he established the Oratory in Birmingham. His rectorship of the Catholic University in Dublin (1854–8) was deemed a failure, though it called forth his *Idea of a University*. His essay of 1859 in the *Rambler* on consulting the faithful was delated for heresy to Rome, which later would not allow him to establish an Oratory at Oxford. He became a public figure again by the triumphant reception of his *Apologia Pro Vita Sua* in 1864 and the conferment of his cardinalate in 1879. His *Grammar of Assent* of 1870 analysed the conditions of religious certitude. His haunting prose works constitute the finest Christian apologetic in English, and his *Dream of Gerontius* about the soul's passage through death was set to music by Edward Elgar (1857–1934).

Sheridan Gilley, *Newman and his Age* (London, 1990).
Ian Ker, *John Henry Newman: A Biography* (Oxford, 1988).

SHERIDAN GILLEY

New Poor Law   The term 'New Poor Law' was used to describe the Poor Law (Amendment) Act of 1834, and also, more generally, the administration of POOR RELIEF in England under the act and its successors. The act changed the arrangements under which poor relief was administered. It required parishes (townships in the north), which had previously been responsible for poor relief (see OLD POOR LAW), to be formed into unions of parishes for this purpose. The Poor Law was to be administered by boards of guardians, elected on a plural franchise that favoured owners and occupiers of large property. Justices of the peace were *ex officio* members of the board. Relief work was to be undertaken by salaried relieving officers. The guardians were under the supervision of three Poor Law commissioners sitting in London and their peripatetic assistant commissioners. Originally, each parish paid the cost of outdoor relief of their own poor and a contribution to the cost of institutional relief for the union as a whole. After the Union Chargeability Act (1865) the cost of all poor relief was borne equally by the component parishes of the union. This was an important change in what was known as a settlement, that is the claim to poor relief in a particular community. The relevant community had been the parish; henceforth it was the union, roughly twenty times as large. This did something to take account of migration. But migration was not confined to the immediate neighbourhood. The difficulties experienced by immigrants in establishing a claim on the community should have acted as a bar to more distant migration; there is little evidence that this was so.

The act cannot be understood apart from the policy prescriptions contained in the report of the Royal Commission on the Poor Laws (1832–4). The most important related to the treatment of able-bodied men. To ensure the discontinuance of the older practice of giving relief in aid of wages, these were not to be relieved except in a workhouse (see WORKHOUSES). To deter applications from all but the destitute, conditions in the workhouse were to be 'less eligible' than those of the poorest independent labourer. In practice, this use of the 'workhouse test' proved impracticable. Relief in the workhouse was more expensive than relief at home. In manufacturing areas guardians were unwilling to build workhouses capable of housing all those who might apply for relief in times of depression. By 1852 they were permitted to provide outdoor relief if combined with a deterrent labour test. This concession did not apply to agricultural areas. Here the seasonal nature of agricultural work, particularly in areas of tillage, also produced numerous applicants for poor relief at certain periods. Research suggests that guardians preferred to relieve them more economically at home and disguised the fact from the central Poor Law authority by including them among the sick. Central-authority control over boards of guardians was far less than had been envisaged by the Royal Commission. The limited powers available did not produce the desired uniformity. It left guardians, among whom employers were strongly represented, much discretion to adapt relief policy to the requirements of the local labour market.

Great emphasis was placed on the classification of paupers with the intention of devising different forms of relief for different categories. Gradually, specific policies were designed to meet the needs of the sick and infirm, at first through the development of a Poor Law medical service and after 1860 increasingly through the separate treatment of the sick in the workhouses. A similar emphasis led to the establishment of workhouse schools in the 1840s and to more dispersed residential provision later. These developments led to increasing expenditure: £4.9 million, or 5s. $5\frac{1}{2}d$. per head of population, in 1852; £8 million, or 6s. $11\frac{1}{2}d$ per head, in 1872. This in turn led to greater insistence on deterrence, not only for the able-bodied but now also the aged and infirm. By the end of the century there was widespread doubt whether deterrence was suited to those who had little control over the circumstances that led to their destitution. The first result was the Medical Relief (Disqualification) Act (1885), which removed the loss of voting rights from those using the Poor Law medical services. But by then deterrence operated not only through external mechanisms. After two generations of Poor Law policy, most of the poor regarded the need to apply for poor relief as a matter of deep shame.

Anne Digby, *The Poor Law in Nineteenth Century England and Wales* (London, 1982).

E. P. HENNOCK

newspapers During the nineteenth century newspapers began to circulate widely and to fulfil their primary function of collecting and reporting the news. This growth of the press reflected significant economic and cultural changes, particularly in the United States and Britain. Literacy expanded greatly in both countries, creating a large potential readership. The technology of PRINTING likewise improved, making possible an increase in the speed and quantity of newspaper production. Expanded consumer demand also created an advertising base which transformed the commercial structure of the press.

At the beginning of the century newspapers were generally restrained in make-up and content. Their circulations were small and they ignored feature stories, concentrating instead on political and international news. Their leader columns occupied a disproportionate amount of space, reflecting a widespread belief in the traditional pedagogical function of journalism. Most of the nineteenth-century innovations in the press occurred first in the United States. There penny daily papers appeared in the 1830s, including James Gordon Bennett's (1795–1872) pioneering *New York Herald*. Bennett won a large circulation for the *Herald* by focusing on extensive coverage of the news. He hired teams of reporters to write about local and national news and emphasized the necessity for speed in getting the information to readers. He also specialized in aggressive crime-reporting, a departure from the accepted model except in the disreputable police gazettes of the period. During the American Civil War a further stimulus was given to news-reporting when hundreds of correspondents were sent to write about battles and war events with a human appeal. For the first time, news was telegraphed extensively, a major breakthrough; it was also frequently printed on the front page, still another innovation.

In Britain changes occurred more slowly, notwithstanding the detailed disseminating of political news in influential papers like *The Times* and the *Morning Chronicle*. The stamp duty on newspapers and other 'taxes on knowledge' hampered the growth of circulation. When the remaining penny duty was finally removed in 1855, numerous cheap provincial and London newspapers sprang into existence, including the *Liverpool Daily Post* and (as a daily newspaper) the *Manchester Guardian*. One of the most significant of the new penny papers was the *Daily Telegraph*, whose concentration on feature-writing and condensed news coverage presaged the emergence of popular journalism. Within a few years it amassed a circulation in the hundreds of thousands. The Crimean War and the Franco-Prussian War of 1870 also gave a stimulus to the expansion of the press. Special correspondents such as William H. Russell (1821–1907) of *The Times* and Archibald Forbes (1838–1900) of the *Daily News* reported from the battle fronts in an iconoclastic style that the public admired.

From the 1870s, significant changes in newspapers began to take place and a popular press came into existence with most of the departures from convention continuing to originate in the United States. The typography and substance of newspapers were revolutionized and their price was lowered, reflecting the interest of an expanding middle-class and working-class readership. Multidecked headlines came to be employed, as did pictorial features. The 'inverted pyramid' method of writing a news story replaced the lengthy, free-flowing, traditional narrative structure. Human interest came to be stressed, with gossip, sport, crime, women's features and personal interviews filling up entire sections of newspapers and increasingly superseding leaders, particularly in the United States. As the size and organizational complexity of newspapers increased, professional reporters and editors were hired to replace the freelance contributors and 'penny-a-liners' who had dominated journalism until then.

Among the foremost creators of this 'new journalism', as it came to be known in Britain ('yellow journalism' was the more common term in the United States), were Joseph Pulitzer (1847–1911), William T. Stead (1849–1912), William Randolph HEARST and Lord NORTHCLIFFE. Pulitzer was the most successful of the four in breaking free from the 'mediocre and conventional', and his innovations in every area of

journalism set a new standard. Like Stead, he fused democratic instincts with an aggressive desire to make profits. His first crusades
against big corporations, urban political corruption and the evils of the
white slave trade paved the way for American newspaper-muckraking,
which was relatively unhindered by the kind of tight libel laws existing
in Britain. Stead's analogous efforts in Britain included a series of
sensational articles exposing child prostitution, which appeared in the
Pall Mall Gazette in 1885. Hearst's contributions to the development
of a mass press in America were even more spectacular. They were
characterized by banner headlines, exaggerated and fabricated news
accounts and a seemingly insatiable penchant for popular sensationalism,
especially crime news. These innovations profoundly influenced the
design and content of newspapers, not only in the United States and
Britain, but throughout the world.

By 1900 newspapers had become transformed out of recognition to
their forebears of a century before. Improvements in technology and
better methods of communicating and distributing news and newspapers made this revolution possible. Press agencies like Reuters, the
Associated Press and Havas (based in Paris) collected and sold news
everywhere. A readership in the millions existed, which encompassed
the full range of social and educational gradation. The Fourth Estate
had come of age at last and the era of mass newspapers had begun.

Lucy Brown, *Victorian News and Newspapers* (Oxford, 1985).
G. A. Cranfield, *The Press and Society: From Caxton to Northcliffe* (London,
  1978).
Edwin Emery and Harry Ladd Smith, *The Press and America* (New York, 1954).

JOEL H. WIENER

new unionism In the late 1880s trade-union organization in Britain
expanded to previously unorganized workers. In 1888 trade unions
were almost entirely confined to the skilled craft workers. There had
been strikes and waves of union organization among the unskilled
workers before – the gas-workers of London conducted a two-week
strike in 1872, for example – but these short-lived efforts did not have
the dramatic impact of the events of 1888–91.

Union organization among unskilled labourers (*see* UNSKILLED LABOUR)
and seamen began in the north-east in 1886. London gas-workers
staged a series of successful strikes in 1886 and 1887 before rapidly
unionizing and achieving the eight-hour day and other concessions in
the summer of 1889. At the same time, a strike of match-girls at
Bryant & May's factory in the summer of 1888, and of seamen in the
north of England in early 1889, encouraged organization among
dockers. The five-week strike of London dockers in the summer of 1889
for a wage increase (the 'docker's tanner'), however, is usually taken
as the real beginning of the new unionism.

The London DOCK STRIKE was conducted with great flair by John Burns (1858–1943), Tom Mann (1856–1941) and Ben Tillett (1860–1943) and the mass demonstrations of orderly dock workers in the centre of London, the public intervention of Cardinal Manning and the obduracy of the dock-owners caught the public imagination. The success of the London gas-workers and dockers sparked a wave of strikes and organization among gas-workers, transport workers, cab drivers and various classes of general labourers in the provinces so that by 1890 the leading new unions were estimated to have 350,000 members.

Four elements seem to have underlain this explosion of militancy and organization. First, the timing owed much to the upswing in the trade cycle beginning c.1886, which lowered unemployment and provided the right conditions to allow workers to act on accumulated grievances. Thus, this period also saw an increasing militancy among coal-miners and railwaymen. Secondly, changes within the division of labour and structure of work created the necessary degree of occupational skill and stability to make union organization feasible among groups like gas-stokers. Thirdly, the issue of poverty and labour-market instability were the subject of much political debate and sociological enquiry. There was a renewed public sympathy for the plight of the poor. And, fourthly, a cadre of socialist militants existed who were eager to lend their organizational talents to the unskilled. Annie Besant (1847–1933) led the match-girls, and the gas-stokers and dockers were led by John Burns and Tom Mann, who were skilled engineers and members of the SOCIAL DEMOCRATIC FEDERATION.

The new unionism, however, was short-lived. After initial concessions, employers mobilized for a counter-attack, which in some cases began as early as 1890 but whose full force was felt by 1892 when worsening economic conditions undermined union membership. The key defeat of the new unions was on the docks, where employers used 'free labour' to break strikes, and by 1893 many of the unions had disappeared and membership had fallen to about 140,000. But other unions were not destroyed, and some even continued to secure gains throughout the 1890s. Those unions that survived did so by abandoning their original objective of GENERAL UNIONISM and retreating into their core strengths of semi-skilled workers with some skill scarcity and occupational stability.

The new unionism, however, had a lasting importance in two ways. First, it opened the debate within the labour movement about socialism and independent labour politics. The new-unionist spokespersons were able to win some significant victories within the TRADES UNION CONGRESS, hitherto dominated by conservative craft unions. At the local level, the new unions began to transform municipal politics by securing representation on school and Poor Law boards. Secondly, it laid the foundations for a permanent expansion of trade-union organization that was to occur again just before the First World War.

H. A. Clegg, Alan Fox and A. F. Thompson, *A History of British Trade Unions since 1889* (Oxford, 1964), pp. 55–96.
John Lovell, *Stevedores and Dockers* (London, 1969).
Henry Pelling, *The Origins of the Labour Party 1880–1900* (Oxford, 1965), pp. 13–39.

RICHARD PRICE

New Zealand Known by the Maoris as Aotearoa, New Zealand was regarded by Britain as an offshoot of New South Wales until 1840, when the North Island was annexed by the TREATY OF WAITANGI and the South Island by right of discovery. In the absence of Maori cartography, European exploration continued into the 1860s. Between 1840 and 1896 the Maori population, already declining, fell from 60,000 to 42,000 while the European population grew from 2,000 to 700,000. Traders, sealers, whalers and missionaries were joined by sheep farmers in the 1850s. Gold discoveries in Otago and on the West Coast in the 1860s added to the South Island's economic dominance.

Systematic colonization by the New Zealand Company in the 1840s brought friction between government and settlers over land (*see* MAORI WARS), but the colony progressed rapidly from representative to responsible government. The 1852 Constitution Act created provincial councils and a central parliament (in which Maoris were allocated four seats from 1867). Financially unstable, provincial governments were abolished, and a development boom hastened centralization under Julius VOGEL. A collapse in export prices brought debt and destitution in the period 1879–95, but in the late 1890s refrigerated shipping enabled dairying to prosper. Near-universal male suffrage was introduced in 1879 and votes for women in 1893. Trade-unionism and the advent of a liberal government in 1891 fostered state involvement in land settlement, industrial protection and social provision. Responding to European dominance, Maoris promoted religious cults, notably Pai Marire and Ringatu. By 1900 young Maoris were reasserting Maori identity while accepting assimilation into the capitalist economy. Economically dependent on Britain, New Zealanders propagated imperialism and their own Pacific role.

Miles Fairburn, *The Ideal Society and its Enemies: The Foundations of Modern New Zealand Society, 1850–1900* (Auckland, 1989).
Keith Sinclair (ed.), *The Oxford Illustrated History of New Zealand* (Auckland, 1990).

MICHAEL C. PUGH

Ney, Michel (*b* Sarrelouis, 10 January 1769; *d* Paris, 7 December 1815) French marshal. His career began as a volunteer in the hussars, but vegetated until the Revolution. He was a general by 1796, fought in southern Germany and Switzerland in 1799 and played a major role in the victory at Hohenlinden, in Prussia, in 1800, which helped consolidate Bonaparte's dictatorship. He was made marshal in 1804, duke in 1808 and prince of Moskwa after the Russian campaign of 1812. He persuaded Napoleon to abdicate at Fontainbleau in 1814, claiming, quite disingenuously, that the troops would no longer fight. At first he served Louis XVIII, and on hearing of Napoleon's escape from Elba promised the king to bring the ogre to Paris 'in an iron cage'. On reading one of Napoleon's proclamations, however, he underwent an emotional crisis and joined him instead. He fought bravely at Waterloo and was shot for treason in December 1815. Napoleon called him the 'bravest of the brave'.

DONALD SUTHERLAND

Nez Percé War (1877) In 1855 the governor of the Washington Territory, Isaac Stevens (1818–62), negotiated a treaty granting the Nez Percé a reservation about half the size of their claimed lands. With the discovery of gold on Orofino creek in 1860, whites swarmed on to Nez Percé lands. In 1863 the government – anxious to protect the miners – purchased the gold-fields, reducing the size of the reservation by three-quarters. Nez Percé cattlemen and buffalo-hunters, approximately a quarter of the tribe, led by Chief Joseph (c. 1840–1907) opposed the treaty and remained off-reservation. Following CUSTER's defeat at Little Big Horn, federal officials and the public clamoured for the return of all native Americans to reservations, and this caused tension with the Nez Percé. In June 1877 young Nez Percé warriors killed nineteen whites, and the commander of the army in the area, Major General Oliver O. Howard (1830–1909), sent Captain David Perry (1841–1908) and two cavalry companies after Chief Joseph's band encamped in White Bird Canyon. Although greatly outnumbered, the Nez Percé soundly defeated Perry's men and, a short while later, a force of 400 men – complete with a howitzer and Gatling guns – led by Howard. The Nez Percé, numbering 145 warriors and 500 non-combatants, resisted capture and fled more than 1,300 circuitous miles in an attempt to reach Canada. On 5 October 1877, over three and a half months after the first hostilities, Chief Joseph finally surrendered to Colonel Nelson A. Miles (1839–1925), just 30 miles from freedom in Canada. 'From where the sun now stands,' Chief Joseph supposedly stated, 'I will fight no more forever.'

Merrill D. Beal, '*I Will Fight No More Forever': Chief Joseph and the Nez Percé War* (Seattle, 1963).
Mark H. Brown, *The Flight of the Nez Percé* (New York, 1967).

JOHN MARTIN

Nien [Nian] Rebellion One of several serious rebellions which almost brought about the collapse of the Ch'ing dynasty in the middle of the nineteenth century, the Nien (Nian) Rebellion was roughly contemporary with the Taiping (*see* TAIPING REBELLION) and Muslim Rebellions of south-west and north-west China. Nien ('band') was the name given to secret-society and bandit gangs living off plunder in northern China in the late eighteenth and early nineteenth centuries. In 1853 uncoordinated Nien bands rose in support of the Taipings. Their most powerful leader was Chang Lo-hsing (*d* 1863), who followed the Taipings' military system and frequently co-operated with them. However, unlike the Taipings, they had no distinctive religious beliefs, clear political goals or ideology, and lacked unified leadership. In 1855 the poorly organized Nien bands were divided into five bands. They employed guerrilla tactics, surprise attacks and swift cavalry movements.

The Ch'ing, having failed over several years of fighting to suppress the Nien, eventually used the formidable Mongolian leader Prince Seng-ko-lin-ch'in (*d* 1865) against them. Although the Nien leader, Chang, was killed in 1863, the movement continued, strengthened by Taiping remnants in 1864. Seng was killed in battle in 1865, being replaced by TSENG KUO-FAN. Tseng's Hunan army, however, failed to defeat the Nien, in over a year's fighting. In 1867 he handed over the operations to LI HUNG-CHANG. By the end of 1867 Li, in a fierce war of attrition, had succeeded in defeating the eastern band of the Nien and in consolidating his own political career. However, it was not until 1868 that the rebellion was completely suppressed by troops under the command of the new imperial commisioner, Tso Tsung-t'ang. (*d* 1865).

Although it was finally suppressed, the rebellion had severely damaged the prestige of the Ch'ing dynasty.

A. Feuerwerker, *Rebellion in Nineteenth Century China* (Ann Arbor, Mich., 1975).

JOHN DAVIES

Nicholas I (*b* Tsarskoe Selo, 25 June 1796; *d* St Petersburg, 18 February 1855) Tsar of Russia (1825–55). The younger brother of Alexander I, he was poorly educated, but was honest and had a strong sense of duty. His reign is remembered for its reactionary character, initially influenced by his savage treatment of the DECEMBRISTS. His suppression of the Polish uprising of 1830–1 and his determination that the revolutions of 1848 would not spread to Russia highlighted his suspicious and repressive behaviour. The powers of the police were increased and censorship intensified. He did, however, codify the laws, improve the economy, prohibit the sale of serfs without land and virtually free all those owned by the crown. His unbending foreign policies were largely successful but ended in the debacle of the CRIMEAN WAR, which proved to many the corruption and inefficiency of his government.

N. V. Riasonovsky, *Nicholas I and Official Nationality in Russia, 1825–55* (Berkeley, Calif., 1955).

A. V. KNOWLES

Nicholas II (*b* St Petersburg, 6 May 1868; *d* Ekaterinburg, 17 July 1918)   Last tsar of Russia (1894–1917). The son of Alexander III and cousin of George V of England, he was a charming, intelligent and extremely patriotic man, but also weak-willed and reactionary. In his speech to the Tver zemstvo on his accession he asserted his intention of upholding the principles of autocracy, but after the revolution of 1905 was forced to grant a constitution with a legislative assembly (Duma). On the outbreak of the First World War he became commander-in-chief of the armed forces and left the government of Russia to his wife. After the February Revolution in 1917 he was asked to abdicate and, to everyone's surprise, agreed. He and his family were assassinated in 1918 by the Bolshevik secret police on the orders of Lenin.

R. Charques, *The Twilight of Imperial Russia* (London, 1958).

A. V. KNOWLES

Nietzsche, Friedrich (*b* Röcken, Saxony, 15 October 1844; *d* Weimar, 25 August 1900)   German philosopher and critic of culture. An incandescent, Faustian personality and an antisystematic, aphoristic thinker, Nietzsche was one of the first to confront honestly the nineteenth-century loss of faith in God and absolute values in the wake of the Enlightenment and empirical science. Perhaps his best-known and most influential work is *Also Sprach Zarathustra* (1883–92), which he himself called 'the deepest book that mankind possesses'. In all his works his critical diagnosis of Western culture is vastly more convincing than his positive doctrines.

He attacked both Christianity as a 'slave mentality' fostering meekness and dependence, and the tradition of corrosive Socratic reason as the destroyer of the tragic grandeur and heroic values of the Greeks; and sounded a fatefully influential antidemocratic note with his scornful dismissal of 'herd values'. The driving force of all human behaviour is 'the will to power'. The modern age requires a 'revaluation of all values' based on the unbridled assertion of their Titanic wills by a series of creative personalities comparable with Goethe, Napoleon, and Cesare Borgia. These indomitable *Übermenschen* will not discover but will freely create values and treat ordinary men and women as material for their schemes. Ever-changing aesthetic and voluntaristic categories thus come to usurp the role traditionally played by those of universal reason and empirical knowledge. Relativism and 'perspectivism' in thought and practice become dominant.

Nietzsche's impact on subsequent European literature has been incalculably great and his emphasis on unconscious forces makes him a precursor of Freud (1856–1939). He was misappropriated by much Fascist and right-wing thought, and a complete edition of his works was presented by Hitler to Mussolini on the Brenner Pass.

ROGER HAUSHEER

Nigeria   The name 'Nigeria' was coined in 1898 by the journalist Flora Shaw (1852–1929) (later wife of Baron Lugard (1858–1945), British governor-general of Nigeria) for the territories acquired by Britain on and adjoining the valley of the River Niger in West Africa. It was officially adopted in 1900. This area was a major focus for British trade, initially for slaves and later (especially after the banning of the slave trade in 1807) for palm oil, the delta of the Niger being known to British traders as the 'Oil Rivers'. It also became an area of British missionary enterprise from the 1840s onwards. The British government was drawn into interference in the area in order to suppress illegal slave-trading, protect missionaries and promote the new trade in palm oil. Britain annexed the port of Lagos (later the capital of Nigeria), on the coast west of the Niger, in 1861, but was initially reluctant to extend its formal authority over the rest of the region. Fears of encroachment by France and Germany, however, led to the declaration of a British protectorate over the entire 'Niger Districts' in 1885. Initially, this region was administered as three separate colonial territories: the Lagos Colony and Protectorate (incorporating YORU-BALAND in the immediate hinterland of Lagos) to the west; the area around the lower Niger, originally known as the Oil Rivers Protectorate (renamed the Niger Coast Protectorate in 1894, and Southern Nigeria in 1900), to the east; and the middle Niger area in the interior, which was originally administered by the Royal Niger Company (granted a charter for this purpose in 1886), but was taken under direct government rule (and renamed the Protectorate of Northern Nigeria) in 1900. Lagos was incorporated into Southern Nigeria in 1906, and Northern and Southern Nigeria amalgamated to form a single colony in 1914.

See also ROYAL NIGER COMPANY.

Michael Crowder, *The Story of Nigeria*, second edn (London, 1966).

ROBIN LAW

Nightingale, Florence (*b* Florence, 12 May 1820; *d* London, 13 August 1910)   English nurse, known as the 'Lady with the Lamp' for her service during the CRIMEAN WAR. She enjoyed a privileged life of ease as the daughter of a wealthy gentleman, but struggled to find a useful career that would also meet with her family's approval. The conflicts generated by her aspirations sometimes plunged her into despair until her 1854 appointment to lead a group of nurses to the Crimea liberated her from her family's demands. After her return, Nightingale's prestige enabled her to transform nursing into a respectable profession for women as well as to do important work on behalf of the cause of army reform. Her *Notes on Hospitals* and *Notes on Nursing*, published in 1859, stood as concise and lucid statements of nursing practice for many years, and she became an emblem of idealized Victorian womanhood.

Cecil Woodham-Smith, *Florence Nightingale, 1820–1910* (London, 1951).

GAIL SAVAGE

Nonconformity Consisting of the Protestant Dissenters of England and Wales who worshipped outside the established Church of England, Nonconformity had traditionally comprised 'the three denominations', the Presbyterians, Independents and Baptists. The Presbyterians had generally become 'rational Dissenters', repudiating Trinitarian orthodoxy, and from 1813 were able to avow themselves UNITARIANS. They formed the elite of Nonconformity, attracting only 0.2 per cent of the population to their services in 1851 but nourishing able civic and intellectual leaders. They stood apart from the orthodox Presbyterians, largely of Scottish origin, who also drew 0.2 per cent. The Independents (attracting 4.4 per cent), who increasingly preferred to be called Congregationalists, drew their names from their belief in the independence from all external authority of individual congregations. Each local church, though led by ordained ministers and lay deacons, was governed by the church meeting, where all members could assemble. The prevailing theology of the Congregationalists gradually shifted during the nineteenth century from a moderate Calvinism to a more liberal form of EVANGELICALISM. The Baptists (drawing 3.3 per cent of the population in 1851) were identical to the Independents except that they practised not infant baptism but the baptism of believers by total immersion. When some Baptist churches began to admit to communion people who had not been baptized as believers and moderated their Calvinism, their more rigid contemporaries became known as Strict and Particular Baptists. The New Connexion of General Baptists, which shared the non-Calvinist theology of METHODISM, merged with the Baptist mainstream in 1891. During the nineteenth century the Methodists, the QUAKERS and a number of smaller groups were also usually regarded as Nonconformists.

Dissent spread in the early years of the century through a vigorous campaign of itinerant evangelism that planted chapels in villages wherever it was not resisted by squire and parson. Its structures were also readily adaptable to the growing towns. Consequently, by 1851 Nonconformity possessed nearly half the church-goers. Despite a slackening recruitment rate later on, in 1901 some 15 per cent of the population still attended the chapels. While Unitarians had only a single congregation in most large towns and popular strength only in Lancashire, Congregationalists and Baptists were particularly powerful in a band from East Anglia through the south Midlands to the West Country and south Wales. Although the lay leaders were often prosperous industrialists and well-to-do shopkeepers, Nonconformity attracted a large number of artisans, and even late in the century many chapels were supported overwhelmingly by the respectable working classes. Men seem to have attended services as much as women, but fewer men took the decisive step of becoming members. Children were catered for by the flourishing Sunday schools, and sometimes, especially in the middle years of the century, by day schools attached to the chapels. Ministers, though usually trained in theology, were generally poorly paid. Their sermons were central to worship, which tended to become more formal as time went on. Chapel life also embraced a range of organizations for evangelism, sick-visiting, charitable work, bazaars, music and self-improvement. Many families found in its plethora of activities their chief social outlet.

The repeal of the TEST AND CORPORATION ACTS in 1828 ended a period when Nonconformity had normally been politically quiescent. Many chapel-goers were enfranchised in 1832, and the Congregational and Baptist Unions, created in 1831 and 1832, were national bodies designed partly to watch public affairs. Throwing off the restrained leadership of the Unitarians, the more radical Nonconformists began to agitate for redress of their grievances. They demanded public registration of births, the opportunity to marry in their own buildings, the right to hold their own burial services in parish graveyards, the abolition of Anglican tests at the ancient universities and (probably most keenly) the ending of rates for the upkeep of parish churches. They also called for DISESTABLISHMENT. All these causes cemented Nonconformist support for the Liberal Party. Chapel-goers were particularly prominent in campaigns such as that of 1876 against Turkish atrocities in Bulgaria, and the loyalty of the great majority to Gladstone survived the test of the Irish Home Rule Bill ten years later. Although Anglican and Roman Catholic influence in education was a matter of concern, the chief causes taken up by the Nonconformist conscience at the end of the century were temperance, anti-gambling and sexual morality. At a time when alternative leisure facilities were undermining the chapels' appeal, they established Free Church Councils during the 1890s both to co-ordinate evangelism and to articulate Nonconformist views on public affairs.

David Bebbington, *Victorian Nonconformity* (Bangor, 1992).
James Munson, *The Nonconformists: In Search of a Lost Culture* (London, 1991).

D. W. BEBBINGTON

North German Confederation (1867–1871)   Established following the defeat of Austria in 1866, the North German Confederation connected Prussia (enlarged by the annexation of Schleswig-Holstein, Hesse-Kassel, Hanover, Frankfurt and Nassau) with the other German states north of the River Main. The Prussian king was president of the confederation, controlling foreign policy and the army. Nominal sovereignty remained with the member states, which together administered the confederation through the federal council (where Prussia had seventeen of forty-three votes). There was a democratically elected parliament. Bismarck hoped the confederation would elicit support in northern and central Germany and prove attractive to south Germans. The confederation did introduce a good deal of liberalizing and unifying economic measures but could not disguise the dominance of autocratic Prussia. It was abolished in 1871 with the establishment of the German Empire, though various of its constitutional features and reforms were preserved.

Gordon Craig, *Germany 1866* (Oxford, 1978).

JOHN BREUILLY

Norway   *see* SCANDINAVIA.

novel   While the form has a long prehistory, reaching back to classical antiquity, the nineteenth century produced an extraordinary flowering of the novel in all the major European cultures, the United States and those cultures of the non-European world touched by colonialism and imperialism – though in some cases, such as China and Japan, there was an indigenous tradition of extended prose narrative. The novel is a remarkably plastic form, capable of being used to articulate the texture of ordinary lives and of sweeping historical change. It typically does so in a language that is vernacular and diverse. The novel was thus the artistic form best placed to exploit the range and variety of subnational 'languages' and dialects that flourished and proliferated in the nineteenth-century world. It became the central form in which nineteenth-century societies in Europe and North America explained themselves to themselves, by reflecting on personal and social realities and possibilities, and by projecting solutions and alternatives. Moreover, it is a form which typically occupies itself with the matter of private and domestic life, though in the most ambitious artistic projects these 'private' matters are linked to wider processes of historical change. The novel is thus a form which especially appeals to women; the nineteenth century witnessed major artistic achievements from a number of women novelists, especially in Britain, France and the United States. The outstanding richness of the nineteenth-century novel remains the prime artistic legacy of the century.

Its great range of possibilities can be gauged by two contrasting

British novelists from the beginning of the century, Jane Austen (1775–1817) and Walter Scott (1771–1832). The former, drawing on a multitude of eighteenth-century predecessors, many of them women, used the form to give careful and morally discriminating accounts of the domestic manners of the English rural governing class. Scott, by contrast, used the novel to dramatize historical change; beginning with *Waverley* (1814), his series of historical novels placed the lives of individuals at the centre of profound historical conflicts. In Britain it was in the 1840s that the full range of possibilities for the novel began to unfold. This decade witnessed mature novels by Charles DICKENS and William Makepeace Thackeray (1811–63), as well as first novels from Charlotte Brontë (1816–55), Elizabeth Gaskell (1810–65) and the only novel by Emily Brontë (1818–48), *Wuthering Heights* (1847). In this remarkable efflorescence, the possibilities of the novel form were extended in a variety of ways. Dickens's *Dombey and Son* (1847–8) gave a panoramic view of contemporary England, seeking to link the highest to the lowest, and achieving a popular audience for writing which both comforted and challenged its readership. Thackeray's *Vanity Fair*, (1847–8), by contrast, whose scope was equally panoramic, subjected its characters and their manners to a relentless satirical scrutiny, frustrating the bonds of social and moral solidarity which bound Dickens to his audience. Gaskell's *Mary Barton* (1848) sought to come to terms with the new historical reality of industrial Manchester; one of the main uses of the novel throughout the nineteenth century was as a means of exploring the lives of people distant from both writer and reader in social, historical, religious or racial terms. Emily Brontë's *Wuthering Heights* was a novel of extreme, entwined, passionate and social conflict; her sister Charlotte Brontë's *Jane Eyre* (1847) radically made a woman's subjectivity its unequivocal centre. The range of writing resists easy summary because of the diversity of the form. In this decade the great formal repertoire of the British novel began to be established, to be extended still further by subsequent novelists, including George Eliot (1819–80), George Meredith (1828–1909), George Gissing (1857–1903), Thomas Hardy (1840–1928) and the American Henry James (1843–1916). This is to mention only those writers who have become canonical for the twentieth century. Throughout the nineteenth century the novel was used as a vehicle for discussing a range of pressing and immediate contemporary problems (such as religious doubt, the woman question and the housing question) and was, of course, a major form of popular entertainment, being the staple of lending libraries and magazines. It drew on a range of differing forms, including Gothic, melodrama, romance, government reports, journalism, popular humour and the developing nineteenth-century languages of PSYCHOLOGY, SOCIOLOGY and DARWINISM.

Similarly, the outstanding novelists who dominated the French novel in the nineteenth century represented only the high points in a rich environment. The dominant figure in the early part of the century was Honoré de Balzac (1799–1850), whose great series of linked novels collectively known as the *Comédie humaine* sought to depict, in minute realistic detail, the lives of French society during the social and political upheavals of the early nineteenth century. His contemporary George Sand – the pseudonym of Amandine Dupin (1804–76) – wrote novels which extended the form towards moral and philosophical reflection and, in such tales as *La Mare au diable* (The Devil's Pool, 1846), towards rural idylls. The ambition of Balzac was to some extent carried forward by Gustave Flaubert (1821–80), who also sought to write about ordinary human lives in their everyday environment; Flaubert's greater self-conscious artistry made for a more objective style, notably in his best-known work, *Madame Bovary* (1857), which treats of the stupidities of provincial bourgeois existence. This more objective style continued, or perhaps reached its terminus, in the naturalist novels of the later decades of the century, above all in the work of Emile Zola (1840–1902) (*see* NATURALISM). As in Britain, nineteenth-century France produced a wide range of novels and novelists writing in a variety of styles. Some, like Victor Hugo (1802–85) and, in a different way, Eugène Sue (1804–57) used Gothic and sensational melodrama to dramatize the disparities and miseries of Paris.

Of the other major European cultures, Russia produced the most remarkable range of great novelists, above all Fyodor Dostoevsky (1821–81) and Lev TOLSTOI. These very different writers emerged from divergent strains in Russian intellectual life, and used the novel form in distinctive ways. Dostoevsky, in such novels as *Crime and Punishment* (1866) and *The Brothers Karamazov* (1880), dramatized the sometimes extreme conflicts of the moral life, always in a carefully realized social context – he was the great novelist of St Petersburg. Tolstoi, by contrast, realized individual lives in the fullest detail, and at the same time retained a sense of underlying historical and social movements, most strikingly in his sweeping historical novel of the Napoleonic war, *War and Peace* (1865–72), but also in his tragedy of domestic life, *Anna Karenina* (1875–6). In these novels the form reached a high point, combining a sense of the importance of individual lives with that of the societies in which such lives were lived.

In other European cultures, too, the century produced novelists who used the form both to explore their changing contemporary societies and to provide a fuller sense of their national histories. In Germany literary life at the beginning of the century was dominated by the figure of GOETHE, whose great *Bildungsroman* (novel of education) *Wilhelm Meisters Lehrjahre* continued to be published at the beginning of the century. The great realist novelists Theodor Fontane (1819–1898) and Wilhelm Raabe (1831–1910) used the form to address

contemporary problems in the context of the history which informed
them. In Italy Alessandro Manzoni (1785–1873) published *I Promessi
Sposi* (The Betrothed) in 1825–7, exploring life in seventeenth-century
Lombardy under Spanish administration. In Spain the novel began to
flourish towards the end of the century. Partly under French influence,
Benito Pérez Galdós (1843–1920), Clarín (1852–1901) and Emilia
Pardo Bazán (1851–1921) produced a series of realist novels exploring
the grave national problems besetting Spain and its transition to modernity, though their 'realism' had to be tempered by the conservative
cultural context in which they were writing. The novel was thus used
in multiple ways in different national contexts.

In the United States realism was less dominant. Writers like Nathaniel
Hawthorne (1804–1864) and Herman Melville (1819–91) gave
powerful and at times symbolic expression to themes from American
history and society. Thus Hawthorne drew on his New England intellectual inheritance to show a world best explained not by the minute
particularization of realism but by its openness to the spiritual world
– his best-known novel *The Scarlet Letter* (1850) turned on the
transfigurative power of spirituality in seventeenth-century New England. Melville's great novel *Moby Dick* (1851) was a mythic story of
the hunting and revenge of a great whale which included realistic
information about whaling. Contemporary with both these novels was
the melodramatic *Uncle Tom's Cabin* (1851–2), by Harriet Beecher
Stowe (1811–96), which had a tremendous impact, in the United States
and elsewhere, as a polemical antislavery tract. Later in the century
the influence of naturalism became more evident in the work of
American novelists.

The novel was the literary form which expressed certain aspects of
the nineteenth-century mentality most fully. It could recognize and
indeed celebrate ordinary human lives; much of the internal development of the form in the course of the century arose from the need to
find new ways of accommodating middle- and working-class experience. Secondly, the form was especially open to history; many of the
great novels of the century were historical, and the historical novel
was one of the great expressions of nineteenth-century historical consciousness. Thirdly, in its attention to private and domestic life, the
novel took the experience of women seriously; many of the greatest
novelists were women, and the attention paid to women's subjectivity
within the novel both contributed to and drew from contemporary
feminism. And finally, in its capacity to absorb other forms of writing,
and submit them to extension, questioning and ridicule – for it could
also be comic – the novel in the nineteenth century showed itself
typical of its time in its restless and relativizing spirit.

See also REALISM.

SIMON DENTITH

Nullification Crisis (1832–1833) An idea first proposed by Thomas Jefferson in his 1798 Virginia and Kentucky Resolutions, nullification attracted new interest from South Carolinian John C. CALHOUN, who proposed it as an alternative to secession in his *South Carolina Exposition and Protest* (1828). Calhoun believed that states possessed the right to nullify, or to refuse to enforce, any federal law they deemed unconstitutional. By the late 1820s many southerners, especially those in economically depressed South Carolina, insisted that the protective tariff benefited only the north, and drained money from the south, which bought many luxury goods from England. They saw nullification as a possibility. Calhoun prevented any rash action in 1828 when the extremely unpopular Tariff of Abominations passed Congress. When the tariff passed in 1832 offered only modest relief, Calhoun led the efforts to convene the convention that nullified both tariffs. President Andrew JACKSON responded swiftly, threatening military force. With the efforts of Henry CLAY, however, a compromise tariff was passed which resolved the crisis.

William W. Freehling, *Prelude to Civil War: The Nullification Controversy in South Carolina, 1816–1836* (New York, 1966).

ALICE E. REAGAN

O

Obrenovich   The Obrenovich dynasty (1815–1903) gave SERBIA five rulers: Milosh (1815–39, 1858–60), Milan I (1839), Michael (1839–42, 1860–8), Milan II (prince, 1868–82; king, 1882–9), Alexander (1889–1903). The founder of the house, Milosh (*b* Srednja Dobrinja, 18 March 1780; *d* Topchider, 26 September 1860), was a wealthy peasant and merchant who joined Kara George (*see* KARA GEORGE) in the first Serbian revolt. As leade. of the second revolt (1815), he secured considerable autonomy for Serbia and was appointed prince (hereditary prince by the assembly in 1817). By skilful and patient diplomacy he secured full autonomy, and during his autocratic reign laid the foundations of a centralized state. The second reign of his son Prince Michael (*b* Kragujevac, 16 September 1823; *d* Kosutnjak, 10 June 1868) was a remarkable period of modernizing reforms in the army, finances, judiciary, education and culture, and also saw an active and successful foreign policy. Under the unpopular rule of Milan II (*b* Maraşeşti, Moldavia, 22 August; *d* Vienna, 11 February 1901) Serbia achieved full independence in 1878, and was proclaimed a kingdom in 1882.

Michael Petrovich, *A History of Modern Serbia, 1804–1918* (New York, 1976).

MARIA TODOROVA

obstetrics   Encompassing all aspects of pregnancy, birth and the consequences of birth, obstetrics developed as a distinct area of gynaecology during the nineteenth century. Traditionally, this area of medical work was the domain of midwives, who provided a service for the majority of women who could not afford the care of physicians. The increasing professionalization of physicians and surgeons in the nineteenth century limited the growth of the mainly female group of midwives (*see* DOCTORS). There were concerns for the regulation of all medical services. In Europe, especially France and Germany, midwives were subject to specific licensing, retaining control over all aspects of pregnancy and childbirth. In Britain midwives had no special status, and registration was not introduced until the 1902 Midwives Act. In the United States the midwifery tradition was established by new immigrants, but as in Britain, there was a movement from the late nineteenth century towards control of pregnancy and childbirth by doctors, and increasing hospitalization for birth. Post-natal obstetric care was recognized during the nineteenth century as a way in which high infant and maternal mortality rates could be reduced (see INFANT MORTALITY, PUERPERAL FEVER). Female health visitors were trained to provide new mothers with information to supplement the primarily medical care provided by the doctors.

J. Lewis, *The Captured Womb: A History of Obstetrics in Britain* (Oxford, 1984).

R. W. and D. C. Wertz, *Lying In: A History of Childbirth in America* (New York, 1979).

SALLY SHEARD

O'Connell, Daniel (*b* near Cahirciveen, County Kerry, 6 August 1775; *d* Genoa, 15 May 1847) Irish political leader, called 'the Liberator'. Ireland's foremost criminal barrister, the energetic O'Connell transformed Catholic politics, successfully leading the movement for CATHOLIC EMANCIPATION in 1829, forcing the issue by his election, as a Roman Catholic, as member of parliament for County Clare in 1828. Having concentrated in the 1830s on winning, with limited success, concrete reforms for Ireland at Westminster, he launched the Repeal Association in 1840 to secure the repeal of the union (see IRISH ACT OF UNION): 1843 was declared 'Repeal Year', but in face of government opposition, O'Connell abandoned the largest of his demonstrations, at Clontarf, planned for 8 October 1843. The decision hastened the rift with the Young Irelanders and reflected O'Connell's pragmatism and constitutionalism. A product of the eighteenth-century Enlightenment, he saw nationalism as a matter of good government rather than a cultural imperative, while his experience of the French Revolution convinced him that no revolution was worth the shedding of human blood.

Oliver MacDonagh, *The Hereditary Bondsman: Daniel O'Connell 1775–1829* (London, 1988).

—— *The Emancipist: Daniel O'Connell 1830–47* (London, 1989).

PATRICK BUCKLAND

O'Connor, Feargus (*b* Connorville, County Cork, 18 July 1796; *d* London, 30 August 1855) Chartism's most influential leader. Trained for a legal career, he served as member of parliament first for County Cork and later for Nottingham (1847–52). He was a gifted orator, and his tours of the industrial districts of England and Scotland, along with his support in London, were crucial to the emergence of CHARTISM. He was the owner of the *Northern Star* (1837–52), Chartism's national journal. He championed open constitutionalist means for winning democratic rights, although he pushed constitutionalism to the verge of violent confrontation. Following Chartism's first mobilization, O'Connor was sentenced to eighteen months' imprisonment. In 1842 he was again tried but acquitted. He subsequently launched the Chartist Land Plan. Following the failure of the third National Petition and the Land Plan, O'Connor lost support but remained a popular leader until his mental health failed.

James Epstein, *The Lion of Freedom: Feargus O'Connor and the Chartist Movement* (London, 1982).

JAMES EPSTEIN

O'Higgins, Bernardo (*b* Chillán, Chile, 20 August 1778; *d* Callao, Peru, 23 October 1842)   Chilean revolutionary. The illegitimate son of an Irishman in Spanish government service, he spent his childhood in Europe. In England he met Francisco de Miranda (1750–1816), a leading Spanish American revolutionary, and returned to CHILE in 1802 already committed to the independence cause. O'Higgins commanded the patriot army fighting the royalists in 1813–14, but following defeat at Rancagua he withdrew to Argentina, where he eventually joined SAN MARTIN. After the patriot victory at Chacabuco in 1817 O'Higgins was nominated as supreme director of Chile. His rule was autocratic yet liberal in intent. He quarrelled with the church and with leading members of the landowning elite, and further undermined his position by appointing an incompetent and corrupt minister of finance. Lacking any real power-base within Chile, O'Higgins was forced to abdicate in 1823. He went into exile in Peru, where he remained until his death.

RORY MILLER

oil   The invention of the kerosene lamp in 1854 created the first mass demand for oil. The United States and Europe were the major producers in the nineteenth century; the major fields of Latin America and the Middle East began to be developed only in the early twentieth century. The first oil well sunk for commercial purposes was at Titusville in Pennsylvania in August 1854, and by the 1870s and 1880s the industry had spread to California and Texas. The development of the European oil industry followed close behind the American. The first oil refinery in the world was built in 1857 at Ploesti, Romania and by the end of the century Russia was producing oil at its Baku fields. Oil did not become a major energy source, however, until the development of the internal combustion engine and its adoption by navies (beginning with the British) in the early twentieth century.

RICHARD PRICE

Old Corruption The phrase 'old corruption' had emerged by the late eighteenth century primarily in reference to the British Whig oligarchy's efforts to retain power by electoral manipulation, bribery and state pensions, the high taxation required to disburse such funds, retention of governmental control over substantial numbers of nominally independent members of parliament and refusal to countenance PARLIAMENTARY REFORM (see WHIGS). When the reform movement revived after 1810, the phrase was widely associated with William COBBETT's *Political Register*. As a concept which purportedly explained economic distress as a result of heavy taxation, it was under attack from 1815 by the OWENITES in particular, for whom competition, unequal exchanges of labour for wages and the manufacturing system were more crucial causes of poverty. With the parliamentary reforms of 1832 and 1867, the phrase fell out of favour.

GREGORY CLAEYS

Old Poor Law Prior to the NEW POOR LAW in 1834, the Old Poor Law operated in England. Each parish or township was responsible for the maintenance of its own settled poor, the cost being met from a local rate. POOR RELIEF was administered by unpaid overseers, appointed annually by the vestry, and was under the general supervision of local justices of the peace. An act of 1780 permitted parishes to unite for the administration of poor relief, the principle imposed on all parishes under the New Poor Law. Relief practice was marked by great geographical diversity and should be considered in relation to the local economy. Historians, like contemporaries, have concentrated particularly on the rural and predominantly arable areas of the south-eastern half of England. There the quarter-century before 1815 was a period of rapid price rises outstripping wages. The consequent distress led parishes to favour relief scales that varied with the price of bread and family size. The best-known of these were recommended by the Berkshire justices and named after Speenhamland, the village in which they had met.

After 1815, with demobilization and continuing population growth, the dominant problem was underemployment. This was also due to the introduction of forms of cultivation which accentuated seasonal fluctuations in labour demand, just when ENCLOSURE of commons made the poor more dependent on wage labour for their subsistence. Parishes responded to this seasonality by methods designed to subsidize the employment of the surplus labour from the rates, whether by a 'labour rate', which left farmers a choice between employing more labour or paying higher rates, or the 'roundsman' system which imposed a quota of surplus labourers on all. Contemporaries were acutely conscious of the steep rise in the absolute amount paid in relief. Set against the rise in population or land values, these figures become much less startling.

G. W. Oxley, *Poor Relief in England and Wales 1601-1834* (Newton Abbot, 1974).

E. P. HENNOCK

Ollivier, Emile (*b* Marseilles, 2 July 1825; *d* St Gervais-les-Bains, 20 August 1913) French politician. The son of an umbrella merchant who was a great admirer of Rousseau (1712-78) and a member of the secret society the Charbonnerie, he became a commissioner of the Provisional Government in the *département* of the Bouches-du-Rhône in 1848. There he lowered the working day to eleven hours and was shortly thereafter dismissed by the new moderate government in Paris. A committed republican, he was a member of secret societies during the reaction of 1849 and was later elected as an opposition deputy in the Second Empire. In an amazing volte-face, however, he became a government minister and later prime minister under Louis Napoleon because, he argued, the empire had become liberal. He authorized a law legalizing trade unions in 1864 but led France into the disastrous war with Prussia in 1870. He spent the rest of his life trying to explain his actions and failures.

T. Zeldin, *Emile Ollivier and the Liberal Empire of Napoleon III* (Oxford, 1963).

DONALD SUTHERLAND

Omdurman, Battle of (2 September 1898) In 1896, alarmed by Italian and French advances in the region, the British government, acting notionally for EGYPT, decided to reconquer the SUDAN. The building of a railway helped the Anglo-Egyptian army, under KITCHENER, to reach the outskirts of Khartoum. Near the twin-town of Omdurman a battle was fought on 2 September 1898, each side showing conspicuous determination, but the Mahdist army suffered heavy casualties and withdrew. After the occupation of Khartoum the British pursued the Mahdist remnants and their leader, the Khalifa, died bravely in a skirmish in Kordofan in 1899. The Battle of Omdurman, which soon passed into the historical mythology of both parties, led to an immediate confrontation between the British and the French at Fashoda on the upper Nile, which effectively halted French advance (*see* FASHODA CRISIS).

P. E. H. HAIR

Open Door Doctrine A demand for equal trading opportunities for all foreign powers throughout China, the Open Door Doctrine was Britain's response to the 'spheres of influence' policy espoused by some powers (including Russia and Japan) in China in the 1890s. Britain eventually persuaded the United States to lead the movement for commercial equality. The doctrine, formulated by W. W. Rockhill (1854–1914) was delivered to those powers with interests in China by the American secretary of state John Hay in 1899. They were asked not to interfere in the free trade of any other power in their sphere. The European powers were reluctant to make this commitment but in 1900 Hay was satisfied that they had done so. During the BOXER RISING the United States extended the doctrine to include the preservation of China's territorial integrity and administrative autonomy. The doctrine was a statement of principle depending for its effectiveness on the co-operation of the powers. There was no military machinery to enforce it.

JOHN DAVIES

opium trade The growing demand in Europe for Chinese tea, silk and porcelain was not matched by a corresponding growth in Chinese demand for Western goods. The West developed a serious balance-of-trade deficit, having to pay for Chinese goods in silver. To offset this, the British began exporting Indian-grown opium to China. By the 1830s over 25,000 chests (each containing 130 to 160 pounds) were arriving each year. As opium-smoking spread throughout all classes the market for the drug grew, despite imperial prohibition on home production and importation. 'Country traders', licensed by the monopoly-holding East India Company, anchored their vessels off the south China coast. The opium was taken ashore by local dealers, the provincial security forces being too weak to prevent its distribution. In response, LIN TSE-HSU was sent to Canton to stamp out the trade. His actions led to the first Anglo-Chinese War (*see* ANGLO-CHINESE WARS).

JOHN DAVIES

Opium War *see* ANGLO-CHINESE WARS.

Orange Free State Following the annexation of Natal in 1843 many Boers looked to the region between the Vaal and Orange Rivers to establish a republic (*see* GREAT TREK). In 1848 Britain annexed the area as the Orange River Sovereignty. Effective autonomy was granted by the Sand River Convention in 1852. When various disputes involving African land rights, the British, Boers living north of the Vaal River and the Sovereignty had been resolved, the British, wanting to minimize responsibilities, imposed independence in 1854, bringing the Orange Free State into being.

The predominantly agrarian state had substantial links with the Cape Colony and, as the mining industry developed, with the Transvaal. Deeply conservative, it was the grass roots of early Afrikaner nationalism. Following defeat in the Boer War, it became the Orange River Colony, then the Orange Free State, in the Union of SOUTH AFRICA, in 1910, providing the Union's judicial capital at Bloemfontein.

SIMON KATZENELLENBOGEN

Orders in Council (1807)   The chief British response to Napoleon's CONTINENTAL SYSTEM, the Orders in Council were a series of regulations introduced in 1807 to control the activities of neutral shipping, and to restrict the supply of colonial goods to France and its allies. In particular, ships from any nation that had acceded to the Continental System were declared to be liable to seizure unless they first put into British ports, paid duties on their cargo and obtained a licence for trade with the enemy. Designed to encourage opposition to Napoleon in Europe, the orders in fact brought such dislocation to British trade that public pressure forced their repeal in 1812 in a move that has been attributed to the increasing power of the new middle classes. Meanwhile, they also led to a reinforcement of the Continental System and contributed to the outbreak of war with the United States in 1812 (*see* WAR OF 1812).

CHARLES ESDAILE

Ottoman Empire   At the beginning of the nineteenth century the Ottoman Empire had sovereignty over Turkey, much of the Balkans and all the Arab lands except Morocco. By 1830, however, the Greek War of Independence (*see* GREECE), salvaged by European intervention, had set the pattern for the dismantling of Ottoman Europe. Before the century was over, the Serbs and Bulgarians had won their freedom and the Armenians in Anatolia were demanding theirs (*see* BULGARIA, SERBIA). In contrast to the internal rebellions of Ottoman Europe, the North African provinces fell as a result of invasion, as first ALGERIA (1830), then TUNISIA (1881), EGYPT (1882) and Libya (1911) were incorporated into the European empires.

As early as the eighteenth century the Ottomans had undertaken military reforms in recognition of their vulnerabilities to European expansionism, indigenous warlordism and the aspirations of their own minorities. It was only in the nineteenth century, however, that they sought broader remedies than mere military reorganization. Under the grand viziers MUSTAFA RESHID PASHA and KEÇECIZADE MEHMED FUAD PASHA, the Ottomans introduced Western-orientated reforms of the political, legal, judicial and educational systems. The reforms were centralizing and secularist. In 1856 an Imperial Rescript proclaimed the equality of non-Muslims, and in 1876 the first Ottoman constitution, guaranteeing representation to non-Muslim as well as Muslim men, provided for the first multidenominational general election in Islamic history. The despotic Abdulhamid II (1876–1908), however, opposed political liberalization of any kind and in 1878 used the war with Russia as a pretext to suspend the constitution. In the Young Turk revolution of 1908 (*see* YOUNG TURKS) the constitution was restored, but democracy and national pluralism soon fell victim to the illiberalism of wartime. The decision to enter the First World War on the side of Germany stripped the Ottomans of their territory outside Turkey, but it was the Turkish War of Independence between 1919 and 1923 that put an and to 600 years of Ottoman dominion.

M. E. Yapp, *The Making of the Modern Near East 1792–1923* (London, 1987).
MADELINE C. ZILFI

Otto-Peters, Louise (*b* Meissen, Germany, 26 March 1819; *d* Leipzig, 13 March 1895)   Novelist and journalist who played a central role in the German women's movement. She was one of the first generation of women who took up writing as a profession, sometimes publishing under the pseudonym of Otto Stern. In 1849 she founded a newspaper, the *Frauen-Zeitung* (Women's Newspaper), which appeared weekly until 1852, when a law forbidding women to participate in political life forced her to abandon it. In 1865 she organized one of the first formal German organizations of women, the Allgemeiner Deutscher Frauen-Verein (National Association of German Women). Essentially a moderate despite her support of the 1848 revolution, Otto-Peters believed that women should have the right to earn a living rather than be forced into prostitution or marriage for economic reasons. In her later career she stressed the need for women's education and successfully pressed for the admission of women to German universities.
GAIL SAVAGE

Owen, Robert (*b* Newtown, Montgomeryshire, 14 May 1771; *d* Newtown, 17 November 1858)   Welsh social reformer, generally accounted the founder of British socialism. At the age of 10 he became a draper's apprentice, but a move to Manchester in 1788 heralded a meteoric career as a cotton-spinner. Owen's reputation was built on the success of the mills he managed at New Lanark, where he combined high profits with experimental efforts to improve the conditions of his workers, especially in housing and infant education. His attempts to extend such ideals to manufactures generally were rebuffed, however. By 1817 he became convinced that only the resettlement of unemployed labourers, and eventually the entire population, in 'cooperative communities' would solve the evils of competition. Thereafter he devoted his life to founding a successful community (of which

New Harmony, Indiana was the best-known example) and to secularism, in the belief that the priesthood widely opposed his chief philosophical doctrine, that human character was chiefly a product of the
environment.

See also OWENITES, UTOPIANISM.

Frank Podmore, *Robert Owen*, second edn (London, 1923).

GREGORY CLAEYS

Owenites   During the early years of the socialist movement in Britain
the followers and associates of the philanthropist and reformer Robert
OWEN were known as Owenites. Many of them disagreed with elements of Owen's strategy – his alleged paternalism, hostility to democracy and especially his criticisms of the Chartist movement – and with
his financial inefficiency during the latter years of the movement
(*c.*1836–45). Owen attracted considerable interest, and some financial
support, between 1815 and 1820, when his plan for co-operative villages to house the poor and unemployed was first developed. Owenism
proper, however, began with the London printer George Mudie (*b*
1788), whose newspaper the *Economist* (1821–2) expounded Owen's
views at length for the first time for a largely artisan and middle-class
reforming public. Mudie also set up an urban community in Spa Fields,
London. Further support focused on the short-lived community at
New Harmony, Indiana, in 1824, while there was similar publicity
attending the first British rural community at Orbiston, near Owen's
New Lanark mills. Thereafter, while several later colonies were founded
in the United States, Owen's views enjoyed a wider circulation in
Britain, and most of his energies after 1830 were concentrated on the
founding of a community there.

By the early 1830s co-operative ideas were discussed, and retail societies organized, on a fairly wide scale in Britain (*see* CO-OPERATION).
Many of the latter, however, were not 'Owenite' in that they did not
seek to house their own workers, or anyone else, in communities on
the land or in cities, but merely sought to reduce consumer costs.
Owen's adherents were instead attracted to his SECULARISM, his proposals to house the population in communities where property would
be held in common and his critique of the greed and inefficiency of
untrammelled capitalism. Owen attracted further attention by his
connections with the trades-union movement in the mid-1830s, and
particularly his link with the first effort to form a general trades union.

The grand phase of his activities, however, was the period 1835–45,
when a new organization, the Association of All Classes of All Nations (AACAN), was formed to buy land and build a model community in Britain. Eventually selecting a site at Queenwood, Hampshire,
the AACAN spent most of the decade raising funds by forming local
branches. Some fifty existed at the peak of the movement, with the

largest at Manchester and many of the rest scattered around the factory districts; there was also considerable representation in Scotland and London. The branches, often housed in buildings known as 'halls of science', also enjoyed a vibrant cultural life, holding lectures, teas and dances, and aiming at cradle-to-grave care for members (*see* POOR RELIEF). At its peak the branches had perhaps 4,000 members, while the movement circulated some 2 million tracts annually. During this period the Owenite movement was organized around a central board, usually headed by Owen himself, and annual congresses to which the branches elected delegates to determine policy. These were generally harmonious occasions where branch members, often artisans, accommodated themselves to the views of Owen's own circle, which included entrepreneurs and capitalists. By the mid-1840s, however, the mounting debts and poor returns of the Queenwood community inspired a revolt by working-class members of the association's branches. Owen was ejected from his central role at the congress of 1844, but by then Queenwood had no means of raising further capital. The AACAN dissolved amid considerable acrimony, with several branches emigrating to the United States, and lawsuits persisting over Queenwood's debts until at least the early 1860s.

Intellectually, the Owenite movement helped to popularize a more interventionist, humanitarian approach to the factory system and Poor Law reform. Building on the influence of Thomas Paine's *Age of Reason* (1794), it gave birth to the modern secularist movement associated with George Jacob Holyoake (1817–1906). It had a considerable impact on the ideas of several Chartist leaders, notably William LOVETT and James 'Bronterre' O'Brien (1805–64) (*see* CHARTISM). Owen's ideas were revived in part with the new wave of socialist activity which began in the early 1880s, notably by William MORRIS.

Gregory Claeys, *Machinery, Money and the Millennium: Form Moral Economy to Socialism, 1815–1860* (Princeton, NJ, 1987).
——, *Citizens and Saints: Politics and Anti-politics in Early British Socialism* (Cambridge, 1989).
J. F. C. Harrison, *Robert Owen and the Owenites in Britain and America* (London, 1969).

GREGORY CLAEYS

Oxford Movement (1833–1845) Nurtured in a romantic cultural atmosphere, the leaders of the Oxford Movement, which reasserted the authority of the Church of England as a branch of the divinely commissioned Catholic Church, looked for their inspiration to the Caroline divines of the seventeenth century and beyond them to the fathers of the early church. They were reacting against the liberal atmosphere associated with CATHOLIC EMANCIPATION and PARLIAMENTARY REFORM. The movement is conventionally dated from 1833, when John Keble

(1792–1866) preached an assize sermon denouncing state suppression of ten Anglican bishoprics in Ireland. Apart from Keble, professor of poetry at Oxford and a village clergyman, the leaders were E. B. Pusey (1800–82), Regius professor of Hebrew, who had turned against the theological liberalism of Germany, and J. H. NEWMAN, vicar of St Mary's, Oxford, whose views had evolved from an early EVANGELICALISM. Together they contended that the apostolic succession of bishops from the days of Christ ensured that his teaching was faithfully transmitted; that the sacraments of baptism and the eucharist were to be revered as channels of divine grace; and that the clergy, as holders of a sacred office, must show great holiness of life. By 1838 it was evident that some adherents were going further, towards expressing Roman Catholic sympathies. In *Tract 90* (1841), the last of a series that gave the movement its alternative name of the Tractarians, Newman himself endorsed many Roman views, and he eventually seceded to Rome in 1845. The influence of the movement nevertheless continued to spread throughout the Anglican communion, encouraging a greater attention to dignity in public worship and, by the 1860s, an imitation of Roman Catholic liturgical practice. The tradition was to carry great weight in the twentieth-century Church of England.

Geoffrey Rowell, *The Vision Glorious: Themes and Personalities of the Catholic Revival in Anglicanism* (Oxford, 1983).

D. W. BEBBINGTON

Oyo Empire   Ruled by a king entitled the alafin, the Oyo, or Yoruba, Empire was until the early nineteenth century the most powerful state in YORUBALAND, and an important supplier of slaves for the transatlantic trade. After the death of Alafin Abiodun (reigned 1774–89), traditionally regarded as its last strong ruler, it was weakened by internal divisions, leading to the rebellion of the important provincial town of Ilorin, under its chief Afonja, and in the 1820s and 1830s it disintegrated in civil war. It also suffered an insurrection of Muslim elements, led by clerics inspired by UTHMAN DAN FODIO, in 1817. Afonja at first allied with the Muslims against the alafin, but they killed him (c.1823) and seized power in Ilorin for themselves. Many captives taken in these disturbances were sold for export, so that the Oyo now became major victims of the transatlantic slave trade (*see* ATLANTIC SLAVE TRADE). Around 1836, after a decisive defeat by Ilorin, the original capital of Oyo (Old Oyo) was abandoned, and has since remained unoccupied.

The kingdom was reconstituted by Alafin Atiba (d 1859), with its capital at the modern city of Oyo (New Oyo) further south, but the alafin's authority was now purely nominal. From the 1830s the real powers in the area were the towns of Ijaye and Ibadan which, although formally acknowledging the alafin as their overlord, were effectively independent, and fought each other for primacy. With the defeat and destruction of Ijaye in 1862, Ibadan emerged as the leading power, but its dominance was resisted by a coalition of rival states. The alafin's role in these conflicts was little more than that of an ineffective mediator. In 1888 the alafin accepted a treaty which made Oyo a virtual British protectorate, and it was subsequently incorporated into NIGERIA.

Robin Law (1977), *The Oyo Empire c.1600–c.1836* (London, 1991).

ROBIN LAW

P

painting Nineteenth-century European painting began with a lingering nostalgia for the ancient world and ended with the dawn of modernism. The intervening transformations were the result of the political, industrial and social revolutions of the previous century which definitively changed Western civilization. Underlying the shifts in subject and style were historicism, egalitarianism, nationalism, secularism, industrialism and pragmatism. France nominally dominated the art world, but the movements were international, enriched by criss-crossing currents.

By 1800 the canons of the return to the antique were entrenched in the academies of Europe. The last unified international style, NEOCLASSICISM, was grounded in Rome, the capital of antiquarianism. The histories and myths of antiquity provided heroic subjects, intended to edify the public. The style was predicated on drawing after ancient art, with an idealized definition of form exemplified by Raphael (1483–1520) and Poussin (1594–1665). It perpetuated the Renaissance techniques of perspective and of modelling (modifying hue with light/dark values). Line was held to be morally superior to colour because it conveyed fact. Great care was taken to be archaeologically correct (although anachronisms abounded). The most famous exponent of this 'True Style' was Jacques Louis David (1748–1825), whose rebellious disciple J. A. D. Ingres (1780–1867) came to epitomize the academic tradition up to the 1860s. While that tradition was eroded by subsequent radical movements, it remained the foundation of the 'official' style into the twentieth century.

ROMANTICISM superseded the classical revival during the early decades of the century. The categorization of the Graeco-Roman world according to time and place initiated historicism. The next step was to apply the concept to European history, which underpinned budding nationalist sentiments (*see* NATIONALISM). Beginning with the Middle

Ages, painters ransacked the past for subjects that illustrated a nation's history. National styles were sacrosanct, and artists emulated their forebears. In response to the crushed ideals of the Enlightenment, the romantics rejected the rational and objective in favour of the emotional and subjective. A pessimistic outlook, in which malevolent forces overpowered human aspirations, predisposed many romantics to themes ranging from the melancholy to the violent. Empowering the imagination, they explored the murky realms of the irrational and the eccentric, brilliantly revealed in the art of Francisco de Goya (1746–1828). In the quest for originality, artists found new topics in contemporary literature. Escapism held more appeal than stoicism. The exotic, removed in time and place, served as a refuge from the excruciatingly mundane. Odalisques and caravanserai heralded the Orientalism which was to remain popular for the next hundred years. Nature provided another avenue of escape. Where the eighteenth century saw nature as collective and universal, the nineteenth saw it as individual and idiosyncratic. Landscape functioned as a metaphor for human nature or for divine revelation.

The style of the romantics was governed by the rules of the Old Masters until the colour experiments of Eugène Delacroix (1798–1863), beginning in the 1820s, introduced a freer, more painterly technique in France. Over the next forty years Delacroix expunged black from his palette, modelling with undiluted hues. His decision to base his choices on aesthetic effect announced 'art for art's sake', a notion that subsequent artists used to justify a preference for the means rather than the subject of their art.

By the 1830s the middle class, made affluent by the industrial revolution, expanded the market for art. Exhibitions and galleries proliferated. The burgeoning press published reviews and articles, promoting, explaining and defending art. Altering patterns of patronage inevitably affected taste. The egalitarian attitudes that accompanied the rise of the middle class encouraged art that was more accessible. Arcane, self-indulgent subjects gave way to those that reassured middle-class values. Small, unpretentious canvases suited the home. The methodologies of science gave credence to the empirical, and an insistence on fact arose from attitudes towards science. The philosophies of positivism and materialism strengthened the merits of the tangible. This translated into the visual arts as a preference for realistic detail, images that could be validated by observation. The urge to record the visible world hastened the invention of PHOTOGRAPHY at the end of the decade, a discovery that challenged the very process of observation and, consequently, of painting.

REALISM encompassed a broad spectrum of works of art, sometimes referring to the technique rather than the subject. It emerged in period genre paintings filled with polished details that were historically accurate;

it spread to picturesque, sometimes moralizing, vignettes of contemporary life. Influenced by realist literature, especially the novels of Honoré de Balzac (1799–1850), painters moved on to more serious social commentary. Paradoxically, the sense of history imbued the present with distinction as a unique temporal span. At mid-century painters responded to what was called 'the heroism of modern life'. The Pre-Raphaelite Brotherhood (*see* PRE-RAPHAELITES) in England declared this to be central to its mission. Adolf Menzel (1815–1905) would carry it into the factory in Germany. Gustave Courbet (1819–77) shocked the French with scenes of rural life on a scale hitherto reserved for history painting. Famous for his dictum that he could not paint an angel because he had never seen one, Courbet made the banal potent. He published the *Realist Manifesto* in 1855. Equally revolutionary was his style, which acknowledged another reality: the material substance of paint. Applying thick layers of paint with the palette knife, he stressed the picture's surface.

In the simplest terms, painting in the second half of the century split into two camps, one that remained faithful to the Old Master style and one that demolished it. While academic-style artists have been denigrated as old-fashioned, dismissed as *pompier*, they shared many of the concerns that motivated the avant-garde, at least at the outset. Both espoused a measure of realism, however differently they defined it. Light and its effects preoccupied artists on both sides of the Atlantic, whatever their school. And compositions might appear less formally structured, more like a snapshot. As Paris replaced Rome as the Mecca for artists, the French led the attack that repudiated the Old Master tradition.

From the 1860s Edouard Manet (1832–83) and Edgar Degas (1834–1917) captured modern life on canvas in fresh ways. They found their subjects in the Paris of their day, sometimes touching the seamier *demi-monde* explored by the novels of Emile Zola (1840–1902). The literary term 'naturalism' can also denote paintings that shared a documentary approach to social realism. Under the influence of photography and the Japanese print, Manet and Degas redefined pictorial space, eliminating Old Master perspective and modelling. Manet built his images through chromatic patches of paint that unified and asserted the surface of the canvas. Degas depicted horse races, cafe concerts and dancers, from odd angles, radically cropped, with flat areas of pure colour. They sought a style that would be as direct and up to date as their subjects. In doing so they brought unprecedented attention to the formal elements of painting; the work of art began to assume an identity independent of the illusion. Both men were associated with the impressionists – Degas actually exhibited with them, but their goals were not identical.

Impressionism grew out of the trend towards painting out of doors (*plein-air*) in order to seize the fleeting effects of light and atmosphere (*see* IMPRESSIONISM AND POST-IMPRESSIONISM). Based on the observation of reality, it reflected the world familiar to the artists – city life, middle-class leisure, the countryside and the seashore. Such non-anecdotal slices of life, devoid of a specific message, still carry implicit social content. The insistence on the visible stemmed from the empirical methods of POSITIVISM. Themes accessible to everyone were inherently democratic. The city served as an emblem of progress. Excursions, made possible by improved transportation, were the leisure pursuits of an urban population. Trade with Japan made its prints and artefacts cheap and abundant. Photography demonstrated a world in motion. The manufacture of oil paints in tubes facilitated the artist's escape from the studio.

The movement owed its name to the painting *Impression: Sunrise*, by Claude Monet (1840–1926), exhibited in 1874. The impressionists exploited optical colour. They applied pure hues with small, comma-like brushstrokes, contrasting warm and cool, juxtaposing complementary colours. They expunged black from their palette. As these artists pursued the transient effects of atmospheric conditions, light became the true subject of impressionism. This explains why Monet painted series, repeating the same motif at varying times of day and seasons. Tangible form dissolved in shimmering veils of light. No one point of reference dominated the pictorial space; rather the focus was diffused across the surface of the canvas through colour and texture. When, during the 1880s, the artistic means took precedence over the observation of nature impressionism proper declined in France, though its international influence had just begun.

The next generation reacted against the constraints of realism and the relentless pragmatism of the industrial world by turning art inward. Out of the innovations of Manet and the impressionists, who had inadvertently dematerialized nature, emerged a greater awareness of the abstract language of art. Its vocabulary could express intangible realms beyond appearances. Artists groped to communicate feelings, dreams, ideas that welled up from the unconscious. While their pursuits coincided with the studies of Sigmund Freud (1856–1939) in the 1880s, they were more immediately influenced by Henri Bergson (1859–1941), who concluded that art resulted from the inner spirit of the artist rather than the observation of nature. SYMBOLISM loosely describes the movement wherein art explored these emotive, irrational, esoteric trends during the last two decades of the century. Echoes of romanticism characterized its aims, but symbolism was distinguished by its disregard for realism, its psychic excesses and its predilection for the perverse. As a style it was incoherent, manifested in a variety of techniques; the most original variants played on the nature of art.

Georges Seurat (1859–1891) undertook a systematic investigation of colour and line, seeking to control the emotional tenor of his paint-ings. His style, under the misnomer neo-impressionism, evoked a mysterious, poetic vision that belied the science of his method. Vincent Van Gogh (1853–90) raised painting to a feverish emotional pitch through an intuitive manipulation of colour and distortion of form. His goal was to communicate feelings directly to the viewer, provok-ing a response equal to his subjective experience.

Similarly, Paul Gauguin (1848–1903) delved into the unconscious. Already at Pont Aven, in Brittany, working among fellow symbolists, he freed colour from its descriptive role. He insisted on the flat surface for the way its iconic power emitted a compelling force rather than mirroring the visible. His fusion of form and colour, synthetism, con-veyed the intuitive through the abstract. Fascinated with the occult and the exotic, and spurred by cultural anthropology, the impover-ished artist moved to the South Seas in 1891. Immersed in his neo-romantic fantasy of paradise, he painted highly personal visions, constructed around a theosophy derived from Christianity, Maori cults and Eastern religions. In a last gasp of Rousseau's philosophy, Gauguin saw the primitive as virtuous. Awkward shapes and coarse definition had an honest boldness. Chemically based paints produced garish col-ours which he combined in clashing and allied harmonies, flirting with the non-representational. The accidental tapped the unconscious. If necessity drove him to substitute gunny sacks for canvas and to mix oils with sand, genius lent these flaws aesthetic merit. However re-moved Gauguin was from Europe, his art exerted a pronounced influ-ence there. His experiments impressed others, notably Edvard Munch (1863–1944), who strove to create an art that transcended mere facts. Fauvism, expressionism and surrealism were indebted to him.

Belgian artists absorbed English and French influences to generate their own version of symbolism, which spread in turn across Europe. Primarily a style of design, art nouveau embodied a hyper-refined elegance through sinuous line and decorative pattern. It may be seen to designate the decadent mood of *fin-de-siècle* painting, evident in artists as diverse as Henri de Toulouse-Lautrec (1864–1901) and the Vienna Secessionist Gustav Klimt (1863–1918).

The great exception to the symbolist tendencies was Paul Cézanne (1839–1906), who sought to regain control over forms in nature. Cézanne constructed his landscapes, portraits and still lifes with flat strokes of paint, reminiscent of Manet's patches. He rendered three-dimensional volumes through two-dimensional planes, balancing the reality of art against that of illusion. The distinction between mass and space was broken down, since both were equal planes of colour; space was no longer a void. Moreover, shapes were no more static than colours; they interacted with each other and with space in dynamic flux. Each touch of the brush recorded a separate moment of seeing, so that the whole documented the artist's process of perception. Thus the fourth dimension, time, was acknowledged as a fundamental component of creation. The explosive composition was held together by a linear grid resulting from the interlocking edges of the planes. Cubism and abstract expressionism were Cézanne's legacy.

While these radical transformations were occurring, the academic tradition remained the mainstream style of the conservative establishment. Nor was it as impervious to change as history subsequently cast it. By the time war broke out in 1914, the avant-garde had redefined art for the new century. Whether in the expressive distortions of a Gauguin or the detached formalism of a Cézanne, priority was given to the artist's vision, one abstracted from nature to assert the reality of the work of art itself.

Albert Boime, *A Social History of Art*, vol. 2: *Art in an Age of Bonapartism, 1800–1815* (New York, 1990).

Françoise Cachin, *Art of the Nineteenth Century*, vol. 2: *1850–1905* (New York, 1992).

Robert Herbert, *Impressionism: Art, Leisure, and Parisian Society* (New Haven, Conn., 1988).

Robert Rosenblum and H. W. Janson, *Nineteenth-Century Art* (New York, 1984).

William Vaughan, *Art of the Nineteenth Century*, vol. 1: *1780–1850* (New York, 1989).

Gabriel P. Weisberg, *The Realist Tradition: French Painting and Drawing, 1830–1900* (Cleveland, 1980).

JUNE ELLEN HARGROVE

Palmerston, Henry John Temple, third Viscount (*b* Broadlands, Hampshire, 20 October 1784; *d* Brocket Hall, Hertfordshire, 18 October 1865) English statesman. As befitted his rank, he entered political office – first as lord of the Admiralty (1807–9) and then secretary at war (1809–28) – out of duty, not as a step to power. Having crossed to the Whigs, he found his *métier* as foreign secretary (1830–41, 1846–51), displaying a forthright (and expert) independence which often infuriated senior colleagues, the queen and foreign statesmen. True to his Canningite origins, he displayed scant regard for party or party grandees. Instead, he cultivated the support of the newspaper-reading public, promoting England as the role model for a liberal Europe, within which nationalist movements were supported if their success altered the balance of power to British advantage. As home secretary (1852–5) and then prime minister from 1855 to 1858 and from 1859 to 1865 (when he died in office), he eclipsed his erstwhile rival Lord John RUSSELL. By combining domestic inaction with forthright rhetoric in foreign affairs, Palmerston, 'the most English minister', established the surest recipe for success in British politics.

JOHN BELCHEM

Panama Canal The acquisition of California by the United States in 1848 and the subsequent gold rush (*see* GOLD RUSHES) encouraged thousands of migrants to cross the Central American isthmus and revived interest in the creation of better transport links between the Atlantic and Pacific Oceans. In 1855 the Panama Railway was completed, after enormous engineering difficulties and at the cost of perhaps 25,000 lives. The real need, though, was for a canal which would remove the need to transship goods. French investors obtained a concession from the Colombian government, which controlled Panama, and in 1880 Ferdinand de LESSEPS, the engineer in charge of the Suez Canal, arrived to begin construction. The project (for a sea-level crossing) was poorly conceived, and expenditure extravagant. Malaria and yellow fever again killed thousands of workers. The French company eventually went bankrupt in 1889, and the canal was completed by American engineers only in 1914.

RORY MILLER

Panjeh Incident The culmination of a series of ever-broadening conflicts over the definition of the Russo-Afghan border after 1884, the Panjeh Incident was not resolved until the Protocol of 1887. Panjeh was a border area claimed by AFGHANISTAN, autonomous and remote, which the British believed had a strategic significance since it controlled the approach to Herat and to British India. When, despite earlier promises, the Russians took the Merv region and, in 1881, delineated a border with Persia that absorbed territory adjacent to Panjeh, the area assumed international significance. After initial British attempts to constitute a boundary commission were thwarted, Afghanistan occupied the area with British support and raised the potential for a conflict involving Russia. Finally, a joint boundary commission was constituted, which awarded the area to Russia in 1887, on a geographic and ethnographic basis, and tensions dissipated.

Pierce Fredericks, *The Sepoy and the Cossack* (New York, 1971).

ROBERT J. YOUNG

Panslavism The term 'Panslavism' first appeared in a work on Slavic languages by the Slovak scholar Jan Herkel (1786–*c.*1850) in 1826. It came to denote the movement of the Slav peoples for political union. Related but not identical to this movement were Slavism and Slavophilism, which both recognized the Slav cultural comity without, however, embracing the idea of political union implicit in Panslavism. There was also Austro-Slavism (the movement to recast the Habsburg Empire as a political union of the Slav peoples within it), but this explicitly excluded the largest Slav nation, RUSSIA, central to most Panslav concepts.

Panslavism began as a movement of intellectuals such as the Slovak poet Jan Kollár (1793–1852), who pleaded in 1830 for the 'mutuality' of Slav relations. There was a Slav congress in Prague in 1848, a second in Moscow in 1867 and another smaller gathering in 1868 in Prague. The various attempts to create Panslav cohesion foundered, however, on the conflicting interests of the various nations. Russian Panslavs like Tyutchev (1803–73) and Danilevski (1838–1923) saw the movement as anti-European, anti-West and pro-Eastern Orthodoxy, an attitude inherited from Russian Slavophilism, while the Russian government usually rejected it as threatening legitimacy. The few in the regime interested in Panslavism – Ignatiev (1832–1908), Skobelev (1843–82) – saw it merely as a tool of Balkan and anti-German policy. Obversely, the other – mostly Catholic – Slav nations, with the Polish example before them, feared Russian dominance as much as they desired the support of Russian numbers. The 1848 Slav Congress met without Russian involvement; and the subjugation of POLAND in 1863 meant that the Poles did not attend the congress in 1867.

Overall, Panslavism was more effective as a rallying cry for anti-Slav sentiment among Germans and Magyars than it was as a movement for Slav unity.

John Erickson, *Panslavism* (London, 1964).

STEVEN BELLER

papacy The nineteenth century saw six pontificates: PIUS VII (1800–23), LEO XII (1823–9), PIUS VIII (1829–30), GREGORY XVI (1831–46), PIUS IX (1846–78) and LEO XIII (1878–1903). Despite the Concordat of 1801, which regularized the church's relations with France after the excesses of the Revolution, Napoleon annexed the Papal States and imprisoned the pope in 1809. Restoration of the pope's estates by the Congress of Vienna (1815) ushered in reactionary measures by the Holy See to strengthen its secular power in central Italy and its spiritual power throughout the world. These measures included a highly centralized administration by clerics, the re-establishment of the Jesuits and the Inquisition and the submission of Catholic missions to complete papal control. The disappearance, after the French Revolution, of clerical political power in national governments and the tendency of governments to strengthen themselves by a closer connection of throne and altar led to increased ULTRAMONTANISM, which Pius IX exploited. The Vatican Council defined as dogma in 1870 the long tradition of papal infallibility, weakening those who wanted a more democratic church and setting off official protests, especially Bismarck's KULTURKAMPF.

After its annexation of Rome in 1870, Italy passed the Law of Guaranties (1871) which granted the pope royal honours and privileges, the freedom to conduct religious affairs and a state subsidy. The pope rejected the offer, pressing for restoration of his temporal sovereignty and maintaining that he was a 'prisoner of the Vatican'. Leo XIII's encyclical 'Immortale Dei' (1880) solemnized Pius IX's earlier call for Italian Catholics to abstain from political life while this 'Roman Question' remained unsettled. But Leo XIII was not as illiberal as his predecessor; he called for increased study of church history and of Thomist philosophy (to show that science and religion were not antithetical), and promulgated 'Rerum Novarum' (1891). This encyclical developed Catholic social teaching concerning the working class, encouraged trade unions and urged the state to work for a just wage and the regulation of working conditions.

See also CATHOLICISM.

Frank Coppa, *Cardinal Giacomo Antonelli and Papal Politics in European Affairs* (Albany, NY, 1990).

LAWRENCE P. ADAMCZYK

Paraguay A remote province of the Spanish Empire in South America, Paraguay effectively achieved independence in 1811 (*see* ARGENTINA). FRANCIA, dictator from 1814 until his death in 1840, kept the country virtually isolated from the outside world. Carlos Antonio López (1792–1862), a landowner and lawyer, then acquired a similar position of personal authority, maintaining tight control over the state and its resources. López was determined to develop a strong military capacity to defend Paraguayan independence. He promoted education, imported European technical experts and encouraged foreign trade in order to obtain arms and machinery. After his death in 1862, his son Francisco Solano López (1827–70) took Paraguay into the disastrous PARAGUAYAN WAR, which ended with his defeat in 1870. Six years of enemy occupation and a decade of political violence and instability followed, before a military coup in 1880 inaugurated twenty-five years of *colorado* rule. Under these administrations Paraguay's agricultural production and trade grew rapidly, but at the cost of enormous social inequalities as a few large landowners came to dominate the economy.

John Hoyt Williams, *The Rise and Fall of the Paraguayan Republic, 1800–1870* (Austin, Tex., 1979).

RORY MILLER

Paraguayan War (1864–1870) The causes of the Paraguayan War lay in the chronic instability of URUGUAY, Francisco Solano López's (1827–70) desire to have PARAGUAY recognized as a major regional power and ARGENTINA's and BRAZIL's fears of Paraguay's ambitions. In 1863–4 Argentina and Brazil allied themselves with *colorado* rebels in Uruguay. The beleaguered *blanco* government appealed for aid to Paraguay. López overestimated his own strength and mistimed his intervention. After successfully invading the Brazilian Mato Grosso late in 1864, he demanded permission to cross Argentine territory to the Brazilian–Uruguayan frontier. When this was refused he invaded the Argentine province of Corrientes; in response, Argentina, Brazil and the Uruguayan *colorados* formed the Triple Alliance in May 1865.

Paraguay quickly suffered naval defeat at Riachuelo, thus becoming isolated from the outside world, and lost many of its forces in Corrientes. Forced back on the defensive, the reconstructed army was destroyed in May 1866 in battles marked by the degree of carnage on both sides. Epidemics of smallpox and cholera also ravaged both the invading armies and the Paraguayan population. Late in 1868 the allies occupied Asunción, but the war did not end until March 1870, when López was killed. Paraguay was devastated. Its population was almost halved, and there were too few able-bodied men to bury the dead.

RORY MILLER

Paris Commune The term 'Paris Commune' refers to both the government of Paris between 18 March and 21 May 1871 and the single largest and bloodiest insurrection in Parisian history. The insurrection was fuelled by the extreme deprivation Parisians had undergone during the Prussian siege of the city in the autumn and winter of 1870–1 (*see* FRANCO-PRUSSIAN WAR), suspicions of betrayal on the part of their military leaders during the war, disgust at the peace THIERS signed with Bismarck and the election of a largely monarchist assembly in February 1871. The republican government, anxious to restore peacetime conditions, hastily ended the moratorium on rents and bills and cancelled pay of the National Guard, on which many working-class families depended.

A minor incident in Montmartre, in which women tried to prevent troops from removing cannons from the area, led to the death of a general, fraternization with troops throughout the city and Thiers's order for the army and government to withdraw from the city. Radicals immediately called elections and many 'socialists' formed the new Paris Commune. An attack on the government troops at Versailles was postponed, which gave Thiers time to reorganize. The commune decreed the abolition of night work in bakeries, a moratorium on rents and bills, the establishment of producers' co-operatives and preferential government contracting to them, the transformation of abandoned businesses into co-operatives and minimum wage and piece rates. The troops of the THIRD REPUBLIC re-entered Paris on 21 May and in the following week, 20,000 to 25,000 Communards were summarily shot while the city burned. Over the next four years military courts ordered the execution or deportation to tropical penal colonies of thousands more.

The Paris Commune has been the subject of great controversy since Marx's *The Civil War in France*, in which he saw the commune as a prototype of a proletarian government. Non-Marxists have retorted that it was in the Jacobin and patriotic tradition, and this view is gaining ground with the sociological study of the background of participants, which scarcely differed from the background of those who revolted in the 1790s. Other studies of the motivation of the Versailles army show that the period can also be viewed as one of competing visions of French nationalism, with the Versailles officers convinced that the Communards were German agents. Another view is that the commune instituted the programme of 1848 (*see* BLANC).

R. Tombs, *The War against Paris 1871* (Cambridge, 1981).

DONALD SUTHERLAND

Paris, Peace of *see* VIENNA, CONGRESS OF.

Paris, Treaty of (30 March 1856) Signed by the representatives of Great Britain, France, Russia, Austria, Sardinia and Turkey, the Treaty of Paris ended the CRIMEAN WAR. The signing of the treaty has long been regarded as a turning-point in nineteenth-century international relations because it ended the alliance system established at the CONGRESS OF VIENNA and inaugurated the era of aggressive nationalist policies dominated by BISMARCK, CAVOUR and Gorchakov (1798–1883).

The treaty's major provisions were: the powers recognized and guaranteed the Ottoman Empire's independence and territorial integrity; Russia returned Kars to the Ottoman Empire, ceded the mouth of the Danube and a small part of Bessarabia to the Turks and agreed to the neutralization of the Black Sea; Russia also relinquished its status as protector of the Danubian principalities (which were placed under the joint guarantee of the powers) and its role as guardian of the Christians living in the Ottoman Empire; and all parties to the treaty recognized freedom of navigation on the Danube.

W. Baumgart, *The Peace of Paris, 1856* (Santa Barbara, Calif., 1981).

GEORGE O. KENT

parliamentary reform Before 1832 approximately 10 per cent of adult males enjoyed the parliamentary vote in Britain. This reflected a multitude of qualifications, some of great antiquity, largely linked to residence and property. In counties the 40 shilling freeholders were typical electors. The boroughs showed much more variation, ranging from those where the vote was restricted to a handful of freemen or members of the corporation to a few where resident householders, some of whom were quite poor, could vote.

The late-eighteenth-century movement for parliamentary reform was stimulated by the revolutionary era, and after 1815 middle-class discontent with Tory policies, which seemed to reflect aristocratic self-interest, fuelled the campaign for change. The reformers regarded the landed aristocracy as the source of the corruption that was endemic in the system. One simple means of curbing this element was the occasional act to disfranchise a few particularly corrupt boroughs. More positively, radicals sought to enfranchise independently minded middle-class men and to correct the huge imbalance of representation which left many seats in small southern towns and few in the industrial northern districts.

The Great Reform Act of 1832 left traditional voting rights largely intact, but in the boroughs it enfranchised owners and tenants of property worth £10 if resident for twelve months and if they paid poor rates; in counties the 40 shilling freeholders were joined by £10 copyholders, £50 tenants, £10 long-leaseholders and £50 medium-leaseholders. Additionally, the act went some way to redistributing representation to reflect population changes. Twenty-two new double-member seats and thirty new single-member seats were created in the boroughs, while sixty-five were awarded to populous counties. Fifty-six existing English boroughs lost their representation and another thirty were deprived of one of their two members.

In many ways, the reforms of 1832 were shrewdly judged. The electorate grew by about 50 per cent to over 700,000. This appeased middle-class pride, but by boosting the dependent sections of the county electorate it did little to undermine landlord influence. Some working men actually lost their vote and for the first time women were legally barred. However, during the mid-Victorian era the political elite saw little reason to give way to pressure for further reform, though some minor changes were made. In 1858 the property qualification for members of parliament was abolished. As a result of the increased electorate, the amount of bribery and treating grew such that by the 1840s a majority of members of parliament were thought to be guilty. A series of acts designed to curb corruption in 1841, 1842, 1852 and 1854 testified to the growing embarrassment, but were largely ineffective.

The 1850s and 1860s also saw some desultory attempts to modify the franchise. Under PALMERSTON the Liberal Party felt broadly content with the *status quo*; but the growing dissatisfaction of the urban radicals, combined with the politicians' confidence in the Liberal loyalties of skilled artisans, prompted GLADSTONE to attempt to lower the borough franchise in 1866. In the event, it was DISRAELI who carried an unexpectedly sweeping measure in 1867. This introduced a new borough franchise for male householders subject to a one-year residence requirement, and a lodger qualification for those occupying rooms of £10 annual value. Together with lesser modifications in the counties, the Second Reform Act increased the electorate from 1.36 million in 1866 to 2.44 million in 1869.

The 1867 measure also stimulated several further reforms. Excessive expenditure at elections from 1868 onwards prompted Gladstone to enact the first effective measure – the 1883 Corrupt and Illegal Practices Prevention Act. This fixed the maximum expenditure in relation to size of constituency, required detailed returns from the agent appointed by every candidate and imposed severe penalties including fines, prison sentences and disqualifications on those found guilty of the offences prescribed. Moreover, the franchise reform of 1867 had been an illogical compromise; it was difficult to justify withholding from the counties the householder and lodger qualifications granted to the boroughs. This was corrected by the Third Reform Act of 1884 which created an electorate of 5.7 million, equivalent to six in ten adult males. However, the complications of registering for a vote and the prohibition on those who received poor relief continued to exclude several millions. In order to pass his bill through the House of Lords, Gladstone had agreed to the Conservative demand for a redistribution of constituencies in 1885. This replaced the traditional two-member system with single-member seats in most of the country. Population units of 50,000 were adopted for the creation of new seats, although in practice the reformed system still fell well short of equally sized constituencies.

See also SECRET BALLOT, ELECTORAL SYSTEMS, FRANCHISE REFORM.

J. A. Cannon, *Parliamentary Reform, 1640–1832* (Cambridge, 1972).
Martin Pugh, *The Evolution of the British Electoral System 1832–1987* (London, 1988).
C. S. Seymour, *Electoral Reform in England and Wales: The Development and Operation of the Parliamentary Franchise, 1832–1885.* (New Haven, Conn., 1951).
F. B. Smith, *The Making of the Second Reform Bill* (Cambridge, 1966).

MARTIN PUGH

Parnell, Charles Stewart (*b* Avondale, County Wicklow, 27 June 1846; *d* Brighton, 6 October 1891)   Irish nationalist leader, 'the Uncrowned King of Ireland'. Inherited nationalist sympathies, physical stature, authoritarian leadership and sensitive political antennae enabled Parnell, a Protestant and landlord, to lead the Catholic and peasant IRISH NATIONAL LAND LEAGUE and the HOME RULE movement. With a vague political programme, Parnell was probably trying to preserve landlord influence by restoring the 1782 constitution. Assisted by able lieutenants, he forced Gladstone to reform the land system and, by 1886, to commit the Liberal Party to home rule. Parnell's reputation soared with the exposure as forgeries of letters supposedly implicating him in murder and outrage in the land war, but his own position was undermined, and the Home Rule movement split, by his refusal to step down from the leadership, even temporarily, after his self-indulgent affair with Kitty O'Shea (1845–1921), the wife of one of his supporters, led to a much publicized divorce.

Paul Bew, *C. S. Parnell* (Dublin, 1980).

PATRICK BUCKLAND

Pasteur, Louis (*b* Dôle, France, 27 December 1822; *d* Saint-Cloud, France, 28 September 1895)   French chemist. His life is filled with major accomplishments in practical chemistry and medicine. He gained initial fame in 1848 for his work on the asymmetry of crystals. In 1849, while trying to determine the cause of wine souring, Pasteur discovered that fermentation involved the work of microbes. He found that gentle heating would kill undesirable microscopic organisms. This process, called pasteurization, is widely used today. Pasteur's work on the diseases of silkworms eventually resulted in his developing the germ theory to account for communicable diseases. Continuing his investigations into disease micro-organisms, Pasteur developed specific vaccines for anthrax in sheep, chicken cholera and rabies. His successful VACCINATION in 1885 of a young boy bitten by a rabid dog was acclaimed world-wide.

Rene Dubos, *Pasteur and Modern Science* (Berlin, 1988).

BARBARA KAPLAN

paternalism   The term 'paternalism' may refer to any social system in which the welfare of the majority is presumed to be a chief concern of their nominal social superiors, such as landlords or a nobility, and where the greater social and political independence and responsibility of the majority is not conceived by the elite as either possible (given, for example, the ostensible inevitability of poverty) or desirable. Feudalism, slavery and patriarchalism are general examples of the doctrine; the movements towards liberalism, democracy and greater social egalitarianism are its antithesis. In the nineteenth-century context the term is used to refer to the widespread belief that, in return for their deference and willingness to accept the existing, divinely established social hierarchy and the elite's right to rule, the poor deserved care from above, including regulation of conditions of labour, food prices, poor relief and the like. In Britain this view, revived by romantic conservatives like Samuel Taylor Coleridge (1772–1834) in the aftermath of 1815, stressed the desirability of an organic unity of church, state and the landowning classes. In the mid-Victorian period it was associated with factory and humanitarian reformers like Richard Oastler (1789–1861) and Lord SHAFTESBURY, as well as with the revival of conservatism by Benjamin DISRAELI, though similar views were shared at least in part by radicals like COBBETT as well as socialists like OWEN. In Britain paternalism was generally less authoritarian than in, for example, Austro-Hungary or Russia, where paternal authority was embodied in the person of the king (although writers like Thomas CARLYLE lent an authoritarian edge to British paternalism too). Often associated with the moral economy ideal of 'the just price and fair wage', which had a long pedigree of Christian charity behind it, paternalism can be said to have been eroded by measures like the NEW

POOR LAW of 1834, which attempted to discourage the receipt of poor relief. But it was reinforced, albeit increasingly in a novel form by which traditional elites were now replaced by a rational bureaucratic state acting in the public interest, by much social reform legislation in the last decades of the nineteenth century, which underlay the modern welfare state.

David Roberts, *Paternalism in Early Victorian England* (London, 1979).

GREGORY CLAEYS

patriarchy The term 'patriarchy' derives from the system embodied in Greek and Roman law that gave the male head of the family absolute power over dependent members of the household, although no consensus now exists as to its precise definition. It is currently used as an analytical concept to describe the structural relationship between men and women. Three distinct elements are commonly brought into play. First, patriarchy implies the systematic subordination of women to men as central to social organization. Institutions, ideology and social practice together serve to maintain the differential power relations between the genders. Secondly, patriarchy suggests a reciprocal and sustaining relationship between the family and the state. Political institutions thus reinforce the power of husbands and fathers in the family circle, and the male-headed family buttress the power of men in society at large. Thirdly, patriarchy always has a historical aspect, displaying a protean capacity for survival over the long term. (*See also* PATERNALISM.)

The nineteenth century witnessed the development of self-conscious political activism by women on their own behalf (*see* FEMINISM). Women also enjoyed during this period an exalted position as the repository of moral virtue. These developments took place, however, in the context of what the historian Lawrence Stone sees as a vigorous revival of patriarchal power. The nineteenth-century idealization of women, as Stone points out, also required from them total submission (*see* DOMESTICITY). In return for this surrender of autonomy, women ostensibly enjoyed a sheltered existence within the home. Statute 213 of the 1804 Napoleonic Code accordingly defined the reciprocal duties of husband and wife: 'A husband owes protection to his wife; a wife obedience to her husband.' Thus a paternalistic transaction, defined and enforced by the state, recognized male obligations and duties as well as female ones. This served to mitigate somewhat the power that privileged the position of men in the home, in the workplace and in public affairs. (*See also* MARRIED WOMEN'S PROPERTY ACT.)

During the late eighteenth and early nineteenth century secular explanations for women's subordinate position within the family developed, with medicine, law and history all providing convenient rationales for patriarchy. The intrinsic biological differences between men and women condemned women to domestic life because the capacity to bear children made a woman too weak to undertake other tasks. This view justified the exclusion of women from the workforce and from higher education. Law, which subsumed the identity and property of wives under that of husbands, exchanged the authority of religion and custom for a different sort of authority based on reason and natural law. Sir Henry Maine (1822–88), a historian of ancient jurisprudence who argued for the universality of the patriarchal family, found its purest expression in Roman law. The German Johann-Jakob Backofen (1815–82) thought that patriarchy superseded an earlier, prehistorical matriarchal society and regarded its emergence as evidence of its superiority.

Patriarchal expressions abounded in contemporary literature. In his poem *The Princess* (1847) Alfred Tennyson (1809–92) echoed the Napoleonic Code with the lines 'Man to command, woman to obey/ All else confusion.' Emile Zola's (1840–1902) novels underlined the widely accepted differentiation of the sexes with his characterization of women as the source of fertility. Patriarchal presumptions did not, however, go unchallenged during the nineteenth century. When the American feminists Henry Blackwell (1825–1909) and Lucy Stone (1814–1900) married in 1855 they drew up a marriage contract that denounced the power over wives granted to husbands by law. Henrik Ibsen's (1828–1906) play *A Doll's House* (1880) vividly portrayed the pernicious effects of patriarchy on the character of both men and women, and depicted Nora courageously leaving her loving and tyrannical husband.

The concept of patriarchy, with its presumption of GENDER as the fundamental salient of analysis, views all aspects of life in light of the subjugation of women to men. This stance raises several large questions that remain to be resolved. The seeming universality of patriarchy makes it difficult to explain either change over time or resistance to male domination. In addition, the relationship between patriarchy and other fundamental divisions within society, social class and race continues to be a matter of controversy. Employing this lens to examine the nineteenth century, however, produces particularly rich results because of the radical differentiation between male and female nature that characterized the period.

Kate Millett, *Sexual Politics* (New York, 1969).
Lawrence Stone, *The Family, Sex and Marriage in England, 1500–1800* (New York, 1977).

GAIL SAVAGE

patriotism The affirmation of unquestioning faith in one's country, often in terms of defending the 'homeland', patriotism is a simple proposition derived from the ordinary peasant's loyalty to his or her village or plot of land. A patriot is one who truly, or ostentatiously and injudiciously, loves and serves his or her country. The French short-story writer Guy de Maupassant (1850–93) thought patriotism a kind of religion, 'the egg from which wars are hatched'. Devotion to one's locality or region was as powerful a force in the nineteenth century as in any other. The problem for nationalists, eager to drive out foreign rulers in Europe, Ireland, South America and elsewhere, was how to convert this local patriotism into a larger sense of nationhood, based on common racial, religious or linguistic identity. For not all patriots of necessity become nationalists, although all nationalists are in origin patriots. NATIONALISM, unlike peasant patriotism, was an urban doctrine, the creation of schoolmasters and journalists who preached it to the new middle class. Wars of liberation against external rulers, such as those of tiny Piedmont against mighty Austria during the Italian Risorgimento (1848–70), served to unify the disparate elements of a potential nation-state. Yet patriotic Sicilian peasants were indifferent to nationhood for years after unification and widely believed 'Italia' to be the name of their new king Victor Emmanuel's wife. The existence of an overarching national identity that transcended local, regional and ethnic identities could not be firmly established even in Britain.

Patriotism was more than the kernel from which movements of national liberation and unification developed in the mid nineteenth century. It also provided the essential driving force, converted into nationalism, behind such major European conflicts as the French Revolutionary and Napoleonic wars (1792–1815) and the Crimean War (1854–6). With the exception of wars of national unification and the Franco-Prussian War (1870–1), the Crimea saw the only major continental clash of the nineteenth century, a conflict between Russia on the one side and France, Britain, Turkey and Piedmont on the other. Newspapers and patriotic entertainments of the day successfully whipped up a fervour of anti-Russian feeling in both France and Britain. Heroic 'Jolly Jack Tar' became the personification of English patriotism on the stage. The credibility of national stereotypes rested on the widespread nineteenth-century view that nations had specific 'characters', as in 'Anglo-Saxon' or 'Celtic', which could be objectively identified. Thus the relative success of any specific patriotism was believed to be ultimately dependent on the 'national character' of the people who subscribed to it. However, the most potent national symbol during wartime, capable of harmonizing the divergent patriotisms of church, chapel, locality, nation, kingdom and empire, was the monarchy. Queen VICTORIA, for example, had become a ubiquitous patriotic icon by the end of the century, when the British fought the Boers in South Africa.

Britain also exemplifies how patriotism slowly lost its links with

RADICALISM and became identified with the right of the political spectrum. Roast beef and plum pudding, the Union Jack, 'Rule Britannia' and John Bull himself were used as part of English radical rhetoric in the 1790s to legitimize opposition. 'Patriots' were those who opposed the governments of the day. The vocabulary of radical patriotism reached a comparable peak with the CHARTISM of the 1840s, in which the state was seen as a tyrant and the working class as patriots fighting for their rights and liberties. The incorporation of patriotic notions into Tory politics did not really become established until the Russo-Turkish war of 1877–8 (see JINGOISM). Gradual liberalization of the English state had made the language of freedom and tyranny less appropriate to domestic politics, while both working-class radicals and Tory nationalists shared a common Russophobia. The English ruling class sought in patriotism a means of defusing the consciousness of the working class; hence the people were constantly exhorted, in an age of overseas colonial possessions (see IMPERIALISM), to show their true patriotism by lending uncritical support to queen and country. Patriotism thus became a key component of the ideological apparatus of the imperialist state, firmly identified in the last quarter of the century with Conservatism, militarism, royalism and racism; opposition to which came only from a small minority of pro-Boers, socialists and liberal internationalists.

Hugh Cunningham, 'The Language of Patriotism', in Raphael Samuel (ed.), *Patriotism: The Making and Unmaking of British National Identity*, vol. 1 (London, 1989), pp. 57–89.

JOHN SPRINGHALL

patronage   The term 'patronage' refers to a mutually satisfactory exchange in which a rich patron or politician, often both, used his influence and resources to provide benefits or preferment for a relative or connection of lower income and status. The client, for his part, reciprocated by offering services or general support to the patron. It was often difficult to distinguish public from private patronage in nineteenth-century Britain. The former not only survived in those salaried areas where it had been the norm in the eighteenth century – the court, central and local government, the Church of England, the armed services and the East India Company – but also, in an increasingly complex urban and industrial society, expanded into new areas as a result of early Victorian reforms in local government, education, public health and finance. Thus Poor Law, ecclesiastical and railway commissioners were all appointed through patronage, as were prison, factory, health and school inspectors.

The American party system that emerged in the 1820s and 1830s saw the politics of patronage flower under the so-called 'spoils system', whereby all the office-holders of a losing party were dismissed when power changed hands in a local, state or national election, their government jobs being taken over by adherents of the new administration. In contrast, the Northcote-Trevelyan Report of 1854 recommended the complete abolition of patronage in the British civil service and its replacement by a system of competitive examinations. The system operated by the Civil Service Commission between 1855 and 1870 was, however, only a limited contest between nominated candidates. Truly competitive examinations based solely on merit awaited further reforms in the 1870s before making any real impression on recruitment.

J. M. Bourne, *Patronage and Society in Nineteenth-Century England* (London, 1986).

JOHN SPRINGHALL

pawnbroking In the nineteenth century pawnbroking was the most important source of credit for the British working-class. By 1870 there were over 3,000 pawnshops in England and Wales, and in 1902 it was estimated that in London there were six per capita pledges each week. Middle-class commentators regarded the practice as evidence of lower-class thriftlessness because of the 100 per cent annual interest rates pawnbrokers charged. Pawning was, in fact, a strategy of managing the high debt ratios and inadequate budgets that were endemic to working-class life. Goods were pawned to meet sudden emergencies or immediate cash needs. Pawnshops were, therefore, the functional equivalent of savings banks. But use of pawnshops was also a status indicator and, while occasional use to avoid pauperism was common within working-class families, recurrent recourse to the local pawnbroker ('uncle') was a sign of low social standing within the community.

RICHARD PRICE

Pedro I (*b* Queluz, 12 October 1798; *d* Queluz, 24 September 1834) Emperor of Brazil (1822–31). The son of João VI (1767–1826) of Portugal, Dom Pedro accompanied his family to BRAZIL in 1807–8, and became regent of the Brazilian kingdom when his father returned to Portugal in 1821. To preserve the Bragança family's control of both countries Pedro declared independence in 1822 and was crowned emperor. Brazil's emancipation was secured by CANNING'S mediation with Portugal, but the price, concessions to Britain over commerce and the slave trade, was high. The authoritarian Constitution of 1824, the unsuccessful war in the Banda Oriental (*see* URUGUAY), Pedro's scandalous private life and his close association with those Portuguese who had remained further increased the emperor's unpop-ularity. After an explosion of nationalist sentiment in Rio de Janeiro he abdicated in 1831. On his return to Europe he led a rebellion against his brother

Dom Miguel (1802–66), who had usurped the Portuguese throne in 1828, but died soon after its successful conclusion.

RORY MILLER

Pedro II (*b* Rio de Janeiro, 2 December 1825; *d* Paris, 5 December 1891)   Emperor of Brazil (1831–89). He became emperor of BRAZIL on his father's abdication in 1831 (*see* PEDRO I). For nine years Brazil was under a regency, but internal conflicts so threatened national unity that Pedro was granted full powers in 1840. A serious man, he was much more sensitive to Brazilian realities than his father, but possessed little control over ministers; when he did use his authority to intervene in 1868 it antagonized the liberals and helped to stimulate a republican revival. His known opposition to slavery, in contrast, caused resentment among many conservatives. The problems aroused by the PARAGUAYAN WAR, increasing discontent within the army, the frustration of elites outside Rio and the unpopularity of Pedro's heir, Isabel (1846–1921), all hastened the end of the imperial system. Pedro II was overthrown in a military coup in November 1889 (*see* DEODORO DA FONSECA) and died in exile in Paris two years later.

RORY MILLER

Peel, Sir **Robert** (*b* Bury, Lancashire, 5 February 1788; *d* London, 2 July 1850)   Leading Tory politician of the early nineteenth century. The son of a cotton manufacturer, he served as Irish secretary, home secretary and as prime minister (1834–5, 1841–5). He believed that administrative and political reform were essential if Britain were to cope successfully with the pressures of urbanization and industrialization, and that these could best be achieved under Conservative rule. He was associated particularly with granting civil rights to Roman Catholics, the establishment of an effective police force (*see* POLICE), the modernization of tax and banking policy and the support of free trade, which led him to repeal the CORN LAWS in 1846, splitting his party and ending his premiership. He represented the Conservative political tradition associated with industry rather than land, with urban rather than rural society and with individualism rather than paternalism.

See also TAMWORTH MANIFESTO.

Norman Gash, *Sir Robert Peel* (London, 1972).

RICHARD PRICE

Peninsular War (1808–1814)   Often referred to as Napoleon BONA-PARTE's 'Spanish ulcer', the Peninsular War of 1808–14 is generally reckoned to have played a major role in the emperor's downfall, by tying down large numbers of troops and encouraging war-weariness. However, its domestic impact was probably more important, leading, as it did, to the emergence of liberalism and the politicization of the Spanish army. From 1796 to 1808 Spain had been an ally of France, but by the latter date Napoleon was becoming increasingly dissatisfied with its backwardness and unreliability. Determined to incorporate it fully into his CONTINENTAL SYSTEM as a reliable satellite state, he made use of the opportunity provided by his decision to send troops into Portugal in 1807 to overthrow the Bourbons and place his brother Joseph (1768–1844) on the throne. The result, however, was a huge popular revolt which embraced both Spain and Portugal, and soon embroiled the French in major difficulties, especially after the humiliating defeat of Bailén (see BATTLE OF BAILEN) and the liberation of Portugal by the British. Personal intervention by Napoleon stabilized the situation, but suppressing Spanish resistance proved extremely difficult, especially given the emergence of numerous guerrilla bands in the interior, Napoleon's refusal to permit a united command and the presence of an increasingly powerful Anglo-Portuguese army under the duke of WELLINGTON in Portugal, which largely remained free of French control despite successive attempts at invasion. With the aid of an endless supply of reinforcements, the task might still have been achieved, but the outbreak of war with Russia diverted French attention elsewhere, and Wellington was able to eject the French armies by means of the decisive Battle of Vitoria in northern Spain (21 June 1813).

Gabriel Lovett, *Napoleon and the Birth of Modern Spain* (New York, 1965).

CHARLES ESDAILE

pensions, old-age In many states old-age pensions for the civil and military service were known for much of the century. Private pensions formed part of informal charity, while endowed charities provided pensions for the aged in many countries. Until 1870 the English aged poor, at least in some rural areas whose records have survived, obtained regular out-relief, for which the term 'old-age pension' would be appropriate. The extension after 1870 of the deterrent principles of 1834 (see NEW POOR LAW) to the aged poor does much to explain the feeling common by the end of the century that the Poor Law was inappropriate for the aged deserving poor. Proposals for the introduction of state pensions for the poor had been made at the beginning of the century, but they gathered momentum after 1870. They can be divided into proposals for compulsory contributions (Blackley, 1878), state subsidies to encourage savings through mutual-aid societies (Chamberlain, 1892) (see FRIENDLY SOCIETIES) and state-financed pensions on easier terms than the Poor Law (Booth, 1891). The 1890s saw much discussion and 1897 the beginning of a broadly based agitation, but no action was taken until 1908. The pioneer in the provision of workers' old-age pensions was the German Empire, where invalidity and old-age pensions were introduced in 1889. These were based on compulsory contributions by both worker and employer, the state contribution being limited to 50 marks per annum. Workers qualified at the age of 70, but could obtain an invalidity pension at an earlier age. Denmark introduced old-age pensions in 1891 as part of its system of poor relief on a discretionary and highly selective basis. New Zealand introduced old-age pensions for the poor in 1898 financed from general taxation.

Pat Thane, 'Non-contributory versus Insurance Pensions 1878–1908', in Pat Thane (ed.), *The Origins of British Social Policy* (London, 1978), pp. 84–105.

E. P. HENNOCK

People's Charter *see* CHARTISM.

periodicals The nineteenth century witnessed an explosion in periodical publishing, both of general magazines and of more specialized academic journals. Indeed, one of the major characteristics of this tremendous growth was the increasing fragmentation of periodical publishing, so that reviews which had functioned as organs of cultural authority at the beginning of the century, and which served a comparatively homogeneous reading public, were largely replaced at the end of the century by popular and general magazines on the one hand, and specialist academic journals with very limited readerships on the other.

In Britain the outstanding quarterly reviews were the Whig *Edinburgh Review* (founded 1802), the Tory *Quarterly Review* (founded 1809) and the radical *Westminster Review* (founded 1824). These provided magisterial reviews of contemporary science and literature. In addition, the first thirty years of the century saw a variety of magazines, often ferociously partisan, which offered a different combination of reviews, fiction, poetry and journalism. As the century progressed, increasingly popular magazines appeared to cater for an expanding reading public, including *Punch* (founded 1841) and Dickens's *Household Words* (1850–59) and *All the Year Round* (founded 1859). The growth and fragmentation of the reading public can be gauged from the almost simultaneous foundation of *Tit-Bits* (founded 1881), a mass-circulation magazine with no educational ambitions, and a number of leading academic journals such as *Mind* (founded 1876), the *English Historical Review* (founded 1886) and the *Classical Review* (founded 1887). General magazines, some with real intellectual distinction such as the *Fortnightly Review* (founded 1865) and the *Nineteenth Century* (founded 1877), continued to be published throughout the latter part of the century.

Comparable patterns of development occurred in North America and Europe, though in Germany especially the growth of specialized academic journals occurred at an earlier date. In all cases periodical publication responded, in different ways in different national contexts, to the growth of a mass reading public and the break-up of a homogeneous public sphere.

SIMON DENTITH

Perovskaia, Sofia Lvovna (*b* St Petersburg, 1 September 1853; *d* St Petersburg, 3 April 1881)   Russion revolutionary. The daughter of a nobleman who held various important government posts, she was educated at home and later attended special courses for women in the capital. She joined the embryo women's movement and then the populist Chaikovskii circle, which was involved in peaceful, political and social propaganda among students, factory workers and the peasantry. Disillusioned at the lack of success of educative methods in the populist movement, she joined the Land and Freedom organization and later the terrorist People's Will (*see* POPULISM (RUSSIA)). She played a leading role in four of the unsuccessful attempts on the life of Alexander II in 1879 and 1880 and organized the final stages of his assassination on 1 March 1881. She was arrested, along with five others, tried and executed.

Barbara Alpern Engel, *Mothers and Daughters* (Cambridge, 1983).

A. V. KNOWLES

Persia   Under the rulership of the Qajar dynasty, which was in power from 1794 to 1925, Persia, or Iran, retreated from its imperial borders to those that now contain twentieth-century Iran. It is difficult to know how much the Qajars might have preserved if they had been better leaders, or merely more interested in the well-being of their subjects. Perhaps there was no leader, given Iran's sparse population and tribal domination, who could have prevented Russia's drive into the northern territories or the parcelling out of 'small sovereignties' to great families, powerful tribes and, increasingly, foreigners. It is certain, however, that many Qajar dynasts treated their domain like enemy territory. In the north their vassals often willingly accepted Russian domination. In 1812 Russian victories forced Iran to renounce its claims to Georgia and Daghestan and to recognize Russian control over Derbend, Baku, Shirvan, Karabagh and portions of Iran on the Caspian. In February 1828, by the Treaty of Turkomanchai, FATH ALI SHAH surrendered to the Russians not only Erivan and Nakhichevan but capitulatory rights within Iran itself.

Unlike Egypt and the Ottoman Empire, which responded to similar shocks with energetic reforms of their military, civil administration and economy, Qajar efforts were shallow and short-lived. Unable to establish an effective standing army, the Qajars relied on factious tribal allies and, increasingly, on diplomatic intervention by Great Britain. Both dependencies only added to domestic antagonisms. In the 1840s and 1850s a number of rebellions, including that of SAYYID ALI MOHAMMED, were put down with great loss of life and more discontent. Although Iran was increasingly affected by the world economy, little was done in education, communications, agriculture or banking to enable it to defend itself, on any level, against Russian and British influence, which by the end of the century served to reinforce the country's general paralysis.

Peter Avery, *Modern Iran* (New York, 1967).

MADELINE C. ZILFI

Peru The independence of Peru from Spain was declared by SAN MARTIN on 28 July 1821, but it was not secured until Marshal Sucre's (1793–1830) victory at Ayacucho in December 1824 (*see* BATTLE OF AYACUCHO). By then government had changed hands four times, presaging the instability that was to dominate nineteenth-century Peru. The next two decades were disastrous. The independence wars caused immense economic disruption, especially to silver-mining. The treasury was bankrupt, and no group could establish overall control in a country where communications were difficult, and ethnic and regional conflicts profound. Santa Cruz's (1792–1865) attempt to establish the Peru-Bolivia Confederation (1836–9) resulted in bitter domestic opposition and invasion by the Chileans, followed by war with Bolivia (1839–41).

Nevertheless, under the presidencies (1845–51, 1855–62) of Ramón Castilla (1799–1867) and aided by revenues from guano exports, both the economy and the political situation improved. Castilla abolished slavery and the Indian head tax, and in 1860 established a constitution which survived the resurgence of *caudillo* struggles. In the late 1860s, however, the guano economy began to fail and, burdened by the massive foreign debts incurred to build railways, government finances fell into disorder. By 1879, when the WAR OF THE PACIFIC broke out, rivalries within the civilian and military elites were again intense. During the war ethnic, regional and personal conflicts reached a new pitch, and the Peruvian state collapsed.

Reconstruction began after 1886 under President Andrés A. Cáceres (1836–1923), who imposed fiscal and monetary reforms and a settlement with Peru's foreign creditors. However, Peru was badly hit by the BARING CRISIS and falling world prices for silver in the early 1890s. In 1895 Cáceres was overthrown by a coalition of the Lima elite and dissident *caudillos*. The new president, Nicolás de Piérola (1839–1913), then began to consolidate a more modern state apparatus, which formed the basis for a successful export-based economy.

David P. Werlich, *Peru: A Short History* (Carbondale, Ill., 1978).

RORY MILLER

Peterloo   The derisive sobriquet 'Peterloo' was coined in bitter mockery of the recent Battle of Waterloo to express public outrage at the 'massacre' on St Peter's Fields, Manchester on 16 August 1819. The day began peaceably, as a crowd, estimated at 60,000, assembled in disciplined manner to attend a radical mass meeting, the latest (and largest) in a series of regional demonstrations of overwhelming popular support. The legal status of such 'monster' meetings was far from secure, but by discipline and order the radicals established a public image of legitimate extraparliamentary behaviour which the authorities had no right to infringe. Dismayed by the government's refusal to introduce special legislation to prohibit the radical mass platform, the Manchester magistrates, much alarmed by reports of preparatory midnight drilling on the moors, decided to take matters into their own hands. On the day they ordered the local yeomanry to arrest Henry HUNT, the star speaker on the platform. Inexperienced in crowd control (and allegedly inebriated), the publicans and shopkeepers of the Manchester and Salford Yeomanry rode roughshod through the assembly, seizing radical banners and flailing their sabres. At least eleven people were killed and many hundreds injured. The area was finally cleared by the 15th Hussars. The Manchester magistrates were officially thanked for their decisive action but the government took utmost care to ensure against any repetition of their bloody deeds.

In the confrontational politics of 1819, 'Peterloo' was a great moral and propaganda triumph for the radicals, but it proved a Pyrrhic victory. The established opposition, not the radicals, benefited from the sense of public outrage, while in the courts the authorities were exonerated without question. As radicals argued over tactics in the aftermath of the 'massacre', the government regained the initiative, introducing the repressive SIX ACTS.

'Peterloo Massacre: Special Issue', *Manchester Region History Review*, 3 (1989).

JOHN BELCHEM

Philanthropy   Among philanthropic activities we need to distinguish between the personal commitment of individuals to care for the needs of others (a long tradition found in all sections of society, not least among the poor) and formally organized commitment to service, paid or unpaid, which required financial resources beyond that of those immediately involved. Such resources were raised by single appeals for the needs of the moment, for example disaster appeals; endowments whose income provided for a regular need in the future; and voluntary societies, membership of which depended on regular subscriptions. Philanthropic or charitable endowments had been known since the Middle Ages and the law relating to them was codified in the 1601 Statute of Uses. Philanthropic societies were greatly developed, if not invented, in the eighteenth century. The nineteenth century thus inherited numerous philanthropic endowments and many philanthropic societies, together with a tradition to associate for such purposes that was of fairly recent origin. Philanthropy in the nineteenth century was marked by large commitment of resources and the identification of and response to new needs.

Two things are clear. First, the enormous amount of resources available for philanthropic purposes. By the mid-1880s the income of the London charities alone exceeded the public revenues of Sweden. Secondly, the difficulties experienced by contemporaries in finding out about them. A survey of the country's public endowed charities, undertaken between 1818 and 1840, identified 28,880, with a total income of £1.2 million. This income was most unevenly distributed. Close on half had an annual income of less than £5, while just over 1 per cent had an income of over £500. A further 4,000 charities that had been overlooked were subsequently identified, quite apart from new ones constantly being founded. The investigation uncovered much maladministration, which it took many decades to rectify, as well as cases where the founders' intention was no longer suited to a changed society. A process of adaptation less lengthy and ruinously expensive than proceedings in the court of Chancery was required. In 1860 the Charity Commissioners (established 1853) were finally able to start dealing with these problems, particularly for the many small charities. This adaptation to changing needs was rarely anything but cautious. The exception was the remodelling after 1869 of the endowed grammar schools to provide a more modern education, and after 1883 of the parochial charities of the City of London.

Once the philanthropic societies maintained by subscriptions are included, there are no usable figures for the country as a whole. There are figures for London, which include the headquarters of many national societies, and these become more reliable at the end of the century. Contributions in 1908 accounted for 45 per cent of a total income of £8.48 million. The lion's share of donations went to medical charities, in particular to hospitals. Apart from education, other significant beneficiaries were the physically handicapped, fallen women, delinquency and particularly the destitute and helpless. Here the century saw important innovations of method in response to the growth of an urbanized society, as well as debates over priorities and objectives. Examples of the former are RAGGED SCHOOLS and other institutions for children at risk, housing associations and in particular the development of district visiting, all of which illustrate the fundamental fact, that organized philanthropy and discipline of the poor were frequently inextricably combined. The body that pursued most consistently the connection between philanthropic means and disciplinary ends was the Charity Organization Society (COS) (founded 1869). It campaigned against fraudulent begging, the tendency to resort to charitable giving to relieve feelings of compassion or guilt without regard for its consequences on the recipient and the use of charity to induce the poor to attend religious services in the hope that this would lead to their moral reformation. Such rationalism as this went counter to many other values current in nineteenth-century society, and the COS never obtained the influence in the philanthropic world to which it aspired.

See also POOR RELIEF.

David Owen, *English Philanthropy 1660–1960* (London, 1965).
F. K. Prochaska, 'Philanthropy', in F. M. L. Thompson (ed.), *The Cambridge Social History of Britain 1750–1950*, vol. 3 (Cambridge, 1990), pp. 357–93.

E. P. HENNOCK

philosophic radicals   *see* UTILITARIANISM.

Phoenix Park murders (6 May 1882)   The grisly assassination in Phoenix Park of the new Irish chief secretary, Lord Frederick Cavendish (1836–82), and the under-secretary, Thomas Burke (1829–82), by members of a Fenian splinter group, the Invincibles, shocked opinion in Britain and Ireland. It threatened to undermine the agreement reached the previous month between Gladstone and PARNELL to restore peace to the Irish countryside, since Cavendish had replaced William Forster (1819–86), the chief secretary responsible for waging war on the Land League. Parnell offered to resign the leadership of the Irish Parliamentary Party, but was persuaded by Gladstone to remain. Subsequent attempts to associate him with the crime, through forged letters published in *The Times*, backfired and instead enhanced his reputation. On the evidence of an informer, later shot dead in revenge, five people were executed and eight imprisoned for the crime.

Tom Corfe, *The Phoenix Park Murders* (London, 1968).

PATRICK BUCKLAND

photography   Forty years before the announcement of photography in Paris on 7 January 1839, Thomas Wedgwood (1771–1805) combined two widely known phenomena – the camera obscura and the light sensitivity of silver nitrate – but achieved only fugitive leaf shadows on paper. Not until 1826 was a permanent camera image secured by Joseph Nicéphore Niépce (1765–1833), but his process, heliography (bitumen on pewter), proved impractical and the image primitive. While Niépce's partner, Louis Jacques Mandé Daguerre (1787–1851) continued with the experiments after his death, William Henry Fox Talbot (1800–77) conceived of photography independently. By 1835 Talbot had fixed silver chloride 'photogenic drawings', employed the negative/positive principle and taken from life the first permanent paper camera negative. Daguerre then encountered a crucial two-stage phenomenon: the latent image – brief exposure to silvered copper plates sensitized with iodine fumes; then amplification by mercury vapour, giving exquisitely detailed, but unique, mirror images – daguerreotypes. Talbot, shocked, published his work in February 1839 and struggled to create a more sensitive paper. By 1841 he had patented the calotype which, employing the latent image and enabling duplication, led to modern photography.

Initally, few perceived photography to be a new art, let alone a cultural revolution unparalleled since printing. 'Among all the mechanical poison that this terrible nineteenth century has poured upon men', lamented John Ruskin, 'it has given us at any rate *one* antidote, the Daguerreotype.' While public imagination propelled the trade of daguerreotype portraiture throughout the developed world, patent restrictions and its coarse-grainedness confined the calotype in England to a handful of amateurs, but in Scotland the remarkable portraiture of David Octavius Hill (1802–70) and Robert Adamson (1821–48) gave early intimations of photography's artistic potential. French enthusiasm for paper processes began with Hippolyte Bayard (1801–87), inventor of a direct positive process and the first to exhibit photographs.

Dramatic expansion, amateur and commercial, occurred from 1851 when Frederick Scott Archer (1813–57) freely published his wet-collodion-on-glass process, which combined advantages of the original processes with near-instantaneous exposure. Some, like Roger Fenton (1819–69), acknowledged master of landscape, deplored the multiplied mediocrity of carte-de-visites avidly collected into albums. Before photographing the Crimean War during 1855, Fenton organized amateur exchange and royal patronage, Queen Victoria becoming a devotee. As painters assimilated the implications for art, 'high art' photographers Oscar Rejlander (1813–75) and Henry Peach Robinson (1830–1901) sought to elevate photography by emulating narrative painting. Amateur portraiture of the 1860s by Lewis Carroll (1832–98), Lady Hawarden (1822–65) and, above all, Mrs Cameron (1815–79) approached greatness, as did Nadar's (1820–1910) record of French celebrities and Mathew Brady's (1823–96) documentation of the Civil War in America, where Eadweard Muybridge (1830–1904) explored, with the new gelatin dry plate, the photography of movement, anticipating cinematography. During the 1880s Peter Henry Emerson (1856–1936) denounced 'high art', advocating naturalism as photography's artistic destiny, while George Eastman (1854–1932) demystified the medium with roll-film snapshot Kodaks.

Helmut Gernsheim, *The Origins of Photography* (London, 1982).
——, *The Rise of Photography* (London, 1988).

GEOFFREY TUCKER

phrenology The study of the correlation of skull types with personality traits, 'phrenology' as a term was coined by T. I. Forster (1789–
1860) to describe the psychological system of F. J. Gall (1758–1828)
and his adherents, especially J. Spurzheim (1776–1832) and the Edinburgh lawyer George Combe (1788–1858). The system asserted that
mind and brain were codeterminate, and that mental powers could be
classed into a number of distinct faculties located in a definite portion
of the surface of the brain. The size of such portions in turn supposedly defined the prominence of its relevant characteristic in the personality of the individual concerned, as measured by external assessments
of the skull.

Gall, who first reduced all mental phenomena, including the emotions, to physiology and biology, was chiefly instrumental in popularizing the system in France shortly after the turn of the century. In
Britain Combe and Spurzheim won support from such prominent
members of the establishment as Archbishop Richard Whately (1787–
1863). Public interest spread rapidly, and by 1832 there were some
twenty-nine phrenological societies in Britain and several journals
devoted to the subject. Gall had been concerned chiefly with the criminal and deviant mind, and assigned names to organs of theft, murder and the like. Spurzheim and Combe followed a different system
by which the mind was divided into two chief categories, the feelings
and intellectual faculties, to give a total of thirty-five propensities
(amativeness, philogenitiveness, concentrativeness, adhesiveness,
combativeness, destructiveness, secretiveness, acquisitiveness and con-
structiveness); lower and superior sentiments, including self-esteem,
benevolence, veneration, wonder; and the perceptive and reflective
faculties, including individuality, form, size, weight, colour, comparison and causality.

While some progress in theories of mental activity may be linked to
the 'science', its claims are now generally regarded as wholly defunct.
Critics like Brougham (1778–1868) and Jeffrey (1773–1850), at the
idealistic extreme, asserted that no discernible connection existed between the mind and any material substance. Even those who conceded the localization of functions in the brain contested the chief
interpretative categories that phrenologists used to describe functions,
as well as the separability of capacities into distinct faculties or organs.
Nor did the description of compound mental states as the effect of the
joint action of various organs find much support after the late-Victorian
period.

Sociologically, though its influence in popular scientific culture was
more long-lasting, the heyday of phrenology was from *c*.1825 to 1850.
During this time it attracted the attention of, among others, Charlotte
Brontë (1816–55), George Eliot (1819–80), Edgar Allan Poe (1809–
49), Walt Whitman (1819–91), J. S. Mill, Samuel Smiles (1812–1904)

and Auguste Comte (1798–1857). Aspects of phrenological doctrine found their way into the sociology of Herbert Spencer and the evolutionary biology of Robert Chambers (1802–71) and A. R. Wallace (1823–1913), and lent an evolutionary focus to the study of mental phenomena well before Darwin. Indeed, it has been claimed that the controversy of George Combe's *The Constitution of Man* (1828) was considerably greater than that which *The Origin of Species* initially encountered. This was in part because of the association of phrenology with a radical and often seemingly infidel or secularist materialism. (But by no means all adherents to the doctrine adopted this view, for phrenology was also linked to a variety of immaterialist doctrines, including Neoplatonism and some forms of romanticism.)

It has been argued that the popularity of phrenology lay in its 'levelling' assumption, parallel to the very different environmentalist theories of early socialists like OWEN, that the ruling groups in society were not themselves necessarily more competent or fit to govern. This meritocratic emphasis helped to link phrenology to various social-reform causes, which also contributed to popular scientific culture, such as water-drinking and animal magnetism.

Where metaphysicians and mental philosophers appeared to support entrenched privilege, phrenology was thus perceived as a science for, as well as of, the people. Widely seen as a demystifying, rational, liberal enterprise, phrenology won applause as a scientific reflection of some of the age's greatest ideological concerns. But in Combe's hands it was also wedded to a wider plea for industry, regularity, cleanliness, individualism, property rights and free trade, indeed the creation of a broadly liberal 'character' akin to the views popularized by Samuel Smiles (*see* SELF-HELP). From this viewpoint, morality rather than politics was rendered scientific, and the formula proved immensely attractive.

Roger Cooter, *The Cultural Meaning of Popular Science: Phrenology and the Organisation of Consent in Nineteenth-Century Britain* (Cambridge, 1984).

GREGORY CLAEYS

physics The discipline of the study of change in nature, physics, in the first half of the nineteenth century, encompassed electricity, magnetism, optics, acoustics and heat, all of which were unified by a series of theoretical developments. Two articles published in 1800, examining disparate phenomena that were ultimately shown to be different effects of a common origin, exemplified the trend towards unification: Thomas Young's (1773–1829) 'Outlines of Experiments and Inquiries respecting Sound and Light' demonstrated light interference and advocated the wave theory of light, while Alessandro Volta's (1745–1827) letter described his creation of a voltaic pile, which subsequently led to the developed of the electric battery.

Isaac Newton (1642–1727) had asserted that light consisted of tiny particles (like darts) emitted from radiating sources, while Christiaan Huygens (1629–93) had in 1678 anticipated Young's proposal that light was propagated by waves. Both theories satisfactorily explained the path, reflection and refraction of light rays. However, the particle explanation required that light travel faster in optically dense media (such as water) than in less dense ones (air), while the wave theory depended on the opposite assumption. In 1850 Jean Foucault (1819–68) actually measured the speed of light in air and in water, demonstrating that light travelled more slowly in water and establishing that light was a wave.

Following Volta's invention, many scientists investigated both the electrochemical processes that produced current and the relationship between electricity, magnetism and light. G. S. Ohm (1789–1854), for instance, formulated the law relating the voltage, resistance and current of a circuit, in 1827. Michael FARADAY's researches on the passage of an electric current through electrolytes revealed the existence of an elementary natural unit of charge. This led to the discovery of the electron by J. J. Thomson (1856–1940) in 1897 and the realization that bodies gained or lost charges by the movement of electrons.

Although the similarity between electric and magnetic attraction had been noted since the Middle Ages, the study of magnetism developed separately from electricity, and flourished in the early nineteenth century, instigated by the idea that the magnetism of the earth could be used as a directional tool in navigation. In 1820 Hans Christian Oersted (1777–1851) first demonstrated a connection between magnetism and electricity, when he showed that a compass may be affected by an electric current – a compass needle brought near a wire carrying current would assume a position parallel to the wire. Shortly thereafter, André Marie AMPERE distinguished between static electricity and electric current, demonstrating that there was a force between two parallel currents, and arguing that both electricity and magnetism were based on circulating currents. In 1831 Faraday and Joseph Henry (1797–1878) independently produced electricity by magnetic induction. They discovered that the most important aspect was the relative motion between a magnet and wire: by merely moving copper wire between the poles of a magnet electricity was induced. These studies produced the essential ideas that led to the electric generator.

That charges acted on each other across distances, even when separated by a vacuum, could not be explained. To address this problem Faraday proposed the concept of the electric field: each charge had an electric field which filled the space around it. Charges acted on each other via their electric field. James Clerk Maxwell (1831–79) developed this field notion into his theory of electromagnetic waves, introducing the hypothesis that magnetic fields could induce a motion of electric charge in ether as well as in conducting wires. Maxwell derived a set of equations linking changes in electric and magnetic fields, and accounting for all known electromagnetic interactions. He argued that electromagnetic fields could travel through the ether, explained visible light as a form of electromagnetic wave and predicted that non-visible electromagnetic waves existed at other frequencies. In 1888 Heinrich Hertz (1857–94) succeeded in generating and detecting low-frequency waves, providing the basis of Guglielmo Marconi's (1874–1937) invention of the radio in 1895 and W. C. Röntgen's (1845–1923) discovery of X-rays in 1895.

Toward the end of the nineteenth century it was recognized that all hot bodies emitted a continuous spectrum of electromagnetic waves, depending only on their temperature and called 'blackbody radiation'. In 1900 Max Planck (1858–1947) used thermodynamics and Maxwell's equations to derive the frequency distribution of this radiation, deriving a formula with the assumption that energy could be emitted only in discrete units – quanta – there by launching modern physics.

See also CHEMISTRY, ENERGY, GAS.

Charles Gillispie, *The Edge of Objectivity* (Princeton, NJ, 1960).

STEVE AMANN

piece-work A wage-payment system, piece-work was often at the centre of nineteenth-century production relationships. Under this system remuneration was calculated according to an individual's measured output of standard tasks. Although long established in putting-out industries, most early-nineteenth-century manufacturers disliked piece-work methods of wage payment (*see* PUTTING-OUT SYSTEM). Since early industrial workers commonly refused to expand their output past a customary limit, manufacturers instead relied on harsh discipline and mechanization, rather than incentives, to increase productivity.

Marking an important shift in attitude, employers of the 1830s showed a growing interest in extending payment by result, a tendency which later led Karl Marx to conclude that piece-work represented the most appropriate mode of wage payment under capitalism. The opposition of craft unions, however, greatly slowed the progress of piece-work. Engineers, carpenters, shipbuilders and others, insisting that piece-work led to sweating, driving, demoralization and impoverishment by rate-cutting, successfully resisted its imposition.

The imperative for employers to extend piece-work intensified during the Great Depression (1873–96) in order to increase productivity in the face of strong foreign competition. The deployment of piece-work, along with speed-ups and changes in the division of labour, allowed manufacturers to challenge craft autonomy and gain closer control over the pace and quality of work. Employers' concern to link labour costs to improved productivity took its ultimate form in the premium-bonus system, widely used by the 1890s. Under that system, unlike straight piece-work, rates paid for successive increments of production declined, automatically reducing wage costs per unit of production. As earlier, craft unions fought the spread of this managerial tool. By the close of the nineteenth century, however, a majority of industrial workers were paid according to piece-work and accepted it as a permanent feature of employment.

Eric Hobsbawm, 'Custom, Wages and Work-load', in *Labouring Men* (London, 1964), pp. 344–70.

RICHARD J. SODERLUND

Piedmont, kingdom of *see* VICTOR EMMANUEL II.

Pierce, Franklin (*b* Hillsborough, New Hampshire, 23 November 1804; *d* Concord, New Hampshire, 8 October 1869) President of the United States (1853–7). He was a lawyer who followed his father into the the Democratic Party, as congressman and senator from New Hampshire. An expansionist who supported the Gadsden Purchase from Mexico, he served in the Mexican War as a brigadier-general. Sectional tensions and the resultant split in the Democratic Party at its convention in 1852 made Pierce an attractive candidate because of his colourless record. Nominated on the forty-ninth ballot, he defeated Winfield Scott (1786–1866) overwhelmingly and became the fourteenth president of the United States. His support of the Kansas-Nebraska Bill (*see* KANSAS-NEBRASKA ACT) to placate the south alienated northern Democrats. A compromise candidate with no leadership ability, Pierce attempted unsuccessfully to reconcile sectional factions with cabinet appointments. He failed to secure the party nomination in 1856 and retired to obscurity.

KEVIN MURPHY

Pinkerton Detective Agency Founded by Allan Pinkerton (1819–84) in the 1850s, the Pinkerton Detective Agency had become nationally famous when they foiled an attempted assassination of President Abraham Lincoln in 1861. Following the Civil War, the agency expanded, with Allan's sons, William (1846–1923) and Robert (1847–1907), taking active roles. In the west the Pinkertons frequently worked for railroads in the battle against outlaw gangs. Detectives were killed by the James gang and the Younger brothers. The Pinkertons were also employed by businessmen in labour disputes. Thus, in 1874 and 1875, they helped ferret out the MOLLY MAGUIRES and in 1892 broke the Homestead Strike in Pittsburgh. Their strikebreaking activities earned them the hatred and hostility of labour unions. The Pinkertons often employed their agents as spies in the unions and some barely escaped with their lives. Following congressional action in 1937 on management spying, the Pinkerton Agency eliminated its industrial division.

JOHN MARTIN

Pius VII [Barnaba Chiaramonti] (*b* Cesena, 14 August 1742; *d* Rome, 20 August 1823) Pope (1800–23). He entered the Benedictine monastery of Santa Maria del Monte (1756), taught theology and canon law at Parma and Rome and became abbot of San Paolo. In 1782 he was made bishop of Tivoli, and in 1785 cardinal bishop of Imola. At Christmas 1797 he preached coexistence between the church and the French Revolution, and in 1800 he was elected pope under Austrian protection at San Giorgio in Venice. In 1801 his CONCORDAT with Napoleon restored the Catholic Church in France, though it was contradicted by the Organic Articles, which were published with it in 1802. Pius came to Paris in 1804 to crown Napoleon emperor, but the emperor crowned himself. The pope's insistence on papal neutrality resulted in the incorporation of Rome into the empire in 1809, when he was taken a prisoner to Savona, and in 1812 to Fontainebleau, where he retracted his signature from a projected concordat. He returned to Italy in 1814, when he restored the Jesuits. He also gave refuge to Napoleon's family. His sufferings were repaid by the restoration at Vienna in 1815 of the Papal States alone among the former ecclesiastical principalities. With Cardinal Consalvi (1757–1824), he divided them into legations with lay advisers, a mark of his political moderation which was also shown in an avoidance of the HOLY ALLIANCE. His portrait by Lawrence shows a face of extraordinary wasted sweetness and the long elegant hands never raised except in blessing.

A. Fliche and V. Martin (eds), *Histoire de l'Eglise*, vol. 20: *La Crise révolutionnaire 1789–1846*, by Jean Leflon (Paris, 1949), bk. 2, pp. 159–376.

SHERIDAN GILLEY

Pius VIII [Francesco Saverio Castiglioni] (*b* Cingoli, Ancona, 20 November 1761; *d* Rome, 30 November 1830) Pope (1829–30). Of noble parents, he became vicar-general of Anagni and then Cingoli, bishop of Montalto in 1800, bishop of Cesena and cardinal in 1816 and bishop of Frascati in 1821. His election was the work of Cardinal Consalvi's (1757–1824) moderate disciple Cardinal Albani (1750–1834), and was a triumph for the *politicanti* against the *zelanti*, but the new pope was ill unto death with a neck abscess, and though he saw CATHOLIC EMANCIPATION carried in the United Kingdom (1829), compromised over Prussian legislation on mixed marriages (1830) and recognized the July Monarchy of Louis-Philippe in France (1830), his pontificate was too brief to leave much mark upon the church.

A. Fliche and V. Martin (eds), *Histoire de l'Eglise*, vol. 20: *La Crise révolutionnaire 1789–1846*, by Jean Leflon (Paris, 1949), bk. 3, pp. 409–25.

SHERIDAN GILLEY

Pius IX (*b* Senigallia, Marches, 13 May 1792; *d* Rome, 7 February 1878) Pope (1846–78). Originally considered a 'liberal', he granted the Papal States a constitution, and was considered a possible leader to unite Italy. Refusal to declare war on Austria cost him the support of liberals. Forced to flee Rome in the revolt of 1848, he became staunchly conservative. He returned to Rome in 1850 with the help of a French garrison which remained until 1870. It was during his pontificate that the papacy lost its temporal dominions at the hand of united Italy. In spiritual matters, Pius defined the dogma of the Immaculate Conception (1854), issued the 'Syllabus errorum' (Syllabus of Errors, 1864), which denounced liberal ideas about God, the church and society, and called the Vatican Council, which defined the dogma of papal infallibility (1870).

Frank Coppa, *Pius IX: Crusader in a Secular Age* (Boston, 1979).

LAWRENCE P. ADAMCZYK

Place, Francis (*b* London, 3 November 1771; *d* London, 1 January 1854) Radical political activist. Active in underground trade-union and political organizations in the 1790s, from 1799 he became a successful tailor and political organizer, at which he proved most effective. He was the self-appointed interpreter of trade-union and working-class political aims in Westminster, maintaining close contacts with radical members of parliament, and in this role worked to represent working-class politics as compatible with Whig liberalism, especially its economic doctrine of *laissez-faire*. He co-ordinated the campaign to repeal the COMBINATION ACTS in 1824 and was a leading organizer of popular demonstrations, in support of the Reform Bill of 1832 (*see* PARLIAMENTARY REFORM). His collected manuscripts and press clippings in the British Museum have shaped our understanding of early-nineteenth-century RADICALISM.

The Autobiography of Francis Place (1771–1854), ed. Mary Thale (London, 1972).

RICHARD PRICE

plantation system *see* SLAVERY (UNITED STATES).

Plekhanov, Georgi Valentinovich (*b* Gudalovka, 29 November 1857; *d* Terioki, 30 May 1918) Russian politician, historian and literary critic, known as the 'Father of Russian Social Democracy'. As a young man he joined the Populist revolutionary group Land and Freedom (see POPULISM (RUSSIA)), and when it split in 1879 he became the leader, along with P. B. Akselrod (1850–1928), of the non-violent organization the Black Redistribution. A year later they emigrated and in 1883 founded the Liberation of Labour group, which played an important role in spreading Marxism in Russia. When the Russian Social Democratic Labour Party was established in 1898 Plekhanov was influential on the orthodox Marxist wing. Although he inclined towards the Bolsheviks on their formation in 1903, he soon became a Menshevik, advocating a broad proletarian party and collaboration with the liberals. After the February Revolution in 1917 he returned to Russia, vehemently opposing Lenin and the Bolsheviks.

S. H. Baron, *Plekhanov: The Father of Russian Marxism* (London, 1963).

A. V. KNOWLES

Plessy versus Ferguson (1896) The crucial United States Supreme Court decision in *Plessy* versus *Ferguson* explicitly sanctioned racial segregation, holding that separate accommodations were not inherently unequal. It was the culmination of a series of practices that gradually eroded the gains AFRICAN-AMERICANS had made since the passage of the fourteenth amendment to the United States constitution which guaranteed freedmen equal protection under the law. Since emancipation, many states and localities in the south had legalized informal segregation in public facilities. The decision, which upheld these 'Jim Crow' laws, opened the way for numerous other forms of legal segregation. Some historians have suggested that the decision in 1896 merely legalized already prevalent social practices, while others believe that the law altered the treatment of African-Americans, who might have made more progress towards equality without it. The Supreme Court issued another ruling in 1955 instructing that state and local laws start desegregation 'with all deliberate speed'.

KEVIN MURPHY

Plombières, Pact of (1858) A secret agreement between NAPOLEON III and Count CAVOUR, prime minister of Piedmont, the Pact of Plombieres planned and co-ordinated the future policies of their countries regarding Austria and Italian unification. Cavour's aim was to expel the Austrians from northern Italy and unify the country under his leadership. Although Napoleon III was sympathetic to ITALY's national aspirations, he preferred to proceed cautiously and in stages. Cavour and Napoleon III agreed that France would join Piedmont in a war against Austria only if such a war could be justified before European and French public opinion and that once Austria had been driven from Italy, the country would be divided into four federal states with the pope as president. In return for France's support, Nice and Savoy were to become French, and the daughter of Victor Emmanuel II (later king of Italy) was to marry a cousin of Napoleon. A formal treaty embodying this agreement was signed by the two men on 10 December 1858.

C. F. Dalzell (ed.), *The Unification of Italy 1859–61* (Malabar, Fla., 1976).

GEORGE O. KENT

poaching In Britain the legal right to take game (for example rabbits, deer, pheasant, partridge, salmon) for sport or pot was confined to landowners and their nominees. Anyone else doing so was poaching, and if caught liable to be fined, imprisoned or (until 1831) transported. From 1844 it was also illegal to take game even on a public highway. The incidence of poaching, which peaked in 1830 and 1843, is widely used by historians as an index of the social and economic plight of agricultural labourers. For many poaching was an economic necessity, or a pardonable lapse given diets where fresh meat was a rarity. Many regarded it as a moral right, criminalized by landowners as part of the extinction of common rights at ENCLOSURE. In 1880 tenant farmers were finally permitted to kill rabbits on land they rented, but for many labourers poaching remained both a sport and a form of social protest.

MALCOLM CHASE

poetry The nineteenth century produced a remarkable range and variety of poetry in all the literate countries of Europe and the Americas, and in the literate countries of Asia. Nevertheless, especially in Europe, poetry was generally displaced from its pre-eminence as the dominant form of literary expression by the continued rise of the NOVEL. Outside Europe, the myriad uses to which poetry was put in traditional and especially oral cultures followed the fortunes of the societies which produced such poetry; the massive extension of colonial rule in the course of the nineteenth century, and the sometimes genocidal replacement of indigenous peoples, meant that much of the traditional poetry of the pre-modern world simply ceased to be.

The history of poetry in Europe in the nineteenth century is in most respects the history of ROMANTICISM, though this is a difficult term to define and has different meanings in different national contexts. In Britain the century opened with a striking constellation of major poets, all different from each other but all fairly described as romantic: William Blake (1757–1827), William Wordsworth (1770–1850), Samuel Taylor Coleridge (1772–1834), Lord BYRON (1788–1824); Percy Bysshe Shelley (1792–1822) and John Keats (1795–1821). These poets wrote in reaction to what they perceived as the excessive rationalism of the eighteenth century, turning instead to the truths of the imagination, the beauty of natural forms or traditional folk poetry such as the ballad. However, many of their contemporaries continued to find neoclassical forms adequate to their needs. French romanticism equally repudiated eighteenth-century rationalsim but the greater influence of Jean Jacques Rousseau (1712–78) produced a more immediately subjective poetry differently implicated in its country's cultural politics, in the writing of Alphonse de LAMARTINE, Alfred de Vigny (1797–1863) and Victor Hugo (1802–85). In both countries the impetus given to poetry by romanticism produced in the course of the century some of the most enduring writing of their respective national literatures, both in direct continuation of the romantic spirit and in opposition to it.

Elsewhere in Europe the century produced poets who have become the dominant figures in their national literatures. In Germany the decisive influence was that of Johann Wolfgang Goethe (1749–1832), whose extensive poetry provided inspiration for succeeding schools of German poets. In Russia the early nineteenth century produced a number of outstanding poets, among whom Alexander Pushkin (1799–1837) was pre-eminent. In both countries the development of poetry was intimately bound up with the development of a national consciousness, and the assimilation or repudiation of western European, and especially French, models. If this was the case with the poetry written in two great imperial languages, it was still more so with the developing national poetries of the subject nations of eastern and southern Europe. Across Europe the nineteenth century saw poetry used as a way of asserting national identity and rediscovering lost and popular cultural traditions, with very different emphases according to different national situations, and drawing on different cultural and linguistic resources.

In the United States, too, the fate of poetry was partly caught up with the question of the articulation of a national identity, in for example the poetry of Henry Wadsworth Longfellow (1807–82) and Walt Whitman (1819–92). Here the more consciously democratic social order, the absence of a suppressed or remote national tradition and the prestige of English cultural models meant that an American poetic tradition had to be self-invented. The greatest American poet of the nineteenth century was perhaps Emily Dickinson (1830–86), whose work demonstrated the extraordinary power that could be achieved in lyrical and religious poetry with the exiguous-seeming cultural resources of provincial New England.

Across the rest of the world the fate of poetry was bound up with the fate of the cultures in which it flourished. In the great literate cultures of the Arabic world, the Indian subcontinent and the Far East, the differing impacts of colonialism and imperialism led variously to poetic revivals, poetic collapses, the adoption of European poetic models and their repudiation. Elsewhere, the assimilation of native and indigenous peoples into European and American empires meant the wholesale disappearance of a vast range of poetic forms, with the disappearance of the languages and sometimes the people who used them. Across North America and Siberia, the Pacific Ocean, Australasia, Africa and Latin America epic poems, songs of praise, religious chants, laments and ritual lyrics disappeared with their occasions, or are now known only by ethnographic records made at the moment of their disappearance. The extraordinary wealth of European poetry in the nineteenth century needs to be set against this background.

See also ARTS AND LITERATURE.

SIMON DENTITH

pogrom see ANTI-SEMITISM.

Poland In the nineteenth century Poland was more a cause than a political reality. As a result of the three partitions at the end of the eighteenth century (1772, 1793, 1795), the independent state of Poland disappeared from the map, swallowed up by Russia, Prussia and Austria. Some semblance of a Polish state was restored by Napoleon in 1807 with the creation of the duchy of Warsaw, but the post-Napoleonic settlement of 1815 saw Poland again partitioned.

Poland was to remain partitioned throughout the nineteenth century, with only the tiny Cracovian Republic serving as a temporary symbol of Polish independence, until annexation by Austria in 1846. Austria ruled the southern sector, Galicia. Prussia's portion was in the west, the grand duchy of Posen, which enjoyed limited autonomy until 1848. The largest share of territory and population was Russia's: the congress kingdom of Poland (Congress Poland). The population of these three territories combined has been estimated at 8.3 million in 1820 and 23.7 million by 1914.

Congress Poland, centred on the former state's capital of Warsaw, acted throughout the century as the main focus of Polish national identity. It began as an autonomous constitutional monarchy within the Russian Empire, with the tsar as king, but possessing a liberal constitution and its own administrative and legal system, parliament (Sejm) and army. Tsars ALEXANDER I and NICHOLAS I, absolutists as they were, paid scant attention to Polish constitutional niceties, and Polish unrest boiled over into the November Insurrection of 1830. The subsequent war led eventually to Russian subjugation of the Poles in September 1831 and mass oppression. The Organic Statute of 1832 suspended the 1815 constitution, replacing it with a true union with Russia, in which Polish autonomy was reduced to a minimum.

The Polish cause, now led from emigration by the moderates around Adam Czartoryski (1770–1861) and the radicals in the Polish Democratic Society, became one of the great liberal *causes célèbres*. The failure of the 1846 insurrection in Galicia weakened the Polish position in the 1848 Revolution (*see* REVOLUTIONS OF 1848). Although Poles were very prominent throughout revolutionary Europe, especially in Hungary and Italy, 1848 ended with Polish disappointment, culminating in the abolition of the autonomy of the grand duchy of Posen.

In Congress Poland, the reign of ALEXANDER II began with a more conciliatory attitude to Polish aspirations, but the attempts at accommodation by his Polish minister, Aleksander Wielopolski (1803–77), fell apart in the January Insurrection of 1863. The resulting war, with Prussia co-operating with Russia, again led, despite heroic resistance, to utter defeat in April 1864. In the aftermath Russia tried to crush Polish resistance once and for all. The peasantry was emancipated partly to cow the Polish gentry. The kingdom of Poland was abolished, the lands to be known henceforth as Vistulaland, and a ruthless Russification employed to expunge Polish national consciousness. Similarly harsh policies of Germanization attempted the same goal in Prussian Poland after 1863. In Galicia, however, Austria's weak position, internally and externally, resulted in the Poles obtaining from Vienna by 1864 a *de facto* autonomy, with the Lvov Sejm controlling, critically, educational policies, and with Polish as the province's official language. Galicia thus became the 'Piedmont' of Polish national aspirations, with Cracow once again the symbolic, cultural capital of Poland.

Congress Poland's position as the leading industrial region of the Russian Empire brought major economic and social transformations. One result was the emergence of new political parties, most notably the Polish Socialist Party (PPS), founded in 1893, eventually to be led by Józef Piłudski (1867–1935); and, on the Right, the Polish League, founded in 1887 and reorganized in 1892–3 by Roman Dmowski (1864–1939) as the National League (later the National Democratic Party). The polarization between Piłudski and Dmowski, which was to become the dominant force in Polish politics, itself had many continuities with the nineteenth-century rivalry between what Polish historiography knows as 'romanticism' and 'positivism'. Romanticism looked back to the multi-ethnic, inclusive Polish 'nation' (state) and saw the national struggle in terms of a liberal Messianism, as articulated most famously by Adam Mickiewicz (1798–1855). Positivism, the dominant force from 1864 to the 1890s, took a more realistic approach, dispensing with dreams of Messianic restoration and instead adopting the minimalist tactic of 'organic work' to improve Poles' material circumstances. Dmowski coupled this realism with a 'scientific', narrow definition of Polish national identity, which excluded the other minority groups, such as the Jews, Lithuanians and Ukrainians, whereas Piłudski adopted romanticism's liberal definition of Polishness. Thus the stage was set for the twentieth century's struggles over Polish identity.

Norman Davies, *God's Playground: A History of Poland*, vol. 2: *1795 to the Present* (New York, 1982).
Adam Zamoyski, *The Polish Way* (New York, 1988).

STEVEN BELLER

police Policing in the leading European nations, France and Britain, reflected the historical differences between the constitutions of the two states. Absolutist France had developed a professional, centralized bureaucracy as early as the seventeenth century. Louis XIV (1638–1715) created the office of *lieutenant général de police* for Paris in 1667, and a national force of mounted police – the *maréchaussée* – under the minister of war had been established in 1720. By the mid eighteenth century Paris was policed by a force of 3,000 men and was thought by many to be the safest city in Europe. Approximately the same number of *maréchaussées* (after 1791, *gendarmes*) patrolled the roads of rural France.

Britain had no comparable institutions, despite periodic concern about public disorder and rising crime, particularly in London. Mindful of the constitutional 'liberties' of their subjects, British monarchs employed a limited number of professional servants and relied, instead, on a decentralized government system staffed by untrained amateurs. Until the mid eighteenth century, day-to-day policing was the exclusive preserve of unpaid local officers – justices of the peace, parish constables, bailiffs and watchmen – exercising uncoordinated and often overlapping jurisdictions. As in France, serious disturbances were usually suppressed by the army. English society, however, had long-standing reservations about the use of troops against civilians, and this fear of military institutions retarded eighteenth-century efforts to introduce French-style, professional police. Some progress was made towards establishing a police force for metropolitan London in 1792 when the Middlesex Justice Act instituted a system of police offices, constables and stipendiary magistrates in metropolitan Middlesex and Surrey. One of the first magistrates appointed under the new legislation was Patrick Colquhoun (1745–1820), who emerged as the most effective publicist for police reform. His *Treatise on the Police of the Metropolis* (1795), which had gone through seven editions by 1807, focused government attention on the related issues of crime and policing. But five parliamentary committees appointed between 1812 and 1822 all balked at recommending the introduction of a new police system inimicable to traditional British liberties.

The 1820s brought major changes in both France and Britain. In France the conviction that the police had become politicized during the revolutionary and imperial regimes led to the introduction in 1829 of a new force of unarmed, civilian police to patrol Paris. Known initially as *sergents de ville*, they were later renamed *agents de la police nationale*. In Britain the home secretary, Sir Robert PEEL, persuaded parliament to appoint a new committee, which finally recommended the creation of a centralized professional police force for London. Legislation setting up the London Metropolitan Police passed in 1829, and the first uniformed, unarmed 'bobbies' entered service six months after the first *sergents* appeared on the streets of Paris. By May 1830, when the London force was fully operational, the 'New Police' comprised 3,200 men.

Police reform in the counties of England and Wales followed slowly. Some provincial towns took advantage of the 1833 Lighting and Watching Act to establish independent police forces, and the City of London obtained its own force in 1839. The Chartist activity of that year prompted new legislation empowering county magistrates to create local forces. Many, objecting to the cost, failed to do so, and by 1841 constabularies had been established in fewer than half the counties of England and Wales. Successive governments made no attempt to encourage the creation of county forces until 1856, when public apprehension about the impact on crime levels of the end of both transportation and the Crimean War stimulated legislation mandating the creation of county constabularies. The government assumed authority to inspect local forces and to contribute financially to those that met minimal standards of efficiency. Control locally was vested in watch committees in the boroughs and in police committees in the counties. Despite further minor reforms in the 1870s, these arrangements set the organizational pattern for policing in England and Wales into the twentieth century.

Patterns of police development in Continental countries other than France varied considerably. The unified Germany, for example, adopted a decentralized system on the British pattern. Italy, on the other hand, closely copied the centralized French model. After unification in 1870, two national police organizations were created – the Guardia di Publica Sicurezza and the Carabinieri, both directed from Rome by the ministry of the interior. However, most Continental states followed the French example in establishing a dual structure of policing. Prussia instituted a *gendarmerie* for the countryside in 1812, the Netherlands in 1814, Spain in 1844 and Austria in 1849.

Policing in the United States in the early nineteenth-century was based largely on the unreformed British system. Hostility towards military institutions was, if anything, even stronger in the United States than in Britain. Nevertheless, some southern cities maintained armed, military-style police to control their African-American populations, while communities elsewhere established vigilance committees which placed policing in the hands of private citizens. Municipal police forces, modelled on the London Metropolitan Police, began to emerge in the larger American cities in the 1840s, and by the end of the century many smaller towns also had locally appointed, uniformed police. Concern for liberty and the rule of law did not prevent most later-nineteenth-century policemen from carrying, and using, firearms. Nor did it prevent the use of NATIONAL GUARD troops (formal state militias) against rioters and, in the 1870s and 1880s, against striking workers as 'the policemen of industry'. The small national army assumed a federal police role: in 1877 the secretary of war asserted that 'The Army is to the United States what a well-disciplined and trained police force is to a city'.

See also PUNISHMENT.

Jacques Aubert et al., L'Etat et sa police en France (1789–1914) [The State and its Police in France] (Geneva, 1979).
Clive Emsley, Policing and its Context 1750–1870 (London, 1983).
Wilbur R. Miller, Cops and Bobbies: Police Authority in New York and London 1830–1870 (Chicago, 1977).
Eric H. Monkkonen, Police in Urban America 1860–1920 (Cambridge, 1981).

J. S. COCKBURN

political economy The name originally given to economics in the seventeenth century, 'political economy', continued to be used well into the nineteenth century. It expressed the belief that most economists continued to hold until the late nineteenth century that economics included understanding economic theory and behaviour in conjunction with social consequences and political advocacies and policies. The idea that economics could be separated from political processes was alien to thinkers like Adam Smith (1723–90) and J. S. MILL. MARX added a historical dimension, arguing that each epoch had its own particular political economic arrangements which reflected the class forces of the period.

But at the same time, the discipline of economics was beginning to be conceptualized as pure theory and science, with no necessary political and social dimensions. Nassau Senior (1790–1864) was the first to attempt an abstract and theoretical model of economics and to emphasize its separation from policy formation, in An Outline of the Science of Political Economy. This trend continued throughout the century, with only Marx standing out against the tendency. Mathematics was introduced into economics in 1838 by the French economist Augustin Cournot. But it was the marginalist revolution in economic thought in the 1870s that established the idea of economics as an aspirant natural science and dismissed the notion of political economy from the discipline.

See also FREE TRADE, LIBERALISM, RICARDO.

RICHARD PRICE

Polk, James Knox (b Mecklenburg County, North Carolina, 2 November 1795; d Nashville, Tennessee, 15 June 1849) President of the United States (1845–9). Admitted to the Bar in Tennessee in 1820, Polk entered the House of Representatives in 1825. As a Democrat, he supported Andrew JACKSON's policies and in 1832 was Jackson's defender on the Bank issue. In 1839 Polk was elected governor of

Tennessee but was defeated in re-election attempts in 1841 and 1843. When Martin VAN BUREN opposed the annexation of Texas in 1844, the Democratic Party dropped him and chose Polk as a dark-horse candidate. An expansionist and 'continentalist', Polk favoured the annexation of Texas and Oregon and the purchase of westward lands from Mexico. He saw the nation nearly double in size and expand to the Pacific Ocean during his presidency. The charge that Polk provoked a war with Mexico to extend slavery lacks substantiation, although he did little to avoid the MEXICAN-AMERICAN WAR.

JOHN MARTIN

poor relief In the nineteenth century poor relief could take many forms, much of it informal and neighbourly: mutual help (*see* FRIENDLY SOCIETIES), charitable relief (*see* PHILANTHROPY) and relief from public funds (*see* OLD POOR LAW, NEW POOR LAW). The Scottish Poor Law, reformed in 1845, differed from the English in continuing to be parish-based and in excluding the able-bodied by law from any relief. The Irish Poor Law dated from 1838.

Beyond Britain, European relief systems were roughly of two kinds. In Scandinavia and the German-speaking areas the local commune was obliged by law to provide poor relief and to levy a compulsory rate for the purpose, if required. This was in many respects similar to the situation in Britain. In the principal Latin countries, France, Belgium, Italy and also in the Netherlands there was no such obligation. Poor relief was provided on a charitable basis from endowments or through the church. In France and Belgium these were administered by committees (*bureaux*) appointed by the local commune under arrangements that dated from the time of the Directory. Elsewhere the control of the church authorities was more direct. There were no compulsory rates for the purpose. However, the Dutch relied on the commune to act as back-up, and elsewhere there was an increasing tendency towards the end of the century for the state to accept an obligation to relieve certain categories of the poor out of tax-provided funds (*see also* OLD-AGE PENSIONS).

Ian Levitt (ed.), *Government and Social Conditions in Scotland 1845–1919* (Edinburgh, 1988).
'Foreign and Colonial Systems of Poor Relief', in 'Royal Commission on the Poor Laws and Relief of Distress', vol. 33, app., British Parliamentary Papers 1910 Cd. 5441.

E. P. HENNOCK

popular culture The term 'popular culture' has multiple, overlapping meanings. The first is descriptive, referring to the complex of belief systems and social activities associated with the peasantry and the WORKING CLASSES. The second is a social definition, referring to culture that is made by 'the people', the opposite of the 'high culture' of the elites to which it is usually subordinate. The contours of popular culture are therefore vague. Sometimes synonymous with folklore, popular culture also remains heavily dependent on region as well as ethnicity and gender.

The nineteenth century witnessed the culmination of a process going back to the Reformation whereby elites withdrew from participation in popular culture to form a separate, learned culture based on print, as opposed to popular culture which remained largely oral. In western Europe and the United States it was rooted in custom and retained a carnivalesque dimension. Drink, violence and licentiousness remained essential elements of popular life, interspersed with occasional periods of religious revivalism. Popular values at work and at play were expressed through folk-song, while festivals (usually on saints' days) were particularly important as opportunities for popular gatherings when the values of the community were asserted. European charivari (the use of rough music to ridicule newly weds or social misfits who were often promenaded in public on a pole) was practised even in the American Midwest. Old supernatural and pagan ideas were still evident. In Britain the last reported case of 'swimming a witch' was in Chelmsford in 1863.

The nineteenth century is often interpreted as a period of eclipse when the authentic folk culture of the labouring poor was remoulded by the discipline of industrial capitalism. Improved communications and transport eroded local customs, and 'rough' culture came under assault from the bourgeoisie who considered it backward but also feared its subversive characteristics. Old community gatherings were suppressed (through the abolition of many saints' days) and remoulded in a respectable, orderly form, as part of the process of creating a supine proletariat. Cruel popular sports such as cock-fighting were forbidden and popular gatherings often required police permission. Cultural provision therefore became an arena of social control.

The shift was also caused by the emergence of a print culture within the working class, related to the increasingly high levels of literacy in Britain, the United States and some parts of Europe. In the second half of the century cheap stories and popular NEWSPAPERS became part of the culture of the proletariat. Print respected no national boundaries. American pulp novels were pirated and found an enthusiastic readership in Russia after the emancipation of the serfs. Popular culture became increasingly commercialized, a phenomenon associated with the coming of 'mass culture' (cultural artefacts created not by the people but for them by heavily capitalized culture industries). Thus, the bullfight in Spain became a major business enterprise. In Britain street FOOTBALL was banned and turned into a commercialized spectator sport – part of a process that amounted to nothing less than the formation of a new British working-class culture based on MUSIC HALL, fish and chips and seaside holidays. Affecting to be 'traditional', its nature was deeply apolitical, stressing the delights of home and immediate forms of pleasure. This was signified by the reinvention of the cockney as a cheery proletarian, addicted to monarchy and the nation.

During the century it was clear to contemporaries that old popular customs were being lost. This led to the folklore movement throughout Europe which was determined to record old customs and songs before it was too late and which located the soul of the nation in popular culture.

Although subject to reform, popular culture was characterized as much by continuity as by disruption. Many of the old customs survived and attempts at social control never truly succeeded. Drink and rough behaviour remained part of everyday life. Even mass culture (then in its infancy before the arrival of cinema and radio) had only a moderate impact because many could not afford to participate in the pleasures it offered. Popular culture was therefore never successfully tamed during the nineteenth century. It retained its ability to shock, embarrass, subvert and maintain the social order all at the same time.

Jeffrey Brooks, *When Russia Learned to Read: Literacy and Popular Culture, 1861–1917* (Princeton, NJ, 1985).

Hugh Cunningham, *Leisure in the Industrial Revolution c.1780–1880* (London, 1980).

ROHAN MCWILLIAM

populism (Russia) An ideological, social and political movement which began among the radical intelligentsia in the 1860s, Russian populism hearkened to HERZEN's call 'to the people, that is where you belong' (hence its Russian name, *narodnichestvo*), and the promptings of the left-wing literary critic and political thinker Chernyshevskii (1828–89). The populists believed that Russia could achieve socialism without passing through a capitalist stage, by means of a peasant revolution and the development of their communes. Influenced largely by BAKUNIN, who mistakenly believed that the peasants were on the point of rising against the landowners, thousands of young people went to the countryside in the mid-1870s with revolutionary propaganda, plans for educating the peasantry and laudable philanthropic ideals (*see* PEROVSKAIA). Others, following more the ideas of Lavrov (1823–1900), joined them in the hope of organizing numbers of leaders from the peasants themselves. When the movement failed, and many of the participants were arrested, imprisoned and exiled, an underground organization called Land and Freedom (Zemlia i volia) was set up but was unsuccessful. In 1879 it split into the People's Will (Narodnaia volia), with its adherence to Tkachev's (1844–86) view that power would have to be seized forcibly by a revolutionary minority, and the

Black Redistribution (Chernyi peredel), which remained loyal to Bakunin and led by PLEKHANOV. The former organization was responsible for the assassination of Alexander II in 1881, while the latter developed into the Russian social democrats. In the 1880s and early 1890s a rather more liberal strain emerged under the leadership of Mikhailovskii (1842–1904), who stressed the more humanitarian and evolutionary aspects of populism's ideals, adhering to the policies and writing of Herzen and Lavrov. The more successful activities of the ZEMSTVA stem from such elements. In 1902 the differing parties amalgamated to form the Social Revolutionary Party.

F. Venturi, *Roots of Revolution* (London, 1960).

A. V. KNOWLES

populism (United States)   The name given to the activities of the People's Party (1892), populism in the United States grew out of the agrarian discontent of southern and western farmers during the nineteenth century. Calling for a more just capitalism, Farmers' Alliance (1875) leaders issued the Ocala Demands (1890), which proposed a government grain bank, state ownership of the railroads, the direct election of senators, an income tax and the unlimited coinage of silver. In 1892 they reorganized the alliance as the People's Party, and unsuccessfully ran General James B. Weaver (1833–1912) of Iowa for president. Most of their success came on the state and local level in the south, but this led to a white backlash, because the populists welcomed African-American voters. The party was already in tatters when the Democrats co-opted their free-silver issue and candidate William Jennings Bryan (1860–1925) in 1896. After disaster in the election populism faded, but many of its programmes were passed during the Progressive period.

Lawrence Goodwyn, *Democratic Promise: The Populist Movement in America* (New York, 1976).

ALICE E. REAGAN

Portales, Diego (*b* Santiago, 15 June 1793; *d* Viña del Mar, 6 June 1837)   Chilean politician. The son of a royal official, he entered business in CHILE during the independence era. Following the exile of Bernardo O'HIGGINS, he came to dominate the opposition to the liberals, and became the leading figure in the conservative government of 1830–1, when he purged the bureaucracy and army, established a national guard dominated by landowners and businessmen and greatly restricted political freedoms. The authoritarian Constitution of 1833, which lasted, in modified form, until 1925, was heavily based on his thinking, though after organizing the election of President Joaquín Prieto (1786–1854) in 1831 he himself retired from office. Portales returned in 1835 as minister of war and of the interior, and managed the initial stages of the conflict with the Peru-Bolivia Confederation (*see* PERU), instituting a period of repression within Chile. He was assassinated by a mutinous army battalion in 1837.

RORY MILLER

Portugal For Portugal the nineteenth century opened with heavy involvement in the Napoleonic wars. In 1801 it was attacked by Spain, and in October 1807 a French army drove out the royal family, which fled to Brazil. However, in June 1808 the populace rose in revolt, the French being driven out on the arrival of a British army under Wellington. The subsequent PENINSULAR WAR had dramatic political effects. Resentment of British influence, the spread of Freemasonry, reduced censorship and wartime reforms all encouraged support for liberalism, while discontent was further encouraged by government repression and João VI's (1767–1826; prince regent 1792–1816; reigned 1816–26) failure to return from America, the result being the outbreak of revolution in August 1820. Forced to return from Brazil, which now broke away in turn, João sanctioned a liberal constitution, only for absolutism to be re-established under his younger son, Miguel (1802–66), in 1828. Liberal exiles based in Britain then invaded northern Portugal in 1832, provoking a two-year civil war that culminated in the overthrow of Miguel and his replacement by Maria II (1826–53). However, the liberal victory did not produce stability. On the contrary, political opinion remained divided between moderates and radicals, while the war had thrown up a clique of powerful generals who were all too ready to intervene in politics.

At the same time, Portugal was bankrupt, attempts to resolve the state's financial problems by expropriating the religious orders leading only to wholesale disorder in the countryside. Revolts were therefore frequent and it was not until the 1850s that a stable parliamentary system emerged. Even then, however, politics were corrupt and Portugal remained backward in Europe, the acquisition of a substantial colonial empire in Africa only adding to the strain on its resources. The consequence was the emergence of a republican movement which by 1900 was threatening the survival of the monarchy.

Harold Livermore, *A History of Portugal* (Cambridge, 1947).

CHARLES ESDAILE

positivism The French philosopher Auguste Comte (1798–1857) coined the term 'positivism' in the 1830s to denote a belief in the certain and distinctive kind of knowledge obtainable by science. According to his general account of human development, knowledge passed through three phases: the theological, the metaphysical or critical and finally the positive, where knowledge was based only on definitely knowable facts and the relations between them; all enquiries about ultimate ends or causes were relegated to the pre-scientific. Positive knowledge in this sense was extended by Comte from the natural and biological sciences to include knowledge of society; 'sociology' was another of his coinages (*see* SOCIOLOGY). However, positivism was developed beyond philosophy to become a scheme of social and political reform, in which, along with many eccentricities, the positive laws of human social development were to act as sole guides to social and political action.

Positivism as a philosophy was widely influential in the mid nineteenth century, especially in Britain, where intellectuals who passed under its influence included the philosopher John Stuart MILL, the novelist George Eliot (1819–80) and the writers Frederic Harrison (1831–1923) and Harriet MARTINEAU. For some, the strongly religious, though antitheological, inspiration of positivism led to the foundation of the Religion of Humanity. Positivism as a scheme of political and social reform was less widely diffused among European intellectuals, though it was strongly influential in the emergent nations of Latin America and in some cases affected the formulation of their constitutions.

These particular senses of positivism, closely associated with the *Positive Philosophy* (1830–42; trans. 1853) and the *Positive Politics* (1851–4) of Comte, need to be distinguished from a less specific meaning for positivism that began to emerge in the nineteenth century, where positivism meant little more than a commitment to the empirical sciences and was thus felt to be inadequate as a guide for the most important areas of human experience.

Walter M. Simm, *European Positivism in the Nineteenth Century* (Ithaca, NY, 1963).

SIMON DENTITH

potato famine   *see* IRISH FAMINE.

Powderly, Terence Vincent (*b* Carbondale, Pennsylvania, 22 January 1849; *d* Washington, DC, 24 June 1924)   Irish-American labour leader. As a young adult he worked on the railroad and as a machinist, where he became involved in the union movement in Pennsylvania. He served as mayor of Scranton as a member of the Greenback-Labor Party from 1878 to 1884, and was elected Grand Master Workman of the KNIGHTS OF LABOR in 1879, a post he held until 1893. A believer in protecting American labour from foreign competition, he was instrumental in passing the Contract Labor Act of 1885, which banned the importation of unskilled foreign workers. He opposed the trade-unionism of Samuel GOMPERS because he believed that skilled workers should help the unskilled. Idealistic and reform-minded rather than pragmatically aggressive, Powderly supported co-operative production rather than a wage system, and did not advocate strikes. He resigned from the Knights because of his opposition to combative unionism.

KEVIN MURPHY

Prempeh I (*b* Ashanti, *c.*1871; *d* Kumasi, 1931)   Ruler of ASHANTI. In 1888, after a period of internecine war, Kwaku Dua Asamu was elected Asantehene, or ruler, of Ashanti, the most powerful traditional state of the region. Entitled Prempeh ('the plump one'), he was enstooled (that is enthroned) only in 1894. In a period of confusion he attempted to reassert Ashanti influence, but when negotiations with the neighbouring British colony of Gold Coast broke down, in 1896 Ashanti was annexed and invaded, and Prempeh sent into exile, ultimately to the Seychelles. The British had long feared Ashanti expansionism but now sought an excuse for action, in order to forestall French advances in the interior. A serious revolt followed in 1900. In exile Prempeh wrote historical accounts of some interest. He was allowed to return from exile in 1924, but only as ruler of the Ashanti capital, Kumasi.

P. E. H. HAIR

Pre-Raphaelites   Formed in 1848, the Pre-Raphaelite Brotherhood was a group of artists and critics with a very distinctive practice of, and attitude to, painting. The brotherhood originally consisted of William Holman Hunt (1827–1910), John Everett Millais (1829–96), Dante Gabriel Rossetti (1828–82), William Michael Rossetti (1829–1919), Frederick George Stephens (1828–1907) and James Collinson (?1825–81). They took their inspiration from medieval art and were strongly antipathetic to contemporary academic art, for which the classicism of Raphael (1483–1520) was an important model. In practice their art showed a striking commitment to the minutely detailed rendition of nature, in treating morally uplifting and often religious topics. This made some of their pictures controversial, such as Millais's *Christ in the House of his Parents* (1849), which appeared to detract from the aura of sacred abstraction conventionally associated with such topics. But Pre-Raphaelite painting was quickly accepted, especially in provincial England, and provided some of the most familiar images of nineteenth-century English art. These include Holman Hunt's *The Light of the World* (1853–6) and *The Awakening Conscience* (1852), Rossetti's *Astarte Syriaca* (1877) and *The Blessed Damozel* (1871–9) and Ford Madox Brown's *Work* (1852–65).

In the 1850s the original brotherhood became a looser association, and attracted other figures such as William MORRIS, Edward Burne-Jones (1833–98), Ford Madox Brown (1821–93) and Henry Wallis (1830–1916). Pre-Raphaelitism thus became a looser term, denoting an artistic practice which combined realism with allegorical, historical and especially medieval subjects. The term can also be extended to include writers who were either members of the group or associated with it. Thus, making due allowances for the differences between visual and written forms, the poetry of William Morris, Dante Gabriel Rossetti, Christina Rossetti (1830–94) and even Algernon Swinburne (1837–1909) can be described as Pre-Raphaelite.

Timothy Hilton, *The Pre-Raphaelites* (London, 1970).

SIMON DENTITH

press *see* NEWSPAPERS.

Pretoria Convention (1881) The agreement reached by Britain and the TRANSVAAL Republic which ended the first Boer War (*see* ANGLO-BOER WARS), the Pretoria Convention established the republic's territorial boundaries and forbade Boer settlement beyond them. The limit of debt the republic could incur was set, along with the size of a British grant-in-aid. A British resident was established in Pretoria, representing Britain's suzerainty. This was a concept never precisely defined; interpreted differently by the Boers and the British, it was the source of considerable friction. Some of the convention's restrictions – for example British control over policy regarding Africans (referred to at the time as 'natives') and over the republic's foreign policy, as well as Britain's right to move troops through the republic without consultation – were rescinded in the London Convention of 1884.

SIMON KATZENELLENBOGEN

Pretorius, Andries Wilhelminus Jacobus (*b* Graaf-Reinet, Cape Colony, 27 November 1798; *d* Pretoria, 23 July 1853) Boer leader. Famous for his part in the BATTLE OF BLOOD RIVER (1838), he is often ranked on a par with Paul KRUGER as a folk hero, and celebrated in the name of the city of Pretoria. In relations with Britain, he favoured negotiation, but a series of rebuffs led him towards armed resistance. He was often in conflict with other Boer leaders and the *volksraads* (literally, people's councils), jealous guardians of the republican pattern of group government against powerful individuals or centralized control. However, his widespread popularity, military prowess and rhetorical powers often forced opponents to give way. His political career – and negotiating skills – culminated in his leading part in the Sand River Convention (*see* ORANGE FREE STATE).

SIMON KATZENELLENBOGEN

Primrose League In 1883 the Primrose League was founded by a group of British Conservative politicians under Lord Randolph Churchill as a means of improving the popular organization of Conservatism, a task made urgent by franchise extension and legal restrictions on electoral expenditure (*see* PARLIAMENTARY REFORM). Its name was intended to highlight the link with Benjamin DISRAELI whose favourite flower was reputedly the primrose.

The league's preferred brand of Conservatism was traditional. It concentrated on maintenance of the established church, support for religious education, preservation of the union with Ireland, expansion of the empire and defence of the House of Lords and private property. It also exploited Queen Victoria's known sympathy for the Conservative Party. This approach made the league acceptable to the party leadership otherwise apprehensive that a mass organization would challenge the parliamentarians' control over policy.

The novelty of the league lay primarily in its activities and membership. Its habitations offered a multitude of social events including musical entertainments, teas, fetes, picnics and railway excursions, and its political propaganda was often attractively conveyed by means of magic-lantern slides and *tableaux vivants*. Moreover, by offering a low membership fee it managed to enrol a much wider range of members than was usual for the Conservative Party, including working men, women, children and Catholics. The league claimed a million members by 1891 and 1.5 million by 1901. Its extensive local network provided a stable base for the sweeping electoral victories enjoyed by the Conservatives between 1886 and 1905, though it was in steady decline after the turn of the century.

See also TORYISM.

Martin Pugh, *The Tories and the People 1880–1935* (Oxford, 1985).
Janet Robb, *The Primrose League 1883–1906* (New York, 1942).

MARTIN PUGH

printing The expansion of NEWSPAPERS and book production in the nineteenth century was made possible by technical advances in printing, the most important since Gutenberg's original invention in the fifteenth century. The greatest innovation, symbolizing the advent of the new industrial age, was the application of steam power to printing. König steam presses, developed in Saxony, were used first on *The Times* in 1814, leading to a quadrupling of the number of copies of an edition produced per hour and a dramatic lowering of costs. In subsequent decades modifications to the steam press created a further revolution in the newspaper industry. By the 1830s advanced presses were turning out 4,000 double-sided impressions of a paper per hour. R. Hoe & Company of New York, the leading manufacturer of printing-presses, produced a type-revolving 'lightning' press which locked individual blocks of type into rotating cylinders, permitting still greater speed and output.

Two additional inventions, spurred by the newspaper industry and cheap book publishers, were stereotyped plates and the Linotype. Stereotyping, widely used for the first time in the 1870s, was a prerequisite to the duplicating and breaking up of individual pages. With the development of web rotary printing-machines, which used stereotyped plates, it became possible for multiple presses to run off unlimited copies of newspapers within a brief period of time. The Linotype was invented by Ottmar Mergenthaler (1854–99) of the *New York Tribune* in the 1880s. It represented an even more striking advance because it mechanized the process of typesetting. By the end of the century electroplating was being employed to cast stereotypes rapidly, and technical improvements in pictorial printing were well under way, including the use of the half-tone photo-engraving process with the rotary press, which enabled newspapers to reproduce photographs. The beginning of colour printing in newspapers during the final decades of the century was further indication that a veritable revolution had been carried out.

See also PERIODICALS.

S. H. Steinberg, *Five Hundred Years of Printing*, second edn (London, 1966).

JOEL H. WIENER

prostitution   During the nineteenth century prostitution underwent significant changes. Contemporaries observed with alarm what they believed to be an enormous increase in the number of prostitutes. Although the numbers reported, often in many thousands for cities such as London and Paris, must be treated with scepticism, the number of women dependent on prostitution for a livelihood probably did grow during the period.

Two cardinal aspects of nineteenth-century historical development fuelled this increase. First, the explosive growth in population, and the increasing concentration of that population in urban areas, augmented the size of the potential supply of prostitutes as well as the size of their potential market. Secondly, as larger numbers became dependent on wage labour, working-class women became more vulnerable to the economic pressure to engage in prostitution during economic downturns that pushed them or their husbands into unemployment. In addition, domestic service, the single largest sphere of female employment during the nineteenth century, left women vulnerable to sexual exploitation. With termination of employment the usual consequence of pregnancy, prostitution became the only alternative to starvation for many. Finally, throughout the period prostitution remained the most remunerative occupation for women.

The actual number of prostitutes varied according to economic conditions, increasing in times of depression and contracting at other times. Working-class women moved into and out of prostitution as their circumstances changed, and a period of prostitution did not necessarily leave a woman stigmatized within her community, although such transitions became more difficult to negotiate during the course of the century. The urban venue of these developments guaranteed that they would be played out before the view of a growing and increasingly politically powerful, respectable middle class, which regarded prostitution not simply as a social problem but also as a challenge to both moral and political order.

The basic outlines of the official response to prostitution first emerged in France, where authorities developed a system of registering prostitutes which required them to submit to medical inspection, remanding those infected by venereal disease to prison hospitals for treatment. Napoleon's concern about the debilitating impact of VENEREAL DISEASE on the efficiency of his armies had been the original impetus for this departure. By the middle of the century similar systems had been adopted at the national level in Prussia, the Netherlands, Belgium and Norway, in some localities in Italy and Denmark, and in most major European cities. England adopted this approach in the 1860s with the passage of a series of CONTAGIOUS DISEASES ACTS.

Fear of venereal disease animated this intervention by the state into what had previously been the province of private life. The public-health menace of syphilis led authorities to protect men seeking an outlet for their sexual impulses, which were believed to be both natural and uncontrollable. Since nineteenth-century medicine regarded overt sexuality on the part of women as dangerous and unnatural, those women who engaged in prostitution thereby rendered themselves liable to state surveillance. Intractable realities of male and female sexual nature made prostitution inevitable and thus necessitated state regulation, according to William Acton, the pre-eminent medical expert on the subject. Acton articulated this point of view in his *Prostitution considered in its Moral, Social and Sanitary Aspects* (1857).

The problem of prostitution also provoked strenuous efforts to achieve moral reform. This took two forms. One focused on the moral reclamation of individual prostitutes, either by rescue work undertaken by many as a recognized form of charitable endeavour or by the founding of Magdalene homes for prostitutes seeking a more respectable life. Secondly, state regulation itself came under attack as an official condonation of sexual vice and as placing an oppressive and inequitable burden on women in order to protect men from the consequences of their sexual adventures. In England the charismatic Josephine BUTLER led the Ladies' National Association in resisting the operation of the Contagious Diseases Acts and in demanding their repeal. This example stimulated similar movements on the Continent, but only in England did the system of regulation succumb to such pressure.

The sentimental depictions of prostitutes found in such popular novels as Charles Dickens's *Oliver Twist* (1839) and Victor Hugo's *Les Miserables* (1862) underlined the saliency of prostitution for the nineteenth-century imagination. The prostitute raised troubling issues about order – moral, political, social – and the controversies over these issues revealed deeply felt attitudes towards GENDER and sexuality.

Alain Corbin, *Les Filles des Noce* (Paris, 1978), transl. by Alan Sheridan as *Women for Hire* (Cambridge, MA, 1990).
Judith Walkowitz, *Prostitution and Victorian Society: Women, Class and the State* (New York, 1980).

GAIL SAVAGE

protectionism The ideology and practice of levying tariffs or customs duties on imported commodities (more rarely on exports) to promote the interests of domestic producers is known as protectionism. At the beginning of the nineteenth century tariffs were customary features of commercial regimes, responding to the revenue needs of governments with primitive fiscal systems as well as to the protectionist doctrine of mercantilism. By the mid nineteenth century the principal apostles of FREE TRADE, Adam Smith (1723–90), David Ricardo and John Stuart Mill, had demonstrated the inconvenience of such obstacles to international trade. None the less, outside Britain free-trade ideas were embraced only briefly, and by the 1880s a new protectionist age had begun.

Although some trade liberalization occurred in Britain in the 1780s, the financial burden of the Napoleonic wars caused British tariff levels to rise, and the move to free trade did not occur decisively until the 1840s. Sir Robert Peel abolished all export duties and greatly reduced import tariffs in 1842 and 1845. Crucially, the CORN LAWS protecting the agrarian interest were dismantled in 1846. Peel's reforms were continued by W. E. Gladstone, such that by 1860 Britain had adopted in effect a completely free and non-discriminatory trade regime, a stance it was not to modify until long after 1900. But the commercial policy perceived as appropriate to the most advanced industrial power did not necessarily meet with approval elsewhere: low-cost manufactures imported from Britain could be represented as an obstacle to the development of domestic manufacturing industry.

In France Napoleon's CONTINENTAL SYSTEM had an avowedly protectionist intent which remained characteristic of French commercial policy to mid-century. This was true also of Austria and Russia. The formation of the ZOLLVEREIN in 1834, eliminating customs duties between the German states and putting in place a relatively low common external tariff, was in no sense a victory for free trade; and in the 1840s (following publication of Friedrich List's (1798–1846) *National System of Political Economy* in 1841, which argued the need to protect the industries of nations vulnerable to competition from more advanced countries) Germany's tariffs on manufactured goods were raised. List, however, had added little of substance to the 'infant industry' arguments of the major precursor of modern protectionism, Alexander Hamilton's (1757–1804) *Report on Manufactures* (1791) to the United States Congress. In fact, the United States had no need of industrial protection while the European powers were at war, but from 1816 to 1832, and again in the 1840s, it maintained an important tariff.

Britain's move to free trade in the late 1840s found some response elsewhere, but it was above all the COBDEN-Chevalier Treaty of 1860 which stimulated liberalization in European trade. Its significance was less the concessions Britain and France accorded each other than the network of similar commercial agreements which followed in the 1860s with other European countries (though not the United States), in which most-favoured-nation clauses gave multilateral effect to bilateral concessions. However, by the late 1870s protectionism was again in the ascendancy, for political as well as economic reasons. Nationalism was an increasingly potent force, with industrial strength (implying self-sufficiency and military capacity) a forceful expression. From the early 1870s a downturn in the long economic cycle (the GREAT DEPRESSION) introduced throughout the international system two decades of weak economic performance, for which imports were a convenient scapegoat. Europe's agriculture did not escape the downturn, with cheap grain from the United States (where the high tariff of the Civil War years had not been reversed) undercutting local production. It is characteristic of tariffs that, although their burden on consumers tends to be diffused, the producers who benefit are well defined and organized. Only in Britain, Denmark and the Netherlands was European agriculture not protected by 1900. Tariffs on manufactures were increased almost universally: in Germany (1879), France (1881, 1892), Italy (1878, 1887), Russia (1868, 1893) and the United States (1890, 1897 following slight reduction in 1883). However, the true extent of the protection resulting from these tariffs is better assessed not by their nominal level (per cent addition to import price), but instead by calculating levels of 'effective protection' (the rate of protection on value added in production after allowing for tariffs on imported inputs as well as on finished goods).

A. G. Kenwood and A. L. Lougheed, *The Growth of the International Economy 1820–1960* (London, 1971).

Sidney Pollard, *Peaceful Conquest: The Industrialization of Europe 1760–1970* (Oxford, 1981).

HENRY FINCH

proto-industrialization Seen as a phase in the development of modern industrial economies, dominated by the spread of commercially organized rural domestic manufacturing for distant markets, proto-industrialization preceded and paved the way for industrialization proper by endorsing regional specialization and by promoting the accumulation of capital, entrepreneurial and work skills. Regions less well favoured agriculturally came to specialize in the production of textiles, metalwares or other traded craft goods. Proto-industry was successful because it used cheap underemployed rural labour. The PUTTING-OUT SYSTEM was prevalent and the role of merchants in organizing production and trade was pivotal. The expansion of extra-agricultural income-earning opportunities for men, women and children is seen to have been a powerful solvent of the agrarian order: promoting proletarianization, freeing marriage from the inheritance of land, stimulating population growth and changing roles and relationships between the sexes and the generations. The concept has stimulated much interdisciplinary research, which has shown that the dynamics of proto-industry were much more varied and complex than the theory allows.

See also INDUSTRIAL REVOLUTION.

L. A. Clarkson, *Proto-industrialization: The First Phase of Industrialization* (London, 1985).

P. Kriedte, H. Medick and J. Schlumbohm, *Industrialization before Industrialization* (Cambridge, 1981).

PAT HUDSON

Proudhon, Pierre Joseph (*b* Besançon, 15 January 1809; *d* Paris, 19 January 1865) French socialist-anarchist theoretician. He became a printer-proofreader in the 1820s. His most famous work, *Qu'est-ce que la propriété?* (What is Property?) appeared in 1840. The answer, 'La propriété, c'est le vol' (Property is theft), caused a sensation, although neither the form of the question nor the answer, which came from the Girondin politician of the 1790s Brissot (1754–93), was his own. He became a journalist and deputy during the Second Republic and attempted to form a popular bank in 1849 but this effort collapsed after his imprisonment for press offences. His writings idealized artisan workshops, were hostile to industrialization and excessive division of labour and demanded absolute equality of incomes. His depiction of the state as the enemy of working people has had a lasting influence on French trade-union traditions.

R. Hoffman, *Revolutionary Justice: The Social and Political Theory of Pierre-Joseph Proudhon* (Urbana, Ill., 1972).

DONALD SUTHERLAND

Prussia On 14 October 1806 the Prussian army was disastrously defeated by Napoleon at Jena (*see* BATTLE OF JENA) and Auerstadt (near Jena, in Thuringia). The king and court fled from Berlin, which was occupied by the French, and the Prussian fortresses quickly surrendered. Clearly, fundamental reforms were required to save the kingdom. The task was entrusted to the baron vom STEIN, an imperial knight who had entered the Prussian service in 1780, and other reformers. An edict of 1807 abolished personal serfdom (but not the peasants' labour services) and permitted commoners to acquire noble estates. The towns were granted a limited form of self-government in 1808. Gerhard von Scharnhorst (1755–1813), the son of a Hanoverian peasant, abolished corporal punishment in the army; commoners were admitted to the officer corps; and, later, general conscription was introduced. In 1812, under Stein's successor, HARDENBERG, compulsory guilds were abolished and the Jews emancipated. These radical reforms enabled Prussia – together with its allies, especially Russia – to defeat the French in the 'War of Liberation' (1813) and to gain large Rhenish territories at the peace of 1815. However, after the victories the reforms were reversed. The royal promise of representative institutions was not kept, and, thanks to strong noble opposition, the agrarian reforms brought the landlords large compensation in land at the peasants' expense. Under the dullard FREDERICK-WILLIAM III (reigned 1797–1840) reaction triumphed, the reformers were dismissed and many victimized. But the creation of the German Customs Union in 1833 (see ZOLL-VEREIN), which Austria did not join, paved the way to the War of 1866 and Austria's expulsion from Germany, and in the new Rhenish provinces and the Ruhr industries began to develop quickly.

Hopes that FREDERICK-WILLIAM IV (reigned 1840–61) would bring about change were not fulfilled. He was a romantic who dreamt of medieval glory. No constitution was granted, and a meeting of the united diet ended in failure in 1847. On 18 March 1848 the revolution reached Berlin (see REVOLUTIONS OF 1848). Barricades were put up and Prussian troops engaged in fierce street fighting but were withdrawn on the 19th. Berlin and other towns were in the hands of the revolutionaries, yet the army was not defeated. The king paid homage to the dead and donned the black, red and gold colours of liberal Germany. A Prussian constituent assembly met in Berlin, which was more radical than the FRANKFURT PARLIAMENT elected by the whole of Germany. A liberal ministry was appointed, against strong conservative opposition, and many remnants of the old system disappeared. But the liberal triumph did not last. In November 1848, after the defeat of the revolution in Vienna, the constituent assembly was adjourned and then dissolved. The Prussian army reoccupied Berlin. A constitution was proclaimed by the king, who retained all executive power and the right of appointing and dismissing the government. The diet consisted of two houses, an upper house modelled on the British House of Lords and a lower house, elected indirectly by a reactionary three-class franchise which favoured the well-to-do. It remained valid until 1918. Military force was triumphant, yet Prussia had a constitution, however limited, and the diet possessed budgetary rights.

Under the next king, WILLIAM I (reigned 1861–88) this led to a new conflict, about the reform of the army desired by William and the generals, to make it ready for offensive operations. The lower house of the diet granted the financial means, at first only 'provisionally', and later refused it altogether. Several dissolutions brought victory to the new liberal and bourgeois Progressive Party, until the hesitant king appointed Otto von BISMARCK prime minister to fight the battle with the deputies. This he did by introducing strict press censorship, dismissing liberal officials and judges and ruling unconstitutionally without a budget. Bismarck deliberately played the military card. In the wars against Denmark (1864) (see SCHLESWIG-HOLSTEIN QUESTION) and against Austria and the other German states (1866) the Prussian army triumphed, and the Progressive Party was decisively defeated. Prussia annexed Hanover, Schleswig, Holstein, Hesse-Kassel, Nassau and Frankfurt, and Bismarck created the NORTH GERMAN CONFEDERATION, dominated by Prussia, with a Reichstag elected by universal male franchise – a further means to defeat the Progressives by mobilization of the loyal peasantry – but in Prussia the three-class franchise remained. The Prussian officer corps and the upper levels of the bureaucracy continued to be headed by the nobility, although the true Prussian JUNKERS were highly critical of Bismarck's revolutionary methods. The Progressive Party split; the new National Liberal Party supported Bismarck's policy, especially when German unification followed the war against France (1870–1) (see UNIFICATION OF GERMANY). Bismarck became the German chancellor and remained Prussian prime minister, supported by changing majorities in the Reichstag and the Prussian diet. The old Prussia dominated the new Germany, but it was transformed by economic changes and rapid industrialization, an odd mixture of the old and the new.

G. A. Craig, *The Politics of the Prussian Army* (Oxford, 1964).
E. J. Feuchtwanger, *Prussia: Myth and Reality* (London, 1970).

                                                                    F. L. CARSTEN

psychology As the nineteenth century began, the chief influences on psychology, the study of the causes and effects of mental activity and the relation of behaviour to mental processes, were philosophical, via the work of René Descartes (1596–1650) and the eighteenth-century British empiricists. Experimental methods were introduced by several nineteenth-century German physiologists, establishing psychology as a scientific enterprise. Johannes Müller (1801–58) conducted experiments to show that stimulation of any particular nerve caused sensations characteristic of that nerve. Hermann von Helmholtz (1821–94) applied similar techniques to ocular focusing, colour vision and neural impulse studies. Gustav Fechner (1801–87), while investigating the connection between stimulus intensity and sensation, invented the methods of average error and constant stimuli – foundational aspects of psychophysical methodology – showing that behaviour could be studied via scientific measurement.

In 1876 Wilhelm Wundt (1832–1920) founded the first laboratory devoted entirely to psychological studies, signifying the birth of psychology as a modern science. Wundt believed psychology involved analysing conscious experience into basic elements, determining connections between those elements and elucidating the laws governing those connections. Concurrently, Hermann Ebbinghaus (1850–1909) began experimental investigations of learning, memory, the formation of associations and consciousness, greatly extending the scope of psychology.

William James's (1842–1910) *Principles of Psychology* (1890) addressed the origin and characteristics of consciousness. Influenced by DARWIN, James viewed mentality and human thinking capabilities as the results of natural selection, rather than of divine origin, arguing that organisms with consciousness could adapt quickly to novel situations – a survival advantage that became a species characteristic. By the end of the century, Sigmund Freud (1856–1939) was stressing *un*conscious mental states as powerful, intentional agents of behaviour. Until 1895, Freud had believed that all mental phenomena were reducible to neurological activity; however, following studies such as the case of 'Anna O.', he rejected this reductionism, claiming that psychological explanations were autonomous from natural science, presaging the development of psychoanalysis.

Owen Flanagan, *The Science of the Mind* (Boston, 1984).

STEVE AMANN

public health Concern about the public health went through a number of phases in the nineteenth century. Initially, the problem was seen primarily as involving the exclusion of epidemic disease through quarantine. In the early nineteenth century society had to be protected against yellow fever and cholera in this manner. By mid-century, the common threat was thought to come from within the city. Epidemic disease was blamed on stagnant and decomposing filth which was thought to generate miasmas (*see* THEORIES OF DISEASE). It could be fought through improving the environment with sanitary engineering. In the late nineteenth century the public-health threat was seen in more individualistic terms. The bacteriological revolution devalued generic miasmatic explanations of disease. An increasing tendency to see health education as the best means of combating sickness made environmentalism seem like a set of excuses for individual failings.

These approaches overlapped to some degree and each left their mark on the health departments of cities and countries. The quarantine strategy remained important in port cities where ships were increasingly subject to careful inspection and rigorous if brief quarantine where infectious cases were discovered. The environmental strategy left health officers in many places empowered to prevent disease by keeping cities and villages clean (*see* CHOLERA). The individualistic approach favoured curative medicine in hospitals, health visitors to the poor (especially poor mothers) and technologically advanced public-health laboratories in larger cities (*see* MEDICINE).

In England the environmental strategy was codified in law with the Public Health Acts of 1848 (largely the work of Edwin Chadwick (1800–90)) and 1875 (principally framed by John Simon (1816–1904)). Chadwick put the engineers in charge of the environmental approach while Simon left more discretion to the medical profession (*see* DOCTORS). This contrast between medical and engineering approaches was common in many other places and was a matter of great controversy at the time.

C. Fraser Brockington, *Public Health in the Nineteenth Century* (Edinburgh, 1965).

GERRY KEARNS

puerperal fever An infection of the uterus normally sustained either during or after delivery, puerperal fever (also known as metria, puerperal septicaemia or puerperal sepsis) remained the major cause of death in childbirth throughout the nineteenth century. Although the pathological cause of death, usually septicaemia or peritonitis, was clear, vehement debate surrounded the contagious nature of the illness. The observations of Gordon (1752–99; Aberdeen, 1795), Holmes (1809–94; Boston, 1843) and Semmelweis (1818–65; Vienna, 1858) showed that doctors and midwives were carriers of infection, and that, by following simple codes of cleanliness, death rates from puerperal fever could be dramatically reduced. Yet the medical profession refused to contemplate that they may have been vehicles for puerperal fever. Partly as a result of this negligence, over 100,000 women died from puerperal fever in the United States as late as the 1920s, many of them needlessly.

See OBSTETRICS.

GRAHAM MOONEY

punishment Forms of punishment underwent a radical transformation during the nineteenth century. Death sentences and other, lesser, physical punishments were greatly curtailed or abandoned altogether; Britain discontinued and France began the practice of transporting criminals to other parts of the world; and in both Europe and North America confinement in state-controlled prisons was established as the standard punishment for most serious offences.

In Britain piecemeal amelioration of the 'Bloody Code' – the widespread use of death and corporal punishments to safeguard property and social stability – began in the eighteenth century when transportation to the American colonies was established as a condition of royal pardon for convicted felons. When transportation was disrupted by the American War in 1776, convicts awaiting shipment were imprisoned in hulks (decommissioned warships moored in the Thames and other harbours) and set to hard labour. This stopgap measure anticipated the nineteenth-century move to imprisonment, and even after transportation (to Australasia) was resumed in 1787 incarceration in the hulks continued. Despite appalling conditions and high mortality, it was not finally phased out until 1857. Transportation continued until 1868. By that date, approximately 160,000 convicts had been sent to Australia and Van Diemen's Land (Tasmania).

Interest in prison reform dates from the late-eighteenth-century investigations of John Howard (1726–90), whose tours of English and Continental prisons focused public attention on the insanitary and irrational nature of prison life. Legislation authorizing the construction of two national penitentiaries in England proved abortive, and the first national institution, at Millbank, was not opened until 1816. However, a number of local prisons, substituting Howard's reformative regime of penitential discipline for the unregulated, corrupting confinement of earlier establishments, were built during the final quarter of the eighteenth century. Most of Howard's reforming ideals were soon abandoned in the face of prisoner indiscipline and increasing public concern about rising crime, and replaced by harsh, deterrent regimes. Diets were reduced, silence was strictly enforced and prisoners were set to repetitive and useless forms of labour. The trends towards increased severity and central control culminated in the opening in 1842 of Pentonville, a new penitentiary modelled on the American 'separate' system of solitary confinement. Ten new prisons on the Pentonville model were built in England during the following decade, in addition to several on the Continent; others were converted to the 'separate' system. Several small local prisons were closed, but full rationalization was delayed until 1877 when local and national prisons were integrated into a unified, government-funded system. Mounting criticism of solitary confinement and of useless hard labour finally led to the passage in 1898 of the Prison Act, which relaxed the 'separate' system and opened the way for the more constructive prison regimes of the twentieth century.

France instituted a centralized prison system in 1810. Several new penitentiaries were built, and a variety of old buildings adapted to the new carceral practices. Influenced by developments in the United States and Britain, the French also experimented with solitary confinement and with various labour and and rehabilitation schemes. In the 1850s, just as England was winding down transportation to Australia, France established overseas penal colonies in Guiana and New Caledonia. These were not permanently closed until the Second World War. After 1840 the science of punishment was increasingly internationalized. Beginning in 1846, European congresses met regularly to debate penal developments in other countries.

Early-nineteenth-century efforts to curtail the use of the death penalty in Britain were impeded by fears aroused by the French Revolution. A parliamentary campaign led by Sir Samuel Romilly (1757–1818) failed to reduce significantly the more than two hundred capital statutes then in force. As imprisonment and transportation assumed a more central role in the criminal justice system, however, the number of offenders actually executed declined. By the 1840s execution for offences other than murder was rare. This trend was formalized in 1861 when the death penalty was abolished for all crimes other than murder and high treason. Belgium, Denmark, Holland, Italy and Portugal all abolished the death penalty entirely before the end of the century but moves to do so in Britain failed.

In keeping with emerging nineteenth-century notions of decency and decorum, most other forms of physical punishment were removed from public view, or wholly abandoned, during the century. In Britain the dissection of executed felons was discontinued in 1832, and two years later the practice of exposing the bodies of malefactors on gibbets was terminated by statute. Public execution was finally discontinued in 1868. France continued to guillotine felons publicly until 1939. In 1837 the pillory, which had been used in England to punish serious public crimes until 1830, was formally abolished. Petty offenders continued to be placed in the stocks until mid-century. Whipping remained the traditional punishment for minor crimes. Statutory approval for private whipping had been granted in 1779, but the public flogging of women was not actually forbidden until 1817. They were whipped in private until 1820. Men were still being publicly flogged as late as 1835, and the abolition of public whipping was not effected until 1862. In the same year, in response to popular apprehension about violent street crime, whipping was introduced as an additional punishment to penal servitude for robbery or attempted robbery with violence. However, further attempts to extend corporal punishment failed. Flogging survived as a disciplinary device in most American and European prisons and in the British armed forces (where its use was abolished in 1881), and as a punishment for a range of adult and juvenile offenders. Almost 600 juveniles were flogged annually in England between 1858 and 1860, 2,900 in 1873 and 3,400 in 1900. Corporal punishment for both juvenile and adult offenders was not abolished until 1948.

See also POLICE.

Clive Emsley, *Crime and Society in England 1750–1900* (New York, 1987).
Michael Ignatieff, *A Just Measure of Pain: The Penitentiary in the Industrial Revolution 1750–1850* (New York, 1978).
Patricia O'Brien, *The Promise of Punishment: Prisons in Nineteenth-Century France* (Princeton, NJ, 1982).
J. A. Sharpe, *Judicial Punishment in England* (London, 1990).

J. S. COCKBURN

putting-out system   In early modern western Europe putting-out was a common method of organizing manufacturing production in textiles (*see* TEXTILE INDUSTRIES), metalwares and other consumer goods. It has also been prevalent in other parts of the world, continues to be widespread in less developed countries and is found in some sectors of advanced economies, notably the clothing trades. The pivotal figure in the putting-out system is the merchant-manufacturer who distributes raw materials to households or workshops (often through intermediaries), collects the semi-finished or finished products and arranges their sale. The success of putting-out usually rests on the cheap labour of women and juveniles in particular, often working at home and paid piece-rates. Overhead costs are low as workers generally provide their own tools and equipment as well as premises. Factory production and powered technology give greater control to employers over the pace and quality of work but the cost advantages of low overheads and cheap labour, plus the ability quickly to contract production in the face of depression, allows putting-out to endure. Putting-out remains common particularly where cheap female labour is required, where technological needs are small-scale and where demand for products is unstable.

L. Benton, *Invisible Factories: The Informal Economy and Industrial Development in Spain* (New York, 1990).
D. Bythell, *The Sweated Trades* (London, 1978).
S. Pennington and B. Westover, *A Hidden Workforce: Homeworkers in England, 1850–1985* (London, 1989).

PAT HUDSON

Q

Qadiriyya *see* ABD AL-QADIR.

Quadrilateral A system of four fortresses set up by the Austrians in northern Italy – Mantua and Peschiera on the Mincio, and Verona and Legnago on the Adige – the Quadrilateral proved a very effective system of mutually reinforcing fortresses, due largely to the naturally strong position of Mantua, and the ability of the Austrians to send troops down the Adige to Verona. The military advantages of the Quadrilateral were used to their greatest effect by RADETZKY in his 1848 campaign against the Italian revolutionary republics, when his withdrawal of the Austrian army within the Quadrilateral in March gave him the breathing-space to launch the counter-attack which resulted in the victory at Custozza. Even in less fortunate campaigns the Quadrilateral continued to prove its worth. In the campaign of 1859 losses at Magenta and Solferino still left the Austrian position in the Quadrilateral intact (*see* BATTLES OF MAGENTA AND SOLFERINO); this remained the case until the Austrian cession of Venetia in 1866.

STEVEN BELLER

Quakers Members of the Society of Friends, the Quakers formed a religious group known for its peculiarities. Worship was conducted in silence until someone felt moved to speak. Members continued to observe seventeenth-century standards of plain speech (using 'thou' rather than 'you'), men were expected never to doff their hats and conventional pagan names for months were rejected. Although so-called 'gay Friends' conformed more to normal contemporary behaviour, the sectarian ethos was enforced by overseers and an efficient hierarchy of business meetings culminating in the London Yearly Meeting. Quaker theology centred on 'the light within' every human being which, if heeded, would lead towards perfection. Although Quietists defended traditional ways within the society, EVANGELICALISM gradually rose to dominate it by the 1840s. The most impatient Evangelicals, particularly in Manchester, broke away in the Beaconite schism of the 1830s; the most entrenched Quietists, based at Fritchley, Derbyshire, seceded in the 1860s. Later in the century, in association with renewed interest in early Quaker history, there was a tendency to embrace a more liberal theology.

Membership fell from some 20,000 in 1800 until the 1860s, when a recovery began after the code of speech and dress became optional and Quakers were first allowed to marry non-members. The society was widespread in England but predominantly urban. Only half the membership was drawn from the lower middle classes or below, and the society was known for its prosperous bankers, merchants and manufacturers. Although men were as numerous as women, most travelling ministers were female. Women played a full part in leading worship and in many business meetings. Quakers were prominent in philanthropic causes, particularly antislavery, peace movements, prison reform and education. Their agitation against tithes and church rates drew them increasingly into Liberal politics alongside other branches of NONCONFORMITY.

Elizabeth Isichei, *Victorian Quakers* (Oxford, 1970).

D. W. BEBBINGTON

quinine The most effective treatment for MALARIA until the development of a synthetic replacement in 1934, quinine is an active alkaloid from the powdered bark of the cinchona tree, which is native to South America. It works by suppressing the action of the malaria parasites, and confers some immunity if taken regularly. In the nineteenth century quinine was imported into Europe on a massive scale, but there were increasing problems with adulteration of the powder. A partial solution was found in 1820 when two French chemists, Pelletier (1788–1842) and Caventou (1795–1877), were able to extract sulphate of quinine from the cinchona bark. This was a purer remedy but more expensive. In the mid nineteenth century, to meet the strong demand from tropical colonies, the Dutch began to grow cinchona trees on plantations in the East Indies.

SALLY SHEARD

R

race, theories of   The continuation and extension of European colonial rule, and the persistence of slavery in the United States *(see* SLAVERY (UNITED STATES))*, produced pervasive notions of racial hierarchy, asserting the natural inferiority of non-white races. Based on the Bible and supposedly on science, such notions were also espoused by many antislavery and 'radical' thinkers.

Quasi-scientific findings of eminent phrenologists, anthropologists, ethnologists and anatomists which demonstrated 'Anglo-Saxon' physical, intellectual and moral superiority found a ready audience among the 'respectable' classes on both sides of the Atlantic. The comte de Gobineau's (1816–82) influential *Essai sur l'inégalité des races humaines* (The Inequality of Human Races, 1853–5) maintained 'Arian' supremacy in human history on the basis of racial determinism, spawning the Louisiana anatomists Josiah Nott's (1804–73) and G. Gliddon's *Types of Mankind* (1855). The Harvard naturalist Louis Agassiz (1807–73) maintained the natural inferiority of 'Negroes' and their incapacity for civilized attainment. Herbert SPENCER's 'survival of the fittest' credo and SOCIAL DARWINISM's distortion of the discovery of 'natural selection' were increasingly marshalled as the century progressed to justify the European oppression and extinction of colonial peoples. In 1865 the eugenicist Francis Galton (1822–1911) proposed differential breeding programmes to cause the eventual disappearance both of inferior races and of the lower social strata within the dominant race (*see* EUGENICS). The catch-all category of 'race' frequently discriminated against not only non-whites but also 'Kelts' (the Irish), Jews and the working and 'lumpen' masses of the industrial nations.

While it is wise to be wary of anachronistic judgements on nineteenth-century racism, it is equally the case that the 'accepted' biblical and scientific views were repudiated by a significant minority of black and white abolitionists, by sections of the radical-liberal intelligentsia and by social scientists. The German psychologist Theodor Waitz (1821–64), for example, showed in *Anthropologie der Naturvölker* (1859–71) that environmental conditions crucially determined the development of civilization and that the capacities of individual races were indistinguishable.

Michael Banton, *Racial Theories* (Cambridge, 1987).

TONY BARLEY AND SIMÓN DENTITH

Radetzky, Count **Johann Joseph** (*b* Třebnice, Bohemia, 2 November 1766; *d* Milan, Italy, 5 January 1858)   Austrian general. He entered the Austrian army in 1784. His valour and skill during the revolutionary and Napoleonic wars made him a war hero, and from 1813 he was chief of staff to Prince Schwarzenberg (1771–1820). In 1831 he was made commander-in-chief of the Austrian army in Italy, in 1836 field marshal. He commanded the Austrian forces in Italy during the 1848 revolution there. Due to Radetzky's masterful strategy, including his use of the QUADRILATERAL, he defeated the Piedmontese and revolutionary Lombard forces, culminating in the great victories in northern Italy of Custozza in July 1848, and Novara in March 1849. These successes in effect saved the Habsburg Empire from dissolution in 1848. From 1849 to 1857 Radetzky was both commander-in-chief of the army in Italy and governor-general of Lombardy-Venetia.

Alan Sked, *The Survival of the Habsburg Empire: Radetzky, the Imperial Army, and the Class War, 1848* (London, 1979).

STEVEN BELLER

radicalism   The term 'radical', in the sense of going to the root, or reforming thoroughly, is applied to several political movements in the nineteenth century. In Britain it described those parliamentary reformers who sought universal adult male suffrage in particular, and also, frequently, equal electoral districts, payment of members of parliament, voting by ballot and similar reforms (*see* FRANCHISE REFORM, PARLIAMENTARY REFORM). 'Radical' as a term of political description arose in the late eighteenth century to describe the reform proposals of opponents of the crown and government. These centred on demands for the reform of parliament, and especially the abolition of 'rotten' boroughs, the bribery of electors and governmental influence over the election of members, in particular. (In all these measures the independence of the Commons was a crucial goal.)

Arising principally through the late-eighteenth-century activities of John Wilkes (1727–97), radicalism was first given a clear programme by Major John Cartwright (1740–1824), whose proposals for universal suffrage and annual parliaments harked back to an ancient

Saxon democracy, but were to become crucial to the radical platform of the nineteenth century. These principles were given tremendous impetus by the American Revolution and its popularizing of democratic ideals, and then the French Revolution. In the 1790s the radical programme was linked widely to Thomas Paine's (1737–1809) *Rights of Man* (1791–2) in particular. After a period of wartime reaction, a revival in the fortunes of the radical movement took place after 1815, led by men like Sir Francis Burdett (1770–1844), Henry HUNT and William COBBETT, which culminated in the most important working-class movement in nineteenth-century Britain, CHARTISM. This focused on the six points of the People's Charter: annual parliaments, payment of members of parliament, equal electoral districts, universal adult male suffrage, abolition of property qualifications for members of parliament and the ballot. Nominally, much of this programme began with Cartwright but, as with Paine, it was associated increasingly with the welfare of the poor and unemployed. During the 1848 revolutions radicalism was consequently intermixed with a variety of socialist and communist doctrines.

By the 1860s the term came to encompass all those, who, aiming at a genuinely meritocratic society, were willing to go considerably further than the parliamentary Liberal Party on such issues as the franchise, church disestablishment, marriage laws, reform of the House of Lords and of the taxation and educational systems, land tenure and much else. As much a frame of mind as a programme, radicalism rallied men of such diverse interests as John Stuart MILL, Charles BRADLAUGH and David Lloyd George (1863–1945). 'Advanced liberals', as they sometimes also termed themselves, were sometimes republicans, and usually sought at least to restrict the powers of the Lords, to limit the sway of the great landed magnates, to make land more widely available, to abolish the game laws, to admit Dissenters to the same rights as Anglicans, to limit imperial aggression, to reduce the civil list, to strengthen local government and to nationalize at least some large-scale resources or services, such as the railways.

At the time of the Second Reform Bill such measures were espoused in a work entitled *The Radical Party* (1867), written by a member of the National Reform Union, D. Brewster, who presumed Mill, COBDEN and BRIGHT to be the leaders of the movement. The devotion of these men, and especially the latter two, to the FREE TRADE doctrines of the Manchester School clearly demonstrates the deeply liberal, even libertarian, cast of the radical imagination. None the less, the individualist biases of most early radicals gave way by the late nineteenth century to a much more interventionist conception of legislation and of the duties of the state, in relation to education, industry and welfare in particular. A further important statement of principles was *The Radical Programme* (1885), which was introduced by Joseph CHAMBERLAIN.

On the Continent, those calling themselves radicals occupied a similar point on the political spectrum, and were of particular importance in France, where in 1848 Alexandre Ledru-Rollin (1807–74) led the more left-leaning non-socialist republicans and helped to reshape the Jacobin tradition in light of rapidly expanding industrialization. Later the Radical Party, led by CLEMENCEAU and GAMBETTA, dominated the Third Republic and pursued a variety of anticlerical and antidynastic policies. Other European and Latin American countries took up the title with similar aims in mind. By the early twentieth century, however, radicals found themselves increasingly marginalized by the creation of large-scale working-class political parties, and by socialists and communists of various types.

W. Harris, *The History of the Radical Party in Parliament* (London, 1885).
C. B. R. Kent, *The English Radicals* (London, 1899).
Leo Loubère, *Radicalism in Mediterranean France: Its Rise and Decline 1848–1914* (Albany, NY, 1974).
Simon Maccoby, *English Radicalism 1785–1886* (London, 1935).

GREGORY CLAEYS

ragged schools The ragged-school movement for poverty-stricken or potentially criminal children is popularly associated with the seventh earl of SHAFTESBURY, though his precursors were John Pounds (1766–1839), a Portsmouth cobbler, and Sheriff Watson (1796–1878) of Aberdeen. Day and Sunday schools for the ragged were intended to inculcate principles of morality and religion, teach reading, writing and a simple trade and develop habits of diligence that would enable their pupils to follow an honest and decent living; some also offered a 'band of hope', mothers' and TEMPERANCE meetings and opportunities for emigration to Australia. Teachers, linked by the Ragged School Union founded in 1846, were volunteers from all classes (well-known examples included Dr Barnardo (1845–1905) and General GORDON); their enterprise provided a model of co-operation ahead of its time, between Anglicans and Nonconformists. The Fees Act of 1891, which enabled children to attend elementary schools free of charge, brought the movement to an end.

C. J. Montague (1904), *Sixty Years in Waifdom* (London, 1969).

ROBIN BETTS

railways Even though inland transportation had already experienced substantial improvement through better road-building and the construction of navigable waterways (*see* CANALS) in Britain, Europe and the United States, railways were the most profoundly transforming innovation of the nineteenth century. By 1830, when the world's first railway opened between Liverpool and Manchester, rails had in fact been in use for several decades for wheeled traffic drawn by horse, generally as feeders from mines to inland or coastal shipping. The significance of 1830 was to demonstrate the viability of a public railway linking centres of population with steam locomotives running on iron rails. The advantages of the railway over other transport modes – faster, more reliable and cheaper – ensured its remarkably rapid and eventually universal adoption. By 1840, 5,500 miles had been built world-wide (of which half were in the United States and a quarter in Britain). The total rose to 66,000 in 1860, 222,000 in 1880 and 466,000 by the end of the century. Construction required the mobilization of unprecedented quantities of capital (amounting to more than half of total investment in Britain in the late 1840s), as well as armies of labour. The enterprises which resulted were vast undertakings, whose scale and geographically dispersed nature demanded the development of new management skills to cope with the organizational problems.

Railways were built to move freight, especially bulky commodities, and passengers. They were built also for strategic or political reasons: to increase national cohesion, to make it easier to move armies or (so much did they come to be identified with civilization) as symbols of progress. The spread of railways was at first confined largely to Europe and North America. Costs varied greatly. In mid-century heavily engineered lines and the expense of land acquisition in Britain raised costs by a factor of two compared to Belgium, and three or four compared to Germany. In the United States, on the other hand, early lines were notoriously primitive, and land was cheap. Even in 1880 the two continents together still accounted for 83 per cent of total mileage; India, and subsequently Australia and Argentina, also developed large systems. Only in Britain were railways an outcome of earlier industrial growth. In Belgium, Germany, France and the northeastern United States they contributed considerably to the growth of industry, especially iron (see IRON AND STEEL) and COAL, for which they were the principal consumers. In Spain, Russia and further afield, railways were built in advance of industry. Indeed, in the primary-producing regions of Latin America, Asia and Africa railways had only a modest domestic component: enterprise, capital, skilled labour and equipment were all imported from the industrial countries, whose markets consumed the commodities which provided the railways with their traffic.

Railways thus contributed, with steamships and the telegraph, to the international division of labour of the late nineteenth century; but the effect of railways universally was to reduce the natural protection of distance and thus promote a regional specialization based on scale effects and more efficient location. Such widespread economic reorganization, with its political and strategic implications, as well as problems of raising capital, encouraged governments to assist or regulate the construction of railways, and to intervene or take over their operation. Other than initial parliamentary approval of construction, this was least true in Britain, whereas in the United States private companies received large public subsidies, and in Belgium and France the state imposed a planned network. State ownership and control quickly became the norm in Continental Europe, whereas in the United States hostility to the natural monopoly of the railways led instead to the regulatory Interstate Commerce Commission in the 1880s, and in Britain there was a reluctance to coerce private companies in safety or rate-fixing until the end of that decade.

In social terms, the effect of railways was liberating in that they offered mobility and communication. They also unified, both territorially and in requiring a standardized system of timekeeping. They were celebrated as the symbol of an age of unparalleled material progress. More soberly, but contentiously, there have been recent attempts to measure their contribution to that progress using the concept of 'social saving', that is the loss of national income that would have occurred over a period of time if railways had been unavailable and alternative transport systems had been used. These studies have in general given a diminished role to railways as an agent of faster economic growth, but the methodology is much criticized.

T. R. Gourvish, *Railways and the British Economy 1830–1914* (London, 1980). Patrick O'Brien, *The New Economic History of Railways* (London, 1977). Jack Simmons, *The Victorian Railway* (London, 1991).

HENRY FINCH

Rammohun Roy *see* ROY, RAM MOHAN.

Ranke, Leopold von (*b* Wiehe, Thuringia, 21 December 1795; *d* Berlin, 25 May 1886) German historian. He was appointed professor of history at the University of Berlin in 1825 on the strength of his *Histories of the Latin and Teutonic Nations from 1494 to 1514* (1824). This work contained programmatic statements on his historical method, which was 'merely' to portray 'how things actually were' (*wie es eigentlich gewesen*). This entailed the historian rigorously and impartially scrutinizing and evaluating the evidence on the past, and allowing it to 'speak for itself'. Ranke rejected HEGEL's notions of historical development and progress, and emphasized instead that every epoch was 'of equal value' and 'stood in immediate proximity to God' (*unmittelbar zu Gott)*. His critical use of documents and his concern with the subject of the state as a prime object for historical investigation were of key importance in setting the agenda for the subsequent development of German historiography in the nineteenth century and beyond.

ELIZABETH HARVEY

rational recreation   The idea of 'rational recreation', a cultural initiative by the British middle and upper classes to 'civilize' the working class through the provision of leisure facilities, emerged in the 1830s at the time of the CONDITION-OF-ENGLAND QUESTION, when fears of revolution were plentiful. Its proponents urged the use of philanthropy to divert the working classes from Chartism in particular. The initiative took the form of providing parks, libraries (*see* LIBRARIES AND ARCHIVES), museums, games, excursions, art galleries, MECHANICS' INSTITUTES, TEMPERANCE associations and the volunteer movement whose purpose was class harmony and the integration of workers into the social order under bourgeois hegemony.

Often supported by churches, rational recreation was a complex movement. Many of its institutions were taken over by the working class, in particular working men's clubs. Furthermore, the sabbatarian movement prevented the provision of leisure facilities on Sundays for much of the century. From the 1870s onwards, the assumptions of rational recreation were evident in municipal provision of leisure, particularly in Birmingham and London. The concern to use leisure to 'elevate' the working class was also echoed in the approach of many socialists, who wanted to use recreation for the creation of a new socialist identity (for example the Clarion Vocal Union).

Historians have often interpreted 'rational recreation' as a form of social control. If it was, it was largely unsuccessful, as POPULAR CULTURE tended to remain defiantly rough and unreconstructed throughout the period.

Peter Bailey (1978), *Leisure and Class in Victorian England: Rational Recreation and the Contest for Control, 1830–1885* (London, 1987).

ROHAN MCWILLIAM

realism   A term with an especially complex history, 'realism' took on its distinctive modern emphases in the nineteenth century. To be a realist in the nineteenth and twentieth centuries has entailed a belief in the possibility of understanding the world which we inhabit. In medieval philosophy to be a realist meant almost the opposite; it meant a believer in the reality of the underlying forms of thought, especially Platonic forms. Yet something of this history persisted into nineteenth-century uses of the words 'realism' and 'realist', for in a complex range of debates about art and philosophy the underlying reality, be it psychological, social or historical, was often contrasted with confusing surface appearances. But in general, a commitment to realism in science, philosophy or literature entailed a commitment to secular rather than theological kinds of explanation for material and social life.

The nineteenth-century literary form most dominated by questions of realism was the NOVEL. In France, Britain, Russia, other European countries and, to a lesser extent, the United States the realist novel became the dominant form in the course of the century. It is important, however, to recognize the variety which characterized this great range of writing, and not to confuse a belief in the local truth-to-life of the writing with the total ambitions of realism. Realism did not confine itself to the desire to render, in recognizable and lifelike detail, the actuality of the world. Though it included such writing, more generally realism was characterized by the desire to relate the multifarious details of personal and social life to the wider movements of the historical process. Thus the novels of Walter Scott (1771–1832), early in the century, sought to connect the lives of typical individuals to the wider shifts of Scottish and English history. The panoramic sequence of realist novels by Honoré de Balzac (1799–1850) not only represented in minute detail the lives of a vast range of characters in Napoleonic and Restoration France, but did so in a way designed to bring out the underlying realities shaping these lives. Lev Tolstoi's great realist novels, such as *War and Peace* (1863–9) and *Anna Karenina* (1873–7), reproduced in compelling lifelikeness the immediacy of people and their lives, but also saw them as symptomatic of wider and more general histories. These representative national novelists were all accompanied by a number of other writers for whom realism was an animating principle of their writing.

In this respect, realism in the novel can be seen as cognate with realism in other areas of nineteenth-century intellectual life, which similarly sought to bring the vast and multifarious data of social life into comprehensible form. The abstractions of political economy, the collection and analysis of statistics, the new study of SOCIOLOGY, the explosion of historical forms of understanding were all in their different ways realist enterprises, which sought to find appropriate non-theological ways of understanding the variety of society and history. Realism in this context has to be understood as one of the characteristic modes of nineteenth-century thought.

See also PAINTING, SCULPTURE.

Georg Lukács, *Studies in European Realism* (London, 1972).

SIMON DENTITH

reconstruction (1863–1877) As early as 1863, President Abraham LINCOLN began to explore how to bring the seceded southern states back into the union. From the beginning, Lincoln believed that the process should be a quick, compassionate one. All that the north must do, he reasoned, was replace a few disloyal individuals with Unionists. In December 1863 Lincoln issued his Proclamation of Amnesty and Reconstruction, which said that a state could ask for readmission after 10 per cent of its 1860 electorate promised future loyalty to the union, and they wrote a new constitution abolishing slavery and repudiating secession. Lincoln hoped to attract a loyal nucleus in Arkansas, Louisiana, Virginia and Tennessee under this programme. Republican members of Congress, especially the radicals, who favoured abolition and some sort of punishment for rebel leaders, believed Lincoln's plan was too moderate, because it only asked about future loyalty. Therefore, when representatives from the four states appeared in Congress to ask for their seats, Congress rejected them.

Instead, congressional radicals proposed the Wade-Davis Bill (1864), which demanded that 50 per cent of the 1860 electorate take an 'ironclad' oath before a state reorganized. The ironclad oath stated that an individual had never given any aid in any form to the Confederates. Lincoln vetoed this bill, claiming that he wanted to leave his options open for the future. When he died in April 1865 reconstruction policy was at a stalemate between Congress and the president.

The new president, Andrew JOHNSON, at first acted as if he would punish the south. From an impoverished background, Johnson hated southern planters, whom he held responsible for the war. His Proclamation of Amnesty and Pardon (1865) permitted most southerners to take an oath of allegiance and get on with their lives. He placed restrictions, however, on several groups of people, including field-grade Confederate officers and anyone who had held $20,000 in property in 1860. Johnson insisted that these individuals must ask him personally for their pardons. Despite his harsh talk, he soon began pardoning people at an alarming rate. When the southern states elected new governments under his plan, the voters refused to abandon old leaders, even if they were unpardoned. These new governments, filled with ex-Confederates, began to pass Black Codes, a series of laws that attempted to reduce AFRICAN-AMERICANS to a second-class status. To make matters worse in northern eyes, these governments made no attempt to protect blacks from white violence. In the minds of many northerners, the south failed to appear the least bit sorry for secession.

When Congress met in December 1865 it appointed a joint committee to study the reconstruction issue. The joint committee proposed two fairly moderate pieces of legislation in early 1866. First, they attempted to extend the life of the FREEDMEN'S BUREAU. They also drew up a Civil Rights Act. Johnson vetoed both of these laws. Congress overrode them after some parliamentary manœuvring. Next, Congress created the fourteenth amendment, which established black citizenship, excluded most Confederate officials from politics temporarily and repudiated the Confederate war debt. Basically, they saw this as a peace treaty. Only Tennessee, now controlled by Johnson's political rivals, approved the amendment and won readmission.

After the Republicans won a resounding victory in the congressional elections of 1866, Congress remanded the south to military rule in early 1867. Each southern state now had to approve African-American suffrage before it was readmitted. At the same time, most traditional southern leaders were not allowed to take part in the process. Many white southerners sat out this stage of reconstruction, calling their action 'masterly inactivity'. The new governments formed under the military plan were, therefore, dominated by the Republican Party which relied on African-American votes (80 per cent of Republican voters). Under this plan, all the Confederate states came back into the union by 1871.

After readmission to the union, few states continued under Republican control for long. White conservative southerners, using the Ku Klux Klan and other similar terrorist organizations, soon reclaimed North Carolina and Georgia, and Virginia never left conservative control. Factionalism between African-Americans, CARPETBAGGERS and native white southern scallywags lost the Republicans control in Alabama, Texas and Arkansas (1874). In Mississippi a taxpayers' revolt and the intimidation by so-called rifle clubs drove Republicans from power. The remaining three states, South Carolina, Louisiana and Florida, returned to conservative control with the Compromise of 1877. Under this agreement, Republican candidate Rutherford B. Hayes (1822–93) received their electoral votes and, in return, agreed to let conservatives regain control over the state governments. Reconstruction ended in failure, not because it was vindictive, as conservatives alleged, but because northerners lost interest in it as they focused their attention on economic development, especially after the Panic of 1873, and they tended to share southern white racist attitudes towards African-Americans.

Eric Foner, *Reconstruction: America's Unfinished Revolution, 1863–1877* (New York, 1988).

John Hope Franklin, *Reconstruction: After the Civil War* (Chicago, 1961).

C. Vann Woodward, *Reunion and Reaction: The Compromise of 1877 and the End of Reconstruction* (Garden City, NY, 1956).

ALICE E. REAGAN

Red Cloud (*b* Blue Creek, Nebraska, *c*.1822; *d* Pine Ridge, South Dakota, 10 December 1909) Prominent leader of the Oglala Sioux. He distinguished himself as a young warrior with raids against the Crow and Pawnee. By the 1860s, his ferocity won him a position as a war leader in the tribe. In 1866 the United States 'negotiated' to open the Bozeman Trail through Sioux lands. Refusing to recognize the treaty, the Sioux waged war on the army protecting the trail. Military successes like the Fetterman massacre led to the growth of Red Cloud's reputation in Washington as the premier Sioux chief, and he was treated as such by the United States peace commission of 1867 which negotiated a temporary peace with the Sioux. In fact, he represented only a minority of the tribe, and because he spoke for conciliation in the war of 1876–7 (*see* CUSTER, SITTING BULL) most Sioux mistrusted him until his death.

JOHN MARTIN

red flag   A symbolic banner, the red flag was also the name of a song. A red flag appeared in Britain during the London seamen's unrest of 1768 and at Merthyr in 1831, and there were intimations during the French Revolution, most notably in the colour symbolism of red for liberty and republicanism. But the general adoption of the red flag as the workers' own symbol occurred in 1848. The flag appeared spontaneously on barricades in Paris, and then everywhere through revolutionary Europe (*see* REVOLUTIONS OF 1848). LAMARTINE diverted a demand for the flag's adoption as the emblem of the Second Republic with the words: 'The *tricolore* has gone around the world in triumph, the red flag [a reference to the massacre of 17 July 1791] has only been dragged through mud and blood in the Champ de Mars.' The red flag, as the symbol of social emancipation, was to go round the world too.

Green was the colour of British Chartism from 1839 to 1848, but in 1850 'Howard Morton' [a pseudonym, possibly for Helen Macfarlane] eulogized red as the colour of social emancipation, and the flag as 'the banner of the future'; meanwhile, Alfred Fennel made it a subject for poetry. The red flag was the 'banner of solidarity' of the All-German Workers' Association from its foundation in May 1863. But it was MAY DAY which firmly institutionalized the emblem and embedded it in the festivals of the workers. The Italian socialists definitely adopted the flag for the first time only after 1892. Red flags bearing the slogan 'Anarchist Communism' were brandished by followers of Kòtoku Shùsui (1871–1911) in Japan at the demonstration of June 1908, and the ensuing disturbances are now referred to as the Red Flag Incident. The red flag emerged as a state emblem with the foundation of the Soviet Union in 1918.

The song 'The Red Flag', published in 1889, was written by Jim Connell (1852–1929), sometime Fenian, Irish Land Leaguer, Social Democratic Federation and Independent Labour Party member. His inspiration was a lecture by Herbert Burrows (1845–1922) and 'the Paris Commune, the heroism of the Russian nihilists, the firmness of the Irish Land Leaguers, the devotion unto death of the Chicago anarchists'. Connell wrote the words to the tune The White Cockade, and was angry when A. S. Headingley set it to Maryland (Tannenbaum), now the most popular version.

JOHN L. HALSTEAD

Redmond, John Edward (*b* Ballytrent, County Wexford, 1 September 1856; *d* London, 6 March 1918)   Irish nationalist leader who was devoid of hostility to the British Empire. Educated at Trinity College, Dublin and a member of parliament from 1881 to 1918, the mild and thoughtful Redmond suffered in reputation in comparison to PARNELL, to whom he was devoted. An able lieutenant and successful fund-raiser for the Home Rule movement in the United States and Australia in the early 1880s, he reunited the Irish Parliamentary Party after the Parnellite split and assisted in Ireland the establishment of democratic local government, land purchase and the National University. Like other Irish nationalists, he never understood and always underesti-mated the determination of Ulster Unionists to resist Home Rule, which eventually undermined his leadership after the introduction of the Third Home Rule Bill in 1912.

Denis Gwynn, *The Life of John Redmond* (London, 1932).

PATRICK BUCKLAND

Reeves, William Pember (*b* Lyttelton, New Zealand, 10 February 1857; *d* London, 16 May 1932)   Intellectual who became a Fabian socialist. His early career spanned journalism and politics. As a minister in the New Zealand Liberal government of the 1890s, he introduced legisla-tion to improve working conditions. His greatest political achievement was the Industrial Conciliation and Arbitration Act (1894), the world's most comprehensive labour-relations code. In 1896 Reeves became New Zealand agent-general in London where he was friendly with G. B. Shaw (1856–1950) and the Webbs. He wrote poetry, a seminal history of New Zealand (*The Long White Cloud*, 1898) and *State Experiments in Australia and New Zealand* (1902). He was director of the London School of Economics (1908–19), and became a prominent champion of Greek causes.

Keith Sinclair, *William Pember Reeves, New Zealand Fabian* (Oxford, 1965).

MICHAEL C. PUGH

Reform Acts 1832, 1867, 1884   *see* PARLIAMENTARY REFORM.

Reform League   Established in London in 1865 to replace the lack-lustre Trade Unionists' Manhood Suffrage and Vote by Ballot Associa-tion, the Reform League exposed divisions within RADICALISM as prospects for PARLIAMENTARY REFORM revived. The 'Junta', the coterie of full-time leaders and bureaucrats who dominated mid-Victorian trade-union politics, entered an accommodation with advanced Liber-als, who provided the funds for agitation to supplement the pressure applied by the middle-class Reform Union for household suffrage. Their control of the league, however, was challenged by industrial militants and extraparliamentary radicals, heirs to the Chartist tradi-tion of democratic independence. Against the advice of Edmond Beales

(1803–81), the middle-class barrister and president of the league, the militants successfully defied the government's ban on demonstrations in Hyde Park, prompting the resignation of the home secretary, but it is doubtful whether such extraparliamentary pressure determined the final nature of the Reform Act of 1867, a matter of 'high politics'.

JOHN BELCHEM

refrigeration   It has long been known that refrigeration preserves perishable foods, as lower temperatures delay the process of chemical change. Arctic explorers packed meat underground in snow and English country mansions had ice houses. Ice was cut from frozen lakes and ponds for food storage in summer. Although traditional forms of preservation, smoking, salting, drying and canning were unreliable and the food itself became unpleasant to taste, refrigeration was not generally used commercially before the nineteenth century.

Rising populations in Europe, higher real incomes, the demand for a more varied diet, improved transportation and the opening up of new sources of supply all combined to encourage artificial refrigeration using compressed air (the Bell-Coleman method) or liquid coolant systems with ammonia (demonstrated by Michael Faraday) to ensure that perishable food could be safely preserved over long distances. The history of mechanized refrigeration is largely that of the frozen and chilled meat trade. Maritime conditions frustrated early experiments from Australia until the 1880s, but ships successfully carried refrigerated meat in insulated chambers from the United States to Britain, followed by the pioneering voyages of the *Frigorique* (using the Tellier system) and the *Paraguay* from South America during the 1870s. Technological changes in refrigeration were profitably applied to other products like fruit, especially apples and bananas, and milk. Although superficially similar, carriage conditions (temperature, packing and journey time from producer to consumer) differed for each product, even each type of meat or fruit, and required strict control.

Improved refrigeration was not confined to ocean shipping but exploited by the railroads for inland transportation, and by dairies and wholesale and retail stores. Consumers also had direct access to domestic refrigeration from the end of the nineteenth century.

Charles Singer et al., *A History of Technology*, vol. 5: *The Late Nineteenth Century, c.1850–c.1900* (Oxford, 1979), pp. 45–51.

ROBERT G. GREENHILL

Reinsurance Treaty (18 June 1887)   Signed between Germany and Russia, the Reinsurance Treaty arose out of Tsar Alexander III of Russia's refusal to renew the THREE EMPERORS' LEAGUE (between Russia, Germany and Austria) due to his dissatisfaction with Austria's policies in the Balkans. The treaty provided for the neutrality of the partners in case of war with a third party, except for German aggression against France or Russian aggression against Austria. The partners confirmed the *status quo* in the Balkans, and Germany also recognized Russia's preponderate influence in Bulgaria and promised to support Russia in its drive toward the Straits. Bismarck's major aim in signing the Reinsurance Treaty was to keep Russia and France from forming an alliance. When the terms of the treaty became known in 1890, after Bismarck's dismissal, they created a sensation because of their conflict with Bismarck's support for the MEDITERRANEAN AGREEMENTS. The debate over the possible conflict between the Reinsurance Treaty and the DUAL ALLIANCE or the Mediterranean Agreements has continued to this day.

B. Waller, *Bismarck at the Crossroad* (London, 1974).

GEORGE O. KENT

republicanism One of the central ideals of political thought and action in nineteenth-century Europe, 'republicanism' is derived from the Latin *res publica*, or common weal. Generally used to denote states where supreme power rests with the people instead of a monarch or aristocracy, and often representing more an ethos than a programme, the concept had a wide variety of meanings by the early nineteenth century. It was associated in part with the classical republicanism of Athens, the more ascetic model of Sparta and the speculative utopia of Plato's *Republic*, then with Rome in its pre-imperial phase, as well as with later polities in Venice, Holland and Switzerland. Much English-language republican writing was indebted to Machiavelli (1469–1527) and his British interpreters, especially James Harrington (1611–77), who stressed the importance of civic virtue and the dangers of corruption for free states.

Central to nineteenth-century republicanism was the model of the United States, which to many proved that considerable social equality, an elected chief executive, representative institutions with a wide franchise and a liberal attitude towards commerce could be combined successfully. (This reconciliation was popularized most widely in Europe at the end of the century by Thomas Paine's *Rights of Man*, 1791–2.) American republicanism, particularly in its federalist form, laid less stress on the need for patriotic zeal to promote social unity, and more on the use of constitutional checks and balances and frequent elections to temper selfish commercial tendencies. The greater concern with direct democracy of, for example, Rousseau (1712–78), however, would be adopted by some more radical strands of republican thought in the nineteenth century. During the French Revolution republican ideals were upheld by moderates like Sieyès (1748–1836) and Condorcet (1743–94), and more extreme Jacobin republicans like Robespierre

(1758–94). Practically, the Revolution first exported republican principles to most parts of Europe. With Babeuf's (1760–97) conspiracy, too, we witness the inception of a much more radical, egalitarian form of republicanism which would be taken up by SOCIALISM.

Many republicans were content to aim at popular control without insisting on the abolition of kingship, though Continental movements against autocracy were more prone to stress the latter doctrine. More at ease with a constitutional monarchy, Britain's republican tradition was combined with the working-class and radical parliamentary reform movements during most of the century, and overlapped with LIBERALISM, for example in the writings of Jeremy Bentham (1748–1832), in a variety of ways, with both doctrines centrally sharing the aim of popular sovereignty. Republicanism also shared much in common with RADICALISM in this period. During the first half of the nineteenth century the Chartist movement in Britain (c.1835–58), which concentrated on the extension of the franchise to all adult males, ensured the widest diffusion of republican aims (see CHARTISM). Thereafter Charles BRADLAUGH was the most prominent representative of the trend.

In France a variety of republican ideals and parties claimed allegiance to the aims of the French Revolution, and anticlerical and centralizing influences tended to be stronger. Despite revolutions in 1830 and 1848, it was only with the foundation of the Third Republic (confirmed by a new constitution in 1875) after France's defeat in the Franco-Prussian War that republican principles were truly triumphant. Here, moreover, with the revolt of the PARIS COMMUNE in 1871, there was soon the challenge of a more directly democratic and socialistic brand of the doctrine. France, too, produced one of the century's greatest sociological tracts, Alexis de TOCQUEVILLE's *De la Démocratie en Amerique* (1835–40), which warned of the dangers of rampant individualism in the United States, and the threat of homogeneity of opinion in a democracy for the long-term interests of liberty.

Italy produced two of the foremost republicans of the period, MAZZINI and GARIBALDI. Instigated by the FRANKFURT PARLIAMENT, Germany witnessed an outpouring of republican sentiment during the REVOLUTIONS OF 1848, led by men like Ruge (1802–80), Hecker (1811–81) and Struve (1805–70). Poland and Hungary contributed notable figures to the republican cause during the revolutions of 1848 in particular.

With the origins of socialism in particular, and especially after 1848, republican assumptions that popular political control, social equality and economic prosperity were interwoven were challenged by the view that rather than merely lessening taxation, more fundamental economic reforms like land nationalization were required to alleviate poverty. 'Red republicans' aimed to combine political reforms with such programmes, and inherited concerns for more direct mechanisms of democracy, with bureaucratic accountability, and the dangers of social inequality for popular sovereignty. But by now many of these doctrines came to be associated with socialism proper, and in this sense 1848 represented the peak of nineteenth-century republican energies in Europe. By the end of the century, France alone among the great European nations was republican in constitution. In Germany the success of Bismarck's unification and industrialization strategies had done much to underpin the monarchy, while in Britain, though the franchise had been extended in three Reform Acts, popular support for the monarchy was considerable.

H. A. L. Fisher, *The Republican Tradition in Europe* (London, 1911).

GREGORY CLAEYS

Republican Party Growing out of sectional tensions over the extension of slavery, the Republican Party was formed in 1854 as a result of the KANSAS-NEBRASKA ACT and its doctrine of 'popular sovereignty', which held that any territory could choose if it would be slave or free. This reversal of the Missouri Compromise was intolerable to some independent members of the DEMOCRATIC PARTY who had briefly been associated with the FREE-SOIL PARTY, and many northern WHIGS who feared a southern 'slave power conspiracy'. Named to commemorate the Democratic-Republican Party of Thomas Jefferson, the organization ran its first candidate for the presidency, John C. Fremont (1813–90), in 1856. Though he lost the election, Fremont carried eleven states.

One persuasive interpretation of the Republican Party during this period holds that the rapid growth of the party in the north and west after 1854 was attributable to the accuracy with which its ideology reflected the north's image of a 'good society'. This ideology centred around the idea of free labour, not only as an attitude towards work but as a justification of northern society. Republicans viewed the slave south as essentially backward, an aberration in a dynamic and expanding capitalist republic. The unifying theme of the party was the value and dignity of labour and the right of the individual to attain economic independence.

The Republicans nominated Abraham LINCOLN in 1860, with a platform that included Free-soil principles, a Homestead Bill, subsidized internal improvements and a protective tariff. The party captured the presidency by appealing to farmers and urban workers in the north and west as well as to those opposing the extension of slavery. Lincoln held together the disparate elements of the party during the war, issuing the Emancipation Proclamation in part to satisfy more radical elements in 1863.

After the war, the radical wing of the party gained control and nearly removed Lincoln's successor, Andrew JOHNSON, from office because of his lenient stance with regard to the defeated southern states. Determined to implement more far-reaching reforms in the south, and espousing their doctrine of an active federal government during RECONSTRUCTION, radicals such as Thaddeus Stephens (1792–1868) and Charles Sumner (1811–74) dominated the committee that wrote the fourteenth amendment to the United States constitution, with its equal-rights clause. Beyond question, the party was an instrument of reform during reconstruction, though the intent of the radicals and the extent of their success has generated controversy ever since.

After 1877 and the return of home rule in the south to the Democratic Party, Republicans turned away from reform and became increasingly identified with business interests, and the party's ethical position gradually eroded. Indian frauds, whisky rings and GRANT's extremely corrupt administration all produced party disaffection and undercut the party's moral leadership.

Republican control of the White House was interrupted only twice (by Grover Cleveland) from 1865 until the turn of the century. Begun as a sectional party, it remained so after the war, its influence confined to the north-east and Midwest. Reconstruction left the nation weary of the 'Negro question', and the party built a workable majority around the tariff issue. Republican figures such as James GARFIELD concentrated on the tariff in key northern states and made it the central question of late-nineteenth-century American politics, branding the Democrats as the party of free trade. Emphasizing the benefits of higher duties to industry, Republican leaders also stressed the advantages of higher wages to workers. By linking the tariff to general prosperity and patriotism, Republicans such as James G. Blaine (1830–93) discovered a means to revive enthusiasm for their party, divide Democrats and lay the basis for a national majority after 1894. Superior organization during this period – the party created the National League of Republican Voters in 1887 to maintain enthusiasm between elections and marshal electoral support – also assisted Republicans in expanding their influence.

The depression of 1893 worked to the Republicans' advantage, as the severity of the economic collapse caused voters to reconsider the role of government in society and the economy. Aided by Grover Cleveland's ineptness in handling the tariff issue, Republican candidates were swept into office in unprecedented numbers in the congressional elections of 1894. Republican advocacy of tariff protection, subsidies and the beginnings of the regulatory state of the twentieth century positioned the party to fend off the agrarian challenge of populism and dominate American politics until the New Deal.

Eric Foner, *Free Soil, Free Labor, Free Men: The Ideology of the Republican Party before the Civil War* (London, 1970).
George H. Mayer, *The Republican Party, 1854–1966* (New York, 1967).

KEVIN MURPHY

Reshid Pasha, Mustafa (*b* Istanbul, 13 March 1800; *d* Istanbul, 17 December 1858)   Ottoman statesman and grand vizier. He is considered to have been the chief author of the Tanzimat, the sweeping Westernizing reforms undertaken by the Ottomans between 1839 and 1876. Proficient in French and an able diplomat, Reshid convinced his sultans of the need for reform, persuaded the European powers that the OTTOMAN EMPIRE was capable of it and then directed the reorganization of the Ottoman administration. As grand vizier in 1848 and five times thereafter, he also institutionalized the training of succeeding generations of bureaucratic reformers, including KEÇECIZADE MEHMED FUAD PASHA.

MADELINE C. ZILFI

revolutions of 1830–1832   The most significant of the revolutions of 1830–2 was the July Revolution in France which occurred because Charles X refused to accept the results of the election of 13 July 1830 which returned a majority liberal opposition to his government. He retaliated by issuing the Four Ordinances, which called new elections, altered the franchise in favour of the rich and further limited press freedom. Street riots on 27–9 July forced his abdication while notables, fearing further disorder, replaced him with his cousin Louis Philippe.

News of these events stoked local resentments elsewhere in Europe. Long-standing grievances against treatment of Catholics and French speakers in the southern Netherlands by the Protestant House of Orange in The Hague, as well as a short-term economic crisis, provoked rioting in Brussels and other towns from August 1830 onwards which eventually led to the creation of the kingdom of BELGIUM. In Poland an inept rising of young officers in Warsaw in November 1830, profiting from fears of being sent west to suppress other revolutions, incited a rising which spread throughout Polish society against the Russian occupiers' violations of the treaties of 1815 on Polish internal government. In Italy rising population, falling prices, structural changes in manufacturing, heavy taxation to finance bloated princely courts and widespread corruption and smuggling were the backdrop for a series of risings in February–March 1831 in Bologna, Modena and the Papal Legations, led by former Bonapartist officers, civil servants and students. This created a short-lived United Provinces of Italy.

Although the revolutions of 1830–2 were repressed (as in Italy and Poland) or constitutional reforms were withdrawn (as in several German states), or governments resisted attempts to turn the revolution in a social direction (as in France), the disappointments of radicals and nationalists had a great influence in stimulating the REVOLUTIONS OF 1848. Elsewhere, in Britain and Denmark, constitutional reforms were more permanent (*see* PARLIAMENTARY REFORM).

Clive H. Church, *Revolution in 1830: Revolution and Political Change* (London, 1983).

DONALD SUTHERLAND

revolutions of 1848 Two major waves of revolution occurred in the first half of the nineteenth century threatening the internal and international order agreed on by the powers at Vienna in 1815. The first came in 1830 (*see* REVOLUTIONS OF 1830–1832). The second, in 1848, was revolution on a much greater scale – both geographically and in terms of the demands made for political and also social reform. Where revolution occurred, it appears that economic and political crises coincided. Governments were blamed for the misery and anxiety which affected most of the population, reinforcing demands for constitutional reform.

In France in 1847 government rejection of an extension of the franchise encouraged those active politicians who despaired of winning electoral victory under the existing system to seek the support of the unenfranchised. The government's decision to ban a demonstration in favour of electoral reform planned for 22 February 1848, together with its failure to disperse protesting crowds and to prevent the upward cycle of violence which resulted from the deployment of the army, were to result in a crisis of confidence within the political leadership and the collapse of its authority. The call for protest and the demands for wider participation in politics were made largely by men already involved in the political system, and mainly drawn from the professional middle classes. Given that they had not wanted revolution, it is hardly surprising that they were rarely found among those killed on the barricades. Those who fought in the streets were small tradesmen and workshop owners and, especially, skilled workers from the small workshops and building industries. They were motivated by a desire for greater material security and an enhanced social status, and by resentment of those (employers, wholesale merchants, landlords, politicians) who exploited them and excluded them from political debate. The news of events in Paris between 22 and 24 February stimulated protest which led to disorder in Vienna on 13 March, and this in its turn encouraged risings in Milan and Venice, and in Berlin on 18 March, as a result of which the Austrian and Prussian monarchs felt obliged to promise constitutional reform, afraid as they were of otherwise being dragged into an uncontrollable, continent-wide crisis. This inevitably weakened resistance in the smaller German states which had looked to Austria and Prussia for support.

Unplanned revolution created a power vacuum into which groups with at least a modicum of organization and authority might step. In France, with monarchy apparently discredited, a small body of bourgeois republicans, well known to the Paris public because of their political and journalistic activities, were able to seize power. They introduced manhood suffrage for the election of the Constituent Assembly which would draft a new republican constitution. In a major radicalizing move, popular sovereignty was thus recognized, together with the 'right to work'. Nevertheless, in France and to an even greater extent in Austria and Prussia, where monarchs simply invited liberal politicians to participate in government, substantial elements of the previous regime remained intact. The moderates who had acceded to power were anxious to avoid further violence and sought compromises acceptable to existing social elites. Initially, these were willing to accept liberal or moderate republican ministers in the hope of avoiding something worse, but in the longer term they were committed to political reaction.

In the mean time, the new governments faced major problems, notably those of securing recognition of their authority and achieving a constitutional settlement. In Germany in 1848 this involved not only liberal reform in the individual states but responding to the demand for greater national unity. There was a need also to respond to demands made by the large numbers thrown out of work because of the renewed crisis of business confidence caused by the revolution. They wanted the restoration of prosperity and, in the mean time, assistance. A small but growing minority proved susceptible to socialist calls for a permanent reorganization of work on the basis of producers' co-operatives. In many regions peasants reacted against the growing capitalist commercialization of agriculture and demanded the restoration of customary rights of usage in forests and on common lands. In eastern Germany and the Austrian Empire they demanded the abolition of the last vestiges of serfdom.

Once concessions were made to liberal demands, a political realignment commenced as the more moderate, especially among the better-off and economically secure, affirmed their fundamental desire to avoid social change. In France this was evident from as early as the April 1848 elections. Traditional elites, including the clergy, were able to exert a considerable influence among an inexperienced electorate. Radicals were bitterly disappointed. Revolt followed the government's announcement in June of the closure of the Paris national workshops. This decision not only threatened the existence of the large numbers of unemployed workers but also had considerable symbolic value. The workshops had appeared to represent the first step in a programme of social reform, all hope of which would now disappear. With its determined leadership and ruthless tactics, the government was assured of military success on the streets against mainly unprepared insurgents. This was a revolt which impressed and frightened the whole of Europe. It was described by Marx as 'the first great battle ... between the two classes that split modern society'. In the same month the

Austrian general WINDISCHGRÄTZ regained control of Prague. September saw the return of the army to Berlin, while in October 2,000 to 5,000 insurgents died in Vienna as the army re-entered the city. As a result, it was possible for the Austrians to deploy substantial forces in 1849, first in northern Italy and subsequently in Hungary, where, with Russian help, resistance was finally crushed between August and October.

The parliament which had convened in Frankfurt in May 1848 (see FRANKFURT PARLIAMENT) had been dominated by jurists and officials. From the beginning, major divisions were apparent on such matters as whether or not to include Austria, with its non-German peoples, within the new German Empire, on the franchise qualification, and social reform. Moreover, it quickly became apparent that the implementation of constitutional measures depended on the goodwill of the major states. When by April 1849 agreement was finally reached to establish a federal union (excluding Austria) with an elected diet, responsible ministers and an emperor with substantial executive power, FREDERICK-WILLIAM IV, the most favoured candidate, was determined not to accept the crown from an elected assembly. In this situation, with most of its members, like other men of property, unwilling to call for resistance to the monarchy and risk radical rebellion, there was little to do but go home. Protest risings in the south-west and in Dresden were easily suppressed. Significantly, too, German and Austro-German liberals were unable to accept that to non-Germans 'freedom' and 'unity' might mean the end of German dominance.

In spite of these successes, conservatives remained gravely concerned. Military repression was not enough to restore self-confidence entirely. Even as governments reasserted their authority and regained control of the major cities, democratic organizations such as Solidarité Républicaine in France or the Zentralmärzverein in Germany continued efforts to propagandize and organize in provincial towns and, increasingly, even in the countryside. Such events as the January 1849 elections in Prussia, and those of May in France, in which liberals in the former and the radical démocrate-socialistes in the latter, appeared to be gaining ground, suggested that opposition groups might one day secure an electoral majority. For the vast majority of both conservatives and liberals, there was an urgent need to ensure that electoral systems were modified in order to prevent this outcome, and to restrict the powers of parliamentary institutions. In France the election of Louis Napoleon Bonaparte (see NAPOLEON III) as president of the republic in December 1848, with the support of most conservative notables, was part of this drive to restore social order, although it also represented a far more widespread popular desire for prosperity and security. With substantial support from all social groups, Bonaparte would launch a *coup d'état* in December 1851. In Austria Prince Felix Schwarzenberg (1800–52), who became chancellor in November 1848, was a man dedicated to the modernization, centralization and Germanization of the monarchy.

The nineteenth-century revolutions were important stages in the development of mass politicization. As such they heightened the sense of anxiety felt by elites since the French Revolution and reinforced by accelerating processes of economic and social change. Mass discontent was, however, soon to be reduced by improvements in living standards. The capacity of states to prevent disorder would be reinforced by improved communications. Fundamentally conservative institutions of socialization were to be established through education and the mass media and limited political reform. War, as the collapse of the Second Empire and the Paris Commune revealed, was to represent the main threat to this stability. Paradoxically, in central and eastern Europe it was to be another legacy of 1848 – growing national discontent – which was to constitute a major cause of the internal and international tensions which eventually led, in 1914, to the war that destroyed the social order created in and after 1848.

M. Agulhon, *The Republican Experiment, 1848–1852* (London, 1983).

F. S. Hamerow, *Restoration, Revolution, Reaction* (London, 1958).

R. Price, *The Revolutions of 1848* (London, 1988).

A. Sked, *The Survival of the Habsburg Empire: Radetzky, the Imperial Army and the Class War, 1848* (London, 1979).

ROGER PRICE

Rhine, Confederation of the   Established on 17 July 1806 by Napoleon in a treaty signed at Paris, the Confederation of the Rhine brought together a number of states in western and southern Germany, including Baden, Bavaria, Hesse-Darmstadt and Württemberg with a population of over 8 million. The confederation was essentially a French satellite, which introduced the CODE NAPOLEON, confirming religious toleration and the abolition of feudal rights. It also introduced a constitution on the French model, and was obliged to supply 63,000 troops to Napoleon's armed forces. Its life-span was determined by the military successes and failures of the Napoleonic wars: it was established after the Battles of Ulm (1805), in Germany, and Austerlitz (1806) (*see* BATTLE OF AUSTERLITZ), and eventually collapsed with the withdrawal of the French after the BATTLE OF LEIPZIG (1813).

TIMOTHY KIRK

Rhodes, Cecil John (*b* Bishop's Stortford, Hertfordshire, 5 July 1853; *d* Muizenburg, Cape Colony, 26 March 1902)   English Financier, politician and ardent imperialist. Having gone to Natal for his health, he moved to Kimberley's diamond-fields, ultimately controlling the industry through De Beers Consolidated. A latecomer to the Witwatersrand (Transvaal) gold-fields, his company, Consolidated Gold

Fields, initially acquired poorer mines. To halt Transvaal expansion northwards and seeking new gold reserves, he formed the BRITISH SOUTH AFRICA COMPANY, chartered by the British government to administer what became the Rhodesias.

As Cape prime minister (1891–5), he sought collaboration between the British and the Dutch (Boers, or Afrikaners), but forfeited success by involvement in the abortive JAMESON RAID (1895) and the subsequent Boer War (*see* ANGLO-BOER WARS). His financial success was due largely to advice and help from friends such as Alfred Beit (1853–1906). His fortune became the basis of the Rhodes Trust which provided scholarships and a library at Oxford.

Robert Rotberg, *The Founder: Cecil Rhodes and the Pursuit of Power* (New York, 1988).

SIMON KATZENELLENBOGEN

Ribbonism   The term 'Ribbonism' was used indiscriminately in the early nineteenth century to describe lower-class combinations in Ireland, including agrarian secret societies. In fact, Ribbonism constituted a network of Catholic secret societies which, while attracting some farmers, was an urban phenomenon, supported by tradesmen. It was confined largely to the northern part of Ireland, including Dublin; the northern countries of Leinster; north Connaught; and south and central Ulster. Its network extended also to Irish communities in different parts of Britain. Their secret signs and internal feuding almost became ends in themselves, but Ribbonmen did have vague political aspirations to overthrow the Protestant religion and the British government, keeping alive a popular tradition of conspiracy and disaffection stemming from the Defenders and United Irishmen in the previous century.

M. R. Beames, 'The Ribbon Societies: Lower-class Nationalism in Pre-famine Ireland', *Past and Present*, 92 (1982), 157–71.

PATRICK BUCKLAND

Ricardo, David (*b* London, 19 April 1772; *d* Gatcombe Park, Gloucestershire, 11 September 1823)   English political economist. The son of a stock-exchange dealer whose training was in his father's business, he began to write on currency problems in 1809, and established his reputation with the *Principles of Political Economy and Taxation* (1817). This focused on the relations between rent, profit and wages and the effects of taxation on them. Ricardo's main disciples, James Mill (1773–1836) and J. R. McCulloch (1789–1864), helped to ensure that the text became the foundation work of classical political economy. Ricardo retired from business in 1813 and served as member of parliament from 1820 until his death, notably supporting the causes of parliamentary reform and the ballot. Ricardo was best known for his opposition to the CORN LAWS and to high rents, which he argued raised food prices and wages unduly; and for his labour theory of value, which assumed that the value of a product was proportionate to the amount of labour embodied in it. This view was later developed in a critical direction by MARX.

GREGORY CLAEYS

Rio de la Plata *see* ARGENTINA.

Risorgimento *see* ITALY.

Rochdale Pioneers *see* CO-OPERATION.

Rockefeller, John Davison (*b* Richford, New York, 8 July 1839; *d* Ormond, Florida, 23 May 1937)   American industrialist and philanthropist. After working with a firm of commission merchants, he became, in 1863, part-owner of an oil refinery which within two years was the largest in Cleveland. By 1865 he had bought out his partners and begun construction on a new refinery. Rockefeller pioneered oligopolistic business methods. Using vertical and horizontal integration, his company made its own barrels, built warehouses and purchased tankers, and Rockefeller began acquiring the competitor's holdings in Cleveland and throughout Ohio. With national expansion under way, he began experimenting with maintaining interstate corporate control: 'trust' formation, interlocking directorates and, in 1899, a holding company – Standard Oil of New Jersey, which became one of the nation's wealthiest firms. Although his company was increasingly under attack by 'muckrakers' such as Ida Tarbell (1857–1944), Rockefeller was almost solely concerned with philanthropy after 1897, creating the Rockefeller Foundation among other philanthropic institutions.

JOHN MARTIN

Roland, Pauline (*b* Falaise, France, 7 June 1805; *d* Lyons, 16 December 1852)   Radical French feminist. Of working-class origin, she moved to Paris in 1832 to join the Saint-Simonians (*see* SAINT-SIMON). A utopian socialist who rejected traditional marriage, Roland lived out her principles by bearing four children fathered by two Saint-Simonian men. The sole support of her family as a teacher and a writer, she found herself reduced to destitution during the 1840s. Her experience led her to question the price of sexual freedom for women handicapped by political inequality and economic disadvantage. Asserting the necessity for women to win political rights, she unsuccessfully attempted to cast a vote in the 1848 elections for the National Assembly. In 1849 she assisted Jeanne DEROIN in efforts to organize workers' associations and to create a united federation of such associations. Arrested in 1850, imprisoned and then exiled to Algeria, Roland died on the voyage back to France after her release.

GAIL SAVAGE

Roman Catholicism *see* CATHOLICISM.

Romania After 1859 the united Danubian principalities Wallachia and Moldavia were known as Romania. Vassals of the Ottoman Empire, they were under Phanariote rule from 1711/1714 to 1821 but retained their own large landowning boyar nobility. The abortive uprising of the Philiki Etairia (1821) put an end to the Phanariote regime, and native princes were appointed after 1824. Under Russian protection (1829–34), the principalities received their first constitution, the *Réglement Organique*. Growing cultural and political nationalism and acute social problems culminated in the revolutions of 1848, which were put down by joint Russo-Turkish military intervention. Following successive occupation by Austria and Russia during the Crimean War, the Treaty of Paris (1856) ended the new Russian protectorate. The national movement for unification effected the union of the principalities with the double election of Alexandru CUZA (1859) which was ratified by the great powers in 1861. Cuza's sweeping reforms precipitated his overthrow in 1866, and from 1866 to 1914 Romania was ruled by CAROL I.

Romania received Dobrudja and attained full independence with the CONGRESS OF BERLIN (1878); in 1881 it was proclaimed a kingdom. Domestic politics until 1888 were dominated by Bratianu's (1864–1927) liberal party, and in the 1890s by conservative and liberal cabinets. There were serious efforts to promote industry and communications, but the chief problem remained the agrarian. Although formally emancipated in 1864, the Romanian peasantry was the most impoverished in the Balkans, and the country remained one of large estates with absentee landlords. Peasant unrest intensified and exploded after the turn of the century. As elsewhere in the Balkans, foreign policy was dominated by an irredentist programme, focused around Transylvania and Bessarabia, but its solution had to wait until the First World War.

R. W. Seton-Watson (1934), *A History of the Roumanians* (Cambridge, 1963).

MARIA TODOROVA

romanticism Works in literature, music and the visual arts that exalt the subjective, emotional, irrational, fantastic, grotesque, horrific or transcendental are characterized as 'romantic'. Their mutual influence gave impetus to the *Gesamtkunstwerk*, the fusion of all these arts into a creative entity. Rooted in the second half of the eighteenth century, romanticism crested in the 1830s. NEOCLASSICISM, once considered the antithesis, is now seen as the preliminary phase of romanticism because it was predicated on nostalgia for the past. Romanticism evolved at a different pace, according to the disciplines, among the countries of Europe and North America.

Edmund Burke (1729–97) anticipated the trend in his *Philosophical Enquiry into the Sublime and the Beautiful* (1757), which stated that the most powerful effects were sublime, inspired by terror or awe. The movement emerged in the English Gothic novel, inspired by medieval romances, whence its name. Similarly, German writers of the *Sturm und Drang* (Storm and Stress), notably Johann Wolfgang von GOETHE, experimented with style and content. The poems and art of William Blake (1757–1827) stressed the imagination and announce an esoteric spiritualism that defied the rational canons of the Enlightenment. Henry Fuseli (1741–1825) heralded bizarre subjects and eccentric style in his paintings. These incipient trends, which coalesced around 1800, are often described as proto-romantic.

A reaction to the 'Age of Reason', romanticism elevated 'sentiment' into a governing objective. In the Preface to the *Lyrical Ballads* (1798) William Wordsworth (1770–1850) defined poetry as 'the spontaneous overflow of powerful feelings'. The work of art was thus highly personal and felt, promoting the perception of the artist as a pre-eminent creator. The artist became the tortured genius, a tragic misfit in a world prone to crass materialism and pragmatism. Originality won status as the hallmark of genius. The very subjectivity of romanticism precluded a consistent definition of style.

Sheer emotional impact distinguished the romantics of the nineteenth century. The surging power of Ludwig van Beethoven (1770–1827), the haunting subtlety of Franz Schubert (1797–1828), the heroic mode of Hector Berlioz (1803–69) all shared an expressive force previously unknown to music. The poems of Lord BYRON, the novels of François René de Chateaubriand (1768–1848), the plays of Victor Hugo (1802–85) all partook of epic emotions set in remote times or distant lands. Painters as different as Francisco de Goya (1746–1828) and Theodore Géricault (1791–1824) found common ground exploring the darker side of human existence. These men themselves became romantic legends, acting out larger-than-life dramas, victims of their genius.

Authors and artists relished extreme psychological states, intertwining madness and genius, tenderness and cruelty, virtue and vice. Excesses of emotion overpowered stoic reason and restraint. Scenes of violence provided a forum to condemn man's inhumanity to man or to lament the futility of man's struggle with the hostile forces of nature.

The growing awareness of distinctions of time and place, first applied to the Graeco-Roman world, resulted in historicism. Fascination with the Middle Ages replaced the 'return to the antique', evidenced in the popular novels of Sir Walter Scott (1771–1832) and troubadour painting. The taste for historic revivals soon spread to an eclectic appreciation of bygone days. Nationalism fuelled the association of the present with the past, reinforcing the notion of separate cultural identities.

Escape from the present appealed to the romantics, who sought refuge in the exotic. Exoticism started with the artistic exploitation of the Levant, which expanded into the phenomenon of Orientalism, and eventually embraced the globe. Such themes as the Crusades brought the diverse threads together. The painter Eugène Delacroix (1799–1863) and the poet Byron merged them with stylistic innovations that had a profound effect on their contemporaries.

Historicism spurred the popularity of post-classical literature; Milton (1608–74), Shakespeare (1564–1616) and Dante (1265–1321) became sources of inspiration for modern creations. Contemporary authors offered a wealth of fresh themes and perspectives to painters and sculptors. Delacroix, for example, borrowed subjects from Byron.

Nature assumed a prominent role as a source for sublime emotions, ranging from melancholy to ecstasy to terror. The English landscape sparkled under the brush of John Constable (1776–1837), echoing the delectation of nature in Wordsworth's poems. J. M. W. Turner (1775–1851) unleashed the awesome forces of nature in fiery orgies of colour. Influenced by transcendental poets, such as Josef von Eichendorf (1788–1857), Caspar David Friedrich (1774–1840) crystallized the rugged northern landscape into intense spiritual revelations of divine power. The animal kingdom provided metaphors for the human condition, exemplified in the sculpture of Antoine Barye (1795–1875).

Full of contradictions, romanticism continued to have an impact long after the movement proper was over. Richard Wagner (1813–83), Paul Gauguin (1848–1903) and Auguste Rodin (1840–1917) were among those who may be described as late manifestations of romanticism.

M. H. Abrams, *The Mirror and the Lamp* (New York, 1953).
Hugh Honour, *Romanticism* (New York, 1979).

JUNE ELLEN HARGROVE

Roosevelt, Theodore (*b* New York, 27 October 1858; *d* Oyster Bay, New York, 6 January 1919) One of the most popular presidents of the United States. He began his political career in the New York state legislature (1881–4). A partisan Republican who nevertheless unnerved party leaders by periodically supporting legislation to limit partisan appointments and to protect organized labour, he gained executive experience as a civil service commissioner (1889–1895), a New York

City police commissioner (1895–7), assistant secretary of the navy (1897–8) and governor of New York (1899–1900). His popular appeal rested on his devotion to 'the strenuous life', which he most vividly demonstrated by serving in the Spanish-American War (1898). Roosevelt's presidency (1901–9) transformed the federal government into an effective, if only occasional, regulator of industry in defence of consumers and workers.

William Harbaugh, *Power and Responsibility* (New York, 1961).

ROBYN MUNCY

Rosas, Juan Manuel de (*b* Buenos Aires, 30 March 1793; *d* Southampton, 14 March 1877) Dominant *caudillo* of early-nineteenth-century ARGENTINA. Although born into a landowning family, he accumulated his own wealth through cattle-ranching in Buenos Aires, and in 1820 participated in the defence of Buenos Aires against provincial armies. In the civil war of 1828–9 he led the federalist opposition to the *unitarios*, and between 1829 and 1832 he served as provincial governor. Re-elected in 1835, he remained in power for the next seventeen years. Rosas demanded absolute authority and ruled Buenos Aires like the owner of a cattle-ranch. He maintained his influence through pacts with provincial leaders, his control of the *gauchos* (cowboys) and the urban populace, and the occasional terror unleashed by the notorious *mazorca*, and successfully resisted two foreign blockades, in 1838–40 and 1845–6. However, in 1852 he was overthrown by a coalition of provincial *caudillos* allied with Uruguay and Brazil, and spent the rest of his life farming outside Southampton.

RORY MILLER

Rosebery, Archibald Philip Primrose, fifth earl of (*b* London, 7 May 1847; *d* Epsom, 21 May 1929) British Liberal Imperialist politician. He did more than anyone to reconcile Liberal opinion to the idea of empire. Rosebery first entered a Liberal government in 1881, joining the cabinet in 1885, but he made his reputation as foreign secretary (1892–4), where he advocated a policy of continuity. He succeeded Gladstone as prime minister in 1894, but his cabinet was perhaps the most divided of the nineteenth century and he resigned in 1895. He never again returned to office, though was often expected to do so, and increasingly saw himself as an independent statesman above the ruck of party politics. He consistently championed the cause of the reform of the House of Lords. Rosebery was also the first chairman of the London county council, a successful racehorse owner and accomplished writer.

Robert Rhodes James, *Rosebery* (London, 1963).

DAVID DUTTON

Rothschild   Probably the wealthiest and best-known bankers of the
nineteenth century, the Rothschild family began its rise during the
Napoleonic wars when Meyer Amschel Rothschild (1743–1812) of
Frankfurt, with his sons Nathan (1777–1836) in London and James
(1792–1868) in Paris, began to specialize in making international bullion
transfers on behalf of princes and governments. Soon the London,
Paris and Vienna branches of the Rothschilds eclipsed their Frankfurt
parent in wealth and influence. Their paths began to diverge even though
the separate branches of the family continued an extensive correspondence. London remained more closely linked to foreign government finance and the bullion trade; Paris invested heavily in railways and
industrial enterprises, not only in France, but also in Belgium, Italy and
Spain; while Vienna developed particularly close ties with the Habsburg
monarchy. Later in the century the London house took a lead in
organizing mining companies to operate in Spain and South Africa.

RORY MILLER

Roy, Ram Mohan (*b* Radhanagar, 22 May 1722; *d* Bristol, 27 September 1833)   Dominant Indian intellectual of his time and prominent social reformer. Working in close co-operation with British
authorities, he advocated the reform of Hinduism and an end to such
widespread abuses as widow-burning (suttee) and child marriage for
which there was no justification in Vedic literature. To achieve these
ends, he founded the Brahmo Samaj (1828), an organization which
became deeply rooted among intellectuals in his native Bengal.

Thoroughly grounded in the major languages of India and in English, he wrote numerous books and pamphlets advocating reform,
challenging Christian missionary activity and helping define modernist
currents in Hinduism. His translations of selected Upanishads were
especially significant in this regard. These and other works represent
the first significant attempt by an Indian intellectual to respond to
positive influences from the West while defending Indian tradition.

See also ARTS AND LITERATURE.

Hiren Mukerjie, *Indian Renaissance and Raja Rammahun Roy* (Poona, 1975).

ROBERT J. YOUNG

Royal Niger Company   Founded in 1886, the Royal Niger Company
represented a stage in the formation of modern NIGERIA. In 1884, British
control having already extended to the lower Niger, the upper Niger
was divided between French and British spheres of influence. When
French traders then withdrew from the middle Niger and its tributary
the Benue, various British trading companies were united by George
Goldie (1846–1925) into the Royal Niger Company, which was given
a 'charter' to administer riverain territories. This was a conventional
form of colonial advance which put the cost on shareholders rather

than on taxpayers. The company fought several small wars and was not a conspicuous commercial success, but it extended British influence and to a limited extent 'developed' what was to become Northern Nigeria. In the delta, however, it harried rival African traders. In 1898 Joseph Chamberlain agreed frontiers for a 'Big Nigeria' with France, and hence in 1900 the company's charter was revoked.

P. E. H. HAIR

rubber The rubber tree, from whose latex rubber is derived, occurs naturally throughout the world's tropical regions. The main species is *Hevea brasiliensis* and, until plantations were established after 1900, wild rubber from the Amazon remained the chief source. Tapping conditions were very primitive and native collectors were badly exploited. Regarded first as a curiosity, rubber became a major modern industry after a chain of innovations. Its erasing qualities were already known when in 1820 Thomas Hancock (1786–1865) developed rubber sheeting; in 1832 Charles Macintosh (1766–1843) found that cloth impregnated with rubber became waterproof; Goodyear's (1800–60) vulcanization process (1839) kept rubber pliable without the adverse effects caused by temperature change. Solid rubber tyres were used on early bicycles (*see* BICYCLE) but Dunlop's (1840–1921) pneumatic tyre in 1888 brought further changes as the age of the motor car dawned.

Colin Barlow, *The Natural Rubber Industry: Its Development, Technology, and Economy in Malaysia* (Oxford, 1978).

ROBERT G. GREENHILL

Ruskin, John (*b* London, 8 February 1819; *d* Coniston, Lancashire, 20 January 1900) English writer and art and social critic. The son of Evangelical parents (his father was a wealthy wine merchant), he made his name defending Turner (1775–1851) and then the PRE-RAPHAELITES in *Modern Painters* (1843–60), a work of art criticism based on a combination of romanticism and Evangelical metaphysics. His distinctively moral conception of art led him to consider its social basis, especially in *The Stones of Venice* (1851–3), where the success of Gothic architecture was ascribed to the freedom of artistic expression allowed its producers. The consequent critique of contemporary nineteenth-century forms of artistic and then manufacturing production was extended, in a series of writings until the 1880s, into a wholesale critique of political economy and the contemporary economic system. This romantic critique of capitalism placed Ruskin in a tradition which included Thomas Carlyle and William Morris. His final work, *Fors Clavigera* (1871–84), was an attempt to communicate his views to labouring men.

SIMON DENTITH

Russell, John, first Earl Russell (*b* London, 18 August 1792; *d* London, 28 May 1878) English statesman. The arch-Whig of nineteenth-century British politics, Russell, the third son of the sixth duke of Bedford, failed to fulfil the promise displayed in his early career when he prepared and introduced the first Reform Bill of 1831. He subsequently held a number of high offices and twice served as prime minister (1846–52, 1865–6), but lacked the administrative talent and constructive policies of contemporaries – Melbourne, Peel and Palmerston – who continually overshadowed him. Having insisted that the Reform Act of 1832 was a final settlement, 'Finality Jack' took up the issue of parliamentary reform again towards the end of his career in the vain hope of recapturing his earlier success. He was raised to the peerage in 1861.

JOHN BELCHEM

Russia At the beginning of the nineteenth century Russia was geographically the world's most extensive country. In the words of the nineteenth-century historian Kliuchevskii, Russia was 'a country which colonizes itself'. This tradition continued, largely in the first half of the century, with the final annexation of Georgia in 1800, the rest of the Caucasus by the 1870s, Bessarabia in 1812, the central Asian areas of Kazakhstan, Uzbekistan and Tadjikistan by the late 1850s and Turkmenistan in 1881. Finland was controlled from 1809 and the duchy of Warsaw subsumed in 1815, while Vladivostok, on the Pacific, was founded in 1860. Russian 'spheres of influence' included northern Persia and Mongolia. The only significant territory to be given up was Alaska, sold to the United States in 1867.

This vast area was, however, thinly populated and the cities, with the exception of Moscow and the capital St Petersburg, small. Whereas the population in 1750 has been estimated at some 17 million, by 1850 it had quadrupled. After that the rate of growth increased markedly. By 1897 there were 124 million inhabitants and in 1914 nearly 170 million. This staggering increase in the second half of the century is only very partially explained by territorial expansion. This, the highest growth rate in Europe, was accompanied by the lowest grain yields, yet the country managed to feed itself with only the occasional localized famine. Agriculture remained primitive, with the three-field system still the norm; the climate was harsh, the soil poor and the main grain was rye, which also happened to be that with the lowest yield. Extensive rather than intensive methods were therefore employed, which produced a meagre though adequate food supply. Even in 1900 four-fifths of the population was still officially classified as peasant.

Although the Russians had a long tradition of successful trade and commerce, their industries generally lagged behind those of other developed countries. For example, in the eighteenth century Russia had

the largest iron-smelting production in Europe and the cotton industry, the first to be mechanized, spun more yarn in 1850 than Germany,
but most ouput was from small cottage industries. The surge in heavy
industry started in the 1890s and so rapid was it that by 1914 Russia's
industrial production was the fifth largest in the world.

The country's political system was autocratic, patrimonial, centralized
and heavily bureaucratic. One of the more striking phenomena within
it was the general lack of interest in political influence by the wealthy.
While the tsars guaranteed their position, they were quite content to
let matters remain as they were. Attempts at modernizing the country
were made by ALEXANDER I, but achieved little. It was not until the
reign of ALEXANDER II that serious consideration was given to reform,
especially in SERFDOM, local government (*see* ZEMSTVA), the judiciary
and the armed forces. The power of the tsar remained virtually un-
diminished until NICHOLAS II was forced to grant a form of limited
constitutional government after the 1905 revolution.

Although there were sporadic peasant disturbances and, latterly,
industrial unrest, opposition to the regime came mainly from the intelligentsia, in spite of their being hampered by the strict censorship
and the police. The unsuccessful revolt by DECEMBRISTS in 1825 inspired succeeding generations of radicals, revolutionaries and terrorists. The great debate between the Slavophiles, who believed in the
uniqueness of Russia and its social institutions, and the Westernizers,
who wished to follow, where appropriate, the example of western
Europe, was succeeded by populism (*see* POPULISM (RUSSIA)). When that
largely peaceful and educative movement failed in the mid-1870s,
terrorism became increasingly prevalent, culminating in the assassination
of Alexander II in 1881. The last two decades of the century saw the
beginnings and growth of Marxism (*see* PLEKHANOV), coinciding with
increasing industrialization and urbanization.

Foreign affairs during the century were dominated by three main
factors. The first twenty years were concerned predominantly with
relations with France and the wars with Napoleon: the defeat at
Austerlitz (*see* BATTLE OF AUSTERLITZ) and the TREATY OF TILSIT, and then
the victory at Borodino (*see* BATTLE OF BORODINO), followed by the
occupation of Paris and the mystical HOLY ALLIANCE and the CONGRESS
SYSTEM. While the successes over Napoleon were succeeded by extreme
reaction and the politically stagnant reign of NICHOLAS I, the disastrous
CRIMEAN WAR opened the way for reform. Problems with the Ottoman
Empire lasted throughout the century, the most serious consequence
being the RUSSO-TURKISH WAR in the 1870s. After this Russia's foreign
policies were generally conciliatory and non-interventionist.

H. Seton-Watson, *The Russian Empire, 1801–1917* (Oxford, 1967).

A. V. KNOWLES

Russo-Turkish War (1877–1878)   As the former mighty Ottoman Empire declined, the European powers vied for control of the Balkans. This was an area which Russia had attempted to influence throughout the nineteenth century. In 1875 there were revolts in Bosnia and then a major insurrection in Bulgaria which was suppressed with savage ferocity by the Turks. In July 1876 Serbia and Montenegro opened hostilities against Turkey and their small armies were on the point of annihilation when Russia proposed a cease-fire. The Turks refused and Russia declared war, somewhat reluctantly, in August 1877. By early 1878 Russian troops were threatening Constantinople. The Turks agreed to an armistice and on 3 March 1878 the TREATY OF SAN STEFANO was concluded. This created an independent and extensively enlarged Bulgaria. Britain, Germany and Austria-Hungary were alarmed and the treaty was considerably modified at the CONGRESS OF BERLIN in July 1878.

A. V. KNOWLES

S

———◆———

Sadowa [Königgrätz], Battle of *see* AUSTRO-PRUSSIAN WAR.

Saigo Takamori (*b* Satsuma, 1828; *d* Satsuma, 1877) Japanese samurai. He was one of a remarkable group of talented young men from samurai families, mainly from the domains of Choshu, Satsuma, and Tosa, who in the 1850s engineered the downfall of the Tokugawa Shogunate after its failure to repel the attempts of the Western powers to open up Japan, and brought about the MEIJI RESTORATION. In so doing they decisively changed the course of Japanese, and ultimately of world, history.

He later played an important role in the Meiji government until his resignation in 1873 over the decision not to invade Korea. Having broken with the oligarchy, he returned to his native Satsuma where in 1877 he eventually led a rebellion of discontented samurai whose feudal privileges had been destroyed by the Meiji government. The rising was suppressed and Saigo died in traditional samurai fashion, committing suicide.

JOHN DAVIES

Saint Monday The custom of observing Monday as a holiday was widespread until 1850, especially among skilled men in small-scale and domestic industry. Typically spent at the alehouse or at popular pastimes like blood sports, this central aspect of traditional work culture reflected a preference for leisure over maximizing earnings. After 1850 workers in many industries came under increasing pressure to adopt more regular work discipline, particularly from employers who used steam power. This pressure coincided with the general introduction of a regular working week of Monday through Friday with a Saturday half-day, a schedule rationalizing the division between work and leisure.

The embracing of the values of independence and respectability by the ARISTOCRACY OF LABOUR, along with improving pastimes, also furthered the erosion of Saint Monday. Although the custom continued to be observed until 1870 or later, it was increasingly viewed as unrespectable behaviour.

Hugh Cunningham, *Leisure in the Industrial Revolution c.1780–c.1880* (London, 1980).

RICHARD J. SODERLUND

Saint-Simon, Claude Henri de Rouvroy comte de (*b* Paris, 17 October 1760; *d* Paris, 19 May 1825) French social reformer. He fought with the French in the American War of Independence and became an enormously rich land speculator in the French Revolution but was reduced to living off his friends afterwards. His ideas and writings were very influential. He argued that scientists should be the new priesthood, that property-holders could protect themselves from the poor only by subsidizing research, that science and technology applied to industry would resolve social problems and that war should be abolished. His followers developed the master's message after his death, calling for the rights of women, for holding property in common and for the abolition of the death penalty.

F. Manuel, *The New World of Henri Saint-Simon* (Cambridge, Mass., 1956).

DONALD SUTHERLAND

Salisbury, Robert Arthur Talbot Gascoigne-Cecil, third marquess of (*b* Hatfield, Hertfordshire, 3 February 1830; *d* Hatfield, 22 August 1903) British Conservative politician. He was member of parliament for Stamford (1853–68) and made his reputation as a formidable parliamentarian through his persistent opposition to further electoral reform. He was twice secretary of state for India, but it was as foreign secretary after 1878 – when he accompanied Disraeli to the CONGRESS OF BERLIN – that his talents really emerged. After Disraeli's death he emerged as the dominant force in Conservative politics and was prime minister three times (1885–January 1886, July 1886–1892, 1895–1902). In his later years he was closely associated with the policy of 'splendid isolation', but progressively lost influence within his own government, especially to Joseph CHAMBERLAIN. Before his final retirement, he saw the country embark on a new course in foreign policy.

Robert Taylor, *Lord Salisbury* (London, 1975).

DAVID DUTTON

Salvation Army Established in London in 1865 (although it was not organized as such until 1878) by William (1829–1912) and Catherine

(1829–90) Booth, the Salvation Army was a denomination devoted to reaching the urban working class. It adopted a military-style structure, ranks and uniforms. Converts were turned into evangelists as soon as they were saved and it was one of the first denominations to engage women preachers. By 1882 there were 400 corps across Great Britain as well as scattered corps in the British Empire. Its unusual methods and dynamic growth made it highly visible and the target of attacks from more established Christian denominations, the press and many of the working-class people it aimed to convert. The publication of William Booth's *In Darkest England and the Way Out* in 1890 marked the beginning of an ambitious social-service programme. These services, including maternity homes for unmarried women and shelters for the homeless, soon gained the army the reputation as an important provider of social services.

PAMELA J. WALKER

Samoa The Samoan Islands in the South Pacific were little known and were considered unimportant until they became the focus of intense rivalry between the United States, Great Britain and Germany in the 1880s. In 1889 these powers recognized the independence of Samoa, but ten years later the United States and Germany occupied the islands and divided the territory between them. The fate of the Samoan Islands was thus closely linked to the imperial rivalries of the powers, and particularly to the expansion of American influence in the Pacific (*see* IMPERIALISM). Samoa was an object of competition among the great powers not for its territorial significance but for reasons of prestige, public opinion and domestic policy.

Paul Kennedy, *The Samoan Tangle* (New York, 1974).

GEORGE O. KENT

San Martín, José de (*b* Yapeyú (Corrientes), 25 February 1778; *d* Boulogne-sur-mer, 17 August 1850) Argentine soldier and statesman. A professional military officer, he fought in Spain against Napoleon. He returned to ARGENTINA in 1812, and took command of its northern army before becoming governor in Mendoza. Having conceived the idea of attacking the Spanish stronghold in Peru through CHILE, in 1817 he led 5,000 men through two narrow Andean passes. His victories at Chacabuco and Maipo (*see* BATTLE OF MAIPO) secured Chile's independence. In 1820 he landed in PERU. By then San Martín had begun to favour the establishment of monarchies in Spanish America; he also preferred to wait for Peruvians to seek independence themselves. This created serious divisions within his forces, while the Peruvian elite remained lukewarm about emancipation. Although he entered Lima and declared independence in July 1821, the city was poverty- stricken and of symbolic rather than strategic importance. Fifteen months later, ill, lacking resources, in disagreement with BOLIVAR and facing increasing opposition in Peru, San Martín left Lima for exile in Europe.

RORY MILLER

San Stefano, Treaty of (3 March 1878) The RUSSO-TURKISH WAR of 1877–8, during which Russian armies advanced to the gates of Constantinople but were too exhausted to occupy it, ended with the Treaty of San Stefano. The peace dictated by Russia would have deprived Turkey of large parts of its empire in Europe and forced it to pay Russia a huge indemnity. Montenegro and Serbia would have been given additional territory and, like Romania, become independent states. Bulgaria, enlarged by the addition of Macedonia and given an outlet to the Aegean Sea, was to become an autonomous state occupied for two years by Russian troops. Bosnia and Hercegovina were to be granted reforms by the sultan, and Russia was to receive Ardahan, Kars, Batum and Bayazid on the Asiatic borders of the Ottoman Empire. However, the powers, and especially Britain, were alarmed at the prospect of such extensive Russian gains and called for a European Congress at Berlin to redress the balance of power (*see* CONGRESS OF BERLIN).

Barbara Jelavich, *A Century of Russian Foreign Policy 1814–1914* (Philadelphia, 1964).

GEORGE O. KENT

Santa Anna, Antonio López de (*b* Jalapa, 21 February 1794; *d* Mexico City, 21 June 1876) President of MEXICO eleven times. His career epitomized the instability of the early republic. After fighting for the royalists he switched sides to support independence, but then abandoned ITURBIDE. Having consolidated power bases in his home state of Veracruz and the national army, Santa Anna enhanced his reputation by defending Tampico against Spanish forces in 1829. Between 1832 and 1834 he led a successful rebellion, became president, relinquished power and carried out a conservative coup against his vice-president. Despite suffering eventual defeat in Texas in 1836, he salvaged his reputation when the French invaded Veracruz in 1837 (losing a leg in the action), but as president he was unsuccessful in defending the country in the Mexican-American War (1846–7). Essentially a political opportunist normally supported by conservatives, the church and the army, Santa Anna achieved little of substance. His last presidency (1853–5) culminated in financial collapse and the success of the liberals after a bloody civil war.

RORY MILLER

Sanusi, Sidi Muhammad ibn Ali al- (*b* Algeria, 1791; *d* 7 September 1859) Founder of the Sanusiya religious brotherhood. In the years after the death of his teacher, the reformist Sufi master Ahmad ibn Idris (*d* 1837), Muhammad ibn Ali established his own movement in what is now Libya. By 1856 his fundamentalist teachings had found particular favour among desert tribesmen, whom he organized into a loose confederation of missionary-training centres. By the time of his death the movement had spread across Libya and into central and west Africa, where each of its lodges possessed a committed army of supporters among surrounding tribespeople. With its antiforeign focus, the movement rallied further support under Muhammad ibn Ali's son Sidi Muhammad al-Mahdi, as the European powers proceeded to carve up Africa. In 1911 the Sanusiya provided the principal opposition against the Italian invasion.

John Voll, *Islam: Continuity and Change in the Modern World* (Boulder, Colo., 1982).

MADELINE C. ZILFI

Savoy *see* VICTOR EMMANUEL II.

Scandinavia In the nineteenth century Scandinavia played an increasingly minor role in international politics. Internally, the Scandinavian kingdoms saw the liberalization of political, economic and social life.

Denmark
During the Napoleonic wars Denmark attempted to remain neutral, but Great Britain, fearing that the Danish fleet might be seized by the French, launched attacks on Copenhagen in 1801 and 1807, driving the Danes into alliance with Napoleon. Having backed the losing side, Denmark had to pay the price and in 1814 ceded its rights to Norway to Sweden by the Treaty of Kiel. The post-war period saw the growth of liberal sentiment. However, the monarchy resisted pressures to liberalize the constitution until 1849 when Frederick VII (reigned 1848–63), alarmed by the 1848 revolutions in France and Germany, summoned a constituent assembly. This abolished the absolute monarchy and created a popularly elected parliament of two chambers, the Folketing (lower house) and the Landsting (upper house), to share legislative power with the king and his ministers. A free press and freedom of association and religious belief were guaranteed by the new constitution, as was an independent judiciary.

The other major influence on Danish political life in this period was nationalism. These feelings inflamed the dispute with the German Confederation over the future of the duchies of Schleswig and Holstein (*see* SCHLESWIG-HOLSTEIN QUESTION). The loss of the duchies following Denmark's defeat by Austria and Prussia in 1864 caused the collapse of the National Liberal Party, which had dominated the government since 1849. The landowner-dominated government that succeeded introduced a new constitution in 1866 which, in effect, gave the Conservative Party an inbuilt majority in the Landsting. However, after 1872, the peasant farmers' party, the United Left, held the majority in the Folketing and a long period of political stagnation followed as the two houses struggled for supremacy. The conservative government eventually resigned in 1901 (by which time it held only eight of the ninety-eight seats in the Folketing), though the constitutional questions raised by the crisis were not solved until 1915.

The late nineteenth century was a period of growing prosperity as Danish farmers specialized in dairy and bacon production for the British market and organized co-operatives to compete more effectively with the big landowners. The political and economic advances of the farmers were undoubtedly aided by the folk high schools, adult education institutions inspired by the pioneering educationalist N. F. S. Grundtvig (1783–1872).

Sweden

Like Denmark, Sweden initially pursued a policy of neutrality in the Napoleonic wars, but in 1805 the deeply conservative Gustav IV (reigned 1792–1809) joined the alliance against Napoleon. However, the TREATY OF TILSIT between France and Russia in 1807 left Sweden isolated and led to a disastrous war with Russia. Great Britain, preoccuppied with the war in Spain, was unable to help, and in 1809 Sweden was forced to surrender Finland and the Åland Islands to Russia. The war also led to the overthrow of Gustav IV and the end of the absolute monarchy. Charles XIII (reigned 1809–18), Gustav's senile and childless uncle, was placed at the head of a constitutional monarchy, but after 1810 the real ruler was Charles's adoptive heir, Bernadotte (1763–1844; king of Sweden and Norway, 1818–44), formerly one of Napoleon's marshals. In 1813 Sweden again joined the war against Napoleon and was rewarded with Denmark's rights to Norway. Ruling under the name Charles XIV, Bernadotte resisted pressures to liberalize the constitution until 1840 when the government ministries were reformed. Further reforms followed, for example compulsory school education (1842), equality of inheritance rights for men and women (1845), the gradual introduction of free enterprise (1846–64), freedom of worship (1860) and local self-government (1862).

Parliamentary reform was slower in coming. Only in 1865–6 was the Riksdag, with its medieval division into the four estates of nobles, clergy, burghers and peasants, replaced by a parliament of two equal chambers. However, the king retained executive power until 1905 when, following the constitutional crisis caused by Norway's declaration of independence, parliament usurped the remaining royal powers. Only towards the end of the century did Sweden begin to industrialize (timber-processing and iron and steel being most important) and modernize its agriculture: for most of the century Sweden remained a poor country which saw large-scale emigration of its surplus rural population to the United States.

Norway
In 1814 the Norwegians declared their independence from Denmark. However, Denmark had ceded Norway to Sweden by the Treaty of Kiel and a Swedish invasion ensured that Norwegian independence was short-lived. The union with Sweden was purely a union of crowns and, though Norway did not have independent diplomatic relations, the country kept its constitution, parliament and government. The union was increasingly resented and in June 1905 the Norwegian parliament declared the union dissolved, an act which was finally accepted by Sweden after three months of negotiation. The Norwegian economy, which depended heavily on fish and timber exports at the beginning of the nineteenth century, was boosted by the rapid development of the shipping industry: by 1900 Norway possessed the world's third largest merchant fleet (after Great Britain and the United States). Nevertheless, economic growth failed to keep pace with population growth and Norway had the highest relative rate of emigration (mainly to the United States) of all European countries after Ireland.

Iceland
Despite Norwegian protests, the Treaty of Kiel allowed Denmark to keep the old Norwegian dependencies of Greenland, the Faeroe Islands (still Danish possessions) and Iceland. Danish rule was unpopular in Iceland, not least because of the unequal terms of trade imposed by Denmark, but demands for home rule were resisted until 1874. Independence under the Danish crown followed in 1918.

Finland
Under Russian rule from 1809, Finland was subject to authoritarian government appointed by the tsar. Opposition to Russian rule increased sharply in the 1890s as attempts were made to incorporate Finland more fully into the Russian Empire. In the aftermath of the 1905 revolution, 'Russianization' was stopped and in 1906 a single-chamber parliament, elected by a universal franchise, was created. The Russian government soon went back on its concessions, however, and Finland was annexed to Russia in 1914.

T. K. Derry, *A History of Scandinavia* (Minneapolis, 1979).

JOHN HAYWOOD

Schleswig-Holstein Question The two duchies of Schleswig and Holstein, which are located between Germany and Denmark, were a source of contention between Denmark (*see* SCANDINAVIA), PRUSSIA (and later Germany), Austria and Great Britain for much of the nineteenth century. The problems raised by the duchies involved the nationality rights of the German minority in Schleswig and the Danish minority in Holstein, as well as the rights of succession of various branches of the Danish royal family.

The national feeling aroused by the Napoleonic wars led the Germans in Schleswig-Holstein to call for the incorporation of the duchies into a united Germany, while the Danes urged that Schleswig become an integral part of Denmark. When unrest in the area turned to open revolt in March 1848, the Frankfurt Parliament authorized Prussia to dispatch federal troops to quell the disturbance. Despite protests by Russia and Great Britain, which were both anxious to keep Prussia away from the entrance of the Baltic Sea, Prussia complied and war with Denmark broke out. Despite several British attempts to mediate the conflict, the war dragged on until 1850 and led eventually to an inconclusive peace, the London Protocol, which temporarily settled the dispute by demanding that the German Confederation return Schleswig-Holstein to Denmark and that Denmark keep the duchies together and exercise loose control over them.

On 30 March 1863, however, King Frederick VII of Denmark violated the London Protocol by announcing a new constitution for Denmark that included the annexation of Schleswig. In response, the diet of the GERMAN CONFEDERATION voted to intervene, and federal troops entered Holstein on 24 December 1863. Bismarck, who was preoccupied with the constitutional conflict at home, saw in these developments an opportunity to arouse German national feeling and to distract public attention. He concluded an alliance with Austria in January 1864, and both powers invaded Schleswig after the Danes had rejected an ultimatum to withdraw the new constitution. Abandoned by Great Britain and overwhelmed by Austro-Prussian forces, the Danes were defeated and, in compliance with the Treaty of Vienna (30 October 1864), surrendered Schleswig-Holstein and the duchy of Lauenburg to Prussia and Austria. At the Convention of Gastein (14 August 1865) Prussia and Austria agreed to a 'provisional' division: Austria was to administer Holstein while Prussia assumed responsibility for Schleswig and acquired the rights to Lauenburg from Austria for 2.5 million thalers. Following its defeat in the Austro-Prussian War, Austria was expelled from the German Confederation and Prussia took over Holstein.

O. Pflanze, *Bismarck and the Development of Germany*, vol. 1 (Princeton, NJ, 1990).

K. A. P. Sandiford, *Great Britain and the Schleswig-Holstein Question, 1848–64* (Toronto, 1975).

GEORGE O. KENT

Schreiner, Olive Emilie Albertina (*b* Herschel, Cape Colony, 24 March 1855; *d* Wynburg, Cape Colony, 11 December 1920)   South African feminist, novelist and political writer. A missionary's daughter, she travelled much, then became governess to various Cape farm families. Her experiences provided the basis of her novels, most notably *The Story of an African Farm* (1883), which have generally been judged more highly by female than male critics. In England she developed a close relationship with Havelock Ellis (1859–1939). Returning to South Africa in 1889, she campaigned for women's equality, particularly their right to independence through employment, and married Samuel Cronwright (1863–1936). She developed a strong dislike of Cecil Rhodes's imperialist ambitions, and bitterly opposed the Boer War. Strongly distrusting politicians, she none the less encouraged Samuel's political career, wrote pamphlets supporting the Boers and attempted to explain South African realities to the British. Active in England throughout the First World War, she returned to South Africa in 1920.

Ruth First and Ann Scott, *Olive Schreiner* (London, 1980).

SIMON KATZENELLENBOGEN

Schumann, Clara Wieck (*b* Leipzig, 13 September 1819; *d* Frankfurt am Main, 20 May 1896)   German pianist and composer. A musical prodigy who began performing at the age of 9, she became one of the foremost concert pianists of the nineteenth century. She premiered the works of Beethoven (1770–1827), Chopin (1810–49) and Brahms (1833–97) as well as those of her husband, Robert Schumann (1810–56), whom she married in 1840. Clara Schumann introduced important innovations in concert programming and performance, such as playing from memory and without supporting musicians, and, later in her life, enjoyed great success as a teacher. Despite the demands of family life (she had seven children), she maintained a busy concert schedule, composed and managed a large and complicated household. Her husband's mental breakdown and subsequent death left her the sole support of her family, but her career as a musician always represented an artistic as well as an economic necessity for her.

Nancy B. Reich, *Clara Schumann: The Artist and the Woman* (Ithaca, NY, 1985).

GAIL SAVAGE

science   The discipline of science, which attempts systematically and unbiasedly to observe nature and thence to classify and explain its structure, forces and effects, probably began as an intellectual enterprise prompted by curiosity and a need to find or create order in our perception and understanding. By the Renaissance, however, the utilitarian aspects of science had come to be recognized; science was seen as a key to power over nature and other nations. In the late nineteenth century science was adopted by many governments as an instrument of policy, as exemplified by the rapid development of the chemical and electrical industry in Germany (see CHEMICAL INDUSTRY, ELECTRICITY AND ELECTRICAL INDUSTRY). This period saw unprecedented development in science, its increasing division into many specialized fields, the unifying power of certain explanatory concepts such as ENERGY and force, the development of science as a profession and the study of science itself.

Initially, the explicit connections between science and technology were relatively few – the most prominent exceptions being the work of James Watt (1736–1819) and the Lunar Society. There were few careers or opportunities for education in science. Furthermore, there was some reaction against the mechanized science of Newton (1642–1727), as exemplified by *Naturphilosophie* in Germany, the writings of Blake (1757–1827) and Coleridge (1772–1834) and natural theology, which was widely accepted throughout Britain. By the end of the nineteenth century science and technology had produced, among other things, the telephone and radio (see TELEGRAPHY AND TELEPHONY).

As science became a part of the culture, more sciences became 'professional' and the number of scientific societies multiplied. For example, in London societies were founded for botany and zoology (1788), geology (1807) and astronomy (1820); while in the United States societies were started for natural history (1830), chemistry (1876) and geology (1888). Some organizations were established to promote the development of science in general: the British Association for the Advancement of Science (1831) and its American counterpart (1848). The emphasis on the development of scientists via university teaching and research, and the awarding of the degree of Doctor of Philosophy, was essentially a German invention, with Justus von LIEBIG being its most prominent advocate.

This development of science also led to attempts to establish the philosophical basis of science. In 1830 Auguste Comte (1798–1857) classified sciences according to the order in which they had emerged from superstition and theology: physics ahead of life sciences, which in turn preceded the social sciences. John Herschel's (1792–1871) *Preliminary Discourse on Natural Philosophy* (1830) introduced the distinction between the 'context of discovery' and the 'context of justification'. He insisted that the means used to formulate or derive a theory were irrelevant to considerations of its acceptability, and sought to determine which criteria were acceptable for use in formulating scientific theories. His list included: the crucial experiment, the discovery of unintended scope and the successful explanation of extreme cases. William Whewell (1794–1866) created a philosophy of science based on the history of science. He argued that the history of science evidenced a river–tributary analogy, which he termed 'consilience of inductions'. Progress was the result of many particular theories being subsumed under a few theories with greater explanatory power. John Stuart Mill's *A System of Logic* (1872) argued that scientific enquiry was the search for causal connections that were both invariable and unconditional, and that history could not be used to demonstrate something invariable; thus, inductive logic must be the basis for scientific practice.

Until the nineteenth century the scientific enterprise was dominated by Isaac Newton whose *Philosophiae naturalis principia mathematica* (1687) argued that the task of science was to fit all material events into a relatively simple framework of mathematically expressible results. It was Newton who first demonstrated a law of physical movement which seemed entirely unrelated to any spiritual order, giving immediacy to the conception of determinance. The phrase 'scientific determinism' and the associated mechanical view of the world were dominant themes during this era. However, it was the geologists and the evolutionary biologists who raised the issues primarily responsible for the developing conflict between religion and science by demonstrating that man had a much different role in nature than had previously been thought (*see* DARWINISM, EVOLUTION, GEOLOGY). At the end of the century Ernst Mach (1838–1916) reformulated Newtonian mechanics away from its 'metaphysical' speculations to the positivism that has influenced most twentieth-century thinkers.

See also CELL THEORY, CHEMISTRY, GAS, PHYSICS.

Charles Coulston Gillispie, *On the Edge of Objectivity* (Princeton, NJ, 1960). John Loose, *Historical Introduction to the Philosophy of Science* (Oxford, 1979).

STEVE AMANN

sculpture The history of sculpture parallels the history of PAINTING in the nineteenth century. NEOCLASSICISM dominated sculpture longer because the prevalence of ancient prototypes made comparisons more obvious. Sculpturs such as Antonio Canova (1757–1822) brought the emulation of antiquity to its zenith with his 'modern classics' and legitimized the exhibiting of plaster models in place of bronze or marble. Bertel Thorvaldsen (1770–1844) and John Flaxman (1755–1826) extended the scope of classicism to the archaic and bridged the transition to ROMANTICISM. Romanticism in sculpture became fully apparent in the 1830s, with works of dynamic energy and emotional fervour, as exemplified by François Rude (1784–1855). The international exchange among artists made reciprocal influence the norm. Historicism was manifested in diverse subjects and styles. Antoine Barye (1796–1875) introduced the vogue for animal sculptures, launching the *animaliers*, whose popularity grew with the interest in zoology and Darwinism.

Sculpture flourished as a result of the attitudes and technology generated by the industrial revolution. Bronze foundries exploited improved casting techniques, for example a machine that reduced or enlarged models for reproduction, which, along with the introduction of cheaper metals, such as zinc, and economical processes, such as electroplating, allowed the market for bronze sculptures to expand. The marriage of art and industry fostered the belief that good taste was within reach of every pocket. Trade fairs, culminating with the world fairs, made art synonymous with consumer goods.

The profession also profited from urban expansion, which encouraged vast sculptural programmes for Architecture. Public monuments embellished the new urban spaces. As the century became increasingly democratic and secular, commemorative sculpture fulfilled a pedagogical mission to instruct the public in its civic and moral obligations. Allegories proclaimed nationalist sentiments and aspirations. The cult of great men, extolling merit over birth, encouraged the erection of statues celebrating individuals as paradigms for a more egalitarian society. Flaxman, Pierre David d'Angers (1788–1856) and Christian Daniel Rauch (1777–1857) were seminal in defining the standard form of such portraits, rendered in historical realism, with identifying attributes. The practice was so widespread by the end of the century (as evidenced on our streets today) that a reaction to 'statuemania' set in. Funerary sculpture followed a similar evolution, as cemeteries moved from churchyards in the city centres to municipal parks on the edge. Likewise, as armies shifted from mercenaries to citizens, collective monuments honouring soldiers who died in battle became common.

The towering genius of the second half of the century was Auguste Rodin (1840–1917), whose sculptures challenged the accepted canons of beauty and taste. He explored inner reality at the expense of superficial detail. He made the fragment as expressive as the whole: awkward stances and unbalanced masses conveyed anguish and uncertainty; compacted poses or thrusting forms spoke of yearning or ecstasy. Eschewing polish and elegance, Rodin communicated the raw vitality of emotions through powerfully modelled surfaces. His effects of light and shadow have been incorrectly associated with impressionism, the one movement that did not have a true sculptural counterpart. However, the probing of the human psyche that was the essence of his creativity was symbolist (*see* Symbolism).

The relationship between sculpture and painting, whatever their differences, went beyond mutual participation in stylistic movements. No prior century had seen more painter-sculptors. These artists, whether they were exponents of the avant-garde, such as Edgar Degas (1834–1917) or members of the conservative academics, such as Léon Gérôme (1824–1904), imbued sculpture with the sensibilities of painting. What Gérôme did for chryselephantine sculpture Max Klinger (1857–1920) effected for polychrome. The disdain for technique, implicit in Degas's waxes, enabled Paul Gauguin (1848–1903) to experiment with colour and unlikely materials. Because these painter-sculptors moved across traditional categories, their creations were highly original. Perhaps the greatest legacy of the nineteenth century was the radical breakdown of categories, fundamental to the ambiguity between painting and sculpture that has stimulated much art of the twentieth century. Ultimately, the dissolution of the boundaries between separate art forms, combined with the acceptance of traditional, even found, materials has provoked the redefinition of art itself.

H. W. Janson, *Nineteenth-Century Sculpture* (New York, 1984).

JUNE ELLEN HARGROVE

Second International First assembled in Paris in 1889 on the centenary of the storming of the Bastille, the Second International last functioned in the shadow of war, at Brussels in July 1914. In between, as well as returning to Brussels and Paris (1891, 1900), it perambulated around Zurich (1893), London (1896), Amsterdam (1904), Stuttgart (1907), Copenhagen (1910) and Basle (1912). It brought together representatives from countries as far north as Scandinavia, as far east as the Balkans, Poland, Russia and Japan and as far south as South Africa and Australasia, as well as the western Europeans. However, until the foundation of the International Socialist Bureau in 1900, it was without even rudimentary organization. Its title was an invention of historians.

The participants represented anarchism, Marxism, social democracy and trade-unionism. Differences of ideological outlook or organizational affiliation, and varying national socio-economic conditions, accounted for disputes and difficulties within the International. The conflict with anarchists led to their exclusion from 1896; but ANARCHISM remained a factor in subsequent debate about the general-strike weapon versus political action. This issue was related to the question of revolutionary versus evolutionary SOCIALISM, brought to a head in 1899 by the French socialist Millerand's (1859–1943) decision to join a radical-republican government. The ensuing theoretical debate was of considerable intellectual interest, but it was widely divorced from the practice of many parties, including that of the Germans who dominated the discussion.

Another major issue, in an age of imperial rivalry, was the colonial question. Socialists could assert the principle of the basic equality of all peoples and races, but the matter was complicated by NATIONALISM.

Socialism versus nationalism was another area of major debate and proved to be the factor on which all the great hopes of the International foundered. For all the internationalism of leaders in debates touching on questions of war, was nationalism a stronger force among ordinary party members?

J. Braunthal, *Geschichte der Internationale*, vol. 1, (Bonn, 1961); *History of the International 1864–1914*, trans. Henry Collins and Kenneth Mitchell (London, 1966).
Georges Haupt, *Socialism and the Great War* (Oxford, 1972).
J. Joll, *The Second International 1889–1914* (London, 1955).

JOHN L. HALSTEAD

secularism The term 'secularist' is usually applied to opponents of established Christianity who seek to supplant orthodox religious practice with moral beliefs and practices not grounded in theology. It should not be confused with 'secularization', the process by which religion in general tends to decrease in importance in modern societies. The secularist movement proper dates from Thomas Paine's *The Age of Reason* (1794), which built on Enlightenment deist efforts to dispute the idea of divine revelation and establish a religion based on nature. This tradition was revived in Britain first by Richard Carlile (1790–1843), but then by the followers of Robert Owen (*see* OWENITES) in particular as well as by some Chartists. The Owenite circle included atheists like Charles Southwell (1814–60) as well as deists like Owen himself.

Organized secularism dates from the decline of Owenism in the mid-1840s and the pursuit of its freethinking aspects by George Jacob Holyoake (1817–1906) in particular, who named his own movement 'Secularism' in 1851. His journal, *The Reasoner*, lasted from 1846 to 1861, and aimed at not only toleration for infidels, but greater democracy and an increased reward for the labouring classes. The movement was lent support by, among others, pleas for toleration of 'blasphemous' opinions by John Stuart Mill, and gained intellectual sustenance with the inception of SOCIAL DARWINISM in the last third of the nineteenth century. From the 1870s onwards, most of its activities in Britain were linked to Charles BRADLAUGH, whose National Secular Society was founded in 1866. Though it never became a mass movement, secularism was also lent support by adherents to Auguste Comte's (1798–1857) 'Religion of Humanity', especially in Britain and France, and was reinforced by the anticlericism of many leading republicans in France in particular.

Edward Royle, *Victorian Infidels: The Origins of the British Secularist Movement 1791–1866* (Manchester, 1974).

GREGORY CLAEYS

Sedan, Battle of *see* FRANCO-PRUSSIAN WAR.

Seddon, Richard John (*b* St Helens, Lancashire, 22 June 1845; *d* at sea out of Sydney, 9 June 1906) Premier of New Zealand (1893–1906). He was a populist politician whose ample girth and autocratic style earned him the sobriquet 'King Dick'. He left England in 1863 for the Melbourne gold-fields and then settled in the mining area of New Zealand's West Coast. He grew successful as a 'bush lawyer' and community leader, and in national politics he helped to establish a liberal-party grouping. His government introduced the vote for women (which he personally fought against), a means-tested old-age pension and measures to protect labour. A Freemason, racist and strident imperialist, Seddon fostered New Zealand's expansion in the Pacific and participation in the Boer War. He also set a pattern of authoritarianism in New Zealand politics.

David Hamer, *The New Zealand Liberals: Years of Power, 1891–1912* (Auckland, 1988).

MICHAEL C. PUGH

Segu Bamana [Ségou Bambara] (*c.*1650–1861) A large west African imperial hegemony, the Segu Bamana State was founded in the mid-seventeenth century. Ruled by Bamana-speaking lineages (Bamana is a Mande language), the state was most associated with Mamari (Biton) Kulubaly (*c.*1712–55), the fama, or chief, during the first half of the eighteenth century.

The integrity of this military state, founded and maintained by state-owned warrior-slaves, was assured by a domestic/religious ideology serving public interests. Despite their military orientation, the Segu Bamana were primarily agriculturalists, while Islamized 'strangers', resident fisherfolk and herders of different ethnic identities, were subject to similar state conventions and protocols. Domestic and foreign commerce were extensive, and markets were integrated into both the domestic and ATLANTIC SLAVE TRADE (*see* SLAVERY (AFRICA)), even during the nineteenth century, although the latter was illegal after 1815. The Segu Bamana State was not entirely dependent on the slave trade, however, and also traded extensively in domestic produce, such as prepared foods and the Segu textiles for which it was famous. Foreign merchandise, such as gold from the south and European and north African manufacture, together with Saharan rock-salt brought south to Timbuktu by desert-side traders, were likewise included in the public and private mercantile inventories. As a military state, it produced a variety of arms; and, like the Ashanti and Ethiopia under Menelik II, it also stockpiled Europeans arms, sometimes in exchange for slaves. Although free men and women worked, a large proportion of the labour force, both public and private, was provided by slave men, women and children.

In 1861 the Segu Bamana state fell to the conquering Umarian armies under the leadership of 'UMAR IBN SA'ID TAL from the Futa Toro in Senegal (west Africa). It was under Umarian dominance, during the SCRAMBLE FOR AFRICA, that the consolidation of French colonial power on the middle and upper Niger was delayed. On destroying the Umarian state (1891–3), the French restored a client-scion of the last-ruling Bamana dynasty to power.

A. S. Kanya-Forstner, *The Conquest of the Western Sudan* (Cambridge, 1968). Louis Tauxier, *Histoire des Bambara* [History of the Bambara] (Paris, 1942).

B. MARIE PERINBAM

self-help   A central tenet in a widespread nineteenth-century middle-class ideology, self-help was given its classic expression in Samuel Smiles's (1812–1904) *Self-help* (1859), but was widely expressed in many other forms both before then and into the twentieth century. Self-help is a fundamentally individualist creed, expressing the view that each individual is responsible for his or her (usually his) social and economic advancement. It is thus critical of paternalistic and conservative views of the social order, in which every man should know his place. But it is equally critical of communal and especially socialist notions of mutuality and co-operation, and can easily relapse into the view that if people do not help themselves they have only themselves to blame. Stories of self-help were widespread in the nineteenth century, both in Britain and the United States; they tended especially to heroic accounts of self-helping individuals, written to encourage emulation by the stories' readers.

See also INDIVIDUALISM.

SIMON DENTITH

Self-strengthening Movement (1861–1895)   At the heart of the Self-strengthening Movement, the programme of limited reform introduced by the Ch'ing dynasty in response to China's defeat by Britain in the Anglo-Chinese Wars, was the 'ti-yung' (essence – practical application) formula of CHANG CHIH-TUNG. The 'essence' of China's culture was to be preserved and only the technology, not the philosophy, of the West, was to be borrowed. This led to a programme of limited reform. A foreign affairs bureau, the Tsungli Yamen, was set up from 1861 to deal with the representatives of foreign powers resident in Peking. The Yamen was effective only up to 1871. It was replaced in 1901 by the ministry of foreign affairs. Two major arsenals, at Kiangnan (Shanghai) and Nanking, and some smaller munitions factories were established. Later there was an attempt to stimulate industrial and commercial development. A leading role was played by provincial officials, notably

LIHUNG-CHANG. Li believed that steamships and guns would of themselves be sufficient to stop foreign aggression. His neglect of Western political systems and culture was symptomatic of the whole movement. His long period of office as governor-general of Chihli and admiral of the northern ocean enabled him to build up quite a considerable industrial empire in north China, notable enterprises being the Nanking arsenal and the China Merchants' Steam Navigation Company. But generally, the reforms introduced as a result of the Self-strengthening Movement were uncoordinated. Consequently, China did not achieve an industrial breakthrough comparable to that of Meiji Japan. The dominant figure in the Ch'ing court, Tz'u-hsi, was at best half-hearted in her commitment to reform. The failure of the Self-strengthening Movement was brutally highlighted by China's defeat by Japan in the Sino-Japanese War (1894–5).

JOHN DAVIES

Seneca Falls Convention (1848) The first national meeting called to discuss women's rights in the United States met at Seneca Falls in 1848. During the early nineteenth century an American woman had few legal rights; she could not vote, collect her own pay cheque, sue for divorce or gain custody of a minor in the event of her husband's death or a divorce. American female abolitionists, refused the right to participate in an international antislavery convention held in London (1840), began to organize to demand more legal rights for women. Led by Lucretia Mott (1793–1880) and Elizabeth Cady STANTON, these middle-class reformers gathered at Seneca Falls, New York in 1848 to discuss their plight. In the 'Declaration of Rights and Sentiment' written at the convention the women compared themselves to the American colonies, and berated American men in the same manner that Thomas Jefferson had attacked King George III. Among other things, the declaration demanded WOMEN'S SUFFRAGE.

Miriam Gurko, *The Ladies of Seneca Falls: The Birth of the Women's Rights Movement* (New York, 1974).

ALICE E. REAGAN

Serbia The Balkan state of Serbia was incorporated in the Ottoman Empire after 1459. Misrule by the janissaries precipitated a spontaneous revolt led by Kara George in 1804. By the Treaty of Bucharest (1812) autonomy was granted, but it was taken back by the Porte which squelched the insurrection in 1813. The second Serbian revolt (1815), led by Milosh Obrenovich achieved considerable autonomy, and Milosh was appointed hereditary prince in 1817. Serbia received full autonomy under Ottoman suzerainty and Russian protection in 1830.

Milosh's land reform created a landowning peasant class. He laid the foundations of legal, police and educational systems, but his despotism clashed with attempts to build up representative institutions, and he abdicated in 1839. After the short reigns of his sons Milan I (reigned 1839) and Michael (reigned 1839–42), the throne was passed to Alexander Karageorge (reigned 1842–58). This period saw the articulation of Serbia's ambitious national programme by Garashanin (1812–74) in 1844, and the oligarchic rule of the state council. In 1858 the national assembly brought back Milosh for a short reign, to be succeeded by the second reign of his able son Michael (reigned 1860–8), who achieved the complete withdrawal of Turkish garrisons from Serbia in 1867. On Michael's assassination, the country was ruled by regency which passed a new constitution (1869) broadening the powers of the assembly. Under the reign of Prince Milan II (1868; king, 1882–9) Serbia fought with Montenegro against the Ottomans, and was given full independence by the CONGRESS OF BERLIN (1878). Milan's defeat in the Serbo-Bulgarian war (1885) and his notorious personal life lost him popularity and he was obliged to pass a more liberal constitution before his abdication in 1889. By the 1880s Serbia had a full-fledged political life dominated by the radical, the progressive and the liberal parties. The last decade of the century saw a regency, constant cabinet shifts and, with the assassination of Alexander (reigned 1889–1903), the extinction of the Obrenovich dynasty.

See also KARAGEORGE, OBRENOVICH.

Michael Petrovich, *A History of Modern Serbia, 1804–1918* (New York 1976).

MARIA TODOROVA

serfdom Institutionalized in Russia under the Legal Code of 1649, serfdom had two sources: slavery proper which had existed since earliest times, and complex economic arrangements between peasants and landowners. The distinction between slaves and peasants gradually disappeared, and under Catherine II (1729–96) both became known as serfs and some 73 per cent of the population were handed over into bondage by the Charter of the Nobility (1775). At the start of the nineteenth century over 90 per cent of the Russian population was 'owned' by the state, the church or private landowners. The masters had almost complete control over their serfs, although they did have certain (largely overlooked) obligations to provide seed in case of crop failure and to support them in times of famine. Nor were they permitted to 'ruin or deal cruelly' with them. The serfs living on the land did, however, have a measure of self-government in the form of the commune, or mir, which was responsible for all peasant households, collection of taxes and periodic redistribution of land. The Russian Slavophiles and populists viewed the mir idealistically, seeing it as a unique Russian phenomenon, and supported its continuance; it remained in force until the reforms of Stolypin (1862–1911) in 1907.

The existence of serfdom was a serious hindrance to both social and economic development and various methods were proposed for its alleviation and abolition, until in 1861 ALEXANDER II issued the Edict of Emancipation by which the serfs were technically freed and allowed to purchase land. To assist them further in this, the Peasant Land Bank was established in 1883 which granted loans on favourable terms. The existence of serfdom and later the memory of its excesses provided much impetus to the growth of radical political activity throughout the nineteenth century.

R. Piper, *Russia under the Old Regime* (London, 1974).

A. V. KNOWLES

servants *see* DOMESTIC SERVANTS.

Seward, William Henry (*b* Florida, New York, 16 May 1801; *d* Auburn, New York, 10 October 1872) Republican leader and American secretary of state (1861–9). A protege of anti-Jacksonian editor Thurlow Weed (1797–1882), he began his career as an antislavery Whig, serving as governor of New York (1839–43) before embarking on lengthy congressional service. In the Senate he opposed the COMPROMISE OF 1850 because of its tough Fugitive Slave Law, warning his opponents that the issue of slavery was governed by 'higher law'. Joining the new Republican Party in 1855, he continued to add to his radical abolitionist reputation by warning of the coming of an 'irrepressible conflict' between the sections (1858). Electing not to run for president in 1856, Seward emerged as the front runner in 1860, only to be passed over for the more moderate Lincoln. Chosen as Lincoln's secretary of state, he served ably during the Civil War, and kept Europe from sending troops to aid the Confederacy. After the war he was responsible for the purchase of Alaska (1867) from Russia.

Glyndon G. Van Deusen, *William Henry Seward* (New York, 1967).

ALICE E. REAGAN

sewing-machine Beginning in the late eighteenth century, a number of inventors attempted to devise a machine that would perform the repetitious movements of sewing. It was only in the 1840s, however, that several inventors, working independently, devised the key elements of the modern sewing-machine. The central technical breakthrough, advocated most forcefully by an American mechanic, Elias Howe (1819–67), was the use of a needle and a shuttle, each carrying its own thread, to produce a 'lock stitch' (rather than the single-thread stitches of hand sewing). By the early 1850s, several inventors had put together the key elements of the modern sewing-machine and had begun manufacturing.

It required the commercial acumen of the American mechanic and entrepreneur Isaac Singer (1811–75) to bring these elements together into a practical machine and the novel marketing techniques required to sell it in large numbers. Further legal acumen was required to form the means to create the Sewing Machine Combination in 1856. The sewing-machine rapidly became the first complex machine sold for both factory and household use. By 1875 the Singer company alone was selling a quarter of a million machines a year. The sewing-machine became the basis for the large garment industry that sprang up in every industrialized country late in the nineteenth century, with its consequent expansion of clothing consumption (through department stores and mail-order catalogues) and its labour abuses (*see* SWEATED TRADES).

ROBERT FRIEDEL

Shaftesbury, Anthony Ashley Cooper, seventh earl of (*b* London, 28 April 1801; *d* Folkestone, 1 October 1885) English social reformer and philanthropist. His aristocratic political pedigree notwithstanding, Lord Ashley (as he was known until his succession to the earldom in 1851) held only minor office in 1828 and 1834. Thereafter, he was drawn whole-heartedly into projects to promote physical and spiritual welfare, driven by a strong Evangelical conscience and paternalist commitment which placed him outside the ranks of the Tory leadership. However, his efforts to ameliorate the lot of working people (factory operatives, underground mining workers, climbing boys and so on) stopped short of political reform: indeed, the passing of the 1867 Reform Act filled him with gloom. Furthermore, the social legislation which his philanthropic work inspired was generally informed by a collectivist spirit alien to his essential individualism, to his aspirations for individual moral and religious development. An indefatigable philanthropist – he was chairman of the Ragged School Union (*see* RAGGED SCHOOLS) for thirty-nine years – Shaftesbury personified the paradoxes of Tory PATERNALISM.

JOHN BELCHEM

Shaka (*b* ?Nguga, Natal, *c*.1787; *d* Dukuza, Natal, 22 September 1828) Founder of Zulu kingdom (*see* ZULUS). Considered illegitimate by his father, Senzngakhona (*c*.1757–1810), he had an unhappy childhood, but defeated his rivals for succession to the clan chieftainship. He established the organization of society into homestead production units. This was supported by the organization of his army into age regiments subject to Spartan training, strict discipline and celibacy. He was something of a military genius, his most significant innovation being the replacement of the thrown spear with a shorter stabbing weapon. Shaka was assassinated by his brother DINGANE, who succeeded him. The European image of Shaka was of a cruel despotic man. While he was undoubtedly very ruthless with regard to potential rivals, this view is certainly exaggerated and served European interests rather than reflecting reality.

Jeff Guy, *The Destruction of the Zulu Kingdom: The Civil War in Zululand, 1879–1884* (London, 1979).
E. A. Ritter, *Shaka Zulu: The Rise of the Zulu Empire* (London, 1955).

SIMON KATZENELLENBOGEN

Sher Ali (*b* Afghanistan, 1823; *d* Balkh, Russia, 21 February 1879) Ruler of Afghanistan (1839–41). The son of DOST MOHAMMED, he laid claim to the throne of AFGHANISTAN. Not until 1869, after a protracted civil war, did he succeed. Deeply embittered by the British delay in recognizing his government, and suspicious of the expansionist policies of Viceroy Lytton (1831–91), he was courted by Russian interests. Fearing Russian expansion less than British, since the Anglo-Russian Agreement of 1873 had successfully delineated Afghanistan's northern border, he became preoccupied with British activities at Quetta (modern Pakistan) and engaged in secret diplomacy with the Russians.

Anti-British bias, attempts to block the British sent to Kabul to negotiate and a call to frontier Muslims to revolt eventually precipitated the second Afghan War (1878–80). Sher Ali, poorly prepared militarily or diplomatically to resist, fled, while the British forces speedily occupied the southern half of Afghanistan and chose his successor.

H. W. Bellew, *Afghanistan and the Afghans* (Lahore, 1979).

ROBERT J. YOUNG

Sherman, William Tecumseh (*b* Lancaster, Ohio, 8 February 1820; *d* New York, 14 February 1891) Leading northern general in the AMERICAN CIVIL WAR. After graduating from the United States Military Academy in 1840, he served in the army until 1853, then entered business until the outbreak of the Civil War in 1861. He succeeded Ulysses S. Grant in 1864 as commander-in-chief of the western Union armies. In September 1864 he captured the key southern city of Atlanta, helping to re-elect Abraham Lincoln in November. With 60,000 soldiers, he then began his famous 'March to the Sea' (or 'March through Georgia'), systematically destroying Confederate sources of food and material supply. He captured Savannah, Georgia on 21 December, then turned north to meet Grant's army, receiving the surrender of Confederate general Joseph E. Johnston (1807–91) in April 1865. After the war he served as commander of the United States army until his retirement in 1884. He is best remembered for his dictum 'War is hell'. His methods of waging total war foreshadowed twentieth-century conflicts.

KEVIN MURPHY

Sherman Anti-trust Act (1890)   Directed against the large monopolistic corporations in the United States, the Sherman Anti-trust Act was designed to make illegal 'every contract, combination . . . or conspiracy in restraint of trade or commerce'. Violators could receive fines of $1,000 or sentences of up to one year and victims could sue for triple damages. Passing with only one nay vote, the legislation assuaged the fears of the American public without posing a real threat to big business. In 1895 the Supreme Court (in *United States* versus *E. C. Knight*) ruled that the American Sugar Refining Company, controlling more than 90 per cent of the industry, did not violate the act. During the 1890s almost half of the eighteen suits the government filed were against labour unions. Not until the twentieth century was the act enforced – although erratically – against big business.

Hans B. Thorelli, *Federal Antitrust Policy: The Origination of an American Tradition* (Baltimore, 1955).

JOHN MARTIN

short story   It is possible to find anticipations of the short story in earlier writing, but the short story as a self-conscious literary form developed in the nineteenth century, and received some of its classic formulations at the end of the century. It is not to be thought of simply as a shorter novel, but as a distinctive form of prose-writing. There are two complementary explanations for the development of the short story in the nineteenth century. On the one had, there were powerful aesthetic reasons why many writers should have wished to adopt the short-story form – its necessary concentration, the requirement to be read at one sitting (like a lyric poem), its ability to focus narrowly on one aspect of a situation or on a moment of transition or revelation. But cruder reasons of the literary market-place also encouraged the form, above all the growth of magazine publication, with its insatiable demand for copy (*see* PERIODICALS). Though the serialized NOVEL was still being written at the end of the century, the short story was an obvious response to this demand.

In Britain earlier writers like Walter Scott (1771–1832), Charles Dickens and Elizabeth Gaskell (1810–65) all published shorter fiction, but it was never their characteristic form. Towards the end of the century, however, many writers used the form in a sustained and self-conscious way. They included Rudyard Kipling (1865–1936), Robert Louis Stevenson (1850–94), Thomes Hardy (1840–1928), Henry James (1843–1916) and Arthur Conan Doyle (1859–1930). In the United States Edgar Allan Poe (1809–49) wrote some powerful short stories in the 1830s and 1840s, continuing a tradition of Gothic uses for the form that ran throughout the century. But the most famous American short-story writer was O. Henry (1862–1910), who began writing stories at the end of the century but did not commence publication until 1904. In France, as in Britain, many of the great novelists of the century also wrote shorter fiction, but here too the short story became a more self-conscious form towards the end of the century, where in the hands of a writer like Guy de Maupassant (1850–93) it became a powerful and sometimes shocking instrument. Similarly, in Russia, though the great masters of the full-length novel, such as Fyodor Dostoevsky (1821–81), wrote short stories, the form received its classic expression in Russian at the hands of Anton Chekhov (1860–1904) in the 1880s and 1890s.

In all these cases, the arbitrariness of terminal dates is especially apparent, for the short story was a characteristically modern form which reached definitive status in the 1880s but continued to be richly produced in the early decades of the twentieth century in an unbroken line from the late nineteenth century onwards.

Valerie Shaw, *The Short Story: A Critical Introduction* (London, 1983).

SIMON DENTITH

Siam The efforts of two outstanding kings, Mongkut, Rama IV (reigned 1851–68) and Chulalongkorn, Rama V (reigned 1868–1910), ensured that Siam maintained its independence and avoided the fate of its south-east Asian neighbours. From China's failure to maintain its isolation in the face of Western pressure, Mongkut drew the conclusion that Siam had no option but to come to terms with the West before change was imposed upon it. Accordingly, in 1855 he concluded a Treaty of Friendship and Commerce with Britain, appointed foreign advisers and began the process of modernization. His successor, Chulalongkorn, developed this process further, introducing reforms which decisively affected every aspect of Siam's life. Slavery was abolished, the army and financial system reformed, education developed and communications improved by the building of railways and modern roads. In contrast to Burma and Vietnam, Siam maintained its independence.

D. G. E. Hall, *A History of South-East Asia* (London, 1964).

JOHN DAVIES

Sidi Muhammad ibn Ali *see* SANUSI, SIDI MUHAMMAD IBN ALI AL-.

Sidmouth, first Viscount *see* ADDINGTON, HENRY.

Siemens, Ernst Werner von (*b* Lenthe, Prussia, 13 January 1816; *d* Charlottenberg, Berlin, 6 December 1892) German electrical engineer, who established one of the world's largest electrical-engineering concerns. He trained as an engineer in the Prussian army, from which he resigned in 1849 to concentrate on managing a telegraphic-equipment factory in Berlin he had founded two years previously with Johann Georg Halske (1814–90). He had successfully developed an electroplating process while still a serving officer. The company was responsible for laying cables across the Mediterranean and between Europe and India. Branches were established in France, Austria, Russia and England, where its interests were handled by Siemens's brother Karl Wilhelm (1823–83), pioneer of regenerative furnaces. Siemens contributed to the development of many branches of electrical engineering, including power generation and electric traction. He invented the self-excited generator in 1866 and demonstrated an electric locomotive at the Berlin Exhibition of 1879. He served as a liberal member of the chamber of deputies.

BARRIE TRINDER

Sierra Leone In 1807 the coastal settlement of Freetown, recently established as a home for free persons of African extraction (*see* AFRICAN-AMERICANS), albeit most of them born as slaves in North America, was transferred from the Sierra Leone Company and became a British colony. The settlers, mainly English-speaking, Christian and literate, thereafter acculturated the 70,000 'Liberated Africans' who, up to the 1870s, were rescued from slave ships and settled at and around Freetown. The resulting 'Creole' community spread modernizing influences along the coast of western Africa, through an educated elite, ranging from clerks to Bishop Samuel CROWTHER. In 1896 the deep hinterland of Freetown was added to the colony, creating modern Sierra Leone.

The extent to which the various interior peoples had been previously subject to European and Creole influence varied, but long-standing social structures and processes had generally been maintained – for instance the spread of Islam. In the 1890s reactions occurred: a limited interior revolt in 1898 directed against colonial taxation and the creoles, and a process of British demotion of Creole influence, partly ideological, that is racist, but more opportunist. British colonial rule had extended to new west African territories which raised up their own educated elites, while more intensive rule demanded updated technical expertise outside Creole experience and instead supplied by white expatriates.

Christopher Fyfe, *A History of Sierra Leone* (London, 1962).

P. E. H. HAIR

Sikhs The term 'Sikh' originally referred to an informal gathering of the followers of the Guru Nanak (1469–1539), both Hindu and Muslim in origin, who sought a personalized religious experience beyond the structures of organized religion. Tacitly rejecting the inequities of caste (varna), emphazising charity and preaching a message of peace and universal brotherhood, the movement spread in the Punjab area and formalized as a separate religious tradition. The compilation of the Adi Granth Sahib, the Sikh holy book, by Guru Arjun (1581–1606) was an especially important development in that direction.

Declining Mughal authority in the late seventeenth and eighteenth centuries, together with victimization, initiated a significant shift to militancy and the creation of a martial organization (Khalsa), in 1699, which increasingly provided leadership for the Sikhs. Persian and Afghan invasions throughout the eighteenth century made militant Sikhism a dominant element.

The creation of a Sikh-dominated state, centred in Punjab, in 1799, was the beginning of a significant period of Sikh political development. Between 1799 and 1839 Sikhs reached beyond Punjab to Peshwar in the west and Kashmir in the north-east. Thereafter a reputation for martial prowess followed them throughout the nineteenth century. At the death of Ranjit Singh (1780–1839) the Sikh state rapidly disintegrated. British authority was quickly established over the remnants of the Sikh empire in a series of wars in the 1840s.

Once integrated into the territories of the English East India Company, Sikhs distinguished themselves as loyal subjects, became a significant element in the Company's military and played a significant role in suppression of the Sepoy Mutiny (see INDIAN MUTINY) in 1857 which earned them a priviledged position in the Indian army as one of the martial races.

W. H. McLeod, *The Sikhs* (New York, 1989).

ROBERT J. YOUNG

Sino-Japanese War (1894–1895) Defeat at the hands of Meiji Japan in the Sino-Japanese War was China's most humiliating defeat in the nineteenth century and final proof that the Self-strengthening programme (see SELF-STRENGTHENING MOVEMENT) pursued by the Ch'ing dynasty since the 1860s was a failure. It was one thing to be defeated by the Western barbarians with their superior military technology but another matter altogether to be defeated by Japan, a tributary and inferior state in Chinese eyes.

The origin of the war lay in Korea, traditionally a tributary state of China, but where China and Japan had been in dispute since the mid-1880s, supporting rival claimants to power. In 1894 a rising of the banned Tonghuk sect was crushed by China. Japan used the opportunity to send troops to Korea. LI HUNG-CHANG hoped to reach a diplomatic settlement with the aid of the Western powers, but his diplomacy served only to delay China's military preparations, already seriously impaired by financial corruption. War was declared on 1 August after the *Kowshing*, carrying Chinese troops to Korea, was sunk. The Chinese were quickly defeated in Korea, the Chinese fleet comprehensively beaten at the Battle of the Yalu in September, and Japan took Port Arthur in November and Weihaiwei in February 1895.

Li was blamed for China's defeat and dismissed, but was recalled to negotiate the Treaty of Shimonoseki in April 1895. China recognized the independence of Korea, paid an indemnity, ceded Taiwan, the Pescadores and the Liaotung peninsula to Japan and opened further TREATY PORTS. The intervention of Germany, France and Russia forced Japan to return the Liaotung peninsula in return for a further indemnity. The war made clear the extreme weakness of China and led to a further surge of foreign imperialism and accelerated the demand for internal reform.

I. C. Y. Hsu, *The Rise of Modern China* (4th edn, Oxford, 1990).

JOHN DAVIES

Sitting Bull (*b* South Dakota, *c.*1831; *d* Standing Rock Reservation, South Dakota, 15 December 1890) Leader of the Teton Sioux at Little Big Horn. Known as Tatanka Iyotake by the Teton Sioux, he won a reputation for fearlessness in youthful battles with the Crow. Although he had only sporadic contact with whites until middle age, he was their unrelenting enemy. These feelings were based more on devotion to traditional Sioux culture than to personal hatred. After the United States peace commission of 1867 negotiated with RED CLOUD, the majority of the Teton Sioux – who mistrusted Red Cloud and his treaty – chose Sitting Bull as their head chief, an unprecedented position. In 1876, following successes against George Custer's Seventh Cavalry, the Sioux fought in smaller groups, each eventually surrendering. Fearing Sitting Bull's possible leadership in the Ghost Dance movement of the 1890s (*see* BATTLE OF WOUNDED KNEE), tribal police attempted to arrest him. Sitting Bull died in the process.

JOHN MARTIN

Six Acts (1819) A comprehensive set of repressive legislation, known as the Six Acts, was passed after parliament was specially convened in November 1819, within a few months of PETERLOO. Taken together, the new laws sought to restrict popular participation in all forms of political debate and activity. Attention has generally focused on restrictions and taxes on the press, but the cornerstone of the Six Acts was the new Seditious Meetings Prevention Act, prohibiting the carrying of banners and flags and restricting attendance to residents of the parish. Reinforced by its new powers, the government launched a sustained campaign of prosecution: by 1820 all leading radical orators, organizers, journalists, publishers and distributors were confined in prison. However, the effects of the Six Acts were largely nullified later in 1820 when the government, much to its embarrassment, was confronted by mass demonstrations and an unlicensed press in support of Queen Caroline's (1768–1821) cause.

JOHN BELCHEM

skilled workers Individuals employed in manufacturing occupations which required manual skill, knowledge and substantial discretion in the planning and execution of tasks, skilled workers were also referred to as artisans. The possession of skill was the basis for greater security of employment, more substantial levels of remuneration and higher status within the working class. Skilled workers protected their privileged position by erecting barriers, chiefly apprenticeship requirements, against the vagaries of the labour market. The enforcement of apprenticeship restrictions helped to defend skilled workers against employers but the tactic of exclusion was also aimed at the immense ranks of unskilled labourers. Exclusion similarly defined women's work as inherently unskilled, gender discrimination which forced women into the worst-paid occupations.

Recent historians have emphasized the centrality of workshop-based manufacture and other 'archaic' forms of production in the industrial revolution. Given the limited extent of technological change, employers remained acutely dependent on human skill throughout the nineteenth century, conceding broad workplace authority to artisans. The ability to control the pace of work, productive output as well as the hours of labour were central aspects of artisan independence.

The absence of constant pressure toward deskilling, however, did not prevent employers from attacking artisans' workplace authority. In the face of unregulated competition, and often dependent on middlemen for credit, employers of skilled workers regularly breached workplace customs and standards, resorting to sweating and driving to remain profitable (*see* SWEATED TRADES). At the same time, by the logic of uneven economic development, skilled workers' retention of a high degree of skill allowed for the organization of resistance to employer encroachments. Thus the early decades of the nineteenth century witnessed the proliferation of artisan unions to further the protection of skilled trades and safeguard artisan independence. Concerned with work rules and output restrictions as much as with wages, these small, locally based and sectional trade unions reflected the centrality of the immediate work group in resisting subordination.

Subjected to similar pressures and threats, skilled workers were the most politically active component of the early-nineteenth-century working class. Alarmed at the threat which unregulated competition posed to their independence, artisans demonstrated great interest in Owenite schemes of co-operative production (*see* CO-OPERATION) and other alternatives to unfettered capitalism. Informed by an ideology which credited productive labour as the only true source of wealth, the nascent class consciousness of skilled workers was evidenced by the move away from sectionalism and attempts at GENERAL UNIONISM. That endeavour collapsed by 1834, ending the attempt at constructing a broader radical working-class alliance. Nevertheless, the artisan initiatives of the 1830s produced a formative critique of capitalism and an inspired legacy of democratic collective action.

The final defeat of Chartism hastened the retreat of the working class from politics and the movement towards greater interclass co-operation. A number of bourgeois-sponsored institutions, including temperance societies, libraries and workingmen's clubs served as cultural bridges, linking the middle class to skilled workers and culturally differentiating the ARISTOCRACY OF LABOUR from the larger working class. Underlying the equilibrium of mid-Victorian society, however, was the stabilization of production relationships. Here, Britain's unilateral economic domination, the persistence of intercapitalist competition and the absence of managerial theory acted to restrain employers from challenging the continued authority which Victorian craftsmen exercised at the workplace. The solidification of new divisions of labour, critical to the security of skilled workers, was further strengthened by the establishment of 'new model unions'. Typified by the Amalgamated Society of Engineers (ASE), new model unions fused the traditions of autonomous regulation exercised by local work groups to a national organizational structure.

The GREAT DEPRESSION (1873–96) and Britain's lagging industrial productivity imposed new imperatives on manufacturers, eroding the structures of authority which had secured the mid-Victorian compromise. Some skilled workers, such as engineers and printers, were faced with the introduction of new technologies which threatened craft traditions. More commonly, however, employers attempted to increase labour productivity by introducing more systematic managerial supervision, including the imposition of PIECE-WORK, and effecting new divisions of labour. Fracturing craft boundaries that had been stable since the mid nineteenth century, the reorganization of labour created the need for whole new classes of semi-skilled work. This change, which was behind the emergence of NEW UNIONISM, blurred the older source of working-class segmentation and allowed for the articulation of a new social identity explicitly based on class.

Richard Price, *Masters, Unions and Men: Work Control in Building and the Rise of Labour, 1830–1914* (Cambridge, 1980).

E. P. Thompson, *The Making of the English Working Class* (New York, 1966).

RICHARD J. SODERLUND

slavery (Africa)   Domestic slavery in Africa was a pre-capitalist institution in place long before the Atlantic slave trade, to which it was subsequently linked. It was likewise integrated into the age-old trans-Saharan slave trade and its shorter-lived Indian Ocean counterpart, and persisted throughout the nineteenth century. Although slaves were a traded commodity, most were 'lineage slaves' who were integrated into free lineages through marriage and concubinage. A differentiation was almost always made between the 'slave' and 'free' lineages. While most domestic slaves were war captives, slavery was sometimes a common punishment for aberrant behaviour. Although no indisputable demographic data exist, slaves made up well over 50 per cent of some African populations, many of whom were women and children. Slaves performed a wide range of functions in addition to domestic and field labour. Some men served as chiefs' counsellors and advisers, as provincial rulers in African imperial hegemonies or, more commonly, in slave armies. Large numbers of women and men slaves engaged in commerce, sometimes on their masters' or mistresses' behalf, sometimes on their own. Some slaves became rich, and it was not uncommon for rich slaves to own slaves.

Suzanne Miers and Igor Kopytoff (eds), *Slavery in Africa: Historical and Anthropological Perspectives* (Madison, Wisc., 1977).

B. MARIE PERINBAM

slavery (United States) During the nineteenth century slavery in the United States reached its mature phase. By the early 1830s, only Cuba and Brazil still also had slavery in the western Hemisphere. The African-American slave population was the only one to reproduce itself in the western hemisphere. In the United States state slave codes supposedly strictly controlled the slaves, outlawing black literacy, large gatherings, and movement without a pass. In reality, state and local officials usually left control of the slaves up to the individual masters. In addition, the local population formed itself into a posse-like organization known as 'the patrol' to control African-American movements after dark.

The slaves' lives depended on each individual master and on the type of work the slaves performed. Some masters were kindly and more lenient, but others were extremely cruel. Approximately 75 per cent of the slaves performed some sort of agricultural work. These field hands worked primarily on large cotton plantations, but some worked for hemp-, sugar- and rice-planters. Those on rice plantations worked under the task system, where they performed a given task and then had time for themselves. This led to a greater autonomy for these slaves. The slaves who worked in cotton performed their labour under the gang system, where workers went to the fields at sun-up and had little time to themselves. Some worked side by side with smaller yeomen farmers. Another 15 per cent of the slaves were house servants, working as cooks, maids, butlers and carriage-drivers. The other 10 per cent worked as skilled craftsmen, often in an urban setting. This last group often worked for people besides their masters, and split their wages with their owners.

No matter what kind of master they had, slaves never lost sight of the fact that whites considered them property or chattel. American slavery was unique in Western history because it operated mainly for the master's profit. Owning slaves was a status symbol in the south because they represented a large investment. Approximately 25 per cent of all white families owned slaves in 1860. This represented a considerable change from the 1830s, when 33 per cent of white families had owned slaves. As the price of slaves and land rose by nearly 70 per cent during the 1850s, fewer southerners, especially young people, owned slaves. Some radical southerners suggested reopening the international slave trade, banned since 1808, to remedy this problem.

Slavery was a system of coercion. Whites used force, often beatings, to enforce their rules and gratify their whims. Only one in 5,000 slaves successfully escaped to the free north, and those who did faced the threat of slave-catchers. Most slaves found ways to force some accommodation with whites. They often slowed down their work, broke tools, faked sick, stole chickens and pigs, committed arson or ran away for brief periods of time. Slaves often showed one face to the master and had another that they used out of the sight of whites.

By 1830 white southerners insisted that slavery was a positive good. They claimed it brought civilization to a backward people by teaching them Christianity and other white ways. These paternal attitudes reinforced white feelings of superiority towards the slaves. They found justification for their opinions, they claimed, in the Bible, in science and by comparing slave society to white wage labour in the north.

Slaves created their own culture in the United States, and by the nineteenth century two institutions stood at the centre of the black community. One was African-American religion. Slaves adopted white Christianity to their own purposes. Their religion promised them deliverance from slavery, and portrayed American slaves as God's chosen people like the Hebrews of the Old Testament. Unlike southern white Protestantism, slave religion was very joyous. Since whites distrusted slave religious meetings, they often had to meet at night in 'hush arbors'. They added ring-shouts and the call and response to Christian rituals. Some masters tried to force their 'people' to attend white religious services or to control the black preachers. They achieved only mixed success.

The other major slave institution was the African-American family. Because of the domestic slave trade, approximately 33 per cent of all African-American families saw members sold away from them. The average slave found himself or herself on the auction block at least once during their life. In order to overcome this problem, slave families adopted newcomers whom their masters bought. These individuals became 'aunts', 'uncles' and 'cousins' to other slaves. Slave families lived usually in the slave 'quarters', a group of cabins located near the plantation house. One of the biggest problems experienced by slaves was their lack of privacy.

See also ABOLITIONISM, AFRICAN-AMERICANS, COMPROMISE OF 1850, FUGITIVE SLAVE ACT, MISSOURI COMPROMISE.

John W. Blassingame, The Slave Community: Plantation Life in the Antebellum South (New York, 1972).

Robert W. Fogel, Without Consent or Contract: The Rise and Fall of American Slavery (New York, 1989).

Eugene D. Genovese, Roll, Jordon, Roll: The World the Slaves Made (New York, 1974).

ALICE E. REAGAN

slave trade, Atlantic In the nineteenth century alone, more than 2 million slaves were shipped to the Americas from Africa. The Atlantic slave trade was one of the crucial forces in creating the nineteenth-century world, and indeed the world of today. In his classic study of the trade Phillip Curtin tentatively estimated that from the fifteenth to the nineteenth centuries a total of 9.6 million slaves landed in the Americas. More recent estimates have usually tended to raise this figure: Inikori and Engerman suggest that the extent of the trade was no less than 12 million or more than 20 million; and Inikori himself suggests 15.4 million. By far the most important destination for slaves in the nineteenth century was Brazil, followed by Cuba; and the chief sources of slaves had shifted from the Guinea coast to west-central Africa (Congo, Angola) and Mozambique. (An account of the African, as opposed to the Atlantic, slave trade should also include slave exportations to the Muslim world – north Africa, the Middle East and the Indian Ocean. That trade became extensive from the ninth century and continued until about 1900.)

In the Americas the nineteenth century saw huge expansion in several major slave regimes – the United States (expansion by natural increase), Cuba and southern Brazil (by importation) – but it also saw the collapse of, first, the Atlantic slave trade, and then of slavery itself. Denmark abolished its slave trade in 1802, Britain and the United States by 1808 and France (after British insistence) in 1815; but the trade to Brazil was not effectively ended until 1850, and that to Cuba not until the 1860s. The Cuban closure meant that the Atlantic trade was ended (except perhaps for some smuggling). The institution of slavery (rather than merely the trade in slaves) ended in the British West Indies in 1833, in French colonies in 1848, in Dutch territories by 1863 and in the United States in 1865. From the 1810s to 1830s the Latin American republics introduced gradual emancipation, but final abolition usually came only in the 1850s and 1860s. Cuba abolished slavery in 1886, and in 1888 slavery was ended in Brazil – which meant that slavery in the Americas (but not discrimination against African-Americans) was ended.

The collapse of slave-trading and slavery in the Americas occurred in the nineteenth century, and the region-by-region timing of this collapse, in the major regimes of the Americas at least, generally coincided locally with the growth of influence of industrial capitalism (either domestic urban-industrial development, or international, especially British, influence). Eric Williams developed a theory of the connections between capitalism and slavery, arguing that profits from the slave trade and the slave colonies of the Americas created the industrial revolution in Europe, and hence established British domination of the West in the nineteenth century. He went on to argue that the slavery system, having been crucial to commercial capitalism, became unprofitable and was attacked as a barrier to free trade and economic progress. Humanitarian influence in the downfall of slavery was downplayed. Recent work has, however, argued that slavery did not die from within (through lack of profits); it collapsed through pressure being placed on slave-holders. The role of slaves and freed blacks (as Williams argued) was crucial in HAITI, and significant elsewhere. A revised version of the Williams thesis (of economic and class self-interest leading to abolition) seems to have much explanatory power. Rising urban interests *perceived* slavery as unprofitable, backward, and a threat to liberal (and middle-class) values.

It is clear that Africa was the great loser from the slave trade; and western Europe, North America and sections elsewhere within the Americas the great gainers. Although special factors (like a non-peasant social structure) help to explain why Britain, and not other West-European countries with slavery connections, led the industrial revolution, the slavery system was crucial across western Europe in developing trade and the potential for industrialization. The slave trade dramatically reduced African population growth (by exportations, mortality before exportation and the dislocation of societies). It encouraged domination by warrior classes with slaving interests, and brought gains to a few members of African elites; but for Africa generally it brought political and economic damage in the long run. (*See* SCRAMBLE FOR AFRICA.) In short, the trade crucially influenced regional inequalities in the modern world, prompting the development of racist myths of white superiority and black inferiority (*see* THEORIES OF RACE). Roughly coinciding with the collapse of slavery in the Americas, the rise of 'scientific' racist ideas in Europe and elsewhere, together with the massive expansion of European imperialism, reinforced these notions of a hierarchy of races.

See also SLAVERY (AFRICA), SLAVERY (UNITED STATES).

Phillip D. Curtin, *The Atlantic Slave Trade* (Madison, Wisc., 1969).
Joseph E. Inikori and Stanley L. Engerman (eds), *The Atlantic Slave Trade* (Durham, NC, 1992).
Eric Williams, *Capitalism and Slavery* (Chapel Hill, NC, 1944).

MICHAEL TADMAN

Smiles, Samuel *see* SELF-HELP.

Smith, Joseph *see* MORMONS.

social Darwinism   An attitude towards race, poverty, nature, history and society, social Darwinism was distinguished by the use of some form of quasi-biological or other naturalist explanation for social evolution and/or the existing distribution of wealth. Often associated with the defence of untrammelled *laissez-faire*, the doctrine none the less appealed to some socialists, as well as those who assumed its chief moral lesson was the need for a more pacific form of society. The crucial question in the doctrine's search for biological analogies to human development was the degree of determinism accorded to natural phenomena in social evolution and, further, the degree of dependence of individual human character on the general character of the species. During the second half of the nineteenth century such questions were linked to Charles DARWIN's *Origin of Species* (1859), whose doctrine of natural selection sought to explain how species characteristics were inherited, and how specific traits affected individual and species survival given limited resources (*see* DARWINISM).

Darwin believed that variation in how characteristics were inherited determined the chances of survival and of the 'selection' or perpetuation of some parts of a species rather than others. Without doubt, this notion helped to create a world-view analogous to a providential government of nature and society and offering a new theory of natural order and design. The adaptation of such themes to social theory was not Darwin's invention, however, and to some degree the label 'social Darwinism' is a misleading one. Many issues similar to those raised by Darwin, especially in relation to population growth, had emerged during the widespread discussion of T. R. Malthus's (1766–1834) *Essay on Population* (1798), which stressed the tendency of human and animal populations alike to outstrip subsistence, and suggested a relation between individual restraint and survival (*see* MALTHUSIANISM). Biological aspects of the new social sciences had been explored by Auguste Comte (1798–1857), Herbert SPENCER and others prior to Darwin. Spencer used the term 'survival of the fittest', widely perceived to be the central dogma of the movement, and in 1852 had suggested in the *Westminster Review* that intraspecific struggle resulted in improvements in individual character or 'type'. This was not necessarily deducible from Darwin's own position, which stressed that population pressure, while promoting evolutionary change, did not necessarily lead to the 'best' types surviving.

Instead, social Darwinists linked notions of 'fitness' to concepts of the desirable and valuable, while emphasizing the Malthusian theory of the harm of unlimited population growth. Although such views were used to bolster conservative and *laissez-faire* ideals, they were also adapted as weapons against the aristocracy as an institution rewarded by status rather than achievement, for example by the economist W. R. Greg (1809–81) and the founder of EUGENICS, Francis Galton (1822–1911), whose *Hereditary Genius* (1869) described a meritocracy as the best means of developing ability. So, too, Walter Bagehot (1826–77) in *Physics and Politics* (1872) contended that liberal democracies offered the best guarantees for evolutionary progress and were most suitable for the higher forms of social development. Bagehot also argued that only those societies which permitted a substantial measure of political freedom would produce the variations required for further, higher evolution, since competition in the world of ideas would produce victory for the best thoughts (a view analogous to J. S. Mill's case for freedom of speech from a non-biological but organic viewpoint in *On Liberty* (1859)). A more collectivist slant, emphasizing progress towards a co-operative ideal, was given to such views by the British 'new liberal' David Ritchie (1853–1903) (*Darwinism and Politics*, 1889), among others, who like many by the 1880s began to turn from the greater stress given to the virtues of competitive individualism of the previous decade, still defended by Spencer. Ritchie thus conceived of the state as a benevolent institution which could assist social evolution by freeing the individual from a perpetual struggle for the means of existence. This view was lent some support by T. H. HUXLEY (*Ethics and Evolution*, 1894) and by Benjamin Kidd's (1858–1916) *Social Evolution* (1894); some socialists took a similar position while trying to avoid the Malthusian implications of Darwin's research, as did anarchists like KROPOTKIN.

In Europe, the United States and elsewhere both social Darwinism and its practical result, the eugenics movement, had a considerable impact. Much of this was easily translated into racialist doctrines, to notions of an ideal race of 'supermen', associated with the philosophy of Friedrich NIETZSCHE, as well as to hostility to working-class 'overbreeding'.

John Burrow, *Evolution and Society* (Cambridge, 1966).
Richard Hofstadter, *Social Darwinism in American Thought* (New York, 1944).
Greta Jones, *Social Darwinism and English Thought* (Brighton, 1980).

GREGORY CLAEYS

social democracy The nineteenth and early twentieth century saw social democracy change from a working-class doctrine espousing Marxism to one concerned with economic growth and social reforms within capitalism. Developments in Germany were central. The German Social Democratic Workers' Party (SDAP) was founded in 1869 advocating Marxist socio-economic principles and a democratic state, reaffirming these at its 1891 Erfurt Congress as the Social Democratic Party (SPD) (*see* SOCIAL DEMOCRATIC PARTY (GERMANY)). The SPD became the largest party in the *Reichstag* in 1912. It espoused revolutionary goals but in the face of practical realities was effectively reformist. Its leaders from 1875, LIEBKNECHT and BEBEL, were democrats. Karl KAUTSKY combined a Marxist economic analysis with a commitment to democratic class struggle. Eduard BERNSTEIN attempted to revise both the economic theory and the politics of Marxism in German social democracy.

In 1864 delegates from across Europe founded an international organization of labour (*see* FIRST INTERNATIONAL). Its inaugural address, written by MARX, condemned the concentration of ownership in private hands and urged the conquest of political power by the working class through the democratic process, a combination of collectivism with democracy which confirmed the social democratic principles of the International.

In Britain the FABIAN SOCIETY founded in 1883 was more influential than Marxism. Sidney and Beatrice WEBB advocated gradual change and the bureaucratic provision of collective goods by enlightened middle-class intellectuals. After 1918 social democracy in the British LABOUR PARTY (founded 1900) and other English-speaking countries combined Fabianism with labourism, the pursuit by organized labour of reforms in its own sectional interests.

In the 1914–18 war national working classes turned against one another. In the 1917 Russian Revolution Lenin's (1870–1924) Bolsheviks overthrew the social democratic government of the Menshevik Kerensky (1881–1970). After these events, social democracy shed the internationalist and Marxist principles it had affirmed at the 1889 SECOND INTERNATIONAL and these became associated with Bolshevism. Social democracy reacted against both Bolshevik tyranny and the economic crises and social effects of liberal capitalism. It became distinguished from Bolshevism by its adherence to liberal democratic institutions. And it now equated working-class interests not with the overthrow of capitalism but with economic growth and social-welfare reforms within it. In this form, social democracy enjoyed parliamentary representation and governmental success in Europe and Australasia in the twentieth century.

G. Lichtheim, *A Short History of Socialism* (London, 1983).

LUKE MARTELL

Social Democratic Federation The first Marxist group in Britain, the Social Democratic Federation (SDF) played a noteworthy role in the late-nineteenth-century revival of SOCIALISM. It began life in 1881 as the Democratic Federation, a motley coalition of advanced liberals and radical London working men. After driving the radicals away with his constant onslaught against Gladstone, the federation's leader, H. M. Hyndman (1842–1921), converted the body to socialism in 1883, renaming it the Social Democratic Federation the following year. A gentleman by birth and of imperialist and radical Tory inclinations in politics, the top-hatted Hyndman adopted Marxism in 1880, introducing it to a larger audience with his *England for All*, published in 1883. Thoroughly dominating the SDF, Hyndman embraced orthodox Marxist economics and the primacy of class struggle, agitating tirelessly for the cause of socialism. The SDF, however, suffered regular secessions, due largely to Hyndman's dictatorial personality. Moreover, with its mechanical insistence on the inevitability of violent revolution and pronounced hostility to the pragmatic trade-union movement, the SDF gained only a handful of followers.

The SDF's most important period of influence commenced in the economically depressed years of 1886–7, after it assumed leadership of the sometimes violent mass demonstrations of the London unemployed. By 1890 the SDF could claim a modest following among enclaves of SKILLED WORKERS in London and Lancashire. It further extended its influence by participating in the establishment of the INDEPENDENT LABOUR PARTY in 1893 and of the Labour Representation Committee (LRC) in 1900. That compromise with pragmatism proved temporary, however, and disatisfied with the labourist orientation of the LRC, the SDF broke with it in 1901, returning to sectarian marginality. Despite its fatal dogmatism, the SDF introduced Marxist vocabulary to Britain and also provided critical experience and training for a number of notable working-class socialist leaders.

Chushichi Tsuzuki, *H. M. Hyndman and British Socialism* (Oxford, 1961).

RICHARD J. SODERLUND

Social Democratic Party (Germany) The Socialist Workers' Party (SAP), which had been formed in 1875 through the merger of LASSALLE'S General Union of German Workers and the Eisenach Party (*see* EISENACH CONGRESS) led by BEBEL and LIEBKNECHT, and which had been driven underground by the ANTI-SOCIALIST LAW between 1878 and 1890, was succeeded by the Social Democratic Party (SPD). The party adopted its new name in 1890; and committed itself to a Marxist analysis of society and the pursuit of revolutionary goals at its Erfurt Congress in 1891. Following the party's legalization, both its membership and its electoral support grew dramatically: in 1912 it had over 1 million members, attracted the support of more than one-third of those who voted in national elections and was the largest party in the Reichstag. This political mobilization was accompanied by the emergence under its aegis of a panoply of workers' social and recreational organizations which came to constitute the institutional framework for a separate workers' subculture. Despite its maintenance of an ostensibly revolutionary stance – confirmed, against the revisionism of BERNSTEIN, at the turn of the century – the SPD came increasingly to adopt a reformist practice. This was in part a consequence of the growing influence of the free trade unions, with which it was closely associated and which contributed handsomely to the party's coffers; and in part a consequence of the burgeoning of bureaucratic structures and practices within what was the largest socialist movement in the world and the mainstay of the SECOND INTERNATIONAL. Yet the apparent contradiction between the party's theory and its practice is perhaps best understood as a reflection of the political environment in which it operated – an environment which was simultaneously 'open' enough to make the struggle for representation and reforms appear worth while and yet still so 'closed' as to make the prospect of dramatic change without revolutionary upheaval seem remote.

See also SOCIAL DEMOCRACY.

R. Fletcher (ed.), *Bernstein to Brandt: A Short History of German Social Democracy* (London, 1987).
C. E. Schorske, *German Social Democracy, 1905–1917* (Cambridge, Mass., 1955).

S. J. SALTER

social housing A variety of social-housing policies evolved during the second half of the nineteenth century in northern Europe and the United States. The dwellings produced by these programmes formed a very small proportion of the total housing provision in any country before the First World War, and their chief interest and importance was as forerunners of the more ambitious state-subsidized house-building programmes after 1919.

In Britain the enlightened self-interest of factory-owners provided a number of show-piece company towns, including Saltaire, Port Sunlight, Bournville and New Earswick. Private PHILANTHROPY (notably that of Peabody (1795–1869), the London-based American financier) provided model tenements. Octavia Hill (1838–1912) pioneered well-publicized attempts to reform the irregular life-styles of slum-dwellers, in a programme which now appears as a highly intrusive form of social engineering.

Local government was drawn into social housing in Britain from rising concern about slums and unhealthy areas in congested cities, public house-building being seen initially in the restricted role of replacing demolished slums (generally providing many fewer new units than were demolished). The Artisans' and Labourers' Dwellings Act 1868, often known as the Torrens Act, first provided powers for the demolition of individual condemned houses; while its Amendment Act, passed in 1879, inserted provisions for compensation and replacement dwellings. The Artisans' and Labourers' Dwellings Improvement Act 1875 (the Cross Act) permitted councils to purchase and clear areas of unfit dwellings, to prepare sites for development and to sell or lease them to builders. Only if it proved impossible to find a developer was the local authority empowered to build dwellings itself (and in this event the dwellings were to be offered for resale within ten years). These limited 'sanitary' measures were followed by the Housing of the Working Classes Act 1890, which consolidated and updated earlier powers and required London local authorities to provide replacements for not less than 50 per cent of the clearances. Part 3 of this most important of nineteenth-century British Housing Acts also gave powers to local authorities to improve, remodel or build 'lodging houses for the working classes'. Local-authority 'lodging houses' were normally the same types of four-, five- or six-storey tenement blocks already being built by philanthropic housing trusts. The London County Council also adopted two-storey terraced 'cottage' housing for its early-twentieth-century suburban projects, thus setting a pattern for the use of low-rise garden-city housing for the much greater subsidized social house-building drives of the interwar years.

In France, too, cottage housing in the 'workers' city' (pioneered at Mulhouse in 1853) was an ideal for many reformers who hoped thereby to channel private finance into affordable housing, and thus to stabilize the working class in property ownership. Financial incentives were provided in the 1894 law on low-cost housing which sought to direct funds from charitable and savings societies into low-cost housing (*see* BUILDING SOCIETIES). Little was achieved in practice, however, and the French housing policies of the late nineteenth century focused on sanitary measures and (unsuccessful) attempts to reform the oppressive private-tenancy laws.

In 1890 German non-profit co-operative building societies were permitted to borrow money on favourable terms from the funds created by the Invalidity and Old Age Insurance Act of the same year, and about 11,000 dwellings were provided in this way by 1914. The German emphasis on co-operatives (by contrast with the growing British reliance on municipal powers) has been explained by comparing the lack of political power of small property owners in the British political system with the strength of this group in the tricameral Prussian parliament. The British Housing of the Working Classes Act of 1890 (providing powers for municipal house-building) would probably have been defeated in Germany. In Britain both options were considered and attempted, but the council-housing solution eventually triumphed, dwarfing the early efforts of the self-build co-operatives and the philanthropic housing trusts.

The United States opted for the encouragement of home ownership. Higher living standards and greater disposable income among the American working class meant that many families were able to invest savings in the Building and Loan Associations (BLAs), and the state proved willing to subsidize the BLAs as a solution to the growing late nineteenth-century housing crisis in the great cities. American housing reformers opposed the spread of the tenement (which was seen as un-American) and promoted construction of affordable owner-occupied single-family homes. In the United States, as in most other countries, the nineteenth-century tenure system was still dominated by private tenancy. However, on the periphery of many American nineteenth-century cities self-build remained an option for those willing to invest their own labour, just as the pioneer farmers built their homes and barns on the prairie. For obvious reasons, opposition to the excessive property taxation of small houses was a concern of the American social-housing movement.

N. Bullock and J. J. Read, *The Movement for Housing Reform in Germany and France 1840–1914* (Cambridge, 1985).

M. J. Daunton (ed.), *Housing the Workers: A Comparative History, 1850–1914* (Leicester, 1990).

SIMON PEPPER

socialism The term 'socialism' emerged as a popular usage during the 1830s, but the ideas it embodied began to gather currency in the later years of the French Revolution. Gracchus Babeuf (1760–97) and the Conspiracy of Equals of 1796 was one source, but more important was the experience of 1793–4, when the Revolution was sustained by an alliance with the lower orders, especially the Paris crowd, and when the regime used its authority to enforce control over the economy in the interests both of equity and of war mobilization. These policies were symbolized by the so-called 'Jacobin maximum', which governed the prices of necessities. This was also, of course, the time of the Terror, a connection that was perhaps not entirely coincidental.

The revolutionary origins of socialism meant that for many the socialist project would be a continuation and an extension of the struggle for democracy. That is certainly how MARX and ENGELS saw it and it was how they acted as well, for the two founders of 'scientific socialism' got their first taste of politics in the democratic upheavals of 1848. It was the basis, moreover, for the distinction they drew between themselves and the various thinkers whom they derisively labelled 'utopian socialists' (*see* UTOPIAN SOCIALISM). It was, however, the so-called 'utopian socialists' like SAINT-SIMON, Robert OWEN and Charles FOURIER whose writings and activities made socialism part of the political discourse during the first half of the nineteenth century.

That discourse was in crucial respects more social than political; hence the sympathetic hearing with which socialism was met in elite circles despite the avowedly reactionary temper of the time. The early socialists were not themselves anti-democratic, but their concern was with social and economic organization. In this they were responding imaginatively to the enormous rupture in economic life portended by the beginnings of industrialization. Though economic historians have recently pointed out the modest nature of the economic growth generated during Britain's first wave of industrialization, contemporaries were rather more impressed. They intuitively grasped both the threat posed by modern industry to traditional ways and its potential for abolishing scarcity and enlarging the scope of human achievement. They believed as well, perhaps naively, that the shape of the new society was still open to debate and subject to rational control, and so sought to guide its development.

All the early socialists – Saint-Simon, Owen, Fourier and others – envisioned a new industrial society that was organized on a more collectivist, communal and egalitarian basis than the society around them. Their programmes differed greatly in detail, of course, and their rhetorics were equally distinct. Owen was a freethinker, a feminist and radical egalitarian who had, despite or perhaps because of these characteristics, made a modest fortune in textiles. His factory in New Lanark was a model; and his subsequent experiments in co-operative production and communal living were intended not only to inspire but to flourish. Saint-Simon was less socially radical and looked more to scientists, financiers and enlightened rulers to build and guide the new society – a reflection possibly of the weakness of French entrepreneurship during these years. Fourier was a wilder, more colourful character whose elaborate plans for a social organization based on phalansteries spanning the globe seem, in retrospect, rather silly but whose vision was at the time extremely appealing. Marx and Engels had little difficulty pinning the label 'utopian' on these thinkers, for it certainly could be argued that none of their plans specified a plausible mechanism by which the new society could be brought into being. It was a moment, however, when the social order seemed very much in flux and proposals for grand schemes of social reorganization very much in order. And in the end, of course, who would argue that Marx and Engels' vision was realistic, let alone scientific?

The ideas of Marx and Engels were, however, more genuinely political than those of fellow socialists. Marx and Engels are often portrayed merely, or primarily, as intellectuals who combined the insights of German philosophy (Hegel in particular) with the analytical rigour of English and Scottish political economy and infused the mixture with a Jacobin radicalism. The theories of Marx and Engels certainly were shaped by these traditions – indeed, it is not unreasonable to regard Marx as simultaneously the culmination of Hegel and of classical political economy – but they were worked out in relation to contemporary political concerns as well. At the centre of Marxism after all, was an argument about the historic tasks, prospects and interests of particular classes. To Marx and Engels the emerging proletariat was distinguished from the bourgeoisie, the peasants and, of course, the old aristocratic interests by both its need for socialism and its capacity to bring it about. This argument, however flawed, was based on a serious reflection on recent history and an equally serious engagement with the political struggles of the moment. Marx focused on the revolutionary potential of the workers only after studying what the bourgeoisie had accomplished during the French Revolution and witnessing what they would and would not do elsewhere, particularly in 1848. Likewise, Marx and Engels' estimate of the revolutionary potential of the peasants was not deduced from theory but came from a reading of recent political history.

That Marxism developed as a reflection on the political and social history of the nineteenth century was part of what made it so compelling. It helped to make sense of what Eric Hobsbawm has called the 'dual revolution' and went beyond interpretation to project a future that, if bloody and turbulent, had nevertheless an alluring goal. It was ironic, however, that despite Marx and Engels' interest in practical politics there was very little opportunity for them to participate in a genuinely socialist political movement in their lifetimes. Socialism became a part of European intellectual life early in the nineteenth century. Between 1848 and the 1870s, and particularly with the publication of Das Kapital in 1867, Marx created an intimidating theoretical edifice. Not until the 1880s, however, did socialist groups and parties begin to gather significant support.

It would appear that socialism was unable to sink roots among the workers until the first great wave of industrial expansion had begun to falter with the Great Depression of 1873–96. By then, capitalism had succeeded in creating a working class, or the beginnings of one, in virtually every country in Europe, but had by no means begun to generate the sustained growth of income that would eventually undermine working-class support for socialist transformation (see WORKING CLASSES). Economic troubles translated quickly into political critique and agitation. The SPD (see SOCIAL DEMOCRATIC PARTY (GERMANY)) was founded in 1875, outlawed in 1878 and began to gather large numbers of votes in the 1880s. By 1890, it attracted close to 1.5 million votes and elected thirty-five representatives to the Reichstag. Elsewhere, progress was less spectacular, but none the less significant, and in

1889 the socialist parties from across Europe gathered in Paris to found the Socialist International (*see* SECOND INTERNATIONAL). From 1889 to 1914 socialist parties grew in strength in every country, gathering support from their association with the growing trade-union movement and benefiting from the democratization of the suffrage.

The socialism that had emerged by 1900 was vaguely Marxist in its theory and its rhetoric, except in Britain (*see* LABOUR PARTY), but there were important national and local inflections. National roots and variations would become more pronounced during the First World War, which effectively shattered socialism's pretensions to being a universalist and internationalist movement. Nevertheless, by the turn of the century socialists across Europe could reasonably claim to be the major party giving voice to ordinary people. In this sense, socialism provided the vehicle through which the working people first came to be represented within modern democratic politics; and the socialist vision and programme would for many years continue to shape, in some cases even to define, working-class interests and aspirations.

Eric Hobsbawm, *Workers: Worlds of Labor* (New York, 1984).
James Joll, *The Second International, 1889–1914* (New York, 1966).
Ira Katznelson and Aristide Zolberg (eds), *Working Class Formation: Nineteenth-Century Patterns in Western Europe and the United States* (Princeton, NJ, 1986).
George Lichtheim, *Marxism* (London, 1967).
David McClelland, *Karl Marx: His Life and Thought* (New York, 1973).

JAMES E. CRONIN

sociology   The term 'sociology' was first used by the French theorist Auguste Comte (1798–1857) in 1830, and was introduced into English in 1843 in reference to his writings. Broadly, it describes the scientific, methodical analysis of society as opposed to political science, the study of politics. Its antecedents lie especially in the emphasis on the need for a science of society by leading writers in the Scottish Enlightenment, such as Ferguson (1723–1816), Smith (1723–90) and Millar (1735–1801), and in France, in the writings of Montesquieu (1689–1755) and Rousseau (1712–78). Sociology gained recognition especially through the growing early-nineteenth-century perception that the sphere of society was governed by laws which were or ought to be largely independent of political interference.

The notion of a 'science of society' was popularized in Britain by the followers of Robert OWEN, while in France the notion of a *science sociale* began to be discussed in the same period by the followers of SAINT-SIMON in particular. The latter's one-time secretary Comte took up the notion that social evolution tended towards an eventual state of equilibrium. Comte's system of thought, called POSITIVISM, distinguished between the structure of society and its related parts, called 'statics'; and 'dynamics', or alterations in ideas and institutions. Comte divided history into three main stages: the theological, when divine causation of all phenomena was largely presumed; the metaphysical, where objects were ascribed powers and entities according to conceptions of their purpose, rather than any verifiable reality; and the positive stage, when pure science analysed objects and described their relations in terms of increasingly abstract laws of development.

Other nineteenth-century sociologists of note included Alexis de TOCQUEVILLE, whose *De la Démocratie en Amerique* (Democracy in America, 1835–40) was a pioneering study of the effects of equality in modern society; Emile Durkheim (1858–1917), who did much to define the disciplinary boundaries of the new science and contributed important studies of religion and the division of labour; Gustave Le Bon (1841–1931), renowned for his work on the crowd; Herbert SPENCER, the leading British sociologist, who was also of great influence in the United States; Ferdinand Tönnies (1855–1936); Karl MARX; and Max Weber (1864–1920).

J. H. Abraham, *The Origins and Growth of Sociology* (Harmondsworth, 1973).
GREGORY CLAEYS

Solferino, Battle of *see* MAGENTA AND SOLFERINO, BATTLES OF.

South Africa Officially used more broadly in the earlier nineteenth century to refer generally to the southern part of the African continent, the term 'South Africa' came effectively to mean the area later known as the Union of South Africa. From 1847 the Governor of the CAPE COLONY was also named high commissioner for South Africa, with general oversight of territories under British 'protection' but not formally annexed, Bechuanaland (Botswana), Basutoland (Lesotho) and Swaziland. The BRITISH SOUTH AFRICA COMPANY territories also came under the high commissioner.

Seeking to reduce its obligations in the region in mid-century, as only the Cape had any strategic importance, the British sought – without success – to achieve a federation of the two Boer republics and the two British colonies. Diamond discoveries at Kimberley in 1867 and viable gold finds in the TRANSVAAL led to major capital inflows, railway and port development and renewed British desire to maintain control over the region. Britain's Pyrrhic victory in the second ANGLO-BOER WAR led to the establishment in 1910 of the Union of South Africa governed essentially by Boers (*see* AFRIKANERS), although economic strength remained for many years in British and other foreign hands.

SIMÒN KATZENELLENBOGEN

South African Republic *see* TRANSVAAL.

South African War *see* ANGLO-BOER WARS.

Spain The history of Spain in the nineteenth century was in large
part conditioned by its experience of the PENINSULAR WAR of 1808–14.
On the one hand, this produced the vigorous liberalism expressed in
the constitution of 1812. On the other, it politicized the army, which
came to identify its own professional interests with those of the nation, restoring absolutism – in the person of FERDINAND VII – to power
by a military coup in 1814. But the king could no more satisfy its
demands than could the liberals, the result being the revolution of
1820 and the restoration of the constitution. In 1823 a French army
reinstated absolutism, but victory was hollow: Spain's American empire, whose retention had been one of the cornerstones of Ferdinand's
policy, was now all but lost, while the king soon discovered that
Spain's financial problems were such that he simply could not follow
the advice of the medievalist 'pure royalists'. Liberal bureaucrats were
therefore restored to favour, and by the time Ferdinand died in 1833
the regime had become openly reformist. Traditionalists were horrified, and from 1827 a series of revolts broke out that culminated in
the first Carlist War (1833–40) (*see* CARLIST WARS), this in turn forcing
the monarchy, now represented by the infant Isabella II (1830–1904),
to appeal to the liberals by means of the 'statute' of 1834. However,
the liberals were divided between moderates and radicals, and, lacking
mass support, both groups sought to advance their cause by forging
links with the army. Already strongly influenced by the legacy of the
Peninsular War, many soldiers were therefore again drawn into politics. A more progressive constitution was introduced as a result of a
military coup in 1837, and from then until 1868, when Isabella II,
now much despised, was overthrown, there were no fewer than nineteen such *pronunciamientos*. As for the downfall of Isabella, this only
produced fresh chaos. Amadeo of Savoy (1845–90; reigned 1870–3)
soon foundered as a substitute for the Bourbons, and as radicalism
became a popular force, a republic was declared in 1873. Immediately,
large areas of the country rose in revolt: Carlism re-emerged in the
north while in the south agricultural labourers, urban workers and
the petty bourgeoisie joined in an inchoate protest against the liberal
state. Order was restored only in 1874 when an alliance of conservative politicians and generals brought ALFONSO XII to the throne. Dedicated to protecting the landed oligarchy which dominated Spanish
society – a combination of the grandees and the bourgeois beneficiaries of the sale of the lands of the church by successive liberal regimes
– and the conciliation of the army, the 'restoration monarchy' ruled
through a system of rigged parliamentarianism. Yet this, too, was
inherently unstable. Anarchism and socialism were gaining ground,
Catalan and Basque separatism was stimulated by industrialization,

and humiliation in the SPANISH-AMERICAN WAR of 1898 disgusted the intelligentsia. At the turn of the century, in short, Spain seemed destined for a turbulent future.

R. Carr, *Spain, 1808–1975* (Oxford, 1982).

CHARLES ESDAILE

Spanish-American War (1898)   More appropriately called the Spanish-American-Cuban-Filipino War, this conflict began in CUBA, where insurgents had long tried to gain independence from imperial Spain. Renewed revolution in 1895 attracted attention from the United States. American interest in Cuba emerged from several concerns. Some policymakers longed for the United States to dominate the western hemisphere, which seemed to require eviction of all European rivals. Others hoped that Cuban independence would facilitate profitable commerce between the two countries, and many genuinely believed in the moral obligation of the world's foremost democracy to aid any fight for self-rule. Some from each camp, furthermore, prescribed war as an antidote to what they saw as diminishing manliness among American men.

Consequently, in April 1898 the United States Congress authorized President William McKinley to force Spain out of Cuba. Soon thereafter, the United States also attacked Spanish rulers in the Philippines. Filipino nationalists and the American navy triumphed in Manila shortly after Spain's forces had disintegrated in the Caribbean. In August 1898 Spain signed an armistice; in the Treaty of Paris, negotiated in December 1898, Spain agreed to free Cuba and to cede Puerto Rico, Guam and the Philippines to the United States. Ratification of the treaty by the United States Senate in February 1899 meant something different to each combatant. For Spain it meant the end of empire; for the United States it signified its emergence as an imperial power; for the Filipinos, it brought devastation from an unsuccessful guerilla war against the United States (1899–1902) and subsequently – as to Puerto Rico and Guam – domination by yet another foreign power; for Cuba it secured an independence severely limited by the military and economic demands of its northern neighbour.

Gerald Linderman, *Mirror of War* (Ann Arbor, Mich., 1974).

ROBYN MUNCY

Spence, Thomas (*b* Newcastle upon Tyne, 21 June 1750; *d* London, 1 September 1814)   English land reformer and radical publisher. He was already a highly original agrarian reformer when he left his native Tyneside for London shortly before the French Revolution. He became deeply involved in RADICALISM and the revolutionary movement, publicizing his theory that private property was the root of all exploitation and inequality. Between 1797 and 1820 revolutionary conspiracies in London were consistently associated with his name or ideas. However, it was as a land reformer, with an alternative social vision to Thomas Paine (1737–1809) and OWEN, that his influence endured. 'Spencean philanthropists' were active and influential members of the early co-operative, socialist and Chartist movements. Thus Spence's ideas remained a central element of continuity in the agrarian tradition within the labour movement, and a bench-mark to which later reformers referred, notably H. M. Hyndman (1842–1921) and Henry George (1839–97).

Malcolm Chase, 'The People's Farm': English Radical Agrarianism, 1775–1840 (Oxford, 1988).

MALCOLM CHASE

Spencer, Herbert (b Derby, 27 April 1820; d Brighton, 8 December 1903) English philosopher. He wrote extensively on biology, psychology, sociology and philosophy, attempting to arrange these various areas by means of the same fundamental principles. In all areas, from the history of matter to the evolution of social forms, he traced the same progression from 'homogeneity' to 'heterogeneity'. This enormously ambitious synthetic philosophy, which had its absurdities as well as its insights, was influential in the nineteenth century and widely translated. Spencer's deep commitment to *laissez-faire* led to his hostility to all forms of government 'interference' and in later life hostility towards socialism. His belief in competition caused him to coin the term 'survival of the fittest' in advance of widespread knowledge of Darwin's theory of evolution; the idea of evolution was central to his work, though he tended to give it moralized expression (*see* SOCIAL DARWINISM). The view of society as an 'organism' was at once the source of the major insights of his work and of its major difficulties.

SIMON DENTITH

spiritualism While a belief in the survival of the human spirit after death and its ability to communicate with the living is a part of many religious traditions, an Anglo-American variety of spiritualism, or spiritism, became popular after 1848 when news of the American Fox sisters' – Ann Leah (? 1818–90), Margaret (? 1833–93) and Catherine (? 1839–92) – ability to communicate with spirits inspired others to learn to receive spirit communications through table-rappings, passive writing and trance utterances. Spiritualism emerged at time when Christians mounted new kinds of challenges to biblical authority and many regarded science as a source of universal truth. Spiritualists strived to employ a scientific method to verify their claims, arguing, for example, that spirit communication was proof of an afterlife. They often took a keen interest in physical purity, promoting hydropathy and vegetarianism. Socially progressive movements, including women's suffrage and plebeian socialism, were also strongly associated with spiritualism.

Alex Owen, *The Darkened Room: Women, Power and Spiritualism in Late Victorian England* (London, 1989).

PAMELA J. WALKER

sport A foreign visitor to Britain in 1899, overwhelmed by the British passion for sport remarked, 'All is sport in England. It is sucked in with the mother's milk.' Organized sport, and gambling which accompanied most sports, played a major part in the leisure activities of men of all classes in Britain, to an extent unknown in other European countries. Some sports, particularly horse-racing, cricket, golf, athletics and rowing, remained popular throughout the nineteenth century, but within these and other sports many changes took place, especially in how they were played, and who played them.

At the start of the century the most popular sporting activities were blood sports, and games such as FOOTBALL which were often played on an intervillage basis. The games were invariably rough, disorderly and contained few, if any, rules. But in the growing urban environment of Victorian Britain the boisterousness and violence engendered in these sports were increasingly objected to on both moral and safety grounds. Most blood sports, apart from HUNTING and shooting, were outlawed, and other games were codified with rules which reduced rough play and emphasized self-discipline. Along with regulation came centralization. By 1890 fifteen sports had such a wide following that they were governed by national bodies whereas fifty years earlier only CRICKET, golf and horse-racing possessed any form of national organization.

Substantial changes occurred around the middle of the century, partly through developments within the public schools, where the belief that organized sport moulded character and developed qualities of courage and loyalty, was one which was adhered to firmly. To achieve this end, it was essential that participants in games played fairly and accepted certain codes of conduct. Consequently, the rules of many games were standardized and written down, and it was from among the ranks of ex-public schoolboys that the chairmen and members of national sporting bodies, and the legislators of Victorian sports, were to be found.

Thomas Hughes (1822–96) and Charles Kingsley (1819–75), leaders of the Muscular Christian movement, argued strongly that if sport was fundamental in developing moral character then opportunities for playing sports should be extended to the working classes. Muscular Christians worked hard through their churches and chapels in providing such opportunities, and it has been estimated that in the 1860s one-quarter of all the organized football teams in the country consisted of church, chapel and Sunday school teams. It is easy, however, to exaggerate the influence of this movement. The major factors which enabled large numbers of working men to participate in or watch sports was a rise in real wages and increased leisure time, particularly after the introduction from the 1850s onwards of half-day Saturday working. Railways, too, played their part by making it possible for the playing of matches between distant teams on a regular basis. But more importantly, especially for the growing numbers of spectators following football teams, was the growth of the urban tram and bus services towards the end of the century.

As well as the desire to bring sport to working men within their own country, the British were largely responsible in the nineteenth century for exporting a large number of sports to different parts of the world. The traditional British games of cricket and football were taken abroad. Other sports which were not British in origin, such as tennis, were codified and repackaged and then played by the British both on the continent of Europe and in various parts of the British Empire.

The last quarter of the century saw an enormous growth in organized sport at all levels. The building of football and cricket grounds in Britain was accompanied by a growth in the number of sporting-goods firms catering for a growing number of participants in a wide variety of games. Newspapers, responding to demand but also stimulating it, gave increasing coverage to sports, and by the 1890s the most popular features were the football and horse-racing tipsters. For although off-course betting on horse-racing had been made illegal in 1853, the street bookmaker still existed and flourished.

Although there was an increasing number of professional players among the top ranks of cricketers and footballers, the idea of the amateur sportsman remained predominant at the end of the century. In some sports amateurs continued to play against professionals, in others (as in rugby) they were separated. It was also on an amateur basis that most of the new sports, such as lawn tennis and badminton, were played. Ironically, at the time that Muscular Christians were extolling team games because they promoted virtues of loyalty and interdependence, many of the new games which were played by the middle classes were individual rather than team games. It is important to note that many of these new sports were taken up by middle-class women. This is true also of cycling, especially after the introduction of the 'safety bicycle' in the 1880s (*see* BICYCLE).

In other parts of the world sport was beginning to figure prominently in the leisure activities of many men. Not only was organized sport being developed within countries but there were moves to develop sport on an international basis and in 1894 the International Olympic Committee was founded.

See also BASEBALL.

R. Holt, *Sport and the British* (Oxford, 1989).
J. Walvin, *Leisure and Society 1830–1950* (London, 1978).

J. M. GOLBY

Stambolov, Stefan (*b* Tîrnovo, 31 January 1854; *d* Sofia, 18 July 1895) Bulgarian revolutionary and statesman. A leader of the national revolution, he participated in the anti-Ottoman revolts and the Russo-Turkish war (1877–8). After 1878 he was elected to the national assembly and became its president (1884). He persuaded Alexander BATTENBERG to accept the union with Eastern Rumelia (1885) despite Russian opposition. On Alexander's abdication, he headed the regency council securing FERDINAND I's election (1887) and became the all-powerful prime minister. His foreign policy was aimed at peaceful penetration of Macedonia through religion and education, rapprochement with Turkey (which won him the enmity of the Macedonian committees), earning the support of the Western powers. He emancipated BULGARIA from Russian interference but at the expense of severing diplomatic relations. This, and his ruthless suppression of political opponents and dictatorial policies, enabled Ferdinand to dismiss him (1894). Stambolov died after a brutal assassination attack.

Richard Crampton, *Bulgaria 1878–1918: A History* (Boulder, Colo., 1983).

MARIA TODOROVA

Standard-of-Living Controversy A long-standing scholarly dispute over the effects of the INDUSTRIAL REVOLUTION on the living standards and quality of life of the British working class (*see* WORKING CLASSES), the Standard-of-Living Controversy has engaged historians concerned with the social dimensions of industrialization and has served as a terrain where critics and defenders of capitalism have waged battle, imparting a sometimes contentious political tone to the debate. The origins of the debate can be traced to the nineteenth-century debate on the CONDITION-OF-ENGLAND QUESTION. Like divisions between contemporaries, the scholarly controversy has ranged optimists, or those who argue for the positive consequences of industrialization, against pessimists, or those who hold that the working class experienced the industrial revolution as a disaster.

Recent debate on the question has pursued three main lines of enquiry. One area of research has addressed the size and distribution of the national income during industrialization. Here, neither side has made a convincing case. Optimists have invoked aggregate statistics on national income which demonstrate growing national wealth, but with no plausible evidence on patterns of distribution. On the other side, current research has undermined the pessimists' contention that high investment demands during early industrialization reduced wage levels. Investment needs were remarkably modest and did not necessarily affect wage levels.

A second line of enquiry in the debate has explored working-class patterns of consumption. Here, too, the evidence is ambiguous but has tended to bolster the pessimists' case. Per capita meat consumption, for example, may have declined between 1780 and 1840 while other basic commodities, such as coffee, tea and sugar, remained infrequent pleasures for most in the working class. Throughout the period the main working-class dietary staple continued to consist of bread and, increasingly in the north of England, potatoes.

The third and most substantial avenue of research concerns trends in wage and price levels, or movement in real wages. The bulwark of the optimists' case for improvement rests on evidence that industrial workers realized significant gains in purchasing power between 1790 and 1850. Optimists insist that on these grounds alone the industrial revolution brought immediate benefits to greater numbers than it harmed. The optimists' approach, however, raises several issues that call for consideration. One problem derives from the erratic fluctuation of both prices and wages between 1790 and 1850, as boom years rapidly gave way to depression. Several participants in the controversy have chosen atypical years for the interval of their analysis, rendering the identification of real-wage trends problematic. Moreover, some price indexes have been compiled from wholesale rather than retail data, sources which tell us little about working-class spending choices. Gathering wage data has proven similarly difficult, with few sources documenting a long series of wage rates for single occupations in specific areas. Optimists have also failed to account satisfactorily for the effects of casual work (*see* CASUAL LABOUR) and UNEMPLOYMENT on real-wage trends. For many, the frequency of both conditions may have prevented higher weekly wages from improving the standard of living.

Given these qualifications, cautious conclusions on real-wage trends are possible. From 1790 to 1815, wages barely kept up with rapid price inflation. Beginning in the early 1820s, substantial price deflation translated to a real wage increase of around 25 per cent, but only for individuals in constant employment. From 1825 to the late 1840s, similar increases spread to the general labour force. Mean averages, however, obscure the immense variety of experience. SKILLED WORKERS, who made the most significant gains, comprised only around 20 per cent of the total labour force. They were greatly outnumbered by the multitudes engaged in SWEATED TRADES whose circumstances remained precarious at all times. In short, optimists have indeed disproven contentions that industrialization subjected the working class to an absolute decline in the standard of living. However, in an era when national wealth grew immensely, improvements for the working class were modest and spread unevenly.

Finally, standards of living entailed more than real-wage trends. The quality of life, an imprecise but unavoidable term, included a variety of elements. Explosive rates of urbanization, with seemingly endless tracts of wretched housing, prevalent conditions of squalor and disease, and the fracturing of traditional family life, advanced traumatic social dislocation. Industrialization likewise imposed fundamental changes in workplace routines, as millions struggled to adapt to the rhythms of machine toil and others, formerly independent, experienced a loss of control over their working lives. Considered together, these central aspects of the period qualified or offset gains made in real earnings.

Arthur J. Taylor (ed.), *The Standard of Living in Britain in the Industrial Revolution* (London, 1975).

RICHARD J. SODERLUND

Stanley, Sir **Henry Morton** (*b* Denbigh, Wales, 28 January 1841; *d* London, 10 May 1904) Welsh journalist and explorer, Liberal-Unionist member of parliament (1895–1900). Born John Rowlands, he escaped a deprived childhood to find work in New Orleans with Henry Stanley, whose name he adopted. Following service on both sides of the American Civil War, he travelled in Turkey, then reported on Indian wars in America. After journalistic success in covering the Abyssinian campaign, he acquired celebrity as leader of the expedition into central Africa which eventually found David LIVINGSTONE at Ujiji (1871). He reported on the Ashanti War (1873), and then led major expeditions to the Nile headwaters and along the Congo (Zaïre) River to the Atlantic, followed by employment by the INDEPENDENT CONGO STATE. In 1887 he led the relief expedition to rescue Emin Pasha (1840–92), one of Gordon's lieutenants, cut off in equatorial Africa after the fall of Khartoum. Lionized, but often criticized, Stanley constantly sought acceptance and approval. Reflecting Victorian attitudes, he considered Africans to be uncivilized children, but whatever his faults, he played a significant role in Europe's penetration of Africa.

SIMON KATZENELLENBOGEN

Stanton, Elizabeth Cady (*b* Johnstown, New York, 12 November 1815; *d* New York, 26 October 1902) One of the founders of the American women's suffrage movement. She helped to organize a convention on women's rights that met in Seneca Falls, New York in 1848 (*see* SENACA FALLS CONVENTION). With Lucretia Mott (1793–1880), Stanton drew up a 'Declaration of Sentiments' modelled after the American Declaration of Independence detailing the 'repeated injuries and usurpations' perpetrated by men to secure their 'absolute tyranny' over women. With her long-time friend Susan B. ANTHONY, Stanton organized the National Women's Suffrage Association in 1869. She continued to be a central figure in the suffrage movement until the 1890s. In the course of a long career in political activism, Stanton espoused a feminism in the equal-rights tradition, and also developed a radical and wide-ranging analysis of the position of women.

Lois Banner, *Elizabeth Cady Stanton: A Radical for Women's Rights* (Boston, 1980).

GAIL SAVAGE

steamships Despite numerous eighteenth-century efforts, the first successful steam vessels appeared only in the first decade of the nineteenth century. Robert Fulton's (1765–1815) *North River* opened up steam commerce on the Hudson River in 1807, and similar efforts followed in Europe and other areas of the world, rapidly transforming the economics of river commerce. The effect was particularly great on such major systems as the Mississippi-Missouri-Ohio, or the Amazon and Congo systems.

The first ocean-going steamships were either adaptations of river craft or hybrids, using steam only to supplement sail. In 1819 the *Savannah* became the first craft to use steam in crossing the Atlantic. It was not until propellors and iron hulls began to be used almost two decades later, however, that steamships began to take the place of sailing vessels on regular ocean runs. Subsequently, ships began to grow steadily in both size, power and speed. Steam cut the voyage from London to Calcutta to six weeks (from several months) in the 1840s, and by the end of the century little more than two weeks were required.

ROBERT FRIEDEL

Stein, Heinrich Friedrich Karl, baron vom (*b* Nassau, 26 October 1757; *d* Cappenberg, Westphalia, 29 June 1831) Prussian statesman. An imperial knight, he had risen to the level of a Prussian minister by the time of the French defeat of 1806. Dismissed by Frederick-William III for 'insolence', Stein was recalled as first minister in October 1807. He presided over a flood of reforms, including peasant emancipation and urban self-government. Dismissed in October 1808 at Napoleon's insistence, Stein continued his anti-French crusade in Austria. He left Austria after the 1809 war to advise Tsar Alexander I. He returned to Germany in 1813–14, in charge of occupied territory. His commitment to destroying much of what Napoleon had created in Germany was set aside by the more pragmatic, state-orientated policy of METTERNICH. After 1815 Stein returned to his Nassau estates and served as marshal to the Westphalian provincial diet. He established the scholarly basis for a proper understanding of German history, the *Monumenta Germaniae Historica*.

James Sheehan, *German History 1770–1866* (Oxford, 1989).

JOHN BREUILLY

Stephenson, George (*b* Wylam, Northumberland, 9 September 1781; *d* Chesterfield, Derbyshire, 12 August 1848) English railway engineer, the most important figure in the beginning of railway engineering. The son of a colliery worker, he learned his trade as a mechanic in the mines of north England. This experience exposed him to the tradition of RAILWAYS that had long been used for hauling heavy mine-loads, and encouraged him in the application of steam power. While in his thirties, Stephenson demonstrated his talent for making improvements in steam engines, and thus received the appointment as engineer for the Stockton and Darlington Railway in 1821. He made this into a model of railway engineering, and thus was made engineer for the pioneering Liverpool and Manchester and Manchester and Leeds Railways in 1825. His design of locomotives, track and other technical elements set the standard for the steam railway technology that was to revolutionize transport in the nineteenth century. Stephenson became one of the most honoured and respected engineers of his day, and founder of the Institution of Mechanical Engineers (1847).

ROBERT FRIEDEL

Straits Question Like the EASTERN QUESTION and closely linked to it, the Straits Question came to the fore repeatedly throughout the nineteenth century as the European powers vied for control of this vital passage from the Black Sea to the Mediterranean. Formed by the Bosporus and the Dardanelles and separating Europe from Asia Minor (with Constantinople, the capital of the Ottoman Empire, on the European side), the Straits are the only outlet from the Black Sea to the Aegean, the Mediterranean and the world's oceans. Since the fifteenth century, the Straits had been controlled by the Ottoman Turks. Free passage through the Straits was, and still is, crucial for Russia's overseas trade and this, along with the tsars' desire to re-establish Constantinople as the capital of the Orthodox Church, led successive Russian governments to try in various ways to conquer Constantinople and to gain control of the Straits.

The strategic location of the Straits made it important not only to Russia and the Turks but also to Great Britain and, to a lesser extent, to France, Austria and Germany. Because Britain wanted to protect its trade routes through the Mediterranean to India and to keep Russia away from the Straits, it supported the declining Ottoman Empire against Russian encroachments in this region for most of the nineteenth century. A long series of treaties, stretching from the late eighteenth century to the 1920s, reflect the importance of the Straits Question to European affairs in this period. Following the Treaty of Kutchuk

Kainarji (1774), Russian merchant vessels were given rights of passage through the Straits, and in 1833 (TREATY OF UNKIAR-SKELESSI) the Ottoman Empire, recently defeated by Russia, was forced to agree to close the Straits to all foreign (that is French and British) warships. A few years later the London Straits Convention of 1841, which was signed by all the major European powers, decreed that transit of the Straits in peacetime would be restricted to the Turks, and this ruling remained in force until the Lausanne Convention of 24 July 1923.

B. Jelavich, *The Ottoman Empire, the Great Powers, and the Straits Question 1870–87* (Bloomington, Ind., 1973).

GEORGE O. KENT

suburbs A suburb is a particular geographical location for home-owning, largely by middle-income families, living in which necessitates commuting to a workplace located in an adjoining urban centre. Suburban or residential development took place on the fringes of major British towns from the 1830s and 1840s, providing access to the cheapest land for those escaping the slums and having sufficient security of employment and leisure to afford the time and money spent travelling. In the United States suburban growth was more a feature of the twentieth century, but the old city of Boston was ringed by expanding suburbs in the second half of the nineteenth century, stimulated by the advent of the tram in 1852 and mainly affecting middle-income families who still worked in the centre of the city. Unlike Paris, the railway did not have a marked affect on Boston's suburban expansion since, as in many British cities, is was too expensive for short trips for all but a few of the wealthiest commuters.

David Thorns, *Suburbia* (London, 1972).

JOHN SPRINGHALL

Sudan 'Bilad-es-Sudan', meaning 'Land of the Blacks', a term long used in the Arab world for a southern zone across Africa, gave rise to the name 'Sudan', as applied to a territory limited to regions on the middle and upper Nile and their hinterlands, after their conquest by Egypt. MUHAMMAD ALI, the new ruler of a resurgent Egypt, conquered minor polities in the northern Sudan that were either Arabic-speaking or at least partly Islamic, and in 1821 he founded Khartoum, at the confluence of the Blue and White Niles. Later rulers of Egypt extended their influence to more southern parts, where the non-Arab 'pagan' peoples were thereafter subject to slave-raiding by northern traders. Egypt being notionally part of the Ottoman Empire and its army and administration being commanded by individuals from all over the empire, the northern Sudanese referred to this colonial rule as the 'Turkiya'.

Grievances against the regime, including its employment of Christians such as the Englishman Charles Gordon, contributed to the Mahdist uprising of the 1880s (*see* MAHDISM; MUHAMMAD AHMAD IBN 'ABDALLAH). The Mahdist regime was not supported by all the many peoples of the Sudan, not even by all Arab tribes, and this eased the transition to British (notionally Anglo-Egyptian) colonial rule. The nineteenth century had created a geopolitical unit, but one whose peoples were divided by historical traditions, ethnic rivalries and extreme cultural diversity.

P. M. Holt, *A Modern History of the Sudan* (London, 1961).

P. E. H. HAIR

suffrage *see* FRANCHISE REFORM.

suffrage, women's *see* WOMEN'S SUFFRAGE.

suffragists *see* WOMEN'S SUFFRAGE.

sweated trades The idea that certain trades were characterized by the 'sweating' of its workers became prominent around 1850 through the writings of Henry Mayhew (1812–87) and Charles Kingsley (1819–75). These dealt with certain London trades where material was 'put out' to be made up at very low wages (*see* PUTTING-OUT SYSTEM). Mayhew identified the cause as lack of wage regulation, but his views were uninfluential. From the 1850s until the late 1880s sweating was thought to be due to particularly unscrupulous middlemen. This view did not survive the select committe of the House of Lords (1888–90). It examined conditions in thirteen trades across the country and reported that sweating was not necessarily connected with subcontracting, and, where it was, the middleman was not himself the cause of the evil. It characterized 'sweating' as a combination of low wages, excessive hours and bad sanitation of workplaces. Since the greater part of sweated workers were women and children, it hoped for improvement from an extension of trade-unionism, and of inspection under factory and workshop legislation. On account of their isolation, 'home workers' were difficult to organize and their workplaces difficult to inspect. Trade-union organizers of women workers and humanitarian philanthropists therefore concentrated on home work as the real source of the problem. In imitation of the Berlin exhibition of 'Home Work' (1905), the *Daily News* organized an exhibition of 'Sweated Labour' in 1906, which led to the formation of an influential Anti-sweating League and the appointment of the 1907 select committee on Home Work. This identified the lack of bargaining power on the part of the workers as the basic problem. Its recommendations were put into effect by the 1909 Trade Board Act which established boards to settle minimum wages in four trades in the first instance. (*See* LABOUR LEGISLATION.)

D. Bythell, *The Sweated Trades* (London, 1978).

E. P. HENNOCK

Sweden   *see* SCANDINAVIA.

Swing, Captain   *see* CAPTAIN SWING.

symbolism   Human cultures universally rely on symbols in most systems of communication, and especially as a means of finding material embodiment for immaterial or spiritual realities. But in the nineteenth century 'symbolism' referred to a particular movement in French poetry which subsequently had a wide influence on other national literatures. French symbolist poetry was essentially a continuation of ROMANTICISM, especially in the value it attached to the imagination, but was distinguished from earlier romantic writing by the high value afforded to poetic craftsmanship and lyrical concentration. Its characteristic form was the lyric, which in symbolist terms was densely suggestive and musical, at times almost esoteric.

SIMON DENTITH

T

Taff Vale   In 1901 a legal decision held trade unions liable for damages which a business suffered as a result of a strike. It was the culmination of a series of anti-union court judgments, and greatly increased trade-union support for independent political organization. The specific case concerned an August 1900 strike at the Taff Vale Railway in south Wales. The railway company, seeking to end the mass picketing organized by the Amalgamated Society of Railway Servants, took out injunctions against two union officials and the society itself. A court granted the injunctions, rendering the union's funds liable for any damages suffered by the company and this judgment was subsequently upheld by the House of Lords. Recognizing that this decisively undermined trade-union legal rights and status, and alarmed at the Liberal Party's indifference, a number of formerly reluctant trade unions pursued affiliation with the Labour Representation Committee (*see* LABOUR PARTY).

RICHARD J. SODERLUND

Tagore, Rabindranath (*b* Calculta, 7 May 1861; *d* Calculta, 7 August 1941)   Indian poet and philosopher. He emerged from a wealthy landed gentry family to become the leading literary figure of the Bengal renaissance at the end of the nineteenth century. He became an internationally acclaimed poet and author, the first Indian to receive a Nobel prize in literature. His most notable work, *Gitanjali*, which immortalized the countryside of Bengal amid exotic imagery, was translated into all the major languages of western Europe where it found a receptive audience. Although fully at home in the Anglicized environment of Calcutta, Tagore advocated the preservation of Indian art and culture. To this end he established Shanti Niketan as an institution to perpetuate Indian arts and culture (*see* ARTS AND LITERATURE).

In the final years of his life, deeply affected by the partition of Bengal in 1905, he embraced the INDIAN NATIONAL CONGRESS and became a leading spokesman for Bengal.

Ernest Rhys, *Ravindranath Tagore: A Biographical Study* (New York, 1970).
ROBERT J. YOUNG

Taiping Rebellion (1850–1864) The most serious rebellion in nineteenth-century China, the Taiping Rebellion affected at various times sixteen of China's eighteen provinces. Originating in Kwangsi, it was led by HUNG HSIU-CH'UAN, a failed scholar. Hung's Society of God-Worshippers' guiding dogma was a potent mixture of Evangelical Christianity and primitive communism. The Hakka minority in Kwangsi proved fertile soil for the doctrine. Population pressures and social tensions in the famine year 1849–50, led to clashes between the imperial authorities and Hung's followers and a declaration of rebellion in 1851. Hung proclaimed himself 'Heavenly King' of a new 'Kingdom of Heavenly Peace', Taiping.

The Taipings proved to be fierce fighters, defeating the imperial forces and driving northwards towards the Yangtze, establishing their capital at Nanking. A northern expedition was repulsed short of Tientsin and a western foray was defeated by TSENG KUO-FAN. The Taipings forbade opium- and tobacco-smoking, alcohol, gambling, ancestor-worship, prostitution and polygamy. Land was to be held in common, surplus produce going to a common storehouse. However, because of constant warfare, common ownership was only spasmodically applied in limited areas. Civil-service examinations were to be based on Christian and biblical tracts, and there was to be equality of the sexes. Initially, the foreign powers remained neutral in the Taiping–Ch'ing struggle but from 1860 they supported the Ch'ing as trade at Shanghai was threatened. The imperial armies having failed to defeat the Taipings, victory was secured only by the provincial armies of Tseng Kuo-fan and LI HUNG-CHANG. Tseng's army broke into Nanking in 1864, by which time Taiping ideals had been destroyed from within by corruption. Hung committed suicide.

V. Y. C. Chih, *The Taiping Ideology: Its Sources, Interpretations and Influence* (Seattle, 1976).
Immanuel C. Y. Hsu, *The Rise of Modern China*, fourth edn (Oxford, 1990).
JOHN DAVIES

Talleyrand-Périgord, Charles Maurice de (*b* Paris, 2 February 1754; *d* Paris, 17 May 1838) French cleric and diplomat. He took up a clerical career after a childhood accident prevented him from going into the military. He became an official in the church and became bishop of Autun in 1788. As a deputy to the Constituent Assembly in 1789, he proposed the secularization of church property and left the church to pursue a diplomatic career. He was foreign minister in 1797 and later under Napoleon, pursuing his master's aggressive foreign policy while in office. There is no corroborating evidence to the claim in his memoirs that he tried to moderate Napoleon's ambition. He was instrumental in the restoration of Louis XVIII in 1814, however, and he represented France at the CONGRESS OF VIENNA. Ultraroyalists drove him from office in 1815 but he played an important role in bringing LOUIS-PHILIPPE to the throne in 1830. He ended his career as ambassador in London. On his deathbed, he is reported to have said, 'Remember, I am a bishop.'

J. F. Bernard, *Talleyrand* (London, 1973).

DONALD SUTHERLAND

Tammany Hall Begun as a patriotic society during the American Revolution, Tammany Hall had by 1850 become the most powerful political organization in the DEMOCRATIC PARTY in New York City. By 1870 'Boss' William Tweed (1823–78) controlled New York state politics through a sophisticated machine headquartered at Tammany. Accompanying extraordinary urban growth, political machines such as Tammany relied on patronage, immigrant votes and an elaborate and effective organization that reached down to the precinct and ward levels. Ward captains ran their organizations through political clubs and were held strictly responsible for the Democratic vote. Even in the GILDED AGE, when political corruption was commonplace, Tammany was noted for its graft and manipulative practices. Although Tammany illustrated much that was undesirable about nineteenth-century American politics, it nevertheless remained a force to be reckoned with because it was one of the few organizations capable of even partially meeting the needs of swelling city populations.

KEVIN MURPHY

Tamworth Manifesto The famous election address by PEEL to his constituents in December 1834, the Tamworth Manifesto was elevated by wide circulation in the press to the unprecedented status of an 'official' party programme, confirming the dominance of party in the newly reformed political system. Ironically, Peel had been called into office after the king's dismissal of Melbourne, the last such act by a monarch. Although lacking a parliamentary majority, Peel was able to consolidate his position as party leader, using the general election of 1835 to widen the party's social base and improve its constituency organization. The manifesto expounded the merits of progressive conservatism to the national electorate, accepting the Reform Bill of 1832 as 'final and irrevocable' and promising a safe haven between radical agitation and negative Tory reaction.

JOHN BELCHEM

Tawfiq Pasha, Muhammad (*b* Cairo, 30 April 1852; *d* Hulwan, Egypt, 7 January 1892)   Khedive of Egypt (1879–92). A great-grandson of MUHAMMAD ALI, the founder of the Egyptian dynasty, he succeeded to the throne on the deposition of his father, ISMAIL PASHA. His failure to repel European demands aroused the opposition of army officers led by AHMAD URABI PASHA. Fearing the movement's nationalist aims, Great Britain occupied Egypt in 1882, quashed Urabi and restored the grateful Tawfiq to the throne. Compliant to the end, he was succeeded by his son ABBAS HILMI II.

P. J. Vatikiotis, *The History of Egypt from Muhammad Ali to Mubarak* (Baltimore, 1986).

MADELINE C. ZILFI

Taylor, Frederick Winslow (*b* Philadelphia, 20 March 1856; *d* Philadelphia, 21 March 1915)   American engineer. Although he had intended to enter Harvard Law School on graduation from Phillips Exeter Academy in 1874, Taylor's failing eyesight – and some say a nervous breakdown – kept him from pursuing a career in law. Instead, he worked in a pump-manufacturing plant in Philadelphia, where by 1884 he had risen to the position of chief engineer. Over the next six years he patented mechanical inventions, developed new methods of manufacturing and studied production processes. In 1893 he opened a consulting firm in Philadelphia specializing in the systemization of management and reduction in cost. His reputation grew so that in 1898 he was employed by the Bethlehem Steel Company for that sole purpose. There he developed his theory of scientific management, known as 'Taylorism', which streamlined workers' actions, cut production costs and waste, and removed decision-making from workers.

JOHN MARTIN

Taylor, Harriet (*b* London, 10 October 1807; *d* Avignon, France, 3 November 1858)   Intimate companion and then wife of John Stuart MILL. She contributed profoundly to writing that appears under Mill's sole name. Coming from a background of Unitarian radicalism, and a friend of William J. Fox (1786–1864), she was habituated to a range of speculation, particularly on matters of equality of the sexes, which went beyond Mill's formation in UTILITARIANISM. Mill himself asserted that *On Liberty* (1859) should be considered as a joint production, while she also contributed substantially to *The Principles of Political Economy* (1848). Her thinking on the question of the relations between the sexes and the position of women went beyond Mill's in some respects, and was expressed in writing of her own.

John Stuart Mill and Harriet Taylor Mill, *Essays on Sex Equality*, ed. Alice S. Rossi (Chicago, 1970).

SIMON DENTITH

Taylor, Zachary (*b* Montebello, Virginia, 24 November 1784; *d* Washington, DC, 9 July 1850)   President of the United States (1849–50). He grew up on a Kentucky plantation and joined the army in 1808, where he distinguished himself in the War of 1812. In 1846, following the annexation of Texas, he led an American force into territory claimed by both Texas and Mexico. After Mexico attacked, Congress declared war and the ensuing conflict placed Taylor, who led the northern campaign, in the headlines. In 1848, the Whig Party ran Taylor for president, calculating that a war hero could ensure victory, as William Henry Harrison had done in 1840. As a political novice, Taylor alienated both southern Democrats with attempts to bring California and New Mexico into the union as free states, and fellow Whigs with his non-partisan appointments. He unexpectedly became ill at a public ceremony and died of cholera five days later.

JOHN MARTIN

Tecumseh (*b* Little Miami River, Ohio, *c.*1768; *d* Moraviantown, Ontario, 5 October 1813)   Native-American chief of the Shawnees. Tecumseh (Tekamthi in Shawnee) began fighting white encroachment as a youth. From around 1805, he and his younger brother Tenskwatawa ('The Prophet'), began advocating intertribal unity against white intrusion, and in 1808 moved their supporters to the mouth of the Tippecanoe River where they established Prophet's Town. From there Tecumseh visited eastern tribes as far away as Florida and Canada. In 1811, while he was seeking the support of distant tribes, William Henry HARRISON led his forces against Tenskwatawa and, although fighting to a draw, burned Prophet's Town. Breaking with his brother, Tecumseh led his warriors in scattered attacks on white settlements. When the War of 1812 broke out, the British commissioned him a brigadier-general. Fighting against the Americans at the Battle of the Thames in 1813, Tecumseh was killed and his dream of native-American unity shattered.

JOHN MARTIN

Tel-al-Kebir, Battle of (13 September 1882)   Government incompetence and the demands of EGYPT's European creditors provoked popular opposition led by the Egyptian army under AHMAD URABI PA-SHA. When Urabi became minister of war, the new government's insistence on Egyptian autonomy convinced the British to intervene. In June

1882 rioting in Alexandria and attacks on Europeans provided the pretext for the invasion. On 13 September Urabi's troops were easily defeated at Tel-al-Kebir and Urabi himself was captured two days later. Although the khedival regime was formally restored, Britain had become Egypt's new sovereign and would remain so, despite Egyptian bitterness and struggle, until after the First World War.

P. J. Vatikiotis, *The History of Egypt: From Muhammad Ali to Mubarak* (Baltimore, 1986).

MADELINE C. ZILFI

telegraphy and telephony The term 'telegraphy' refers to the use of apparatus for sending messages over distances via codes. Although the word 'telegraph' was first used in 1792 by Claude Chappe (1763–1805) to describe a visual signalling system he implemented in France, it came to denote transmissions via electric wires. 'Telephony' refers to the art and practice of reproducing articulate speech across distances by utilizing electric waves.

The first breakthrough in electrical communications was Paul Schilling's demonstration in 1832 that the deflection of a compass needle by an electric current could transmit information. A system for railway communication was made operational in 1838 by William Cooke (1806–79) and Charles Wheatstone (1802–75), using two current-bearing wires to deflect compass needles towards selected letters. In 1837 Samuel Morse (1791–1872) devised a means to pass the arriving current through an electromagnet, a significant improvement which, among other things, required only one wire between stations. While Morse provided the necessary ideas, his assistant, Alfred Vail (1807–59), provided the mechanical knowledge, inventing the telegraph key in 1840 and refining their signal code to create Morse Code. They were further aided by Joseph Henry (1797–1878) who in 1842 invented a relay that could restore weak signals across long distances. Morse and Vail built the first long-distance telegraph line from Baltimore to Washington, DC in 1844. Telegraph operators interpreted the signals from the sound of the movements of the armature, thus eliminating the need for written recording.

Although Morse experimented with laying cables under New York harbour in 1842, telegraphy was initially restricted to crossing land. The first successful submarine cable was laid under the English Channel in 1850, and the first transatlantic cable was completed in 1858. Another restriction was that only one message could be sent at a time. In 1853 Wilhelm Cintel invented the duplex system, which allowed two messages to be sent simultaneously in opposite directions over the same line; this was further developed by Thomas EDISON in 1874. At the same time Emile Baudot (1845–1903) developed the time-division multiplex system, which allowed several operators to share one line, and this was deployed widely by 1880. Electric telegraphs provided the only means of fast long-distance communication until the introduction of long-distance telephone lines in the late 1890s.

The production of an undulatory current corresponding to a speech wave was the foundation for all telephony. C. G. Page, in 1837, and Charles Bourseul (1829–1912), in 1845, devised methods for transmitting the pitch of sounds, but not articulate speech, across distance. In 1874 Alexander Graham BELL created a system consisting of a strip of iron attached to a membrane which, when actuated by a voice, would vibrate in front of an electomagnet, inducing an electric current capable of transmitting speech. In 1876, assisted by Thomas Watson (1854–1934), Bell devised a receiver and transmitter containing a voice -actuated diaphragm which varied the electrical resistance (and hence the current) and transmitted the first audible complete sentence via electronic means. Bell filed his patent just hours before Elisha Gray (1835–1901) filed a notice of pending patent application for an electric telephone, involving a liquid transmitter similar to the one used by Bell. In view of his prior filing, Bell was issued the patent for the telephone; however, priority claims by Gray, Daniel Drawbaugh and others led to extensive and prolonged litigation. Bell's patents were upheld, leading to the creation of the Bell system telephone network.

Bell's original electromagnetic transmitter also served as the receiver. Separate inventions in 1877 by Emile Berliner (1851–1929) and Thomas Edison of superior transmitters utilizing variable contact resistance between two solid electrodes led to the separation of the receiver and transmitter. The first handset (transmitter and receiver in the same handle) was developed by Robert Brown in 1878. Two problems that plagued telephony were the limitation of available lines and the poor transmission efficiency of the speech currents over long distances. Fran Jacob in 1882 and John Carty in 1886 addressed the first problem, developing the idea of 'phantoming', deriving three telephone circuits from two sets of wires. Vashy (1889) and Oliver Heaviside (1850–1925), in 1893, demonstrated the theoretical possibility of diminishing attenuation by increasing inductance. Independently, Michael Pupin (1858–1935) and George Campell discovered that increased inductance could be achieved by the proper spacing of loading coils, depending on the highest frequency to be transmitted. By 1900 the United States, Great Britain and most European countries had extensive telephone systems, mostly under complete or at least partial government control.

Ronald Brown, *Telecommunications: The Booming Technology* (New York, 1970).

Arthur W. Page, *The Bell Telephone System* (New York, 1941).

STEVE AMANN

temperance   The temperance movement was a reaction to the increasing consumption of alcohol by the working class during the late eighteenth and early nineteenth centuries. Originating in the United States, it spread through Europe and Australasia. Alcohol was perceived as a threat to social and industrial discipline, the Protestant work ethic and the Enlightenment ideal of the rational individual. Arguments for temperance varied. Some favoured abstention from spirits and moderate use of beer and wine while others (teetotallers) renounced all forms of alcohol. In Britain and the United States teetotalism tended to dominate the movement, whereas moderate drinking was preferred in Europe.

One of the earliest temperance advocates in the United States was Dr Benjamin Rush (1746–1813), a signatory of the Declaration of Independence, who counselled in 1784 that distilled spirits would cause mental degeneration. The first major temperance organization was the Massachusetts Association for the Suppression of Intemperance, founded in Boston in 1813. Spreading quickly, the movement favoured moderate consumption of alcohol and had an elite membership. The American Temperance Society (1826) repudiated moderation and adopted a teetotal pledge. For the most part, it considered the drunkard to be unreclaimable and urged others not to follow this path. The next wave of temperance reform was led by the 'Washingtonians', formed in Baltimore (1840). Less socially elitist, they attempted to reclaim drunkards and used ex-drunks to witness to the virtues of temperance.

Most groups followed a policy of persuasion, but by 1850 it was clear that this had failed and advocates then looked to prohibition. The 'Maine Law' of 1851 banned the sale or manufacture of liquor in the state of Maine. Within three years, thirteen states had adopted similar statutes (although these often proved temporary). After the Civil War, demands were made for a prohibition amendment to the constitution or for Local Option (whereby electors would vote on whether to permit alcohol in each licensing district). Local Option was introduced in much of the United States, Europe and Australasia, proving the most effective form of temperance control.

The English and Irish movements followed the American shift from persuasion to coercion. Temperance was imported from the United States in the late 1820s, taking root in the industrial north of England. In 1832 teetotalism became the chief stance of the movement which was originally bourgeois in composition but was taken over by the working class, for whom temperance was an important aspect of SELF-HELP. Nonconformists, especially Methodists, were key supporters (see NONCONFORMITY). Inspired by the Maine Law, the United Kingdom Alliance (1853) vainly lobbied parliament for Local Option. Disappointed by Gladstone's licensing legislation of 1872, temperance reformers were nevertheless associated with the Liberal Party up to 1914. In Ireland temperance originated with Ulster Protestants inspired by the American Temperance Society, but in the 1840s Father Theobald Mathew (1790–1856) led an effective campaign to persuade Catholics to abandon drink. His achievements proved temporary. Reformers thereafter looked to parliament for legislation but were thwarted by the antipathy of the Conservative and Home Rule Parties.

The German movement was also directly influenced by the American experience but found that consumption of schnapps was vital to labourers as part of their diet. It promoted beer and wine as temperance beverages and never attempted to become a major force in parliamentary politics. Temperance in France and Russia began relatively late. In France anti-alcoholism became part of the panic that followed the PARIS COMMUNE of 1871. The consequence was the 'loi Roussel' of 1873 which prohibited public drunkenness but temperance never became a major part of French life. Fears of national degeneration also led the Russian government to sponsor a temperance movement in 1895, which took the form of the supervision of liquor sales by local elites and the advocacy of moderation.

Temperance reform can be interpreted as a reactionary endeavour – a vain attempt to preserve status and social discipline by the middle class and the 'respectable' working class. It is better seen as part of the liberal reform tradition. Drink was a real problem and many labour organizations accepted temperance as one solution to social ills. Furthermore, temperance movements were particularly characterized by the active participation of women. Often considered a failure, the success of temperance is more striking. With its high public profile, the movement reduced popular consumption of alcohol in some countries and everywhere ensured that drunkenness could not be considered respectable.

Jack S. Blocker, *American Temperance Movements: Cycles of Reform* (Boston, 1989).
Brian Harrison, *Drink and the Victorians: The Temperance Question in England, 1815–1872* (London, 1971).

ROHAN MCWILLIAM

Ten Hours Act (1847) A British statute limiting the work of children and women in textile factories to no more than ten hours a day, or fifty-eight hours a week, the Ten Hours Act altered the provisions of the 1833 and 1844 FACTORY ACTS. Although it did not restrict the hours of adult men, the intent of reformers was to achieve this end indirectly, as children and women's labour was essential to production.

The act marked the culmination of a sustained struggle both within and outside parliament to regulate working hours. The campaign which started in 1830 was centred in the industrial districts of northern England and Scotland, where short-time committees were formed. The factory movement brought together leaders from divergent backgrounds, united in a humanitarian concern transcending the principles of *laissez-faire* economics. Thus, Richard Oastler (1789–1861), Michael Sadler (1780–1835), Lord Ashley (the seventh earl of SHAFTESBURY), the Revds J. R. Stephens (1805–79) and G. S. Bull (1799–1864) were Tories or Tory-radicals moved by Evangelical Christianity; John Doherty (1798–1854) was a prominent radical and trade-unionist; John Fielden (1784–1849) and Charles Hindley (1800–50) were liberal-radical factory-owners. During the 1830s, stirred by the impassioned rhetoric of Oastler and Stephens, the cause assumed a violent edge.

Supported by an impressive petitioning campaign, Fielden, who took over the measure's parliamentary direction from Ashley, finally secured a majority, based on Tory votes, the softening of Whig opposition and the Peelites' abstention. But having failed to specify the time at which work should cease relative to when it commenced, the act was evaded by employers who merely staggered shifts, keeping women and children at factories for more than ten hours but not continuously working. The Factory Act of 1850 closed this loophole but established a sixty-hour week based on ten and a half hours' daily and seven and a half hours' Saturday work.

J. T. Ward, *The Factory Movement, 1830–1855* (London, 1962).

JAMES EPSTEIN

Test and Corporation Acts, repeal of the (1828)   Passed respectively in 1673 and 1661, the Test and Corporation Acts had laid down that office-holders, and particularly members of town councils, must qualify by taking communion in the Church of England. Although there were annual Indemnity Acts and few attempts at enforcement, the legislation was seen by Protestant Dissenters as a symbol of their treatment as social inferiors. In 1827 a united committee was formed to manage a campaign for repeal. Led by William Smith (1756–1835), a Unitarian member of parliament, it prompted large-scale petitioning of the Commons but was careful to adopt a moderate stance and conciliatory tactics. In a tolerant political atmosphere the Repeal Bill was carried during 1828, providing an important precedent for CATHOLIC EMANCIPATION in the following year.

T. W. Davis (ed.), *Committees for Repeal of the Test and Corporation Acts: Minutes 1786–90 and 1827–8* (London, 1978).

D. W. BEBBINGTON

Tewodorus [Theodore] **II** (*b* Gonder, *c.*1818; *d* Maqdala, Ethiopia, 13 April 1868)   Emperor of ETHIOPIA (1855–68). A former local ruler with limited power, Kasa Haylu was a bandit for many years before being crowned emperor. As Tewodorus II, he initiated a major programme of military reform, economic modernization and political centralization, but large-scale desertion, the result of extremely harsh military discipline, left him unable to suppress internal political dissent. Protestant (as against French-supported Catholic) missionaries, although keen to facilitate the introduction of European technology, were unwillingly coerced into assisting him in the manufacture of heavy armaments. He looked to Britain for help, but its interests were directed towards Egypt, Tewodorus's prime enemy. Insulted by Queen Victoria's failure to reply to a letter, he imprisoned the British consul and subsequently some sixty other Europeans. Sent to secure their release, Lord Napier (1810–90) and 32,000 men, assisted by dissident local rulers, moved easily to Maqdala (Magdala) where, deserted by most of his army and facing inevitable defeat, Tewodorus committed suicide.

SIMON KATZENELLENBOGEN

textile industries Cotton-manufacturing spearheaded and sustained industrialization in Britain, the first industrial nation, and in several of its early followers. The industry's essential components – a machine technology, factory organization and a complex array of trading networks – were all consolidated and expanded in the nineteenth century.

In Britain the cotton manufacture concentrated in south-east Lancashire and the margins of Cheshire and Yorkshire. The advantages of an equable climate, high rainfall and humidity, swift-flowing streams and abundant supplies of soft water in the Pennine foothills and the presence of coal in south-east Lancashire, plus the disadvantage of poor agricultural soils in the east, help to explain its location. So, too, did Liverpool's port facilities, the canal and road links of the eighteenth century, Manchester's long textile tradition and the relative freedom of the region's towns from manorial, guild or corporate restrictions. With concentration came horizontal specialization: while spinning characterized towns in the south, weaving predominated to the north. Specialization was even more intense than this, however, as each community, led by entrepreneurs such as John Rylands (1801–88) found its own niche. For example, in spinning Bolton led the fine-spinning section and Oldham the coarse; in weaving Blackburn centred on shirtings and, later, dhotis; Burnley's pre-eminence in weaving by the end of the century rested on plain cloths, exported to India for printing. Finishing (bleaching, dyeing, printing) was widely dispersed over the region's eastern section where water was plentiful and soft. Textile-machine-building emerged in the major towns, the largest firm being Platts of Oldham. Communications across the region improved with the coming of railway networks from 1825 and the opening of the Manchester Ship Canal in 1894 (*see* CANALS, RAILWAYS). Liverpool merchants nevertheless retained their hold of the raw-cotton market. The completion of a world-wide telegraph-cable network by Manchester merchant John Pender (1816–96) in the 1870s 'decisively centralized the world market in cotton goods in Manchester' (Farnie, p. 64).

The nineteenth-century growth of the British cotton industry was phenomenal. Between 1801 and 1901 total employees rose from 242,000 to 544,000; factory spindles from under 4 million to over 45 million; annual raw-cotton consumption from 53 million pounds to 1,570 million pounds; and exports from £6.9 million to £73.7 million. Growth came in three periods. The heroic age, from the 1780s until 1840, saw cotton dislodge the centuries-old woollen industry from its primacy in export markets, with cotton exports first overhauling (in value) woollen exports in 1803. Maturity came in the middle period 1840–72 when, facilitated by the newly adopted FREE TRADE policies of the Manchester School, raw cotton was the country's most valuable import and re-export and cotton manufactures the most valuable export. The industry had, however, become export-dependent, with over half its production being exported by 1840. In this period the cotton-spinning industries of Europe and the the United States began catching up and in the third phase, one of deceleration from the 1870s, the world of Asia began retrieving its traditional supremacy in cotton-manufacturing.

By the end of the nineteenth century Lancashire still commanded the international cotton-manufacturing industry. While the United States had 17 million spindles, Germany 8 million, Russia 7 million, France 6 million and Japan under 1.5 million, Britain had over 45 million and over 45 per cent of the world's total spindleage.

Lancashire's most innovative rival was the United States. Factory forms of the cotton and woollen industries spread from Britain, diffused by skilled mechanics and sponsored by American merchant capitalists early in the nineteenth century. Given the shortage of skilled operatives in the United States, the imported textile technology was modified in the direction of saving labour and skill. From the New England cotton industry came the ring spindle (1828) and the Northrop automatic power loom (1892). By the early 1830s the United States had 1.2 million cotton spindles and in 1860 (when Britain had about 30 million) 5.2 million. The next forty years saw that figure more than treble. In large part this reflected population growth and urbanization (with the American population rising from 31 to 76 million between 1860 and 1900). Expansion was also due to the rise of a cotton-manufacturing industry in the South, with 3.8 million spindles as compared to New England's 13.2 million by 1900. The shift was part of the South's post-Civil War reconstruction: southern agricultural communities looked for diversifying opportunities; northern entrepreneurs were attracted by the cheaper land, labour and power and the proximity of raw cotton in the South.

The woollen industry also grew in the nineteenth century and the

United Kingdom remained ahead, with 4 million worsted spindles in 1910, compared to 2 million in France and a similar number in the United States. In the United Kingdom the two distinct branches of the industry, woollen and worsted, were heavily concentrated in the West Riding of Yorkshire, each boosted by new fibre sources, new technology, factory organization and new products. From the early 1800s short-fibred merino wool from Australia fed the woollen industry. In contrast, long-fibred wools, which made a hard, smooth worsted yarn and cloth, were augmented by alpaca (sheep's wool) from Peru and mohair (goat's wool) from the Ottoman Empire. Cotton technology was applied to woollen carding, spinning and weaving by the 1820s. Worsted-combing was much more difficult to mechanize. By the late 1850s, however, three machines, associated with the names of Samuel Lister (1815–1906), James Noble (*fl* 1805–50s) and Isaac Holden (1807–97), removed the technical bottleneck. In France an alternative system, based on the Heilmann comb, processed shorter fibres. Synthetic dye-stuffs in the 1860s gave all textiles a greater colour range, as fashion allowed. Factory organization spread rapidly in the latter half of the century, deciding the fate of hand weavers and hand combers (*see* FACTORIES). By 1902 the United Kingdom had 1,538 woollen mills and 841 worsted mills, employing (in 1905) 163,000 in the woollen industry and 120,000 in the worsted. The major new products of the century were worsteds made from alpaca and mohair, pioneered from the 1830s by Titus Salt (1803–76) at Saltaire near Bradford, and shoddy or recycled woollens.

D. A. Farnie, *The English Cotton Industry and the World Market, 1815–1896* (Oxford, 1979).

D. T. Jenkins and K. G. Ponting, *The British Wool Textile Industry, 1770–1914* (London, 1982).

Akio Okochi and Shin'ichi Yonekawa, *The Textile Industry and its Business Climate* (Tokyo, 1982).

DAVID J. JEREMY

theatre and performing arts The nineteenth century witnessed a remarkable spread of theatres, opera-houses and music halls throughout Europe and the United States. At the beginning of the century the capital cities of Europe and the large provincial cities boasted a small number of theatres, often very large, playing a classic repertoire, as in the Comédie-Française in Paris or Drury Lane and Covent Garden in London. By the end of the century a massive programme of theatre-building meant that large cities like London, Paris and New York boasted an enormously extended number of theatres arranged as part of a system of largely middle-class entertainment and culture (the West End, Broadway); in addition, they possessed innumerable suburban houses and a network of music halls and vaudeville theatres playing

to popular audiences. The history of theatre in Europe and the United
States in the nineteenth century is the history of the growth and regeneration of high-art theatre; of its transformation and indeed displacement by popular forms, especially the melodrama; of the massive growth
of popular theatrical forms, from music hall through burlesque, pan-
tomime, vaudeville and boulevard; and of the regeneration of theatre
at the end of the century, by a shift towards various forms of REALISM
or NATURALISM, a shift effected with very different emphases in different national contexts but invariably reinforcing divisions between elite
or avant-garde forms and popular art.

The first three-quarters of the century were dominated, in both
Europe and the United States, by melodrama. Melodrama was a theatrical mode which, in London and Paris, emerged from the 'illegitimate' stage and made its way up the cultural hierarchy, so that by the
1830s even elite theatrical forms drew on its distinctive style. Melodramatic theatre was dominated by the effect; it used the full technical
resources of the theatre of music, lighting and scenery, to dramatize
moral and spiritual conflicts. It is thus not fairly represented by its
surviving scripts, but has to be judged by the total theatrical experience it provided. Moreover, it was in effect an international style;
there was massive interchange between Paris and London, and indeed
versions of French and English melodramas, or plays in a melodramatic style, dominated theatres as far apart as the United States and
Russia. Technical advances in theatre (gas lighting in the 1820s, electric lighting in the 1870s, gradual adoption of auditorium black-out)
were thus seized on by melodrama in the large commercial theatres.
But melodrama remained a truly popular style also, being the staple
of the innumerable small-scale travelling theatre companies that persisted, certainly in England and the United States, throughout the
century.

Later in the century European theatre saw the gradual and partial
transformation of dominant theatrical styles. Change came from various directions. From the 1850s, Charles Kean (1811–68) in London
and then the Meininger Company in Germany, developed a production style which attempted historical accuracy in costume and set design
and naturalistic handling of crowds. These were influential on the
production styles of both André Antoine (1858–1943) in Paris and
Konstantin Stanislavsky (1863–1938) in Moscow; both sought to
transform theatre in the direction of greater naturalism not only in the
external matters of costume and setting but also in ways of presenting
the inner life of character.

But the crucial transformation came perhaps from the range of writers
for the theatre who emerged towards the end of the century and
whose naturalist style involved a fundamental change in the way theatre presented the relationship between character and environment. The

Norwegian Henrik Ibsen (1828–1906) produced a series of plays from the 1860s onwards which searchingly explored pressing human and social problems in a theatrical idiom at once sober, contemporary and ambitious. In Russia Anton Chekhov (1860–1904) wrote a series of plays at the end of the century which, while in a very different idiom, also presented people's lives in the immediacy of their social surroundings. The Swede August Strindberg (1849–1912) and the German Gerhart Hauptmann (1862–1946) wrote powerful naturalist dramas that were first produced at the end of the century. Productions of the work of these dramatists, especially of Ibsen in the 1890s, heralded a widespread series of analogous changes not only in their native countries but also in London, Paris and New York – changes that meant a partial move towards a greater seriousness and intellectual ambition in one section of the theatre but which reinforced growing cultural splits between elite and popular art.

Nevertheless, popular theatrical art flourished in the nineteenth century, unsurprisingly perhaps in an era of massive urbanization but before the advent of the cinema (first commercially developed in the 1890s). In Britain MUSIC HALL originated in the 1840s; by the end of the century there were hundreds of music halls, with a developed star system and a tremendous variety of acts. Comparable developments in American vaudeville occurred from the 1860s onwards; by the end of the century there were circuits for established acts and headline stars. In Continental Europe the great range of indigenous and traditional popular theatrical forms persisted alongside the larger commercial theatrical enterprises that sought to provide popular entertainment. These traditional theatrical forms (such as puppet shows in southern and eastern Europe, or dialect theatre in Italy) variously waxed and waned, depending on the advance of urbanization and the relationship of these forms to newly establishing national cultural norms.

See also POPULAR CULTURE.

Michael R. Booth, *The Revels History of Drama in English*, vol. 6: *1750–1880* (London, 1975).

SIMON DENTITH

Thérèse of Lisieux, Saint [Marie Françoise Thérèse Martin] (*b* Alençon, 2 January 1873; *d* Lisieux, 30 September 1897) French mystic and saint. The youngest daughter of a successful watchmaker Louis Martin, she entered the Discalced Carmelite convent in Lisieux in 1888 and died of tuberculosis in 1897. She achieved an international cultus, a 'hurricane of glory', through the posthumous circulation and publication of her autobiography *L'Histoire d'une âme*, (The History of a Soul), which taught a 'little way', a pattern of holiness by everyday acts of love and renunciation. She was beatified in 1923 and canonized in 1925 as Saint Teresa of the Child Jesus and the Holy Face, with the popular title of 'The Little Flower'. A vast basilica in Lisieux (begun 1926) also preserves her memory.

Autobiography of a Saint: Thérèse of Lisieux, trans. Ronald Knox (London, 1958).

SHERIDAN GILLEY

Thibaw (*b* 1858; *d* 1916)   King of Burma (1878–85). He was a weak ruler, who was manipulated by his forceful wife, Supayalet. His disputed succession to the throne in 1878 was followed by the murder of eighty members of the royal family at the instigation of the queen, on the grounds that they were allegedly plotting rebellion. It seemed possible that Britain would intervene to protect British citizens and commercial interests. Britain did not do so but relations with Thibaw deteriorated. His attempt to oust a British company from the teak industry in favour of French rivals led to an ultimatum from the government of India. The ultimatum was rejected and a British expeditionary force was sent to Mandalay, forcing the surrender and abdication of Thibaw in 1885 and the annexation of Burma as a province of British India in 1886.

JOHN DAVIES

Thiers, Louis Adolphe (*b* Marseilles, 18 April 1797; *d* St Germain-en-Laye, 3 September 1877)   French historian and politician. As a minister under Louis-Philippe, he savagely repressed rebellions of royalists and republicans, and later became prime minister (1836, 1840). He was a major supporter of Louis Napoleon's candidacy for president in 1848 because he, wrongly, believed himself more clever than the prince. Jailed for a time under the Second Empire, he became an opposition deputy. He later became convinced that a conservative republic would best serve the cause of order, and became the first president (1871–3) of the THIRD REPUBLIC. He was responsible for the cruel repression of the PARIS COMMUNE in 1871. He failed to rally monarchists to the conservative republic but it turned out to be France's longest-lasting regime since 1789. His histories of the Revolution and the empire are part of the classic historiography of the French Revolution.

J. M. S. Allison, *Thiers and the French Monarchy* (London, 1926).

DONALD SUTHERLAND

Third Republic (1871–1940)   France's longest-lasting regime since the Revolution, the Third Republic was unlike the other five republican regimes since 1792, for it had no formal constitution or declaration of rights. It was formed by a series of enabling laws in 1875 by an assembly of monarchists, following the failure of talks with the comte de Chambord (1820–83) (*see* LEGITIMISTS) and in the face of an electoral resurgence of republicans and Bonapartists. The 'constitution' was designed to protect large property-owners but electoral victories by republicans in 1876 and 1877 signalled the final defeat of the notables. The republicans did little to alter existing institutions but the Third Republic none the less had a troubled history. The Panama scandal (*see* LESSEPS), and the BOULANGER and DREYFUS Affairs convinced the republican elites that the political culture of the country was not republican. The consequence was a series of waves of anticlericalism, the republicanization of the educational system and the establishment of embryonic welfare and wage-protection measures.

The republican elite was also haunted by their defeat by Prussia in 1870 and the consequent fears of national decline. Demographers denounced the popular taste for luxury, thought to be the source of the declining birth rate; criminologists and sociologists debated the sources of the decadence of the lower classes, whether it was alcoholism or the distractions of urban life; and historians fashioned a national history designed to inculcate patriotism at a time when 'Frenchness' was a matter of debate. The Third Republic received little credit for the victory in the First World War, and with the depression in the 1930s, an extremely unstable series of governments and the attraction of Fascism and communism abroad, institutions once more came to be questioned. Not until the defeat of 1940, however, did the politicians elected in 1936 vote the Third Republic out of existence.

R. Anderson, *France, 1870–1914: Politics and Society* (London and Boston, 1974).
Ruth Harris, *Murders and Madness* (New York, 1989).

DONALD SUTHERLAND

Three Emperors' League There were two agreements in the nineteenth century between Germany, Russia and Austria-Hungary. The first, of 6 May and 6 June 1873, emphasized monarchical solidarity in the face of revolutionary movements and pledged support for Germany in the event of a war with France. The second, of 18 June 1881 (also known as the Three Emperors' Alliance), was initiated by Bismarck to reassure Russia after the signing of the DUAL ALLIANCE between Germany and Austria.

The league also reflected the continuing feud between Bismarck and Gorchakov (1798–1883), the Russian chancellor; in the words of A. J. P. Taylor, 'The basis of the agreement was the Austrian belief that Germany would automatically support her, and the Russian belief that she would not.' The main article, which was secret, was the stipulation that two of the partners would remain neutral if the third partner went to war with a fourth power. In addition, Russia agreed to recognize the position Austria had gained at the CONGRESS OF BERLIN; the three partners guaranteed that the Straits should be closed to all warships (*see* STRAITS QUESTION); and Germany and Russia agreed that Austria could annex BOSNIA-HERCEGOVINA at its pleasure. Other provisions of the agreement dealt with the interests of the three governments in the Balkans and at the Straits.

B. Waller, *Bismarck at the Crossroads* (London, 1974).

GEORGE O. KENT

Tientsin, Treaty of (1858)   After the second Anglo-Chinese War (*see* ANGLO-CHINESE WARS), Britain achieved the long-desired right of diplomatic representation in Peking through the Treaty of Tientsin. Christian missionaries were allowed to travel and settle in all parts of China. Ten new TREATY PORTS were to be opened. Foreigners with passports issued by their consuls could travel throughout China. Travel within 30 miles of the treaty ports required no passports. The inland transit duty, likin, was not to exceed 2.5 per cent *ad valorem* and standard weights and measures were to be used throughout China. The Chinese were to pay an indemnity of 4 million taels to Britain and 2 million to France. A supplementary clause legalized the importing of opium.(*see* OPIUM TRADE). The treaty was not ratified by the Chinese court, and to enforce it Britain and France launched an expedition which took Peking in 1860. The terms of the treaty were reaffirmed in the Convention of Peking.

JOHN DAVIES

Tilak, Bal Ganghadar (*b* Ratnagiri, 23 July 1856; *d* Bombay, 1 August 1920)   Militant Indian nationalist. Originally with a political base in the Bombay presidency among the Marathi-speaking population, he emerged as a militant figure in the INDIAN NATIONAL CONGRESS. He clashed with British authorities over issues such as the Age of Consent Bill of 1891 and forced inoculations during the smallpox epidemics of the 1890s, denouncing these as attacks on Hindu religious traditions. Opposition to British policies led to his imprisonment in 1897 on charges of advocating violence, and to his elevation as a nationalist martyr. During the latter portion of his life Tilak played a significant role in shifting the Indian National Congress away from conservatism to militancy. Many militant policies which he advocated, such as economic independence and boycott, were later used as effective weapons by Mahatma Gandhi (1869–1948) and the National Movement.

Stanley Wolpert, *Tilak and Gokhale: Revolution and Reform in the Making of Modern India* (Berkeley, Calif., 1962).

ROBERT J. YOUNG

Tilsit, Treaty of (7–9 July 1807)   After defeating the Prussian and Russian armies at Jena (*see* BATTLE OF JENA), Auerstadt, Eylau and

Friedland, Napoleon I arranged to meet Tsar Alexander I of Russia and King Frederick-William IV of Prussia on a raft in the Niemen River to sign a peace treaty. By the Treaty of Tilsit, Russia agreed to recognize the grand duchy of Warsaw, the kingdoms of Naples, Holland and Westphalia and the Confederation of the Rhine. The tsar also agreed, in a secret article, to enter an alliance with Napoleon against Great Britain should that become necessary. Prussia relinquished to Napoleon the territories between the Rhine and the Elbe, Danzig and all the lands acquired by Prussia from Poland since 1772. Prussia also agreed to recognize the kingdoms of Naples, Holland and Westphalia, and to close its harbours to British trade until Britain signed a peace treaty with France. In addition, Prussia's army was reduced to 42,000 men and it was forced to pay France an indemnity of 120 million francs.

H. Butterfield, *The Peace Tactics of Napoleon 1806–1807* (New York, 1972).

GEORGE O. KENT

Tipu Sultan (*b* Mysore, 10 November ?1750; *d* Seringapatam, 4 May 1799)   Sultan of Mysore. The son and successor to Hyder Ali (1728–82), the ruler of Mysore who had replaced Hindu rule with Muslim, he inherited an expanding state which rivalled MARATHA power in south India and challenged English East India Company attempts to expand its sphere of influence inland from Madras. Eventual confrontation with the British resulted in a series of three wars – the first outbreak of hostilities (1783) only months after Tipu Sultan came to power. The second Mysore War, ending in 1792, resulted in a decisive victory which forced Mysore to cede districts west of Madras, ensuring both the greater security of Madras and future British expansion. The third Mysore War (1799) ended the power of Mysore, led to the death of Tipu Sultan and opened the way for rapid expansion outward from Madras.

Lewin B. Bowring, *Haidar Ali and Tipu Sultan* (Delhi, 1969).

ROBERT J. YOUNG

Tirpitz, Alfred von (*b* Küstrin, Brandenburg, 19 March 1849; *d* 6 March, 1930)   German state secretary for the navy (1897–1916) and father of the German navy. Harnessing the enthusiasm of Emperor William II for the creation of a German high-seas battle fleet, Tirpitz was the architect of the Navy Laws of 1898 and 1900 which led to a massive increase in German naval construction. He originally saw his creation as a 'risk fleet', sufficiently large to force Britain to make colonial concessions to the German Empire, but was willing after 1900 to accept a naval race with Britain. During the First World War he was a forceful advocate of unrestricted submarine warfare.

J. Steinberg, *Yesterday's Deterrent: Tirpitz and the Birth of the German Battle Fleet* (Cambridge, 1966).

S. J. SALTER

Tisza, Count Kálmán (*b* Fekete-Geszt, Hungary, 10 December 1830; *d* Budapest, 23 March 1902)   Hungarian statesman. From a Calvinist noble family, he took part in the 1848 revolution in a minor capacity and was forced into brief exile. He rose to prominence in 1859 as a defender of religious freedom. Elected to the Hungarian diet in 1861, he became a leader of the independence-minded Left, rejecting the COMPROMISE OF 1867. Political developments and his own ambition soon led him, however, to become prime minister of Hungary in 1875, a position he was to hold, off and on, until 1890, thus becoming the dominant figure of the Hungarian establishment and a major pillar of Austro-Hungarian dualism. Tisza's government modernized Hungary's finances and administrative, judicial and educational systems. His pro-railway policies also encouraged Hungary's economic upswing during these years. He resigned in March 1890 as a result of a controversy over control of the Hungarian army.

STEVEN BELLER

Tocqueville, Alexis de (*b* Paris, 29 July 1805; *d* Cannes, 16 April 1859)   French historian, political philosopher and politician. He became a principal drafter of the constitution of 1848 and, for a brief period in 1849, foreign minister. He is best known for *De la Démocratie en Amerique* (Democracy in America, 1835–40) and *L'Ancien Régime et la Révolution* (The Old Regime and the French Revolution, 1856). Both books reflect his lifelong intellectual quest for working out the consequences for society of the principle of equality. In the first book he argued that democracy risked becoming a slave to mediocrity and to lethargic dictatorship. In the second he argued that the French monarchy collapsed because of its despotism, which permitted the emergence of a class of irresponsible intellectuals who feasted on abstract ideas. The Revolution was a culmination of centuries of French history, not a break, and it continued the work of the kings of France of increasing centralization and undermining liberty.

R. R. Palmer (ed.), *The Two Tocquevilles* (Princeton, NJ, 1987).

DONALD SUTHERLAND

Tolpuddle Martyrs   In March 1834 six agricultural labourers from Tolpuddle in Dorset were sentenced to seven years' transportation for administering an 'unlawful oath' of initiation into a trade union. Shadowy forms of trade-union organization among the labourers of the south-west had existed for some years, and in 1833 a wages agreement was signed with local farmers which they subsequently repudiated.

George (1797–1874) and James (1808–73) Loveless attempted to organize to secure its enforcement. The recent CAPTAIN SWING movement and explosion of union organization led the farmers to react fiercely. Within a month, the leaders of the union were brought to trial and transported. The harsh sentence and the piety of the men – two of whom were Methodist preachers – caused the case to receive national attention. A campaign was organized by the Grand National Consolidated Trades Union (which the men had been in contact with) to protest the sentence, and two years later the victims were pardoned.

Joyce Marlow, *The Tolpuddle Martyrs* (London, 1971).

RICHARD PRICE

Tolstoi, Count Lev Nikolaevich (*b* Yasnaia Poliana, 28 August 1828; *d* Astapovo, 7 November 1910) Russian writer. He was a prolific author, his collected works running to ninety volumes. His most well-known works were the novels *War and Peace* (1863–9) and *Anna Karenina* (1873–7). Snobbish, puritanical, ascetic and aristocratic, he devoted the latter part of his life to an attempt to improve the lot of his fellow countrymen. He denounced the church and the state, espoused the peasantry, vegetarianism and teetotalism, yet rejected socialism and bourgeois values alike. His fiction displayed clarity of vision, striking psychological analysis, outstanding powers of description and originality of viewpoint. His style was wide-ranging, panoramic and extremely detailed. His novels and stories deal with the values of family life, religion, death, relations between the sexes, history, the superiority of the country over the town, of Russia over the West and of simplicity over sophistication.

H. Troyat, *Tolstoy* (Harmondsworth, 1970).

A. V. KNOWLES

Toryism   The word 'Tory' – originally a term of abuse used to describe an Irish papist outlaw – was coined as a political title to denote a supporter of the legitimate heir to the throne, the Catholic James (1633–1701), duke of York, during the exclusion crisis of 1679–81. But for most of the eighteenth century, though the words 'Whig' and 'Tory' continued to be used, they did not provide a useful basis for distinguishing one politician from another or for defining how politicians organized themselves in the quest for political power. Though there was no Tory party at the beginning of the nineteenth century – all who aspired to office tended to describe themselves as WHIGS – the word 'Tory' continued to convey a set of attitudes. These included an instinctive respect for the established order, support for government and the crown, a leaning towards the landed interest and, notwithstanding the earlier Catholic association, loyalty to the Church of England.

The rebirth of Toryism as a more active political movement is best traced to the diversity of English responses to the French Revolution and, more particularly, to the writings of Edmund Burke (1729–97), principally his *Reflections on the Revolution in France* (1790). The Revolution provoked a lively debate between those impressed by the libertarian spirit of the revolution and those who were already wary of reform. Out of reaction to the Revolution Burke produced an important statement of fundamental Tory (and later Conservative) attitudes. Aware that human nature could be weak, ignorant and indeed evil, Burke argued for the imposition of discipline through an ordered society which would liberate the best elements and hold back the worst. But Toryism was not synonymous with total reaction. As Burke argued, 'a state without the means of some change is without the means of its conservation'.

In political terms Toryism re-emerged through the followers of William Pitt the Younger (1759–1806), though he too would have rejected the nomenclature. Party names came back into use at the general election of 1807, with Tories being recognized as supporters of the action of George III (1738–1820) in removing the Government of All the Talents. Lord LIVERPOOL's administration (1812–27) was widely described as Tory by contemporaries even though its own members rarely used this appellation. At this date the notion of a Tory party still involved little more than a group of men in office and those who adhered to them in parliament on personal or public grounds.

The word 'Conservative' was first used as an alternative to 'Tory' in an article in the *Quarterly Review* in January 1830: 'We are now, as we always have been, decidedly and conscientiously attached to what is called the Tory, and which might with more propriety, be called the Conservative Party.' There was no striking change in 'Conservative' as compared with 'Tory' principles and attitudes, with both names remaining in use. But 'Conservative' was increasingly used after the Great Reform Act of 1832 to liberate the party from some of its old associations and to emphasize a more sympathetic attitude to reform, particularly after Robert PEEL delivered his TAMWORTH MANIFESTO in 1834. But Peel gravely damaged his party through his determination to repeal the CORN LAWS. The result was a major split, the relegation of Toryism to a generation in opposition and the equation of the movement with unqualified reaction. Such a stance was unrealistic in the context of an expanding electorate, particularly after the Second Reform Act (1867), and it was left to Benjamin DISRAELI to revamp the party's image and make it electorally viable again. Though Disraeli was sometimes stronger on rhetoric than achievement, under his leadership Toryism became associated with national unity, nationalism, a vigorous foreign policy, imperialism and a greater sympathy towards measures of social reform. This period also witnessed the beginnings of many of the institutions of the modern party. Not surprisingly, many present-day Tories look back to Disraeli as their founder figure. By the end of the nineteenth century his successors were well on the way to establishing the Tory Party as the natural governing party, no small achievement in a country which was moving slowly but progressively towards a democratic franchise.

Though the terms 'Tory' and 'Conservative' were – and are – generally used interchangeably, 'Tory' is sometimes employed to stress a particular strain within the party which emphasizes the traditions of an organic society, authority and paternalism, and a general concern for all social questions. Harold Macmillan once described Toryism as 'paternal socialism'.

See also CONSERVATISM, PATERNALISM.

Robert Blake, *The Conservative Party from Peel to Thatcher* (London, 1985).
Bruce Coleman, *Conservatism and the Conservative Party in Nineteenth-Century Britain* (London, 1988).

DAVID DUTTON

trade cycles Also known in economic parlance as business cycles, trade cycles are characteristic of industrialized economies. They are to be distinguished from commercial fluctuations in the pre-industrial period by their all-pervading nature. Their causes are the subject of much debate among economists, but may be generally understood as a function of uneven rates of growth and development in one sector leading to crises that spread throughout the whole economy.

Trade cycles were identified by socialists in the early nineteenth century as the basic rhythm of industrial CAPITALISM, and their periodicity first began to be studied and measured by economists in the 1860s. There are two kinds of cycles that regulate economic fluctuations: the long waves, known as Kondratieff cycles, of forty to fifty years which are marked by periods of structural economic change and decay, and the short-term fluctuations caused by a variety of internal and external influences on particular economies.

The nineteenth century saw two long waves, from c.1787 to 1842 and from 1843 to 1897, and short waves generally of four to seven years' duration. The timing of these latter waves varied to a lessening degree between different countries, with the United States following its own distinctive pattern until the early twentieth century. In general terms, what happened in Britain during the nineteenth century was the most important determinant of world fluctuations in the trade cycle and the following account refers mainly to the British experience.

Until the 1840s AGRICULTURE remained the most important influence on the trade cycle and this continued the pattern of the eighteenth century. Bad harvests caused a decline in purchasing power and an outflow of bullion to pay for corn imports, which further increased domestic deflationary pressures and often led to the collapse of credit and banking crises. This pattern in its purest form was last experienced in the depression of the late 1830s, but by the 1840s the growing influence of trade and investment on economic fluctuations began to be felt. The depression of 1842–3 was a result of the coincidental collapse of the speculative railway boom and of foreign textile markets. The crisis of 1845–7 was the last economic collapse in which agricultural collapse played a major role, with important political consequences throughout Europe. The next depression came with the collapse of 1857, which is usually regarded as the first world-wide trade-cycle crisis.

The remaining peaks of trade-cycle activity in Britain were 1865, 1873, 1882, 1890 and 1899 and the troughs were 1869, 1879, 1886 and 1893. The pattern of this activity reflected the key role of exports in determining fluctuations in the British economy. The major downturns in the economy were all associated with interruptions to exports, as a very high proportion of British goods depended on overseas markets after the introduction of FREE TRADE. Thus, it was said by Beveridge that the secret of the trade cycle was to be found 'not in bankers' parlours or the board rooms of industry, but on the prairies and plantations, in the mines and oil wells'. This was increasingly true as the export of goods and the export of capital from Britain were closely connected. The boom of the mid-Victorian years rested on these twin pillars. Capital was exported for developmental purposes which would then stimulate the purchase of British goods. A local crisis or the collapse of a speculative boom reverberated throughout the export markets. Thus, the BARING CRISIS in 1890 directly influenced economic collapse in Argentina which choked off British exports to that country.

After c.1890 the central role of Britain as the sole supplier of capital and manufacturing goods was diminished, with the rise of alternative suppliers such as Germany and the United States and the determinants of the trade cycle became more complex.

Sir William Beveridge, 'The Trade Cycle in Britain before 1850', *Oxford Economic Papers*, 3 (1940), 74–109.

W. Arthur Lewis, *Growth and Fluctuations 1870–1913* (London, 1978).

R. C. O. Matthews, *The Trade Cycle* (Cambridge, 1959).

RICHARD PRICE

Trades Union Congress   A national body of trade unions, founded in 1868, the Trades Union Congress (TUC) sought to advance the common interests of organized labour. In its earliest years the TUC devoted itself to gaining legal reforms that would safeguard trade-union status and activities. Determined to secure a place of respectability for trade unions within capitalist society, the leaders of the TUC's guiding body, the parliamentary committee, pursued a politically moderate course for more than two decades. By 1890, however, the cautious Lib-Lab leadership of the TUC was challenged by the growing influence of socialists in the trade-union movement (*see* SOCIALISM). In 1900, pressured by an employers' offensive and a series of unfavourable legal decisions, segments of the TUC reluctantly agreed to pursue an alliance with the socialist societies for the purpose of electing independent labour members to parliament. Together, they sponsored the Labour Representation Committee, the forerunner of the LABOUR PARTY.

RICHARD J. SODERLUND

trade unions *see* AMERICAN FEDERATION OF LABOR; GENERAL CONFEDERATION OF FRENCH LABOUR; GENERAL UNIONISM; NEW UNIONISM.

Trafalgar, Battle of (21 October 1805) Perhaps the most famous naval battle of all time, Trafalgar was the sequel to a series of unavailing French attempts to open the way for an invasion of Britain. Having abandoned this plan in favour of marching against Austria, Napoleon BONAPARTE ordered the large Franco-Spanish fleet trapped in Cádiz under Villeneuve (1763–1806) to break out and enter the Mediterranean in support. Attempting this manoeuvre, however, Villeneuve was caught by NELSON's fleet off Cape Trafalgar, on the coast of southwest Spain, and annihilated in a close-range action that gave weight to superior British seamanship and gunnery. In the process Nelson was killed, but the victory put an end to Napoleon's hopes of challenging the British at sea for many years to come, thereby forcing him to adopt his costly and counter-productive Continental blockade (*see* CONTINENTAL SYSTEM). At the same time, too, SPAIN's sea power was shattered and with it the security of its colonial empire.

CHARLES ESDAILE

tramping system Craft societies used the tramping system to provide for the geographic mobility of members, primarily as a mode of UNEMPLOYMENT relief. Skilled men (*see* SKILLED WORKERS) on the tramp travelled from town to town, seeking work at their trade among local craft societies or clubs. The presentation of a 'blank' or certificate of membership at a society's house of call entitled a tramp to food, accommodation and a small money allowance. If no work was available, the migratory craftsman travelled on to the next destination. Originating in the eighteenth century, the system was adopted by virtually every skilled trade during the early nineteenth century as a response to the chronic unemployment of that economically tumultuous period. After 1850, however, it gradually lost favour as most trades adopted static unemployment relief, a change reflecting recognition of the national character of TRADE CYCLES and economic fluctuations. The practice had disappeared by 1914.

R. A. Leeson, *Travelling Brothers* (London, 1979).

RICHARD J. SODERLUND

trams The street tramway, or streetcar, was first introduced in November 1832 in New York. It was simply an application of railroad technology (at first horse-drawn) to urban roads. By 1842 something similar was to be seen in Vienna, but the 'Chemin de fer Américain' was really first established in Europe when a line was opened in Paris in 1853.

Although cars ran over the goods lines of the Mersey Docks and Harbour Board in Liverpool for a few months in 1859, it was an American who first laid down purpose-built tramlines, opening a line, with some panache, in Birkenhead on 30 August 1860. But his rails were not set flush with the road surface, and subequent lines built, without authority, in London were forcibly removed. The American promoter, aptly named G. F. Train (1829–1904), retired in disgust, but local enterprise in Birkenhead relaid the line with slot rails, and the new system caught on.

To avoid the expensive procedure of obtaining parliamentary powers, as for a railway, the Tramways Act 1870 enabled lines to be built with local-authority consent (and they were most often built by local authorities, who then franchised an operating company). In 1879 a further act permitted the use of mechanical power, and while this was initially steam in most cases, cable-cars were also introduced, most notably in Edinburgh. Electric traction was first used at Anhalt in Germany in 1881, and on 4 August 1883 Magnus Volk (1851–1937) opened the electric railway along the front at Brighton, which runs to this day. The first electric street tramway in Britain was opened in Blackpool in September 1885, and this also continues to exist.

The nineteenth-century tramways brought cheap and frequent travel nearer to the mass market. Many lines were under-financed, so that by the end of the century local authorities were obtaining powers to operate the cars themselves. But private enterprise remained significant, usually through investment trusts such as the British Electric Traction Company, formed in 1896, after the Light Railways Act of that year simplified further the process of obtaining authority to build a line.

J. HIBBS

transport *see* BICYCLE; CANALS; RAILWAYS; STEAMSHIPS; TRAMS.

Transvaal As a result of the GREAT TREK, European occupation extended to the area north of the Vaal River. Unsuccessful attempts were made to unite the region with the Orange River Sovereignty. Transvaal unity was achieved in 1860, but civil unrest delayed the establishment of the South African republic for four years. The area was annexed by the British in 1877 but regained autonomy in 1881 as the Transvaal, with Britain retaining suzerainty, an ill-defined concept which caused considerable friction. The discovery of gold on the Witwatersrand led to a rush of Uitlanders ('foreigners') and foreign capital, and made the Transvaal economically more important than the Cape. The desire to bring Transvaal wealth under British control increased antagonism to the point where Cecil Rhodes arranged the unsuccessful JAMESON RAID, 1895. Joseph Chamberlain and Sir Alfred Milner subsequently provoked the second Boer War (see ANGLO-BOER WARS). The Transvaal gained responsible government in 1906 and became a province of the Union of South Africa in 1910.

SIMON KATZENELLENBOGEN

treaty ports Following the first Anglo-Chinese War, the TREATY OF NANKING stipulated that five ports, including Shanghai and Canton, be opened to British trade. These were the first treaty ports. Successive treaties between China and the foreign powers led to the opening of many dozens of ports by the end of the century. The ports became enclaves outside Chinese jurisdiction as foreigners enjoyed extraterritoriality (the right to be subject not to Chinese law but to that of their own country). The most notable example was the international settlement in Shanghai. In the ports foreigners established the beginnings of a modern economic infrastructure, developing banking, insurance, commercial services and industrial enterprises, an infrastructure also of benefit to the Chinese business community growing up alongside foreign industry and commerce. However, the modernizing impact of foreign economic activity remained confined to the treaty ports, and did not extend to the Chinese rural economy which remained a subsistence peasant economy.

See also TREATY OF TIENTSIN.

JOHN DAVIES

Triple Alliance The agreement of 1882 between Germany, Austria-Hungary and Italy established one of the two main alliance systems of Europe leading up to the First World War (the other being the Triple Entente). The Triple Alliance tied each country into a mutual-defence pact. It protected Germany against Russian and French aggression by guaranteeing aid from Austria-Hungary and Italy; for Austria-Hungary, it ensured Italy's neutrality in the event of a war with Russia; and it protected Italy in case of an unprovoked attack from France.

The alliance was of considerable benefit to Italy: Germany and Austria pledged non-interference in its internal affairs, and it conferred great-power status on Italy. The alliance was renewed at regular intervals and lasted until 1915. It fell apart when Italy joined the First World War on the Anglo-French side.

GEORGE O. KENT

Tristan, Flora (*b* Paris, 7 April 1803; *d* Bordeaux, 14 November 1844)   French socialist and feminist. Descended from Inca nobility on her father's side, she was an engraver-lithographer by trade. After she returned from Peru in an unsuccessful attempt to claim her inheritance, she published *Péréginations d'une Paria (1833–1838)* in 1838 in which she argued that the emancipation of women (and slaves) could be achieved only in a general social liberation. She was a strong opponent of the death penalty and, because of her own unhappy marriage, argued for the reinstitution of divorce, which had been abolished in 1816. Her most important book, *L'Union ouvrière* (1843) called for the joining together of all working classes irrespective of craft or nationality in a general emancipation to be achieved by peaceful means. She died on a speaking tour in 1844 while promoting her ideas. She was the grandmother of the painter Gauguin (1848–1903).

D. Desanti, *A Woman in Revolt: A Biography of Flora Tristan* (New York, 1976).

DONALD SUTHERLAND

Troppau, Congress of   *see* CONGRESS SYSTEM.

Tseng Kuo-fan [Xeng Guofan] (*b* Hunan, 1811; *d* 1872) Chinese scholar-official. He rose to prominence as the most respected official of the period during the TAIPING REBELLION. The imperial army having proved no match for the Taipings, Tseng raised a militia in his native province of Hunan. The Hunan army, committed to the defence of Confucianism, was in essence a private provincial army. The soldiers were recruited by their officers, to whom they pledged allegiance and through them to Tseng himself. After initial set-backs, Tseng took charge of the entire operation against the Taipings as imperial commissioner in 1860. After the fall of the Taiping capital, Nanking, in 1864, Tseng was created a marquis. His later career was inevitably something of an anticlimax. Although later reviled by Marxists for having saved the Ch'ing dynasty, he became in the Nationalist era (1927–49) the model of the upright, cultivated public official.

JOHN DAVIES

Tuan, Prince (*b* c.1860; *d* 1911)   Reactionary member of the Ch'ing court. He recommended the empress dowager, TZ'U-HSI, to use the Boxer movement, originally anti-Ch'ing as well as antiforeign, to expel the foreigners from China (*see* BOXER RISING). As the Boxer attacks mounted in northern China, the foreign powers responded by taking the Taku Forts, protecting the entrance to Tientsin. Tuan urged Tz'u-hsi to unleash the Boxers in an all-out attack on the foreign legations in Peking to wipe out the humiliating legacy of Western intervention in China. In the attack on the legations Tuan himself led one of the Boxer contingents. After the defeat of the Boxers by the foreign expeditionary force, the imperial court fled to Sian, where Tuan pressed for a continuation of the war against the foreigners. In the settlement imposed by the foreign powers on China in 1901 Tuan was banished to life imprisonment in Sinkiang.

JOHN DAVIES

Tucumán, Congress of (1816) Called to concentrate minds on the emancipation struggle against the Spaniards rather than the internecine conflicts dividing the creoles in ARGENTINA, the Congress of Tucumán was convoked by the government of Buenos Aires. Although it met at Tucumán in the north-west of Argentina, many provinces sent no representatives. It was notable chiefly for its declaration of the independence of 'the United Provinces of South America' on 9 July 1816, which provided a basis for SAN MARTIN to undertake the invasion of Chile. With Tucumán under threat from Spanish forces in Upper Peru, the congress eventually retreated to Buenos Aires, where in 1819 it produced an extremely centralist constitution. This provoked widespread opposition, leading rapidly to the defeat of the Buenos Aires *unitarios* and declarations of independence by provincial *caudillos*.

RORY MILLER

Tunisia The north African country of Tunisia was part of the Ottoman Empire but effectively autonomous until about 1835 when Ottoman power was reasserted in neighbouring Libya. There was also a tacit French threat from Algeria. Some rulers sought to Westernize without losing control of the country. An international commission was created to supervise finances when Tunisia became bankrupt in 1869. The assumption of control by France was subsequently authorized by the CONGRESS OF BERLIN (1878). The French found a pretext to invade and impose military occupation on Tunisia in 1881, and a full-scale 'protectorate' by the Convention of Marsa in 1883. Under French rule, an elite, Western-educated group, the Young Tunisians, pressed for greater Westernization, but also for more Tunisian participation in government. Although independence was not specifically mentioned, even these early signs of protonationalism were suppressed.

SIMON KATZENELLENBOGEN

Samori Turay, Almami (*b* Manyambaladugu in the Konyan region of present-day Guinea, *c.*1830; *d* Gabon, 2 June 1900) Dyula warrior statesman. Small militant Muslim principalities began emerging among the southern Malinké people in the 1830s. In the 1860s Samori emerged as an outstanding leader, drawing on pagan and Muslim connections, reforming and improving local military techniques, importing and manufacturing firearms and facilitating trade. Following initial contact in 1881, the French attacked Samori in 1882 and recurrent fighting followed. In 1884 Samori took the Islamic title 'almami' (Arabic *alimam*), encouraging Islamization. When revolt errupted in 1888 he restricted his Islamic policy, military achievement being his priority. He eventually suppressed the rebels, but encroaching French power was now technologically irresistible. Samori abandoned Malinké country and withdrew eastwards, becoming, like 'Umar ibn Sa'id Tal, a colonial conqueror, ruling as far as the Volta River. After a short respite, French and British expansion undermined the new state. The French captured Samori on 29 September 1898.

Yves Person, *Samori: une révolution dyula [Samori: a Dyula revolution]*, 3 vols (Dakar, 1968–73).

HUMPHREY J. FISHER

Turkey *see* OTTOMAN EMPIRE.

Turner, Nat (*b* Southampton County, Virginia, 2 October 1800; *d* Jerusalem, Virginia, 11 November 1831) African-American preacher and leader. Born a slave, he became a favourite of his master's family, who taught him to read. As an adult, he emerged as a slave preacher, who claimed he had visions in which the Lord told him he was the one chosen to lead his people to freedom. Gathering a group of conspirators to him, he planned to liberate slaves in the surrounding area. On 22 August 1831, after killing Turner's master and family, the conspirators swept through the neighbourhood killing fifty-one other whites in two days. Captured six weeks later, Turner was hanged. The rebellion sent shock waves through the south. The Virginia assembly debated slavery, and voted to keep it. Other states outlawed black literacy and placed restrictions on black gatherings and preachers. Turner's revolt led southerners to stifle the debate over slavery, and insist as never before that it was a positive good.

Stephen B. Oates, *The Fires of Jubilee: Nat Turner's Fierce Rebellion* (New York, 1975).

ALICE E. REAGAN

Tyler, John (*b* Charles City County, Virginia, 29 March 1790; *d* Richmond, Virginia, 18 January 1862) President of the United States (1841–5). Educated at the College of William and Mary, he read law with his father and began practising law in 1809. Shortly after, he won a seat in the Virginia house of delegates and served there until elected to the House of Representatives in 1816. He campaigned for the Senate as an anti-Jackson Democrat and in 1832 cast the only recorded vote against the Force Bill. In 1840 Tyler ran for vice-president with Whig candidate William Henry Harrison. When Harrison died shortly after inauguration, Tyler became the first president by right of succession. Philosophically a Democrat, Tyler vetoed key Whig legislation and his Whig cabinet – with the exception of Daniel WEBSTER – resigned. Effectively a president without a party, he was none the less able to accomplish much, including the Webster-Ashburton Treaty and the annexation of Texas.

JOHN MARTIN

typewriter As early as the mid eighteenth century, clockmakers and other mechanics designed and built writing-machines. This tradition continued in the nineteenth century, and from these efforts emerged all the key individual elements of the mechanical typewriter. The first commercially viable machine was the 'writing ball' of Malling Hansen of Denmark, in moderate use from 1870 until the early years of the twentieth century.

Commercial success awaited the introduction of the Model Two 'Type-Writer', based on the designs of Christopher Sholes (1819–90), whose most notorious legacy is the much cursed Q W E R T Y keyboard, by the Remington Arms Company in 1878. Further improvements made the typewriter an important addition to the growing offices of insurance companies, mail-order companies and others of the expanding bureaucratic culture of the 1880s. The broader social effects of the typewriter are a matter of some controversy, and the suggestion that its use in offices was somehow 'liberating' to nineteenth-century women is a considerable over-simplification, at best. None the less, the machine rapidly came to be viewed as a new tool of 'women's work'.

Michael A. Adler, *The Writing Machine* (London 1973).

ROBERT FRIEDEL

Tz'u-hsi [Cixi] (*b* Peking, 1835; *d* Peking, 1908) Empress dowager of China. She was the only woman to exercise political power during the Ch'ing period. Although she lacked formal education, her guile and determination sustained her during her domination of Chinese politics from 1861 until 1908. Her power was derived from her position as Emperor Hsien-feng's (1831–61) concubine and later his wife. After his death in 1861 she dominated the regency of her son T'ungchih (1856–74) until 1873 and that of her nephew KUANG HSU from 1875 to 1889. From her coup during the HUNDRED DAYS REFORM until her death in 1908 her power was unchallenged. Lukewarm towards the SELF-STRENGTHENING MOVEMENT, she became actively xenophobic in her encouragement of the BOXER RISING against the foreign presence in China (1899–1900). Politically conservative, she has been held responsible for the CH'ING DYNASTY's failure to regenerate China.

Marina Warner, *The Dragon Empress: The Life and Times of T'zu-hsi, Empress Dowager of China, 1835–1908* (London, 1972).

JOHN DAVIES

U

Uganda The country of Uganda in east Africa came within the British sphere of influence as part of the Anglo-German settlement of rival interests in the SCRAMBLE FOR AFRICA. Considered essential to the protection of British involvement in Egypt by its position of control over the headwaters of the Nile, it was included in the grant to the Imperial British East Africa Company, a chartered company which, in addition to its commercial interests, acted as surrogate for British colonialism. The company's failure was largely due to the financial burden imposed by its Ugandan obligations.

The dominant African group in the area was the Baganda who, as their power waned, sought, more or less successfully, to manipulate the European presence to help sustain their position. A British protectorate was first declared in 1894, with a more formal, detailed agreement being reached in 1900.

SIMON KATZENELLENBOGEN

Uitlanders The term 'Uitlanders' (literally 'foreigners') was and is applied specifically to the people of British, German and other nationalities who went to the TRANSVAAL in large numbers in the wake of gold discoveries on the Witwatersrand. Resented by the Boers (of Dutch origin, later known as Afrikaners), they used their grievances against President Paul Kruger and his government, most notably the length of residence required for the right to vote, as one pretext for the JAMESON RAID and the second ANGLO-BOER WAR.

SIMON KATZENELLENBOGEN

ultramontanism The belief in centralized papal authority over the Roman Catholic Church, ultramontanism derives from the doctrines of the Pope's infallibility in teaching in faith and morals and of his universal jurisdiction. Both doctrines were made binding on Roman Catholics by the decrees of the First Vatican Council of 1869–70. 'Ultramontane' northern European Catholics looked to Roman authority *ultra montes*, beyond the mountains. Ultramontanism invokes the scriptural primacy of St Peter, inherited by the bishops of Rome, but was countered by medieval conciliarism and seventeenth-century Gallicanism, or cisalpinism, which limited infallibility to general ecumenical councils and regarded national churches as independent under a titular papal primacy.

The nineteenth-century triumph of ultramontanism was partly the work of conservative Catholics like Count Joseph de Maistre (1754–1821) who rallied to the pope against the French Revolution and, later, against the Italian nationalist attacks on the Papal States. Ultramontane liberal Catholics like Félicité de LAMENNAIS wanted Rome to sanction liberty against the modern state. This liberal ultramontanism was alienated by the antiliberal papal 'Syllabus errorum' (Syllabus of Errors, 1864) (*see* PIUS IX). Papal authority also grew as the pope created dioceses and appointed bishops over vast new territories evangelized by nineteenth-century missionary Catholicism.

See also PAPACY.

Dom Cuthbert Butler, *The Vatican Council*, 2 vols (London, 1930).

SHERIDAN GILLEY

Ulundi, Battle of (4 July 1879)   One of the battles of the ZULU WARS noted particularly for the burning of king CETSHWAYO's homestead, the Battle of Ulundi was long considered an act of revenge for the earlier annihilation of the British at Isandlwana in January 1879 and subsequent near-defeat at Rorke's Drift. An alternative view is that Lord Chelmsford (1827–1905), mirroring the general feelings of the British government, wanted a victory to salvage his military reputation and that the Zulu forces 'melted away' as they could not sustain a long fight. Cetshwayo's ultimate fate was sealed by a second battle at Ulundi which was part of the Zulu civil war in which the forces led by Zibhebu (*c*.1842–1904) killed many of the king's most able supporters. Unusually, the Zulus were allowed to keep their land, highly significant for their future relationship with whites.

Jeff Guy, *The Destruction of the Zulu Kingdom: The Civil War in Zululand, 1879–1884* (London, 1979).

SIMON KATZENELLENBOGEN

'Umar ibn Sai'd Tal, al-Hajj (*b* Futa Toro, Senegal, *c*.1796; *d* Golo, Sudan 12 February 1864)   Islamic religious-political reformer. Of the Tijaniyya brotherhood (a Sufi, or mystical religious order), he founded an imperial hegemony – by conquest – which extended over large sections of the western Sudan. This Umarian state, in existence for approximately four decades (*c.*1851–2 to 1891–3), delayed the French consolidation of power on the middle and upper Niger for several years. Scion of a clerical lineage from the Futa Toro, 'Umar Tal, a man of considerable learning and religious zeal, was also the author of several theological works (*see* ARTS AND LITERATURE). His life-span overlapping those of UTHMAN DAN FODIO and MUHAMMAD AHMAD IBN 'ABDALLAH AL-MAHDI, Tal visited both the Sokoto caliphate and the Egyptian state on his pilgrimage hají to Mecca (1826–46). He began his jihad or holy war (1851–2), against the Bamana of Kaarta and Segu, and likewise waged a jihad against the French (1857–64). These wars were continued after his death by his sons, one of whom, Ahmadu Tijani Tal (*c.*1833–98) succeeded to his father's Segu sultanate. Tal allegedly died in battle in 1864.

David Robinson, *The Holy War of 'Umar Tal: The Western Sudan in the Mid-Nineteenth Century* (Oxford, 1985).

B. MARIE PERINBAM

unemployment   Throughout the nineteenth century unemployment was a common experience, especially for manual workers. The word was occasionally used in the 1840s, and in the 1860s and 1870s there was a literature that distinguished between different categories of unemployed workers. However, the history of unemployment as a concept has focused on the last two decades of the nineteenth century. In 1886 a Fabian Society report distinguished between seasonal, cyclical and casual unemployment. That kind of analysis was taken further in 1893 by Hubert Llewellyn Smith (1864–1945), labour commissioner at the board of trade, who superimposed it on the earlier preoccupation with the classification of unemployed workers. He devised a two-dimensional system, distinguishing between eight types of trade fluctuation and four types of unemployed workers. This took account of what had become apparent to thoughtful observers, that workers were unemployed on account of both changes in the demand for labour and their personal qualities. The types of trade fluctuations were subdivisions of the three main categories of seasonal, cyclical and technological unemployment. The additional classification of the unemployed distinguished those who were between periods of short-term employment from the so-called unemployables, and from those suffering from oversupply of labour in their trade. The classification was complex and difficult to apply in practice. It was modified in 1908–9 by William Beveridge (1879–1963), who regarded any classification of the unemployed as, strictly speaking, an impossibility and hence confined himself to classifying the causes of unemployment. In his view, personal qualities were secondary; they determined who was to be unemployed, not the extent of unemployment.

Little information exists on the extent of unemployment in Britain in the nineteenth century. Our knowledge is based on the records of those trade unions that gave financial support to their members when unemployed. For such unions it is possible to calculate an unemployment percentage going back, in a few cases, to 1851. However, even at the end of the century these records related to fewer than a third of all trade-unionists in the country and fewer than one-twelfth of all industrial workers. They were unrepresentative of the workforce as a whole but in ways that are impossible to estimate, and therefore provide no information on the extent of unemployment at any one time. At best they enable comparisons to be made between different years and thus serve as an indicator of fluctuations.

They existed because certain unions pursued a policy of financial support for their resident unemployed members or of support for those travelling to seek work in other places (*see* TRAMPING SYSTEM). Both measures were intended to strengthen the bargaining position of the union by preventing the unemployed from undercutting wage rates. Apart from the policy pursued by the unions in the interests of solidarity, it is possible to find a public policy towards the unemployed that differed from the more general policy towards the able-bodied poor pursued under the NEW POOR LAW. It was one of temporary employment by public authorities on so-called public relief works. Its purpose was to save those normally in regular employment but laid off during a period of 'bad trade' from the harshness of the Poor Law, and might be called one of safeguarding the quality of the regular labour force. It found its most prominent expression during the Lancashire COTTON FAMINE of 1862–3. On that occasion the Treasury made special loans available to local authorities to engage in useful public works, but it was not the first time that local authorities had pursued such a policy. After 1886 it enjoyed the official support of the local government board, but the board was able neither to enforce its views nor to provide any financial incentives. The policy of public relief works for the unemployed reached its climax in the 1905 Unemployed Workmen's Act, which compelled local authorities in larger towns to set up distress committees and made a small amount of finance available from the Treasury for the organization of public relief works. Although the Labour Party pressed for its extension, the policy was to be seriously discredited in 1908–9 by Beveridge's analysis of the operations of that act. After 1909 British unemployment policy emphasized national insurance and the establishment of labour exchanges to facilitate the search for work.

Information about unemployment in the nineteenth century elsewhere is, if anything, less complete. Germany, France, Denmark and the United States occasionally attempted to take censuses of the unemployed, but their reliability is not great. Policies pursued at the end of the century were municipal relief works, municipal labour exchanges and occasional municipal subsidies for trade-union unemployment relief.

See also CASUAL LABOUR.

José Harris, *Unemployment and Politics 1886–1914* (Oxford, 1972).

E. P. HENNOCK

Unitarians A development of eighteenth-century Presbyterianism, Unitarianism was a small but important sect in both Britain and the United States, especially New England. Doctrinally, it is distinguished by its denial of the Trinity and its insistence on the unity of God. But its importance is more social and cultural than doctrinal, for Unitarianism appealed especially to leading and enlightened sections of the middle class, especially in London and provincial cities like Leicester, Manchester and Liverpoool, and, in the United States, in Boston and New York. In England a number of leading intellectuals were either Unitarian or profoundly influenced by Unitarianism; the list includes William Godwin (1756–1836), William Hazlitt (1778–1830), Harriet Martineau, William J. Fox (1786–1864), Robert Browning (1812–89), Harriet Taylor, George Eliot (1819–80) and Elizabeth Gaskell (1810–65). In the United States Unitarianism was perhaps the dominant sect among New England intellectuals.

See NONCONFORMITY.

SIMON DENTITH

United States of America During the nineteenth century the United States of America underwent several important transformations. Territorially, it grew from a small republic between the Atlantic Ocean and the Mississippi River, to a continental nation with an overseas empire. By the time of the Civil War, it had acquired nearly all its continental possessions. In 1803 it bought Louisiana from France, and it later (1819) acquired Florida from Spain. The TREATY OF GUADALUPE HIDALGO (1848) gave it the Mexican Cession, and in 1853 it bought the Gadsden Purchase from Mexico. After the Civil War, the United States obtained Alaska and Midway Island (1867); Hawaii, the Philippines, Guam and Puerto Rico (1898); and American Samoa (1899). (*See* MANIFEST DESTINY.)

Economically, the United States transformed itself from an agricultural nation to one of the world's leading industrial powers. Its industrial revolution began shortly after the War of 1812, with the introduction of the factory system in the textile industry. With the aid of better machinery, and electricity after the Civil War, American industries such as oil, steel and textiles rivalled or surpassed European output.

The United States became a more diverse nation with the arrival of numerous European immigrants. Before the Civil War, the majority of newcomers were from Ireland, Germany and Scandinavia. After the war, more came from southern and eastern Europe. They provided a cheap source of labour for American industry. The arrival of millions of immigrants from Europe, coupled with a high birth rate, especially in rural areas, caused the population to expand from 5.3 million (1800) to 76 million (1900). (*See also* AFRICAN-AMERICANS.) The population shifted increasingly towards the city: in 1800 only 5 per cent of all Americans lived in cities, but 40 per cent were urban dwellers by 1900. The Civil War (*see* AMERICAN CIVIL WAR) changed how Americans viewed their nation. Before the war, the United States was regarded in the plural, but afterwards it was seen as an entity.

William Barney, *The Passage of the Republic: An Interdisciplinary History of Nineteenth-Century America* (Lexington, Mass., 1987).

ALICE E. REAGAN

universities The nineteenth century proved to be a great turning-point in university development. Through state and other intervention ancient universities were reformed and many new ones founded, some in parts of the world where facilities for higher education were previously unknown. In 1808 the French government assumed control of all university and higher-education studies. Two years later the University of Berlin was established with financial aid from the Prussian government. As the industrial revolution spread, universities both old and new were required to engage in applied research. In England, Oxford and Cambridge, under critical attack in the 1850s, preserved their independence, but following the Devonshire Commission Reports (1870–5) they developed scientific studies. Manchester (1851) and other cities established university colleges to meet both the needs of local industry and commerce and the challenge of the polytechnics and technical universities of the new German Empire. European universities provided models for new institutions in Canada, India and elsewhere. In the United States, to augment the pre-independence universities, colleges for the agricultural and mechanical arts were established in each state following the MORRILL ACT (1862).

For women to attend universities before the mid nineteenth century was practically unknown; and even where they were permitted to attend, they were often not granted full status or admitted to degrees, as was the case at Oxford and Cambridge. It was the 1860s before women were admitted to universities on the same terms as men, in the United States the lead being taken by the Universities of Iowa and Wisconsin. In Europe the University of Zurich was the first to admit women to lectures in 1872. New Zealand produced the first woman graduate in the British Empire in 1877.

Konrad H. Jarausch, *The Transformation of Higher Learning 1860–1930* (Chicago, 1983).

SYLVIA HARROP AND ROBIN BETTS

Unkiar-Skelessi, Treaty of (8 July 1833) Signed by Russia and the Ottoman Empire, the Treaty of Unkiar-Skelessi reflected the sultan's need for continued Russian support against the rebellious MUHAMMAD ALI of Egypt, who a year earlier had attacked the sultan's forces and been defeated only with the aid of the Russians. As a result of the treaty, Russia withdrew its forces and promised to come to the aid of the sultan if his empire were attacked. In return, the sultan promised to keep the Straits closed to all foreign (that is British and French) warships (*see* STRAITS QUESTION).

GEORGE O. KENT

unskilled labour A convenient definition of nineteenth-century unskilled workers would be those who possessed neither craft skill nor union. They were known generically as 'general labourers', although in reality there was quite a high degree of job specialization: dock labourers tended to work only in the docks, for example. Accurate measurement is impossible, but it is likely that at mid-century in Britain this group included at least 60 to 80 per cent of the working class. Their working conditions were characterized by low earnings, irregular work due to economic fluctuations or seasonality of employment, job insecurity and interchangeability of employment (*see* CASUAL LABOUR, UNEMPLOYMENT).

Every industry was stratified, often in very complicated and detailed ways. Those industries with the lowest number of unskilled included the heavy industries, textiles and the old craft trades, and those with the highest proportion of unskilled workers included chemicals, food and clothing. Wage differentials between the skilled and unskilled also varied greatly, from 200 pre cent between iron puddlers and their labourers to 30 to 40 per cent in the building trades. Until *c.*1890 this differential tended to widen.

Unskilled labourers were recruited from a variety of sources, including adolescent boys entering the labour market for the first time and skilled workers reduced to unskilled jobs due to old age, accidents and other causes. But the largest category of unskilled workers in the nineteenth century were women. Jobs became increasingly gender-specific and the growing number of women in industry were relegated to unskilled work. The replacement of women spinners by men, which accompanied mechanization of the industry, was the most dramatic example of this, but it was a common experience.

By the end of the century, a new occupational stratification was emerging. Technological and organizational changes in industry were creating a distinct category of semi-skilled workers, particularly in new industries like electrical engineering, who were partially recruited from the ranks of the unskilled.

See also GENERAL UNIONISM.

Angela V. John (ed.), *Unequal Opportunities: Women's Employment in England 1800–1918* (London, 1986).

Charles More, *Skill and the English Working Class, 1870–1914* (London, 1980).

Louise A. Tilly and Joan W. Scott, *Women, Work and Family* (New York, 1987).

RICHARD PRICE

Urabi Pasha, Ahmad (*b* 1841; *d* Cairo, 21 September 1911) Egyptian army officer and popular leader. Government bankruptcy, crop failures and the demands of Egypt's creditors in 1881 aroused widespread discontent that found a spokesman in Urabi Pasha, a young army colonel. Although Urabi's protest was initially taken on behalf of aggrieved army officers, it gained a large following when Urabi demanded an end to the privileges of 'non-Egyptians', particularly resident Europeans and Turco-Circassians. In early 1882 Urabi Pasha became minister of war, but the new government aroused the fears of the khedive MUHAMMAD TAWFIQ PASHA as well as of the European powers. When Urabi refused to resign and riots broke out in Alexandria, the British invaded Egypt and defeated the Egyptian army at Tel-al-Kebir (*see* BATTLE OF TEL-AL-KEBIR). Urabi and his followers were exiled to Ceylon, Tawfiq restored to authority and the British installed in Egypt.

Alexander Schölch, *Egypt for the Egyptians! The Socio-political Crisis in Egypt, 1878–1882* (London, 1981).

MADELINE C. ZILFI

urbanization Urban growth was seen from an early date as a distinctive feature of the nineteenth century. Despite the numerous city problems which accompanied growth and increasingly concerned reformers (disease, poverty, crime and slums), urbanization was seen by boosters and civic leaders as the triumphant product of industrialization, commerce and new transport systems, as well as the focus of modern civilization. For good or ill, large-scale urbanization was a relatively new phenomenon.

In 1800 about 3 per cent of the world's inhabitants lived in places of more than 5,000 inhabitants, while the whole of Europe contained only nine cities with populations of more than 100,000. Only two European cities (London and Paris) contained between 500,000 and 1 million (although the Far East then boasted twenty-three cities of 100,000 population and one of more than a million). By 1900 there were ninety-six European cities with more than 100,000 inhabitants, eight between 500,000 and 1 million, and seven over 1 million. Asia now lagged behind. England, the most heavily urbanized country, had 80 per cent of its people living in towns of more than 5,000 and the London area contained between 5 and 6 million. The American statistics are particularly striking, for all these cities were of recent origin. The first federal census of 1790 revealed twenty-four places with more than 2,500 inhabitants, representing 5 per cent of the American population. By 1860 this figure was 20 per cent and by 1900 it had reached 46 per cent. At the end of the century the United States contained 3 'million' cities (Philadelphia, Chicago and San Francisco) while the urban complex of New York counted almost 5 million people.

Everywhere urban expansion was fuelled by migration from rural to urban areas under the twin pressures of increased agricultural efficiency (which drove workers from the farms) and the attraction of urban employment opportunities. The pattern of migration was generally one of small, local moves from farm to village, village to town and town to city: although late in the nineteenth century a number of the very largest American cities experienced direct entry of peasant migrants from eastern and southern Europe. Migration generally involves young people, and it was the combination of high fertility and high mobility in essentially rural populations which accounted for the most dramatic instances of rapid nineteenth-century urbanization.

Richard Lawton (ed.), *The Rise and Fall of Great Cities* (London, 1989).
Adna Ferrin Weber, *The Growth of Cities in the Nineteenth Century* (Ithaca, NY, 1899).

SIMON PEPPER

Uruguay   During the period of Spanish American independence (*see* ARGENTINA) a separatist movement led by José Gervasio Artigas (1764– 1850) developed in Uruguay, the region situated on the eastern shore of the Plate estuary. Artigas was defeated by Portuguese forces from Brazil, backed by Buenos Aires, in 1820. Independence did not arrive until 1828 when the British mediated between Argentina and Brazil to create a buffer state.

Uruguay's political history was tumultuous. The *gaucho* (cowboy) and the mounted soldier were indistinguishable. Divisions between the Montevideo elite and landowners in the interior, among individual *caudillos*, and within the two principal parties, the *colorados* and *blancos*, were exacerbated by persistent interference from Argentina and Brazil. Only after 1876 did a succession of authoritarian *colorado* presidents, aided by technological developments in weapons and communications, begin to establish Montevideo's authority over the interior, the military giving way to civilian rulers in 1890.

Uruguay contained fertile but underpopulated pampas, and the civil wars delayed economic growth. After 1851, however, exports (jerked beef, hides, wool) began to increase, and from the 1860s foreign investment and immigration accelerated the process. By 1900 income per head was probably comparable to that of the United States, although the accumulation of wealth by landowners and foreign capitalists was impoverishing the rural masses.

RORY MILLER

Uthman dan Fodio (*b* Maratta, Gobir, 15 December 1754; *d* Sokoto, 20 April 1817). Revered west African Muslim leader, ruler of Hausaland. He was a Fulani, educated locally in traditional Islamic sciences; his piety, learning, charisma and simplicity early attracted attention, and even disciples. Deploring deficient Islamic faith and practice, particularly of the Hausa people, among whom the Fulani lived in what is roughly modern-day northern Nigeria, Uthman began preaching repentance and reform around 1774. Mystical experiences followed, such as the vision in 1794 in which the twelfth-century founder of the Qadiriyya Sufi brotherhood gave him the 'sword of truth'. Deteriorating relations with the Hausa ruler of Gobir prompted Uthman's hegira (1804), after which a revolutionary jihad commenced. Uthman sought to justify violence against backsliding, yet professing, fellow Muslims. A unified state, Fulani-dominated and dedicated to reformed Islam, with its capital at Sokoto, replaced the area's traditional Hausa kingdoms. Uthman's son MUHAMMAD BELLO succeeded him.

Mervyn Hiskett, *The Sword of Truth* (New York, 1973).

HUMPHREY J. FISHER

utilitarianism Popularly associated with the phrase 'the greatest happiness of the greatest number', which was probably first used by Francis Hutcheson (1694–1746), the doctrine arose primarily in late-eighteenth-century Britain in the writings of Hume (1711–76), Priestley (1733–1804), Revd. John Brown (1715–66), Godwin (1756–1836) and others. Its main argument was that actions were to be judged by their consequences, and were not themselves intrinsically right or wrong. Though utilitarianism has been understood as providing a secular religion like Comte's (1798–1857), some types of theological utilitarianism (for example William Paley's (1743–1805)) attempted to ground morality in divine command, not solely in happiness. In the nineteenth century the theory, sometimes also called philosophical radicalism, was especially linked to the writings of Jeremy Bentham (1748–1832) and his chief followers, a Scottish East India Company official, James Mill (1773–1836), and his precocious son John Stuart MILL.

Utilitarianism posited three main principles: (1) the notion, sometimes called psychological egoism, that all mankind was governed by the pursuit of pleasure and avoidance of pain; (2) the corollary that actions were to be judged good or otherwise not on the grounds of, for example, motive, but solely on the basis of consequences, specifically whether they produced pleasure and avoided pain for the individual as well as the community, defined in terms of the sum of individual interests; and (3) the notion that government and/or society should be so organized as to guarantee the greatest happiness of the population. The latter ideal in turn might be accomplished in part by a spontaneous harmony of interests, growing for example from the pursuit of self-interest in a market society; and/or by an artificial harmony of interests which reconciled individual and social happiness, enforced by legislators and systems of education, law and punishment.

Critics have argued that there is no necessary connection between the psychological fact of individuals desiring their own well-being and the more radical notion that societies must be judged by their capacity to provide for the needs of all. They have also pointed out that there may be a considerable distance between happiness based on our present desires, and that defined by desires which a more rational or perfect being might possess.

The chief initial development of the doctrine came with Bentham's *Introduction to the Principles of Morals and Legislation* (1776) and James Mill's *Essay on Government* (1819). Bentham emphasized that analysing the consequences of actions, and their tendency to produce pleasure, could be the only basis of a scientific approach to ethics which would supersede intuitionist, natural law, moral sense and other concepts of morality. Bentham's main aim was legal reform, and the construction of a code which would punish criminals according to the actual harm they did, rather than merely subjective perception. Accordingly, he sought a simple, quantitative measure for pleasure which made no fundamental distinction between, to use his famous example, push-pin and poetry. (Critics in turn contended that pleasures were fundamentally incommensurable and thus immeasurable.)

Neither Bentham nor James Mill ever clearly established why we should seek the happiness of others, however. It was left to J. S. Mill's *Utilitarianism* (1863), the most important mid-nineteenth-century exposition of the doctrine, to argue that society conditions us to associate our own happiness with that of others, whereby we learn to treat others' happiness as an end in itself rather than solely a means to our own happiness. Mill, however, innovated in one crucial way in his interpretation of the meaning of the utilitarian philosophy. Partly influenced by Macaulay's (1800–59) famous attack on his father in 1829, he conceded that the more materialistic hedonism associated with Bentham – the 'pig philosophy', as Carlyle termed it – was inadequate. Instead, seeking a defence of the ideal of self-cultivation and spiritual perfection, Mill proposed a distinction between 'higher' and 'lower' pleasures, by which the former were intrinsically more desirable than the latter. But this also implied against Bentham that each person was not necessarily the best judge of his or her own interest, since, Mill argued, only those who had experienced both higher and lower pleasures could understand the distinction clearly. This also meant (taking a cue from TOCQUEVILLE) that the pursuit of more vulgar pleasures might debase society generally and foster mental decline. Individuality, genius and creativity thus needed special protection against the pressures of social conformity, the case for which was central to *On Liberty* (1859).

It was J. S. Mill, in fact, who made virtually a 'religion' of the doctrine 'in one of the best senses of the word', as his *Autobiography* put it. In his youth, he founded a Utilitarian Society to debate his principles, and closely assisted his father in the editing of the *Westminister Review*, founded in 1824, which became the great organ of Benthamite RADICALISM. For by now, though Bentham had earlier wavered over the issue of democracy, utilitarianism was associated with demands for the extension of the franchise (and J. S. Mill, against his father and Bentham, urged that women possess the right as well); the abolition of parliamentary corruption, primogeniture and entail; the creation of a meritocratic society through educational reform and the provision of greater equality of opportunity; and the reform of aristocratic and monarchical abuses of all types. J. S. Mill remained a stalwart defender of David RICARDO's classical political-economy principles and freedom of trade until 1848, when he began to consider that a more co-operative, socialistic economy might some day prevail. Later he was much interested in land-tenure issues and conceded the case for land nationalization.

After Mill, utilitarianism continued to attract criticism, notably by James Fitzjames Stephen (1829–94), whose *Liberty, Equality, Fraternity* appeared in 1874. But it was also developed by, among others, the philosopher G. E. Moore (1873–1958), and has remained controversial in the twentieth century.

Elie Halevy, *The Growth of Philosophical Radicalism* (London, 1928).
Leslie Stephen, *The English Utilitarians*, 3 vols (London, 1900).

GREGORY CLAEYS

utopianism   The concept of 'utopianism' refers in the first instance to Thomas More's (1478–1535) *Utopia* (1516), which described an imaginary land where considerably greater social harmony and order and egalitarianism prevailed than in the England of More's time, and where property was held in common. From this period, it referred primarily to both literary texts that embodied ideals or models of a more perfect future or past society, and practical efforts to construct such a society. These were described as 'utopian' pejoratively by those who viewed such schemes as impossible or contrary to human nature; but also positively by those who viewed the utopian impulse as crucial to human progress and improvement. In the nineteenth century the concept referred initially to the writings and activities of Robert OWEN, Charles FOURIER, Henri de SAINT-SIMON, Etienne CABET and their followers, the so-called utopian socialists (*see* UTOPIAN SOCIALISM). Among this group, only Cabet wrote a literary utopia, the *Voyage en Icarie* (1840).

The concept was also applied to the other great literary utopias of the period, such as William MORRIS's *News from Nowhere* (1890), Edward Bellamy's (1850–98) *Looking Backward* (1888), Theodor Hertzka's *Freiland* (1890), H. G. Wells's (1866–1946) *When the Sleeper Awakes* (1899) and *A Modern Utopia* (1905). These described varied images of the future, socialist (Morris), 'nationalist' (Bellamy) and so on. It was their literary form which linked them as a genre rather than a specific programme. Many would include the writings of the most important nineteenth-century socialists, Karl Marx and Frederick Engels, in this category, owing to the seeming impossibility of establishing their ideal of communist society. Some would also add a few of the classic anarchist texts of this period, such as Max Stirner's (1806–56) *The Ego and its Own* (1845).

See also UTOPIAS.

Krishan Kumar, *Utopianism* (Milton Keynes, 1991).

GREGORY CLAEYS

utopian socialism The phrase 'utopian socialism', derived from Marxist sources and especially Frederick Engels's pamphlet *Socialism: Utopian and Scientific* (1880), is usually applied in two senses: first, to describe chronologically all forms of SOCIALISM prior to the 'scientific socialism' of MARX and ENGELS, and especially the writings of Cabet, Owen, Fourier, Saint-Simon and their followers (*see* UTOPIANISM); and secondly, to relegate these earlier forms of socialism to an inferior doctrinal status compared to MARXISM. The first meaning of the phrase is unproblematic, though 'early socialism' is a less ideological or tele-ological rendering of the chronological development of socialism. The second use refers primarily to three doctrines which Marx and Engels presumed separated them from their predecessors: (1) a historical analysis of the development of capitalism to a final stage of crisis which would result in a socialist revolution and the creation of a new communist society, as opposed to imaginative or 'utopian' portrayals (in reference to Thomas More's *Utopia*, 1516) of an ideal future society; (2) the belief that only the industrial proletariat or working class was capable of bringing about such a revolution, instead of a coalition of well-meaning philanthropists, labour reformers and the like; and (3) a willingness to use violence, instead of persuasion, to effect these ends. The case has been made that Marx and Engels's socialism is itself 'utopian' in the sense that the goal of a future communist society, with all property held in common, the alienation of labour superseded and economic specialization greatly reduced, is very unrealistic if not contrary to human nature.

George Lictheim, *The Origins of Socialism* (London, 1969).
Keith Taylor, *The Political Ideas of the Utopian Socialists* (London, 1982).

GREGORY CLAEYS

utopias The social and political upheavals of the nineteenth century prompted numerous proposals for idealized communities, and a much larger number of experiments – mostly short-lived – attempting to put such ideas into practice. The utopian literary tradition went back to Plato, the genre taking its name from Sir Thomas More's (1478–1535) *Utopia* (1516), its title derived from the Greek *ou topos*, no place. Religious freedoms, social reform and new economic regimes all featured in the nineteenth-century utopian prospectus and were often combined, particularly in the more radical co-operative experiments inspired by Charles FOURIER, notably Brook Farm in Massachusetts (1841–7), and the various sectarian communities established in North America (the Amana settlements in Iowa, the Shakers, the Onieda community in New York state). As the century wore on, the boundary between radical social experiments and reformist industrial and communal housing enterprises became increasingly blurred (*see* CO-OPERATION, SOCIAL HOUSING). Utopian idealism and enlightened self-interest yielded model factory villages and company towns throughout Europe and North America. Novels such as Edward Bellamy's (1850–98) *Looking Backward 2000–1887* (1888) and William MORRIS's *News from Nowhere* (1890) maintained the romantic tradition, satirized in Samuel Butler's (1835–1902) *Erewhon* (1872). The genre also yielded practical proposals such as Ebenezer Howard's (1850–1928) *Tomorrow: A Peaceful Path to Real Reform* (1898) which initiated the garden-city movement.

W. H. G. Armytage, *Heavens Below* (London, 1961).
John McKelvie Whitworth, *God's Blueprints: A Sociological Study of Three Utopian Sects* (London, 1975).
Lewis Mumford, *The Story of Utopias: Ideal Commonwealths and Social Myths* (London, 1923).

SIMON PEPPER

V

vaccination The discovery of immunization through vaccination is most commonly associated with the disease smallpox and the English physician Edward Jenner (1749–1823). He used material from the lesion of a bovine infection, cowpox, to confer immunity from a human disease, smallpox. This signalled a departure from the hazards of inoculation. With inoculation, a controlled dose of smallpox normally produced a minor, non-fatal infection resulting in immunity during later life. But since smallpox is a droplet contagion, it was also possible that the infected person could pass on the disease to another, if not actually develop a full-blown case.

The knowledge of Jenner's discovery, after its publication in 1798, was rapidly disseminated on an international scale and vaccinations had been performed in most European countries and the United States by 1800. Spain actually sent out vaccination teams to Mexico in 1803. Voluntary vaccination was common, but it gradually became compulsory in a number of European countries: Bavaria (1807), Norway and Denmark (1810), Russia (1812), Baden (1815), Sweden (1816) and England and Wales (1853). But prosecutions under what was often defective legislation were not always enacted, and a final major smallpox epidemic struck Europe as late as the 1870s.

Vaccination should be studied in the particular political context of central–local relations. In some cases, it provided the first state-run, comprehensive public-health activity. For example, in Sweden the national medical board established a number of vaccination depots as early as 1803. In England and Wales, vaccination was eventually provided free through the Poor Law. But antivaccination movements everywhere riled against compulsory measures and retarded their effectiveness. It was claimed that compulsory vaccination bypassed local feeling and represented an imposition by central government on individual freedom.

Despite this, smallpox vaccination had important implications for the overall decline of mortality and the rise of population during the second half of the nineteenth century, though the exact contribution to this improvement remains an area of contentious debate.

See also THEORIES OF DISEASE, PUBLIC HEALTH.

GRAHAM MOONEY

Van Buren, Martin (*b* Kinderhook, New York, 5 December 1782; *d* Kinderhook, 24 July 1862)　President of the United States (1837–41). He formed one of the nation's earliest political machines, the Albany Regency, during the early 1820s. Like other politicians of his generation, Van Buren saw politics as a profession, rather than a hobby for only the landed elite. Throwing his support behind Andrew JACKSON in 1828, he used his organizing ability to carry the election for Jackson. During the Jackson administration he became the president's main adviser or, in the eyes of some, evil genius. Outmanœuvring John C. Calhoun, he replaced the South Carolinian as vice-president in 1832. As Jackson's hand-picked successor, he won the presidential election in 1836. He accomplished little as president because of the Panic of 1837. Beaten by the Whigs in 1840, he failed to gain renomination in 1844 because he opposed the annexation of Texas, and in 1848 he ran as the antislavery Free-soil candidate (*see* FREE-SOIL PARTY).

John Niven, *Martin Van Buren: The Romantic Age of American Politics* (New York, 1983).

ALICE E. REAGAN

Vanderbilt, Cornelius (*b* Port Richmond, New York, 27 May 1794; *d* New York, 4 January 1877)　American financier. He began building his huge fortune by gaining control of the shipping routes along the New York coast, then opening a route from New York to California in the early 1850s. Using capital from his shipping interests, the 'Commodore' Vanderbilt became an early railroad magnate. He acquired control of the New York Central and extended his empire by purchasing numerous smaller railways, unifying them into one profitable network. His epic battle with Daniel Drew (1797–1879) for control of the Erie Railroad drew national attention. Vanderbilt's estate totalled $100 million when he died. Prudent as well as bold, he was one of the first modern American captains of industry, though his query 'What do I care about the law? Hain't I got the power?' was a singular comment on the ruthless business practices of the GILDED AGE.

KEVIN MURPHY

venereal disease　Gonorrhoea was widely known in Europe and was acknowledged to be spread through sexual intercourse, its symptoms being clearly identified in many of the regulations relating to the control of brothels in fourteenth-century France and Italy. Two things confused the picture by the nineteenth century. First, the devastating epidemics of a lethal strain of syphilis in the early fifteenth century eclipsed the old practices relating to the causes and treatment of gonorrhoea. Over time the balance between syphilis and its human host changed, and by the nineteenth century the disease was a self-limiting infection which was rarely fatal and cleared up in a few years. However, this milder experience of syphilis served further to confuse the issue when, in 1767, John Hunter (1728–93), the great student of the circulation of the blood, inoculated himself with matter from a gonorrhoeal patient and contracted both syphilis and gonorrhoea since, unknown to him, the patient was suffering from both. Hunter's claim that the two diseases were identical stood until Phillipe Ricord (1800–89) inoculated 2,500 patients with gonnorhoeal discharges without producing syphilis in any and concluded, in 1838, that the diseases were distinct.

The treatment of venereal disease was very limited. On the theory that one violent action was needed to drive out another, people were persuaded to swallow or apply mercury, since the salivation which resulted would drive out the humoral affliction of the venereal disease. The discomfort which the therapy produced was, it seemed, no more than the sinful deserved. Preventive measures were largely restricted to the regulation of PROSTITUTION through such measures as the CONTAGIOUS DISEASES ACTS. In the early 1880s Karl Sigmund Franz Crede (1819–92) showed that a silver-nitrate solution dropped into the eyes of newborn babies would prevent the blindness with which the gonorrhoeal discharges of the mother sometimes afflicted the baby.

Allan M. Brandt, *No Magic Bullet: A Social History of Venereal Disease in the United States since 1880* (Oxford, 1985).

GERRY KEARNS

Venezuela In 1829 Venezuela left the Federation of Gran Colombia (*see* BOLIVAR, BATTLE OF CARABOBO). José Antonio Páez (1790–1873), the *caudillo* who led the secession, dominated the country for almost twenty years. However, Venezuela had few stable exports (coffee, the most important, periodically experienced severe crises), and regional and social differences were profound. Rebellion and civil war were thus endemic. In 1848 Páez was exiled by José Tadeo Monagas (1784–1868), whom he had nominated as president. The corrupt rule of the Monagas brothers was ended by the Federal Wars of 1858–63, but order was not restored until Antonio Guzmán Blanco (1829–99) took power in 1870. Despite two significant revolts against him, Guzmán Blanco re-mained in control for almost two decades by skilfully manipulating the regional *caudillos* and repressing the opposition, but he also attempted to modernize the country by improving communications and stimulating foreign trade and investment. When he relinquished power in 1887, regional and personal rivalries brought a return of disorder, only partially alleviated by the presidency (1892–8) of General Joaquín Crespo (1845–98).

J. V. Lombardi, *Venezuela: The Search for Order, the Dream of Progress* (New York, 1982).

RORY MILLER

Verona, Congress of *see* CONGRESS SYSTEM.

Victor Emmanuel II (*b* Turin, Piedmont, 14 March 1820; *d* Rome, 9 January 1878)　King of Sardinia-Piedmont (1849–61) and Italy (1861–78). A prince of the house of Savoy, he accepted the constitution of 1848 granted by his father. Although a constitutional monarch, he retained much power, especially his prerogative in military and foreign affairs. Overseeing the unification of ITALY in 1861, Victor Emmanuel was proclaimed the first 'king of Italy' but continued in the Piedmontese style as Victor Emmanuel 'II', obscuring whether this was a new Italian monarchy or simply an enlarged Piedmont. A brash and bellicose monarch, he sought to improve Italy's reputation through war and was, therefore, often at odds with his ministers. After his unexpected death, he was hailed throughout Europe in hagiography as a great ruler and unifier of Italy.

Denis Mack Smith, *Victor Emmanuel, Cavour, and the Risorgimento* (London, 1971).

LAWRENCE P. ADAMCZYK

Victoria (*b* London, 24 May 1819; *d* Osborne, 22 January 1901) Queen of Great Britain and Ireland (1837–1901). Her long reign co-incided with Britain's industrial and imperial hegemony. Victoria scrupulously carried out her monarchical duties and took an informed interest in the details of governance. Her views influenced government policy through the 1890s. Happily married to Prince ALBERT of Saxe-Coburg and the mother of nine children, Victoria in her family life embodied the values of domesticity idealized during the nineteenth century. Her withdrawal from public life after the death of Prince Albert in 1861, however, provoked some hostility towards the institution of monarchy. This began to dissipate during the 1870s with Disraeli's tactful creation of a new title, 'empress of India', for her. By the end of her life, Victoria's name had become synonymous with the central values and characteristics of her time.

Elizabeth Longford, *Queen Victoria: Born to Succeed* (London, 1965).

GAIL SAVAGE

Vienna, Congress of (September 1814–June 1815)　To end the wars against Revolutionary and Napoleonic France, the victorious allies called the Congress of Vienna. Delegates from France and all the states that had fought Napoleon were represented at the congress, but the principal negotiators were Metternich (Austria), Hardenberg and Humboldt (Prussia), Castlereagh and Wellington (Great Britain) and Tsar Alexander I (Russia). When the allies became deadlocked over the Saxon–Polish dispute and war was threatened, Austria and Britain brought the French foreign minister, Talleyrand, into the negotiations and agreement was finally reached on 8 June 1815.

The congress approved the final peace treaty with France (limiting it to its 1792 borders, with some minor additional territorial adjustments in the north-east and in Savoy), established a GERMAN CONFEDERATION to take the place of the Holy Roman Empire, awarded Austria and Prussia some additional territories (Lombardy and Venetia to the former and Posen, Danzig, Pomerania and part of the west bank of the Rhine to the latter), gave the former grand duchy of Warsaw (renamed Congress POLAND) to Russia, re-established Switzerland as an independent confederation and restored the legitimate dynasties to the thrones of Spain, Sardinia, Tuscany, Modena, the Papal States and Naples.

The terms of the Congress of Vienna endured for almost fifty years, and Europe avoided a general war for nearly a century thereafter. A hundred years later, the British looked back to the Congress of Vienna in the hope that it would serve as a model for the Paris Peace Conference of 1919, but the intensely nationalistic strivings of the many participants at the latter made any attempt to replicate the earlier congress futile.

D. Dakin, 'The Congress of Vienna 1814–15, and its Antecedents', in Alan Sked (ed.), *Europe's Balance of Power* (New York, 1979), pp. 14–33.
H. Nicolson, *The Congress of Vienna* (New York, 1946).

GEORGE O. KENT

Vogel, Sir Julius (*b* London, 24 February 1835; *d* East Molesey, Surrey, 12 March 1899)   New Zealand statesman. Regarded as New Zealand's first statesman, he was prime minister (1873–5, 1876) and New Zealand agent-general in London (1876–81). Born into a Jewish merchant family, he combined gold-prospecting and journalism, first in Australia and then in Otago. He became colonial treasurer of New Zealand in 1869 and, at a time of severe economic depression, expanded the colony's economy and infrastructure (especially railways), mainly by borrowing for public works. His immigration schemes helped to double New Zealand's population during the 1870s. However, borrowing power and prosperity failed in 1887 and, highly unpopular, Vogel retired to England.

Raewyn Dalziel, *Julius Vogel: Business Politician* (Auckland, 1986).

MICHAEL C. PUGH

Wahhabis A puritanical Islamic sect based on the Hanbali school of Sunni Islamic jurisprudence, the Wahhabi movement arose in northern Arabia around 1750 when its missionary founder, Muhammad ibn Abd al-Wahhab (1703–92), formed an alliance with the tribal chief Muhammad ibn Saud to uproot what they regarded as corrupt practices in contemporary Islam. Gathering adherents among the tribes of Arabia, Saudi-led armies attacked not only local shrines and tombs but the pilgrimage caravans to Mecca, killing without mercy. In 1801 they destroyed the Shi'ite holy city of Karbala and in 1803–4 captured Mecca and Medina. Although the Wahhabis were especially antagonistic toward Shi'ism, their chief political adversary was the Sunni Ottoman Empire, the nominal sovereigns of Arabia and guardians of Islam's holy places. Ottoman efforts to re-establish order in the peninsula were unsuccessful until the armies of their Egyptian viceroy, MUHAMMAD ALI, scattered the Wahhabi forces and captured the Saudi Prince Abdullah in 1818. Abdullah was executed and the Wahhabi brethren were forced to retreat to the interior. In 1902, again as champions of Wahhabi puritanism, the Saudis began their drive to conquer Arabia. The task was completed after the first World War, when the Saudi kingdom was proclaimed with Wahhabism as its official faith.

John Voll, *Islam: Continuity and Change in the Modern World* (Boulder, Colo.,1982).

MADELINE C. ZILFI

Waitangi, Treaty of (1840) The poorly drafted Treaty of Waitangi remains a controversial symbol of NEW ZEALAND race relations and national identity. In the late 1830s Britain decided to legitimize, through the consent of Maori chiefs, British sovereignty over New Zealand, and to regulate land purchases by speculators and the New Zealand

Company. As lieutenant-governor designate, Captain William Hobson RN (1793–1842) wrote the text in the Bay of Islands in consultation with missionaries and the British resident. Imperfectly translated overnight, it was signed by northern chiefs on 6 February 1840 and then hawked around the country. It contained ambiguities and contradictions regarding the transfer of sovereignty to the crown; guarantees of Maori chieftainship over lands, settlements and possessions; the crown's pre-emptive right to buy Maori land; and the extension of British-subject status to the Maoris. (*See* MAORI WARS.)

I. K. Kawharu (ed.), *Waitangi* (Auckland, 1989).
Claudia Orange, *The Treaty of Waitangi* (Wellington, 1987).

MICHAEL C. PUGH

Wakefield, Edward Gibbon (*b* London, 20 March 1796; *d* Wellington, New Zealand, 18 May 1862)   Colonization theorist, land speculator and colonial politician. His early diplomatic career was marred by his three-year term in Newgate prison for abducting a schoolgirl heiress. He wrote *A Letter from Sydney* (1829) in Newgate, and subsequently *A View of the Art of Colonization* (1849), to advocate colonial land sales as a way of financing systematic emigration. He founded the National Colonization Society in 1830 and influenced the development of Canada, Australia and New Zealand. He became an adviser to Lord Durham (1792–1840) in 1838 and was elected to Canada's legislative assembly. After directing the New Zealand Company and promoting the Canterbury settlement, he arrived in New Zealand in 1853 where he briefly entered politics. A power-hungry intriguer, usually in conflict with officialdom, Wakefield agitated for self-governing colonies in which labourers would buy land and speculators prosper.

MICHAEL C. PUGH

Waldeck-Rousseau, Pierre Marie (*b* Nantes, 2 December 1846; *d* Corbeil, 10 August 1904)   French politician. A barrister by training, he entered the chamber of deputies in 1879 and served as minister of the interior under Gambetta and Ferry. He was responsible for the law of 1884 which bears his name legalizing trade unions. After over 200 anti-Semitic and anti-Dreyfusard riots had broken out in France and Algeria, he formed a government of republican defence in June 1899 which included a broad spectrum of republican opinion, including the socialist Millerand. His government arranged a pardon for DREYFUS in the hopes of diffusing the affair. He also removed the remaining restrictions on freedom of association, except for religious congregations.

DONALD SUTHERLAND

warfare   The art of war was transformed in the nineteenth century. In 1800 its technology remained characterized by the smooth-bore musket and cannon on land and the wooden sailing ship at sea, but by 1900 the industrial revolution had long since ushered in a new age. Before that could occur, however, the military establishments of Europe were provided with a model that was to remain influential throughout the century. Between 1800 and 1815 Europe was dominated by the military might of France, and, in particular, the genius of Napoleon (*see* Napoleon BONAPARTE). Thanks to the new-found ability of the French to field large armies, the guiding principle of land warfare became, not the manœuvre of the eighteenth century, but the decisive battle, the object being to seek out and destroy the main concentration of the enemy's strength. Indeed, it was not until his adversaries succeeded in bettering Napoleon's mastery of this art that he was finally overcome.

Yet, decisive though the influence of Napoleon was, military thinkers were divided on his message. For the Swiss theorist Jomini (1779–1869), battles were decided by the movements that proceeded them. Manœuvre therefore retained a great importance, Jomini in consequence favouring the small professional army. By contrast, the Prussian, Karl von Clausewitz (1780–1831), argued that what mattered was mass (in that the greater the mass the greater the chance of destroying the enemy). Underlying these differences was a more fundamental point: whereas Jomini dreamed of the limited wars of the eighteenth century, Clausewitz seemed to presage an age in which war would aim at the complete subjugation of the enemy through the total mobilization of the nation and all its resources.

The industrial revolution ensured that war did indeed tend to become total. From the Napoleonic wars onwards, technological advances brought great changes to the battlefield. Field guns grew more powerful, while the rifled percussion musket replaced the old smooth-bore flintlock, and these developments alone soon rendered the relatively small quasi-professional armies still retained by most states obsolete. Though Napoleonic warfare enjoyed one last 'hurrah' in the Franco-Austrian war of 1859, in the CRIMEAN WAR of 1854–6 the Franco-British armies that attacked Sevastopol found themselves bogged down in a trench warfare that they simply did not have the strength to sustain. And in the AMERICAN CIVIL WAR of 1861–5, not to mention the even more terrible PARAGUAYAN WAR of 1864–70, even relatively poorly armed and badly outnumbered states were able to hold greatly superior adversaries at bay for several years at the cost to both sides of appalling casualties. War, in short, seemed likely to become a matter of attrition and total mobilization.

Meanwhile, the latter was in turn being rendered more attainable by the acceleration of industrialization: not only could factories produce all the physical requirements of warfare in ever-greater quantity but railways facilitated reliance on mass armies. Weapons grew still more powerful: by 1870 European armies were armed with breech-loading rifles, the first machine-guns, and artillery that in striking power and range far outclassed anything seen hitherto. Nevertheless, the generals remained mesmerized by the decisive battle. In 1866 and 1870 exceptional circumstances – essentially the technical imbalance that existed between the Prussians and their adversaries – had produced such victories at Sadowa and Sedan (see AUSTRO-PRUSSIAN WAR, FRANCO-PRUSSIAN WAR), and from then on the main aim of all commanders was to replicate them in a future war. Universal CONSCRIPTION was introduced in most European states and, in the face of the still more deadly weapons that were being introduced, it was argued that numbers and élan would prevail. It was not to be, of course: though few perceived it in 1900, a future European – or world – war was likely to be a stalemate that would be resolved by industrial muscle.

Finally, if naval matters have not featured here, it is because the character of a future conflict was decided by developments in land warfare. In brief, however, the introduction of steam propulsion and armour-plating produced a naval race that lasted throughout the nineteenth century and ultimately neutralized the battle-fleet as a factor of decisive importance. Though few admirals accepted it, by 1900 the future belonged to weapons of blockade – above all, the submarine and the torpedo – thus reinforcing the likelihood of a war of attrition. (See NAVIES.)

H. Strachan, *European Armies and the Conduct of War* (London, 1983).

CHARLES ESDAILE

War of 1812 (1812–1814)   In June 1812, ostensibly because of the British disregard of commercial neutrality and the impressment of American sailors, Congress declared war on Britain. In addition, western and southern congressmen believed that Britain was instigating native-American troubles (see TECUMSEH) and that in a war with Britain the United States could acquire territory in Canada and Florida. Although American privateers struck early at the British, by 1813 the Royal Navy had control over the American coastline. Although the Americans scored minor victories in Canada and on the Great Lakes, the British invaded and burned Washington, DC, forcing President James Madison to flee. Weeks after the TREATY OF GHENT (1814), which ended the war but left unresolved the disputes between the two nations, General Andrew JACKSON's forces – unaware of the treaty – soundly defeated the British at New Orleans, redeeming the country's battered pride and turning Jackson into a national hero.

JOHN MARTIN

War of the Castes (1847–1855)   The Yucatán peninsula in the early nineteenth century was peopled by a small 'white' landowning elite and an indigenous population descended from the Maya. Growing exports of henequen (sisal) put the region into closer contact with New Orleans than the national capital. From 1835 it was effectively independent of MEXICO. Labour conditions on the henequen plantations, though, were harsh, and the elite failed to keep its bargain with the Mayan leaders, who had supplied troops to defend the state, over the reduction of church fees, the abolition of the head tax and access to public land. A full-scale ethnic revolt, which began in 1847, devastated the plantations and confined the terrified whites to a few towns. Their request for annexation into the United States was rejected, and they relied on Mexican troops, after the Mexican-American War had ended, to suppress the rebellion in exchange for reincorporation into Mexico.

RORY MILLER

War of the Pacific (1879–1883) The origins of the War of the Pacific, fought by CHILE against PERU and BOLIVIA, lay in the growth of nitrate production in the disputed Atacama Desert, and the *casus belli* in Bolivian attempts to tax the Chilean-owned Antofagasta Nitrate and Railway Company. In February 1879, frustrated by the company's resistance, Bolivia cancelled its concession. Chile occupied Antofagasta and two months later declared war on Peru, claiming that Peru had encouraged Bolivia in order to protect its own nitrate interests from competition.

Bolivian forces were irrelevant. The outcome depended on the clash between Chilean and Peruvian warships (the first significant conflict between ironclads). After Chile's victory at Angamos in October 1879, the Peruvian coast was left undefended. Chilean forces captured Peru's nitrate resources and then, in January 1881, Lima itself. However, although the Peruvian state had collapsed, the Chileans faced increasing resistance from guerrillas in the Andean highlands. In October 1883 they negotiated the Treaty of Ancón with Miguel Iglesias (1830–1909), one of three rival presidents, who recognized Chile's annexation of the nitrate region. A formal armistice with Bolivia, which had lost its access to the Pacific Ocean as a result of the war, was not agreed until 1904.

William F. Sater, *Chile and the War of the Pacific* (Lincoln, Nebr., 1986).

RORY MILLER

Washington, Booker Taliaferro (*b* Hale's Ford, Virginia, 5 April 1856; *d* Tuskegee, Alabama, 14 November 1915) African-American educationist. The son of a black slave and a white father, he was educated at Hampton Institute. He founded Tuskegee Institute as an industrial school (1881), where he served as principal. At Tuskegee he preached a doctrine of thrift, sobriety and self-reliance. One of the most influential

African-American leaders of his time, Washington argued in his address at the Atlanta Exposition in 1895 that economic equality for AFRICAN-AMERICANS would inevitably lead to social equality. He urged them to acquire their own homes, to enter business when possible and to rely on the trades to become economically indispensable. His acceptance of temporary racial segregation, welcomed by southern and northern whites alike, was challenged by younger African-American intellectuals such as W. E. B. Du Bois (1868–1963), who urged more immediate equality and civil rights through higher education of a 'talented tenth' of the African-American population.

KEVIN MURPHY

Waterloo, Battle of (18 June 1815) The duke of WELLINGTON's greatest victory, Waterloo has been described as the classic decisive battle, and as such influenced military thought throughout the nineteenth century. Returning from exile on Elba, Napoleon (*see* Napoleon BONAPARTE) attacked the allied Anglo-Dutch and Prussian armies in Belgium in the hope of securing a rapid victory that would overawe the great powers. With the French badly outnumbered, success depended on separating the allies and keeping them divided, but Napoleon was in poor health and poorly served by his subordinates. An early victory over Blücher's (1742–1819) Prussians at Ligny was not fully exploited, and, when Wellington's troops were attacked in the strong defensive position they had adopted near the village of Waterloo, Blücher was able to march to their aid. By the time his forces were fully deployed, however, the French had spent themselves in a series of fruitless attacks, and, following the repulse of the imperial guard, collapsed in rout, Napoleon subsequently being forced to surrender.

CHARLES ESDAILE

Webb, Sidney (*b* London, 13 July 1855; *d* Passfield Corner, Hampshire, 13 October 1947) and **Webb, Beatrice** (*b* Standish House, Gloucester, 22 January 1858; *d* Passfield Corner, Hampshire, 30 April 1943) English writers, politicians and historians, dedicated to collectivist social reform. Married in 1892 and best conceived of as a partnership, the Webbs were leading participants in the late-nineteenth-century socialist revival. Their socialism, however, was distinguished by its elitism, aversion to trade-unionism and links to Benthamite utilitarianism. Advocates of state intervention and municipal reform, the Webbs and their associates in the FABIAN SOCIETY believed that existing institutions allowed for the evolutionary development of SOCIALISM. The Webbs sought to influence public policy with their professional expertise, infiltrating existing political parties. After the First World War, however, Sidney in particular played a notable role in Labour Party politics. As part of their reform agenda, they also pioneered the historical study of English institutions and founded the London School of Economics.

RICHARD J. SODERLUND

Webster, Daniel (*b* Salisbury, New Hampshire, 18 January 1782; *d* Marshfield, Massachusetts, 24 October 1852)   American statesman and orator. The greatest of the ante-bellum orators, he began his career as a Federalist who opposed the War of 1812. Gradually, he became a consistent supporter of the union and nationalism, first emerging as a spokesman for national supremacy during the Webster–Hayne Debate (1830), in which he condemned the idea of nullification (*see* NULLIFICATION CRISIS). Serving as secretary of state (1841–3), he negotiated the Webster-Ashburton Treaty (1842) settling the boundary of Maine. Returned to the Senate, he supported Clay's COMPROMISE OF 1850, which angered many of his constituents. Webster, like Clay and Calhoun, sought but never won the presidency. Just before his death he broke with the Whigs, because their candidate in 1852, Winfield Scott (1786–1866), refused to endorse the Compromise of 1850. As a protest, some southern Whigs voted for him in November, although he had died in October.

Robert F. Dalzell, *Daniel Webster and the Trial of American Nationalism, 1843–1852* (Boston, 1972).

ALICE E. REAGAN

Wellington, Arthur Wellesley, duke of (*b* Dublin, 1 May 1769; *d* Walmer Castle, Kent, 14 September 1852)   British soldier, statesman and, ultimately, national institution. He joined the army in 1787, serving in Ireland, Flanders and India. Returning to England in 1805, he served in the Portland administration, before fighting in Denmark and then, most famously, the Peninsular War, winning a series of victories against the French, and eventually invading France. Following Napoleon's abdication, Wellington served as British representative at the CONGRESS OF VIENNA and then commanded the Anglo-Dutch army at the BATTLE OF WATERLOO. There followed a long series of military and civil appointments, including two periods as prime minister, the first of which was distinguished by Catholic emancipation. Despite this, however, Wellington on the whole remained a rigid conservative, and it is in this light that his later career is largely remembered.

CHARLES ESDAILE

Whig Party (1834–1853)   Organized as the opposition to President Andrew JACKSON, the Whigs were the brainchild of Henry CLAY of Kentucky. Adopting his economic programme, the 'American System', as their platform, the Whigs called for a weak executive and a harmonious society. Whigs believed in inequality, but also thought that everyone had their place in society. Believing that men must learn to control their emotions and vices in order to succeed, they promoted education, temperance and other reforms. In the north many were middle-class Evangelicals with commercial ties. They found allies in the south among large planters and mercantile city-dwellers. Although they managed to elect only two presidents, William Henry HARRISON (1840) and Zachary TAYLOR (1848), they provided a viable alternative to the Democrats during the Second Party System. Despite their best efforts, the Whigs failed to withstand pressures over the expansion of slavery, and collapsed after the election of 1852 when their candidate refused to endorse the COMPROMISE OF 1850.

Daniel Walker Howe, *The Political Culture of the American Whigs* (Chicago, 1979).

ALICE E. REAGAN

Whigs A group of intermarried aristocratic families centred around the Bedfords, Russells, Devonshires, Granvilles, Spencers and Westminsters, the Whigs dominated nineteenth-century liberal politics (*see* LIBERALISM) until the late 1860s. Whiggism was more a philosophy of governing than a political ideology. Whigs were patrician leaders who traced their political lineage to the role their families had played in the Glorious Revolution of 1688 and whose commitment to constitutional and religious liberties allowed them to reconcile political change with political and social stability. They were not democrats, but believed that the aristocracy ruled in trust for the people. The Whigs were not a political party – there were few back-bench Whigs – but an interrelated leadership whose connections with the commercial interests of the City of London, part of the provincial manufacturing elite and Old Dissent allowed them to serve as intermediaries between the parliamentary and public political worlds. Whigs held an uneasy relationship to middle-class liberalism because of their greater sympathy for an interventionist central government.

In the early nineteenth century, after many years out of power, the demand for constitutional reform in the 1830s gave the Whigs the chance to recapture the political initiative. They co-operated with the Benthamites and middle-class radicals to carry the Reform Bill of 1832 (*see* PARLIAMENTARY REFORM), the NEW POOR LAW, the Municipal Corporations Act and other reforms designed to reconcile constitutional change with the preservation of aristocratic hierarchy. They were sympathetic to the need for factory reform (and passed the first Factory Act in 1833) and in the 1840s supported attempts at public-health reform. Although this style of Whiggism was displaced after the early 1850s, they remained a key group in the emerging Liberal Party until the late 1860s when the growing democratization of politics destroyed the possibility of patrician rule. The final break with liberalism came over Irish HOME RULE in 1886.

Peter Mandler, *Aristocratic Government in the Age of Reform: Whigs and Liberals, 1830–1852* (Oxford, 1990).
Donald Southgate, *The Passing of the Whigs 1832–1886* (London, 1962).

RICHARD PRICE

Whiteboys *see* RIBBONISM.

Whitney, Eli (*b* Westborough, Massachusetts, 1765; *d* 8 December New Haven, Connecticut, 8 January 1825) American inventor. After graduation from Yale, he sought a teaching position in Georgia where he could read law, but this failed to materialize. Instead, he became tutor to the late General Nathanael Greene's (1742–86) children. At the Greene plantation he invented the cotton gin (1793), a device that cleaned the seeds from short-staple cotton with great efficiency, overcoming a barrier to cotton production. Before this, sticky green seeds made the cotton time-consuming to clean, limiting profits. After the creation of the gin, cotton spread throughout the lower south, taking slavery with it. Newly profitable, slavery was preserved. Returning to New England, Whitney made a contract with the government to manufacture 10,000 muskets (1798). In order to meet his quota, Whitney introduced dies that produced interchangeable parts, creating the principles for the machine-tools industry.

Constance M. Green, *Eli Whitney and the Birth of American Technology* (Boston, 1956).

ALICE E. REAGAN

Wilberforce, William (*b* Hull, Yorkshire, 24 August 1759; *d* London, 29 July 1833) Evangelical politician. Born into a prosperous commercial family and educated at St John's College, Cambridge, he sat as member of parliament for Hull (1780–4), Yorkshire (1784–1812) and Bramber, Sussex (1812–25). During 1784–5 he was converted to Evangelicalism, for which his book, *A Practical View* (1797), was an apologia. From 1789 he led the parliamentary campaign against the slave trade, which was formally abolished in 1807. Thereafter he pressed for enforcement of the ban, for European agreement to prohibit the trade and for improvement of the conditions of slaves in British territories. As the leader of the CLAPHAM SECT, he urged moral reform and the defence of Evangelical interests. A loyal Tory, he skilfully deployed his charm, tact and influence with other politicians to further the causes in which he believed.

John Pollock, *Wilberforce* (London, 1977).

D. W. BEBBINGTON

William I (*b* Berlin, 22 March 1797; *d* Berlin, 9 March 1888) Emperor of Germany. He succeeded to the Prussian throne in 1861 after acting as regent for his brother Frederick-William IV since 1857. Devoted to military traditions, and rarely seen out of military uniform, he sought to embody 'Prussian virtues' of loyalty to duty and unsparing asceticism. He had opposed all concessions to liberalism in the 1840s, but later adapted, within limits, to an age of constitutional politics and of rising German national aspirations. William's personal role in policy-making diminished after he appointed Otto von BISMARCK as minister-president in 1862 to resolve the constitutional crisis in Prussia. Despite his suspicions of Bismarck's adventurism and fears concerning the fate of Prussia in a united Germany, he supported the wars engineered by Bismarck which were to bring German unification in 1870–1 (*see* UNIFICATION OF GERMANY). After accepting, with some qualms, the title of emperor of Germany, he went on to function as an important integrative symbol of the new German nation-state.

ELIZABETH HARVEY

William II (*b* Berlin, 27 January 1859; *d* Doorn, Holland, 4 June 1941) Emperor of Germany. The grandson of William I, he succeeded his father, Frederick III (1831–88), as emperor when Frederick died in June 1888 following a three-month reign. William's fanatical belief in his unlimited powers as a monarch was matched by a violent and erratic temperament, possibly associated with brain damage and physical disability sustained at birth. Unlike William I, he was not content to leave policy-making to his ministers; he dismissed Bismarck in March 1890 and by 1900 had gone a long way towards implementing a system of personal rule. Seeking to establish Germany as a world power, William backed the building of a massive navy to rival that of Britain, and pressed on his ministers an aggressive foreign policy which provoked conflicts with other colonial powers. Following Germany's defeat in the First World War, William abdicated in November 1918 and went into exile in Holland.

ELIZABETH HARVEY

William IV (*b* London, 21 August 1765; *d* Windsor, 20 June 1837) King of Great Britain and Ireland (1830–7). A naval man who enjoyed a twenty-year liaison with an actress who bore him ten children, William, third son of George III (1738–1820), settled down to a quiet family life with Adelaide (1792–1849) of Saxe-Coburg-Meiningen whom he married in 1818. On succeeding his brother George IV in 1830, he displayed sound political sense, using his influence to secure the passage of the Reform Bill, thereby enhancing the popularity of the monarchy. Relations with the WHIGS deteriorated thereafter, not to the queen's displeasure. William dismissed MELBOURNE in 1834, the last such act by a British monarch, but when PEEL failed to secure a parliamentary majority, the king was compelled to reinstate the Whigs. By the time of his death, when he was succeeded by his niece Victoria, his two legitimate daughters having died in infancy, the monarchy was seemingly declining in popularity and power.

JOHN BELCHEM

Windischgrätz, Prince Alfred (*b* Brussels, 11 May 1787; *d* Vienna, 21 March 1862) Austrian general. Born in the then Austrian Netherlands, he grew up in Bohemia and Vienna. In 1804 he entered the army, and by the end of the Napoleonic wars he was the commander of a regiment. In command of the army in Bohemia by 1840, he was the conservative choice to restore order in the early days of the 1848 revolution in Vienna. Foiled by the new revolutionary ministry, Windischgrätz withdrew, only to join his army in Bohemia. In June he took the opportunity of a revolt in Prague to launch a counter-revolution, first subduing Prague, and then, in October, subduing Vienna after a further revolt there, in effect ending the revolution. Windischgrätz's next move was against the Hungarians, but his failure quickly to subdue the Hungarian revolutionaries led to his resignation as commander-in-chief in April 1849, and his retirement from public life. (*See* REVOLUTIONS OF 1848.)

STEVEN BELLER

Wiseman, Nicholas Patrick Stephen (*b* Seville, 2 August 1802; *d* London, 15 February 1865) English cardinal. Descended from an Irish merchant family and educated at Ushaw, County Durham and Rome, he became a Syriac scholar and rector of the English College at Rome (1828–40), co-adjutor to Bishop Thomas Walsh in the Central district and president of Oscott College (1840–7) and pro-vicar apostolic and vicar apostolic of the London district (1847–50). In 1850 he was appointed the first cardinal archbishop of Westminster at the head of a restored English Catholic hierarchy, and recast the Roman Catholic Church in England in the ultramontane model of the Church in Rome. A universal polymath who was good at everything except administration, he shaped the Catholic revival stemming from a vast increase in Irish immigration and from a wave of educated converts from the Church of England, notably Henry Edward MANNING and John Henry NEWMAN.

Richard J. Schiefen, *Nicholas Wiseman and the Transformation of English Catholicism* (Shepherdstown, W. Va., 1984).

SHERIDAN GILLEY

Wolseley, Garnet Joseph, Viscount (*b* Golden Bridge, Ireland, 4 June 1833; *d* Mentone, France, 26 March 1913) British field marshal. After an early career in Burma, China, the Crimean War and the

Indian Mutiny, his logistical brilliance in putting down Riel's (1844–85) rebellion in Manitoba (1871) established him as Britain's leading soldier. His staff officers in this campaign became known as the 'Wolseley Ring' and were to form the leadership of the late-Victorian army. Later campaigns included the Ashanti War (1874), the defeat of Arabi Pasha in Egypt (1881), and the abortive attempt to rescue Gordon in 1884. His work as quartermaster-general (1880), adjutant-general (1882) and commander-in-chief (1895–1901) was marked by modernizing reforms. Satirized by Gilbert and Sullivan in *The Pirates of Penzance* as the 'very model of a modern major-general', he is best known for his command of armies in imperial wars and his meticulous organizational methods. He was also the author of the manual of military conduct *The Soldier's Pocket Book*.

RICHARD PRICE

Women's Christian Temperance Union Founded by American women in 1874, the Women's Christian Temperance Union (WCTU) became one of the most important reform organizations of the Gilded Age. TEMPERANCE appealed to many evangelical women because they believed that consumption of alcohol fostered domestic violence and absorbed families' scarce financial resources. Arguing that women could protect their homes from these threats and thus fulfil their duties as wives and mothers only by joining the public fight for temperance legislation, leaders of the WCTU drew thousands of women into their organization and concomitantly into political life. Indeed, from 1879 to 1898, under president Frances Willard (1839–98), the WCTU became the largest women's organization in the United States and, ultimately, a broad-based reform organization affiliated with the KNIGHTS OF LABOR. Committees within the organization devoted themselves to women's suffrage, public-health measures, labour legislation and prison reform.

Ruth Bordin, *Women and Temperance* (Philadelphia, 1981).

ROBYN MUNCY

Women's Co-operative Guild Founded in 1884, the Women's Co-operative Guild (WCG) was a British working-class organization with roots in the co-operative movement originally inspired by the English variant of UTOPIAN SOCIALISM associated with Robert OWEN. Margaret Llewelyn Davies (1861–1944), who served as secretary of the WCG from the 1880s until her retirement in 1922, made the group her life's work. Originally intended to promote domestic education among working-class wives, the WCG's focus was shifted to social reform. Under Davies's influence, it collected petitions in support of women's suffrage and worked to establish minimum wages, to promote divorce-law reform and to improve the living conditions of working-class women and children. *Maternity: Letters from Working Women* (1915) is an important collection of letters from guild members which gives a vivid glimpse of domestic life among the working class at the end of the nineteenth century.

Naomi Black, *Social Feminism* (Ithaca, NY, 1989).

GAIL SAVAGE

women's movements *see* FEMINISM.

women's suffrage Throughout the nineteenth century women's suffrage remained a controversial political issue. The press for universal manhood suffrage began to achieve results towards the end of the period (*see* FRANCHISE REFORM), but the contentious question of whether women also ought to have the right to vote had to wait until the twentieth century for an answer. Indeed, women's suffrage had at first figured among the most revolutionary of political demands, although it later became the centre of a moderate political movement dominated by middle-class women.

The idea that women as well as men should enjoy the right to vote first emerged as a serious proposal during the French Revolution. Revolutionary leaders did not prove receptive to this departure and instead banned political activism on the part of women. The 1848 revolutions again stimulated calls for women's right to vote. Again this demand met with an unsympathetic response even among revolutionaries, who often shared with conservatives the idea that women's sphere should be restricted to the home, leaving the conduct of political life to men. The British sought to avoid the excesses of revolution by passing the 1832 Reform Act (*see* PARLIAMENTARY REFORM), which admitted middle-class property-owners to the franchise and explicitly defined the vote as a male prerogative. CHARTISM, a movement provoked in part by the failure of the act to extend the franchise to the working class, listed universal manhood suffrage on the great charter of reforms because including women in the franchise appeared to many as too radical a demand.

Although these early initiatives failed, they introduced the principle that women ought to vote on equal terms with men into the political arena. The mid-1860s saw a renewed interest in suffrage in England as a consequence of the passage of the 1867 Reform Act, which further extended the franchise for men. Parliament voted down the amendment suggested by J. S. MILL that would have given the vote to women as well. In the wake of this episode, Englishwomen organized two suffrage societies, one in London and one in Manchester. These groups decided to campaign for equal suffrage, which would include women within the franchise however that might be defined, rather than pursue the more radical and threatening goal of universal suffrage. In many countries a broad-based mass movement coalesced around the demand for women's suffrage in the last decade of the century. This phase of political agitation drew on women's previous experience in social reform. The popular appeal of the increasingly narrow focus on suffrage developed as a consequence of the growing realization that women could not depend on male goodwill in order to achieve legal reforms on behalf of women. The strength of the movement, however, varied considerably from place to place.

In the United States the National American Women's Suffrage Association, which combined the forces of the two leading American suffrage organizations in 1890, claimed 2 million members by 1915. In Britain the National Union of Women's Suffrage Societies, also formed in 1890 under the leadership of Millicent FAWCETT, served as an umbrella organization for various suffrage organizations and commanded a large membership. Suffrage did not become the central issue for feminists on the Continent as it had done for women in Britain and the United States. In France active suffrage supporters numbered perhaps 100,000. Women's suffrage in France provoked an especially virulent hostility because of the fear that religious women would vote under the influence of the church and thereby pose a threat to the secular Third Republic. In Germany only with the formation of the Bund Deutscher Frauenvereine (Union of German Women's Associations) in the 1890s did feminists there begin to take an interest in suffrage. The international congress convened in Berlin in 1904 to form the International Women's Suffrage Alliance signified the maturation of the movement, as well as served to provide an impetus for further agitation.

Finnish women became the first in Europe entitled to vote in national elections and to hold national office in 1906. Norwegian women received the right to vote in 1913, followed by Russian women in 1917. In the aftermath of the First World War women in Britain, the United States, Germany, Sweden, Austria and the Netherlands all won the right to vote. Women in France, Italy and Switzerland, however, did not receive the franchise until much later in the twentieth century.

Steven C. Hause and Anne R. Kenney, 'The Limits of Suffragist Behavior: Legalism and Militancy in France, 1876–1922', *American Historical Review*, 86 (1981), 781–806.

Jill Liddington and Jill Norris, *One Hand Tied behind Us: The Rise of the Women's Suffrage Movement* (London, 1978).

GAIL SAVAGE

workhouses Under the OLD POOR LAW, workhouses played only a secondary role in providing assistance to the indigent. In contrast, the Benthamite-inspired NEW POOR LAW (1834) urged that all able-bodied paupers receive relief only in Poor Law Union workhouses. Intended as a deterrent to the improvident and wayward, the 'workhouse test' compelled inmates to accept living standards below those of the worst-paid independent labourer. In addition to meagre provisions, entry into the workhouse meant separation from family members, segregation from the opposite sex, monotonous labour and dreary regimentation. However, despite Poor Law board attempts at establishing uniformity, workhouse conditions continued to vary substantially in practice. Over the course of the nineteenth century, local authorities also gradually softened the early rigour and austerity of the workhouses. Nevertheless, the fear of workhouse 'bastilles' remained a central working-class anxiety into the twentieth century.

Anne Digby, *Pauper Palaces* (London, 1978).

RICHARD J. SODERLUND

working classes The term 'working class' was invented in the nineteenth century to refer to wage workers. In this age of capitalism as a world system, the working classes were created through a process of labour recruitment and the proletarianization of artisans and other craft workers (*see* SKILLED WORKERS). In Europe alone the number of workers doubled between 1800 and 1900, rising to 200 million. These were years when labour mobilizations and trade-unionism presented challenges to powerful economic and political interests.

In England, home of the first industrial revolution, the early working class fought simultaneously for economic rights in the workplace and the extension of political democracy, summed up in the demand for universal male suffrage. United States workers early won access to the ballot-box and formed by the 1830s a series of workingmen's parties. French skilled workers in the artisanal trades led the way in the formation of trade unions and utopian movements, and in 1871 launched a struggle for state power in the short-lived insurrectionary experiment, the PARIS COMMUNE. Even though strikes were illegal in France until 1864 their known numbers soared from roughly fifty a year in the late 1820s to over 1,000 in 1900. Countries of later industrialization, such as Italy, saw a similar rise in a shorter period: between 1880 and 1900 the annual number of strikes climbed from approximately twenty-five to 300.

By the late nineteenth century workers in the most advanced industrial-capitalist countries had created new forms of political and economic organization. In North America and elsewhere the KNIGHTS OF LABOR organized skilled and unskilled workers, black and white, men and women, in what came to be known as the Great Upheaval. British workers began to organize 'new model' unions that offered unskilled workers (*see* UNSKILLED LABOUR) and general labourers a home in the workers' movement (*see* GENERAL UNIONISM). Movements for shorter hours (*see* EIGHT-HOUR DAY, TEN HOURS ACT) led to strikes and demonstrations in the United States, Canada, Great Britain, Australia and other countries over the course of the 1860s, 1870s and 1880s.

As the number of wage-earners in the United States jumped from 2.7 to 4.5 million between 1880 and 1900, conflict escalated. Over 7,300 strikes took place in the 1880s, and almost 12,500 in the 1890s.

CO-OPERATION, SOCIALISM, and syndicalism captivated the hearts and minds of many workers, especially in Continental Europe. The percentage of the German electorate voting for the Social Democratic Party rose from 3.2 in 1871 to 27.2 in 1898. Populist mobilizations in the American south and Midwest and rural Russia threatened to bring the plebeian masses together in opposition to ruling authority (*see* POPULISM (RUSSIA), POPULISM (UNITED STATES)).

Class victories such as the 1889 London dockers' strike (*see* DOCK STRIKE) reverberated around the world, and as reform advocates such as Henry George (1839–97) courted working-class communities in various continents, labour's ideas, organizations and connections took on an increasingly internationalist tone. Migrants and militants carried the cause of the working class far and wide. As capitalism penetrated under-developed areas such as China, India, southern Africa and Latin America, working classes emerged that faced special oppressions and intensified exploitation. Often cultural modernism and national liberation crossed over into the workers' movement, as in Cuba, where the son of a ropemaker, José MARTI, died in the 1895 Cuban War for Independence after promoting his cause among tobacco workers. As early as the 1850s an artisan-army alliance known as Sociedades Democràticas seized power in a coup in Colombia. The resulting repression and bloodshed prefaced a century of violence in this Latin American country.

Life itself was often a struggle for mere existence. UNEMPLOYMENT and the forced reduction of hours wiped out any sense of working-class security; death or desertion of the family 'breadwinner' worsened an already bad situation. Women were pulled out of the domestic realm and into the waged arena, but at rates of remuneration distinctly less than those of men. Child labour, widespread throughout the century, robbed the young of education and locked their adulthood into rounds of routinized work. For every adult male working in the cotton mills of Great Britain or the United States in the 1830s there were four women and children or youths under the age of 18. Real wages may actually have declined in certain periods, especially the 'Hungry Forties', but probably rose incrementally over the course of the century. However, the intensification of work also increased. (*See* CHILD-LABOUR LAWS, LABOUR LEGISLATION.)

Cities seemed the obvious home of the working classes (*see* URBANIZATION). Whereas between 1800 and 1900 the European rural proletariat grew from 90 to 125 million, city proletarians mushroomed from 10 to 75 million. The burgeoning industries and impersonality of urban contexts provided the setting for class formation. Much productive activity was still embedded in regions that remained more country than city, however, and as late as 1900 Belgian miners launched 'potato strikes' to look after their gardens, just as striking weavers in Lancashire in 1859 could sustain themselves haymaking. From Argentina to Australia, however, cities grew rapidly, encroaching on and integrating with rural life in ways that allowed workers to remain half-agricultural. But the city lacked the space of the country, and housing and the use of the streets became contested class terrain. Berlin, Paris, London, New York and Melbourne grew phenomenally between 1850 and 1900, supporting a vast array of working-class institutions, from fraternal orders and benefit societies to newspapers, choirs and saloons, not to mention unions and political associations.

In the New World the growth of cities and the rise of the working class and its diverse cultural life were both related to transatlantic migration: trade-unionism in Buenos Aires, with its working class 80 per cent foreign-born, grew directly out of the mutual-benefit societies formed in the late nineteenth century. German immigrants in Detroit boasted a debating society known as the Dialectical Union and a workers' militia known as the Rifles. Chicago's anarcho-communist workers sustained a rich counter-culture throughout the 1870s and 1880s which left no doubt that as workers gathered in huge cosmopolitan centres they posed a threat to order. In 1886, after a strike at an agricultural-implements works and a protest over the hours of labour, Chicago's Haymarket tragedy resulted in death when a bomb exploded, police opened fire and the state responded with legal executions of immigrant radicals and American socialists (*see* HAYMARKET MASSACRE). Around the world protests were launched by a militant minority of labour activists who pointed out that an injury to any worker must be the concern of all.

Yet many mainstream trade-union figures opposed extending a hand of sympathy to the Haymarket martyrs, just as the American Federation of labor leader, Samuel GOMPERS, avoided backing the radical Eugene Debs (1855–1926) when he led the massive boycott of the Pullman corporation in 1894. The workers' movement at the close of the century was divided ideologically and by the everyday experience of workers as a class. While the working classes on a world scale were being economically homogenized, the forging of a unified class was a difficult undertaking. Inhibiting it were divisions of nationality, ethnicity, race, gender, skill and life-style. Workers straddled many identities and often privileged one part of their being – Irishness or occupation – over their class place. Attachments to God and country, neighbourhood and family, respectability and advancement up the socioeconomic ladder often kept workers apart, as did lack of finances, the coercive and repressive might of employers, the state and the business cycle, and rudimentary communication systems. Combating this state of affairs and improving the lot of the working class was the essential aim of nineteenth-century labour, a legacy to the more materially advanced, but no less fractured, twentieth-century years.

E. J. Hobsbawm, *The Age of Capital, 1848–1875* (New York, 1975).

Jurgen Kuczynski, *The Rise of the Working Class* (New York, 1967).

David Levine, (ed.), *Proletarianization and Family History* (Orlando, Fla., 1984).

E. P. Thompson, *The Making of the English Working Class* (Harmondsworth, 1970).

Charles Tilly, Louise Tilly and Richard Tilly, *The Rebellious Century, 1830–1930* (Cambridge, Mass., 1975).

Marcel Van Der Linden and Jurgen Rojahn (eds), *The Formation of Labour Movements, 1870–1914*, 2 vols (Leiden, 1990).

BRYAN D. PALMER

Workingmen's Party (1829–1830)   Formed as an early labour group by unemployed New York City artisans, the Workingmen's Party sought electoral and banking reform as a prelude to a more radical programme of wealth redistribution in American society. Supported by Robert Dale Owen (1801–77) and the feminist Frances Wright (1795–1852), the Workingmen's Party was an early attempt to rectify urban class inequality. It grew out of labour unrest in April 1829, amid attempts to extend the working day. A committee of fifty journeymen discussed a programme for a new political movement, and its report was informed by the thought of Thomas Skidmore (1790–1832), a non-journeymen member. His book *The Rights of Man to Property!* (1829) attacked inheritance laws and asserted the rights of all people to property. Skidmore held that all property laws were illegitimate, as they fostered an initial maldistribution of wealth in capitalist society. Internal divisions led to the party's break-up.

KEVIN MURPHY

Wounded Knee, Battle of (1890)   Assembled on Wounded Knee Creek in December 1890, the Miniconjou Sioux planned to celebrate the ghost dance, an Indian religious movement which promised that whites would fall into holes in the earth and that the native American dead would return to be with the living. Fearing that the gathering would turn violent, the Seventh Cavalry (*see* CUSTER) under Colonel James Forsyth attempted to disarm the Sioux. Unwilling to comply with Forsyth's orders, and dressed in 'ghost shirts' believed to protect them from the white man's bullets, the Sioux resisted. After bitter hand-to-hand fighting, some Sioux broke through the army's perimeter only to be met with the army's rapid-firing Hotchkiss guns. In this last major military encounter with native Americans in the nineteenth century, twenty-five soldiers and 146 Sioux men, women and children died.

Robert Utley, *The Last Days of the Sioux Nation* (New Haven, Conn., 1963).

JOHN MARTIN

Y

yellow press *see* NEWSPAPERS.

Yiddish   The language of Ashkenazi Jews from the early Middle Ages, Yiddish was based predominantly on dialects of medieval Middle High German, but also on Hebrew and various Slavonic languages, as well as developing its own usages over time. By the beginning of the nineteenth century Western Yiddish was on the decline, being replaced in western and central Europe by French, Dutch and especially German, due to the influences of emancipationist ideologies. In eastern Europe, however, Eastern Yiddish experienced a great literary revival. Writers such as Mendele (1835–1917), Shalom Aleichem (1859–1916) and I. L. Peretz (1852–1915) developed a modern Yiddish literature, making it the language of modern eastern European Jewish experience. There was a flourishing Yiddish press, and the BUND adopted Yiddish as its medium of communication with the Russian Jewish proletariat. Yiddish was rejected, however, as a 'corrupt' language by the Zionists, in preference for a modern form of the 'purer' Hebrew.

See also JEWS AND JUDAISM.

STEVEN BELLER

Yorubaland   From 1842 Yorubaland, in coastal west Africa, became a major focus of British missionary activity, especially the 'Yoruba Mission' of the Church Missionary Society. 'Yoruba' was strictly an alternative name for Oyo (*see* OYO EMPIRE), but was adopted by the missionaries as a general name for the linguistic group to which Oyo belonged, which included several separate indigenous states. Following the disintegration of Oyo, Yorubaland suffered a prolonged period of internecine warfare. The British authorities at Lagos on the coast regarded these wars as injurious to trade, and intervened to end them.

A peace treaty among the major Yoruba states, negotiated with British assistance in 1886, was only partially effective, and peace was eventually imposed through the assertion of effective British control over the interior in 1892–3. Most of Yorubaland then became part of NIGERIA, although some western groups were incorporated into the French colony of Dahomey (modern Benin).

Robert S. Smith, *Kingdoms of the Yoruba*, third edn (London, 1988).

ROBIN LAW

Young Turks By turns Ottoman protest movement, political party and governing regime, the Young Turks, or the Committee of Union and Progress (CUP) as they called themselves, were a clandestine movement that arose in the late nineteenth century to oppose the autocratic regime of Abdulhamid II (1842–1918; reigned 1876–1909). In July 1908 the principal CUP cells, those within the army stationed in Macedonia, marched on Istanbul and compelled Abdulhamid to recognize the constitution of 1876. A year later Abdulhamid was replaced after attempting a counter-coup. As an official party, the CUP sought to build a single Ottoman nationality out of the diverse peoples of the empire, but the goal proved futile given the uninterrupted warfare after 1911 and the heightened separate nationalisms of the population. As the party in power in 1914, the Young Turks entered the First World War on the side of Germany and, to the distress of Ottoman Arabs, increasingly promoted Turkish language and culture. The CUP collapsed when the war ended, and a number of its leaders were tried on war-crime charges by later Turkish courts.

See also OTTOMAN EMPIRE.

Bernard Lewis, *The Emergence of Modern Turkey* (Oxford, 1968).

MADELINE C. ZILFI

youth movements Non-political, often religious, adult-led organizations were prepared to admit unlimited numbers of children, adolescents and young adults into membership, with the aim of propagating some sort of Christian ethos or manly code of living. Youth movements also encouraged the participation of members as leaders and organizers, allowed for the possibility of competing for awards and badges, and provided a specific identity or status in the form of a uniform. Boys' clubs do not meet the latter criteria but derived from a similar middle-class concern to keep young men off the streets, and grew out of the pastoral work of churches in the mid nineteenth century. The purely recreational function of the club idea was spread by the British university and public-school settlement movement which, after 1886, also adopted cadet companies as a method of controlling unruly working-class boys. The late-nineteenth-century origin of youth movements proper, through agencies of Evangelical religion and methods of military training and discipline, coincided with recognition of the new 'problem' of adolescence in British cities.

The world's first voluntary, uniformed youth movement was the church-based Boys' Brigade, founded in 1883 in Glasgow by William Alexander Smith (1854–1914), a Volunteer and Free Church businessman. The Boy Scouts were not started by Robert Baden-Powell (1857–1941) until a quarter of a century later. The Boys' Brigade was dedicated to 'the advancement of Christ's Kingdom among Boys, and the promotion of habits of Obedience, Reverence, Discipline, Self-respect, and all that tends towards a true Christian Manliness'. There followed the (Anglican) Church Lads' Brigade (1891), the Jewish Lads' Brigade (1895), a short-lived Catholic Boys' Brigade (1896), a non-military Boys' Life Brigade (1899) and the Girls' Guildry (1900), forerunner of the Girls' Brigade (1965).

John Springhall, *Youth, Empire and Society: British Youth Movements, 1883–1940* (London, 1977).

JOHN SPRINGHALL

Z

———◆———

Zanzibar After the Napoleonic wars, the Omani rulers of Zanzibar, an island off the east coast of Africa, accepted Britain's reassertion of dominance, expecting more understanding regarding the cultural as well as economic importance of the slave trade. The 1822 Moresby Treaty began a gradual restriction of the trade, which finally ended in 1890. Under Sayyid Said (reigned 1804–56), Zanzibar became the effective capital of Oman, serving as a base for reasserting control over tributary rulers on the mainland. Sayyid encouraged economic development, most notably the plantation production of cloves for export. This increased the demand for slaves, often supplied by traders flying the French flag, France agreeing to allow British inspection of vessels only in 1888.

British influence in Zanzibar increased after Sayyid Said's death, especially after the appointment of Sir John Kirk (1832–1922) as British consul there. As wider European interest in the region developed, Britain and Germany reached agreement in 1890 on their respective spheres of influence. Germany recognized Britain's dominance over Zanzibar in exchange for British recognition of Germany's claims to Heligoland in the North Sea. Britain's hegemony over what became Kenya was agreed, as was Germany's over German East Africa, later Tanganyika. Zanzibar remained independent, but only nominally. (*See* SCRAMBLE FOR AFRICA.)

SIMON KATZENELLENBOGEN

Zasulich, Vera Ivanovna (*b* Mikhailovka, 27 July 1849; *d* Petrograd, 8 May 1919) Russian revolutionary. The daughter of an impoverished nobleman, she was brought up by relations and educated at boarding school. She was first employed as a clerk and later joined a women's collective. On its collapse, she went to St Petersburg and became involved in a terrorist organization which led to her arrest. Although denying involvement in any conspiracy she was sentenced to imprisonment and exile. She later joined Land and Freedom (*see* POPULISM (RUSSIA)). In January 1878 she shot and seriously wounded the governor-general of St Petersburg, General F. F. Trepov (1812–89). Her trial, followed eagerly by the women's movement, revolutionaries and general public alike, was sensational. Although the evidence against her was incontrovertible, the jury acquitted her and she became a heroine in Russia and abroad, and the use of terrorist methods to change the regime in Russia was considerably encouraged.

A. V. KNOWLES

zemindar A term derived from the Persian word for land (*zamin*) which had numerous and subtle nuances over time and across India, 'zemindar' denotes a right to collect land revenues. The right might be hereditary, bestowed for a period of years or for a lifetime tenure. In situations where the zemindar had a hereditary right, he often emerged as a dominant local authority and power-broker between land-tiller and government. Under Mughal rule, and indigenous states which succeeded it during the eighteenth century, there was a clear understanding that the zemindar was officially the collector of land taxes. In 1793 the role of the Bengal zemindar was redefined by Lord Cornwallis (1738–1805) in the Permanent Land Settlement. By East India Company fiat, the Bengal zemindar was transformed into a landowner with the right to buy and sell land, dispossess tenants and so on, a pattern that led to a notable destabilization of Bengali society.

Chittabrata Palit, *Perspectives on Agrarian Bengal* (Calcutta, 1982).

ROBERT J. YOUNG

zemstva In 1864 ALEXANDER II established a system of local government in Russia, popularly known as the zemstva. Each zemstvo was an assembly at county level, elected on a limited franchise, with an executive board; each of these elected another at provincial level. Having no executive powers, they depended on the central government – and the police – to enforce their decisions. They were responsible for local public works, means of communication, trade and industry, education and health, but were, however, seriously under-funded and subject to bureaucratic interference from central government. The zemstva were initially welcomed by both the radicals and the wider public, whose enthusiasm quickly faded into indifference when their limitations became more and more apparent. Their difficulties were amply illustrated by the experience of Levin in Tolstoi's novel *Anna Karenina*. They were replaced after the 1917 revolution by the soviets.

C. L. Black (ed.), *The Transformation of Russian Society* (Cambridge, Mass., 1960).

A. V. KNOWLES

Zetkin, Clara Eissner (*b* Niederaus, Saxony, 5 July 1857; *d* Moscow, 20 June 1933)   German communist leader. The daughter of the village schoolmaster, she lived, in the 1880s, in Switzerland and France, where she married the Russian *émigré* Ossip Zetkin, who died young. Returning to Germany in 1891, she became editor of the socialist women's journal *Gleichheit* (Equality) and prominent on the left wing of the SPD (*see* SOCIAL DEMOCRATIC PARTY (GERMANY)), a close friend of Rosa Luxemburg (1871–1919). Sharply opposed to the First World War, she organized an international women's antiwar conference (1915) and joined the extreme-left Spartacus League and the Independent Social Democratic Party, which she left in 1920 to join the German Communist Party.

F. L. CARSTEN

Zionism   *see* JEWS AND JUDAISM.

Zollverein (German Customs Union)   The Zollverein, which came into force on 1 January 1834, was intended to ease the expansion of commerce by abolishing complicated intra-German tariffs. It ended more than a decade of proposals for tariff reform and, in the absence of the GERMAN CONFEDERATION taking a lead, of smaller-scale tariff union initiatives by individual member states of the confederation. Prussia, an advocate of low tariffs, was the driving force behind the Zollverein, which by the 1850s included most members of the German Confederation except for the Hanseatic cities, the two Mecklenburgs and the protectionist Habsburg monarchy. The founding of the Zollverein benefited German commercial development, though it did not remove all hindrances to trade between its members – different currencies, for instance, remained in force. It has often been seen as a landmark on the road to German unification, though historians in recent times have stressed that what the Zollverein actually promoted was pragmatic co-operation between sovereign German states, not visions of political unity.

ELIZABETH HARVEY

Zulus   In the eighteenth century the Zulus were a small clan within the Nguni peoples of eastern/south-eastern Africa. In a period of conflict arising in large part out of population pressure on available land, under SHAKA's leadership, they became a kingdom in which they dominated a large number of other groups. Their military was highly organized and efficient, the army being an integral part of the wider social structure, and they were able to resist both Boer and British encroachment more effectively than any other African people. Effective resistance continued under Shaka's successors, and by the late 1870s the British government was coming to the view that the complete defeat of the Zulu would be too costly, but the BATTLE OF ULUNDI enabled them to save face.

Europeans seem to have considered the Zulu the 'noblest of savages', tending to romanticize and/or exaggerate both their nobility and their savagery.

SIMON KATZENELLENBOGEN

Zulu Wars As Europeans advanced into Africa beyond the Cape Colony and sought to establish their authority in Natal, there arose a series of conflicts between them and the ZULUS. The 'Zulu Wars' generally refer to British conflicts, but can also refer to conflicts between the Boers and the Zulus (*see* BATTLE OF BLOOD RIVER, CETSHWAYO, BATTTLE OF ULUNDI).

SIMON KATZENELLENBOGEN

Chronology

MAJOR POLITICAL, CONSTITUTIONAL, DIPLOMATIC AND MILITARY EVENTS IN EUROPE		MAJOR POLITICAL, CONSTITUTIONAL, DIPLOMATIC AND MILITARY EVENTS OUTSIDE EUROPE	

1800–1809

		1800	Washington, DC becomes capital of the United States
1801	Act of Union (Great Britain and Ireland)	1801	Georgia annexed by Russia
1801	Peace of Lunéville	1801	French evacuate Egypt
1802	Peace of Amiens	1802–5	Maratha War, India
1803	Britain declares war on France	1803	Louisiana purchased by the United States from France
1803	Robert Emmet's insurrection and execution, Ireland	1803	Britain acquires Tobago and St Lucia
1804	Napoleon crowned emperor	1804	Independence of Haiti
1804	Code Napoléon inaugurated in France		
1804–12	Serbian uprising		
1805	Battle of Trafalgar	1805	Wellesley recalled from India
1805	Battle of Austerlitz	1805	Muhammad Ali appointed governor of Egypt
1806	Battle of Jena	1806	Lewis and Clark expedition
1806	End of Holy Roman Empire	1806	British occupy Cape Colony
1806	Berlin decrees establish Continental System		
1807	Emancipation of Prussian serfs	1807	Portugese royal court exiled to Brazil
1807	Treaty of Tilsit		
1807	Stein begins reforms in Prussia		

	CULTURAL, RELIGIOUS, INTELLECTUAL AND SOCIAL DEVELOPMENTS		SCIENTIFIC, TECHNOLOGICAL, MEDICAL, AGRICULTURAL AND ECONOMIC DEVELOPMENTS
1800	Library of Congress founded	1800	Owen's 'model factory' at New Lanark founded
		1800	Volta produces electricity from cell
1801	Elgin Marbles brought to London	1801	Bichat, *Anatomie généralé*
1801	Beethoven, 'Moonlight' Sonata	1801	First accurate censuses in Italy, Spain, Britain and the United States
1802	*Christian Observer* founded	1802	Thornton, *An Enquiry into the Nature and Effects of the Paper Credit of Great Britain*
1802	*Edinburgh Review* founded		
1802	Bentham, *Civil and Penal Legislation*	1802	Herschel discovers revolution of stars
1803	Lancaster, *Improvements in Education*	1803	Second edition of Malthus, *Essay on the Principle of Population*
1803	Pestalozzi, *How Gertrude Teaches her Children*	1803	First steamboat launched
1804	British and Foreign Bible Society founded		
1804	Beethoven, Third ('Eroica') Symphony		
1804–5	Fichte's lectures on 'The Characteristics of the Present Age' (published in English, 1844)		
1807	Saint-Simon, *Introduction to the Work of Science in the Nineteenth Century*	1807	Humphry Davy isolates sodium and potassium
		1807	Compulsory vaccination introduced in Bavaria

MAJOR POLITICAL, CONSTITUTIONAL, DIPLOMATIC AND MILITARY EVENTS IN EUROPE	MAJOR POLITICAL, CONSTITUTIONAL, DIPLOMATIC AND MILITARY EVENTS OUTSIDE EUROPE

1808–14	Peninsular War	1808	Revolution in Turkey
1808	Battle of Bailén	1808	Importation of slaves
1808	Spanish uprising against Napoleon begins		into the United States prohibited
1808	Ferdinand VII of Spain forced to abdicate; Godoy dismissed		
1809	Metternich becomes chief minister in Austria	1809	United States cuts off trade with Britain and France
		1809	Revolt in Peru against Spain
		1809	Treaty of friendship between British and Sikhs

1810–1819

1810	Hardenberg continues Stein's reforms in Prussia	1810	Rebellion in Mexico against Spain
1811	George, prince of Wales, becomes prince regent	1811	British occupy Java
		1811	Muhammad Ali acquires supreme authority in Egypt
		1811	Venezuela and Paraguay declare independence from Spain
1812	Spanish Cortes passes liberal constitution	1812	United States declares war on Britain
1812	Napoleon invades Russia; Battle of Borodino		
1812	Assassination of Spencer Perceval, British prime minister		
1813	France withdraws from Spain	1813	Simón Bolívar becomes dictator in Venezuela
1813	Battle of Leipzig	1813	Persia cedes Caucasus district to Russia

CULTURAL, RELIGIOUS, INTELLECTUAL AND SOCIAL DEVELOPMENTS		SCIENTIFIC, TECHNOLOGICAL, MEDICAL, AGRICULTURAL AND ECONOMIC DEVELOPMENTS	
1807	Hegel, *Phenomenology of Mind*		
1808	Inquisition abolished in Spain and Portugal	1808	Malus discovers polarization of light by reflection
1808	Goethe, *Faust*, part 1		
1808	Beethoven, Fifth and Sixth ('Pastoral') Symphonies		
1808	Goya, *Execution of the Citizens of Madrid*		
1809	*Quarterly Review* founded	1809	First street gas-lighting, Pall Mall, London
		1809	Repeal of statutes regulating English woollen trade
1810	Berlin University founded	1810	Krupp works founded at Essen
1810	Secession of Primitive Methodists		
1811	Jane Austen, *Sense and Sensibility*	1811–17	Luddism in England
1811	Nash begins work on Regent Street, London		
1812	Jacob and Wilhelm Grimm, *Fairy Tales*	1812	Cylinder-press printing invented
1812	Waltz introduced into England	1812	Orders in Council revoked
1812–16	Hegel, *Science of Logic*	1812	Central London streets lit by gas
1813	Owen, *A New View of Society*	1813	Repeal of Statute of Artificers in England
		1813	Abolition of trade monopoly of English East India Company

MAJOR POLITICAL, CONSTITUTIONAL, DIPLOMATIC AND MILITARY EVENTS IN EUROPE		MAJOR POLITICAL, CONSTITUTIONAL, DIPLOMATIC AND MILITARY EVENTS OUTSIDE EUROPE	
		1813–15	War against the Wahabists in Mecca and Medina
1814	Treaty of Kiel; Norwegian independence and constitution	1814	Treaty of Ghent between Britain and the United States
1814	Ferdinand VIII of Spain abolishes constitution	1814	British acquire Demerara, Essequibo and Berbice
1814	Napoleon exiled to Elba; Louis XVIII restored First Peace of Paris	1814	Cape of Good Hope (Cape Colony) becomes British colony
1814–15	Congress of Vienna; creation of Holy Alliance	1814–16	Gurkha War
1815	Napoleon returns to France – 'Hundred Days'	1815	Morelos's rebellion in Mexico
1815	Battle of Waterloo	1815	British defeated at New Orleans
1815	Napoleon deported to St Helena	1815	British declare war on king of Kandy, Ceylon
1815	Second Peace of Paris	1815	Brazil made an empire under João, prince regent of Portugal
1815–17	Serbian uprising against Ottoman rule		
1816	Diet of German Confederation opens	1816	Congress of Tucumán declares independence of the United Provinces of South America
		1816	Java restored to the Netherlands
1817	German student radicalism; Wartburg Festival	1817–18	Third Maratha War
1818	Congress of Aix-la-Chapelle	1818	Battle of Maipo: independence of Chile secured
1818	Allied troops evacuate France		

CULTURAL, RELIGIOUS, INTELLECTUAL AND SOCIAL DEVELOPMENTS	SCIENTIFIC, TECHNOLOGICAL, MEDICAL, AGRICULTURAL AND ECONOMIC DEVELOPMENTS
1814 Dulwich Picture Gallery opens to public	1814 First railway steam engine
1815 Bible Christians formed 1815–21 Construction of Nash's Royal Pavilion, Brighton	1815 Fresnel discovers theory of the frequency of light 1815 Davy invents miners' safety lamp
1816 William Cobbett publishes cheap edition of *Political Register*, 'twopenny trash'	
1817 First exhibition of Constable's landscapes 1817 *Blackwood's Magazine* founded 1817 Hegel, *Encyclopaedia of the Philosophical sciences* 1817 Jefferson designs University of Virginia 1817 *Scotsman* founded	1817 Ricardo, *Principles of Political Economy and Taxation*
1818 Prado Museum opens in Madrid 1818 Church Building Act, England; John Soane designs model churches	1818 First steamer crosses Atlantic in twenty-six days 1818 Berzelius determines atomic weights

MAJOR POLITICAL, CONSTITUTIONAL, DIPLOMATIC AND MILITARY EVENTS IN EUROPE		MAJOR POLITICAL, CONSTITUTIONAL, DIPLOMATIC AND MILITARY EVENTS OUTSIDE EUROPE	
1819	'Peterloo Massacre', Manchester; Six Acts	1819	Formation of Gran Colombia under Bolívar as president
1819	Carlsbad Decrees establish cultural and political censorship in Germany	1819	British found Singapore
		1819	United States purchases Florida from Spain

1820–1829

1820	Murder of duc de Berry	1820	Missouri Compromise on slavery in the United States
1820	Cato Street Conspiracy, London		
1820–1	Revolutions in Naples, Portugal and Spain	1820–2	Muhammad Ali conquers Sudan and founds Khartoum
1820–1	Congress of Troppau and Laibach against revolutionary movements		
1821	Insurrection in Piedmont; Victor Emmanuel I abdicates	1821	Battle of Carabobo: defeat of Spanish by Bolívar
1821	Ultraroyalists come to power in France	1821	Mexico, Colombia, Guatemala and Peru declare independence from Spain
1821–9	Greek War of Independence	1821	Britain acquires Gold Coast, Sierra Leone and Gambia
1822	Congress of Verona	1822	Independence of Brazil from Portugal
1822	Canning becomes British foreign secretary after Castlereagh's suicide		
1823	French intervention in Spain	1823	Monroe Doctrine declared by the United States
1823	Irish Catholic Association established by O'Connell	1823	Secession of the United Provinces of Central America from Mexico
1824	Accession of Charles X; repression of civil liberties in France	1824	Battle of Ayacucho; Spanish army leaves South America

CULTURAL, RELIGIOUS, INTELLECTUAL AND SOCIAL DEVELOPMENTS		SCIENTIFIC, TECHNOLOGICAL, MEDICAL, AGRICULTURAL AND ECONOMIC DEVELOPMENTS	
1818	Mary Wollstonecraft Shelley, *Frankenstein*		
1819	Schubert, 'Trout' Quintet	1819	Laennec invents stethoscope
1819	James Mill, *Essay on Government*	1819	Electromagnetism discovered
1819	Byron, *Don Juan*		
1820	Sir Walter Scott, *Ivanhoe*	1820	First iron steamship launched
1820	Malthus, *Principles of Political Economy*		
1821	Hegel, *Philosophy of Right*	1821	Bank cash payments resume in Britain
1821	*Manchester Guardian* first published	1821	James Mill, *Elements of Political Economy*
1821	Ecole des Chartes established	1821	Faraday discovers electromagnetic rotation
1821–2	Saint-Simon, *Du système industriel*		
1822–3	Construction of Altes Museum, Berlin		
1823	Death penalty for 100 crimes abolished in Britain	1823	Macintosh patents waterproof garment
1823	Traditional origins of Rugby football		
1824	Beethoven, Ninth ('Choral') Symphony	1824	Establishment of Owenite community at New Harmony, Indiana
1824	Cherokee alphabet invented	1824	Portland cement invented

MAJOR POLITICAL, CONSTITUTIONAL, DIPLOMATIC AND MILITARY EVENTS IN EUROPE	MAJOR POLITICAL, CONSTITUTIONAL, DIPLOMATIC AND MILITARY EVENTS OUTSIDE EUROPE
	1824–6 First Anglo-Burmese War: Britain acquires western Burma outside Irrawaddy delta
1825 Decembrist revolt, Russia	1825 Declaration of independence of Bolivia
	1825 War between Brazil and Argentina over Uruguay
1826 Liberal constitution in Portugal	1826–8 War between Russia and Persia
1827 Battle of Navarino: defeat of Turkish and Egyptian fleets by Britain, France and Russia	1827 Russia conquers Armenia
1827 Dom Miguel usurps Portuguese throne	
1828 Protocol of London issued by France, Britain and Russia recognizing Greek independence	1828 Working Men's Party founded in New York
1828 Repeal of Test and Corporation Acts, Britain	
1828 O'Connell elected member of parliament for County Clare	

CULTURAL, RELIGIOUS, INTELLECTUAL AND SOCIAL DEVELOPMENTS		SCIENTIFIC, TECHNOLOGICAL, MEDICAL, AGRICULTURAL AND ECONOMIC DEVELOPMENTS	
1824	National Gallery of Art founded in London	1824–5	Repeal of Combination Laws, Britain
1824	Ranke, *History of the Latin and Teutonic Peoples*		
1824	*Westminster Review* founded		
1824	Society for the Prevention of Cruelty to Animals founded		
1824	Byron dies at Missolonghi		
1824–47	Construction of British Museum		
		1825	First steam locomotive railway, Stockton–Darlington
		1825–9	Pierre Louis publishes studies of tuberculosis and typhoid fever
1826	Froebel, *The Education of Man*	1826	Telford's Menai Bridge opens
1826	Fenimore Cooper, *The Last of the Mohicans*	1826	Brettoneau establishes the clinical entity of diphtheria
1826	London Zoological Society founded	1826	Niepce produces first permanent photograph camera image
1827	Society for the Diffusion of Useful Knowledge founded	1827	Ohm establishes law of electrical currents
1828	Noah Webster's *Dictionary*		
1828	Protestant Methodists formed		
1828	Combe, *The Constitution of Man*		
1828	Buonarroti, *History of Babeuf's Conspiracy of Equals*		

MAJOR POLITICAL, CONSTITUTIONAL, DIPLOMATIC AND MILITARY EVENTS IN EUROPE		MAJOR POLITICAL, CONSTITUTIONAL, DIPLOMATIC AND MILITARY EVENTS OUTSIDE EUROPE	
1828–9	Russo-Turkish War	1828–9	Civil war in Argentina
1829	Metropolitan Police established in London		
1829	Catholic Emancipation, Britain	1829	Foundation of Swan River Colony (Western Australia)
1829	Treaty of Adrianople ends Russo-Turkish War		

1830–1839

1830	France: July Revolution; Charles X abdicates	1830	France invades Algiers
1830	Louis-Philippe chosen as king of the French	1830	Disintegration of Gran Colombia into republics of Ecuador, Venezuela and New Granada
1830	Belgium proclaims its independence from the Netherlands		
1831	Polish insurrection, crushed by Russia	1831	Annexation of Mysore by English East India Company
1831	Austria suppresses revolutions in Modena, Parma and Papal States	1831	Pedro I of Brazil abdicates
1831	Constitutions granted in Hanover and Saxony		
1831	Formation of Young Italy		
1831	Revolt of Lyons's silk-weavers		
1831	Leopold of Saxe-Coburg becomes king of the Belgians		
1832	Otto of Bavaria elected as king of Greece	1832	British sovereignty proclaimed over Falkland Islands
1832	Polish constitution abolished	1832–3	Turkish-Egyptian War
1832	First Reform Act, Britain		
1833	Treaty of Münchengratz	1833	Whig Party formed, United States
1833	Treaty of Unkiar-Skelessi	1833	Muhammad Ali made pasha of Egypt
1833–40	First Carlist War		

CULTURAL, RELIGIOUS, INTELLECTUAL AND SOCIAL DEVELOPMENTS	SCIENTIFIC, TECHNOLOGICAL, MEDICAL, AGRICULTURAL AND ECONOMIC DEVELOPMENTS
1829 Rossini, *William Tell*	
1829 Fourier, *Le Nouveau Monde industriel et sociétaire*	
1829 First Oxford and Cambridge boat race	
1830 First use of the term 'sociology'	1830 Opening of Liverpool–Manchester railway
1830 Lyell, *Principles of Geology*	
1830 Stendhal, *Le Rouge et le noir*	
1830–42 Comte, *Course of Positive Philosophy* (English translation, 1853)	
1831 Garrison establishes the *Liberator*	1831 British Association for Advancement of Science founded
1831 Darwin begins voyage on the *Beagle*	1831 Faraday establishes law of electrical induction
	1831 Cholera epidemic reaches Europe
	1832 First railway in Continental Europe
	1832 First streetcar in New York
1833 Gogol, *The Government Inspector*	1833 Faraday discovers electrolysis
1833 Carlyle, *Sartor Resartus*	1833 Factory Act in Britain appoints first factory inspectors
1833 First state grant for education in Britain	

MAJOR POLITICAL, CONSTITUTIONAL, DIPLOMATIC AND MILITARY EVENTS IN EUROPE	MAJOR POLITICAL, CONSTITUTIONAL, DIPLOMATIC AND MILITARY EVENTS OUTSIDE EUROPE
	1833 Abolition of slavery in British West Indies
1834 Dom Miguel of Portugal abdicates	1834 Settlement at Port Phillip Bay (Melbourne)
1834 Revolt of Lyons's silk-weavers	1834–48 Great Trek by Boers, South Africa
1834 Formation of Young Europe	
1834 Quadruple Alliance (Britain, France, Spain and Portugal) in favour of liberal governments in Spain and Portugal	
1834 Revolt in Paris ('Massacre of Rue Transnonain')	
	1835 Juan de Rosas becomes dictator of Argentina
	1836 Britain acquires South Australia
	1836 Texas declares independence from Mexico
1837 Liberal constitution in Spain	1837–8 Canadian rebellion
1838 Formation of Anti-Corn Law League, Manchester	1838 Battle of Blood River: Boers defeat Zulus
1838 People's Charter initiates Chartist movement in Britain	1838–42 First Afghan War

CULTURAL, RELIGIOUS, INTELLECTUAL AND SOCIAL DEVELOPMENTS	SCIENTIFIC, TECHNOLOGICAL, MEDICAL, AGRICULTURAL AND ECONOMIC DEVELOPMENTS
1833 Oxford Movement begins	1833 Formation of Zollverein by Prussia
	1833–4 General unionism in Britain; Tolpuddle martyrs
1834 Lammenais, *Paroles d'un croyant*	1834 Hansom cabs appear in London
	1834 Poor Law Amendment Act, England and Wales (New Poor Law)
	1834 Braille develops system for blind to read
1835 Polka first danced in Prague	1835 Colt invents revolver
1835 Gautier's preface to *Mademoiselle de Maupin*, early manifesto of aestheticism	
1835–6 Strauss, *Life of Jesus* (English translation, 1846)	
1835–9 Construction of Euston Station	
1835–40 Tocqueville, *Democracy in America*	
1835–61 Andersen, Fairy Tales	
1836–7 Pugin's publications on Gothic revival	
1836–7 Dickens, *Pickwick Papers*	1837 Morse builds first telegraph
	1838 Steamship service between Britain and the United States established
1838 National Gallery, London, opened	1838 Schleiden's theory on cell structure
1838 Public Records Act establishes system of central national records in Britain	

MAJOR POLITICAL, CONSTITUTIONAL, DIPLOMATIC AND MILITARY EVENTS IN EUROPE		MAJOR POLITICAL, CONSTITUTIONAL, DIPLOMATIC AND MILITARY EVENTS OUTSIDE EUROPE	
1839	Treaty of London guarantees independence of Belgium	1839	Durham Report on Canada
1839	Luxemburg becomes an independent grand duchy	1839	Britain acquires Aden
		1839	New Zealand proclaimed a colony, incorporated into New South Wales
1839	Armed conspiracy by Society of the Seasons, Paris	1839–41	Turkish-Egyptian War: Egypt loses Syria
		1839–42	First Anglo-Chinese ('Opium') War
1840–1849			
		1840	Upper and Lower Canada united
		1840	Treaty of Waitangi, New Zealand
1841	Straits Convention	1841	Egyptian independence from Turkey
		1841	Second Anglo-Afghan War
		1841	Responsible government established in Canada
1842	Foundation of the *Nation*, organ of Young Ireland	1842	Webster-Ashburton Treaty defines United States–Canadian frontier
1842	General strike in Britain	1842	Treaty of Nanking: Hong Kong ceded to Britain
1843	O'Connell's 'Repeal Year' in Ireland	1843	Natal proclaimed British colony
		1843	British conquer Sind, India

CULTURAL, RELIGIOUS, INTELLECTUAL AND SOCIAL DEVELOPMENTS		SCIENTIFIC, TECHNOLOGICAL, MEDICAL, AGRICULTURAL AND ECONOMIC DEVELOPMENTS	
1839	Blanc, *L'Organisation du travail*	1839	Daguerreotypes invented
1839	Henley Royal Regatta instituted	1839	Nasmyth designs steamhammer
1839	First Grand National run at Aintree	1839	Goodyear vulcanizes rubber
1840	Cabet, *Voyage en Icarie*	1840	Kew Botanical Gardens opened
1840	Proudhon, *What is Property?*	1840	Penny postage introduced in Britain
1840	Invention of saxophone		
1840–65	Reconstruction of Houses of Parliament, Westminster		
1841	*Punch* founded	1841	*Bradshaw's Railway Guide* begins monthly publication
1841	Feuerbach, *The Essence of Christianity* (English translation, 1854)	1841	Talbot patents caloytpe photographic process
		1841	Invention of battery
		1841	List, *National System of Political Economy*
		1841	Liebig discovers artificial fertilizers
1842	Mudie's Lending Library opens in London		
1842	Bakunin, *Reaction in Germany*		
1843	Dickens, *A Christmas Carol*	1843	*Economist* founded to promote free trade
1843	Wagner, *The Flying Dutchman*		
1843	Free Church of Scotland secedes in 'Disruption'		

MAJOR POLITICAL, CONSTITUTIONAL, DIPLOMATIC AND MILITARY EVENTS IN EUROPE		MAJOR POLITICAL, CONSTITUTIONAL, DIPLOMATIC AND MILITARY EVENTS OUTSIDE EUROPE	
1845	Formation of Sonderbund, Switzerland	1845	Texas enters the United States
		1845–6	Anglo-Sikh War
1846	Repeal of Corn Laws splits Tory Party, Britain	1846	Britain acquires Labuan, Malaya
1846	Election of liberal Pope Pius IX	1846	Oregon Treaty between Britain and the United States
1846	Austria annexes Cracow after uprising		
1847	Reform banquets in France	1847	War of the Castes (Yucatán peninsula)
1847	Agitation for liberal constitutions in Hungary, Germany, France and Piedmont; attempted revolutions in Italy crushed by Austria	1847	Liberia becomes independent republic
1847	Sonderbund War between the cantons in Switzerland		
1847	Uprisings in Messina and Reggio, Italy		
1848	(*January–March*) Revolutions in Sicily, Naples, Paris, Vienna, Venice, Milan, Warsaw and Cracow	1848	Treaty of Guadalupe Hidalgo ends Mexican-American War, establishes American rule over south-western and western states

CULTURAL, RELIGIOUS, INTELLECTUAL AND SOCIAL DEVELOPMENTS	SCIENTIFIC, TECHNOLOGICAL, MEDICAL, AGRICULTURAL AND ECONOMIC DEVELOPMENTS
1843–60 Ruskin, *Modern Painters*	
1844 British Anti-State Church Association (renamed Liberation Society, 1853)	1844 Foundation of the pioneering New York Pathological Society
1844 Heine, *Deutschland*	1844 Rochdale Pioneers establish modern co-operative movement
	1844 British Bank Charter Act
1845 Newman converts to Roman Catholicism	1845 Layard begins excavation at Nineveh
1845 Engels, *The Condition of the Wording Class in England*	1845–51 Irish famine
1845 Stirner, *The Ego and its Own* (English translation, 1912)	
1845 Wagner, *Tannhäuser*	
1845 Disraeli, *Sybil*	
1846 Evangelical Alliance formed	1846 Liverpool Sanitary Act leads to appointment of first medical officer of health in England
1846–51 Holyoake, *Reasoner* (secularist journal)	1846 Repeal of British Corn Laws
1847 Charlotte Brontë, *Jane Eyre*	1847 Ten Hours Act, Britain
1847 Mormons found Salt Lake City	1847 Chloroform first used as an anaesthetic
1848 Pre-Raphaelite Brotherhood formed	1848 J. S. Mill, *Principles of Political Economy*
1848 Christian Socialists formed	1848 Public Health Act, England

MAJOR POLITICAL, CONSTITUTIONAL, DIPLOMATIC AND MILITARY EVENTS IN EUROPE		MAJOR POLITICAL, CONSTITUTIONAL, DIPLOMATIC AND MILITARY EVENTS OUTSIDE EUROPE	
1848	(*March–April*) Frankfurt Parliament (*April–July*) Suppression of revolutions in Poland, France, Prague and Italy (*August*) Treaty of Malmo over Schleswig-Holstein (*September*) Louis Kossuth declared president of Hungary (*October*) Suppression of revolution in Vienna (*December*) Louis Napoleon elected president of French republic	1848–9	Second Sikh War
1848	Second Carlist War		
1849	Frederick-William IV rejects imperial German crown	1849	British annexation of Punjab
1849	Proclamation of Roman Republic; French troops take Rome		
1849	Austrian victory at Novara; Charles Albert abdicates		
1849	Termination of revolution in Venice		
1849	Hungarian insurgents capitulate to Russia		

1850–1859

1850	Convention of Olmütz	1850	Australian Constitution Act
1850	Prussian constitution granted	1850–64	Taiping Rebellion, China
1850	Pius IX restored in Rome		

CULTURAL, RELIGIOUS, INTELLECTUAL AND SOCIAL DEVELOPMENTS	SCIENTIFIC, TECHNOLOGICAL, MEDICAL, AGRICULTURAL AND ECONOMIC DEVELOPMENTS
1848 Marx and Engels, *Manifest der Kommunistischen Partei* (English translation, *Manifesto of the Communist Party*, 1850)	1848 Gold discovered in California
1849 Millais, *Christ in the House of his Parents* 1849 Dickens, *David Copperfield* 1848–61 Macaulay, *History of England*	1849 Repeal of British Navigation Laws
1850 Restoration of Catholic hierarchy in England 1850 Tennyson becomes British Poet Laureate 1850 Falloux Law extends church influence in French education 1850 Public Libraries Act, England and Wales 1850–1 Construction of Crystal Palace	1850 Royal Meteorological Society founded 1850 Bunsen burner invented

MAJOR POLITICAL, CONSTITUTIONAL, DIPLOMATIC AND MILITARY EVENTS IN EUROPE		MAJOR POLITICAL, CONSTITUTIONAL, DIPLOMATIC AND MILITARY EVENTS OUTSIDE EUROPE	
1851	*Coup d'état* of Louis Napoleon		
1851	Austrian constitution abolished		
1852	Cavour becomes premier of Piedmont	1852	Rosas deposed in Argentina
1852	Treaty of London, guaranteeing integrity of Denmark	1852	Responsible government established in New Zealand
1852	Napoleon III proclaimed emperor of the French	1852	Beginning of 'Umar Tal's jihad
		1852	Second Anglo-Burmese War: Britain acquires Irrawaddy delta
		1853	France annexes New Caledonia
		1853	Responsible government established in Cape Colony
		1853	Britain acquires Nagpur
		1853	'Umar Tal conquers Tamba
		1853–68	Nien Rebellion, China
1854	Liberal revolt in Spain; Queen Christina has to leave	1854	Eureka Stockade, Australia
1854–6	Crimean War	1854	Foundation of Republican Party, United States
		1854	Kansas-Nebraska Act
		1854	Treaty of Kanagawa between the United States and Japan
1855	Denmark introduces single transferable vote		

CULTURAL, RELIGIOUS, INTELLECTUAL AND SOCIAL DEVELOPMENTS		SCIENTIFIC, TECHNOLOGICAL, MEDICAL, AGRICULTURAL AND ECONOMIC DEVELOPMENTS	
1850–9	*Household Words*, edited by Dickens		
1851	Herman Melville, *Moby-Dick*	1851	Sewing-machine invented
1851	Verdi, *Rigoletto*	1851	Gold discovered in Australia
1851–3	Ruskin, *The Stones of Venice*	1851	First submarine cable, Dover–Calais
1851–4	Comte, *The System of Positive Polity*	1851	Great Exhibition, London
		1852	Livingstone's expedition to Zambezi
		1852	French Crédit Mobilier founded
1853	Herbert Spencer coins the term 'evolution'		
1853	Verdi, *Il trovatore* and *La traviata*		
1853–5	Gobineau, *Essai sur l'inégalité des races humaines*		
1854–7	Construction of Reading Room, British Museum	1854	First United States–Japan commercial treaty
1855	*Daily Telegraph* founded	1855	Turret lathe invented
		1855	Paris Exposition
1855	Harriet Martineau, *Autobiography*	1855	Abolition of stamp duty on British newspapers
		1855	Livingstone discovers Victoria Falls

MAJOR POLITICAL, CONSTITUTIONAL, DIPLOMATIC AND MILITARY EVENTS IN EUROPE		MAJOR POLITICAL, CONSTITUTIONAL, DIPLOMATIC AND MILITARY EVENTS OUTSIDE EUROPE	
1856	Peace of Paris ends Crimean War	1856	British annexation of Oudh
1856	Counter-revolution in Spain	1856	Tasmania made self-governing colony
		1856–8	Anglo-French war against China
		1857	Speke discovers source of Nile
		1857–8	Indian Mutiny
1858	Foundation of Irish Republican Brotherhood	1858	Dissolution of English East India Company
1858	Karageorge deposed; Obrenovich declared Serbian king	1858	Britain acquires British Columbia
1858	Orsini attempts to assassinate Napoleon III	1858	Ottawa declared capital of Canada
1858	Plombières meeting: Napoleon III and Cavour to plan for Italian unification	1858–64	French conquest of Cochin-China
1859–60	Franco-Piedmontese war against Austria; Peace of Zurich: Austria retains Venetia, France gains Lombardy	1859	John Brown's raid on Harpers Ferry
		1859–60	Spanish-Moroccan War

1860–1869

1860	Italian unification achieved by invasions of Garibaldi from the south and Victor Emmanuel from the north	1860	Outbreak of Maori Wars
		1860	Lincoln elected president of the United States
1861	Capitulation of Gaeta; downfall of Bourbon Monarchy in southern Italy	1861	'Umar Tal conquers Segu
1861	Victor Emmanuel II proclaimed king of Italy	1861	Britain acquires Kowloon, Hong Kong
1861	Moldavia and Wallachia unite as Romania	1861	Self-strengthening Movement begins in China

	CULTURAL, RELIGIOUS, INTELLECTUAL AND SOCIAL DEVELOPMENTS		SCIENTIFIC, TECHNOLOGICAL, MEDICAL, AGRICULTURAL AND ECONOMIC DEVELOPMENTS
1856	G. Flaubert, *Madame Bovary*	1856	Bessemer discovers process of converting iron into steel
1856	First Thomas Cook tour	1856	Victoria Cross inaugurated
1856	Henry Irving's debut	1856	Burton and Speke expedition to search for Nile sources
1857	Science Museum, London, opens	1857	Otis invents first safety elevator
1857	Baudelaire, *Les Fleurs du mal*	1857–65	Laying of Atlantic cable begun
1858	Ringstrasse begun in Vienna	1858	Brunel's 'Great Eastern' launched
1858	Apparition of Virgin Mary at Lourdes	1858	Virchow's *Cellularpathologie* formulates the theory of cell pathology
		1858	Darwin and Wallace present paper on variation of species
		1858	Anglo-Japanese Commercial Treaty
1859–71	Waitz, *Anthropologie der Naturvölker*	1859	Darwin, *The Origin of Species*
1859	J. S. Mill, *On Liberty*	1859	Construction of Suez Canal begins
1859	Dickens, *A Tale of Two Cities*	1859	First oil well drilled in Pennsylvania
1859	Smiles, *Self-help*		
1860	Last boxing contest with bare fists	1860	Cobden-Chevalier Treaty
1860	Wilberforce–Huxley debate on origins of life		
1860	Open golf championship started		
1861	Herzen, *My Past and Thoughts*	1861	Pasteur develops germ theory of disease
1861	Beeton, *Book of Household Management*	1861	Siemens develops open-hearth steelmaking process
1861–2	First English cricket tour of Australia	1861–4	Lancashire cotton famine

MAJOR POLITICAL, CONSTITUTIONAL, DIPLOMATIC AND MILITARY EVENTS IN EUROPE		MAJOR POLITICAL, CONSTITUTIONAL, DIPLOMATIC AND MILITARY EVENTS OUTSIDE EUROPE	
1861	Emancipation of serfs in Russia	1861–5	American Civil War
1862	Rising in Greece: King Otto abdicates	1862	'Umar Tal conquers Messina
1862	Bismarck appointed Prussian premier	1862	Sioux uprising in Minnesota
		1862	'Alabama' dispute between Britain and the United States
		1862	French annexation of Cochin-China
1863	Polish uprising against Russia		
1863	William, prince of Denmark, recognized as George I of Greece		
1863	Lassalle forms General Union of German Workers		
1863	Danish annexation of Schleswig		
1864	*Zemstva* instituted in Russia	1864–70	War between Paraguay and Argentina, Brazil and Uruguay
1864	Prussian-Danish war		
1865	New democratic constitutions for Sweden	1865	End of transportation of convicts to Australia
1865	Bismarck and Napoleon III meet at Biarritz		
1865	Convention of Gastein on Schleswig-Holstein		
1866	Charles Hohenzollern replaces dethroned Alexander Cuza as king of Romania	1866	Fenian 'invasion' of Canada
1866	Austro-Prussian war		
1866	Austro-Italian war; pro-unification plebiscite in Venetia		

CULTURAL, RELIGIOUS, INTELLECTUAL AND SOCIAL DEVELOPMENTS		SCIENTIFIC, TECHNOLOGICAL, MEDICAL, AGRICULTURAL AND ECONOMIC DEVELOPMENTS	
1862	Gilbert Scott designs the Albert Memorial	1862	London Exposition
1862	Notts County founded, oldest club in Football League		
1862–75	Construction of Paris Opéra		
1863	J. S. Mill, *Utilitarianism*	1863	First international postal congress, Paris
1863	Football Association formed		
1863	Manet, *Déjeuner sur l'herbe*		
1863–5	Construction of St Pancras Station		
1863–9	Tolstoi, *War and Peace*		
1864	Pius IX issues 'Syllabus of Errors'	1864	First International founded
		1864	Maxwell provides theoretical foundation of electrical engineering
		1864	Red Cross founded
		1864–9	Contagious Diseases Acts, England and Wales
1865	*Fortnightly Review* founded	1865	First international telegraph congress, Paris
1866	National Secular Society founded	1866	Cholera epidemic
1866	Mary Baker Eddy founds Christian Science	1866	Mendel develops laws of heredity
1866	St Joseph's Society for Foreign Missions founded		

MAJOR POLITICAL, CONSTITUTIONAL, DIPLOMATIC AND MILITARY EVENTS IN EUROPE		MAJOR POLITICAL, CONSTITUTIONAL, DIPLOMATIC AND MILITARY EVENTS OUTSIDE EUROPE	
1866	Parliamentary reform in Sweden		
1866–7	Fenian terrorist campaign, Ireland and Britain		
1867	Ausgleich: Austro-Hungarian dual monarchy with common foreign and military policies	1867	United States purchases Alaska from Russia
		1867	British North America Act; Canadian unification
1867	Garibaldi defeated in his third march on Rome	1867	Execution of Maximilian in Mexico
1867	London Conference guarantees neutrality of Luxemburg		
1867	Formation of North German Confederation		
1867	Second Reform Act, Britain		
1867	Second Panslav Congress, Moscow		
1868	Revolution in Spain led by Prim; Queen Isabella flees	1868	Meiji Restoration in Japan
		1868	British expedition against Tewodorus of Ethiopia
1869	Eisenach Congress: formation of Social Democratic Workers' Party	1869	Wyoming introduces women's suffrage
		1869	Opening of Suez Canal

1866	Amateur Athletics Association founded		
1867	Marquis of Queensbury adopts rules of boxing	1867	Nobel invents dynamite
1867	Zola, *Thérèse Raquin*, first naturalist novel	1867	Monier invents reinforced concrete
1867	Marx, *Das Kapital*, volume 1	1867	Paris Exposition
1867	French poets form the Parnassians to pursue aestheticism	1867	Diamonds discovered at Kimberley
		1867	Illinois introduces eight-hour-day legislation
		1867–9	Collotype printing and typewriter invented
1868	Royal Historical Society founded	1868	Trades Union Congress established in Manchester
1868	First professional baseball club founded		
1868	Society of Missionaries for Africa founded		
1868	Renoir and Manet begin to paint outdoors		
1868–74	Construction of St Pancras Hotel by George Gilbert Scott		
1868–77	Construction of Manchester Town Hall by Waterhouse		
1869	Galton, *Hereditary Genius*	1869	Margarine invented
1869	Arnold, *Culture and Anarchy*	1869	Periodic system of elements formulated
1869	Girton College, Cambridge, founded for women students	1869	Knights of Labor founded

MAJOR POLITICAL, CONSTITUTIONAL, DIPLOMATIC AND MILITARY EVENTS IN EUROPE	MAJOR POLITICAL, CONSTITUTIONAL, DIPLOMATIC AND MILITARY EVENTS OUTSIDE EUROPE

1870–1879

1870	Italians enter Rome; Italian unification proclaimed		
1870–1	Franco-Prussian War		
1870–6	Third Carlist War		
1870	Prim assassinated in Madrid		
1871	Spanish Socialist Party founded by Lafargue	1871	Livingstone and Stanley meet at Ujiji
1871	Germany united, with William I of Prussia proclaimed emperor at Versailles	1871	Abolition of feudal order in Japan
1871	Peace of Frankfurt ends Franco-Prussian War; France cedes Alsace and Lorraine; Paris Commune; Thiers elected president in France		
1871	*Kulturkampf* begins in Germany		
1872	Three Emperors' League (Germany, Russia and Austria-Hungary)	1872	Introduction of military conscription in Japan
1872	Ballot introduced in Britain	1872	Rebellion in Philippines against Spain
1873	Proclamation of republic in Spain	1873	Russia seizes Khiva and Bokhara
1873	*Narodnik* phase of Russian populism begins	1873–4	Ashanti War
1873	Irish Home Rule League founded		
		1874	Britain annexes Fiji Islands

CULTURAL, RELIGIOUS, INTELLECTUAL AND SOCIAL DEVELOPMENTS	SCIENTIFIC, TECHNOLOGICAL, MEDICAL, AGRICULTURAL AND ECONOMIC DEVELOPMENTS
1869 J. S. Mill, *The Subjection of Women*	
1869–70 First Vatican Council	
1870 Doctrine of papal infallibility	1870 Gramme invents dynamo
1870 Wagner, *The Valkyrie*	1870 Rockefeller founds Standard Oil
1870 Dilke, *Greater Britain*	1870 Schliemann begins excavations at Troy
1871 English Football Association Cup established	1871 Germany adopts gold standard
1871 G. Eliot, *Middlemarch*	1871 Mount Cenis tunnel opened
1871–84 Ruskin, *Fors Clavigera*	
1872 First international football match	
1872 Monet, *Impression: Mist*	
1873 English County Cricket Championship founded	1873 Brunner, Mond & Company begin alkali production
1873 Pater, *The Renaissance*	1873 Vienna Exposition
1873 J. S. Mill, *Autobiography*	1873–96 Great Depression
1873–7 Tolstoi, *Anna Karenina*	
1874 J. Strauss, *Die Fledermaus*	1874 Women's Trade Union League formed in Britain
1874 First impressionist exhibition, Paris	
1874–9 Construction of Metropolitan Museum of Art, New York	

MAJOR POLITICAL, CONSTITUTIONAL, DIPLOMATIC AND MILITARY EVENTS IN EUROPE		MAJOR POLITICAL, CONSTITUTIONAL, DIPLOMATIC AND MILITARY EVENTS OUTSIDE EUROPE	
1875	German Socialist Workers' Party founded	1875	Russo-Japanese agreement over Sakhalin and the Kuriles
1875	Proclamation of Third Republic, France		
1875	Alfonso XII recognized as king of Spain		
1875–8	Risings in Bosnia-Hercegovina against Turkish rule		
1876	Serbia and Montenegro declare war on Turkey	1876	British-French dual control in Egypt
1876	Bulgarian massacres by Turks		
1877–8	Russo-Turkish War	1877	Queen Victoria proclaimed empress of India
		1877	British annexation of Transvaal
		1877	Uprising in Japan under Saigo Takamori
		1877–8	Cape-Xhosa War
1878	Congress of Berlin	1878	Britain, Germany and United States make commercial treaties with Samoa
1878	Anti-socialist Law passed, Germany		
		1878–9	Second Afghan War
1879	Austro-German Dual Alliance founded	1879	Conquest of Zulus by British
1879	Fédération du Parti des Travailleurs founded, France	1879	Transvaal Republic proclaimed by Boers
		1879–80	Third Afghan War
1879	Russian terrorist organization Land and Freedom splits into People's Will and Black Redistribution	1879–83	War of the Pacific, or 'Nitrate War'

1880–1889

1880	Bradlaugh Affair, Britain	1880	France annexes Tahiti
		1880	Capture and execution of Ned Kelly, Australia

	CULTURAL, RELIGIOUS, INTELLECTUAL AND SOCIAL DEVELOPMENTS		SCIENTIFIC, TECHNOLOGICAL, MEDICAL, AGRICULTURAL AND ECONOMIC DEVELOPMENTS
1875	*Trial by Jury* begins Gilbert and Sullivan partnership	1875	Plimsoll's Merchant Shipping Act
1875	Foundation of Liberty & Company	1875	Universal Postal Union established
1875	First crossing of English Channel by swimmer	1875	Trade-union legislation in Britain
1876	Zola, *Le Roman expérimental*	1876	Philadelphia Exposition
1876	Dewey's decimal system of classification for libraries	1876	Otto invents four-cycle gas engine
		1876	Bell patents telephone
		1876	Chromosomes first observed
1877	*Nineteenth Century* (periodical) established	1877	Edison invents the phonograph
1877	Guild of St Matthew founded	1877	Frozen meat first shipped from Argentina to France
1877	First All-England Lawn Tennis championship at Wimbledon	1877	First public telephone
1878	Tchaikovsky, *Swan Lake*	1878	Paris Exposition
1878	Salvation Army founded	1878	Eddison and Swan invent the light bulb
1879	H. George, *Progress and Poverty*	1879	German protectionist legislation
1879	Ibsen, *A Doll's House*	1879	Siemens exhibits electric locomotive
1880	Zola, *Nana*		
1880	Tchaikovsky, *1812 Overture*		

MAJOR POLITICAL, CONSTITUTIONAL, DIPLOMATIC AND MILITARY EVENTS IN EUROPE		MAJOR POLITICAL, CONSTITUTIONAL, DIPLOMATIC AND MILITARY EVENTS OUTSIDE EUROPE	
		1880–1	Transvaal declares independence from Britain; first Anglo-Boer War
1881	Irish National Land League	1881	Political parties established in Japan
1881	Assassination of Alexander II of Russia	1881	Rising of Urabi Pasha in Egypt
		1881	French protectorate over Tunisia
		1881	Pretoria Convention recognizes independence of Transvaal and Orange Free State
1882	Phoenix Park murders, Dublin	1882	Establishment of British protectorate over Egypt
1882	Parti Ouvrier Français founded	1882–5	Mahdi uprising drives Britain and Egypt from Sudan
1882	Milan Obrenovich assumes title king of Serbia		
1882	Italy joins Austro-German alliance (Triple Alliance)		
1883	Social Democratic Federation founded, Britain	1883	French protectorate over Annam and Tonkin
1884	Third Reform Act, Britain	1884	Germany occupies south-west Africa, Togoland and Cameroons
1884	Society for German Colonization founded		
1884	Three Emperors' League renewed	1884–5	Conference of Berlin meets to mediate European claims in Africa
1884	Fabian Society founded, Britain		
1885	Belgian Social Democratic Party founded	1885	Independent Congo State established by Leopold II

CULTURAL, RELIGIOUS, INTELLECTUAL AND SOCIAL DEVELOPMENTS		SCIENTIFIC, TECHNOLOGICAL, MEDICAL, AGRICULTURAL AND ECONOMIC DEVELOPMENTS	
1881	*Tit-Bits* founded		
1881	H. James, *Portrait of a Lady*		
1881	Machado de Assis, *Epitaph of a Small Winner*		
1881–8	Ranke, *World History* (seven volumes)		
1882	Berlin Philharmonic Orchestra founded	1882	Commercial domestic lighting first used, Central Station, New York
1883	Seeley, *The Expansion of England*	1883	Women's Co-operative Guild, Britain
1883	Boys' Brigade founded in Glasgow	1883	Orient Express runs for the first time
1883	Opening of Vatican archives	1883	Galton coins the term 'eugenics'
1883–5	Construction of first skyscraper, Chicago	1883–6	Trans-Caspian railway built
1883–92	Nietzsche, *Thus Spake Zarathustra*	1883–9	German social legislation for sickness, accident, old age
1884	Oxford English Dictionary begins	1884	Machine-gun invented
1884	Gaelic Athletic Association founded	1884	Parsons invents steam generator
1884	Art Workers' Guild	1884	Trade-union legislation in France
1884–6	Seurat, *Sunday on the Grande-Jatte*	1884	Petrol engine invented
		1884	Koch discovers the cholera bacillus
1885	Zola, *Germinal*	1885	Mannesman invents seamless pipes
1885	*Dictionary of National Biography* begins		

MAJOR POLITICAL, CONSTITUTIONAL, DIPLOMATIC AND MILITARY EVENTS IN EUROPE	MAJOR POLITICAL, CONSTITUTIONAL, DIPLOMATIC AND MILITARY EVENTS OUTSIDE EUROPE
1885 Redistribution Act introduces single-member constituencies in Britain	1885 British protectorate established in Nigeria
1885 Serbian invasion of Bulgaria defeated at Slivnitza	1885 British control established over Bechuanaland
	1885 French establish control over Madagascar
	1885 Panjeh Incident
	1885 Germany annexes northern New Guinea and Bismarck Archipelago
	1885-6 Third Anglo-Burmese War; British annexation of Burma
1886 Conflict over Army Bill in German Reichstag	1886 Abolition of slavery in Cuba
1886 Gladstone's Irish Home Rule Bill defeated	1886 Foundation of Indian National Congress
1886-9 Boulangist movement in France	
1887 Attempted coup in France by General Boulanger	1887 Union of Indo-China established by France
1887 Suffrage reform in the Netherlands	
1887 Ferdinand of Saxe-Coburg elected king of Bulgaria	
1887 Reinsurance Treaty between Germany and Russia	
1888 Austrian Social Democratic Party founded	1888 Manhood suffrage in New Zealand
1888 William II becomes *Kaiser* of Germany	1888 British protectorate over north Borneo, Brunei and Sarawak
1888 Swiss Social Democratic Party founded	1888 Abolition of slavery in Brazil

CULTURAL, RELIGIOUS, INTELLECTUAL AND SOCIAL DEVELOPMENTS		SCIENTIFIC, TECHNOLOGICAL, MEDICAL, AGRICULTURAL AND ECONOMIC DEVELOPMENTS	
		1885	Motor car invented
		1885	First electric tramway in Britain at Blackpool
		1885	Gold discovered in Transvaal
1886	English Historical Review founded	1886	Canadian Pacific railway completed
1886	First amateur golf championship	1886	Haymarket Massacre, Chicago
		1886	American Federation of Labor founded
		1886	First international copyright law agreed
1887	Verdi, Otello		
1888	First beauty contest, Spa, Belgium	1888	Kodak box camera invented
1888	Bellamy, Looking Backward	1888	Dunlop patents pneumatic tyre
1888	Arts and Crafts Exhibition Society	1888	Nansen crosses Greenland
1888	Guild of Handicraft founded	1888	Glasgow Exposition
		1888-9	Strike wave in Britain; Dock Strike; new unionism

MAJOR POLITICAL, CONSTITUTIONAL, DIPLOMATIC AND MILITARY EVENTS IN EUROPE	MAJOR POLITICAL, CONSTITUTIONAL, DIPLOMATIC AND MILITARY EVENTS OUTSIDE EUROPE
1889 Naval rearmament begins in Britain	1889 Brazil declared a republic
	1889 Constitution granted in Japan
	1889 Battle of Metemma, Sudan
	1889 Treaty of Ucciali, implying Italian protectorate over Ethiopia

1890–1899

1890 Parti Ouvrier Socialiste Révolutionnaire founded, France	1890 Britain exchanges Heligoland for Zanzibar and Pemba
1890 Grand Duchy of Luxemburg separates from the Netherlands	
1890 Bismarck dismissed	
1890 Socialist Workers' Party in Germany renamed Social Democratic Party and adopts new programme	
1892 Panama scandal in France	
1892 Witte becomes Russian minister of finance	
1893 Agrarian League founded, Germany	1893 Matabele Rising
1893 Independent Labour Party founded in Bradford, England	1893 Franco-British agreement on Siam
	1893 Female enfranchisement in New Zealand

CULTURAL, RELIGIOUS, INTELLECTUAL AND SOCIAL DEVELOPMENTS	SCIENTIFIC, TECHNOLOGICAL, MEDICAL, AGRICULTURAL AND ECONOMIC DEVELOPMENTS
1889 Christian Social Union founded	1889 Second International established at Paris
1889 Eiffel Tower opens	1889 Paris Exposition
1889 *Fabian Essays*, edited by G. B. Shaw	
1890 Ibsen, *Hedda Gabler*	1890 First entirely steel-framed building constructed in Chicago
1890 –1915 Frazer, *The Golden Bough* (twelve volumes)	1890 Initiation of May Day celebrations
	1890 Failure of Baring's Bank
	1890 First corridor train
	1890–1 'Great Strikes' in Australia
1891 Morris, *News from Nowhere*	1891 –1904 Trans-Siberian railway
1891 Oscar Wilde, *The Picture of Dorian Gray*	
1891 Conan Doyle, *The Adventures of Sherlock Holmes*	
1891 Leo XIII issues 'Rerum novarum'	
1892 Hauptmann, *The Weavers*, naturalist drama	1892 French protective tariffs
	1892 Last major European outbreak of cholera, in Hamburg
	1892 First automatic telephone exchange
1893 Gaelic League founded in Ireland	1893 Chicago Exposition
1893 Frank Lloyd Wright's Winslow residence built	1893 Diesel engine
1893 Huxley, *Evolution and Ethics*	

MAJOR POLITICAL, CONSTITUTIONAL, DIPLOMATIC AND MILITARY EVENTS IN EUROPE		MAJOR POLITICAL, CONSTITUTIONAL, DIPLOMATIC AND MILITARY EVENTS OUTSIDE EUROPE	
1893	House of Lords rejects second Irish Home Rule Bill		
1894	French president killed by anarchist bomb	1894	Britain declares protectorate of Uganda
1894	Dutch Social Democratic Party founded	1894	Armenian rising and massacres
		1894	Italian war with Ethiopia
1894	German *rapprochement* with Boers		
1894 –1906	Dreyfus Affair	1894–5	Sino-Japanese War
		1895	Jameson Raid, South Africa
		1896	France annexes Madagascar
		1896	Franco-Italian agreement over Tunisia
		1896	Italians defeated at Adowa; Treaty of Addis Ababa: Italian protectorate over Ethiopia withdrawn
		1896–7	Ndebele Rising
1897	Tirpitz appointed German naval secretary	1897	King of Korea proclaims himself emperor
1897	Queen Victoria's Diamond Jubilee		
1897	First Zionist World Congress, Basle		
1897	Spanish premier assassinated by anarchists		
1897	Greco-Turkish war		
1898	Zola, 'J'accuse'	1898	Spanish-American War
1898	Action Française founded	1898	Old-age pensions introduced in New Zealand
1898	First German Navy Bill passed		

CULTURAL, RELIGIOUS, INTELLECTUAL AND SOCIAL DEVELOPMENTS		SCIENTIFIC, TECHNOLOGICAL, MEDICAL, AGRICULTURAL AND ECONOMIC DEVELOPMENTS	
1893	Tiffany's Favrile glass first manufactured		
1894	Kidd, Social Evolution	1894	Industrial Conciliation and Arbitration Act, New Zealand
1894	International Olympic Committee founded		
1895	Oscar Wilde trial	1895	Lumière invents cinematograph
1895	London School of Economics and Political Science founded	1895	Confédération Générale du Travail founded
1895	National Trust formed	1895	Röntgen discovers X-rays
		1895	Lorentz propounds electron theory
1896	First modern Olympics	1896	Rutherford detects electrical waves
1896	Chekhov, The Seagull		
1896	Herzl, The Jewish State	1896	Nobel prizes established
1896	National Portrait Gallery, London, opens	1896–7	Strikes in St Petersburg
1896	Daily Mail first published		
1896	Puccini, La Bohème		
		1897	Gold discovered in the Klondyke
		1897	Wireless invented
		1898	M. and P. Curie discover radium

MAJOR POLITICAL, CONSTITUTIONAL, DIPLOMATIC AND MILITARY EVENTS IN EUROPE	MAJOR POLITICAL, CONSTITUTIONAL, DIPLOMATIC AND MILITARY EVENTS OUTSIDE EUROPE
	1898 Fashoda Crisis
	1898 Battle of Omdurman: reconquest of Sudan
	1898 United States annexes Hawaii
	1898 Spanish-American War: Guam, Puerto Rico, Philippines and Cuba ceded to the United States
	1898 French capture Samori Turay
	1898 Hundred Days Reform, China; empress dowager Tz'u-hsi seizes supreme power
	1898 Russia obtains lease for Port Arthur
1899 Hague Peace Conference	1899 Revolt against American rule in Philippines
1899 Belgium introduces proportional representation	1899 First labour government, Queensland, Australia
	1899 Settlement of British Guiana–Venezuela boundary dispute
	1899
	–1902 Second Anglo-Boer War

CULTURAL, RELIGIOUS, INTELLECTUAL AND SOCIAL DEVELOPMENTS		SCIENTIFIC, TECHNOLOGICAL, MEDICAL, AGRICULTURAL AND ECONOMIC DEVELOPMENTS	
1899	Machado de Assis, *Dom Casmurro*	1899	Aspirin invented
1899	H. G. Wells, *When the Sleeper Wakes*	1899	First magnetic recording of sound

Appendix: Maps

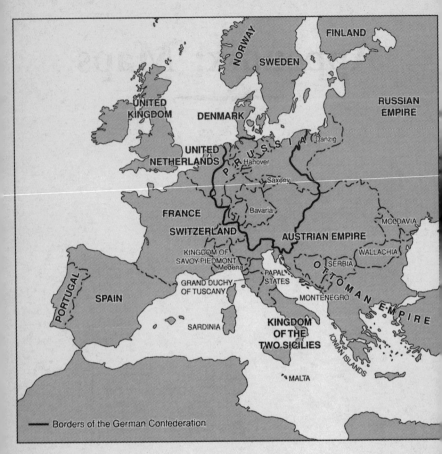

Map 1: Europe in 1815

Map 2: *Europe in 1914*

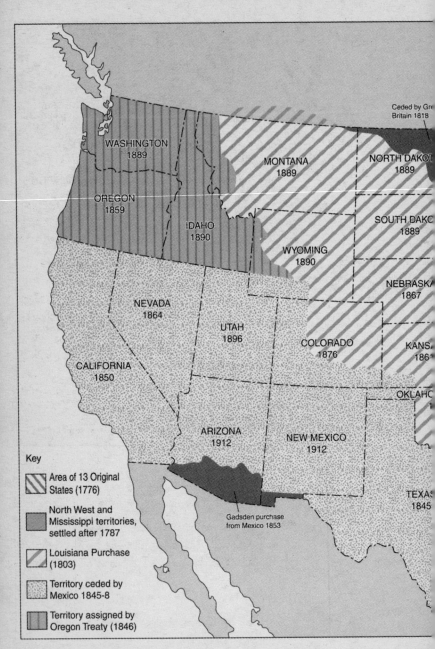

Key

Area of 13 Original
States (1776)

North West and
Mississippi territories,
settled after 1787

Louisiana Purchase
(1803)

Territory ceded by
Mexico 1845-8

Territory assigned by
Oregon Treaty (1846)

WASHINGTON
1889

OREGON
1859

IDAHO
1890

MONTANA
1889

NORTH DAKOT
1889

Ceded by Gr
Britain 1818

SOUTH DAKC
1889

WYOMING
1890

NEBRASK/
1867

NEVADA
1864

UTAH
1896

COLORADO
1876

KANS/
186

CALIFORNIA
1850

OKLAHO
1

ARIZONA
1912

NEW MEXICO
1912

TEXA
1845

Gadsden purchase
from Mexico 1853

Map 3: The United States of America: Westward Expansion

Gained from
Great Britain
1842

MAINE
1820

NNESOTA
1858

VERMONT

NEW
HAMPSHIRE

WISCONSIN
1848

MICHIGAN
1837

NEW YORK

MASSACHUSETTS
RHODE ISLAND
CONNECTICUT

IOWA
1846

PENNSYLVANIA

NEW
JERSEY

MARYLAND

DELAWARE

ILLINOIS
1818

INDIANA
1816

OHIO
1803

WEST
VIRGINIA
1863

VIRGINIA

MISSOURI
1821

KENTUCKY
1792

TENNESSEE
1796

NORTH
CAROLINA

ARKANSAS
1836

SOUTH
CAROLINA

GEORGIA

MISSISSIPPI
1817

ALABAMA
1819

LOUISIANA
1812

Annexed 1812

Purchased from
Spain 1819

FLORIDA
1845

Note: dates indicate year of admission to the Union

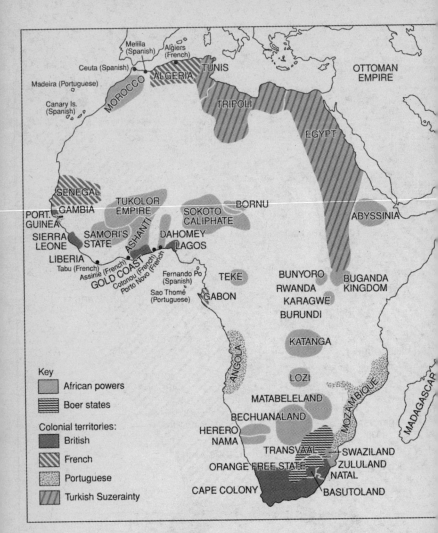

Map 4: Africa Before the Scramble (c.1870)

Key

Possessions:

- British
- French
- German
- Italian
- Portuguese
- Spanish
- Belgian

Map 5: Africa After the Scramble (1914)

Map 6: *Latin America in 1830*

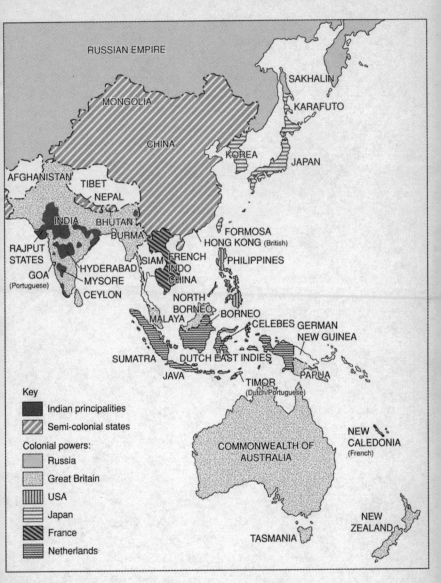

Map 7: *Colonial Powers in Asia and Australasia (1914)*

Index

References to Friedrich Engels, Karl Marx, John Stuart Mill and Robert Owen may be found in the main text under the organizations, people and philosophies concerned. Page references in **bold** type indicate biographical articles in the text.

CHRISTINE HEADLEY

READ MORE IN PENGUIN

In every corner of the world, on every subject under the sun, Penguin represents quality and variety – the very best in publishing today.

For complete information about books available from Penguin – including Puffins, Penguin Classics and Arkana – and how to order them, write to us at the appropriate address below. Please note that for copyright reasons the selection of books varies from country to country.

In the United Kingdom: Please write to *Dept. EP, Penguin Books Ltd, Bath Road, Harmondsworth, West Drayton, Middlesex UB7 ODA*

In the United States: Please write to *Consumer Sales, Penguin USA, P.O. Box 999, Dept. 17109, Bergenfield, New Jersey 07621-0120.* VISA and MasterCard holders call 1-800-253-6476 to order Penguin titles

In Canada: Please write to *Penguin Books Canada Ltd, 10 Alcorn Avenue, Suite 300, Toronto, Ontario M4V 3B2*

In Australia: Please write to *Penguin Books Australia Ltd, P.O. Box 257, Ringwood, Victoria 3134*

In New Zealand: Please write to *Penguin Books (NZ) Ltd, Private Bag 102902, North Shore Mail Centre, Auckland 10*

In India: Please write to *Penguin Books India Pvt Ltd, 706 Eros Apartments, 56 Nehru Place, New Delhi 110 019*

In the Netherlands: Please write to *Penguin Books Netherlands bv, Postbus 3507, NL-1001 AH Amsterdam*

In Germany: Please write to *Penguin Books Deutschland GmbH, Metzlerstrasse 26, 60594 Frankfurt am Main*

In Spain: Please write to *Penguin Books S. A., Bravo Murillo 19, 1° B, 28015 Madrid*

In Italy: Please write to *Penguin Italia s.r.l., Via Felice Casati 20, 1–20124 Milano*

In France: Please write to *Penguin France S. A., 17 rue Lejeune, F–31000 Toulouse*

In Japan: Please write to *Penguin Books Japan, Ishikiribashi Building, 2–5–4, Suido, Bunkyo-ku, Tokyo 112*

In South Africa: Please write to *Longman Penguin Southern Africa (Pty) Ltd, Private Bag X08, Bertsham 2013*

READ MORE IN PENGUIN

HISTORY

Citizens Simon Schama

The award-winning chronicle of the French Revolution. 'The most marvellous book I have read about the French Revolution in the last fifty years' – Richard Cobb in *The Times*

The Lure of the Sea Alain Corbin

Alain Corbin's wonderful book explores the dramatic change in Western attitude towards the sea and seaside pleasures that occured between 1750 and 1840. 'A compact and brilliant taxonomy of the shifting meanings of the sea and shore' – *New York Review of Books*

The Tyranny of History W. J. F. Jenner

A fifth of the world's population lives within the boundaries of China, a vast empire barely under the control of the repressive ruling Communist regime. Beneath the economic boom China is in a state of crisis that goes far deeper than the problems of its current leaders to a value system that is rooted in the autocratic traditions of China's past.

The English Bible and the Seventeenth-Century Revolution
Christopher Hill

'What caused the English civil war? What brought Charles I to the scaffold?' Answer to both questions: the Bible. To sustain this provocative thesis, Christopher Hill's new book maps English intellectual history from the Reformation to 1660, showing how scripture dominated every department of thought from sexual relations to political theory ... 'His erudition is staggering' – *Sunday Times*

Fisher's Face Jan Morris

'*Fisher's Face* is funny, touching and informed by wide reading as well as wide travelling' – *New Statesman & Society*. 'A richly beguiling picture of the Victorian Navy, its profound inner security, its glorious assumptions, its extravagant social life and its traditionally eccentric leaders' – *Independent on Sunday*